Advances in Fractional Differential Operators and Their Applications

Advances in Fractional Differential Operators and Their Applications

Editors

Angelo B. Mingarelli
Leila Gholizadeh Zivlaei
Mohammad Dehghan

Basel • Beijing • Wuhan • Barcelona • Belgrade • Novi Sad • Cluj • Manchester

Editors
Angelo B. Mingarelli
Carleton University
Ottawa, ON, Canada

Leila Gholizadeh Zivlaei
Carleton University
Ottawa, ON, Canada

Mohammad Dehghan
Carleton University
Ottawa, ON, Canada

Editorial Office
MDPI
St. Alban-Anlage 66
4052 Basel, Switzerland

This is a reprint of articles from the Special Issue published online in the open access journal *Fractal and Fractional* (ISSN 2504-3110) (available at: https://www.mdpi.com/journal/fractalfract/special_issues/fract_diff_operator).

For citation purposes, cite each article independently as indicated on the article page online and as indicated below:

Lastname, A.A.; Lastname, B.B. Article Title. *Journal Name* **Year**, *Volume Number*, Page Range.

ISBN 978-3-0365-8904-6 (Hbk)
ISBN 978-3-0365-8905-3 (PDF)
doi.org/10.3390/books978-3-0365-8905-3

© 2023 by the authors. Articles in this book are Open Access and distributed under the Creative Commons Attribution (CC BY) license. The book as a whole is distributed by MDPI under the terms and conditions of the Creative Commons Attribution-NonCommercial-NoDerivs (CC BY-NC-ND) license.

Contents

About the Editors vii

Preface ix

Arshad Ali, Khursheed J. Ansari, Hussam Alrabaiah, Ahmad Aloqaily and Nabil Mlaiki
Coupled System of Fractional Impulsive Problem Involving Power-Law Kernel with Piecewise Order
Reprinted from: *Fractal Fract.* 2023, 7, 436, doi:10.3390/fractalfract7060436 1

Fahad Alsidrani, Adem Kılıçman and Norazak Senu
Approximate Solutions for Time-Fractional Fornberg–Whitham Equation with Variable Coefficients
Reprinted from: *Fractal Fract.* 2023, 7, 260, doi:10.3390/fractalfract7030260 27

Ravshan Ashurov and Sergei Sitnik
Identification of the Order of the Fractional Derivative for the Fractional Wave Equation
Reprinted from: *Fractal Fract.* 2023, 7, 67, doi:10.3390/fractalfract7010067 45

Gerd Baumann and Norbert Südland
Sinc Numeric Methods for Fox-H, Aleph (ℵ), and Saxena-I Functions
Reprinted from: *Fractal Fract.* 2022, 6, 449, doi:10.3390/fractalfract6080449 59

Oana Brandibur and Éva Kaslik
Stability Properties of Multi-Term Fractional-Differential Equations
Reprinted from: *Fractal Fract.* 2023, 7, 117, doi:10.3390/fractalfract7020117 83

Aliaa Burqan, Aref Sarhan and Rania Saadeh
Constructing Analytical Solutions of the Fractional Riccati Differential Equations Using Laplace Residual Power Series Method
Reprinted from: *Fractal Fract.* 2023, 7, 14, doi:10.3390/fractalfract7010014 99

Mohammad Dehghan and Angelo B. Mingarelli
Fractional Sturm–Liouville Eigenvalue Problems, II
Reprinted from: *Fractal Fract.* 2022, 6, 487, doi:10.3390/fractalfract6090487 109

Leila Gholizadeh Zivlaei and Angelo B. Mingarelli
On the Basic Theory of Some Generalized and Fractional Derivatives
Reprinted from: *Fractal Fract.* 2022, 6, 672, doi:10.3390/fractalfract6110672 125

Adel R. Hadhoud, Faisal E. Abd Alaal, Ayman A. Abdelaziz and Taha Radwan
A Cubic Spline Collocation Method to Solve a Nonlinear Space-Fractional Fisher's Equation and Its Stability Examination
Reprinted from: *Fractal Fract.* 2022, 6, 470, doi:10.3390/fractalfract6090470 141

Asad Khan, Azmat Ullah Khan Niazi, Waseem Abbasi, Faryal Awan and Anam Khan
Fractional-Order Nonlinear Multi-Agent Systems: A Resilience-Based Approach to Consensus Analysis with Distributed and Input Delays
Reprinted from: *Fractal Fract.* 2023, 7, 322, doi:10.3390/fractalfract7040322 153

Maksim V. Kukushkin
Cauchy Problem for an Abstract Evolution Equation of Fractional Order
Reprinted from: *Fractal Fract.* 2023, 7, 111, doi:10.3390/fractalfract7020111 169

Chong Li, Yingjie Yang and Xinping Zhu
Stability of Time Series Models Based on Fractional-Order Weakening Buffer Operators
Reprinted from: *Fractal Fract.* 2023, 7, 554, doi:10.3390/fractalfract7070554 191

Nguyen Hoang Luc, Donal O'Regan and Anh Tuan Nguyen
Solutions of a Nonlinear Diffusion Equation with a Regularized Hyper-Bessel Operator
Reprinted from: *Fractal Fract.* 2022, 6, 530, doi:10.3390/fractalfract6090530 215

Eylem Öztürk and Joseph L. Shomberg
Well-Posedness and Global Attractors for Viscous Fractional Cahn–Hilliard Equations with Memory
Reprinted from: *Fractal Fract.* 2022, 6, 505, doi:10.3390/fractalfract6090505 225

Davood Jabari Sabegh, Reza Ezzati, Omid Nikan, António M. Lopes and Alexandra M. S. F. Galhano
Hybridization of Block-Pulse and Taylor Polynomials for Approximating 2D Fractional Volterra Integral Equations
Reprinted from: *Fractal Fract.* 2022, 6, 511, doi:10.3390/fractalfract6090511 253

Apassara Suechoei, Parinya Sa Ngiamsunthorn, Waraporn Chatanin, Chainarong Athisakul, Somchai Chucheepsakul and Danuruj Songsanga
Analysis of a Fractional Variational Problem Associated with Cantilever Beams Subjected to a Uniformly Distributed Load
Reprinted from: *Fractal Fract.* 2023, 7, 141, doi:10.3390/fractalfract7020141 265

Jorge L. Suzuki, Maryam Naghibolhosseini and Mohsen Zayernouri
A General Return-Mapping Framework for Fractional Visco-Elasto-Plasticity
Reprinted from: *Fractal Fract.* 2022, 6, 715, doi:10.3390/fractalfract6120715 283

Hari M. Srivastava and Jose Vanterler da Costa Sousa
Multiplicity of Solutions for Fractional-Order Differential Equations via the $\kappa(x)$-Laplacian Operator and the Genus Theory
Reprinted from: *Fractal Fract.* 2022, 6, 481, doi:10.3390/fractalfract6090481 305

Mengrui Xu
Influences of the Order of Derivative on the Dynamical Behavior of Fractional-Order Antisymmetric Lotka–Volterra Systems
Reprinted from: *Fractal Fract.* 2023, 7, 360, doi:10.3390/fractalfract7050360 333

Kaihong Zhao
Existence, Stability and Simulation of a Class of NonlinearFractional Langevin Equations Involving Nonsingular Mittag–Leffler Kernel
Reprinted from: *Fractal Fract.* 2022, 6, 469, doi:10.3390/fractalfract6090469 347

About the Editors

Angelo B. Mingarelli

Angelo B. Mingarelli was a doctoral student of the late Prof. F. V. Atkinson (Toronto), who was part of the Hardy–Littlewood school via E.C. Titchmarsh. He has published over 130 papers in various fields, spanning the history of art and mathematics, to fuzzy cellular automata and differential equations. Starting at Pennsylvania State University (State College), he then moved on to the University of Ottawa and finally Carleton University, where he has been Professor of Mathematics since 1990.

Leila Gholizadeh Zivlaei

Leila Gholizadeh Zivlaei is a doctoral student of Prof. Angelo B. Mingarelli (Ottawa) in the School of Mathematics and Statistics at Carleton University. She has published 12 papers in the fields of fixed point theory and fractional Sturm–Liouville differential equations. Starting her career as a tutor and researcher at various universities in her home country of Iran, she then moved to Carleton University and has been a Ph.D. student at the university since 2020.

Mohammad Dehghan

Mohammad Dehghan is currently a doctoral student of Prof. Angelo B. Mingarelli in the School of Mathematics and Statistics at Carleton University. He has published eight papers in the fields of linear programming and classical and fractional Sturm–Liouville differential equations. Starting his career at the Azad University of Sari branch in Iran, he then moved to Carleton University as a visiting researcher and is now working in the Canadian Intellectual Property Office (CIPO) as a data scientist.

Preface

This Special Issue comprises 20 articles from well-known researchers in the general field of differential equations with fractional derivatives, integral equations, and systems theory. The content of the papers is diverse, from purely theoretical investigations to numerical simulations and real-world applications. Of course, an overlap between these three areas is possible, indeed desirable and necessitated by the nature of the subject itself. The various designations are not intended to be mutually exclusive.

Angelo B. Mingarelli, Leila Gholizadeh Zivlaei, and Mohammad Dehghan
Editors

Article

Coupled System of Fractional Impulsive Problem Involving Power-Law Kernel with Piecewise Order

Arshad Ali [1,*], Khursheed J. Ansari [2], Hussam Alrabaiah [3,4], Ahmad Aloqaily [5,6] and Nabil Mlaiki [5]

1. Department of Mathematics, University of Malakand, Chakdara Dir (L), Chakdara P.O. Box 18800, Khyber Pakhtunkhwa, Pakistan
2. Department of Mathematics, College of Science, King Khalid University, Abha 61413, Saudi Arabia; ansari.jkhursheed@gmail.com
3. College of Engineering, Al Ain University, Al Ain P.O. Box 64141, United Arab Emirates; hussam.alrabaiah@aau.ac.ae
4. Mathematics Department, Tafila Technical University, Tafila P.O. Box 66110, Jordan
5. Department of Mathematics and Sciences, Prince Sultan University, Riyadh 11586, Saudi Arabia; maloqaily@psu.edu.sa (A.A.); nmlaiki@psu.edu.sa or nmlaiki2012@gmail.com (N.M.)
6. School of Computer, Data and Mathematical Sciences, Western Sydney University, Sydney 2150, Australia
* Correspondence: arshad.swatpk@gmail.com

Abstract: In this research paper, we study a coupled system of piecewise-order differential equations (DEs) with variable kernel and impulsive conditions. DEs with variable kernel have high flexibility due to the freedom of changing the kernel. We study existence and stability theory and derive sufficient conditions for main results of the proposed problem. We apply Scheafer's fixed point theorem and Banach fixed point theorem for the result of at least one and unique solution, respectively. In addition, stability results based on the Ulam–Hyers concept are derived. Being a coupled system of piecewise fractional-order DEs with variable kernel and impulsive effects, the obtained results have multi-dimension applications. To demonstrate the applications, we apply the derived results to a numerical problem.

Keywords: fractional piecewise order derivative; variable kernel; existence of solution; stability results

1. Introduction

Fractional calculus has become an active area of research. In the last two to three decades, fractional calculus has given much importance by researchers due to the non-local and global nature of the differential operators it involves. These operators have the ability to describe the dynamical behavior of a natural phenomena with a high degree of accuracy which have successfully been applied in numerous directions as in [1–5]. For its basic history and some applications, we recommend the books [6,7]. In view of the aforementioned importance fractional differential equations (FDEs) and, more specifically, the coupled systems of FDEs, these are considered as key tools of applied mathematics which are used to develop differential models for high complex systems. For instance, we refer to quantum evolution of complex systems [8], Duffing system [9], anomalous diffusion [10], fractional Lorenz system [11], secure communication and control processing [12]. Similarly, their applications can be observed in applied electrical engineering, mathematical biology, chemical theory, static dynamics, etc.

Here, it should be kept in mind that many real-world phenomena do not have a unique behavior and, rather, exhibit a variety of behaviors, including economic fluctuations, comparable molecular dynamics behaviors, earthquakes, etc. To achieve better results in the aforementioned process, researchers have increasingly used various operators for the mathematical modeling of such processes. In this regard, researchers have introduced various fractional differential operators to describe the crossover behaviours of different phenomenons more comprehensively. For example, author [13] has investigated some classes of impulsive fractional-order problems and discussed the exact solutions, and short-memory cases. In the same way, short memory fractional-order DEs were introduced for the first time [14]: variable-order DEs are the natural extension of classical DEs and were also given much attention in subsequent years (see [15,16]). Here, one thing should kept in mind that fractional derivatives include memory and genetic effects, which play a crucial part in investigations of many real world dynamical problems (see [17]). Almost all the definitions of fractional derivative have different kernels which are either singular or non-singular. For instance, the Caputo derivative and Riemann–Liouville derivative have a singular kernel, the Caputo–Fabrizio derivative has a non-singular exponential decay kernel [18], and the Atangana–Baleanu–Caputo derivative has a non-singular Mittag–Leffler kernel [19]. In all these definitions, the kernels are constant. On the other hand, the usual fractional calculus has long memory effects which result in difficulties with long-term calculation. In addition, the long memory with power law is described using the mathematical tools of usual fractional calculus which contains the fractional-order derivatives and integrals.

Motivated from the above discussion, researchers have introduced the concept of piecewise fractional-order derivatives to address the problem with short memory. Therefore, researchers are using two stages to deal the memory process. One stage is devoted to permanent retention of short memory. The second stage is related to a simple model of fractional derivative. Here, it is interesting that short memory can be applied to improve performance and efficiency to explain physical phenomena more brilliantly (see [20]). Therefore, the concept of piecewise derivative with fractional-order has been used recently in many papers; we refer to [21–23]. Recently, a new concept of fractional derivative with piecewise-order and variable kernel has been introduced. This concept has high flexibility due to the freedom of changing the kernel [24]. These definitions are suitable in physical systems whose properties are based on the dynamics with memory effects which show change in their behavior across the time interval. The mentioned concept has been extended to boundary value problems in [25].

On other hand, differential equations with impulsive behavior have acquired applications in many applied fields of sciences; for example, physical problems that keep instantaneous changes and discontinuous jumps are modeled via impulsive DEs. The existence theory of DEs with impulsive effects has been enticing to many researchers. For instance, authors [26] investigated the three-point boundary value problem (BVP) with impulsive conditions using a fixed-point approach. In addition, a coupled system of BVPs with impulsive conditions has been studied via fixed theory in [27]. The impulsive problem of fractional-order evolution equations has been investigated using the tools of nonlinear functional analysis (see [28]). In the same way, multi-point BVP of FDEs with impulsive conditions has been studied for the existence theory in [29]. All the mentioned studies indicate that researchers have studied various impulsive problems by using fixed-point theory and tools of functional analysis under the fixed fractional-order derivative.

We first convert the considered system to an equivalent variable-order integral system. We use fixed-point theorems due to Banach and Scheafer's to develop sufficient conditions for the existence and uniqueness of solution to the considered problem. Also, stability is an important consequence of optimization theory and numerical functional analysis, therefore we also establish some results by using Ulam-Hyers (UH) concept. The mentioned stability was introduced by Ulam in 1940, and explained further by Hyers in 1941 (see [30]). Later on the aforesaid stability was increasingly studied by other researchers for different problems (see [31–34]).

2. Presentation of our Problem

Here, we remark that coupled systems have been considered in many investigations of real world problems. For instance, authors [35] studied network-based leader-following consensus of nonlinear multi-agent coupled systems by using distributed impulsive control. In the same way, researchers [36] used coupled systems under impulsive conditions to investigate a process of saturated control problems. Moreover, a coupled system with impulsive conditions addressing networks problems has been studied for stability theory in [37]. Therefore, motivated from the aforementioned discussion, in this paper, we investigate a coupled system of Caputo fractional piecewise-order impulsive problem with a variable kernel, as given in (1). Here, the order is piecewise and the kernel has an variable power. The considered problem is described as the following:

$$\begin{cases} {}^cD_{[x]}^{\varrho(x)}w(x) = f(x,u(x),w(x)), & x \in \mathbb{S} = [0,T], x \neq x_i, \\ w(0) = w_0 + \rho(w), \\ \Delta w(x)\,|_{x=x_i} = w(x_i^+) - w(x_i^-) = w(x_i^+) - w(x_i) \\ \quad = \mathcal{I}_i w(x_i^-), \; i = 1,\ldots m, \\ {}^cD_{[x]}^{\varrho(x)}u(x) = \mathcal{F}(x,w(x),u(x)), & x \in \mathbb{S} = [0,T], x \neq x_i, \\ i = 1,\ldots,\aleph, \quad 0 < \varrho(x) \leq 1, \\ u(0) = u_0 + \phi(u), \\ \Delta u(x)\,|_{x=x_i} = u(x_i^+) - u(x_i^-) = u(x_i^+) - u(x_i) \\ \quad = \overline{\mathcal{I}}_i u(x_i^-), \; i = 1,\ldots m. \end{cases} \quad (1)$$

The variable-order $\varrho(x)$ is defined as a finite sequence of real numbers in the interval $(0,1]$ as

$$\varrho(x) = \begin{cases} \varrho_0, & 0 < x \leq x_1 \\ \varrho_1, & x_1 < x \leq x_2 \\ \vdots \\ \varrho_m, & x_m < x \leq T \end{cases} \quad (2)$$

The Caputo derivative, ${}^cD_{[x]}^{\varrho_i, g_i} u(x)$ of order ϱ_i of function $u(x)$ with respect to a finite sequence of nonnegative increasing functions g_i; $(i = 0, 1, \ldots, m)$, is defined by

$${}^cD_{[x]}^{\varrho(x)} u(x) = \begin{cases} {}^cD_{[x]}^{\varrho_0, g_0} u(x), & 0 < x \leq x_1 \\ {}^cD_{[x]}^{\varrho_1, g_1} u(x), & x_1 < x \leq x_2 \\ \vdots \\ {}^cD_{[x]}^{\varrho_m, g_m} u(x), & x_m < x \leq T \end{cases} \quad (3)$$

$f, \mathcal{F} : \mathbb{S} \times \mathbb{R} \times \mathbb{R} \to \mathbb{R}$ are given piecewise continuous functions, $\mathcal{I}_\ell, \overline{\mathcal{I}}_\ell : \mathbb{R} \to \mathbb{R}$, are impulsive continuous functions, $u_0 \in \mathbb{R}$, x_ℓ satisfy $0 = x_0 < x_1 < \ldots < x_m < x_{m+1} = T$, $\Delta w\,|_{x=x_\ell} = w(x_\ell^+) - w(x_\ell^-) = w(x_\ell^+) - w(x_\ell)$, $w(x_\ell^+) = \lim_{\nu \to 0^+} w(x_\ell + \nu)$, $w(x^-) = \lim_{\nu \to 0^-} w(x_\ell + \nu)$ and $\Delta u\,|_{x=x_\ell} = u(x_\ell^+) - u(x_\ell^-) = u(x_\ell^+) - u(x_\ell)$, $u(x_\ell^+) = \lim_{\nu \to 0^+} u(x_\ell + \nu)$, $u(x^-) = \lim_{\nu \to 0^-} u(x_\ell + \nu)$. Also, $[x] = x_\ell$ if $x \in (x_\ell, x_{\ell+1}]$, $\ell = 0, 1, \ldots$ and $x_0 = 0$.

The rest of the paper is organized as follows: A detailed introduction is given in Section 1. The presentation of the problem is given in Section 2. Section 3 is devoted to the existence theory. Section 4 is related to stability results. Section 5 is devoted to application and its discussion. Section 6 consists of the conclusion. Preliminaries results are given in Appendix A. Appendix B is devoted to the proof of Lemma 1.

3. Existence Theory

This part is devoted to derive sufficient results for the existence theory.

We define the Banach spaces by

$$\mathcal{E}_1 = \Big\{ w : \mathbb{S} \to \mathbb{R} : w \in C(\mathbb{S}_\Bbbk, \mathbb{R}) \text{ and } w(x_\Bbbk^+),\ w(x_\Bbbk^-),$$

$$\text{there exists } \Delta w(x_\Bbbk) = w(x_\Bbbk^+) - w(x_\Bbbk^-) \text{ for } \Bbbk = 1, 2, \ldots, \aleph \Big\},$$

and

$$\mathcal{E}_2 = \Big\{ u : \mathbb{S} \to \mathbb{R} : u \in C(\mathbb{S}_\Bbbk, \mathbb{R}), \text{and } u(x_\Bbbk^+),\ u(x_\Bbbk^-),$$

$$\text{there exists } \Delta u(x_\Bbbk) = u(x_\Bbbk^+) - u(x_\Bbbk^-) \text{ for } \Bbbk = 1, 2, \ldots, \aleph \Big\}$$

with respect to the norms $\|w\| = \max_{x \in \mathbb{S}} |w(x)|$ and $\|u\| = \max_{x \in \mathbb{S}} |u(x)|$. Then, the product space, denoted by $\mathcal{E}$, i.e, $\mathcal{E}_1 \times \mathcal{E}_2 = \mathcal{E}$, is also a Banach space with the norm given by $\|(w, u)\| = \|w\| + \|u\|$. We set $\mathbb{S}' := \mathbb{S} \setminus \{x_1, \ldots, x_\aleph\}$.

Lemma 1. *Let $\varrho \in (0, 1]$ and let $\varphi : \mathbb{S} \to \mathbb{R}$ be continuous. A function $w \in \mathcal{E}$ is solution of the fractional integral equation*

$$w(x) = \begin{cases} w_0 + \rho(w) + \dfrac{1}{\Gamma(\varrho_0)} \displaystyle\int_0^x h_0'(z)(h_0(x) - h_0(z))^{\varrho_0-1} \varphi(z) dz, & \text{if } x \in [0, x_1], \\[1em] w_0 + \rho(w) + \dfrac{1}{\Gamma(\varrho_0)} \displaystyle\int_0^{x_1} h_0'(z)(h_0(x_1) - h_0(z))^{\varrho_0-1} \varphi(z) dz \\[0.5em] \quad + \dfrac{1}{\Gamma(\varrho_1)} \displaystyle\int_{x_1}^x h_1'(z)(h_1(x) - h_1(z))^{\varrho_1-1} \varphi(z) dz + \mathcal{I}_1 w(x_1^-), & \text{if } x \in (x_1, x_2], \\[0.5em] \vdots \\[0.5em] w_0 + \rho(w) + \displaystyle\sum_{i=1}^{\Bbbk} \mathcal{I}_i w(x_i^-) + \displaystyle\sum_{i=1}^{\Bbbk} \dfrac{1}{\Gamma(\varrho_{i-1})} \displaystyle\int_{x_{i-1}}^{x_i} h_{i-1}'(z)(h_{i-1}(x_i) - h_{i-1}(z))^{\varrho_{i-1}-1} \varphi(z) dz \\[0.5em] \quad + \dfrac{1}{\Gamma(\varrho_\Bbbk)} \displaystyle\int_{x_\Bbbk}^x h_\Bbbk'(z)(h_\Bbbk(x) - h_\Bbbk(z))^{\varrho_\Bbbk-1} \varphi(z) dz, & \text{if } x \in (x_\Bbbk, x_{\Bbbk+1}],\ \Bbbk = 1, \ldots, \aleph. \end{cases} \quad (4)$$

if and only if it is a solution of the impulsive problem:

$$^c D_{[x]}^{\varrho(x)} w(x) = \varphi(x),\ x \in \mathbb{S},$$
$$t \neq x_\Bbbk,\ \Bbbk = 1, \ldots, \aleph, \quad (5)$$

$$\Delta w(x_\Bbbk) = w(x_\Bbbk^+) - w(x_\Bbbk^-) = w(x_\Bbbk^+) - w(x_\Bbbk) = \mathcal{I}_\Bbbk w(x_\Bbbk^-),\ \Bbbk = 1, \ldots, \aleph, \quad (6)$$

$$w(0) = w_0 + \rho(w), \quad (7)$$

where $[x] = x_\Bbbk$ if $x \in (x_\Bbbk, x_{\Bbbk+1}]$, $\Bbbk = 0, 1, \ldots$ and $x_0 = 0$.

Proof. The proof is given in Appendix B. □

Corollary 1. *As a consequence of Lemma 1, the solution of the coupled system (1) is given by*

$$w(x) = \begin{cases} w_0 + \rho(w) + \dfrac{1}{\Gamma(\varrho_0)} \int_0^x h_0'(z)(h_0(x) - h_0(z))^{\varrho_0-1} f(z, u(z), w(z)) dz, & \text{if } x \in [0, x_1], \\ w_0 + \rho(w) + \dfrac{1}{\Gamma(\varrho_0)} \int_0^{x_1} h_0'(z)(h_0(x_1) - h_0(z))^{\varrho_0-1} f(z, u(z), w(z)) dz \\ \quad + \dfrac{1}{\Gamma(\varrho_1)} \int_{x_1}^x h_1'(z)(h_1(x) - h_1(z))^{\varrho_1-1} f(z, u(z), w(z)) dz + \mathcal{I}_1 w(x_1^-) & \text{if } x \in (x_1, x_2], \\ \vdots \\ w_0 + \rho(w) + \sum_{i=1}^{\Bbbk} \mathcal{I}_i w(x_i^-) + \sum_{i=1}^{\Bbbk} \dfrac{1}{\Gamma(\varrho_{i-1})} \int_{x_{i-1}}^{x_i} h_{i-1}'(z)(h_{i-1}(x_i) - h_{i-1}(z))^{\varrho_{i-1}-1} \\ \quad \times f(z, u(z), w(z)) dz + \dfrac{1}{\Gamma(\varrho_{\Bbbk})} \int_{x_{\Bbbk}}^x h_{\Bbbk}'(z)(h_{\Bbbk}(x) - h_{\Bbbk}(z))^{\varrho_{\Bbbk}-1} f(z, u(z), w(z)) dz, \\ \text{if } x \in (x_{\Bbbk}, x_{\Bbbk+1}], \ \Bbbk = 1, \dots, \aleph. \end{cases}$$

$$u(x) = \begin{cases} u_0 + \phi(u) + \dfrac{1}{\Gamma(\varrho_0)} \int_0^x h_0'(z)(h_0(x) - h_0(z))^{\varrho_0-1} \mathcal{F}(z, u(z), w(z)) dz, & \text{if } x \in [0, x_1], \\ u_0 + \phi(u) + \dfrac{1}{\Gamma(\varrho_0)} \int_0^{x_1} h_0'(z)(h_0(x_1) - h_0(z))^{\varrho_0-1} \mathcal{F}(z, u(z), w(z)) dz \\ \quad + \dfrac{1}{\Gamma(\varrho_1)} \int_{x_1}^x h_1'(z)(h_1(x) - h_1(z))^{\varrho_1-1} \mathcal{F}(z, u(z), w(z)) dz + \mathcal{I}_1 u(x_1^-) & \text{if } x \in (x_1, x_2], \\ \vdots \\ u_0 + \phi(u) + \sum_{i=1}^{\Bbbk} \mathcal{I}_i u(x_i^-) + \sum_{i=1}^{\Bbbk} \dfrac{1}{\Gamma(\varrho_{i-1})} \int_{x_{i-1}}^{x_i} h_{i-1}'(z)(h_{i-1}(x_i) - h_{i-1}(z))^{\varrho_{i-1}-1} \\ \quad \times \mathcal{F}(z, u(z), w(z)) dz + \dfrac{1}{\Gamma(\varrho_{\Bbbk})} \int_{x_{\Bbbk}}^x h_{\Bbbk}'(z)(h_{\Bbbk}(x) - h_{\Bbbk}(z))^{\varrho_{\Bbbk}-1} \mathcal{F}(z, u(z), w(z)) dz, \\ \text{if } x \in (x_{\Bbbk}, x_{\Bbbk+1}], \ \Bbbk = 1, \dots, \aleph. \end{cases} \tag{8}$$

Now to go ahead for the main results, we define the following operators

$$\mathcal{N} = \left(\mathcal{N}_1, \mathcal{N}_2\right) : \mathcal{E}_1 \times \mathcal{E}_2 \to \mathcal{E}_1 \times \mathcal{E}_2$$

by

$$\mathcal{N}(w, u) = \left(\mathcal{N}_1 w, \mathcal{N}_2 u\right).$$

Which may be expressed as

$$(\mathcal{N}_1 w)(x) = \begin{cases} w_0 + \rho(w) + \dfrac{1}{\Gamma(\varrho_0)} \int_0^x h_0'(z)(h_0(x) - h_0(z))^{\varrho_0-1} f(z, u(z), w(z)) dz, & \text{if } x \in [0, x_1], \\ w_0 + \rho(w) + \dfrac{1}{\Gamma(\varrho_0)} \int_0^{x_1} h_0'(z)(h_0(x_1) - h_0(z))^{\varrho_0-1} f(z, u(z), w(z)) dz \\ \quad + \dfrac{1}{\Gamma(\varrho_1)} \int_{x_1}^x h_1'(z)(h_1(x) - h_1(z))^{\varrho_1-1} f(z, u(z), w(z)) dz + \mathcal{I}_1 w(x_1^-) & \text{if } x \in (x_1, x_2], \\ \vdots \\ w_0 + \rho(w) + \sum_{i=1}^{\Bbbk} \mathcal{I}_i w(x_i^-) + \sum_{i=1}^{\Bbbk} \dfrac{1}{\Gamma(\varrho_{i-1})} \int_{x_{i-1}}^{x_i} h_{i-1}'(z)(h_{i-1}(x_i) - h_{i-1}(z))^{\varrho_{i-1}-1} \\ \quad \times f(z, u(z), w(z)) dz + \dfrac{1}{\Gamma(\varrho_{\Bbbk})} \int_{x_{\Bbbk}}^x h_{\Bbbk}'(z)(h_{\Bbbk}(x) - h_{\Bbbk}(z))^{\varrho_{\Bbbk}-1} f(z, u(z), w(z)) dz, \\ \text{if } x \in (x_{\Bbbk}, x_{\Bbbk+1}], \ \Bbbk = 1, \dots, \aleph, \end{cases} \tag{9}$$

and

$$(\mathcal{N}_2 u)(x) = \begin{cases} u_0 + \phi(u) + \dfrac{1}{\Gamma(\varrho_0)} \displaystyle\int_0^x h_0'(z)(h_0(x) - h_0(z))^{\varrho_0 - 1} \mathcal{F}(z, u(z), w(z)) dz, & \text{if } x \in [0, x_1], \\[6pt] u_0 + \phi(u) + \dfrac{1}{\Gamma(\varrho_0)} \displaystyle\int_0^{x_1} h_0'(z)(h_0(x_1) - h_0(z))^{\varrho_0 - 1} \mathcal{F}(z, u(z), w(z)) dz \\[4pt] \quad + \dfrac{1}{\Gamma(\varrho_1)} \displaystyle\int_{x_1}^x h_1'(z)(h_1(x) - h_1(z))^{\varrho_1 - 1} \mathcal{F}(z, u(z), w(z)) dz + \mathcal{I}_1 u(x_1^-) & \text{if } x \in (x_1, x_2], \\[4pt] \vdots \\[4pt] u_0 + \phi(u) + \displaystyle\sum_{i=1}^{\Bbbk} \mathcal{I}_i u(x_i^-) + \sum_{i=1}^{\Bbbk} \dfrac{1}{\Gamma(\varrho_{i-1})} \int_{x_{i-1}}^{x_i} h_{i-1}'(z)(h_{i-1}(x_i) - h_{i-1}(z))^{\varrho_{i-1} - 1} \\[4pt] \quad \times \mathcal{F}(z, u(z), w(z)) dz + \dfrac{1}{\Gamma(\varrho_{\Bbbk})} \displaystyle\int_{x_{\Bbbk}}^x h_{\Bbbk}'(z)(h_{\Bbbk}(x) - h_{\Bbbk}(z))^{\varrho_{\Bbbk} - 1} \mathcal{F}(z, u(z), w(z)) dz, \\[4pt] \text{if } x \in (x_{\Bbbk}, x_{\Bbbk+1}], \ \Bbbk = 1, \ldots, \aleph. \end{cases} \qquad (10)$$

Prior to proving the main results, we give the following accompanying hypotheses:

Hypothesis 1. *For $f, \mathcal{F} : \mathbb{S} \times \mathbb{R} \times \mathbb{R} \to \mathbb{R}$, let there exist constants $k_f, k_\mathcal{F} > 0$, so that for any $x \in \mathbb{S}$ and $(u, w), (u^*, w^*) \in \mathcal{E}_1 \times \mathcal{E}_2$, we have*

$$|f(x, u, w) - f(x, u^*, w^*)| \leq k_f \left(|u - u^*| + |w - w^*| \right),$$

and

$$|\mathcal{F}(x, u, w) - \mathcal{F}(x, u^*, w^*)| \leq k_\mathcal{F} \left(|u - u^*| + |w - w^*| \right).$$

Hypothesis 2. *For $\mathcal{I}_{\Bbbk}, \overline{\mathcal{I}}_{\Bbbk} : \mathbb{R} \to \mathbb{R}$, and any $(w, u), (w^*, u^*) \in \mathcal{E}_1 \times \mathcal{E}_2$,, let there exist constants $k_\mathcal{I}, k_{\overline{\mathcal{I}}} > 0$, so that*

$$|\mathcal{I}_{\Bbbk}(w) - \mathcal{I}_{\Bbbk}(w^*)| \leq k_\mathcal{I} |w - w^*|$$

and

$$|\overline{\mathcal{I}}_{\Bbbk}(u) - \overline{\mathcal{I}}_{\Bbbk}(u^*)| \leq k_{\overline{\mathcal{I}}} |u - u^*|, \ \Bbbk = 1, \ldots, \aleph.$$

Hypothesis 3. *There exist bounded functions $\mathbb{B}_w, \mathbb{C}_w, \mathbb{D}_w, \mathbb{B}_u, \mathbb{C}_u, \mathbb{D}_u \in C(\mathbb{S}, \mathbb{R})$, so that*

$$|f(x, u, w)| \leq \mathbb{B}_w(x) + \mathbb{C}_w(x)|u| + \mathbb{D}_w(x)|w|, \textit{for each } (x, u, w) \in \mathbb{S} \times \mathbb{R} \times \mathbb{R}$$

and

$$|\mathcal{F}(x, u, w)| \leq \mathbb{B}_u(x) + \mathbb{C}_u(x)|u| + \mathbb{D}_u(x)|w|, \textit{for each } (x, u, w) \in \mathbb{S} \times \mathbb{R} \times \mathbb{R}.$$

Hypothesis 4. *There exist η_1, η_2 and $\eta_3, \eta_4 > 0$, so that*

$$|\mathcal{I}_{\Bbbk}(w)| \leq \eta_1 + \eta_2 |w|,$$

$$|\overline{\mathcal{I}}_{\Bbbk}(u)| \leq \eta_3 + \eta_4 |u|; \ \Bbbk = 1, \ldots, \aleph, \ u \in \mathbb{R}.$$

Hypothesis 5. *There exist constants $k_\rho, k_\phi > 0$, so that*

$$|\rho(w(x))| \leq k_\rho$$

and

$$|\phi(u(x))| \leq k_\phi.$$

Hypothesis 6. *There exist constants $k_\rho^*, k_\phi^* > 0$, so that*

$$|\rho(w(x)) - \rho(w^*(x))| \leq k_\rho^* |w - w^*|$$

and

$$|\phi(u(x)) - \phi(u^*(x))| \leq k_\phi^* |u - u^*|.$$

Theorem 1. *Let $f : \mathbb{S} \times \mathbb{R} \times \mathbb{R} \to \mathbb{R}$ be continuous and $(H_3) - (H_4)$ hold. If*

$$\zeta \geq \max\left(\frac{\Delta_0 + k + \mathbb{BP}}{1 - \xi\mathbb{P}}, \frac{\Delta_0 + k + \aleph\eta + \mathbb{QB}}{1 - (\aleph\eta^* + \xi\mathbb{Q})}\right), \quad (11)$$

then the impulsive problem (1) has a solution in $\mathcal{E}$.

Proof. We apply Theorem A1 to show that $\mathcal{N}$ as defined in 9 has a fixed point. We set $\mathcal{B} = \{(w, u) \in \mathcal{E}_1 \times \mathcal{E}_2 : \|(w, u)\| \leq \zeta\}$. This operator, $\mathcal{N}$, is a closed, bounded and convex subset of $\mathcal{B}$, and it is verified in the following steps.

Step 1: In every step, we discuss two cases.

Case I

According to (9), for $(w, u) \in \mathcal{B}_\zeta$ and $x \in [0, x_1]$, we have

$$\begin{aligned}
|\mathcal{N}_1 w(x)| &\leq |w_0| + |\rho(w(x))| + \frac{1}{\Gamma(\varrho_0)} \int_0^x h_0'(z)(h_0(x) - h_0(z))^{\varrho_0 - 1} |f(z, u(z), w(z))| dz \\
&\leq |w_0| + k_\rho + \frac{\left(\mathbb{B}_w + \mathbb{C}_w \|u\| + \mathbb{D}_w \|w\|\right)}{\Gamma(\varrho_0)} \int_0^x h_0'(z)(h_0(x) - h_0(z))^{\varrho_0 - 1} dz \\
&\leq |w_0| + k_\rho + \left(\mathbb{B}_w + \mathbb{C}_w \|u\| + \mathbb{D}_w \|w\|\right) \frac{(h_0(x_1) - h_0(0))^{\varrho_0}}{\Gamma(\varrho_0 + 1)} \\
&\leq |w_0| + k_\rho + \left(\mathbb{B}_w + \mathbb{C}_w \|u\| + \mathbb{D}_w \|w\|\right) \frac{(h_0(T) - h_0(0))^{\varrho_0}}{\Gamma(\varrho_0 + 1)}
\end{aligned} \quad (12)$$

Similarly, using (10), for $(w, u) \in \mathcal{B}_\zeta$ and $x \in [0, x_1]$, we have

$$|\mathcal{N}_2 u(x)| \leq |u_0| + k_\phi + \left(\mathbb{B}_u + \mathbb{C}_u \|u\| + \mathbb{D}_u \|w\|\right) \frac{(h_0(T) - h_0(0))^{\varrho_0}}{\Gamma(\varrho_0 + 1)} \quad (13)$$

From (12) and (13), we have

$$\begin{aligned}
\|\mathcal{N}_1(w, u)\| + \|\mathcal{N}_2(w, u)\| &\leq |w_0| + |u_0| + k_\rho + k_\phi + \Big(\mathbb{B}_u + \mathbb{B}_w + (\mathbb{C}_u + \mathbb{C}_w)\|u\| \\
&\quad + (\mathbb{D}_u + \mathbb{D}_w)\|w\|\Big) \frac{(h_0(T) - h_0(0))^{\varrho_0}}{\Gamma(\varrho_0 + 1)}.
\end{aligned} \quad (14)$$

Or

$$\begin{aligned}
\|\mathcal{N}(w, u)\|_{\mathcal{E}} &\leq \Delta_0 + k + \mathbb{B}\frac{(h_0(T) - h_0(0))^{\varrho_0}}{\Gamma(\varrho_0 + 1)} + \xi\|(w, u)\|\frac{(h_0(T) - h_0(0))^{\varrho_0}}{\Gamma(\varrho_0 + 1)} \\
&\leq \zeta,
\end{aligned} \quad (15)$$

where

$$\zeta \geq \frac{\Delta_0 + k + \mathbb{BP}}{1 - \xi\mathbb{P}}.$$

Thus, $\mathcal{N}(w, u)$ is bounded, and hence, $\mathcal{N}(w, u) \in \mathcal{B}$, which implies that $\mathcal{N}(\mathcal{B}) \subseteq \mathcal{B}$.

Case II

In addition, for interval $(x_\Bbbk, x_{\Bbbk+1}], \Bbbk = 1, \ldots, \aleph$, we have

$$
\begin{aligned}
|\mathcal{N}w(x)| &\leq |w_0| + |\rho(w(x))| + \sum_{0 < x_\Bbbk < x} |\mathcal{I}_\Bbbk w(x_\Bbbk^-)| \\
&+ \sum_{i=1}^{\Bbbk} \frac{1}{\Gamma(\varrho_{i-1})} \int_{x_{i-1}}^{x_i} h'_{i-1}(z)(h_{i-1}(x_i) - h_{i-1}(z))^{\varrho_{i-1}-1} |f(z, u(z), w(z))| dz \\
&+ \frac{1}{\Gamma(\varrho_\Bbbk)} \int_{x_\Bbbk}^{x} h'_\Bbbk(z)(h_\Bbbk(x) - h_\Bbbk(z))^{\varrho_\Bbbk-1} |f(z, u(z), w(z))| dz
\end{aligned}
\quad (16)
$$

Using assumption (H$_3$), (H$_5$) and result (16), we have

$$
\begin{aligned}
|\mathcal{N}_1 w(x)| &\leq |w_0| + k_\rho + \sum_{0 < x_\Bbbk < x} (\eta_1 + \eta_2 |w(x_\Bbbk^-)|) \\
&+ \sum_{i=1}^{\Bbbk} \frac{\left(\mathbb{B}_w + \mathbb{C}_w \|u\| + \mathbb{D}_w \|w\|\right)}{\Gamma(\varrho_{i-1})} \int_{x_{i-1}}^{x_i} h'_{i-1}(z)(h_{i-1}(x_i) - h_{i-1}(z))^{\varrho_{i-1}-1} dz \\
&+ \frac{\left(\mathbb{B}_w + \mathbb{C}_w \|u\| + \mathbb{D}_w \|w\|\right)}{\Gamma(\varrho_\Bbbk)} \int_{x_\Bbbk}^{x} h'_\Bbbk(z)(h_\Bbbk(x) - h_\Bbbk(z))^{\varrho_\Bbbk-1} dz \\
&\leq |w_0| + k_\rho + \aleph(\eta_1 + \eta_2 \|w\|) + \left(\mathbb{B}_w + \mathbb{C}_w \|u\| + \mathbb{D}_w \|w\|\right) \\
&\times \left(\sum_{i=1}^{\Bbbk} \frac{(h_{i-1}(x_i) - h_{i-1}(x_{i-1}))^{\varrho_{i-1}}}{\Gamma(\varrho_{i-1}+1)} + \frac{(h_\Bbbk(x) - h_\Bbbk(x_\Bbbk))^{\varrho_\Bbbk}}{\Gamma(\varrho_\Bbbk+1)}\right).
\end{aligned}
\quad (17)
$$

Similarly, we obtain the following result for the second operator

$$
\begin{aligned}
|\mathcal{N}_2 u(x)| &\leq |u_0| + k_\phi + \aleph(\eta_1 + \eta_2 \|w\|) + \aleph(\eta_3 + \eta_4 \|u\|) + \left(\mathbb{B}_u + \mathbb{C}_u \|u\| + \mathbb{D}_u \|w\|\right) \\
&\times \left(\sum_{i=1}^{\Bbbk} \frac{(h_{i-1}(x_i) - h_{i-1}(x_{i-1}))^{\varrho_{i-1}}}{\Gamma(\varrho_{i-1}+1)} + \frac{(h_\Bbbk(x) - h_\Bbbk(x_\Bbbk))^{\varrho_\Bbbk}}{\Gamma(\varrho_\Bbbk+1)}\right).
\end{aligned}
\quad (18)
$$

Using the notations as used in Case I, we have, from (17) and (18),

$$
\begin{aligned}
\|\mathcal{N}_1(w,u)\| &+ \|\mathcal{N}_2(w,u)\| \leq \Delta_0 + k + \aleph\eta \\
&+ \mathbb{B}\left(\sum_{i=1}^{\Bbbk} \frac{(h_{i-1}(x_i) - h_{i-1}(x_{i-1}))^{\varrho_{i-1}}}{\Gamma(\varrho_{i-1}+1)} + \frac{(h_\Bbbk(x) - h_\Bbbk(x_\Bbbk))^{\varrho_\Bbbk}}{\Gamma(\varrho_\Bbbk+1)}\right) \\
&+ \aleph\eta^* \|(w,u)\|_\mathcal{E} + \left(\sum_{i=1}^{\Bbbk} \frac{(h_{i-1}(x_i) - h_{i-1}(x_{i-1}))^{\varrho_{i-1}}}{\Gamma(\varrho_{i-1}+1)} + \frac{(h_\Bbbk(x) - h_\Bbbk(x_\Bbbk))^{\varrho_\Bbbk}}{\Gamma(\varrho_\Bbbk+1)}\right) \xi \|(w,u)\| \\
&\leq \Delta_0 + k + \aleph\eta + \mathbb{B}\left(\sum_{i=1}^{\Bbbk} \frac{(h_{i-1}(x_i) - h_{i-1}(x_{i-1}))^{\varrho_{i-1}}}{\Gamma(\varrho_{i-1}+1)} + \frac{(h_\Bbbk(x) - h_\Bbbk(x_\Bbbk))^{\varrho_\Bbbk}}{\Gamma(\varrho_\Bbbk+1)}\right) \\
&+ \left(\aleph\eta^* + \xi\left(\sum_{i=1}^{\Bbbk} \frac{(h_{i-1}(x_i) - h_{i-1}(x_{i-1}))^{\varrho_{i-1}}}{\Gamma(\varrho_{i-1}+1)} + \frac{(h_\Bbbk(x) - h_\Bbbk(x_\Bbbk))^{\varrho_\Bbbk}}{\Gamma(\varrho_\Bbbk+1)}\right)\right) \zeta \\
&\leq \zeta,
\end{aligned}
\quad (19)
$$

where $\eta = \eta_1 + \eta_3$ and $\eta^* = \max(\eta_2, \eta_4)$.

Now for sake of simplicity, let us denote $\sum_{i=1}^{\Bbbk} \frac{(h_{i-1}(x_i)-h_{i-1}(x_{i-1}))^{\varrho_{i-1}}}{\Gamma(\varrho_{i-1}+1)} + \frac{(h_{\Bbbk}(x)-h_{\Bbbk}(x_{\Bbbk}))^{\varrho_{\Bbbk}}}{\Gamma(\varrho_{\Bbbk}+1)}$ by $\mathbb{Q}$. Then, we have

$$\|\mathscr{N}(w,u)\|_{\mathcal{E}} \leq \frac{\Delta_0 + k + \aleph\eta + \mathbb{QB}}{1-(\aleph\eta^* + \xi\mathbb{Q})} \leq \zeta, \tag{20}$$

Now if

$$\zeta \geq \max\left(\frac{\Delta_0 + k + \mathbb{BP}}{1-\xi\mathbb{P}}, \frac{\Delta_0 + k + \aleph\eta + \mathbb{QB}}{1-(\aleph\eta^* + \xi\mathbb{Q})}\right),$$

then, $\|\mathscr{N}(w,u)\|_{\mathcal{E}} \leq \zeta$. This means that $\mathscr{N}$ maps $\mathcal{B}_\zeta$ onto itself.

Step 2: $\mathscr{N}$ is continuous.

Let $\{w_s\}_{s\in\mathbb{N}}$ be a sequence, so that $w_s \to w$ on $\mathcal{B}_\zeta$. The continuity of $f(\cdot, u, w)$, $\mathcal{F}(\cdot, u, w)$, $\mathcal{I}_{\Bbbk}(w)$, $\overline{\mathcal{I}}_{\Bbbk}(w)$, $\rho(w)$ and $\phi(u)$ imply that $f(\cdot, u_s, w_s) \to f(\cdot, u, w)$, $\mathcal{F}(\cdot, u_s, w_s) \to \mathcal{F}(\cdot, u, w)$, $\mathcal{I}_{\Bbbk}(w_s) \to \mathcal{I}_{\Bbbk}(w)$, $\overline{\mathcal{I}}_{\Bbbk}(w_s) \to \overline{\mathcal{I}}_{\Bbbk}(w)$, $\rho(w_s) \to \rho(w)$ and $\phi(u_s) \to \phi(u)$ as $s \to \infty$. Moreover, for each $x \in [0, x_1]$,

$$|\mathscr{N}_1(w_s(x), u_s(x)) - \mathscr{N}_1(w(x), u(x))| \leq |\rho(w_s(x)) - \rho(w(x))|$$
$$+ \frac{1}{\Gamma(\varrho_0)} \int_0^x h_0'(z)(h_0(x)-h_0(z))^{\varrho_0-1}|f(z, u_s(z), w_s(z)) - f(z, u(z), w(z))|dz.$$

Using the assumptions and simplifying, we have

$$\|\mathscr{N}_1(w_s, u_s) - \mathscr{N}_1(w, u)\|$$
$$\leq k_\rho^* \|w_s - w\| + \frac{k_f}{\Gamma(\varrho_0)} \int_0^x h_0'(z)(h_0(x)-h_0(z))^{\varrho_0-1}\left(\|u_s - u\| + \|w_s - w\|\right)dz$$
$$\leq k_\rho^* \|w_s - w\| + \frac{k_f(h_0(x_1)-h_0(0))^{\varrho_0}}{\Gamma(\varrho_0+1)}\left(\|u_s - u\| + \|w_s - w\|\right). \tag{21}$$

Similarly, we obtain

$$\|\mathscr{N}_2(w_s, u_s) - \mathscr{N}_2(w, u)\|$$
$$\leq k_\phi^* \|u_s - u\| + \frac{k_f(h_0(x_1)-h_0(0))^{\varrho_0}}{\Gamma(\varrho_0+1)}\left(\|u_s - u\| + \|w_s - w\|\right). \tag{22}$$

Looking at the inequalities (21) and (22), we see that as $s \to \infty$, w_s and u_s converge to w and u, respectively. This implies that $\mathscr{N}_1(w_s, u_s) \to \mathscr{N}_1(w, u)$ and $\mathscr{N}_2(w_s, u_s) \to \mathscr{N}_2(w, u)$. This means that $\mathscr{N}_1$ and $\mathscr{N}_2$ are continuous. Consequently, the operator $\mathscr{N}$ is continuous at $x \in [0, x_1]$. In the same way, we may show that $\mathscr{N}$ is continuous at $x \in (x_{\Bbbk}, x_{\Bbbk+1}]$, $\Bbbk = 1, \ldots, \aleph$.

Step 3: $\mathscr{N}$ maps bounded sets onto equi-continuous sets of $\mathcal{E}$.

Case I

Assume that $\mathcal{B}_\zeta$ is a bounded set as in Steps 1 and 2, and $w \in \mathcal{B}_\zeta$. For arbitrary $\tau_1, \tau_2 \in [0, x_1]$, $\tau_1 < \tau_2$, we obtain

$$|\mathcal{N}_1(w,u)(\tau_2) - \mathcal{N}_1(w,u)(\tau_1)| \leq |\rho(w(\tau_2)) - \rho(w(\tau_1))|$$
$$+ \frac{1}{\Gamma(\varrho_0)} \int_0^{\tau_1} h_0'(z) \Big((h_0(\tau_2) - h_0(z))^{\varrho_0 - 1} - (h_0(\tau_1) - h_0(z))^{\varrho_0 - 1} \Big) |f(z, u(z), w(z))| dz$$
$$+ \frac{1}{\Gamma(\varrho_0)} \int_{\tau_1}^{\tau_2} h_0'(z) (h_0(\tau_2) - h_0(z))^{\varrho_0 - 1} |f(z, u(z), w(z))| dz$$

$$\leq \|\rho(w(\tau_2)) - \rho(w(\tau_1))\| + \frac{\Big(\mathbb{B}_w + \mathbb{C}_w \|u\| + \mathbb{D}_w \|w\|\Big)}{(\Gamma(\varrho_0))}$$
$$\times \int_0^{\tau_1} h_0'(z) \Big((h_0(\tau_1) - h_0(z))^{\varrho_0 - 1} - (h_0(\tau_2) - h_0(z))^{\varrho_0 - 1} \Big) dz$$
$$+ \frac{\Big(\mathbb{B}_w + \mathbb{C}_w \|u\| + \mathbb{D}_w \|w\|\Big)}{\Gamma(\varrho_0)} \int_{\tau_1}^{\tau_2} h_0'(z) (h_0(\tau_2) - h_0(z))^{\varrho_0 - 1} dz$$

$$\leq \|\rho(w(\tau_2)) - \rho(w(\tau_1))\| + \frac{\Big(\mathbb{B}_w + \mathbb{C}_w \|u\| + \mathbb{D}_w \|w\|\Big)}{\Gamma(\varrho_0 + 1)}$$
$$\times \Big((h_0(\tau_2) - h_0(\tau_1))^{\varrho_0} + (h_0(\tau_1) - h_0(0))^{\varrho_0} - (h_0(\tau_2) - h_0(0))^{\varrho_0} \Big)$$
$$+ \frac{\Big(\mathbb{B}_w + \mathbb{C}_w \|u\| + \mathbb{D}_w \|w\|\Big)}{\Gamma(\varrho_0 + 1)} (h_0(\tau_2) - h_0(\tau_1))^{\varrho_0}$$

$$\leq \|\rho(w(\tau_2)) - \rho(w(\tau_1))\| + \frac{2\Big(\mathbb{B}_w + \mathbb{C}_w \|u\| + \mathbb{D}_w \|w\|\Big)}{\Gamma(\varrho_0 + 1)} (h_0(\tau_2) - h_0(\tau_1))^{\varrho_0}. \quad (23)$$

Similarly, we obtain

$$|\mathcal{N}_2(w,u)(\tau_2) - \mathcal{N}_2(w,u)(\tau_1)|$$
$$\leq \|\phi(u(\tau_2)) - \phi(u(\tau_1))\| + \frac{2\Big(\mathbb{B}_w + \mathbb{C}_w \|u\| + \mathbb{D}_w \|w\|\Big)}{\Gamma(\varrho_0 + 1)} (h_0(\tau_2) - h_0(\tau_1))^{\varrho_0}. \quad (24)$$

Since h_0 is continuous, $|\mathcal{N}_1 w(\tau_2) - \mathcal{N}_1 w(\tau_1)| \to 0$ and $|\mathcal{N}_2 w(\tau_2) - \mathcal{N}_2 w(\tau_1)| \to 0$ as $\tau_2 \to \tau_1$.

Case II

By and large, for $x \in (x_\Bbbk, x_{\Bbbk+1}]$, $\Bbbk = 1, \ldots, \aleph$, we get the accompanying inequality

$$|\mathcal{N}_1(w,u)(\tau_2) - \mathcal{N}_1(w,u)(\tau_1)| \leq |\rho(w(\tau_2)) - \rho(w(\tau_1))| + \sum_{0 < x_\Bbbk < \tau_2 - \tau_1} |\mathcal{I}_\Bbbk w(x_\Bbbk^-)|$$

$$+ \frac{1}{\Gamma(\varrho_\Bbbk)} \int_{x_\Bbbk}^{\tau_1} h'_\Bbbk(z) \left((h_\Bbbk(\tau_1) - h_\Bbbk(z))^{\varrho_\Bbbk - 1} - (h_\Bbbk(\tau_2) - h_\Bbbk(z))^{\varrho_\Bbbk - 1} \right)$$

$$\times |f(z, u(z), w(z))| dz + \frac{1}{\Gamma(\varrho_\Bbbk)} \int_{\tau_1}^{\tau_2} h'_\Bbbk(z) (h_\Bbbk(\tau_2) - h_\Bbbk(z))^{\varrho_\Bbbk - 1} |f(z, u(z), w(z))| dz$$

$$\leq \|\rho(w(\tau_2)) - \rho(w(\tau_1))\| + \aleph(\tau_2 - \tau_1)(\eta_1 + \eta_2 \zeta) + \frac{\left(\mathbb{B}_w + \mathbb{C}_w \|u\| + \mathbb{D}_w \|w\|\right)}{\Gamma(\varrho_\Bbbk + 1)}$$

$$\times \left((h_\Bbbk(\tau_2) - h_\Bbbk(\tau_1))^{\varrho_\Bbbk} + (h_\Bbbk(\tau_1) - h_\Bbbk(x_\Bbbk))^{\varrho_\Bbbk} - (h_\Bbbk(\tau_2) - h_\Bbbk(x_\Bbbk))^{\varrho_\Bbbk} \right)$$

$$+ \frac{\left(\mathbb{B}_w + \mathbb{C}_w \|u\| + \mathbb{D}_w \|w\|\right)}{\Gamma(\varrho_\Bbbk + 1)} [(h_\Bbbk(\tau_2) - h_\Bbbk(\tau_1))^{\varrho_\Bbbk}]$$

$$\leq \|\rho(w(\tau_2)) - \rho(w(\tau_1))\| + \aleph(\tau_2 - \tau_1)(\eta_1 + \eta_2 \zeta) + \frac{2\left(\mathbb{B}_w + \mathbb{C}_w \|u\| + \mathbb{D}_w \|w\|\right)}{\Gamma(\varrho_\Bbbk + 1)}$$

$$\times (h_\Bbbk(\tau_2) - h_\Bbbk(\tau_1))^{\varrho_\Bbbk}. \tag{25}$$

Similarly, we obtain

$$|\mathcal{N}_2(w,u)(\tau_2) - \mathcal{N}_2(w,u)(\tau_1)| \leq \|\phi(u(\tau_2)) - \phi(u(\tau_1))\| + \aleph(\tau_2 - \tau_1)(\eta_3 + \eta_4 \zeta)$$

$$+ \frac{2\left(\mathbb{B}_u + \mathbb{C}_u \|u\| + \mathbb{D}_u \|w\|\right)}{\Gamma(\varrho_\Bbbk + 1)} (h_\Bbbk(\tau_2) - h_\Bbbk(\tau_1))^{\varrho_\Bbbk}. \tag{26}$$

Since $h_\Bbbk$ ($\Bbbk = 1, 2, ..., \aleph$) is continuous, that is

$$|\mathcal{N}_1(w,u)(\tau_2) - \mathcal{N}_1(w,u)(\tau_1)| \to 0$$

and

$$|\mathcal{N}_2(w,u)(\tau_2) - \mathcal{N}_2(w,u)(\tau_1)| \to 0 \text{ as } \tau_2 \to \tau_1.$$

Hence, $\mathcal{N}_1(w,u)$, $\mathcal{N}_2(w,u)$ are equi-continuous. Consequently $\mathcal{N}(w,u)$ is equi-continuous on $\mathbb{S}$.

On the other hand, according to Step 1, $\mathcal{N}\mathcal{B}_\zeta \subset \mathcal{B}_\zeta$ is uniformly bounded. Hence, applying the Ascoli–Arzela theorem, the family $\{\mathcal{N}(w,u) : (w,u) \in \mathcal{B}_\zeta\}$ is a relatively compact subset of $\mathcal{E}$. Thus, $\mathcal{N} : \mathcal{PC} \to \mathcal{PC}$ is completely continuous. As a consequence of Steps 1–3 together with the Ascoli–Arzela theorem, we conclude that $\mathcal{N}$ has a fixed point in $\mathcal{B}_\zeta$ which indicates that the impulsive problem (1) has a solution in $\mathcal{E}$. □

Theorem 2. *If* (H_1), (H_2) *and* (H_6) *hold with the following condition*

$$\max(\chi_1, \chi_2) < 1, \tag{27}$$

where

$$\chi_1 = k_\rho^* + k_\phi^* + 2(k_f + k_\mathcal{F}) \frac{(h_0(x_1) - h_0(0))^{\varrho_0}}{\Gamma(\varrho_0 + 1)},$$

and

$$\chi_2 = k_\rho^* + k_\phi^* + \aleph(k_\mathcal{I} + k_{\overline{\mathcal{I}}}) + 2(k_f + k_\mathcal{F}) \sum_{i=0}^{\Bbbk} \frac{(h_i(T) - h_i(x_i))^{\varrho_i}}{\Gamma(\varrho_i + 1)},$$

then, the impulsive problem (1) has a unique solution in $\mathcal{E}$.

Proof. Let $\mathcal{N}$ be the operator defined by (9). Then, $\mathcal{N} : \mathcal{PC} \to \mathcal{PC}$ is well defined by Theorem 1. Next, we will utilize Banach's contraction theorem to demonstrate that $\mathcal{N}$ has a fixed point.

Case I

For arbitrary $(w, u), (w^*, u^*) \in \mathcal{E}$ and $x \in [0, x_1]$, we obtain

$$
\begin{aligned}
&|\mathcal{N}_1(w, u)(x) - \mathcal{N}_1(w^*, u^*)(x)| \leq |\rho(w(x)) - \rho(w^*(x))| + \frac{1}{\Gamma(\varrho_0)} \int_0^x h_0'(z)(h_0(x) - h_0(z))^{\varrho_0 - 1} \\
&\times |f(z, u(z), w(z)) - f(z, u^*(z), w^*(z))| dz \\
&\leq k_\rho^* |w(x) - w^*(x)| + \frac{k_f}{\Gamma(\varrho_0)} \int_0^x h_0'(z)(h_0(x) - h_0(z))^{\varrho_0 - 1} \\
&\times \left(|u - u^*| + |w - w^*| \right) dz \\
&\leq \left(k_\rho^* + \frac{k_f (h_0(x_1) - h_0(0))^{\varrho_0}}{\Gamma(\varrho_0 + 1)} \right) \|w - w^*\| + \frac{k_f (h_0(x_1) - h_0(0))^{\varrho_0}}{\Gamma(\varrho_0 + 1)} \|u - u^*\|.
\end{aligned}
\tag{28}
$$

Thus, we have

$$
\begin{aligned}
&|\mathcal{N}_1(w, u)(x) - \mathcal{N}_1(w^*, u^*)(x)| \\
&\leq \left(k_\rho^* + \frac{k_f (h_0(x_1) - h_0(0))^{\varrho_0}}{\Gamma(\varrho_0 + 1)} \right) \|w - w^*\| + \frac{k_f (h_0(x_1) - h_0(0))^{\varrho_0}}{\Gamma(\varrho_0 + 1)} \|u - u^*\|.
\end{aligned}
\tag{29}
$$

Similarly

$$
\begin{aligned}
&|\mathcal{N}_2(w, u)(x) - \mathcal{N}_2(w^*, u^*)(x)| \\
&\leq \left(k_\phi^* + \frac{k_\mathcal{F} (h_0(x_1) - h_0(0))^{\varrho_0}}{\Gamma(\varrho_0 + 1)} \right) \|u - u^*\| + \frac{k_\mathcal{F} (h_0(x_1) - h_0(0))^{\varrho_0}}{\Gamma(\varrho_0 + 1)} \|w - w^*\|.
\end{aligned}
\tag{30}
$$

From (29) and (30), we have

$$
\begin{aligned}
&\|\mathcal{N}(w, u) - \mathcal{N}(w^*, u^*)\| \\
&\leq \left(k_\rho^* + k_\phi^* + 2(k_f + k_\mathcal{F}) \frac{(h_0(x_1) - h_0(0))^{\varrho_0}}{\Gamma(\varrho_0 + 1)} \right) \left(\|w - w^*\| + \|u - u^*\| \right).
\end{aligned}
\tag{31}
$$

Case II

For $x \in (x_\Bbbk, x_{\Bbbk+1}]$, $\Bbbk = 1, \ldots, \aleph$, we have

$$\begin{aligned}
&|\mathscr{N}_1 w(x) - \mathscr{N}_1 w^*(x)| \\
&\leq |\rho(w(x)) - \rho(w^*(x))| + \sum_{0<x_{\Bbbk}<x} |\mathcal{I}_{\Bbbk} w(x_{\Bbbk}^-) - \mathcal{I}_{\Bbbk} w^*(x_{\Bbbk}^-)| \\
&\quad + \sum_{i=1}^{\Bbbk} \frac{1}{\Gamma(\varrho_{i-1})} \int_{x_{i-1}}^{x_i} h'_{i-1}(z)(h_{i-1}(x_i) - h_{i-1}(z))^{\varrho_{i-1}-1} |f(z,u(z),w(z)) - f(z,u^*(z),w^*(z))| dz \\
&\quad + \frac{1}{\Gamma(\varrho_{\Bbbk})} \int_{x_{\Bbbk}}^{x} h'_{\Bbbk}(z)(h_{\Bbbk}(x) - h_{\Bbbk}(z))^{\varrho_{\Bbbk}-1} |f(z,u(z),w(z)) - f(z,u^*(z),w^*(z))| dz \\
&\leq k_\rho^* |w(x) - w^*(x)| + \sum_{0<x_{\Bbbk}<x} k_{\mathcal{I}} |w(x_{\Bbbk}^-) - w^*(x_{\Bbbk}^-)| \\
&\quad + \sum_{i=1}^{\Bbbk} \frac{k_f}{\Gamma(\varrho_{i-1})} \int_{x_{i-1}}^{x_i} h'_{i-1}(z)(h_{i-1}(x_i) - h_{i-1}(z))^{\varrho_{i-1}-1} \left(|u - u^*| + |w - w^*|\right) dz \\
&\quad + \frac{k_f}{\Gamma(\varrho_{\Bbbk})} \int_{x_{\Bbbk}}^{x} h'_{\Bbbk}(z)(h_{\Bbbk}(x) - h_{\Bbbk}(z))^{\varrho_{\Bbbk}-1} \left(|u - u^*| + |w - w^*|\right) dz \\
&\leq k_\rho^* \|w - w^*\| + \aleph k_{\mathcal{I}} \|w - w^*\| + k_f \left(\|u - u^*\| + \|w - w^*\|\right) \\
&\quad \times \left(\sum_{i=1}^{\Bbbk} \frac{(h_{i-1}(x_i) - h_{i-1}(x_{i-1}))^{\varrho_{i-1}}}{\Gamma(\varrho_{i-1}+1)} + \frac{(h_{\Bbbk}(x) - h_{\Bbbk}(x_{\Bbbk}))^{\varrho_{\Bbbk}}}{\Gamma(\varrho_{\Bbbk}+1)} \right) \\
&\leq k_\rho^* \|w - w^*\| + \aleph k_{\mathcal{I}} \|w - w^*\| + k_f \sum_{i=0}^{\Bbbk} \frac{(h_i(T) - h_i(x_i))^{\varrho_i}}{\Gamma(\varrho_i+1)} \left(\|u - u^*\| + \|w - w^*\|\right).
\end{aligned} \quad (32)$$

Thus

$$\|\mathscr{N}_1(w,u) - \mathscr{N}_1(w^*,u^*)\| \leq k_f \sum_{i=0}^{\Bbbk} \frac{(h_i(T) - h_i(x_i))^{\varrho_i}}{\Gamma(\varrho_i+1)} \|u - u^*\|$$
$$+ \left(k_\rho^* + \aleph k_{\mathcal{I}} + k_f \sum_{i=0}^{\Bbbk} \frac{(h_i(T) - h_i(x_i))^{\varrho_i}}{\Gamma(\varrho_i+1)} \right) \|w - w^*\|. \quad (33)$$

Similarly

$$\|\mathscr{N}_2(w,u) - \mathscr{N}_2(w^*,u^*)\| \leq k_{\mathcal{F}} \sum_{i=0}^{\Bbbk} \frac{(h_i(T) - h_i(x_i))^{\varrho_i}}{\Gamma(\varrho_i+1)} \|w - w^*\|$$
$$+ \left(k_\phi^* + \aleph k_{\overline{\mathcal{I}}} + k_{\mathcal{F}} \sum_{i=0}^{\Bbbk} \frac{(h_i(T) - h_i(x_i))^{\varrho_i}}{\Gamma(\varrho_i+1)} \right) \|u - u^*\|. \quad (34)$$

From (33) and (34), we have

$$\|\mathscr{N}(w,u) - \mathscr{N}(w^*,u^*)\| \leq \left(k_\rho^* + k_\phi^* + \aleph(k_{\mathcal{I}} + k_{\overline{\mathcal{I}}}) \right. \quad (35)$$
$$\left. + 2(k_f + k_{\mathcal{F}}) \sum_{i=0}^{\Bbbk} \frac{(h_i(T) - h_i(x_i))^{\varrho_i}}{\Gamma(\varrho_i+1)} \right) \left(\|w - w^*\| + \|u - u^*\| \right).$$

Now if

$$\max(\chi_1, \chi_2) < 1,$$

where

$$\chi_1 = k_\rho^* + k_\phi^* + 2(k_f + k_{\mathcal{F}}) \frac{(h_0(x_1) - h_0(0))^{\varrho_0}}{\Gamma(\varrho_0+1)},$$

and
$$\chi_2 = k_\rho^* + k_\phi^* + \aleph(k_\mathcal{I} + k_{\overline{\mathcal{I}}}) + 2(k_f + k_\mathcal{F}) \sum_{i=0}^{\Bbbk} \frac{(h_i(T) - h_i(x_i))^{\varrho_i}}{\Gamma(\varrho_i + 1)},$$

then, $\mathcal{N}$ is strict contraction on $\mathcal{E}$. It follows from Banach's contraction theorem that the impulsive FDE (1) has a unique solution on $\mathbb{S}$. □

4. Stability Analysis of Problem (1)

In this main section, we derive some results about stability analysis for the proposed problem (1). Prior to the proof of main results, we give definitions of Hyers–Ulam (H–U) stability and some remarks.

Consider an operator $\mathcal{N} : \mathcal{E} \to \mathcal{E}$, defined by

$$\mathcal{N}(w) = w; \quad w \in \mathcal{E}. \tag{36}$$

Definition 1. *The solution w of problem (36) is H–U stable. If we find a constant $\mathbf{C} > 0$, so that for any $\epsilon > 0$ and any solution $w \in \mathcal{E}$ of the inequality*

$$\{|w - \mathcal{N}(w)| \leq \epsilon, \tag{37}$$

there exists unique solution $\overline{w}$ of Equation (36) in $\mathcal{E}$, so that the following relation satisfies

$$\|\overline{w} - w\| \leq \mathbf{C}\epsilon.$$

Definition 2. *The solution of problem (36) is G–H–U stable if we find*

$$\theta : (0, \infty) \to (0, \infty), \theta(0) = 0$$

so that for any solution of the inequality (37), the following relation satisfies

$$\|\overline{w} - w\| \leq \mathbf{C}\theta(\epsilon).$$

Remark 1. *w is the solution in $\mathcal{E}$ for the inequality (37), iff there exists a function $\varkappa \in \mathcal{E}$ which is independent of solution (w, u), so that for any t*

(i) $|\varkappa(x)| \leq \epsilon, |\varkappa_n| \leq \epsilon,$
(ii) ${}^cD_{[x]}^{\varrho(x)} w(x) = f(x, u(x), w(x)) + \varkappa(x),$
(iii) ${}^cD_{[x]}^{\varrho(x)} u(x) = \mathcal{F}(x, u(x), w(x)) + \varkappa(x),$
(iv) $\Delta w(x_i) = \mathcal{I}_i(w(x_i^-)) + \varkappa_n, \quad n = 1, \ldots, k.$
(v) $\Delta u(x_i) = \overline{\mathcal{I}}_i(u(x_i^-)) + \varkappa_n, \quad n = 1, \ldots, k.$

By Remark 1, we have the following perturbed problem

$$\begin{cases} {}^cD_{[x]}^{\varrho(x)} w(x) = f(x, u(x), w(x)) + \varkappa(x), & x \in \mathbb{S} = [0,T], x \neq x_i, \\ w(0) = w_0 + \rho(w), \\ \Delta w(x_i) = \mathcal{I}_i(w(x_i^-)) + \varkappa_n, \; i = 1,\ldots m, \\ {}^cD_{[x]}^{\varrho(x)} u(x) = \mathcal{F}(x, w(x), u(x)) + \varkappa(x), & x \in \mathbb{S} = [0,T], x \neq x_i, \\ i = 1, \ldots, \aleph, \quad 0 < \varrho(x) \leq 1, \\ u(0) = u_0 + \phi(u), \\ \Delta u(x_i) = \overline{\mathcal{I}}_i(u(x_i^-)) + \varkappa_n, \; i = 1,\ldots m. \end{cases} \tag{38}$$

Lemma 2. *The solution of the perturbed problem (38) satisfies the following relations*

$$\begin{cases} \left| w(x) - \left(w_0 + \rho(w) + \dfrac{1}{\Gamma(\varrho_0)} \int_0^x h_0'(z)(h_0(x) - h_0(z))^{\varrho_0 - 1} f(z, u(z), w(z)) dz \right) \right| \\ \leq \dfrac{\epsilon (h_0(x_1) - h_0(0))^{\varrho_0}}{\Gamma(\varrho_0 + 1)}, \; \text{if } x \in [0, x_1], \\ \vdots \\ \left| w(x) - \left(w_0 + \rho(w) + \sum_{i=1}^{\Bbbk} \mathcal{I}_i w(x_i^-) + \sum_{i=1}^{\Bbbk} \dfrac{1}{\Gamma(\varrho_{i-1})} \int_{x_{i-1}}^{x_i} h_{i-1}'(z)(h_{i-1}(x_i) - h_{i-1}(z))^{\varrho_{i-1} - 1} \right. \right. \\ \left. \left. \times f(z, u(z), w(z)) dz + \dfrac{1}{\Gamma(\varrho_\Bbbk)} \int_{x_\Bbbk}^x h_\Bbbk'(z)(h_\Bbbk(x) - h_\Bbbk(z))^{\varrho_\Bbbk - 1} f(z, u(z), w(z)) dz \right) \right| \\ \leq \left(\Bbbk + \sum_{i=0}^{\Bbbk} \dfrac{(h_i(T) - h_i(x_i))^{\varrho_i}}{\Gamma(\varrho_i + 1)} \right) \epsilon, \\ \text{if } x \in (x_\Bbbk, x_{\Bbbk+1}], \; \Bbbk = 1, \ldots, \aleph, \end{cases} \quad (39)$$

and

$$\begin{cases} \left| u(x) - \left(u_0 + \phi(u) + \dfrac{1}{\Gamma(\varrho_0)} \int_0^x h_0'(z)(h_0(x) - h_0(z))^{\varrho_0 - 1} \mathcal{F}(z, u(z), w(z)) dz \right) \right| \\ \leq \dfrac{\epsilon (h_0(x_1) - h_0(0))^{\varrho_0}}{\Gamma(\varrho_0 + 1)}, \; \text{if } x \in [0, x_1], \\ \vdots \\ \left| u(x) - \left(u_0 + \phi(u) + \sum_{i=1}^{\Bbbk} \overline{\mathcal{I}}_i u(x_i^-) + \sum_{i=1}^{\Bbbk} \dfrac{1}{\Gamma(\varrho_{i-1})} \int_{x_{i-1}}^{x_i} h_{i-1}'(z)(h_{i-1}(x_i) - h_{i-1}(z))^{\varrho_{i-1} - 1} \right. \right. \\ \left. \left. \times \mathcal{F}(z, u(z), w(z)) dz + \dfrac{1}{\Gamma(\varrho_\Bbbk)} \int_{x_\Bbbk}^x h_\Bbbk'(z)(h_\Bbbk(x) - h_\Bbbk(z))^{\varrho_\Bbbk - 1} \mathcal{F}(z, u(z), w(z)) dz \right) \right| \\ \leq \left(\Bbbk + \sum_{i=0}^{\Bbbk} \dfrac{(h_i(T) - h_i(x_i))^{\varrho_i}}{\Gamma(\varrho_i + 1)} \right) \epsilon, \\ \text{if } x \in (x_\Bbbk, x_{\Bbbk+1}], \; \Bbbk = 1, \ldots, \aleph. \end{cases} \quad (40)$$

Proof. The proof can be obtained by applying Lemma A2 repeatedly as in the proof of Lemma 1. □

Theorem 3. *If* (H_1), (H_2) *and* (H_6) *hold with the following condition*

$$\max(\chi_1, \chi_2) < 1,$$

where

$$\chi_1 = k_\rho^* + k_\phi^* + 2(k_f + k_\mathcal{F}) \dfrac{(h_0(x_1) - h_0(0))^{\varrho_0}}{\Gamma(\varrho_0 + 1)},$$

and

$$\chi_2 = k_\rho^* + k_\phi^* + \aleph(k_\mathcal{I} + k_{\overline{\mathcal{I}}}) + 2(k_f + k_\mathcal{F}) \sum_{i=0}^{\Bbbk} \dfrac{(h_i(T) - h_i(x_i))^{\varrho_i}}{\Gamma(\varrho_i + 1)},$$

then, problem (1) *is H–U stable.*

Proof. Let w^* be any solution of set of inequalities (37) and w be the unique solution of problem (1). Then, from integral Equations (8) and (39), we have

$$|w(x) - w^*(x)| \leq |\rho(w(x)) - \rho(w^*(x))| + \frac{1}{\Gamma(\varrho_0)} \int_0^x h_0'(z)(h_0(x) - h_0(z))^{\varrho_0 - 1}$$
$$\times |f(z, u(z), w(z)) - f(z, u^*(z), w^*(z))| dz + \frac{1}{\Gamma(\varrho_0)} \int_0^x h_0'(z)(h_0(x) - h_0(z))^{\varrho_0 - 1} |\varkappa(z)| dz$$
$$\leq \left(k_\rho^* + \frac{k_f(h_0(x_1) - h_0(0))^{\varrho_0}}{\Gamma(\varrho_0 + 1)} \right) \|w - w^*\| + \frac{k_f(h_0(x_1) - h_0(0))^{\varrho_0}}{\Gamma(\varrho_0 + 1)} \|u - u^*\| \quad (41)$$
$$+ \frac{\epsilon(h_0(x_1) - h_0(0))^{\varrho_0}}{\Gamma(\varrho_0 + 1)}.$$

Thus, for $x \in [0, x_1]$, we have

$$\|w - w^*\| \leq \left(k_\rho^* + \frac{k_f(h_0(x_1) - h_0(0))^{\varrho_0}}{\Gamma(\varrho_0 + 1)} \right) \|w - w^*\| + \frac{k_f(h_0(x_1) - h_0(0))^{\varrho_0}}{\Gamma(\varrho_0 + 1)} \|u - u^*\|$$
$$+ \frac{\epsilon(h_0(x_1) - h_0(0))^{\varrho_0}}{\Gamma(\varrho_0 + 1)}. \quad (42)$$

Similarly, for $x \in [0, x_1]$, we have

$$\|u - u^*\| \leq \left(k_\phi^* + \frac{k_\mathcal{F}(h_0(x_1) - h_0(0))^{\varrho_0}}{\Gamma(\varrho_0 + 1)} \right) \|w - w^*\| + \frac{k_\mathcal{F}(h_0(x_1) - h_0(0))^{\varrho_0}}{\Gamma(\varrho_0 + 1)} \|u - u^*\|$$
$$+ \frac{\epsilon(h_0(x_1) - h_0(0))^{\varrho_0}}{\Gamma(\varrho_0 + 1)}. \quad (43)$$

Adding (42) and (43), we have

$$\|w - w^*\| + \|u - u^*\| \leq \left(k_\rho^* + \frac{k_f(h_0(x_1) - h_0(0))^{\varrho_0}}{\Gamma(\varrho_0 + 1)} \right) \|w - w^*\| + \frac{k_f(h_0(x_1) - h_0(0))^{\varrho_0}}{\Gamma(\varrho_0 + 1)} \|u - u^*\|$$
$$+ \frac{\epsilon(h_0(x_1) - h_0(0))^{\varrho_0}}{\Gamma(\varrho_0 + 1)}$$
$$\leq \left(k_\rho^* + k_\phi^* + 2(k_f + k_\mathcal{F}) \frac{(h_0(x_1) - h_0(0))^{\varrho_0}}{\Gamma(\varrho_0 + 1)} \right) \left(\|w - u\| + \|w^* - u^*\| \right) + \frac{\epsilon(h_0(x_1) - h_0(0))^{\varrho_0}}{\Gamma(\varrho_0 + 1)}. \quad (44)$$

That implies

$$\|w - w^*\| + \|u - u^*\| \leq \left(k_\rho^* + k_\phi^* + 2(k_f + k_\mathcal{F}) \frac{(h_0(x_1) - h_0(0))^{\varrho_0}}{\Gamma(\varrho_0 + 1)} \right) \left(\|w - u\| + \|w^* - u^*\| \right)$$
$$+ \frac{\epsilon(h_0(x_1) - h_0(0))^{\varrho_0}}{\Gamma(\varrho_0 + 1)}. \quad (45)$$

From which we obtain

$$\|(w, u) - (w^*, u^*)\| \leq \frac{\frac{\epsilon(h_0(x_1) - h_0(0))^{\varrho_0}}{\Gamma(\varrho_0 + 1)}}{1 - \chi_1}, \quad (46)$$

where $\chi_1 = \left(k_\rho^* + k_\phi^* + 2(k_f + k_\mathcal{F}) \frac{(h_0(x_1) - h_0(0))^{\varrho_0}}{\Gamma(\varrho_0 + 1)} \right)$ is assumed to be less than one.

By and large, for $x \in (x_\Bbbk, x_{\Bbbk+1}]$, $\Bbbk = 1, \ldots, \aleph$, we have

$$\begin{aligned}
&|w(x) - w^*(x)| \\
&\leq |\rho(w(x)) - \rho(w^*(x))| + \sum_{0 < x_{\Bbbk} < x} |\mathcal{I}_{\Bbbk} w(x_{\Bbbk}^-) - \mathcal{I}_{\Bbbk} w^*(x_{\Bbbk}^-)| \\
&+ \sum_{i=1}^{\Bbbk} \frac{1}{\Gamma(\varrho_{i-1})} \int_{x_{i-1}}^{x_i} h'_{i-1}(z)(h_{i-1}(x_i) - h_{i-1}(z))^{\varrho_{i-1}-1} |f(z, u(z), w(z)) - f(z, u^*(z), w^*(z))| dz \\
&+ \sum_{i=1}^{\Bbbk} \frac{1}{\Gamma(\varrho_{i-1})} \int_{x_{i-1}}^{x_i} h'_{i-1}(z)(h_{i-1}(x_i) - h_{i-1}(z))^{\varrho_{i-1}-1} |\varkappa(z)| dz \\
&+ \frac{1}{\Gamma(\varrho_{\Bbbk})} \int_{x_{\Bbbk}}^{x} h'_{\Bbbk}(z)(h_{\Bbbk}(x) - h_{\Bbbk}(z))^{\varrho_{\Bbbk}-1} |f(z, u(z), w(z)) - f(z, u^*(z), w^*(z))| dz \\
&+ \frac{1}{\Gamma(\varrho_{\Bbbk})} \int_{x_{\Bbbk}}^{x} h'_{\Bbbk}(z)(h_{\Bbbk}(x) - h_{\Bbbk}(z))^{\varrho_{\Bbbk}-1} |\varkappa(z)| dz \\
&\leq k_\rho^* \|w - w^*\| + \aleph k_{\mathcal{I}} \|w - w^*\| + k_f \Big(\|u - u^*\| + \|w - w^*\| \Big) \\
&\times \left(\sum_{i=1}^{\Bbbk} \frac{(h_{i-1}(x_i) - h_{i-1}(x_{i-1}))^{\varrho_{i-1}}}{\Gamma(\varrho_{i-1} + 1)} + \frac{(h_{\Bbbk}(x) - h_{\Bbbk}(x_{\Bbbk}))^{\varrho_{\Bbbk}}}{\Gamma(\varrho_{\Bbbk} + 1)} \right) + \left(\Bbbk + \sum_{i=0}^{\Bbbk} \frac{(h_i(T) - h_i(x_i))^{\varrho_i}}{\Gamma(\varrho_i + 1)} \right) \epsilon \\
&\leq k_\rho^* \|w - w^*\| + \aleph k_{\mathcal{I}} \|w - w^*\| + k_f \sum_{i=0}^{\Bbbk} \frac{(h_i(T) - h_i(x_i))^{\varrho_i}}{\Gamma(\varrho_i + 1)} \Big(\|u - u^*\| + \|w - w^*\| \Big) \\
&+ \left(\Bbbk + \sum_{i=0}^{\Bbbk} \frac{(h_i(T) - h_i(x_i))^{\varrho_i}}{\Gamma(\varrho_i + 1)} \right) \epsilon.
\end{aligned} \quad (47)$$

Thus, we have

$$\begin{aligned}
&\|w - w^*\| \\
&\leq k_f \sum_{i=0}^{\Bbbk} \frac{(h_i(T) - h_i(x_i))^{\varrho_i}}{\Gamma(\varrho_i + 1)} \|u - u^*\| + \left(k_\rho^* + \aleph k_{\mathcal{I}} + k_f \sum_{i=0}^{\Bbbk} \frac{(h_i(T) - h_i(x_i))^{\varrho_i}}{\Gamma(\varrho_i + 1)} \right) \|w - w^*\| \\
&+ \left(\Bbbk + \sum_{i=0}^{\Bbbk} \frac{(h_i(T) - h_i(x_i))^{\varrho_i}}{\Gamma(\varrho_i + 1)} \right) \epsilon.
\end{aligned} \quad (48)$$

Similarly, we have

$$\begin{aligned}
&\|u - u^*\| \\
&\leq k_{\mathcal{F}} \sum_{i=0}^{\Bbbk} \frac{(h_i(T) - h_i(x_i))^{\varrho_i}}{\Gamma(\varrho_i + 1)} \|w - w^*\| + \left(k_\phi^* + \aleph k_{\overline{\mathcal{I}}} + k_{\mathcal{F}} \sum_{i=0}^{\Bbbk} \frac{(h_i(T) - h_i(x_i))^{\varrho_i}}{\Gamma(\varrho_i + 1)} \right) \|u - u^*\| \\
&+ \left(\Bbbk + \sum_{i=0}^{\Bbbk} \frac{(h_i(T) - h_i(x_i))^{\varrho_i}}{\Gamma(\varrho_i + 1)} \right) \epsilon.
\end{aligned} \quad (49)$$

From (48) and (49), we have

$$\begin{aligned}
\|w - w^*\| + \|u - u^*\| &\leq \left(k_\rho^* + k_\phi^* + \aleph(k_{\mathcal{I}} + k_{\overline{\mathcal{I}}}) + 2(k_f + k_{\mathcal{F}}) \sum_{i=0}^{\Bbbk} \frac{(h_i(T) - h_i(x_i))^{\varrho_i}}{\Gamma(\varrho_i + 1)} \right) \\
&\times \Big(\|w - w^*\| + \|u - u^*\| \Big) + \left(\Bbbk + \sum_{i=0}^{\Bbbk} \frac{(h_i(T) - h_i(x_i))^{\varrho_i}}{\Gamma(\varrho_i + 1)} \right) \epsilon.
\end{aligned} \quad (50)$$

Which implies that

$$\|(w,u) - (w^*, u^*)\| \leq \frac{\left(\Bbbk + \sum_{i=0}^{\Bbbk} \frac{(h_i(T) - h_i(x_i))^{\varrho_i}}{\Gamma(\varrho_i + 1)}\right) \epsilon}{1 - \chi_2}. \tag{51}$$

Where $\chi_2 = \left(k_\rho^* + k_\phi^* + \aleph(k_\mathcal{I} + k_{\overline{\mathcal{I}}}) + 2(k_f + k_\mathcal{F}) \sum_{i=0}^{\Bbbk} \frac{(h_i(T) - h_i(x_i))^{\varrho_i}}{\Gamma(\varrho_i + 1)}\right)$ is assumed to be less than one. Equivalently, (51) can be written as

$$\|(w,u) - (w^*, u^*)\| \leq \mathbf{C}\epsilon,$$

where

$$\mathbf{C} = \frac{\left(\Bbbk + \sum_{i=0}^{\Bbbk} \frac{(h_i(T) - h_i(x_i))^{\varrho_i}}{\Gamma(\varrho_i + 1)}\right)}{1 - \left(k_\rho^* + k_\phi^* + \aleph(k_\mathcal{I} + k_{\overline{\mathcal{I}}}) + 2(k_f + k_\mathcal{F}) \sum_{i=0}^{\Bbbk} \frac{(h_i(T) - h_i(x_i))^{\varrho_i}}{\Gamma(\varrho_i + 1)}\right)}.$$

This shows that problem (1) is H–U stable. □

Lemma 3. *By setting* $\theta(\epsilon) = \mathbf{C}(\epsilon)$; $\theta(0) = 0$, *problem* (1) *becomes G–H–U stable.*

5. Application and Discussion

In this section, we apply our main results to the following numerical problem to verify the applications of the main results. We also plot graphs for its solution and functions ϱ and h for illustration purposes.

Example 1.

$$\begin{cases} {}^c D^{\varrho(x)}_{[x]} w(x) = \frac{e^{-\pi x}}{20} + \frac{(x - \frac{1}{5})}{28}\Big(|u(x)| + \sin(|w(x)|)\Big), \\ x \in [0,1], \, x \neq x_k, \, k = 1, 2, \ldots, 9. \\ {}^c D^{\varrho(x)}_{[x]} u(x) = \frac{e^{-\pi x}}{25} + \frac{(x - \frac{1}{5})}{20}\Big(|w(x)| + \cos(|u(x)|)\Big), \\ x \in [0,1], \, x \neq x_k, \, k = 1, 2, \ldots, 9. \\ \Delta w\Big(x_k\Big) = \frac{1}{25} w(x_k^-), \quad \Delta u\Big(x_k\Big) = \frac{1}{40} u(x_k^-), \\ w(0) = \frac{w}{22 + |w|} + 0.025, \quad u(0) = \frac{u}{30 + |u|} + 1, \end{cases} \tag{52}$$

where $\varrho = \frac{1}{2}$, $\mathbb{S}_0 = [0, \frac{1}{5}]$, $\mathbb{S}_1 = (\frac{1}{5}, 1]$.
Set

$$f(x, u(x), w(x)) = \frac{e^{-\pi x}}{20} + \frac{(x - \frac{1}{3})}{30}\Big(|u(x)| + \sin(|w(x)|)\Big); u, w \in \mathrm{R}^+,$$

and

$$\mathcal{F}(x, u(x), w(x)) = \frac{e^{-\pi x}}{25} + \frac{(x - \frac{1}{5})}{20}\Big(|w(x)| + \cos(|u(x)|)\Big),$$

$$\mathcal{I}_i(w) = \frac{1}{50} w; w \in \mathrm{R}^+, i = 1, 2,$$

and

$$\rho(w) = \frac{w}{22 + |w|}, \quad \phi(u) = \frac{u}{30 + |u|}.$$

Assuming $\aleph = 2$ ($\Bbbk = 1, 2$), we have

$$^cD_{[x]}^{\varrho(x)}w(x) = \begin{cases} ^cD_{[x]}^{\varrho_0,h_0}w(x), & 0 < x \leq x_1, \\ ^cD_{[x]}^{\varrho_1,h_1}w(x), & x_1 < x \leq x_2 \\ ^cD_{[x]}^{\varrho_2,h_2}w(x), & x_2 < x \leq 1, \end{cases}$$

$$^cD_{[x]}^{\varrho(x)}u(x) = \begin{cases} ^cD_{[x]}^{\varrho_0,h_0}u(x), & 0 < x \leq x_1, \\ ^cD_{[x]}^{\varrho_1,h_1}u(x), & x_1 < x \leq x_2 \\ ^cD_{[x]}^{\varrho_2,h_2}u(x), & x_2 < x \leq 1; \end{cases}$$

$$\varrho(x) = \begin{cases} \varrho_0 = \frac{1}{4}, & 0 < x \leq \frac{1}{3}, \\ \varrho_1 = \frac{1}{3}, & \frac{1}{3} < x \leq \frac{1}{2}, \\ \varrho_2 = \frac{1}{2}, & \frac{1}{2} < x \leq 1. \end{cases}$$

$$h(x) = \begin{cases} h_0(x) = \frac{x}{3}, & 0 < x \leq \frac{1}{3}, \\ h_1(x) = 2^x, & \frac{1}{3} < x \leq \frac{1}{2}, \\ h_2(x) = e^x, & \frac{1}{2} < x \leq 1. \end{cases}$$

Let $w, \overline{w} \in \mathrm{R}^+$ and $x \in [0,1]$. Then,

$$\begin{aligned} |f(x, u(x), w(x)) - f(x, \overline{u}(x), \overline{w}(x))| \\ \leq \frac{(x - \frac{1}{5})}{28}\left(\left||u(x) - \overline{u}(x)\right|\right| + \left|\sin(|w(x)|) - \sin(\overline{w}(x))\right|\right) \\ \leq \frac{1}{35}\left(\left||u(x) - \overline{u}(x)\right|\right| + \left|\sin(|w(x)|) - \sin(\overline{w}(x))\right|\right). \end{aligned} \quad (53)$$

Similarly, we have

$$\begin{aligned} |\mathcal{F}(x, u(x), w(x)) - \mathcal{F}(x, \overline{u}(x), \overline{w}(x))| \\ \leq \frac{(x - \frac{1}{5})}{20}\left(\left||w(x) - \overline{w}(x)\right|\right| + \left|\cos(|u(x)|) - \cos(\overline{u}(x))\right|\right) \\ \leq \frac{1}{25}\left(\left||w(x) - \overline{w}(x)\right|\right| + \left|\cos(|u(x)|) - \cos(\overline{u}(x))\right|\right). \end{aligned} \quad (54)$$

Using (H_1), from (53) and (54), we obtain $k_f = \frac{1}{35}$ and $k_\mathcal{F} = \frac{1}{25}$. By (H_2),

$$|\mathcal{I}_i(w) - \mathcal{I}_i(\overline{w})| \leq \frac{1}{25}|w - \overline{w}|,$$

$$|\overline{\mathcal{I}}_i(u) - \overline{\mathcal{I}}_i(\overline{u})| \leq \frac{1}{40}|u - \overline{u}|.$$

Using (H_2), we get $k_\mathcal{I} = \frac{1}{25}$, $k_{\overline{\mathcal{I}}} = \frac{1}{40}$,

By (H_6), *we have*

$$\begin{aligned}|\rho(w) - \rho(\overline{w})| &= \left|\frac{w}{22+|w|} - \frac{\overline{w}}{22+|\overline{w}|}\right| \\ &\leq \frac{22|w-\overline{w}|}{(22+|w|)(22+|\overline{w}|)} \leq \frac{1}{22}|w-\overline{w}|,\end{aligned}$$

$$\begin{aligned}|\phi(u) - \phi(\overline{u})| &= \left|\frac{u}{30+|u|} - \frac{\overline{u}}{30+|\overline{u}|}\right| \\ &\leq \frac{30|u-\overline{u}|}{(30+|u|)(30+|\overline{u}|)} \leq \frac{1}{30}|u-\overline{u}|.\end{aligned}$$

Which implies $k_\phi^* = \frac{1}{30}$. *Using the derived values, one may show that*

$$\max(\chi_1, \chi_2) < 1,$$

where

$$\chi_1 = k_\rho^* + k_\phi^* + 2(k_f + k_\mathcal{F})\frac{(h_0(x_1) - h_0(0))^{\varrho_0}}{\Gamma(\varrho_0 + 1)},$$

and

$$\chi_2 = k_\rho^* + k_\phi^* + \aleph(k_\mathcal{I} + k_{\overline{\mathcal{I}}}) + 2(k_f + k_\mathcal{F})\sum_{i=0}^{\Bbbk}\frac{(h_i(T) - h_i(x_i))^{\varrho_i}}{\Gamma(\varrho_i + 1)}.$$

Hence, by Theorem 2, the numerical problem (52) has a unique solution, and by Theorem 3, it is H–U stable. We have presented the piecewise graphs of function ϱ in Figure 1. The graph looks like a stair function. Moreover, the piecewise variable-order graphs for different pieces have been presented in Figure 2. The solution under the impulsive conditions and having piecewise variable-order has been plotted in Figure 3. The impulsive points are given as $0.1, 0.2, 0.3, 0.4, 0.5, 0.6, 0.7, 0.8, 0.9$. From the graph of solution, the crossover behaviors in the dynamics of the considered problem can be observed clearly at the given impulsive points. Hence, DEs with variable kernel have high flexibility due to the freedom of changing the kernel. This manuscript has a multiple stage structure. The problem investigated here has Caputo-type piecewise fractional-order derivative and a variable kernel. It can prove interesting for to readers and researchers working in this area.

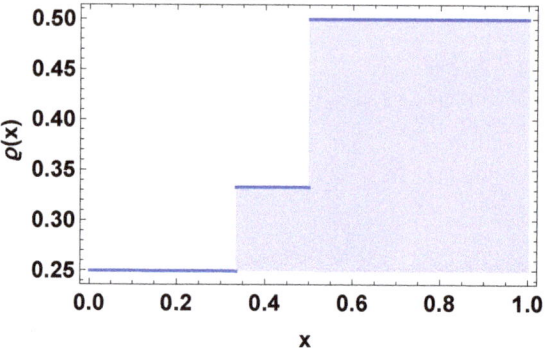

Figure 1. Plot for function ϱ in Example 1.

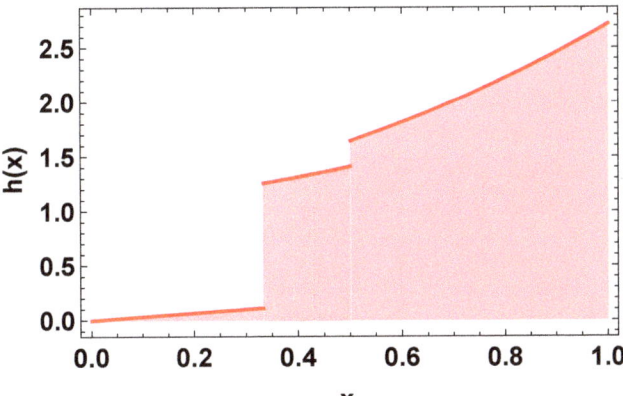

Figure 2. Plot for function h in Example 1.

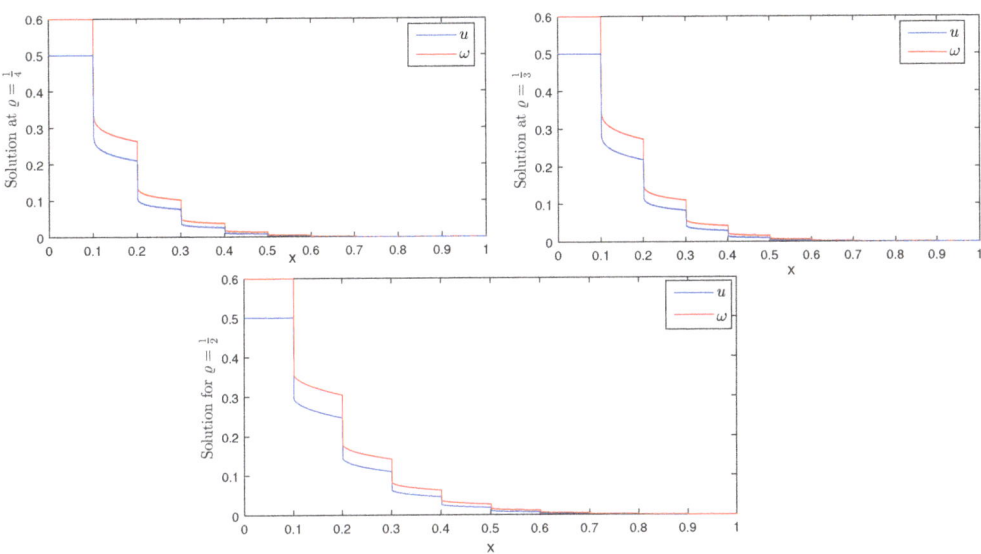

Figure 3. Solution representation of problem (52) in Example 1.

6. Conclusions

In this work, we have studied a coupled system of piecewise-order differential equations (DEs) with a variable kernel and impulsive conditions. The theoretical analysis is based on Scheafer's and Banach fixed-point theorems. For stability results, H–U's concept has been applied. The derived results have been applied to a numerical problem which illustrates the applicability of the main results. The contents of the paper generalize many results already studied in the literature. For the future, the reader should easily extend the results studied in [38,39] under the variable-order with a kernel of variable exponents. In addition, this concept can be extended to various problems of FDEs involving Caputo–Fabrizio or Atangana–Baleanu fractional differential operator with impulsive conditions and variable exponents.

Author Contributions: Conceptualization, A.A. (Arshad Ali); Methodology, K.J.A. and A.A. (Ahmad Aloqaily); Validation, H.A. and N.M.; Formal analysis, A.A. (Ahmad Aloqaily); Resources, K.J.A.; Data curation, H.A.; Writing—original draft, A.A. (Arshad Ali); Writing—review & editing, N.M. All authors have read and agreed to the published version of the manuscript.

Funding: This research received no external funding.

Data Availability Statement: Not applicable.

Acknowledgments: The authors extend their appreciation to the Deanship of Scientific Research at King Khalid University for funding this work through large group Research Project under grant number RGP2/371/44. Ahmad Aloqaily, Nabil Mlaiki are thankful to Prince Sultan University for paying the APC and support through the TAS research lab.

Conflicts of Interest: The authors declare no conflict of interest.

Appendix A

In this section, we give some definitions and preliminary results.

Definition A1 ([6]). *The RL integral of fractional-order ϱ, of function $w(x)$ is given by*

$$\mathcal{I}_{a^+}^{\varrho} w(x) = \frac{1}{\Gamma(\varrho)} \int_a^x (x-s)^{\varrho-1} w(s) ds. \tag{A1}$$

Definition A2 ([24,40]). *The RL integral of fractional-order ϱ, of function $w(x)$ w.r.t $h(x)$ is given by*

$$\mathcal{I}_{a^+}^{\varrho,h} w(x) = \frac{1}{\Gamma(\varrho)} \int_a^x h'(s)(h(x)-h(s))^{\varrho-1} w(s) ds; \tag{A2}$$

the function h is increasing and differentiable such that $h(x) > 0$, for all $x > 0$.

Definition A3 ([6]). *The Caputo fractional derivative (CFD) of function $w(x)$ is given by*

$$^c D_{a^+}^{\varrho} w(x) = \mathcal{I}_{a^+}^{n-\varrho} w^{(n)}(x), \tag{A3}$$

where $n-1 < \varrho < n$ and $w^{(n)}(x) = (\frac{d}{dx})^n w(x)$.

Definition A4 ([24,40]). *The CFD of function $w(x)$ w.r.t $h(x)$ is given by*

$$^c D_{a^+}^{\varrho,h} w(x) = \mathcal{I}_{a^+}^{n-\varrho,h} w_h^{(n)}(x), \tag{A4}$$

where $n-1 < \varrho < n$ and $w_h^{(n)}(x) = (\frac{1}{h'(x)} \frac{d}{dx})^n w(x)$.

Lemma A1 ([40]). *Let $\varphi \in C[a,b]$, $a < b$, so that the CFD exists. Then*

$$^c D_{a^+}^{\varrho,h} \mathcal{I}_{a^+}^{\varrho,h} \varphi(x) = \varphi(x),$$

and

$$\mathcal{I}_{a^+}^{\varrho,h} \, ^c D_{a^+}^{\varrho,h} \varphi(x) = \varphi(x) - \varphi(a),$$

for $0 < \varrho \leq 1$. And $^c D_{a^+}^{\varrho,h} \varphi(x) = 0$ if $\varphi(x)$ is constant function.

Lemma A2 ([40]). *For $\varrho \in (0,1]$, the solution of the following problem*

$$\begin{aligned} ^c D_{a^+}^{\varrho,h} w(x) &= \Phi(x), \\ w(a) &= w_0 \end{aligned} \tag{A5}$$

is given by
$$w(x) = w_0 + \frac{1}{\Gamma(\varrho)} \int_a^x h'(s)(h(x)-h(s))^{\varrho-1}\Phi(z)dz.$$

Theorem A1. *(Schaefer's fixed-point theorem) [41] Let $\mathcal{W}$ be a convex subset of a norm-linear space S with $0 \in \mathcal{W}$ and let $\mathfrak{B} : \mathcal{W} \to \mathcal{W}$ is a completely continuous operator. Then the set $\mathcal{X} = \{w \in \mathcal{W} : w = \varsigma \mathfrak{B} w; 0 < \varsigma < 1\}$ is either unbounded or $\mathfrak{B}$ has a fixed point in $\mathcal{W}$.*

Appendix B

The proof of Lemma 1 is received by using Lemma A2 for number of times. Assume w satisfies (5)–(7). If $x \in [0, x_1]$, then
$$^cD_{[x]}^{\varrho_0,h_0}w(x) = \varphi(x), \quad [x] = 0.$$

Using Lemma A2, we get
$$w(x) = w_0 + \rho(w) + \frac{1}{\Gamma(\varrho_0)}\int_0^x h'_0(z)(h_0(x)-h_0(z))^{\varrho_0-1}\varphi(z)dz.$$

This gives
$$w(x_1^-) = w_0 + \rho(w) + \frac{1}{\Gamma(\varrho_0)}\int_0^{x_1} h'_0(z)(h_0(x_1)-h_0(z))^{\varrho_0-1}\varphi(z)dz.$$

Applying the impulse $w(x_1^-) = w(x_1^+) - \mathcal{I}_1 w(x_1^-)$, we get
$$w(x_1^+) = w_0 + \rho(w) + \frac{1}{\Gamma(\varrho_0)}\int_0^{x_1} h'_0(z)(h_0(x_1)-h_0(z))^{\varrho_0-1}\varphi(z)dz + \mathcal{I}_1 w(x_1^-).$$

If $x \in (x_1, x_2]$, then
$$^cD_{[x]}^{\varrho_1,h_1}w(x) = \varphi(x), \quad [x] = x_1.$$

Using Lemma A2, we get
$$\begin{aligned}
w(x) &= w(x_1^+) + \frac{1}{\Gamma(\varrho_1)}\int_{x_1}^x h'_1(z)(h_1(x)-h_1(z))^{\varrho_1-1}\varphi(z)dz \\
&= w(x_1^-) + \mathcal{I}_1 w(x_1^-) + \frac{1}{\Gamma(\varrho_1)}\int_{x_1}^x h'_1(z)(h_1(x)-h_1(z))^{\varrho_1-1}\varphi(z)dz \\
&= w_0 + \rho(w) + \frac{1}{\Gamma(\varrho_0)}\int_0^{x_1} h'_0(z)(h_0(x_1)-h_0(z))^{\varrho_0-1}\varphi(z)dz \\
&\quad + \frac{1}{\Gamma(\varrho_1)}\int_{x_1}^x h'_1(z)(h_1(x)-h_1(z))^{\varrho_1-1}\varphi(z)dz + \mathcal{I}_1 w(x_1^-).
\end{aligned}$$

This gives
$$\begin{aligned}
w(x_2^-) &= w_0 + \rho(w) + \frac{1}{\Gamma(\varrho_0)}\int_0^{x_1} h'_0(z)(h_0(x_1)-h_0(z))^{\varrho_0-1}\varphi(z)dz \\
&\quad + \frac{1}{\Gamma(\varrho_1)}\int_{x_1}^{x_2} h'_1(z)(h_1(x_2)-h_1(z))^{\varrho_1-1}\varphi(z)dz + \mathcal{I}_1 w(x_1^-).
\end{aligned}$$

Applying the impulse $w(x_2^-) = w(x_2^+) - \mathcal{I}_2 w(x_2^-)$, we get
$$\begin{aligned}
w(x_2^+) &= w_0 + \rho(w) + \frac{1}{\Gamma(\varrho_0)}\int_0^{x_1} h'_0(z)(h_0(x_1)-h_0(z))^{\varrho_0-1}\varphi(z)dz \\
&\quad + \frac{1}{\Gamma(\varrho_1)}\int_{x_1}^{x_2} h'_1(z)(h_1(x_2)-h_1(z))^{\varrho_1-1}\varphi(z)dz + \mathcal{I}_1 w(x_1^-) + \mathcal{I}_2 w(x_2^-).
\end{aligned}$$

If $x \in (x_2, x_3]$, then
$$^cD_{[x]}^{\varrho_2, h_2} w(x) = \varphi(x), \; [x] = x_2.$$

Using Lemma A2, we get

$$\begin{aligned}
w(x) &= w(x_2^+) + \frac{1}{\Gamma(\varrho_2)} \int_{x_2}^{x} h_2'(z)(h_2(x) - h_2(z))^{\varrho_2-1} \varphi(z) dz \\
&= w(x_2^-) + \mathcal{I}_2 w(x_2^-) + \frac{1}{\Gamma(\varrho_2)} \int_{x_2}^{x} h_2'(z)(h_2(x) - h_2(z))^{\varrho_2-1} \varphi(z) dz \\
&= w_0 + \rho(w) + \frac{1}{\Gamma(\varrho_0)} \int_{0}^{x_1} h_0'(z)(h_0(x_1) - h_0(z))^{\varrho_0-1} \varphi(z) dz \\
&\quad + \frac{1}{\Gamma(\varrho_1)} \int_{x_1}^{x_2} h_1'(z)(h_1(x_2) - h_1(z))^{\varrho_1-1} \varphi(z) dz \\
&\quad + \frac{1}{\Gamma(\varrho_2)} \int_{x_2}^{x} h_2'(z)(h_2(x) - h_2(z))^{\varrho_2-1} \varphi(z) dz + \mathcal{I}_1 w(x_1^-) + \mathcal{I}_2 w(x_2^-).
\end{aligned}$$

This gives

$$\begin{aligned}
w(x_3^-) &= w_0 + \rho(w) + \frac{1}{\Gamma(\varrho_0)} \int_{0}^{x_1} h_0'(z)(h_0(x_1) - h_0(z))^{\varrho_0-1} \varphi(z) dz \\
&\quad + \frac{1}{\Gamma(\varrho_1)} \int_{x_1}^{x_2} h_1'(z)(h_1(x_2) - h_1(z))^{\varrho_1-1} \varphi(z) dz \\
&\quad + \frac{1}{\Gamma(\varrho_2)} \int_{x_2}^{x_3} h_2'(z)(h_2(x_3) - h_2(z))^{\varrho_2-1} \varphi(z) dz \\
&\quad + \mathcal{I}_1 w(x_1^-) + \mathcal{I}_2 w(x_2^-).
\end{aligned}$$

Applying the impulse $w(x_3^-) = w(x_3^+) - \mathcal{I}_3 w(x_3^-)$, we get

$$\begin{aligned}
w(x_3^+) &= w_0 + \rho(w) + \frac{1}{\Gamma(\varrho_0)} \int_{0}^{x_1} h_0'(z)(h_0(x_1) - h_0(z))^{\varrho_0-1} \varphi(z) dz \\
&\quad + \frac{1}{\Gamma(\varrho_1)} \int_{x_1}^{x_2} h_1'(z)(h_1(x_2) - h_1(z))^{\varrho_1-1} \varphi(z) dz \\
&\quad + \frac{1}{\Gamma(\varrho_2)} \int_{x_2}^{x_3} h_2'(z)(h_2(x_3) - h_2(z))^{\varrho_2-1} \varphi(z) dz \\
&\quad + \mathcal{I}_1 w(x_1^-) + \mathcal{I}_2 w(x_2^-) + \mathcal{I}_3 w(x_3^-).
\end{aligned}$$

Let

$$\begin{aligned}
w(x_\Bbbk^+) &= w_0 + \mathcal{I}_1 w(x_1^-) + \mathcal{I}_2 w(x_2^-) + \mathcal{I}_3 w(x_3^-) + \cdots + \mathcal{I}_\Bbbk w(x_\Bbbk^-) \\
&\quad + \int_{0}^{T} \frac{(T-z)^{\delta-1}}{\Gamma(\delta)} g(w(z)) dz + \frac{1}{\Gamma(\varrho_0)} \int_{0}^{x_1} h_0'(z)(h_0(x_1) - h_0(z))^{\varrho_0-1} \varphi(z) dz \\
&\quad + \frac{1}{\Gamma(\varrho_1)} \int_{x_1}^{x_2} h_1'(z)(h_1(x_2) - h_1(z))^{\varrho_1-1} \varphi(z) dz + \frac{1}{\Gamma(\varrho_2)} \int_{x_2}^{x_3} h_2'(z)(h_2(x_3) - h_2(z))^{\varrho_2-1} \varphi(z) dz \\
&\quad + \cdots + \frac{1}{\Gamma(\varrho_{\Bbbk-1})} \int_{x_{\Bbbk-1}}^{x_\Bbbk} h_{\Bbbk-1}'(z)(h_{\Bbbk-1}(x_\Bbbk) - h_{\Bbbk-1}(z))^{\varrho_{\Bbbk-1}-1} \varphi(z) dz.
\end{aligned}$$

Then, inductively, for $x \in (x_\Bbbk, x_{\Bbbk+1}]$, we have

$$^cD_{[x]}^{\varrho_\Bbbk, h_\Bbbk} w(x) = \varphi(x), \; [x] = x_\Bbbk.$$

Using Lemma A2, the solution becomes

$$\begin{aligned}
w(x) &= w(x_\Bbbk^+) + \frac{1}{\Gamma(\varrho_\Bbbk)} \int_{x_\Bbbk}^{x} h'_\Bbbk(z)(h_\Bbbk(x) - h_\Bbbk(z))^{\varrho_\Bbbk - 1} \varphi(z) dz \\
&= w_0 + \rho(w) + \sum_{i=1}^{\Bbbk} \mathcal{I}_i w(x_i^-) \\
&\quad + \sum_{i=1}^{\Bbbk} \frac{1}{\Gamma(\varrho_{i-1})} \int_{x_{i-1}}^{x_i} h'_{i-1}(z)(h_{i-1}(x_i) - h_{i-1}(z))^{\varrho_{i-1} - 1} \varphi(z) dz \\
&\quad + \frac{1}{\Gamma(\varrho_\Bbbk)} \int_{x_\Bbbk}^{x} h'_\Bbbk(z)(h_\Bbbk(x) - h_\Bbbk(z))^{\varrho_\Bbbk - 1} \varphi(z) dz.
\end{aligned}$$

Hence (4) holds. Conversely, let w satisfies the Equation (4). If $x \in [0, x_1]$, then $w(0) = w_0$. Since ${}^c D_{[x]}^{\varrho(x)}$ is the left inverse of $\mathbb{I}_{[x]}^{\varrho(x)}$ thus using Lemma A1, we have

$$ {}^c D_0^{\varrho_0, h_0} w(x) = \varphi(x), \quad x \in [0, x_1]. $$

If $x \in [x_\Bbbk, x_{\Bbbk+1})$, $\Bbbk = 1, ..., \aleph$. Then for constant function $\sigma(\cdot)$, we have ${}^c D_{[x]}^{\varrho(x)} \sigma(\cdot) = 0$. Thus

$$ {}^c D_{[x]}^{\varrho_\Bbbk, h_\Bbbk} w(x) = \varphi(x), \text{ for each } x \in [x_\Bbbk, x_{\Bbbk+1}). $$

As well, we can simply infer that

$$ w(x_\Bbbk^+) - w(x_\Bbbk^-) = \mathcal{I}_\Bbbk w(x_\Bbbk^-), \; \Bbbk = 1, ..., \aleph. $$

References

1. ALazopoulos, K.A. Non-local continuum mechanics and fractional calculus. *Mech. Res. Commun.* **2006**, *33*, 753–757. [CrossRef]
2. Cottone, G.; Paola, M.D.; Zingales, M. Fractional mechanical model for the dynamics of non-local continuum. *Adv. Numer. Methods* **2009**, *2009*, 389–423.
3. Carpinteri, A.; Cornetti, P.; Sapora, A. A fractional calculus approach to nonlocal elasticity. *Eur. Phys. J. Spec. Top.* **2011**, *193*, 193. [CrossRef]
4. Riewe, F. Mechanics with fractional derivatives. *Phys. Rev.* **1997**, *E55*, 3581. [CrossRef]
5. Rossikhin, Y.A.; Shitikova, M.V. Application of fractional calculus for dynamic problems of solid mechanics: Novel trends and recent results. *Appl. Mech. Rev.* **2010**, *63*, 010801. [CrossRef]
6. Podlubny, I. *Fractional Differential Equations*; Academic Press: San Diego, CA, USA, 1999.
7. Samko, S.G.; Kilbas, A.A.; Marichev, O.I. *Fractional Integrals and Derivatives: Theory and Applications*; Gordon and Breach: New York, NY, USA, 1993.
8. Kusnezov, D.; Bulgac, A.; Dang, G.D. Quantum Levy processes and fractional kinetics. *Phys. Rev. Lett.* **1999**, *82*, 1136–1139. [CrossRef]
9. Arena, P.; Caponetto, R.; Fortuna, L.; Porto, D. Chaos in a fractional order Duffing system. In Proceedings of the 1997 European Conference on Circuit the Ory and Design (ECCTD97), Budapest, Hungary, 30 August–3 September 1997; Technical University of Budapest: Budapest, Hungary, 1997; pp. 1259–1262.
10. Metzler, R.; Klafter, J. The random walks guide to anomalous diffusion: A fractional dynamics approach. *Phys. Rep.* **2000**, *339*, 1–77. [CrossRef]
11. Grigorenko, I.; Grigorenko, E. Chaotic dynamics of the fractional Lorenz system. *Phys. Rev. Lett.* **2003**, *91*, 034101. [CrossRef]
12. Matignon, D. Stability results for fractional differential equations with applications to control processing. In Proceedings of the International IMACS IEEE-SMC Multi Conference on Computational Engineering in Systems Applications, Lille, France, 9–12 July 1996; GERF, Ecole Centrale de Lille: Lille, France, 1996; pp. 963–968.
13. Wu, G.C.; Zeng, D.Q.; Baleanu, D. Fractional impulsive differential equations: Exact solutions, integral equations and short memory case. *Fract. Calc. Appl. Anal.* **2019**, *22*, 180–192. [CrossRef]
14. Wu, G.C.; Luo, M.; Huang, L.L.; Banerjee, S. Short memory fractional differential equations for new memristor and neural network design. *Nonlinear Dyn.* **2020**, *100*, 3611–3623. [CrossRef]
15. Huang, L.L.; Park, J.H.; Wu, G.C.; Mo, Z.W. Variable-order fractional discrete-time recurrent neural networks. *J. Comput. Appl. Math.* **2020**, *370*, 112633. [CrossRef]
16. Wu, G.C.; Deng, Z.G.; Baleanu, D.; Zeng, D.Q. New variable-order fractional chaotic systems for fast image encryption. *Chaos* **2019**, *29*, 083103. [CrossRef] [PubMed]

17. Du, M.; Wang, Z.; Hu, H. Measuring memory with the order of fractional derivative. *Sci. Rep.* **2013**, *3*, 3431. [CrossRef] [PubMed]
18. Caputo, M.; Fabrizio, M. A new definition of fractional derivative without singular kernel. *Progr. Fract. Differ. Appl.* **2015**, *1*, 73–85.
19. Atangana, A.; Baleanu, D. New fractional derivatives with nonlocal and non-singular kernel: Theory and application to heat transfer model. *Therm. Sci.* **2016**, *20*, 763–769. [CrossRef]
20. Wu, G.C.; Gu, C.Y.; Huang, L.L.; Baleanu, D. Fractional differential equations of variable order: Existence results, numerical method and asymptotic stability conditions. *Miskolc Math. Notes* **2022**, *23*, 485–493. [CrossRef]
21. Shah, K.; Abdeljawad, T.; Ali, A. Mathematical analysis of the Cauchy type dynamical system under piecewise equations with Caputo fractional derivative. *Chaos Solitons Fractals* **2022**, *161*, 112356. [CrossRef]
22. Zeb, A.; Atangana, A.; Khan, Z.; Djillali, S. A robust study of a piecewise fractional order COVID-19 mathematical model. *Alex. Eng. J.* **2022**, *61*, 5649–5665. [CrossRef]
23. Ansari, K.J.; Asma; Ilyas, F.; Shah, K.; Khan, A.; Abdeljawad, T. On new updated concept for delay differential equations with piecewise Caputo fractional-order derivative. *Waves Random Complex Media* **2023**, *2023*, 1–20. [CrossRef]
24. Abdeljawad, T.; Mlaiki, N.; Abdo, M.S. Caputo-type fractional systems with variable order depending on the impulses and changing the kernel. *Fractals* **2022**, *30*, 2240219. [CrossRef]
25. Shah, K.; Ali, G.; Ansari, K.J.; Abdeljawad, T.; Meganathan, M.; Abdalla, B. On qualitative analysis of boundary value problem of variable order fractional delay differential equations. *Bound. Value Probl.* **2023**, *2023*, 55. [CrossRef]
26. Tian, Y.; Bai, Z. Existence results for the three-point impulsive boundary value problem involving fractional differential equations. *Comput. Math. Appl.* **2010**, *59*, 2601–2609. [CrossRef]
27. Ali, A.; Shah, K.; Jarad, F.; Gupta, V.; Abdeljawad, T. Existence and stability analysis to a coupled system of implicit type impulsive boundary value problems of fractional-order differential equations. *Adv. Differ. Equ.* **2019**, *2019*, 101. [CrossRef]
28. Wang, J.; Fečkan, M.; Zhou, Y. On the new concept of solutions and existence results for impulsive fractional evolution equations. *Dynam. Part. Differ. Equ.* **2011**, *8*, 345–361.
29. Shah, K.; Bahaaeldin A.; Abdeljawad T.; Gul R. Analysis of multipoint impulsive problem of fractional-order differential equations. *Bound. Value Probl.* **2023**, *1*, 1. [CrossRef]
30. Ibrahim, R.W. Generalized Ulam-Hyers stability for fractional differential equations. *Int. J. Math.* **2012**, *23*, 1250056. [CrossRef]
31. Khan, H.; Abdeljawad, T.; Aslam, M.; Khan, R.A.; Khan, A. Existence of positive solution and Hyers-Ulam stability for a nonlinear singular-delay-fractional differential equation. *Adv. Differ. Equ.* **2019**, *2019*, 104. [CrossRef]
32. Shah, K.; Abdeljawad, T.; Abdalla, B.; Abualrub, M.S. Utilizing fixed point approach to investigate piecewise equations with non-singular type derivative. *AIMS Math.* **2022**, *7*, 14614–14630. [CrossRef]
33. Chen, C.; Bohner, M.; Jia, B. Ulam-Hyers stability of Caputo fractional difference equations. *Math. Methods Appl. Sci.* **2019**, *42*, 7461–7470. [CrossRef]
34. Sousa, J.V.D.C.; Oliveira, E.C.D. Ulam-Hyers stability of a nonlinear fractional Volterra integro-differential equation. *Appl. Math. Lett.* **2018**, *81*, 50–56. [CrossRef]
35. He, W.; Chen, G.; Han, Q.L.; Qian, F. Network-based leader-following consensus of nonlinear multi-agent systems via distributed impulsive control. *Inf. Sci.* **2017**, *380*, 145–158. [CrossRef]
36. Wu, S.; Li, X.; Ding, Y. Saturated impulsive control for synchronization of coupled delayed neural networks. *Neural Netw.* **2021**, *141*, 261–269. [CrossRef] [PubMed]
37. Suo, J.; Sun, J.; Zhang, Y. Stability analysis for impulsive coupled systems on networks. *Neurocomputing* **2013**, *99*, 172–177. [CrossRef]
38. Shah, K.; Khalil, H.; Khan, R.A. Investigation of positive solution to a coupled system of impulsive boundary value problems for nonlinear fractional order differential equations. *Chaos Solitons Fractals* **2015**, *77*, 240–246. [CrossRef]
39. Wang, J.; Feckan, M.; Zhou, Y. Fractional order differential switched systems with coupled nonlocal initial and impulsive conditions. *Bull. Sci. Mathématiques* **2017**, *141*, 727–746. [CrossRef]
40. Almeida, R. A Caputo fractional derivative of a function with respect to another function. *Commun. Nonlinear Sci. Numer. Simul.* **2017**, *44*, 460–481. [CrossRef]
41. Schaefer, H. Über die Methode der a priori-Schranken. *Math. Ann.* **1955**, *129*, 415–416. [CrossRef]

Disclaimer/Publisher's Note: The statements, opinions and data contained in all publications are solely those of the individual author(s) and contributor(s) and not of MDPI and/or the editor(s). MDPI and/or the editor(s) disclaim responsibility for any injury to people or property resulting from any ideas, methods, instructions or products referred to in the content.

Article

Approximate Solutions for Time-Fractional Fornberg–Whitham Equation with Variable Coefficients

Fahad Alsidrani [1,2], Adem Kılıçman [2,3,*] and Norazak Senu [2,3]

[1] Department of Mathematics, College of Science and Arts, Qassim University, Al Methnab 51931, Qassim, Saudi Arabia
[2] Institute for Mathematical Research, Universiti Putra Malaysia, Serdang 43400, Selangor, Malaysia
[3] Department of Mathematics and Statistics, Faculty of Science, Universiti Putra Malaysia, Serdang 43400, Selangor, Malaysia
* Correspondence: akilic@upm.edu.my

Abstract: In this research, three numerical methods, namely the variational iteration method, the Adomian decomposition method, and the homotopy analysis method are considered to achieve an approximate solution for a third-order time-fractional partial differential Equation (TFPDE). The equation is obtained from the classical (FW) equation by replacing the integer-order time derivative with the Caputo fractional derivative of order $\eta = (0,1]$ with variable coefficients. We consider homogeneous boundary conditions to find the approximate solutions for the bounded space variable $l < \chi < L$ and $l, L \in \mathbb{R}$. To confirm the effectiveness of the proposed methods of non-integer order η, the computation of two test problems was presented. A comparison is made between the obtained results of the (VIM), (ADM), and (HAM) through tables and graphs. The numerical results demonstrate the effectiveness of the three numerical methods.

Keywords: fractional Fornberg–Whitham equation; approximate solution; partial differential equation; Riemann–Liouville derivatives; Caputo's derivatives; variational iteration method; Adomian decomposition method; homotopy analysis method

1. Introduction

The concept of fractional partial differential equations (FPDEs) has been the focus of many studies and an essential topic in computational mathematics due to their various applications in scientific fields. The fractional derivative allows for a more accurate description of the diffusion process, considering the effects of long-range interactions and memory effects in most biological systems and phenomena in physics [1]. In recent years, researchers have demonstrated that many phenomena are successfully described by mathematical models of non-integer order using mathematical tools, for example, the Keller–Segel model for chemotaxis [1], fractional Riccati differential equations [2], and diffusion wave equations [3,4]. The cost of solving large nonlinear systems and related large linear systems after linearization can vary depending on various factors, including the complexity of the system and the method used for solving the system. It is worth noticing that different discretization methods for fractional diffusion equations (FDEs) have been proposed to solve a large linear system. In [5], Donatelli et al. have studied the diffusion equation, which arises in many applications that involves fractional derivatives in the case of variable coefficients (FDE). The proposed method was based on spectral analysis and structure preserving preconditioners for solving the (FDE). The method involves discretization in the space of the fractional diffusion equation, which leads to a linear system with coefficient matrices having a Toeplitz-like structure. In addition, they have shown that the variable coefficient matrix sequence belongs to the generalized locally Toeplitz (GLT) sequences. In [6], Donatelli et al. have implemented a finite volume (FV) method to discretize the space-fractional diffusion Equation (SFDE) with variable coefficients and obtain a large linear system resulting in a

sequence of coefficient matrices. The fractional derivative is considered in the Riesz-space fractional derivative. They showed that the resulting sequence of coefficient matrices belongs to the generalized locally Toeplitz (GLT) sequences. They also developed a good preconditioner and multigrid method to efficiently solve the obtained linear system of equations. In [7], Lin et al. developed fast algorithms for solving the linear systems that arise from the discretized time-dependent space-fractional diffusion Equation (SFDE) with non-constant coefficients. They also proved the convergence of two iteration schemes, one pre-smoother and the other post-smoother. In [8], Bu et al. presented a numerical method for solving a large linear system of the multi-term time-fractional advection–diffusion Equation (MTADE) using the finite element multigrid method. The method is based on the fractional derivative in the Riesz–Caputo sense, and the finite element approximation is considered in the space direction and time direction, respectively. They also discussed the stability and convergence of fully discrete schemes of (MTADE) in two situations.

The fractional derivative (FD) is even more significant in modeling real-life situations; for example, the fractional partial nonlinear Fornberg–Whitham (FPNFW) equation is a mathematical model that describes the evolution of nonlinear dispersive waves in fluid dynamics and the behavior of waves in plasmas.

Consider the nonlinear time-fractional Fornberg–Whitham equation

$$\psi_\zeta^\eta(\chi,\zeta) - \psi_{\chi\chi\zeta}(\chi,\zeta) + \psi_\chi(\chi,\zeta) + \psi(\chi,\zeta)\psi_\chi(\chi,\zeta) - \psi(\chi,\zeta)\psi_{\chi\chi\chi}(\chi,\zeta) - 3\psi_\chi(\chi,\zeta)\psi_{\chi\chi}(\chi,\zeta) = 0 \qquad (1)$$

where $\psi(\chi,\zeta)$ is the fluid velocity, $0 < \eta \leq 1$ is the order of fractional equation, $\zeta > 0$ is the time, and χ is the spatial coordinate. In addition, when $\eta = 1$, Equation (1) is reduced to the original Fornberg–Whitham equation, which was first proposed by Whitham in 1967 for studying the qualitative behavior of wave breaking [9]. In 1978, Fornberg and Whitham [10] obtained a peaked solution of the form $\psi(\chi,\zeta) = \mathcal{K}exp\left(-1/2|\chi - 4\zeta/3|\right)$, where $\mathcal{K}$ is an arbitrary constant. In the literature, several mathematical methods have been implemented to obtain the approximate solutions of fractional differential equations, such as the Adomian decomposition method (ADM), variational iteration method (VIM), homotopy analysis method (HAM), homotopy perturbation method (HPM), Hermite wavelet method (HWM), optimal homotopy asymptotic method (OHAM), Shehu decomposition method (SDM), variational iteration transform method (VITM), Laplace decomposition method (LDM), direct power series method (DPSM), and others.

In [11], Kumar et al. solved the time-fractional Fornberg–Whitham equation involving the Atangana–Baleanu (AB) fractional derivative of non-integer order of the function $\psi(\chi,\zeta)$ by using the Laplace decomposition method (LDM). This method is a mix of Adomian's decomposition method and the Laplace transform approach. The existence of the solution and the uniqueness of the solution of the nonlinear Fornberg–Whitham equation of fractional order were examined. In [12], Gupta and Singh used the homotopy perturbation method (HPM) to find the approximate numerical solution of the time-fractional Fornberg–Whitham equation where the derivatives are taken in the Caputo sense. In [13], Merdan et al. implemented a differential transformation method (DTM) to obtain an approximate analytical solution of the fractional Fornberg–Whitham equation. In [14], Alderremy et al. used the natural transform decomposition method (NTDM) to obtain the approximate numerical solution of the fractional Fornberg–Whitham equation in view of the Caputo operator. In [15], Fayçal and Omrani used two powerful techniques, namely the homotopy analysis method (HAM) and the Adomian's decomposition method (ADM) to obtain an approximate analytical solution of the nonlinear Fornberg–Whitham equation, where $\eta = 1$, and concluded that these methods have perfect accuracy and reductions in the size of calculations. In [16], Wang et al. combined He's (HPM) and the fractional complex transform to find an approximate solution to the nonlinear time-fractional Fornberg–Whitham equation. Recently, in [17], Sartanpara et al. used the p-Homotopy analysis Shehu transform method for the time-fractional Fornberg–Whitham equation with the derivative of the fractional-order in the Caputo sense to obtain the approximate analytical solution.

In [18], Hijaz et al. numerically solved the Fornberg–Whitham classical type and modified type equations via the variational iteration algorithm-I. They used an auxiliary parameter to speed up the convergence rate to the exact solution. In [19], Shah et al. implemented modified techniques, namely the Shehu decomposition method (SDM) and the variational iteration transform method (VITM), to achieve an approximate analytical solution for the time-fractional Fornberg–Whitham equation. The fractional derivative is considered in the Caputo sense. In [20], Iqbal et al. successfully applied two modified methods to investigate the approximate solutions of the fractional Fornberg–Whitham equation. There was agreement between the numerical results obtained by the modified decomposition method (MDM) and modified variational iteration method (MVIM) involving fractional-order derivatives with Mittag–Leffler kernel.

In this paper, we consider the third-order time-fractional partial differential Equation (TFPDE) with variable coefficients

$$\frac{\partial^\eta \psi(\chi,\zeta)}{\partial \zeta^\eta} - \alpha(\chi)\frac{\partial^3 \psi(\chi,\zeta)}{\partial \chi^2 \partial \zeta} + 2\kappa(\chi)\frac{\partial \psi(\chi,\zeta)}{\partial \chi} + \beta(\chi)\psi(\chi,\zeta)\frac{\partial \psi(\chi,\zeta)}{\partial \chi}$$
$$- \gamma(\chi)\psi(\chi,\zeta)\frac{\partial^3 \psi(\chi,\zeta)}{\partial \chi^3} - \omega(\chi)\frac{\partial \psi(\chi,\zeta)}{\partial \chi}\frac{\partial^2 \psi(\chi,\zeta)}{\partial \chi^2} = 0, \quad l < \chi < L, \quad l,L \in \mathbb{R} \quad (2)$$

with the initial and homogeneous boundary conditions

$$\psi(\chi,0) = \phi(\chi)$$
$$\psi(l,\zeta) = 0, \quad \psi(L,\zeta) = 0, \quad \zeta > 0 \quad (3)$$

where $\alpha(\chi), \kappa(x), \beta(\chi), \gamma(\chi), \omega(\chi)$ are the variable coefficients and $p-1 < \eta \leq p, (p \in \mathbb{N})$ is a parameter describing the order of the time-fractional equation. The reason behind including variable coefficients in the time-fractional Fornberg–Whitham equation is that it becomes a more accurate model for the propagation of waves. This makes it a useful tool for studying a variety of phenomena, including fluid dynamics, plasma physics, and others. It is important to note that Equation (2) contains different interesting nonlinear equations. In particular, for $\eta = 1$, when $\beta = 6\gamma = -1$ and $\alpha = \kappa = \omega = 0$ in Equation (2), we obtain the well-known Korteweg–de Vries Equation (KdV), as given in [21]

$$\psi_\zeta + 6\psi\psi_\chi + \psi_{\chi\chi\chi} = 0, \quad \chi \in \mathbb{R}, \quad \zeta > 0. \quad (4)$$

When $\alpha = \gamma = 1, \kappa = 0, \beta = 4$, and $\omega = 3$ in Equation (2), we obtain the Degasperis–Procesi equation (DPE), as given in [22]

$$\psi_\zeta - \psi_{\chi\chi\zeta} + 4\psi\psi_\chi - \psi\psi_{\chi\chi\chi} - 3\psi_\chi\psi_{\chi\chi} = 0, \quad \chi \in \mathbb{R}, \quad \zeta > 0. \quad (5)$$

When $\alpha = \omega = 1, \beta = 3, \gamma = 2$ in Equation (2), and $\kappa \in \mathbb{R}$ is a parameter related to the critical shallow water speed, we obtain the Camassa–Holm Equation (CHE), as given in [21]

$$\psi_\zeta - \psi_{\chi\chi\zeta} + 2\kappa\psi_\chi + 3\psi\psi_\chi - 2\psi\psi_{\chi\chi\chi} - \psi_\chi\psi_{\chi\chi} = 0, \quad \chi \in \mathbb{R}, \quad \zeta > 0. \quad (6)$$

When $\alpha = \beta = \gamma = 1, \kappa = \frac{1}{2}$ and $\omega = 3$ in Equation (2), we obtain the Fornberg–Whitham Equation (FWE), as given in [9]

$$\psi_\zeta - \psi_{\chi\chi\zeta} + \psi_\chi + \psi\psi_\chi - \psi\psi_{\chi\chi\chi} - 3\psi_\chi\psi_{\chi\chi} = 0, \quad \chi \in \mathbb{R}, \quad \zeta > 0 \quad (7)$$

We organize the paper as follows. Section 2 defines preliminary definitions and some properties of the Riemann–Liouville integral and Caputo fractional derivative. In Section 3, the analysis of (VIM) for the nonlinear fractional equation is established. In Section 4, the analysis of (ADM) for the nonlinear fractional equation is established. In Section 5, the analysis of (HAM) for the nonlinear fractional equation is established. Section 6 illustrates the methods for solving time-fractional partial differential equations (TFPDEs) with suitable initial conditions.

2. Problem Formulation and Preliminaries

In this section, we present the definitions of partial Riemann–Liouville integrals, partial Riemann–Liouville derivatives, and Caputo time-fractional derivatives with some properties of the Caputo fractional derivatives, which will be used later.

Definition 1 ([23]). *Let $\eta \in (0,1)$ and $\psi \in L^{-1}(D)$. The partial Riemann–Liouville fractional integrals of order η of a function $\psi(\chi, \zeta)$ with respect to ζ are defined as*

$$_a^{RL}\mathcal{I}_\zeta^\eta(\psi(\chi, \zeta)) = \frac{1}{\Gamma(\eta)} \int_a^\zeta (\zeta - \xi)^{\eta-1} \psi(\chi, \xi) d\xi, \tag{8}$$

for almost all $(\chi, \zeta) \in D$ and $\Gamma(\eta)$ is the well-known Gamma function.

Definition 2 ([23]). *Let $p - 1 < \eta \leq p, p \in \mathbb{N}$ and $\psi \in L^{-1}(D)$. The partial Riemann–Liouville fractional derivatives of order η of a function $\psi(\chi, \zeta)$ with respect to ζ are defined as*

$$_a\mathcal{D}_\zeta^\eta(\psi(\chi, \zeta)) = \frac{\partial^p}{\partial \zeta^p} {_a\mathcal{I}_\zeta^{p-\eta}}(\psi(\chi, \zeta)) = \frac{\partial^p}{\partial \zeta^p} \left(\frac{1}{\Gamma(p-\eta)} \int_a^\zeta (\zeta - \xi)^{p-\eta-1} \psi(\chi, \xi) d\xi \right) \tag{9}$$

for almost all $(\chi, \zeta) \in D$.

For $\psi \in C_\mu$, $\mu \geq -1$, $\gamma > -1$ and $\eta, \beta \geq 0$, the operator $_a\mathcal{I}_\zeta^\eta$ satisfies the following properties [24].

(1) $_a\mathcal{I}_\zeta^\eta {_a\mathcal{I}_\zeta^\beta}(\psi(\zeta)) = {_a\mathcal{I}_\zeta^\beta} {_a\mathcal{I}_\zeta^\eta}(\psi(\zeta)) = {_a\mathcal{I}_\zeta^{\eta+\beta}}(\psi(\zeta))$

(2) $_a\mathcal{I}_\zeta^\eta (\zeta - a)^\gamma = \frac{\Gamma(\gamma+1)}{\Gamma(\eta+\gamma+1)} (\zeta - a)^{\eta+\gamma}$

Definition 3 ([25]). *Let p be the smallest integer that exceeds η, and the Caputo time-fractional derivative operator of order $\eta > 0$ of a function $\psi(\chi, \zeta)$ is defined as*

$$^C\mathcal{D}_\zeta^\eta(\psi(\chi, \zeta)) = \begin{cases} \mathcal{I}_\zeta^{p-\eta}\left(\frac{\partial^p \psi(\chi, \zeta)}{\partial \zeta^p}\right) = \frac{1}{\Gamma(p-\eta)} \int_0^\zeta (\zeta - \xi)^{p-\eta-1} \frac{\partial^p \psi(\chi, \xi)}{\partial \xi^p} d\xi, & p-1 < \tau < p \\ \frac{\partial^p \psi(\chi, \zeta)}{\partial \zeta^p} & \eta = p \in \mathbb{N} \end{cases} \tag{10}$$

The operator $\mathcal{D}_\zeta^\eta$ satisfies the following properties [24]. Let $\zeta > 0$, $p - 1 < \eta \leq p$, $(p \in \mathbb{N})$, then

(1) $\mathcal{I}_\zeta^\eta \mathcal{D}_\zeta^\eta(\psi(\chi, \zeta)) = \psi(\chi, \zeta) - \sum_{k=0}^{p-1} \frac{\zeta^k}{k!} \frac{\partial^k}{\partial \zeta^k} \psi(\chi, \zeta)\big|_{\zeta=0}$

(2) $\mathcal{D}_\zeta^\eta \mathcal{I}_\zeta^\eta(\psi(\chi, \zeta)) = \psi(\chi, \zeta)$

3. Analysis of Variational Iteration Method

In this section, we discuss the (VIM) solution for the time-fractional partial differential Equation (TFPDE) with variable coefficients. This method can reduce the size of calculations and directly handle both linear and nonlinear equations, homogeneous or non-homogeneous [26,27].

We consider the following time-fractional partial differential equation

$$\mathcal{D}_\zeta^\eta \psi(\chi, \zeta) + \mathcal{L}\psi(\chi, \zeta) + \mathcal{N}\psi(\chi, \zeta) = \mathcal{G}(\chi, \zeta) \tag{11}$$

where $\mathcal{D}_\zeta^\eta$ is the Caputo fractional derivative of order $p - 1 < \eta \leq p$, $(p \in \mathbb{N})$, $\mathcal{L}$ is the linear operator, $\mathcal{N}$ is the nonlinear operator, and $\mathcal{G}(\chi, \zeta)$ is a known analytical function. According to the variational iteration method [28,29], to solve the third-order time-fractional partial differential Equation (TFPDE) with variable coefficients in Equation (2), the correction functional can be constructed as follows

$$\psi_{k+1}(\chi,\zeta) = \psi_k(\chi,\zeta) + \mathcal{I}_\zeta^\gamma\left[\lambda\left(\mathcal{D}_\zeta^\eta \psi_k(\chi,\zeta) + \mathcal{L}\tilde{\psi}_k(\chi,\zeta) + \mathcal{N}\tilde{\psi}_k(\chi,\zeta)\right)\right]$$

$$= \psi_k(\chi,\zeta) + \frac{1}{\Gamma(\gamma)}\int_0^\zeta (\zeta-\xi)^{\gamma-1}\lambda(\xi)\left(\frac{\partial^\eta \psi_k(\chi,\xi)}{\partial \xi^\eta} - \alpha(\chi)\frac{\partial^3 \tilde{\psi}_k(\chi,\xi)}{\partial \chi^2 \partial \xi} + 2\kappa(\chi)\frac{\partial \tilde{\psi}_k(\chi,\xi)}{\partial \chi}\right.$$
$$\left. + \beta(\chi)\tilde{\psi}_k(\chi,\xi)\frac{\partial \tilde{\psi}_k(\chi,\xi)}{\partial \chi} - \gamma(\chi)\tilde{\psi}_k(\chi,\xi)\frac{\partial^3 \tilde{\psi}_k(\chi,\xi)}{\partial \chi^3} - \omega(\chi)\frac{\partial \tilde{\psi}_k(\chi,\xi)}{\partial \chi}\frac{\partial^2 \tilde{\psi}_k(\chi,\xi)}{\partial \chi^2}\right)d\xi \qquad (12)$$

where $\mathcal{I}_\zeta^\gamma$ denotes the Riemann–Liouville integral operator of order $\gamma = \eta + 1 - p$, subject to the initial and boundary conditions in Equation (3), where λ is a general Lagrange multiplier which can be identified by variational theory, ψ_k is the kth approximate solution and $\tilde{\psi}_k$ is considered as a restricted variation, i.e., $\delta\tilde{\psi}_k = 0$. This method first requires determining the Lagrange multiplier λ, and it can be easily identified as

$$\lambda(\xi) = \frac{(-1)^p(\xi-\zeta)^{p-1}}{(p-1)!} \qquad (13)$$

where p is the highest order of the differential equation. By determining the value of Lagrange multiplier λ, the successive approximations ψ_{k+1} will be calculated using the given initial function ψ_0.

Making the above correction functional stationary and noticing that $\delta\tilde{\psi}_k = 0$, we obtain

$$\delta\psi_{k+1}(\chi,\zeta) = \delta\psi_k(\chi,\zeta) + \frac{1}{\Gamma(\gamma)}\delta\int_0^\zeta (\zeta-\xi)^{\gamma-1}\lambda(\xi)\left(\frac{\partial^\eta \psi_k(\chi,\xi)}{\partial \xi^\eta} - \alpha(\chi)\frac{\partial^3 \tilde{\psi}_k(\chi,\xi)}{\partial \chi^2 \partial \xi} + 2\kappa(\chi)\frac{\partial \tilde{\psi}_k(\chi,\xi)}{\partial \chi}\right.$$
$$\left. + \beta(\chi)\tilde{\psi}_k(\chi,\xi)\frac{\partial \tilde{\psi}_k(\chi,\xi)}{\partial \chi} - \gamma(\chi)\tilde{\psi}_k(\chi,\xi)\frac{\partial^3 \tilde{\psi}_k(\chi,\xi)}{\partial \chi^3} - \omega(\chi)\frac{\partial \tilde{\psi}_k(\chi,\xi)}{\partial \chi}\frac{\partial^2 \tilde{\psi}_k(\chi,\xi)}{\partial \chi^2}\right)d\xi$$
$$= \delta\psi_k(\chi,\zeta) + \frac{1}{\Gamma(\gamma)}\delta\int_0^\zeta (\zeta-\xi)^{\gamma-1}\lambda(\xi)\left(\frac{\partial^p \psi_k(\chi,\xi)}{\partial \xi^p}\right)d\xi \qquad (14)$$

This yields the Lagrange multipliers $\lambda(\xi) = -1$ for $p = 1$, and substituting this value of the Lagrange multiplier into the corrections functional Equation (12) gives the iteration formula for $0 < \eta \leq 1$

$$\psi_{k+1}(\chi,\zeta) = \psi_k(\chi,\zeta) - \mathcal{I}_\zeta^\eta\left(\frac{\partial^\eta \psi_k(\chi,\zeta)}{\partial \zeta^\eta} - \alpha(\chi)\frac{\partial^3 \psi_k(\chi,\zeta)}{\partial \chi^2 \partial \zeta} + 2\kappa(\chi)\frac{\partial \psi_k(\chi,\zeta)}{\partial \chi}\right.$$
$$\left. + \beta(\chi)\psi_k(\chi,\zeta)\frac{\partial \psi_k(\chi,\zeta)}{\partial \chi} - \gamma(\chi)\psi_k(\chi,\zeta)\frac{\partial^3 \psi_k(\chi,\zeta)}{\partial \chi^3} - \omega(\chi)\frac{\partial \psi_k(\chi,\zeta)}{\partial \chi}\frac{\partial^2 \psi_k(\chi,\zeta)}{\partial \chi^2}\right) \qquad (15)$$

Considering the given initial condition values, $\psi_0(\chi,\zeta) = \phi(\chi)$, and using this selection in Equation (15), we obtain the following successive approximations for $k = 0, 1, \cdots$

$$\psi_1(\chi,\zeta) = \psi_0(\chi,\zeta) - \mathcal{I}_\zeta^\eta\left(\frac{\partial^\eta \psi_0(\chi,\zeta)}{\partial \zeta^\eta} - \alpha(\chi)\frac{\partial^3 \psi_0(\chi,\zeta)}{\partial \chi^2 \partial \zeta} + 2\kappa(\chi)\frac{\partial \psi_0(\chi,\zeta)}{\partial \chi}\right.$$
$$\left. + \beta(\chi)\psi_0(\chi,\zeta)\frac{\partial \psi_0(\chi,\zeta)}{\partial \chi} - \gamma(\chi)\psi_0(\chi,\zeta)\frac{\partial^3 \psi_0(\chi,\zeta)}{\partial \chi^3} - \omega(\chi)\frac{\partial \psi_0(\chi,\zeta)}{\partial \chi}\frac{\partial^2 \psi_0(\chi,\zeta)}{\partial \chi^2}\right) \qquad (16)$$

$$\psi_2(\chi,\zeta) = \psi_1(\chi,\zeta) - \mathcal{I}_\zeta^\eta\left(\frac{\partial^\eta \psi_1(\chi,\zeta)}{\partial \zeta^\eta} - \alpha(\chi)\frac{\partial^3 \psi_1(\chi,\zeta)}{\partial \chi^2 \partial \zeta} + 2\kappa(\chi)\frac{\partial \psi_1(\chi,\zeta)}{\partial \chi}\right.$$
$$\left. + \beta(\chi)\psi_1(\chi,\zeta)\frac{\partial \psi_1(\chi,\zeta)}{\partial \chi} - \gamma(\chi)\psi_1(\chi,\zeta)\frac{\partial^3 \psi_1(\chi,\zeta)}{\partial \chi^3} - \omega(\chi)\frac{\partial \psi_1(\chi,\zeta)}{\partial \chi}\frac{\partial^2 \psi_1(\chi,\zeta)}{\partial \chi^2}\right) \qquad (17)$$

$\vdots$

Thus, the corrections' functional Equation (15) will give a sequence of approximations $\psi_k(\chi, \zeta) = \sum_{m=0}^{k-1} \psi_m(\chi, \zeta)$.

Therefore, the solution of Equation (2) is given by

$$\psi(\chi, \zeta) = \lim_{k \to \infty} \psi_k(\chi, \zeta) \tag{18}$$

4. Analysis of Adomian Decomposition Method

In this section, we discuss the (ADM) solution for the time-fractional partial differential Equation (TFPDE) with variable coefficients. This method provides an analytical approximation to a rather wide class of nonlinear and stochastic equations without linearization, perturbation, closure approximations, or discretization methods resulting in massive numerical computation [30,31].

We consider the following time-fractional partial differential equation

$$\mathcal{D}_\zeta^\eta \psi(\chi, \zeta) + \mathcal{L}\psi(\chi, \zeta) + \mathcal{N}\psi(\chi, \zeta) = \mathcal{G}(\chi, \zeta) \tag{19}$$

where $\mathcal{D}_\zeta^\eta$ is the Caputo fractional derivative of order $p-1 < \eta \leq p$, ($p \in \mathbb{N}$), $\mathcal{L}$ is the linear operator, $\mathcal{N}$ is the nonlinear operator, and $\mathcal{G}(\chi, \zeta)$ is a known analytical function. To solve the third-order time-fractional partial differential Equation (TFPDE) with the variable coefficients shown in Equation (2), by Adomin decomposition method, we express this equation in the operator form as

$$\mathcal{D}_\zeta^\eta \psi(\chi,\zeta) - \alpha(\chi)\mathcal{L}_{\chi\chi\zeta}\psi(\chi,\zeta) + 2\kappa(\chi)\mathcal{L}_\chi\psi(\chi,\zeta) + \beta(\chi)\psi(\chi,\zeta)\mathcal{L}_\chi\psi(\chi,\zeta) \\ - \gamma(\chi)\psi(\chi,\zeta)\mathcal{L}_{\chi\chi\chi}\psi(\chi,\zeta) - \omega(\chi)\mathcal{L}_\chi\psi(\chi,\zeta)\mathcal{L}_{\chi\chi}\psi(\chi,\zeta) = 0 \tag{20}$$

with the initial and boundary conditions shown in Equation (3), which are equivalent to

$$\mathcal{D}_\zeta^\eta \psi(\chi,\zeta) - \alpha(\chi)\mathcal{L}_{\chi\chi\zeta}\psi(\chi,\zeta) + 2\kappa(\chi)\mathcal{L}_\chi\psi(\chi,\zeta) + \mathcal{N}\psi(\chi,\zeta) = 0 \tag{21}$$

Solving Equation (21) for $\mathcal{D}_\zeta^\eta \psi(\chi,\zeta)$, we obtain

$$\mathcal{D}_\zeta^\eta \psi(\chi,\zeta) = \alpha(\chi)\mathcal{L}_{\chi\chi\zeta}\psi(\chi,\zeta) - 2\kappa(\chi)\mathcal{L}_\chi\psi(\chi,\zeta) - \mathcal{N}\psi(\chi,\zeta) \tag{22}$$

where $\alpha(\chi), \kappa(\chi), \beta(\chi), \gamma(\chi)$, and $\omega(\chi)$ are continuous functions, η is the parameter describing the order of the time-fractional derivative, the notations $\mathcal{D}_\zeta^\eta = \frac{\partial^\eta}{\partial \zeta^\eta}$, $\mathcal{L}_{\chi\chi\zeta} = \frac{\partial^3}{\partial \chi^2 \partial \zeta}$, $\mathcal{L}_\chi = \frac{\partial}{\partial \chi}$, $\mathcal{L}_{\chi\chi} = \frac{\partial^2}{\partial \chi^2}$, and $\mathcal{L}_{\chi\chi\chi} = \frac{\partial^3}{\partial \chi^3}$ are the symbolize of the linear operators, and $\mathcal{N}\psi(\chi,\zeta) = \beta(\chi)\psi(\chi,\zeta)\mathcal{L}_\chi\psi(\chi,\zeta) - \gamma(\chi)\psi(\chi,\zeta)\mathcal{L}_{\chi\chi\chi}\psi(\chi,\zeta) - \omega(\chi)\mathcal{L}_\chi\psi(\chi,\zeta)\mathcal{L}_{\chi\chi}\psi(\chi,\zeta)$ symbolizes the nonlinear operators. Applying the operator $\mathcal{I}_\zeta^\eta$ on both sides of Equation (22), with the basic properties of the operator $\mathcal{D}_\zeta^\eta$, we obtain

$$\mathcal{I}_\zeta^\eta \mathcal{D}_\zeta^\eta \psi(\chi,\zeta) = \mathcal{I}_\zeta^\eta [\alpha(\chi)\mathcal{L}_{\chi\chi\zeta}\psi(\chi,\zeta) - 2\kappa(\chi)\mathcal{L}_\chi\psi(\chi,\zeta) - \mathcal{N}\psi(\chi,\zeta)] \tag{23}$$

$$\psi(\chi,\zeta) - \sum_{k=0}^{p-1} \frac{\zeta^k}{k!} \frac{\partial^k}{\partial \zeta^k}\psi(\chi,\zeta)\bigg|_{\zeta=0} = \mathcal{I}_\zeta^\eta[\alpha(\chi)\mathcal{L}_{\chi\chi\zeta}\psi(\chi,\zeta) - 2\kappa(\chi)\mathcal{L}_\chi\psi(\chi,\zeta) - \mathcal{N}\psi(\chi,\zeta)] \tag{24}$$

$$\psi(\chi,\zeta) = \sum_{k=0}^{p-1} \frac{\zeta^k}{k!} \frac{\partial^k}{\partial \zeta^k}\psi(\chi,\zeta)\bigg|_{\zeta=0} + \mathcal{I}_\zeta^\eta[\alpha(\chi)\mathcal{L}_{\chi\chi\zeta}\psi(\chi,\zeta) - 2\kappa(\chi)\mathcal{L}_\chi\psi(\chi,\zeta) - \mathcal{N}\psi(\chi,\zeta)] \tag{25}$$

Since the Adomain decomposition method is in the form of an infinite series

$$\psi(\chi,\zeta) = \sum_{m=0}^{\infty} \psi_m(\chi,\zeta) \tag{26}$$

and the nonlinear term $\mathcal{N}\psi(\chi,\zeta)$ can be decomposed into an infinite series of polynomials given by

$$\mathcal{N}\psi(\chi,\zeta) = \sum_{m=0}^{\infty} \mathcal{A}_m(\chi,\zeta) \qquad (27)$$

where $\mathcal{A}_m(\chi,\zeta)$ are the Adomain polynomials of $\psi_0, \psi_1, \cdots, \psi_m$ defined by

$$\mathcal{A}_m(\psi_0, \psi_1, \cdots, \psi_m) = \frac{1}{m!} \frac{d^m}{d\lambda^m} \left[\mathcal{N}\left(\sum_{j=0}^{\infty} \lambda^j \psi_j \right) \right]_{\lambda=0}, \quad m = 0, 1, \ldots \qquad (28)$$

Therefore, the first Adomain polynomials for $\mathcal{N}\psi(\chi,\zeta)$ are defined by

$$\begin{aligned}
\mathcal{A}_0 &= \mathcal{N}(\psi_0) \\
\mathcal{A}_1 &= \psi_1 \left(\frac{d\mathcal{N}(\psi_0)}{d\psi_0} \right) \\
\mathcal{A}_2 &= \psi_2 \left(\frac{d\mathcal{N}(\psi_0)}{d\psi_0} \right) + \frac{\psi_1^2}{2!} \left(\frac{d^2\mathcal{N}(\psi_0)}{d\psi_0^2} \right) \\
\mathcal{A}_3 &= \psi_3 \left(\frac{d\mathcal{N}(\psi_0)}{d\psi_0} \right) + \psi_1 \psi_2 \left(\frac{d^2\mathcal{N}(\psi_0)}{d\psi_0^2} \right) + \frac{\psi_1^3}{3!} \left(\frac{d^3\mathcal{N}(\psi_0)}{d\psi_0^3} \right) \\
\mathcal{A}_4 &= \psi_4 \left(\frac{d\mathcal{N}(\psi_0)}{d\psi_0} \right) + \psi_1 \psi_3 \left(\frac{d^2\mathcal{N}(\psi_0)}{d\psi_0^2} \right) + \frac{\psi_2^2}{2!} \left(\frac{d^2\mathcal{N}(\psi_0)}{d\psi_0^2} \right) + \frac{\psi_1^2 \psi_2}{2!} \left(\frac{d^3\mathcal{N}(\psi_0)}{d\psi_0^3} \right) + \frac{\psi_1^3}{4!} \mathcal{N}^{(4)}(\psi_0) \\
&\vdots
\end{aligned} \qquad (29)$$

Substituting Equations (26) and (27) into Equation (25), we obtain

$$\sum_{m=0}^{\infty} \psi_m(\chi,\zeta) = \sum_{k=0}^{p-1} \frac{\zeta^k}{k!} \frac{\partial^k}{\partial \zeta^k} \psi(\chi,\zeta) \bigg|_{\zeta=0} + \mathcal{I}_\zeta^\eta \left[\alpha(\chi) \mathcal{L}_{\chi\chi\zeta} \sum_{m=0}^{\infty} \psi_m(\chi,\zeta) - 2\kappa(\chi) \mathcal{L}_\chi \sum_{m=0}^{\infty} \psi_m(\chi,\zeta) - \sum_{m=0}^{\infty} \mathcal{A}_m(\chi,\zeta) \right] \qquad (30)$$

The Adomain decomposition method transforms Equation (30) into a set of recursive relations given by

$$\psi_0(\chi,\zeta) = \sum_{k=0}^{p-1} \frac{\zeta^k}{k!} \frac{\partial^k}{\partial \zeta^k} \psi(\chi,\zeta) \bigg|_{\zeta=0} \qquad (31)$$

$$\psi_{m+1}(\chi,\zeta) = \mathcal{I}_\zeta^\eta \left[\alpha(\chi) \mathcal{L}_{\chi\chi\zeta} \psi_m(\chi,\zeta) - 2\kappa(\chi) \mathcal{L}_\chi \psi_m(\chi,\zeta) - \mathcal{A}_m(\chi,\zeta) \right], \quad m \geq 0$$

Let the expression

$$\psi_m(\chi,\zeta) = \sum_{k=0}^{m-1} \psi_k(\chi,\zeta) \qquad (32)$$

be the m-term approximation of ψ. Using the above recursive relation Equation (31), we can obtain the first terms of (ADM) series solution for $m = 0, 1, \cdots$

$$\psi_1(\chi,\zeta) = \mathcal{I}_\zeta^\eta \left[\alpha(\chi) \mathcal{L}_{\chi\chi\zeta} \psi_0(\chi,\zeta) - 2\kappa(\chi) \mathcal{L}_\chi \psi_0(\chi,\zeta) - \mathcal{A}_0(\chi,\zeta) \right] \qquad (33)$$

$$\psi_2(\chi,\zeta) = \mathcal{I}_\zeta^\eta \left[\alpha(\chi) \mathcal{L}_{\chi\chi\zeta} \psi_1(\chi,\zeta) - 2\kappa(\chi) \mathcal{L}_\chi \psi_1(\chi,\zeta) - \mathcal{A}_1(\chi,\zeta) \right] \qquad (34)$$

$$\vdots$$

Therefore, the approximate solution is

$$\psi(\chi,\zeta) = \lim_{m \to \infty} \psi_m(\chi,\zeta) \qquad (35)$$

5. Analysis of Homotopy Analysis Method

In this section, we discuss the (HAM) solution for the time fractional partial differential Equation (TFPDE) with variable coefficients. Liao proposed a powerful and efficient method for nonlinear problems [32–34].

We consider the following time-fractional partial differential equation

$$\mathcal{D}^\eta_\zeta \psi(\chi, \zeta) + \mathcal{L}\psi(\chi, \zeta) + \mathcal{N}\psi(\chi, \zeta) = \mathcal{G}(\chi, \zeta) \qquad (36)$$

where $\mathcal{D}^\eta_\zeta$ is the Caputo fractional derivative of order $p - 1 < \eta \leq p$, $(p \in \mathbb{N})$, $\mathcal{L}$ is the linear operator, $\mathcal{N}$ is the nonlinear operator, and $\mathcal{G}(\chi, \zeta)$ is a known analytical function. To solve the third-order time-fractional partial differential Equation (TFPDE) with variable coefficients Equation (2) by homotopy analysis method, we consider the nonlinear operator

$$\mathcal{N}[\varphi(\chi, \zeta; \rho)] = \frac{\partial^\eta \varphi(\chi, \zeta; \rho)}{\partial \zeta^\eta} - \alpha(\chi) \frac{\partial^3 \varphi(\chi, \zeta; \rho)}{\partial \chi^2 \partial \zeta} + 2\kappa(\chi) \frac{\partial \varphi(\chi, \zeta; \rho)}{\partial \chi} + \beta(\chi) \varphi(\chi, \zeta; \rho) \frac{\partial \varphi(\chi, \zeta; \rho)}{\partial \chi}$$
$$- \gamma(\chi) \varphi(\chi, \zeta; \rho) \frac{\partial^3 \varphi(\chi, \zeta; \rho)}{\partial \chi^3} - \omega(\chi) \frac{\partial \varphi(\chi, \zeta; \rho)}{\partial \chi} \frac{\partial^2 \varphi(\chi, \zeta; \rho)}{\partial \chi^2} = 0, \quad \zeta > 0 \qquad (37)$$

and the linear operator

$$\mathcal{L}[\varphi(\chi, \zeta; \rho)] = \mathcal{D}^\eta_\zeta [\varphi(\chi, \zeta; \rho)] = \frac{\partial^\eta \varphi(\chi, \zeta; \rho)}{\partial \zeta^\eta} \qquad (38)$$

subject to the initial and boundary conditions Equation (3), with the property $\mathcal{D}^\eta_\zeta (k) = 0$, where k is the integration constant. According to Liao [33], we can construct the zero-order deformation equation

$$(1 - \rho)\mathcal{D}^\eta_\zeta [\varphi(\chi, \zeta; \rho) - \psi_0(\chi, \zeta)] = \rho \hbar \mathcal{H}(\chi, \zeta) \mathcal{N}[\varphi(\chi, \zeta; \rho)] \qquad (39)$$

where $\rho \in [0, 1]$ is an embedding parameter, $\mathcal{D}^\eta_\zeta$ is an auxiliary linear operator, $\varphi(\chi, \zeta; \rho)$ is a mapping function for $\psi(\chi, \zeta)$, $\psi_0(\chi, \zeta)$ is an initial guess of $\psi(\chi, \zeta)$, $\hbar$ is a nonzero auxiliary parameter, and $\mathcal{H}(\chi, \zeta)$ is a nonzero auxiliary function. Obviously, for $\rho = 0$ and $\rho = 1$, we have

$$\varphi(\chi, \zeta; 0) = \psi_0(\chi, \zeta)$$
$$\varphi(\chi, \zeta; 1) = \psi(\chi, \zeta) \qquad (40)$$

Thus, as ρ moves from 0 to 1, the solution $\varphi(\chi, \zeta; \rho)$ varies from the initial guess $\psi_0(\chi, \zeta)$ to the solution $\psi(\chi, \zeta)$. Expanding $\varphi(\chi, \zeta; \rho)$ into the Taylor series with respect to the embedding parameter ρ, we obtain

$$\varphi(\chi, \zeta; \rho) = \psi_0(\chi, \zeta) + \sum_{m=1}^{\infty} \psi_m(\chi, \zeta) \rho^m \qquad (41)$$

where

$$\psi_m(\chi, \zeta) = \frac{1}{m!} \left. \frac{\partial^m \varphi(\chi, \zeta; \rho)}{\partial \rho^m} \right|_{\rho=0} \qquad (42)$$

If the auxiliary linear operator, the initial guess, the auxiliary parameter $\hbar$, and the auxiliary function are so properly chosen, the series Equation (41) converges at $\rho = 1$, then we have

$$\varphi(\chi, \zeta; 1) = \psi(\chi, \zeta) = \psi_0(\chi, \zeta) + \sum_{m=1}^{\infty} \psi_m(\chi, \zeta) \qquad (43)$$

which must be one of the solutions of the original nonlinear equation, as proven by Liao [35]. For $\hbar = -1$ and $\mathcal{H}(\chi, \zeta) = 1$, Equation (39) becomes

$$(1 - \rho)\mathcal{D}^\eta_\zeta [\varphi(\chi, \zeta; \rho) - \psi_0(\chi, \zeta)] + \rho \mathcal{N}[\varphi(\chi, \zeta; \rho)] = 0 \qquad (44)$$

According to Equation (42), the governing equation can be deduced from the zero-order deformation Equation (39).

Define the vector
$$\vec{\psi}_m = \{\psi_0(\chi, \zeta), \psi_1(\chi, \zeta), \ldots, \psi_m(\chi, \zeta)\}$$

By differentiating Equation (39) m number of times with respect to the embedding parameter ρ then setting $\rho = 0$, and finally dividing them by $m!$, we obtain the so-called mth-order deformation equation

$$\mathcal{D}_\zeta^\eta[\psi_m(\chi, \zeta) - \chi_m \psi_{m-1}(\chi, \zeta)] = \hbar \mathcal{H}(\chi, \zeta) \mathcal{R}_m[\vec{\psi}_{m-1}(\chi, \zeta)] \tag{45}$$

where

$$\mathcal{R}_m[\vec{\psi}_{m-1}(\chi, \zeta)] = \frac{1}{(m-1)!} \frac{\partial^{m-1} \mathcal{N}[\varphi(\chi, \zeta; \rho)]}{\partial \rho^{m-1}}\bigg|_{\rho=0} \tag{46}$$

and

$$\chi_m = \begin{cases} 0 & m \leq 1 \\ 1 & m > 1 \end{cases} \tag{47}$$

Applying the operator $\mathcal{I}_\zeta^\eta$ on both sides of Equation (45), with the basic properties of the operator $\mathcal{D}_\zeta^\eta$, we obtain the solution of the above mth-order deformation equation, with the assumption $\mathcal{H}(\chi, \zeta) = 1$

$$\psi_m(\chi, \zeta) = \chi_m \psi_{m-1}(\chi, \zeta) + \hbar \mathcal{I}_\zeta^\eta \mathcal{R}_m[\vec{\psi}_{m-1}(\chi, \zeta)] \tag{48}$$

where

$$\begin{aligned}
\mathcal{R}_m[\vec{\psi}_{m-1}(\chi, \zeta)] &= \frac{\partial^\eta \psi_{m-1}(\chi, \zeta)}{\partial \zeta^\eta} - \alpha(\chi) \frac{\partial^3 \psi_{m-1}(\chi, \zeta)}{\partial \chi^2 \partial \zeta} + 2\kappa(\chi) \frac{\partial \psi_{m-1}(\chi, \zeta)}{\partial \chi} \\
&+ \sum_{k=0}^{m-1} \left(\beta(\chi) \psi_k(\chi, \zeta) \frac{\partial \psi_{m-1-k}(\chi, \zeta)}{\partial \chi} - \gamma(\chi) \psi_k(\chi, \zeta) \frac{\partial^3 \psi_{m-1-k}(\chi, \zeta)}{\partial \chi^3} - \omega(\chi) \frac{\partial \psi_k(\chi, \zeta)}{\partial \chi} \frac{\partial^2 \psi_{m-1-k}(\chi, \zeta)}{\partial \chi^2} \right)
\end{aligned} \tag{49}$$

By using the above relation Equation (48) with the initial and boundary conditions Equation (3), we can obtain the first terms of the (HAM) series solution for $m = 1, 2, \cdots$

$$\begin{aligned}
\psi_1(\chi, \zeta) &= \chi_1 \psi_0(\chi, \zeta) + \hbar \mathcal{I}_\zeta^\eta \mathcal{R}_1[\vec{\psi}_0(\chi, \zeta)] \\
&= \hbar \mathcal{I}_\zeta^\eta \bigg[\frac{\partial^\eta \psi_0(\chi, \zeta)}{\partial \zeta^\eta} - \alpha(\chi) \frac{\partial^3 \psi_0(\chi, \zeta)}{\partial \chi^2 \partial \zeta} + 2\kappa(\chi) \frac{\partial \psi_0(\chi, \zeta)}{\partial \chi} \\
&+ \beta(\chi) \psi_0(\chi, \zeta) \frac{\partial \psi_0(\chi, \zeta)}{\partial \chi} - \gamma(\chi) \psi_0(\chi, \zeta) \frac{\partial^3 \psi_0(\chi, \zeta)}{\partial \chi^3} - \omega(\chi) \frac{\partial \psi_0(\chi, \zeta)}{\partial \chi} \frac{\partial^2 \psi_0(\chi, \zeta)}{\partial \chi^2} \bigg]
\end{aligned} \tag{50}$$

$$\begin{aligned}
\psi_2(\chi, \zeta) &= \chi_2 \psi_1(\chi, \zeta) + \hbar \mathcal{I}_\zeta^\eta \mathcal{R}_2[\vec{\psi}_1(\chi, \zeta)] \\
&= \psi_1(\chi, \zeta) + \hbar \mathcal{I}_\zeta^\eta \bigg[\frac{\partial^\eta \psi_1(\chi, \zeta)}{\partial \zeta^\eta} - \alpha(\chi) \frac{\partial^3 \psi_1(\chi, \zeta)}{\partial \chi^2 \partial \zeta} + 2\kappa(\chi) \frac{\partial \psi_1(\chi, \zeta)}{\partial \chi} \\
&+ \beta(\chi) \psi_0(\chi, \zeta) \frac{\partial \psi_1(\chi, \zeta)}{\partial \chi} - \gamma(\chi) \psi_0(\chi, \zeta) \frac{\partial^3 \psi_1(\chi, \zeta)}{\partial \chi^3} - \omega(\chi) \frac{\partial \psi_0(\chi, \zeta)}{\partial \chi} \frac{\partial^2 \psi_1(\chi, \zeta)}{\partial \chi^2} \\
&+ \beta(\chi) \psi_1(\chi, \zeta) \frac{\partial \psi_0(\chi, \zeta)}{\partial \chi} - \gamma(\chi) \psi_1(\chi, \zeta) \frac{\partial^3 \psi_0(\chi, \zeta)}{\partial \chi^3} - \omega(\chi) \frac{\partial \psi_1(\chi, \zeta)}{\partial \chi} \frac{\partial^2 \psi_0(\chi, \zeta)}{\partial \chi^2} \bigg]
\end{aligned} \tag{51}$$

⋮

Therefore, we obtain an accurate approximation of Equation (2)

$$\psi(\chi,\zeta) = \sum_{k=0}^{m} \psi_k(\chi,\zeta) \qquad (52)$$

6. Applications and Results

In this section, we apply (VIM), (ADM), and (HAM) to obtain the approximate solutions to the third-order time-fractional partial differential Equation (TFPDE) with variable coefficients and suitable initial conditions.

Example 1. *Consider the third-order time-fractional partial differential Equation (TFPDE) with variable coefficients*

$$\frac{\partial^\eta \psi(\chi,\zeta)}{\partial \zeta^\eta} - \chi \frac{\partial^3 \psi(\chi,\zeta)}{\partial \chi^2 \partial \zeta} + 2\chi \frac{\partial \psi(\chi,\zeta)}{\partial \chi} + \chi \psi(\chi,\zeta) \frac{\partial \psi(\chi,\zeta)}{\partial \chi} \\ - \chi \psi(\chi,\zeta) \frac{\partial^3 \psi(\chi,\zeta)}{\partial \chi^3} - \chi \frac{\partial \psi(\chi,\zeta)}{\partial \chi} \frac{\partial^2 \psi(\chi,\zeta)}{\partial \chi^2} = 0, \quad \zeta > 0, \quad 0 \leq \chi \leq 1, \quad 0 < \eta \leq 1 \qquad (53)$$

and the initial and boundary conditions

$$\psi(\chi,0) = e^\chi \\ \psi(0,\zeta) = 0, \quad \psi(1,\zeta) = 0, \quad \zeta > 0 \qquad (54)$$

Applying VIM: the iteration formula for Equation (53) can be constructed as

$$\psi_{k+1}(\chi,\zeta) = \psi_k(\chi,\zeta) - \mathcal{I}_\zeta^\eta \left(\frac{\partial^\eta \psi_k(\chi,\zeta)}{\partial \zeta^\eta} - \chi \frac{\partial^3 \psi_k(\chi,\zeta)}{\partial \chi^2 \partial \zeta} + 2\chi \frac{\partial \psi_k(\chi,\zeta)}{\partial \chi} \right. \\ \left. + \chi \psi_k(\chi,\zeta) \frac{\partial \psi_k(\chi,\zeta)}{\partial \chi} - \chi \psi_k(\chi,\zeta) \frac{\partial^3 \psi_k(\chi,\zeta)}{\partial \chi^3} - \chi \frac{\partial \psi_k(\chi,\zeta)}{\partial \chi} \frac{\partial^2 \psi_k(\chi,\zeta)}{\partial \chi^2} \right) \qquad (55)$$

Considerin the given initial condition values, and using this selection in Equation (55), we obtain the following successive approximations

$$\psi_0(\chi,\zeta) = e^\chi \\ \psi_1(\chi,\zeta) = e^\chi \left(1 + \frac{\chi(e^\chi - 2)\zeta^\eta}{\Gamma(\eta+1)}\right) \\ \psi_2(\chi,\zeta) = e^\chi \left(1 + \frac{\chi(e^\chi - 2)\zeta^\eta}{\Gamma(\eta+1)} + \frac{2\chi(2\chi e^\chi + 2e^\chi - \chi - 2)\zeta^{2\eta-1}}{\Gamma(2\eta)} - \frac{4\chi(-3\chi e^{2\chi} - 4e^{2\chi} + 2\chi e^\chi + 3e^\chi - \chi - 1)\zeta^{2\eta}}{\Gamma(2\eta+1)} \right. \\ \left. - \frac{\Gamma(2\eta+1)\chi e^\chi(24e^\chi\chi^2 - 14\chi^2 e^{2\chi} + 52\chi e^\chi - 23\chi e^{2\chi} - 4\chi^2 + 12e^\chi - 4e^{2\chi} - 20\chi - 8)\zeta^{3\eta}}{\Gamma(3\eta+1)\Gamma(\eta+1)^2}\right) \qquad (56)$$

Hence, the approximate solution for Equation (53) is

$$\psi_2(\chi,\zeta) = e^\chi \left(3 + \frac{2\chi(e^\chi - 2)\zeta^\eta}{\Gamma(\eta+1)} + \frac{2\chi(2\chi e^\chi + 2e^\chi - \chi - 2)\zeta^{2\eta-1}}{\Gamma(2\eta)} - \frac{4\chi(-3\chi e^{2\chi} - 4e^{2\chi} + 2\chi e^\chi + 3e^\chi - \chi - 1)\zeta^{2\eta}}{\Gamma(2\eta+1)} \right. \\ \left. - \frac{\Gamma(2\eta+1)\chi e^\chi(24e^\chi\chi^2 - 14\chi^2 e^{2\chi} + 52\chi e^\chi - 23\chi e^{2\chi} - 4\chi^2 + 12e^\chi - 4e^{2\chi} - 20\chi - 8)\zeta^{3\eta}}{\Gamma(3\eta+1)\Gamma(\eta+1)^2}\right) \qquad (57)$$

Applying ADM: The recursive relations for Equation (53) can be constructed as

$$\psi_0(\chi,\zeta) = \sum_{k=0}^{p-1} \frac{\zeta^k}{k!} \frac{\partial^k}{\partial \zeta^k} \psi(\chi,\zeta) \bigg|_{\zeta=0} \\ \psi_{m+1}(\chi,\zeta) = \mathcal{I}_\zeta^\eta \left[\chi \mathcal{L}_{\chi\chi\zeta} \psi_m(\chi,\zeta) - 2\chi \mathcal{L}_\chi \psi_m(\chi,\zeta) - \mathcal{A}_m(\chi,\zeta) \right], \quad m \geq 0 \qquad (58)$$

Using the above recursive relations, we can obtain the first terms of the (ADM) series solution

$$\psi_0(\chi, \zeta) = e^\chi$$
$$\psi_1(\chi, \zeta) = \frac{\chi e^\chi (e^\chi - 2)\zeta^\eta}{\Gamma(\eta + 1)}$$
$$\psi_2(\chi, \zeta) = \chi e^\chi \left(\frac{(4\chi e^\chi + 4e^\chi - 2\chi - 4)\zeta^{2\eta-1}}{\Gamma(2\eta)} + \frac{(2\chi e^{3\chi} + e^{3\chi} - 4\chi e^{2\chi} - 2e^{2\chi} - 4\chi e^\chi - 2e^\chi + 4\chi + 4)\zeta^{2\eta}}{\Gamma(2\eta + 1)} \right) \tag{59}$$

Hence, the (ADM) series solution for Equation (53) is

$$\psi(\chi, \zeta) = e^\chi \left(1 + \frac{\chi(e^\chi - 2)\zeta^\eta}{\Gamma(\eta + 1)} + \frac{\chi(4\chi e^\chi + 4e^\chi - 2\chi - 4)\zeta^{2\eta-1}}{\Gamma(2\eta)} + \frac{\chi(2\chi e^{3\chi} + e^{3\chi} - 4\chi e^{2\chi} - 2e^{2\chi} - 4\chi e^\chi - 2e^\chi + 4\chi + 4)\zeta^{2\eta}}{\Gamma(2\eta + 1)} \right) \tag{60}$$

Applying HAM: the mth-order deformation equation for Equation (53) is given by

$$\psi_m(\chi, \zeta) = \chi_m \psi_{m-1}(\chi, \zeta) + \hbar \mathcal{I}_\zeta^\eta \left(\frac{\partial^\eta \psi_{m-1}(\chi, \zeta)}{\partial \zeta^\eta} - \chi \frac{\partial^3 \psi_{m-1}(\chi, \zeta)}{\partial \chi^2 \partial \zeta} + 2\chi \frac{\partial \psi_{m-1}(\chi, \zeta)}{\partial \chi} \right.$$
$$\left. + \sum_{k=0}^{m-1} \left(\chi \psi_k(\chi, \zeta) \frac{\partial \psi_{m-1-k}(\chi, \zeta)}{\partial \chi} - \chi \psi_k(\chi, \zeta) \frac{\partial^3 \psi_{m-1-k}(\chi, \zeta)}{\partial \chi^3} - \chi \frac{\partial \psi_k(\chi, \zeta)}{\partial \chi} \frac{\partial^2 \psi_{m-1-k}(\chi, \zeta)}{\partial \chi^2} \right) \right) \tag{61}$$

where

$$\chi_m = \begin{cases} 0 & m \leq 1 \\ 1 & m > 1 \end{cases} \tag{62}$$

Using the above relation Equation (61), we can obtain the first terms of (HAM) series solution

$$\psi_0(\chi, \zeta) = e^\chi$$
$$\psi_1(\chi, \zeta) = -\frac{\chi e^\chi (e^\chi - 2)\hbar \zeta^\eta}{\Gamma(\eta + 1)}$$
$$\psi_2(\chi, \zeta) = \chi e^\chi \left(-\frac{(e^\chi - 2)(\hbar + 1)\hbar \zeta^\eta}{\Gamma(\eta + 1)} + \frac{4(3\chi e^{2\chi} + 4e^{2\chi} - 2\chi e^\chi - 3e^\chi + \chi + 1)\hbar^2 \zeta^{2\eta}}{\Gamma(2\eta + 1)} + \frac{4((\chi+1)e^\chi - \frac{\chi}{2} - 1)\hbar^2 \zeta^{2\tau-1}}{\Gamma(2\eta)} \right) \tag{63}$$

Hence, the (HAM) series solution for Equation (53) is

$$\psi(\chi, \zeta) = e^\chi \left(1 - \frac{\chi(e^\chi - 2)\hbar^2 \zeta^\eta}{\Gamma(\eta + 1)} + \frac{4\chi(3\chi e^{2\chi} + 4e^{2\chi} - 2\chi e^\chi - 3e^\chi + \chi + 1)\hbar^2 \zeta^{2\eta}}{\Gamma(2\eta + 1)} + \frac{4\chi(\chi e^\chi + e^\chi - \frac{\chi}{2} - 1)\hbar^2 \zeta^{2\tau-1}}{\Gamma(2\eta)} \right) \tag{64}$$

Example 2. *Consider the third-order time-fractional partial differential Equation (TFPDE) with variable coefficients*

$$\frac{\partial^\eta \psi(\chi, \zeta)}{\partial \zeta^\eta} - \chi^2 \frac{\partial^3 \psi(\chi, \zeta)}{\partial \chi^2 \partial \zeta} + 2 \frac{\partial \psi(\chi, \zeta)}{\partial \chi} + \psi(\chi, \zeta) \frac{\partial \psi(\chi, \zeta)}{\partial \chi}$$
$$- \psi(\chi, \zeta) \frac{\partial^3 \psi(\chi, \zeta)}{\partial \chi^3} - \frac{\partial \psi(\chi, \zeta)}{\partial \chi} \frac{\partial^2 \psi(\chi, \zeta)}{\partial \chi^2} = 0, \quad \zeta > 0, \quad 0 \leq \chi \leq 1, \quad 0 < \eta \leq 1 \tag{65}$$

and the initial and boundary conditions

$$\psi(\chi, 0) = \chi^2$$
$$\psi(0, \zeta) = 0, \quad \psi(1, \zeta) = 0, \quad \zeta > 0 \tag{66}$$

Applying VIM: the iteration formula for Equation (65) can be constructed as

$$\psi_{k+1}(\chi,\zeta) = \psi_k(\chi,\zeta) - \mathcal{I}_\zeta^\eta \left(\frac{\partial^\eta \psi_k(\chi,\zeta)}{\partial \zeta^\eta} - \chi^2 \frac{\partial^3 \psi_k(\chi,\zeta)}{\partial \chi^2 \partial \zeta} + 2\frac{\partial \psi_k(\chi,\zeta)}{\partial \chi} \right.$$
$$\left. + \psi_k(\chi,\zeta) \frac{\partial \psi_k(\chi,\zeta)}{\partial \chi} - \psi_k(\chi,\zeta) \frac{\partial^3 \psi_k(\chi,\zeta)}{\partial \chi^3} - \frac{\partial \psi_k(\chi,\zeta)}{\partial \chi} \frac{\partial^2 \psi_k(\chi,\zeta)}{\partial \chi^2} \right) \quad (67)$$

Considering the given initial condition values, and using this selection in Equation (66), we obtain the following successive approximations

$$\psi_0(\chi,\zeta) = \chi^2$$
$$\psi_1(\chi,\zeta) = \chi^2 - \frac{(2\chi^3 - 8\chi)\zeta^\eta}{\Gamma(\eta+1)} \quad (68)$$
$$\psi_2(\chi,\zeta) = \chi^2 - \frac{(2\chi^3 - 8\chi)\zeta^\eta}{\Gamma(\eta+1)} + \frac{12\chi^3 \zeta^{2\eta-1}}{\Gamma(2\eta)} + \frac{(-10\chi^4 + 132\chi^2 - 32)\zeta^{2\eta}}{\Gamma(2\eta+1)} + \frac{\Gamma(2\eta+1)(12\chi^5 - 304\chi^3 + 448\chi)\zeta^{3\eta}}{\Gamma(3\eta+1)\Gamma(\eta+1)^2}$$

Hence, the approximate solution for Equation (65) is

$$\psi(\chi,\zeta) = 3\chi^2 - \frac{2(2\chi^3 - 8\chi)\zeta^\eta}{\Gamma(\eta+1)} + \frac{12\chi^3 \zeta^{2\eta-1}}{\Gamma(2\eta)} + \frac{(-10\chi^4 + 132\chi^2 - 32)\zeta^{2\eta}}{\Gamma(2\eta+1)} + \frac{\Gamma(2\eta+1)(12\chi^5 - 304\chi^3 + 448\chi)\zeta^{3\eta}}{\Gamma(3\eta+1)\Gamma(\eta+1)^2} \quad (69)$$

Applying ADM: the recursive relations for Equation (65) can be constructed as

$$\psi_0(\chi,\zeta) = \sum_{k=0}^{p-1} \frac{\zeta^k}{k!} \frac{\partial^k}{\partial \zeta^k} \psi(\chi,\zeta) \Big|_{\zeta=0}$$
$$\psi_{m+1}(\chi,\zeta) = \mathcal{I}_\zeta^\eta \left[\chi^2 \mathcal{L}_{\chi\chi\zeta} \psi_m(\chi,\zeta) - 2\mathcal{L}_\chi \psi_m(\chi,\zeta) - \mathcal{A}_m(\chi,\zeta) \right], \quad m \geq 0 \quad (70)$$

Using the above recursive relations, we can obtain the first terms of the (ADM) series solution

$$\psi_0(\chi,\zeta) = \chi^2$$
$$\psi_1(\chi,\zeta) = -\frac{(2\chi^3 - 8\chi)\zeta^\eta}{\Gamma(\eta+1)} \quad (71)$$
$$\psi_2(\chi,\zeta) = \frac{4(3\chi^5 - 18\chi^3 + 3\chi^2 + 24\chi - 4)\zeta^{2\eta}}{\Gamma(2\eta+1)} - \frac{12\chi^3 \zeta^{2\eta-1}}{\Gamma(2\eta)}$$

Hence, the (ADM) series solution for Equation (65) is

$$\psi(\chi,\zeta) = \chi^2 - \frac{(2\chi^3 - 8\chi)\zeta^\eta}{\Gamma(\eta+1)} + \frac{4(3\chi^5 - 18\chi^3 + 3\chi^2 + 24\chi - 4)\zeta^{2\eta}}{\Gamma(2\eta+1)} - \frac{12\chi^3 \zeta^{2\eta-1}}{\Gamma(2\eta)} \quad (72)$$

Applying HAM: the mth-order deformation equation for Equation (65) is given by

$$\psi_m(\chi,\zeta) = \chi_m \psi_{m-1}(\chi,\zeta) + \hbar \mathcal{I}_\zeta^\eta \left(\frac{\partial^\eta \psi_{m-1}(\chi,\zeta)}{\partial \zeta^\eta} - \chi^2 \frac{\partial^3 \psi_{m-1}(\chi,\zeta)}{\partial \chi^2 \partial \zeta} + 2\frac{\partial \psi_{m-1}(\chi,\zeta)}{\partial \chi} \right.$$
$$\left. + \sum_{k=0}^{m-1} (\psi_k(\chi,\zeta) \frac{\partial \psi_{m-1-k}(\chi,\zeta)}{\partial \chi} - \psi_k(\chi,\zeta) \frac{\partial^3 \psi_{m-1-k}(\chi,\zeta)}{\partial \chi^3} - \frac{\partial \psi_k(\chi,\zeta)}{\partial \chi} \frac{\partial^2 \psi_{m-1-k}(\chi,\zeta)}{\partial \chi^2}) \right) \quad (73)$$

where

$$\chi_m = \begin{cases} 0 & m \leq 1 \\ 1 & m > 1 \end{cases} \quad (74)$$

Using the above relation Equation (73), we can obtain the first terms of (HAM) series solution

$$\psi_0(\chi, \zeta) = \chi^2$$
$$\psi_1(\chi, \zeta) = \frac{(2\chi^3 - 8\chi)\hbar \zeta^\eta}{\Gamma(\eta + 1)}$$
$$\psi_2(\chi, \zeta) = \frac{2\chi(\chi - 2)(\chi + 2)(\hbar + 1)\hbar \zeta^\eta}{\Gamma(\eta + 1)} + \frac{2(5\chi^4 - 66\chi^2 + 16)\hbar^2 \zeta^{2\eta}}{\Gamma(2\eta + 1)} - \frac{12\chi^3 \hbar^2 \zeta^{2\eta - 1}}{\Gamma(2\eta)}$$
(75)

Hence, the (HAM) series solution for Equation (65) is

$$\psi(\chi, \zeta) = \chi^2 + \frac{2\chi(\chi - 2)(\chi + 2)(\hbar + 2)\hbar \zeta^\eta}{\Gamma(\eta + 1)} + \frac{2(5\chi^4 - 66\chi^2 + 16)\hbar^2 \zeta^{2\eta}}{\Gamma(2\eta + 1)} - \frac{12\chi^3 \hbar^2 \zeta^{2\eta - 1}}{\Gamma(2\eta)}$$
(76)

7. Conclusions

This paper presents three numerical methods considered to achieve an approximate solution for a third-order time-fractional partial differential equation (TFPDE). The equation is obtained from the classical (FW) equation by replacing the integer-order time derivative with the Caputo fractional derivative of order $\eta = (0, 1]$ with variable coefficients. The numerical results and graphs have been implemented using Maple 2022. In Figures 1–4 the graphical simulations for the approximate series solutions and the comparison in the form of absolute errors were presented to show the rate of change of the solutions when $\eta = 0.75$ and $\hbar = -1$. In Figures 5–8 we have shown the behavior of the solution with respect to the different values of η. As we can see in Tables 1 and 2, as ζ increases to 1, and χ increases to 1, the absolute errors slowly decrease. The agreement between the numerical results obtained by variational iteration method (VIM), Adomian decomposition method (ADM), and homotopy analysis method (HAM) involves fractional-order derivatives.

Table 1. This table shows the absolute errors for $\mathcal{W}$ = Abso.Error(VIM,ADM), $\mathcal{U}$ = Abso.Error(VIM,HAM), and $\mathcal{V}$ = Abso.Error(ADM,HAM) for Example 1.

	ζ	χ	$\mathcal{W}$	$\mathcal{U}$	$\mathcal{V}$
	0	0	2	2	0
	0.1	0.1	2.541025554	1.991394551	0.549631003
	0.2	0.2	3.977083804	1.738334153	2.238749651
	0.3	0.3	7.163139295	1.104283175	6.058856120
	0.4	0.4	14.00596958	0.26301164	13.74295794
$\eta = 0.25$	0.5	0.5	28.80747376	0.69271694	28.11475682
	0.6	0.6	61.19402329	7.56126741	53.63275588
	0.7	0.7	132.1993350	35.0418419	97.15749309
	0.8	0.8	286.4869258	117.4884319	168.9984939
	0.9	0.9	616.2555191	331.9641125	284.2914066
	1	1	1306.952037	842.2302549	464.7217817
	0	0	2	2	0
	0.1	0.1	2.289636497	2.099416352	0.190220145
	0.2	0.2	3.053697547	2.085683315	0.968014232
	0.3	0.3	4.954885502	1.897138477	3.057747025
	0.4	0.4	9.382828821	1.54535058	7.837478241
$\eta = 0.50$	0.5	0.5	19.47518759	1.73147878	17.74370881
	0.6	0.6	42.52650372	5.62861132	36.89789240
	0.7	0.7	95.44637321	23.41453671	72.03183650
	0.8	0.8	216.6411190	82.8281667	133.8129523
	0.9	0.9	490.9981703	252.3203983	238.6777720
	1	1	1100.897757	689.6370408	411.2607162

Table 1. *Cont.*

	ζ	χ	$\mathcal{W}$	$\mathcal{U}$	$\mathcal{V}$
	0	0	2	2	0
	0.1	0.1	2.219088227	2.152357150	0.066731077
	0.2	0.2	2.628656823	2.243794656	0.384862167
	0.3	0.3	3.627226957	2.269200185	1.358026772
	0.4	0.4	6.084771319	2.229972343	3.854798976
$\eta = 0.75$	0.5	0.5	11.96807065	2.40088841	9.567182238
	0.6	0.6	25.89804802	4.30750395	21.59054406
	0.7	0.7	58.93797052	13.61183285	45.32613767
	0.8	0.8	137.4703988	47.6301328	89.84026597
	0.9	0.9	323.2302447	153.3892413	169.8410034
	1	1	756.9909123	448.5531203	308.4377920

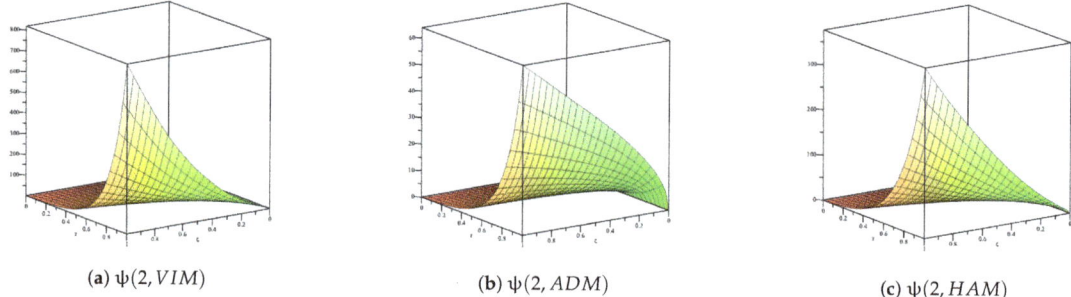

(a) $\psi(2, VIM)$ (b) $\psi(2, ADM)$ (c) $\psi(2, HAM)$

Figure 1. Graphical simulation of the second-level approximate solution $\psi_2(\chi, \zeta)$ when $\eta = 0.75$ and $\hbar = -1$ for Example 1.

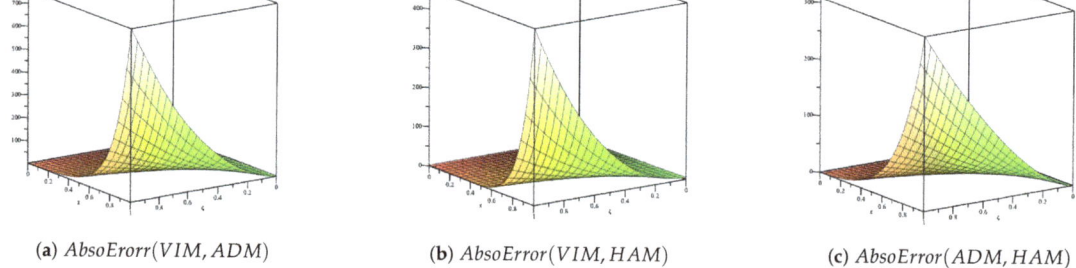

(a) $AbsoErorr(VIM, ADM)$ (b) $AbsoError(VIM, HAM)$ (c) $AbsoError(ADM, HAM)$

Figure 2. Graphical simulation of the absolute error when $\eta = 0.75$ and $\hbar = -1$ for Example 1.

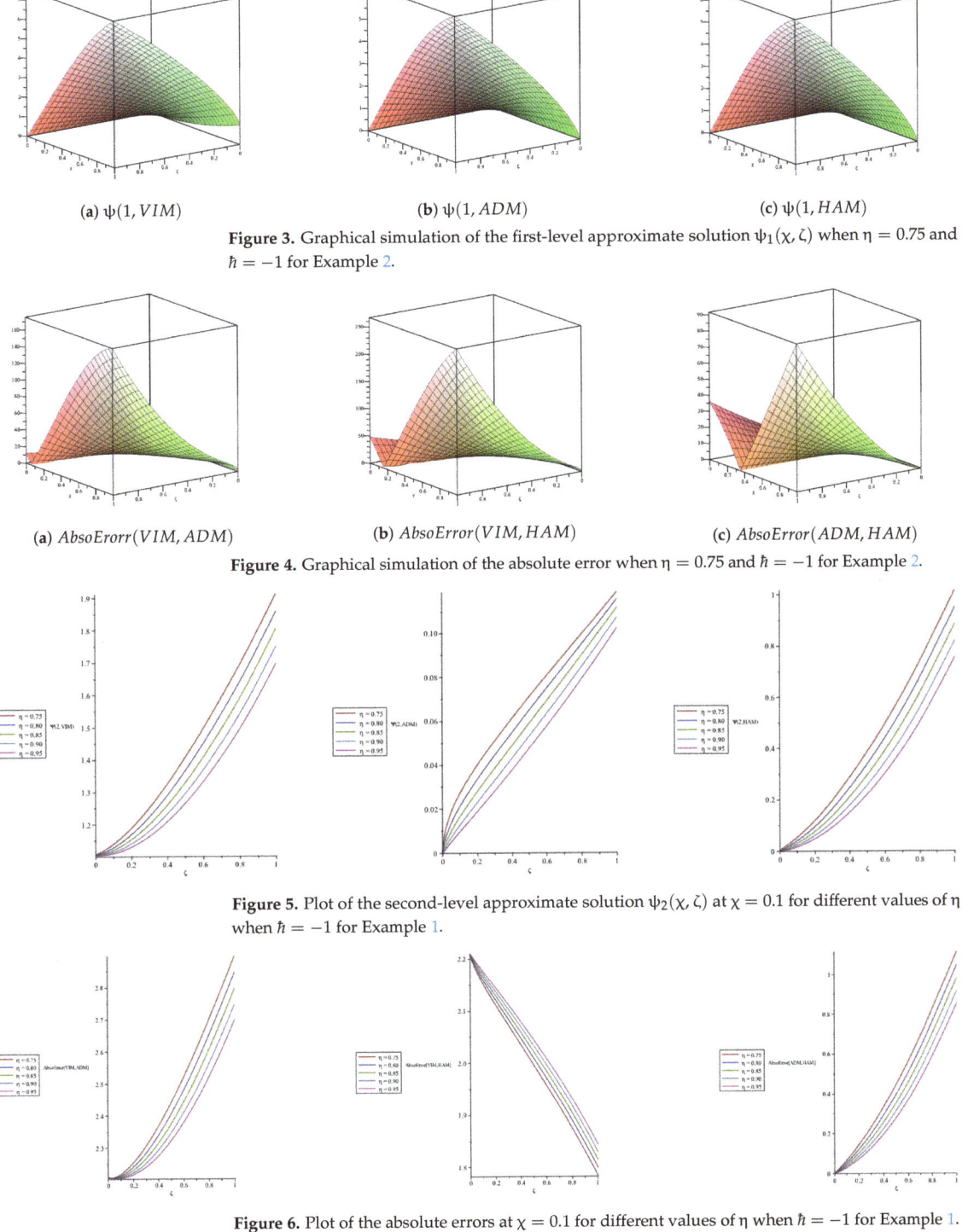

(a) $\psi(1, VIM)$ **(b)** $\psi(1, ADM)$ **(c)** $\psi(1, HAM)$

Figure 3. Graphical simulation of the first-level approximate solution $\psi_1(\chi, \zeta)$ when $\eta = 0.75$ and $\hbar = -1$ for Example 2.

(a) $AbsoErorr(VIM, ADM)$ **(b)** $AbsoError(VIM, HAM)$ **(c)** $AbsoError(ADM, HAM)$

Figure 4. Graphical simulation of the absolute error when $\eta = 0.75$ and $\hbar = -1$ for Example 2.

Figure 5. Plot of the second-level approximate solution $\psi_2(\chi, \zeta)$ at $\chi = 0.1$ for different values of η when $\hbar = -1$ for Example 1.

Figure 6. Plot of the absolute errors at $\chi = 0.1$ for different values of η when $\hbar = -1$ for Example 1.

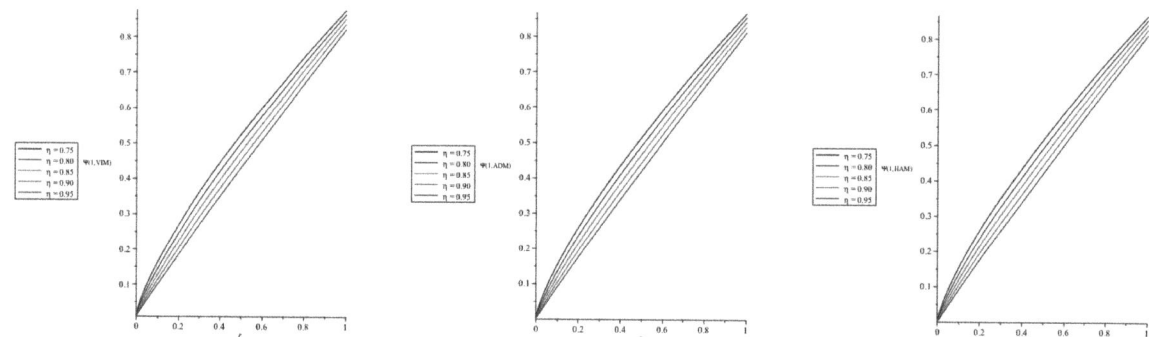

Figure 7. Plot of the first-level approximate solution $\psi_1(\chi, \zeta)$ at $\chi = 0.1$ for different values of η when $\hbar = -1$ for Example 2.

Table 2. This table shows the absolute errors for $\mathcal{W}$ = Abso.Error(VIM,ADM), $\mathcal{U}$ = Abso.Error(VIM,HAM), and $\mathcal{V}$ = Abso.Error(ADM,HAM) for Example 2.

	ζ	χ	$\mathcal{W}$	$\mathcal{U}$	$\mathcal{V}$
	0	0	0	0	0
	0.1	0.1	1.163766699	12.05048415	13.21425085
	0.2	0.2	17.02984022	5.10644444	11.92339578
	0.3	0.3	42.93553452	37.84546649	5.090068030
	0.4	0.4	76.65912143	82.86707406	6.20795263
$\eta = 0.25$	0.5	0.5	115.6963634	137.0397754	21.34341200
	0.6	0.6	157.0968959	196.8876146	39.79071872
	0.7	0.7	197.4322793	258.4945593	61.06227998
	0.8	0.8	232.7973816	317.5061666	84.70878500
	0.9	0.9	258.8244368	369.1656052	110.3411684
	1	1	270.7035747	408.3658330	137.6622584
	0	0	0	0	0
	0.1	0.1	0.7564569989	4.459744999	3.703288000
	0.2	0.2	2.570402463	2.155229537	4.725632000
	0.3	0.3	12.49304336	10.02229136	2.470752000
	0.4	0.4	30.39666054	33.87621254	3.479551997
$\eta = 0.50$	0.5	0.5	56.60474123	69.97974123	13.37500000
	0.6	0.6	90.31573016	117.6308022	27.31507200
	0.7	0.7	129.5188924	174.7947804	45.27588800
	0.8	0.8	170.9122578	238.0579858	67.14572800
	0.9	0.9	209.8305525	302.5997445	92.76919200
	1	1	240.1867606	362.1867606	122
	0	0	0	0	0
	0.1	0.1	0.2413076664	1.122257724	0.8809500575
	0.2	0.2	0.1238826704	1.465903435	1.589786105
	0.3	0.3	2.829465294	1.811451685	1.018013609
	0.4	0.4	9.761568790	11.41702283	1.655454036
$\eta = 0.75$	0.5	0.5	22.59293105	29.70740172	7.114470668
	0.6	0.6	42.43691686	58.35320436	15.91628749
	0.7	0.7	69.50572834	98.00145900	28.49573066
	0.8	0.8	102.7699335	147.9479522	45.17801869
	0.9	0.9	139.6218079	205.8265090	66.20470108
	1	1	175.5469776	267.3218165	91.77483894

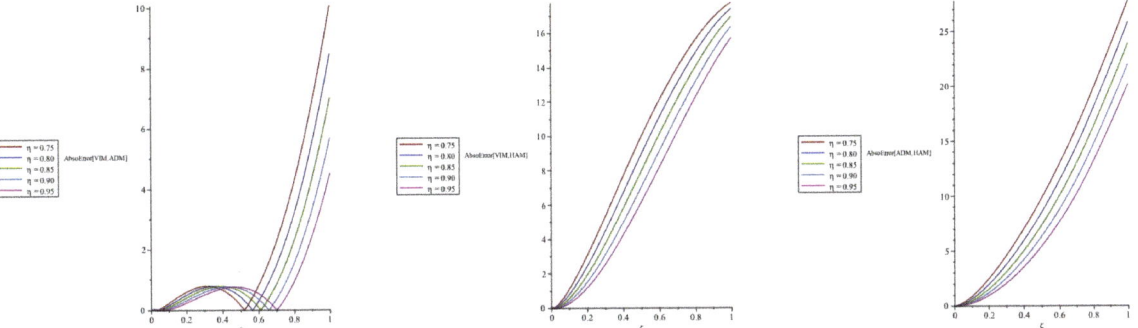

Figure 8. Plot of the absolute errors at $\chi = 0.1$ for different values of η when $\hbar = -1$ for Example 2.

Author Contributions: Methodology, F.A.; Validation, A.K.; Investigation, A.K.; Writing—original draft, F.A.; Writing—review & editing, A.K.; Supervision, A.K. and N.S. All authors have read and agreed to the published version of the manuscript.

Funding: This research received no external funding.

Data Availability Statement: Not applicable.

Conflicts of Interest: The authors declare no conflict of interest.

References

1. Azevedo, J.; Cuevas, C.; Henriquez, E. Existence and asymptotic behaviour for the time-fractional Keller–Segel model for chemotaxis. *Math. Nachr.* **2019**, *292*, 462–480. [CrossRef]
2. Zabidi, N.A.; Abdul Majid, Z.; Kilicman, A.; Rabiei, F. Numerical Solutions of Fractional Differential Equations by Using Fractional Explicit Adams Method. *Mathematics* **2020**, *8*, 1675. [CrossRef]
3. Jafari, H.; Seifi, S. Homotopy analysis method for solving linear and nonlinear fractional diffusion-wave equation. *Commun. Nonlinear Sci. Numer. Simul.* **2009**, *14*, 2006–2012. [CrossRef]
4. Jafari, H.; Golbabai, A.; Seifi, S.; Sayevand, K. Homotopy analysis method for solving multi-term linear and nonlinear diffusion-wave equations of fractional order. *Comput. Math. Appl.* **2010**, *59*, 1337–1344. [CrossRef]
5. Donatelli, M.; Mazza, M.; Serra-Capizzano, S. Spectral analysis and structure preserving preconditioners for fractional diffusion equations. *J. Comput. Phys.* **2016**, *307*, 262–279. [CrossRef]
6. Donatelli, M.; Mazza, M.; Serra-Capizzano, S. Spectral analysis and multigrid methods for finite volume approximations of space-fractional diffusion equations. *SIAM J. Sci. Comput.* **2018**, *40*, A4007–A4039. [CrossRef]
7. Lin, X.l.; Ng, M.K.; Sun, H.W. A multigrid method for linear systems arising from time-dependent two-dimensional space-fractional diffusion equations. *J. Comput. Phys.* **2017**, *336*, 69–86. [CrossRef]
8. Bu, W.; Liu, X.; Tang, Y.; Yang, J. Finite element multigrid method for multi-term time fractional advection diffusion equations. *Int. J. Model. Simul. Sci. Comput.* **2015**, *6*, 1540001. [CrossRef]
9. Whitham, G.B. Variational methods and applications to water waves. *Proc. R. Soc. Lond. Ser. A Math. Phys. Sci.* **1967**, *299*, 6–25.
10. Fornberg, B.; Whitham, G.B. A numerical and theoretical study of certain nonlinear wave phenomena. *Philos. Trans. R. Soc. Lond. Ser. A Math. Phys. Sci.* **1978**, *289*, 373–404.
11. Kumar, D.; Singh, J.; Baleanu, D. A new analysis of the Fornberg-Whitham equation pertaining to a fractional derivative with Mittag–Leffler-type kernel. *Eur. Phys. J. Plus* **2018**, *133*, 1–10. [CrossRef]
12. Gupta, P.K.; Singh, M. Homotopy perturbation method for fractional Fornberg–Whitham equation. *Comput. Math. Appl.* **2011**, *61*, 250–254. [CrossRef]
13. Merdan, M.; Gökdoğan, A.; Yıldırım, A.; Mohyud-Din, S.T. Numerical simulation of fractional Fornberg-Whitham equation by differential transformation method. In *Abstract and Applied Analysis*; Hindawi: London, UK, 2012; Volume 2012.
14. Alderremy, A.; Khan, H.; Shah, R.; Aly, S.; Baleanu, D. The analytical analysis of time-fractional Fornberg–Whitham equations. *Mathematics* **2020**, *8*, 987. [CrossRef]
15. Abidi, F.; Omrani, K. The homotopy analysis method for solving the Fornberg–Whitham equation and comparison with Adomian's decomposition method. *Comput. Math. Appl.* **2010**, *59*, 2743–2750. [CrossRef]
16. Wang, K.L.; Liu, S.Y. He's fractional derivative and its application for fractional Fornberg-Whitham equation. *Therm. Sci.* **2017**, *21*, 2049–2055. [CrossRef]
17. Sartanpara, P.P.; Meher, R.; Meher, S. The generalized time-fractional Fornberg–Whitham equation: An analytic approach. *Partial. Differ. Equ. Appl. Math.* **2022**, *5*, 100350. [CrossRef]

18. Ahmad, H.; Seadawy, A.R.; Ganie, A.H.; Rashid, S.; Khan, T.A.; Abu-Zinadah, H. Approximate Numerical solutions for the nonlinear dispersive shallow water waves as the Fornberg–Whitham model equations. *Results Phys.* **2021**, *22*, 103907. [CrossRef]
19. Shah, N.A.; Dassios, I.; El-Zahar, E.R.; Chung, J.D.; Taherifar, S. The Variational Iteration Transform Method for Solving the Time-Fractional Fornberg–Whitham Equation and Comparison with Decomposition Transform Method. *Mathematics* **2021**, *9*, 141. [CrossRef]
20. Iqbal, N.; Yasmin, H.; Ali, A.; Bariq, A.; Al-Sawalha, M.M.; Mohammed, W.W. Numerical methods for fractional-order Fornberg-Whitham equations in the sense of Atangana-Baleanu derivative. *J. Funct. Spaces* **2021**, *2021*, 1–10. [CrossRef]
21. Lenells, J. Traveling wave solutions of the Camassa-Holm and Korteweg-de Vries equations. *J. Nonlinear Math. Phys.* **2004**, *11*, 508–520. [CrossRef]
22. Chen, J. The stability of solutions for the generalized degasperis-procesi equation with variable coefficients. *Math. Probl. Eng.* **2015**, *2015*, 207427. [CrossRef]
23. Jiang, J.; Feng, Y.; Li, S. Variational Problems with Partial Fractional Derivative: Optimal Conditions and Noether's Theorem. *J. Funct. Spaces* **2018**, *2018*, 1–14. [CrossRef]
24. Singh, B.K.; Kumar, P. Fractional variational iteration method for solving fractional partial differential equations with proportional delay. *Int. J. Differ. Equ.* **2017**, *2017*, 5206380. [CrossRef]
25. Dehghan, M.; Manafian, J.; Saadatmandi, A. Solving nonlinear fractional partial differential equations using the homotopy analysis method. *Numer. Methods Partial Differ. Equ. Int. J.* **2010**, *26*, 448–479. [CrossRef]
26. Wazwaz, A.M. The variational iteration method: A reliable analytic tool for solving linear and nonlinear wave equations. *Comput. Math. Appl.* **2007**, *54*, 926–932. [CrossRef]
27. Wazwaz, A.M. The variational iteration method for analytic treatment for linear and nonlinear ODEs. *Appl. Math. Comput.* **2009**, *212*, 120–134. [CrossRef]
28. He, J.H. Variational iteration method–a kind of non-linear analytical technique: Some examples. *Int. J. Non-Linear Mech.* **1999**, *34*, 699–708. [CrossRef]
29. He, J. A new approach to nonlinear partial differential equations. *Commun. Nonlinear Sci. Numer. Simul.* **1997**, *2*, 230–235. [CrossRef]
30. Adomian, G. A review of the decomposition method in applied mathematics. *J. Math. Anal. Appl.* **1988**, *135*, 501–544. [CrossRef]
31. Adomian, G. *Solving Frontier Problems of Physics: The Decomposition Method*; Springer Science & Business Media: New York, NY, USA, 2013; Volume 60.
32. Liao, S.J. The Proposed Homotopy Analysis Technique for the Solution of Nonlinear Problems. Ph.D. Thesis, Shanghai Jiao Tong University Shanghai, Shanghai, China, 1992.
33. Liao, S. On the homotopy analysis method for nonlinear problems. *Appl. Math. Comput.* **2004**, *147*, 499–513. [CrossRef]
34. Liao, S. Comparison between the homotopy analysis method and homotopy perturbation method. *Appl. Math. Comput.* **2005**, *169*, 1186–1194. [CrossRef]
35. Liao, S. *Beyond Perturbation: Introduction to the Homotopy Analysis Method*; Chapman and Hall/CRC: Boca Raton, FL, USA, 2003.

Disclaimer/Publisher's Note: The statements, opinions and data contained in all publications are solely those of the individual author(s) and contributor(s) and not of MDPI and/or the editor(s). MDPI and/or the editor(s) disclaim responsibility for any injury to people or property resulting from any ideas, methods, instructions or products referred to in the content.

Article

Identification of the Order of the Fractional Derivative for the Fractional Wave Equation

Ravshan Ashurov [1,2] and Sergei Sitnik [3,*]

1 Institute of Mathematics, Uzbekistan Academy of Science, Student Town Str., Tashkent 100174, Uzbekistan
2 AU Engineering School, Akfa University, 264, Milliy Bog Str., Tashkent 111221, Uzbekistan
3 Department of Applied Mathematics and Computer Modelling, Belgorod State National Research University, Pobedy St. 85, Belgorod 308015, Russia
* Correspondence: mathsms@yandex.ru

Abstract: A fractional wave equation with a fractional Riemann–Liouville derivative is considered. An arbitrary self-adjoint operator A with a discrete spectrum was taken as the elliptic part. We studied the inverse problem of determining the order of the fractional time derivative. By setting the value of the projection of the solution onto the first eigenfunction at a fixed point in time as an additional condition, the order of the derivative was uniquely restored. The abstract operator A allows us to include many models. Several examples of operator A are discussed at the end of the article.

Keywords: fractional wave equation; Riemann–Liouville derivatives; inverse problem; determination of the order of derivative; Fourier method

1. Introduction

In applied fractional modeling, the order of the fractional derivative is often unknown, and determining this order is an important inverse problem (see, for example, the review article [1]). In this paper, we consider the inverse problem of determining the order of the fractional time derivative in the wave equation. The method proposed in the article is based on the classical Fourier method. This allows us to consider an arbitrary self-adjoint operator with a discrete spectrum as the elliptic part of the equation.

Since a precise statement of our main result requires several definitions, here (in the introduction) we formulate the corresponding result on the example of the following simple initial-boundary value problem. Let $1 < \rho < 2$ be an unknown number to be determined. Consider the time-fractional string vibration equation with the Riemann–Liouville fractional derivative (see the next Section for the definition) of order ρ:

$$\partial_t^\rho u(x,t) - u_{xx}(x,t) = f(x,t), \quad x \in (-\pi, \pi], \quad t > 0,$$

and attach the 2π-periodical boundary conditions and the following initial conditions

$$\lim_{t \to 0} \partial_t^{\rho-1} u(x,t) = \varphi(x), \quad \lim_{t \to 0} \partial_t^{\rho-2} u(x,t) = \psi(x),$$

where φ, ψ and $f(\cdot, t)$ are 2π-periodical given functions (for the motivation to consider periodic boundary conditions, see the fundamental book by Courant and Hilbert [2] and the solution methods for the case $\rho = 2$ see the book [2], for the case $\rho \in (1,2)$ see [3,4]). Under certain conditions on these functions, there is a unique solution to this problem. Obviously, this solution depends on the choice of the order of the derivative ρ. Now let us ask a question: is there any additional information about the solution at a fixed moment of time that allows us to uniquely determine the parameter ρ?

As it follows from the main result of this paper, the answer is "yes". As for additional information at a fixed time instant t_0, one may consider the following:

$$\int_{-\pi}^{\pi} u(x,t_0)dx = d_0. \tag{1}$$

Knowledge of the value of this integral determines the parameter ρ and, moreover, if one has two pairs of solutions $\{u_1(x,t), \rho_1\}$ and $\{u_2(x,t), \rho_2\}$, then $u_1(x,t) \equiv u_2(x,t)$ and $\rho_1 = \rho_2$.

It should be noted that the first eigenfunction of the corresponding spectral problem is equal to $(2\pi)^{-1/2}$. Therefore, integral (1) is in fact, the projection of the solution onto the first eigenfunction.

This result can be interpreted as follows. The vibration of a string is usually perceived by us by the sound made by the string. The sound of a string is an overlay of simple tones corresponding to standing waves, into which vibration is decomposed. The above result states: having heard only one standing wave, one can uniquely determine the order ρ of the fractional derivative in the corresponding equation of string vibrations.

Usually, inverse problems in the theory of partial differential equations are called problems in which, along with the solution of a differential equation, it is also necessary to determine a certain coefficient of the equation or the right side or the initial or boundary function. Naturally, in this case, in order to find a new unknown function, additional information (redefinition condition) is required on the solution to the differential equation. Moreover, the redefinition condition must ensure both the existence and uniqueness of the solution to the inverse problem. Since inverse problems have important applications in many areas of modern science, including mechanics, seismology, medical tomography, geophysics, and much more (see, for example, refs. [5,6] and references therein), interest in their study is constantly growing.

As noted above, in this paper we study another inverse problem, namely, the problem of restoring the order of a fractional derivative in partial differential equations. This inverse problem has been studied in many papers ([1,7–13]). It should be noted that in all these publications the unknown order of the derivative is less than one (that is, $\rho < 1$), and the following equality was considered as a redefinition condition

$$u(x_0, t) = h(t), \ 0 < t < T, \tag{2}$$

at the observation point $x_0 \in \overline{\Omega}$. Since the goal is to find the order of the derivative in time, it seems natural to have information about the solution on a large time scale. However, this condition, as a rule (an exception is paper [13] by J. Janno, where both uniqueness and existence are proved, see below), can ensure only the uniqueness of the solution to the inverse problem. However, as the main result of this paper states, condition (1) guarantees both the existence and uniqueness of a solution.

The problem concerning the uniqueness of the solution to the inverse problem with condition (2) was studied in papers [7–10]. The authors of [7,8] considered subdiffusion equations with the Gerasimov–Caputo derivative (see next Section for definition). The problems for multi-term time-fractional diffusion equations and distributed order fractional diffusion equations were considered in papers by Li et al. [9,10], correspondingly. In the paper by J. Cheng et al. [7], the authors showed, in addition to the uniqueness of the order ρ, the uniqueness of the diffusion coefficient $p(x)$.

As far as we know, the only paper [13] by J. Janno deals with the existence problem. The author considered a subdiffusion equation with the Gerasimov–Caputo derivative. By setting an additional boundary condition $Bu(\cdot,t) = h(t), 0 < t < T$, with some functional B, the author proved the existence of an unknown order of the derivative and the kernel of the integral operator involved in the equation. The complexity of the proof of existence is due to the fact that the function $h(t)$ cannot be given arbitrarily; since t changes where the equation takes place, the function $h(t)$ must somehow be related to the equation. This circumstance is evident from the formulation of the corresponding theorem (see Theorem 7.2 of the work, which is formulated on more than one page of the journal).

In paper [14], Hatano et al., the equation $\partial_t^\rho u = \triangle u$ is considered with the Dirichlet boundary condition and the initial function $\varphi(x)$. The authors proved the following property of the parameter ρ: if $\varphi \in C_0^\infty(\Omega)$ and $\triangle \varphi(x_0) \neq 0$, then

$$\rho = \lim_{t \to 0} \left[t \partial_t u(x_0, t) [u(x_0, t) - \varphi(x_0)]^{-1} \right].$$

It should be noted that the problem considered and solved in the present article was formulated as open in the "Open Problems" section of the recent review [1] (p. 440) by Z. Li et al.: "The studies on inverse problems of the recovery of the fractional orders ... are far from satisfactory since all the publications either assumed the homogeneous boundary condition or studied this inverse problem by the measurement on $t \in (0, \infty)$. It would be interesting to investigate inverse problem by the value of the solution at a fixed time as the observation data".

In references [15–22], this problem is discussed for various equations of mathematical physics. We note right away that in these works the authors prove not only the uniqueness of the solution to the inverse problem but also its existence. The method used in this paper was first proposed in a recent paper [15], where similar questions are investigated for the subdiffusion equation with a fractional Riemann–Liouville derivative of order $0 < \rho < 1$. The elliptic part of the equation considered in [15] is a second-order differential operator. The authors of [15] instead of the redefinition condition (2), considered a condition that meets the requirements formulated in the open problem formulated above. Namely, as a redefinition condition, they took the projection of the solution onto the first eigenfunction of the elliptic part of the equation at a fixed point in time. However, note that the method of [15] requires the first eigenvalue to be zero. This limitation was lifted in recent works by Alimov and Ashurov [16,17]. The authors of these papers, taking an additional condition in the form $||u(x, t_0)||^2 = d_0$ and the boundary condition not necessarily homogeneous, proved both the existence and uniqueness of a solution to the inverse problem. In this case, the norm $||u(x, t_0)||^2$ is a part of the potential energy. Indeed, if, for example, the elliptic part of the equation has the form $Au = -\Delta u + k^2 u$, then the potential energy is equal to the sum of the norms $||\nabla u||^2 + k^2 ||u||^2$.

In reference [12,18], the inverse problem was studied, where it is required to determine, along with the solution to the equation, both the order of the derivative and the right-hand side of the equation. The authors of [12] proved only the uniqueness of the solution to the inverse problem, while the authors of [18] proved the existence and uniqueness theorem.

The authors of [19] have studied the subdiffusion equations, the elliptic part of which has a continuous spectrum. In this work, along with other problems, the inverse problem of determining the order of the derivative with respect to both space and time is solved.

As far as we know, the inverse problem under consideration for a mixed-type equation was first studied in [20]. The inverse problem for the fractional wave equation was studied in [21]. In this work, in contrast to the present work, the fractional derivative is taken in the Gerasimov–Caputo sense. Without additional restrictions on the spectrum of operator A, the authors present a solution to the problem posed in the review [1] for the fractional order wave equation.

We note one more paper [22], where a system of subdiffusion equations is considered, the elliptic part of which is elliptic pseudodifferential operators. The authors managed to find such additional conditions for solving the inverse problem of restoring the order of fractional derivatives, which guarantees both the uniqueness and the existence of a solution. It should be specially noted that the desired order of the fractional derivative in this work is a vector.

We also note the recent work [23], where the uniqueness of the inverse problem for the simultaneous determination of the coefficient of the equation and the order of the fractional derivative is proved.

In order to not be distracted by the technical aspects of the issue, connected with the uniform convergence of the Fourier series, we first consider an abstract statement of the problem. Then, at the end of the paper, we will make the necessary remarks for the transition to the classical setting.

This article is organized as follows. In the next section, we give the necessary definitions and formulate the main result. Note that the elliptic part of our fractional wave equation is an arbitrary self-adjoint operator A in a Hilbert space. Section 2 proves the existence and uniqueness of a solution to the direct problem. This result will be used to prove the main result in Section 3. Section 4 gives various examples of operator A for which the main result of the paper is valid. The article ends with a conclusion.

2. Main Result

Consider an arbitrary nonnegative self-adjoint operator A in a separable Hilbert space H. Let $(\cdot, \cdot)$ be a scalar product and $||\cdot||_H$ a norm in H. Assume that A has a compact inverse and denote by $\{v_k\}$ the complete system of orthonormal eigenfunctions and by $\{\lambda_k\}$ a countable set of nonnegative eigenvalues: $\lambda_k \leq \lambda_{k+1}$.

For vector functions (or just functions) $f : \mathbb{R}_+ \to H$, fractional analogs of integrals and derivatives are defined using the definition of strong integral and strong derivative (see, for example, [24]). In this case, the known formulas and properties of fractional integrals and derivatives are preserved. Thus, fractional integration in the Riemann–Liouville sense of order $\rho < 0$ is defined as

$$\partial_t^\rho f(t) = \frac{1}{\Gamma(-\rho)} \int_0^t \frac{f(\xi)}{(t-\xi)^{\rho+1}} d\xi, \quad t > 0,$$

provided the right-hand side exists as an element of H. Here the symbol $\Gamma(\rho)$ denotes the Euler gamma function. By this definition, we define the fractional derivative of order ρ, $k-1 < \rho \leq k, k \in \mathbb{N}$, in the Riemann–Liouville sense as

$$\partial_t^\rho f(t) = \frac{d^k}{dt^k} \partial_t^{\rho-k} f(t).$$

If in this equality the fractional integral and derivative are interchanged, then we obtain the definition of the Gerasimov–Caputo fractional derivative.

It is easy to see that for $\rho = k$ the fractional derivative coincides with the classical derivative of integer order: $\partial_t^k f(t) = \frac{d^k}{dt^k} f(t)$. For general information on fractional integro-differential operators of different classes with many applications cf. [3,25,26].

Let $\rho \in (1,2)$ be an unknown constant number and let $C((a,b); H)$ stand for a set of continuous functions $u(t)$ of $t \in (a,b)$ with values in H. Consider the Cauchy-type problem:

$$\partial_t^\rho u(t) + Au(t) = f(t), \quad 0 < t \leq T, \tag{3}$$

$$\lim_{t \to 0} \partial_t^{\rho-1} u(t) = \varphi, \quad \lim_{t \to 0} \partial_t^{\rho-2} u(t) = \psi, \tag{4}$$

where the limit is taken in H norm, $f(t)$, φ, and ψ are given elements of H.

Definition 1. *If a function $u(t)$ has the properties*
1. *$\partial_t^\rho u(t), Au(t) \in C((0,T]; H)$,*
2. *$\partial_t^{\rho-1} u(t), \partial_t^{\rho-2} u(t) \in C([0,T]; H)$*

and satisfies conditions (3) *and* (4)*, then it is called **the (generalized) solution** to problems* (3) *and* (4)*.*

We first prove that for any given functions $\varphi, \psi \in H$, and $t^{2-\rho} f(t) \in C([0,T]; H)$, the solution of this problem exists and it is unique. This solution obviously will depend on ρ. To determine this number we use the additional condition:

$$U(\rho; t_0) \equiv (u(t_0), v_1) = d_0, \quad t_0 \geq T_0, \tag{5}$$

where T_0 is defined later.

We call problem (3) and (4) *the forward problem*. Problem (3) and (4) together with extra condition (5) is called *the inverse problem*.

Let us denote by $E_{\rho,\mu}(t)$ the Mittag-Leffler function of the form

$$E_{\rho,\mu}(t) = \sum_{k=0}^{\infty} \frac{t^k}{\Gamma(\rho k + \mu)}.$$

On Mittag-Leffler functions cf. [4,25,27,28].

Theorem 1. *For any $\varphi, \psi \in H$ and $f(t)$ with $t^{2-\rho} f(t) \in C([0,T]; H)$ forward problem (3) and (4) has a unique solution and this solution has the form*

$$u(t) = \sum_{j=1}^{\infty} \left[\varphi_j t^{\rho-1} E_{\rho,\rho}(-\lambda_j t^\rho) + \psi_j t^{\rho-2} E_{\rho,\rho-1}(-\lambda_j t^\rho) + \int_0^t f_j(t-\xi) \xi^{\rho-1} E_{\rho,\rho}(-\lambda_j \xi^\rho) d\xi \right] v_j, \tag{6}$$

where the series converges in H, $f_j(t)$, φ_j and ψ_j are corresponding Fourier coefficients.

Forward problems for fractional linear wave equations and systems of such equations, involving various elliptic operators and the properties of their solutions have been studied by many authors. Since the main purpose of this article is the solution to the inverse problem, without dwelling on these papers, we refer interested readers to review papers [29,30]. We also note that in a number of papers, initial boundary value problems and the properties of their solutions for nonlinear fractional wave equations are also studied (see, for example, ref. [31] and the literature therein).

Definition 2. *Let $u(t)$ be the solution to problems (3) and (4), and the parameter $\rho \in (1,2)$. Then we call a pair $\{u(t), \rho\}$ the (generalized) solution to the inverse problems (3)–(5).*

Let us describe the proposed method for solving the inverse problem when the following conditions are satisfied

$$\lambda_1 = 0, \quad f_1(t) \equiv 0, \quad \varphi_1^2 + \psi_1^2 \neq 0. \tag{7}$$

If these conditions are not satisfied, then the method becomes technically cumbersome. Further, let parameter T_0 in (5) be defined as

$$T_0 = \begin{cases} 2, & \varphi_1 \cdot \psi_1 \geq 0, \\ 2 \cdot \max\left\{1, \dfrac{|\psi_1|}{|\varphi_1|}\right\}, & \varphi_1 \cdot \psi_1 < 0. \end{cases}$$

Let us formulate a result on the inverse problem.

Theorem 2. *Let $\varphi, \psi \in H$ and $t^{2-\rho} f(t) \in C([0,T]; H)$. Moreover, assume that the conditions (7) are satisfied and $t_0 \geq T_0$ is any fixed number. Then for the inverse problem (3)–(5) to have a unique solution $\{u(t), \rho\}$ it is necessary and sufficient that condition*

$$\min\{\varphi_1, \varphi_1 t_0 + \psi_1\} < d_0 < \max\{\varphi_1, \varphi_1 t_0 + \psi_1\}$$

be satisfied.

Remark 1. *Theorem 2 asserts the existence of a unique solution of equation (5) with respect to ρ. If we set the condition (5) at another point t_1, then we can obtain a new solution ρ_1, i.e., $U(\rho_1; t_1) = d_1$. However, then from the equality $U(\rho_1; t_0) = d_0$, by Theorem 2 we have $\rho_1 = \rho$.*

3. Forward Problem

In this section, we prove Theorem 1. In accordance with the Fourier method, we will seek the solution to the problem (3) and (4) as a series:

$$u(t) = \sum_{j=1}^{\infty} T_j(t) v_j, \tag{8}$$

where functions $T_j(t)$ are solutions to the Cauchy-type problem

$$\partial_t^\rho T_j + \lambda_j T_j = f_j(t), \quad \lim_{t \to 0} \partial_t^{\rho-1} T_j(t) = \varphi_j, \quad \lim_{t \to 0} \partial_t^{\rho-2} T_j(t) = \psi_j. \tag{9}$$

The unique solution of problem (9) has the form (see, for example, [32], p. 173)

$$T_j(t) = \varphi_j t^{\rho-1} E_{\rho,\rho}(-\lambda_j t^\rho) + \psi_j t^{\rho-2} E_{\rho,\rho-1}(-\lambda_j t^\rho) + \int_0^t f_j(t-\xi)\xi^{\rho-1} E_{\rho,\rho}(-\lambda_j \xi^\rho) d\xi. \tag{10}$$

The uniqueness of the forward problem's solution can be proved by the standard technique based on the completeness in H of the set of eigenfunctions $\{v_j\}$. For convenience, we present a proof here (see, for example [33], for the case $\rho \in (0,1)$).

Proof. Assume the opposite, i.e., let the problem (3) and (4) have two solutions $u_1(t)$ and $u_2(t)$. Let us prove that $u(t) = u_1(t) - u_2(t) \equiv 0$. Due to the linearity of the problem, to determine $u(t)$ we obtain the homogeneous problem:

$$\partial_t^\rho u(t) + Au(t) = 0, \quad t > 0; \tag{11}$$

$$\lim_{t \to 0} \partial_t^{\rho-1} u(t) = 0, \quad \lim_{t \to 0} \partial_t^{\rho-2} u(t) = 0. \tag{12}$$

Let $u(t)$ be a solution of problem (11) and (12) and v_k be an arbitrary eigenfunction with the corresponding eigenvalue λ_k. Consider the function

$$w_k(t) = (u(t), v_k). \tag{13}$$

By definition of the solution, we may write

$$\partial_t^\rho w_k(t) = (\partial_t^\rho u(t), v_k) = -(Au(t), v_k) = -(u(t), Av_k) = -\lambda_k(u(t), v_k) = -\lambda_k w_k(t), \quad t > 0.$$

Therefore, we have the Cauchy problem for $w_k(t)$:

$$\partial_t^\rho w_k(t) + \lambda_k w_k(t) = 0, \quad t > 0; \quad \lim_{t \to 0} \partial_t^{\rho-1} w_k(t) = 0, \quad \lim_{t \to 0} \partial_t^{\rho-2} w_k(t) = 0.$$

This problem has a unique null solution: $w_k(t) \equiv 0$ (see (10)). Due to the completeness of systems of eigenfunctions $\{v_k\}$, this means that $u(t) = 0$ for all $t > 0$ (see (13)). Hence the uniqueness is proved.

We turn to the proof of the existence of a solution to the forward problem. For this, we recall the following estimate for the Mittag-Leffler function with a negative argument (see, e.g., [32], p. 29)

$$|E_{\rho,\mu}(-t)| \le \frac{C}{1+t}, \quad t > 0. \tag{14}$$

Therefore, for any positive eigenvalues λ_j one has

$$|t^{\rho-1}E_{\rho,\rho}(-\lambda_j t^\rho)| \leq \frac{Ct^{\rho-1}}{1+\lambda_j t^\rho} \leq \frac{C}{\lambda_j t}(t^\rho \lambda_j)^{\varepsilon/\rho}, \quad t > 0, \qquad (15)$$

with $0 < \varepsilon < \rho$. Indeed, if $t^\rho \lambda_j < 1$, then

$$\frac{1}{\lambda_j t}(t^\rho \lambda_j)^{\varepsilon/\rho} > \frac{1}{\lambda_j t} t^\rho \lambda_j > t^{\rho-1},$$

and if $t^\rho \lambda_j > 1$, then

$$\frac{1}{\lambda_j t}(t^\rho \lambda_j)^{\varepsilon/\rho} > \frac{1}{\lambda_j t}.$$

The fact that function (6) formally satisfies Equation (3) follows from the definition of functions T_j (see (9)). Therefore, by Definition 1, we first need to prove that function (6) satisfies $Au(t) \in C((0, T]; H)$. Consider the sum

$$S_k(t) = \sum_{j=1}^{k} [\varphi_j t^{\rho-1} E_{\rho,\rho}(-\lambda_j t^\rho) + \psi_j t^{\rho-2} E_{\rho,\rho-1}(-\lambda_j t^\rho)$$

$$+ \int_0^t f_j(t-\xi)\xi^{\rho-1} E_{\rho,\rho}(-\lambda_j \xi^\rho) d\xi] v_j.$$

By virtue of the Parseval equality, we may rewrite

$$||AS_k(t)||_H^2 = \sum_{j=1}^{k} \lambda_j^2 [\varphi_j t^{\rho-1} E_{\rho,\rho}(-\lambda_j t^\rho) + \psi_j t^{\rho-2} E_{\rho,\rho-1}(-\lambda_j t^\rho)$$

$$+ \int_0^t f_j(t-\xi)\xi^{\rho-1} E_{\rho,\rho}(-\lambda_j \xi^\rho) d\xi]^2. \qquad (16)$$

Using the inequality $(a+b+c)^2 \leq 3(a^2+b^2+c^2)$ we have three sums on the right side.

For the first sum, one has

$$\sum_{j=1}^{k} \left| \lambda_j \varphi_j t^{\rho-1} E_{\rho,\rho}(-\lambda_j t^\rho) \right|^2 \leq Ct^{-2} \sum_{j=1}^{k} |\varphi_j|^2 \leq Ct^{-2} ||\varphi||_H. \qquad (17)$$

Here, we use estimate (14) and inequality $\lambda t^{\rho-1}(1+\lambda t^\rho)^{-1} < t^{-1}$.

Function $E_{\rho,\rho-1}(-\lambda_j t^\rho)$ in the second sum has the same estimate as $E_{\rho,\rho}(-\lambda_j t^\rho)$. Therefore, the second sum also has an estimate similar to (17).

Now let us consider the third sum in (16). Since operator A is nonnegative, then $\lambda_{j_0} > 0$ for some $j_0 \geq 1$. Further, if $f(t)$ satisfies the condition of the theorem, then $t^{2-\rho}||f(t)||_H \leq C_f$. Therefore, taking into account estimate (15) and the generalized Minkowski inequality, one has

$$\sum_{j=j_0}^{k} |\int_0^t \lambda_j f_j(t-\xi)\xi^{\rho-1} E_{\rho,\rho}(-\lambda_j \xi^\rho) d\xi|^2$$

$$= \sum_{j=j_0}^{k} |\int_0^t \lambda_j (t-\xi)^{\rho-2} f_j(t-\xi)(t-\xi)^{2-\rho} \xi^{\rho-1} E_{\rho,\rho}(-\lambda_j \xi^\rho) d\xi|^2$$

$$\leq C \left(\int_0^t \xi^{\varepsilon-1}(t-\xi)^{\rho-2} \Big(\sum_{j=j_0}^k (t-\xi)^{2(2-\rho)} |f_j(t-\xi)|^2 \Big)^{1/2} d\xi \right)^2 \leq C \cdot C_f^2 \cdot (\varepsilon^{-2} + (\rho-1)^{-2}).$$

Hence, summing up the estimates of all three terms in (16), we obtain $Au(t) \in C((0, T]; H)$.

Further, Equation (3) implies $\partial_t^\rho S_k(t) = -AS_k(t)$. Therefore, from the above reasoning, we finally have $\partial_t^\rho u(t) \in C((0, T]; H)$.

A simple calculation shows the fulfillment of the initial conditions (4) (see (9)).

Thus, Theorem 1 is proved. □

4. Inverse Problem

First, we study some properties of the projection of the forward problem's solution onto the first eigenfunction, i.e., $U(\rho; t_0)$ (see (5)) as a function of $\rho \in (1, 2)$. Let T_0 be a number, defined above.

Lemma 1. *Let conditions (7) be satisfied and $t_0 \geq T_0$. Then function $U(\rho; t_0)$ is strictly monotonic in the variable $\rho \in (1, 2)$ and*

$$\lim_{\rho \to 1} U(\rho; t_0) = \varphi_1, \quad U(2; t_0) = \varphi_1 t_0 + \psi_1. \tag{18}$$

Proof. Since eigenfunctions $\{v_j\}$ are orthonormal, then from (6) by virtue of conditions (7), one may obtain

$$U(\rho; t_0) = \varphi_1 t_0^{\rho-1} E_{\rho,\rho}(0) + \psi_1 t_0^{\rho-2} E_{\rho,\rho-1}(0),$$

or, by definition of the Mittag-Leffler function,

$$U(\rho; t_0) = \varphi_1 y(\rho) + \psi_1 y(\rho-1), \quad y(\rho) = \frac{t_0^{\rho-1}}{\Gamma(\rho)}.$$

Denote by $\Psi(\rho)$ the logarithmic derivative of the gamma function $\Gamma(\rho)$ (see [34] for the definition of this function and its properties). We have $\Gamma'(\rho) = \Gamma(\rho)\Psi(\rho)$ and, then,

$$y'(\rho) = \frac{t_0^{\rho-1}}{\Gamma(\rho)} \big[\ln t_0 - \Psi(\rho) \big].$$

Let $\gamma \approx 0.57722$ be the Euler–Mascheroni constant, then $-\gamma < \Psi(\rho) < 1 - \gamma$ and $\Psi(\rho-1) < 0$ for $\rho \in (1, 2)$. Hence, if $t_0 \geq 2$, then $y'(\rho) > 0$ and $y'(\rho-1) > 0$. Therefore, if $\varphi_1 \cdot \psi_1 \geq 0$ and $t_0 \geq 2$, then $U(\rho; t_0)$ is strictly monotonic in the variable ρ.

Let now $\varphi_1 \cdot \psi_1 < 0$ and prove that t_0 can be chosen in such a way that

$$|\varphi_1 y'(\rho)| > |\psi_1 y'(\rho-1)|. \tag{19}$$

In order to show this, we will rewrite the function $U'(\rho; t_0)$, taking into account the equations

$$\frac{1}{\Gamma(\rho-1)} = \frac{\rho-1}{\Gamma(\rho)}, \quad \Psi(\rho-1) = \Psi(\rho) - \frac{1}{\rho-1},$$

in the form

$$U'(\rho; t_0) = \frac{t_0^{\rho-1}}{\Gamma(\rho)} \left(\frac{\varphi_1}{2} [2\ln t_0 - 2\Psi(\rho)] + \frac{\psi_1}{t_0} [(\rho-1)\ln t_0 + 1 - \Psi(\rho)] \right). \tag{20}$$

It is easy to see that

$$2\ln t_0 - 2\Psi(\rho) > (\rho-1)\ln t_0 + 1 - \Psi(\rho)$$

for all $t_0 \geq 2$. Indeed, this inequality is equivalent to the following

$$2\ln t_0 > (3-\rho)\ln t_0 > \Psi(\rho) + 1 > -\gamma + 1 > \frac{2}{5},$$

that is $\ln t_0 > 1/5$. Therefore, if $t_0 > e^{\frac{1}{5}} > \frac{6}{5}$, or $t_0 \geq 2$, then we obtain the required estimate.

Therefore, for the validity of estimate (19), it is sufficient to simultaneously fulfill two inequalities $t_0 \geq 2$ and $t_0|\varphi_1| \geq 2|\psi_1|$ (see (20)), or which is the same, one inequality $t_0 \geq 2\max\{1, \frac{|\psi_1|}{|\varphi_1|}\}$.

Thus, if $t_0 \geq T_0$, then $U(\rho; t_0)$ is strictly monotonic in the variable ρ. The equalities (18) are easy to check. □

Now let us go to the proof of the Theorem 2.

Proof. The fact that $u(x,t)$ exists for any $\rho \in (1,2)$ follows from Theorem 1. Let the given number d_0 be such that

$$\min\{\varphi_1, \varphi_1 t_0 + \psi_1\} < d_0 < \max\{\varphi_1, \varphi_1 t_0 + \psi_1\}.$$

Then it immediately follows from Lemma 1 that there exists a unique number ρ satisfying the condition (5). Obviously, if the opposite inequalities hold, then such a number ρ does not exist.

We turn to the proof of the uniqueness of the solution to the inverse problem (3)–(5). Let there be two pairs of solutions $\{u_1, \rho_1\}$ and $\{u_2, \rho_2\}$ such that $1 < \rho_k < 2$ and

$$\partial_t^{\rho_k} u_k(t) + Au_k(t) = f(t), \quad 0 < t \leq T; \tag{21}$$

$$\lim_{t \to 0} \partial_t^{\rho_k - 1} u_k(t) = \varphi, \quad \lim_{t \to 0} \partial_t^{\rho_k - 2} u_k(t) = \psi, \tag{22}$$

where $k = 1, 2$.

Consider the following functions

$$w_k^j(t) = (u_k(t), v_j) \quad k = 1, 2; \quad j = 1, 2, \cdots$$

Then Equations (21) and (22) imply

$$\partial_t^{\rho_k} w_k^j(t) + \lambda_j w_k^j(t) = f_j(t), \quad \lim_{t \to 0} \partial_t^{\rho_k - 1} w_k^j(t) = \varphi_j, \quad \lim_{t \to 0} \partial_t^{\rho_k - 2} w_k^j(t) = \psi_j.$$

Solutions to these Cauchy-type problems can be represented as (10). Then, (5) implies $w_1^1(t_0) = w_2^1(t_0) = d_0$, or, since $f_1 = 0$,

$$\varphi_1 t_0^{\rho_1 - 1} E_{\rho_1, \rho_1}(0) + \psi_1 t_0^{\rho_1 - 2} E_{\rho_1, \rho_1 - 1}(0) = \varphi_1 t_0^{\rho_2 - 1} E_{\rho_2, \rho_2}(0) + \psi_1 t_0^{\rho_2 - 1} E_{\rho_2, \rho_2 - 1}(0) = d_0.$$

As we have seen above (see Lemma 1), it follows from these equations that $\rho_1 = \rho_2$. However, in this case, $w_1^j(t) = w_2^j(t)$ for all t and j. Hence

$$(u_1(t) - u_2(t), v_j) = 0$$

for all j. Finally, from the completeness of the set of eigenfunctions $\{v_j\}$ in H, we have $u_1(t) = u_2(t)$. Hence, Theorem 2 is completely proved. □

5. Examples of Operator A

Consideration of the abstract operator A allows us to explore many different models. In this section, we provide several examples of operator A, to which our results apply.

First, we obtain an interesting example if we take a square matrix with constant elements as the operator A: $A = \{a_{i,j}\}$ and $H = \mathbb{R}^N$. In this case, the problem (3) and (4) becomes the Cauchy problem for a linear system of differential equations of fractional order.

As an example of operator A, one can also take any of the physical examples considered in Section 6 of the article by M. Ruzhansky et al. [33]. In particular, the authors considered differential models with involution, fractional Laplacian, and fractional Sturm–Liouville operators, anharmonic and harmonic oscillators, Landau Hamiltonians, and many other operators with a discrete spectrum. If the first eigenvalue λ_1 of the operator A is not zero, then the operator $A - \lambda_1 I$ with zero first eigenvalue should be considered as required in Theorem 2. Here, I is the identity operator.

The solution to the problem in this work, as well as in our work, is understood in a generalized sense (see Definition 1).

Now, let us show how similar results as in this paper can be obtained for classical solutions (see also [15]).

Let $A(x, D) = \sum\limits_{|\alpha| \leq m} a_\alpha(x) D^\alpha$ be an arbitrary non-negative formally self-adjoint elliptic differential operator of the order $m = 2l$ defined in N-dimensional bounded domain Ω with boundary $\partial \Omega$.

Assume that $1 < \rho < 2$ is an unknown parameter that needs to be determined and that the initial-boundary value problem has the form

$$\partial_t^\rho u(x,t) + A(x,D)u(x,t) = f(x,t), \quad x \in \Omega, \quad 0 < t \leq T, \tag{23}$$

$$B_j u(x,t) = \sum_{|\alpha| \leq m_j} b_{\alpha,j}(x) D^\alpha v(x) = 0, \ j = 1,2,...,l; \ x \in \partial\Omega, \quad 0 < t \leq T, \tag{24}$$

$$\lim_{t \to 0} \partial_t^{\rho-1} u(x,t) = \varphi(x), \quad \lim_{t \to 0} \partial_t^{\rho-2} u(x,t) = \psi(x), \quad x \in \overline{\Omega} \tag{25}$$

where $f(x,t)$, $\varphi(x)$ and $\psi(x)$ are given sufficiently smooth functions from $L_2(\Omega)$.

In the paper by S. Agmon [35], it is considered the spectral problem

$$\begin{cases} A(x,D)v(x) = \lambda v(x), & x \in \Omega; \\ B_j v(x) = 0, \ 0 \leq m_j \leq m-1, \ j = 1,2,...,l; \ x \in \partial\Omega. \end{cases} \tag{26}$$

The author found sufficient conditions on the boundary of domain Ω and operators $A(x,D)$ and B_j that guarantee the compactness of the corresponding inverse operator, i.e., the existence of a complete system $\{v_k(x)\}$ of orthonormal eigenfunctions and a countable set $\{\lambda_k\}$ of non-negative eigenvalues of the spectral problem (26).

As the next example, instead of A we take operator $A(x,D)$ with boundary conditions B_j and set $H = L_2(\Omega)$. In this case, an additional condition (5) for determining ρ will have the form:

$$\int_\Omega u(x,t_0) v_1(x) dx = d_0, \quad t_0 \geq T_0, \tag{27}$$

where T_0 is defined as above. Let g_k stand for the Fourier coefficient of a function $g(x) \in L_2(\Omega)$ by the system of eigenfunctions $\{v_k(x)\}$.

Definition 3. *A pair $\{u(x,t), \rho\}$ of the function $u(x,t)$ and the parameter ρ with the properties*
1. *$\rho \in (1,2)$,*
2. *$\partial_t^\rho u(x,t), A(x,D)u(x,t) \in C(\overline{\Omega} \times (0,\infty))$,*
3. *$\partial_t^{\rho-1} u(x,t), \partial_t^{\rho-2} u(x,t) \in C(\overline{\Omega} \times [0,\infty))$*

and satisfying all the conditions of problems (23)–(25), (27) in the classical sense is called **the classical solution** of inverse problem (23)–(25), (27).

Theorem 3. *Let f, φ, ψ be sufficiently smooth functions. Further, let conditions (7) be satisfied and $t_0 \geq T_0$ be any fixed number. Then for the inverse problem (23)–(25), (27) to have a unique solution $\{u(x,t), \rho\}$ it is necessary and sufficient that condition*

$$\min\{\varphi_1, \varphi_1 t_0 + \psi_1\} < d_0 < \max\{\varphi_1, \varphi_1 t_0 + \psi_1\}$$

be satisfied.

The theorem is proved using similar arguments presented above (see, also [15]). In order to reduce the study of uniform convergence to the study of convergence in L_2-norm, we apply Lemma 22.1 of the monograph [36] (p. 453).

Remark 2. *Let $A_0(x, D) = \sum_{0<|\alpha|\leq m} a_\alpha(x) D^\alpha$ be an elliptic operator and $B_{0,j} = \sum_{0<|\alpha|\leq m_j} b_{\alpha,j}(x) D^\alpha$ be boundary operators. Then the first eigenfunction of the spectral problem (26) is a constant and $\lambda_1 = 0$.*

6. Conclusions

The problem of determining the fractional order of a model has been considered by many authors because of its importance to the application. The authors mainly considered subdiffusion equations in which the Gerasimov–Caputo fractional derivative is involved.

As far as we know, the inverse problem of determining the order of the fractional derivative for the fractional wave equation was considered only in [1]. As a fractional derivative, the authors took the Gerasimov–Caputo derivative.

In the present work, by studying the abstract wave equation with the Riemann–Liouville derivative, the open problem formulated in the review article [1] for the considered inverse problems is positively solved. Since the problem is solved on the basis of the classical Fourier method, the explicit form of the elliptic part is not fundamental. Therefore, an arbitrary non-negative self-adjoint operator A in a separable Hilbert space H is taken as the elliptic part. If $H = L_2(\Omega)$, where Ω is an N-dimensional bounded domain with a smooth boundary, then as the operator A we can take the Laplacian with the Neumann condition. In this case, the first eigenvalue is equal to zero, as required in Theorem 2.

Author Contributions: Conceptualization, R.A.; methodology, S.S.; software, R.A.; validation, S.S.; formal analysis, S.S.; investigation, R.A.; resources, S.S.; data curation, S.S.; writing—original draft preparation, R.A.; writing—review and editing, S.S.; visualization, R.A.; supervision, R.A.; project administration, S.S. All authors have read and agreed to the published version of the manuscript.

Funding: This research received no external funding.

Data Availability Statement: The data presented in this study are available upon request from the corresponding author.

Acknowledgments: The authors thank Sh. A. Alimov for the discussions about the results.

Conflicts of Interest: The authors declare no conflict of interest.

References

1. Li, Z.; Liu, Y.; Yamamoto, M. Inverse problems of determining parameters of the fractional partial differential equations. In *Handbook of Fractional Calculus with Applications*; DeGruyter: Berlin, Germany, 2019; Volume 2, pp. 431–442.
2. Courant, R.; Hilbert, D. *Methods of Mathematical Physics*; John Wiley & Sons: Hoboken, NJ, USA, 1989; Volume 1.
3. Samko, S.G.; Kilbas, A.A.; Marichev, O.I. *Fractional Integrals and Derivatives. Theory and Applications*; Gordon and Breach Science Publishers: Philadelphia, PA, USA, 1993.
4. Gorenflo, R.; Kilbas, A.A.; Mainardi, F.; Rogosin, S. *Mittag–Leffler Functions, Related Topics and Applications*, 2nd ed.; (Springer Monographs in Mathematics); Springer: New York, NY, USA, 2020.

5. Machado, J.A.T. (Ed.) *Handbook of Fractional Calculus with Applications*; DeGruyter: Berlin, Germany, 2019; Volume 1–2.
6. Kravchenko, V.V. *Direct and Inverse Sturm-Liouville Problems: A Method of Solution*; Birkhäuser: Cham, Switzerland; Springer Nature: Berlin, Germany, 2020.
7. Cheng, J.; Nakagawa, J.; Yamamoto, M.; Yamazaki, T. Uniqueness in an inverse problem for a one-dimensional fractional diffusion equation. *Inverse Probl.* **2009**, *25*, 115002. [CrossRef]
8. Tatar, S.; Ulusoy, S. A uniqueness result for an inverse problem in a space-time fractional diffusion equation. *Electron. J. Differ. Equ.* **2013**, *257*, 1–9.
9. Li, Z.; Yamamoto, M. Uniqueness for inverse problems of determining orders of multi-term time-fractional derivatives of diffusion equation. *Appl. Anal.* **2015**, *94*, 570–579. [CrossRef]
10. Li, Z.; Luchko, Y.; Yamamoto, M. Analyticity of solutions to a distributed order time-fractional diffusion equation and its application to an inverse problem. *Comput. Math. Appl.* **2017**, *73*, 1041–1052. [CrossRef]
11. Zheng, X.; Cheng, J.; Wang, H. Uniqueness of determining the variable fractional order in variable-order time-fractional diffusion equations. *Inverse Probl.* **2019**, *35*, 125002. [CrossRef]
12. Yamamoto, M. Uniqueness in determining fractional orders of derivatives and initial values. *Inverse Probl.* **2021**, *37*, 57–71. [CrossRef]
13. Janno, J. Determination of the order of fractional derivative and a kernel in an inverse problem for a generalized time-fractional diffusion equation. *Electron. J. Differ.* **2016**, *216*, 1–28.
14. Hatano, Y.; Nakagawa, J.; Wang, S.; Yamamoto, M. Determination of order in fractional diffusion equation. *J. Math-for-Ind.* **2013**, *5A*, 51–57.
15. Ashurov, R.; Umarov, S. Determination of the order of fractional derivative for subdiffusion equations. *Fract. Calc. Appl. Anal.* **2020**, *23*, 1647–1662. [CrossRef] [PubMed]
16. Alimov, S.; Ashurov, R. Inverse problem of determining an order of the Caputo time-fractional derivative for a subdiffusion equation. *J. Inverse Ill-Posed Probl.* **2020**, *28*, 651–658. [CrossRef]
17. Alimov, S.; Ashurov, R.R. Inverse problem of determining an order of the Riemann-Liouville time-fractional derivative. *Progr. Fract. Differ. Appl.* **2022**, *8*, 1–8.
18. Ashurov, R.; Fayziev, Y. Determination of fractional order and source term in a fractional subdiffusion equation. *Eur. Math. J.* **2022**, *13*, 19–31. [CrossRef]
19. Ashurov, R.R.; Zunnunov, R. Initial-boundary value and inverse problems for subdiffusion equation in R^N. *Fract. Differ. Calc.* **2020**, *10*, 291–306.
20. Ashurov, R.R.; Zunnunov, R. Inverse Problem for Determining the Order of the Fractional Derivative in Mixed-Type Equations. *Lobachevskii J. Math.* **2021**, *42*, 2714–2729. [CrossRef]
21. Ashurov, R.R.; Fayziev, Y.E. Inverse problem for determining the order of a fractional derivative in a wave equation. *Math. Notes* **2021**, *110*, 824–836. [CrossRef]
22. Ashurov, R.R.; Umarov, S.R. An inverse problem of determining orders of systems of fractional pseudo-differential equations. *Fract. Calc. Appl. Anal.* **2022**, *25*, 109–127. [CrossRef]
23. Jing, X.; Yamamoto, M. Simultaneous uniqueness for multiple parameters identification in a fractional diffusion-wave equation. *Inverse Probl. Imaging* **2022**, *16*, 1199–1217. [CrossRef]
24. Lizama, C. Abstract linear fractional evolution equations. In *Handbook of Fractional Calculus with Applications*; DeGruyter: Berlin, Germany, 2019; Volume 2, pp. 465–497.
25. Shishkina, E.L.; Sitnik, S.M. *Transmutations, Singular and Fractional Differential Equations with Applications to Mathematical Physics*, 1st ed.; Series: Mathematics in Science and Engineering; Elsevier: Amsterdam, The Netherlands; Academic Press: Cambridge, MA, USA, 2020.
26. Urinov, A.K.; Sitnik, S.M.; Shishkina, E.L.; Karimov, S.T. *Fractional Integrals and Derivatives (Generalizations and Applications)*; Fargona Publishing: Fergana, Uzbekistan, 2020.
27. Dzhrbashian, M.M. *Integral Transforms and Representation of Functions in the Comples Domain*; Nauka: Moscow, Russia, 1966.
28. Paneva-Konovska, J. *From Bessel to Multi-Index Mittag-Leffler Functions: Enumerable Families, Series in Them and Convergence*; World Scientific Publishing: Singapore, 2016.
29. Kochubei, A.N. Fractional-hyperbolic equations and systems. Cauchy problem. In *Handbook of Fractional Calculus with Applications*; DeGruyter: Berlin, Germany, 2019; Volume 2, pp. 19–223.
30. Atanacković, T.N.; Konjik, S.; Pilipović, S. Wave equation involving fractional derivatives of real and complex fractional order. In *Handbook of Fractional Calculus with Applications*; DeGruyter: Berlin, Germany, 2019; Volume 2, pp. 327–353.
31. Ahmad, B.; Alsaedi, A.; Berbiche, M.; Kirane, M. Global Existence and Blow-up of Solutions for a System of Fractional Wave Equations. *Taiwanese J. Math.* **2022**, *26*, 103–135. [CrossRef]
32. Gorenflo, R.; Kilbas, A.A.; Mainardi, F.; Rogozin, S.V. *Mittag-Leffler Functions, Related Topics and Applications*; Springer: Berlin/Heidelberg, Germany, 2014.
33. Ruzhansky, M.; Tokmagambetov, N.; Torebek, B.T. Inverse source problems for positive operators. I: Hypoelliptic diffusion and subdiffusion equations. *J. Inverse Ill-Possed Probl.* **2019**, *27*, 891–911. [CrossRef]
34. Bateman, H. *Higher Transcendental Functions*; McGraw-Hill: New York, NY, USA, 1953.

35. Agmon, S. On the eigenfunctions and on the eigenvalues of general elliptic boundary value problems. *Commun. Pure Appl. Math.* **1962**, *15*, 119–141. [CrossRef]
36. Krasnoselski, M.A.; Zabreyko, P.P.; Pustilnik, E.I.; Sobolevski, P.S. *Integral Operators in the Spaces of Integrable Functions*; M. NAUKA: Moscow, Russia, 1966. (In Russian)

Disclaimer/Publisher's Note: The statements, opinions and data contained in all publications are solely those of the individual author(s) and contributor(s) and not of MDPI and/or the editor(s). MDPI and/or the editor(s) disclaim responsibility for any injury to people or property resulting from any ideas, methods, instructions or products referred to in the content.

Article

Sinc Numeric Methods for Fox-H, Aleph (ℵ), and Saxena-I Functions

Gerd Baumann [1,*] and Norbert Südland [2]

1 Faculty of Natural Sciences, University of Ulm, D-89069 Ulm, Germany
2 Aage GmbH, 73431 Aalen, Germany
* Correspondence: gerd.baumann@uni-ulm.de

Abstract: The purpose of this study is to offer a systematic, unified approach to the Mellin-Barnes integrals and associated special functions as Fox H, Aleph ℵ, and Saxena I function, encompassing the fundamental features and important conclusions under natural minimal assumptions on the functions in question. The approach's pillars are the concept of a Mellin-Barnes integral and the Mellin representation of the given function. A Sinc quadrature is used in conjunction with a Sinc approximation of the function to achieve the numerical approximation of the Mellin-Barnes integral. The method converges exponentially and can handle endpoint singularities. We give numerical representations of the Aleph ℵ and Saxena I functions for the first time.

Keywords: Mellin-Barnes integrals; Sinc methods; Sinc quadrature; Fox functions; Aleph functions; Saxena function; definite integrals; fractional calculus

1. Introduction

In the past 40 years, the field of fractional calculus has undergone extraordinary development. The analytic and numeric approaches in fractional calculus created tremendous progress, especially the analytic side generated diverse directions which increased the improvement tremendously [1]. A large number of methods and approaches were developed, generating a consistent framework for analysis and symbolic computations [1,2]. However, the numeric developments are far behind the analytic achievements especially the numeric representation of special functions like Fox H, Aleph (ℵ), and Saxena I functions [3]. Such kinds of functions exist nowadays utilized in the analysis of fractional calculus. The special functions also found its way to applications in physics, engineering, and computer science [4]. It turned out during the years that linear transforms like Laplace-, Fourier-, and Mellin transforms play a vital role to generate special functions like Fox-H, ℵ, and Saxena's I function [1]. For the generation of such function, it is always essential to use the inverse of linear transforms which analytically exists but finally are difficult to compute numerically. The issue with unknown functions is that they could have previously unknown singularities. Naturally, this affects both the choice of the numerical method and the convergence at these singularities. The convergence of the employed numerical technique itself may also be a concern. This was the case if the approximation was calculated using an inverse Laplace transform, as mentioned in [5,6]. In a recent paper, we demonstrated by using Sinc methods that it becomes pretty efficient when Mittag-Leffler functions, a subset of Fox H functions, are the target in connection with an inverse Laplace transform [7]. Mittag-Leffler functions are frequently used in representing solutions of fractional differential or integral equations [8,9]. However, these functions are only a subset of the analytic functions needed to represent the large assortment of possible solutions to fractional equations.

Generalizations of Fox H functions are ℵ functions which also include the class of Saxena I functions [10]. These exceptional functions, which have been investigated analytically but are difficult to obtain numerically, are still a painstaking foundation for fractional calculus today. We aim to offer a numerical technique that solves most numerical difficulties like convergence and the occurrence of singularities by applying Sinc methods to the computation of these functions. Sinc methods initially introduced by Frank Stenger are a powerful numerical tool that allows representing nearly any calculus operation in an efficient and exponentially converging way [11]. For example, Sinc methods allow for computing of definite or indefinite integrals, convolution integrals, linear integral transforms and their inverse, to solve fractional differential and integral equations, and many other practical computations [12,13]. One essential characteristic of Sinc methods is the use of a small number of computing aids; i.e., small programs, a small number of discretization points, less memory, etc., in connection with a high precision output of numerical results [14]. We shall apply these approaches to the numerical computation of Mellin-Barnes integrals used in the presentation of special functions.

Next, we will introduce the definition of Fox, ℵ, and Saxena I functions. In Section 2, we shall introduce the approximation methods needed for this work. The application of these Sinc methods is demonstrated in Section 3. Section 4 summarizes the results and addresses open problems with the current approach.

1.1. The Fox H Function

The Fox H function was introduced by Charles Fox in connection with dual integral equations in 1965 [15]. As he stated at that time "These H functions contain Bessel functions as special cases and my aim is to show that, with the help of a suitable terminology, it is possible to write down a solution by inspection". Today we know that Fox H functions are a remarkably broad set of functions and include the elementary as well as special functions. The application of these functions is versatile and permits to derive solutions just by "inspection" as Fox noted. A collection of such applications are comprised in the book by Mathai et al. [4] which extends the classical text by Mathai and Saxena [16]. Both monographs concentrate on the part of getting solutions "by inspection". However, since then there exists a tremendous need and pressure to boil down the solutions to numbers; i.e., to represent the symbolic Fox H solutions as numerical estimations at least or as accurate numbers. Our aim here is to use the analytic and symbolic ideas of Fox and his successors to evaluate such kinds of solutions numerically. To this end let us introduce some notations for these functions.

A Fox function $H_{p,q}^{m,n}(z)$ is defined via a Mellin-Barnes type integral using integers m, n, p, q such that $0 \leq m \leq q$, $0 \leq n \leq p$, for $a_i, b_j \in \mathbb{C}$ with $\mathbb{C}$, the set of complex numbers, and for $\alpha_i, \beta_j \in \mathbb{R}^+ = (0, \infty)$ $(i = 1, 2, \ldots, p; j = 1, 2, \ldots, q)$ in the form

$$H_{p,q}^{m,n}\left(z \left| \begin{array}{c} (a_i, \alpha_i)_{1,p} \\ (b_j, \beta_j)_{1,q} \end{array} \right. \right) = \frac{1}{2\pi i} \int_C \mathcal{H}_{p,q}^{m,n}(s)\, z^{-s} ds \qquad (1)$$

with

$$\mathcal{H}_{p,q}^{m,n}\left(\begin{array}{c} (a_i, \alpha_i)_{1,p} \\ (b_j, \beta_j)_{1,q} \end{array} \middle| s \right) = \frac{\prod_{j=1}^m \Gamma(b_j + \beta_j s) \prod_{j=1}^n \Gamma(1 - a_j - \alpha_j s)}{\prod_{j=m+1}^q \Gamma(1 - b_j - \beta_j s) \prod_{j=n+1}^p \Gamma(a_j + \alpha_j s)}. \qquad (2)$$

Here

$$z^{-s} = \exp[-s\{\log |z| + i \arg z\}], \; z \neq 0, \; i = \sqrt{-1}, \qquad (3)$$

where $\log |z|$ represents the natural logarithm of $|z|$ and $\arg z$ is not necessarily the principal value. An empty product in (2), if it occurs, is taken to be one, and the poles

$$b_{j,l} = \frac{-b_j - l}{\beta_j} \; (j = 1, \ldots, m; l = 0, 1, 2, \ldots) \qquad (4)$$

of the gamma function $\Gamma(b_j + \beta_j s)$ and the poles

$$a_{i,k} = \frac{1 - a_i + k}{\alpha_i} \; (i = 1, \ldots, n; k = 0, 1, 2, \ldots) \qquad (5)$$

of the gamma function $\Gamma(1 - a_i - \alpha_i s)$ do not coincide:

$$\alpha_i(b_j + l) \neq \beta_j(a_i - k - 1) \quad (i = 1, \ldots, n; j = 1, \ldots, m; l, k = 0, 1, 2, \ldots). \tag{6}$$

The contour $\mathcal{C}$ in (1) is the infinite contour which separates all the poles $b_{j,l}$ in (4) to the left and all the poles $a_{i,k}$ in (5) to the right of $\mathcal{C}$. In fact there are many ways to define $\mathcal{C}$ in the complex plane. However, we will concentrate on the cases where $\mathcal{C}$ is parallel to the imaginary axis in the complex plane. For this reason let $s = \gamma + i\sigma$, where γ and σ are real; then the contour $\mathcal{C}$ along which the integral of (1) is taken is the straight line whose equation is $\gamma = \gamma_0$, where γ_0 is a constant. This line is parallel to the imaginary axis in the complex s plane and separates the poles.

For numeric integration we take $\mathcal{C}$ as a contour starting at the point $\gamma - i\infty$ and terminating at the point $\gamma + i\infty$, where $\gamma \in \mathbb{R} = (-\infty, \infty)$. To simplify the integration we use the substitutions $s = \gamma + i\sigma$ and $ds = id\sigma$ which delivers

$$\begin{aligned}
H_{p,q}^{m,n}\left(z \left|\begin{array}{c}(a_i, \alpha_i)_{1,p} \\ (b_j, \beta_j)_{1,q}\end{array}\right.\right) &= \frac{1}{2\pi i}\int_{\mathcal{C}} \mathcal{H}_{p,q}^{m,n}(s)\, z^{-s}ds = \frac{1}{2\pi i}\int_{\gamma - i\infty}^{\gamma + i\infty} \mathcal{H}_{p,q}^{m,n}(s)\, z^{-s}ds \\
&= \frac{1}{2\pi}\int_{-\infty}^{\infty} \mathcal{H}_{p,q}^{m,n}(\gamma + i\sigma)\, z^{-\gamma - i\sigma}d\sigma
\end{aligned} \tag{7}$$

allowing a direct integration to represent the Fox H function at points $z \in \mathbb{C}$. Note that the rightmost integral in (7) is a highly oscillating integral. Such kinds of integrals need special care if treated by standard quadrature methods. We will deal with this problem by using the Sinc quadrature discussed in Section 2. The absolute convergence of the integral can be guaranteed under certain conditions on the parameters of the Fox H function; for details see [3].

1.2. The ℵ Function

The ℵ function was introduced by the authors during the examination of fractional differential equations particularly the drift less Fokker-Planck equation [17,18]. The function is a generalization of Fox H function and allows to handle different initial conditions. Today, the ℵ function is well established and in use in several applications [19–23].

An ℵ function $\aleph_{p_k,q_k}^{m,n}(z)$ is defined via a Mellin-Barnes type integral using integers m, n, p_k, q_k such that $0 \leq m \leq q_k$, $0 \leq n \leq p_k$, for $a_i, b_j, a_{i,k}, b_{i,k} \in \mathbb{C}$ with $\mathbb{C}$, the set of complex numbers, and for $\alpha_i, \beta_j, \alpha_{i,k}, \beta_{i,k} \in \mathbb{R}^+ = (0, \infty)$ $(i = 1, 2, \ldots, p_k; j = 1, 2, \ldots, q_k)$, $\tau_k \in \mathbb{R}$ for $k = 1, \ldots, r$. The integration path $\mathcal{C}$ extends from $\gamma - i\infty$ to $\gamma + i\infty$, and is such that the poles of the gamma functions in the numerator $\Gamma(1 - a_j - \alpha_j s)$, $j = 1, \ldots, n$ do not coincide with the poles of the gamma functions $\Gamma(b_j + \beta_j s)$, $j = 1, \ldots, m$. The parameters p_k and q_k are non-negative integers satisfying $0 \leq n \leq p_k$, $0 \leq m \leq q_k$. All the poles of the integrand (8) are often assumed to be simple, and the empty product is interpreted as unity. The ℵ function is defined as follows

$$\aleph_{p_k,q_k,\tau_k;r}^{m,n}\left(z \left|\begin{array}{c}(a_i, \alpha_i)_{1,p} \\ (b_j, \beta_j)_{1,q}\end{array}\right.\right) = \frac{1}{2\pi i}\int_{\mathcal{C}} \mathcal{A}_{p_k,q_k,\tau_k;r}^{m,n}(s)\, z^{-s}ds \tag{8}$$

with the Mellin representation of the kernel $\mathcal{A}_{p_k,q_k,\tau_k;r}^{m,n}(s)$

$$\mathcal{A}_{p_k,q_k,\tau_k;r}^{m,n}\left(\begin{array}{c}(a_i, \alpha_i)_{1,p} \\ (b_j, \beta_j)_{1,q}\end{array}\bigg| s\right) = \frac{\prod_{j=1}^{m}\Gamma(b_j + \beta_j s)\prod_{j=1}^{n}\Gamma(1 - a_j - \alpha_j s)}{\sum_{k=1}^{r}\tau_k \prod_{j=m+1}^{q_k}\Gamma(1 - b_{j,k} - \beta_{j,k}s)\prod_{j=n+1}^{p_k}\Gamma(a_{j,k} + \alpha_{j,k}s)}. \tag{9}$$

Here

$$z^{-s} = \exp[-s\{\log|z| + i\arg z\}],\ z \neq 0,\ i = \sqrt{-1}. \tag{10}$$

Note that the Fox H function follows from the ℵ function in case when $r = 1$ and $\tau_k = 1$. If $\tau_k = 1$ for $k = 1, \ldots, r$ the Aleph function reduces to a Saxena I function [10].

According to the definition of $\mathcal{C}$ we are numerically dealing with a Bromwich integral in the form

$$\aleph_{p_k,q_k,\tau_k;r}^{m,n}\left(z \left|\begin{array}{c}(a_i,\alpha_i)_{1,p}\\(b_j,\beta_j)_{1,q}\end{array}\right.\right) = \frac{1}{2\pi i}\int_\mathcal{C}\mathcal{A}_{p_k,q_k,\tau_k;r}^{m,n}(s)\,z^{-s}ds$$
$$= \frac{1}{2\pi i}\int_{\gamma-i\infty}^{\gamma+i\infty}\mathcal{A}_{p_k,q_k,\tau_k;r}^{m,n}(s)\,z^{-s}ds \qquad (11)$$
$$= \frac{1}{2\pi}\int_{-\infty}^{\infty}\mathcal{A}_{p_k,q_k,\tau_k;r}^{m,n}(\gamma+i\sigma)\,z^{-\gamma-i\sigma}d\sigma.$$

The Aleph function in the present form is the result of solving integral and differential equations using linear transform techniques and is now considered the most generalized special function of a function representation [22].

1.3. The Saxena $\mathcal{I}$ Function

A Saxena I function $I_{p_k,q_k,1;r}^{m,n}(z)$ is similarly defined as an $\aleph$ function via a Mellin-Barnes type integral using integers m, n, p_k, q_k such that $0 \leq m \leq q_k$, $0 \leq n \leq p_k$, for $a_i, b_j, a_{i,k}, b_{j,k} \in \mathbb{C}$ with $\mathbb{C}$, the set of complex numbers, and for $\alpha_i, \beta_j, \alpha_{i,k}, \beta_{j,k} \in \mathbb{R}^+ = (0,\infty)$ ($i = 1,2,\ldots,p_k; j = 1,2,\ldots,q_k$), and $k = 1,\ldots,r$ [10], in the form

$$I_{p_k,q_k,1;r}^{m,n}\left(z\left|\begin{array}{c}(a_i,\alpha_i)_{1,p}\\(b_j,\beta_j)_{1,q}\end{array}\right.\right) = \frac{1}{2\pi i}\int_\mathcal{C}\mathcal{I}_{p_k,q_k,1;r}^{m,n}(s)\,z^{-s}ds, \qquad (12)$$

with the Mellin representation of the kernel $\mathcal{I}_{p_k,q_k,1;r}^{m,n}(s)$

$$\mathcal{I}_{p_k,q_k,1;r}^{m,n}\left(\begin{array}{c}(a_i,\alpha_i)_{1,p}\\(b_j,\beta_j)_{1,q}\end{array}\bigg|s\right) = \frac{\prod_{j=1}^m \Gamma(b_j+\beta_j s)\prod_{j=1}^n \Gamma(1-a_j-\alpha_j s)}{\sum_{k=1}^r \prod_{j=m+1}^{q_k}\Gamma(1-b_{j,k}-\beta_{j,k}s)\prod_{j=n+1}^{p_k}\Gamma(a_{j,k}+\alpha_{j,k}s)}. \qquad (13)$$

Here

$$z^{-s} = \exp[-s\{\log|z|+i\arg z\}],\ z\neq 0,\ i=\sqrt{-1}. \qquad (14)$$

The conditions for the contour $\mathcal{C}$ are the same as for the $\aleph$ function.

2. Approximations

The approaches for approximating using Sinc functions are discussed in this section. First, the basic concepts of Sinc approximations are introduced describing the terms and notion. The second part deals with approximations of definite integrals. Based on these definitions we introduce the approximation of Mellin-Barnes integrals in the next step. We use the properties of Sinc functions allowing a stable and accurate approximation based on Sinc points [24]. For a detailed representation we refer the reader to [11,13].

2.1. Sinc Basis

To start with we first introduce some definitions and theorems allowing us to specify the space of functions, domains, and arcs for a Sinc approximation.

Definition 1. *Domain and Conditions.*

Let $\mathcal{D}$ be a simply connected domain in the complex plane and $z \in \mathbb{C}$ having a boundary $\partial\mathcal{D}$. Let a and b denote two distinct points of $\partial\mathcal{D}$ and ϕ denote a conformal map of $\mathcal{D}$ onto $\mathcal{D}_d$, where $\mathcal{D}_d = \{z \in \mathbb{C} : |\mathcal{I}m(z)| < d\}$, such that $\phi(a) = -\infty$ and $\phi(b) = \infty$. Let $\psi = \phi^{-1}$ denote the inverse conformal map, and let Γ be an arc defined by $\Gamma = \{z \in \mathbb{C} : z = \psi(x), x \in \mathbb{R}\}$. Given ϕ, ψ, and a positive number h, let us set $z_k = \psi(kh)$, $k \in \mathbb{Z}$ to be the Sinc points, let us also define $\rho(z) = e^{\phi(z)}$.

Note the Sinc points are an optimal choice of approximation points in the sense of Lebesgue measures for Sinc approximations [24].

Definition 2. *Function Space.*

Let $d \in (0, \pi)$, and let the domains $\mathcal{D}$ and $\mathcal{D}_d$ be given as in Definition 1. If d' is a number such that $d' > d$, and if the function ϕ provides a conformal map of $\mathcal{D}'$ onto $\mathcal{D}_{d'}$, then $\mathcal{D} \subset \mathcal{D}'$. Let α and β denote positive numbers, and let $\mathbf{L}_{\alpha,\beta}(\mathcal{D})$ denote the family of functions $u \in \mathbf{Hol}\,(\mathcal{D})$, for which there exists a positive constant c_1 such that, for all $z \in \mathcal{D}$. Let $\mathbf{L}_{\alpha,\beta}(\mathcal{D})$ be the set of all analytic functions, for which there exists a constant c_1, such that

$$|u(z)| \leq c_1 \frac{|\rho(z)|^\alpha}{(1+|\rho(z)|)^{\alpha+\beta}}. \tag{15}$$

Now let the positive numbers α and β belong to $(0,1]$, and let $\mathbf{M}_{\alpha,\beta}(\mathcal{D})$ denote the family of all functions $g \in \mathbf{Hol}\,(\mathcal{D})$, such that $g(a)$ and $g(b)$ are finite numbers, where $g(a) = \lim_{z \to a} g(z)$ and $g(b) = \lim_{z \to b} g(z)$, and such that $u \in \mathbf{L}_{\alpha,\beta}(\mathcal{D})$ where

$$u(z) = g(z) - \frac{g(a) + \rho(z)g(b)}{1 + \rho(z)}. \tag{16}$$

These definitions directly allow the formulation of an algorithm for a Sinc approximation. Let $\mathbb{Z}$ denote the set of all integers. Select positive integers N and $M = [\beta N/\alpha]$ so that $m = M + N + 1$. The step length is determined by $h = (\pi d/(\beta N))^{1/2}$ where α, β, and d are real parameters. In addition assume there is a conformal map ϕ and its inverse ψ such that we can define Sinc points $z_j = \psi(jh), j \in \mathbb{Z}$ [25]. The following relations define the basis of a Sinc approximation:

$$\text{Sinc}\,(z) = \frac{\sin(\pi z)}{\pi z}. \tag{17}$$

The shifted Sinc is derived from relation (17) by translating the argument by integer steps of length h and applying the conformal map to the independent variable

$$S(k,h) \circ (z) = \sin(\pi(z/h - k))/(\pi(z/h - k)) = \text{Sinc}\,(z/h - k). \tag{18}$$

The approximation of a function $f(z)$ results to the representation

$$C_{h,M,N}[f](z) = \sum_{k=-M}^{N} f(z_k) \text{Sinc}\left(\frac{\phi(z)}{h} - k\right) = \sum_{k=-M}^{N} f(z_k) S(k,h) \circ \phi(z), \tag{19}$$

using the set of orthogonal functions

$$B_S = \{S(k,h) \circ \phi(z)\}_{k=-M}^{N}, \tag{20}$$

where $\phi(z)$ is the conformal map. This type of approximation allows to represent a function $f(z)$ on an arc Γ with an exponential decaying accuracy [11]. As proved in [11,13] the approximation works effectively for analytic functions. The approximations (19) allow us to formulate the following theorem for Sinc approximations.

Theorem 1. *Sinc Approximation [25].*

Let $u \in \mathbf{L}_{\alpha,\beta}(\mathcal{D})$ for $\alpha > 0$ and $\beta > 0$, take $M=[\beta N/\alpha]$, where $[x]$ denotes the greatest integer in x, and then set $m = M + N + 1$. If $u \in \mathbf{M}_{\alpha,\beta}(\mathcal{D})$, and if $h = (\pi d/(\beta N))^{1/2}$ then there exist positive constants K_1 and k_1 independent of N, such that

$$\epsilon_N = \|f(z) - C_{h,M,N}[f](z)\| = K_1 N^{1/2} \exp\left(-k_1 N^{1/2}\right). \tag{21}$$

with w_k the base function (see (22)).

The proof of this theorem is given in [13]. Note the choice $h = (\pi d/(\beta N))^{1/2}$ is close to optimal for an approximation in the space $M_{\alpha,\beta}(\mathcal{D})$ in the sense that the error bound in Theorem 1 cannot be appreciably improved regardless of the basis [25]. It is also optimal in the sense of the Lebesgue measure achieving an optimal value less than Chebyshev approximations [24].

Here $z_k = \psi(kh) = \phi^{-1}(kh)$ are the discrete points based on Sinc points kh. Note that the discrete shifting allows us to cover the approximation interval (a,b) in a dense way while the conformal map is used to map the interval of approximation from an infinite range of values to a finite one. Using the Sinc basis we are able to represent the basis functions as a piecewise defined function $w_j(z)$ by

$$w_j = \begin{cases} \frac{1}{1+\rho(z)} - \sum_{k=-M+1}^{N} \frac{1}{1+e^{kh}} S(k,h) \circ \phi(z) & j = -M \\ S(k,h) \circ \phi(z) & j = -M+1, \ldots, N-1 \\ \frac{\rho(z)}{1+\rho(z)} - \sum_{k=-M}^{N-1} \frac{e^{kh}}{1+e^{kh}} S(k,h) \circ \phi(z) & j = N \end{cases} \qquad (22)$$

where $\rho(z) = \exp(\phi(z))$. This form of the Sinc basis is chosen as to satisfy the interpolation at the boundaries. The basis functions defined in (22) suffice for purposes of uniform−norm approximation over (a,b).

This notation allows us to define a row vector $\boldsymbol{V}_m(S)$ of basis functions

$$\boldsymbol{V}_m(S) = (w_{-M}, \ldots, w_N) \qquad (23)$$

with w_j defined as in (22). For a given vector $\boldsymbol{V}_m(u) = (u_{-M}, \ldots, u_N)^T$ we now introduce the dot product as an approximation of the function $u(z)$ by

$$u(z) \approx \boldsymbol{V}_m(S) \cdot \boldsymbol{V}_m(u) = \sum_{k=-M}^{N} u_k w_k. \qquad (24)$$

Based on this notation, we will introduce in the next subsection approximations of definite integrals [13].

2.2. Definite Integral Approximation

In this section, we pose the query of how to approximate definite integrals on a domain over $\mathbb{R}$. The approximation will use our basis system introduced in Section 2.1. It turns out that for the basis systems (20), we can get an approximation converging exponentially. Specifically, we are interested in a quadrature formula for definite integrals of the type

$$J(f) = \int_a^b f(t)\,dt, \qquad (25)$$

where a and b can be finite or infinite. If the function f is approximated by the approximation given in Section 2.1, we write for $J(f)$,

$$J(f) = \int_a^b f(t)\,dt \approx$$

$$J_{h,M,N}[f](x) = \int_a^b \sum_{k=-M}^{N} f(t_k) S(k,h) \circ \phi(t)\,dt \qquad (26)$$

$$= \sum_{k=-M}^{N} f(t_k) \int_a^b S(k,h) \circ \phi(t)\,dt. \qquad (27)$$

Scaling the variable $\xi = t/h$ and collocating the expression with respect to ξ, we end up with the representation

$$J(f) \approx h \sum_{k=-M}^{N} f(t_k) \frac{1}{\phi'(t_k)}, \text{ with } t_k = \psi(kh). \tag{28}$$

Equation (28) represents a quadrature formula applicable to different domains. Compared with a Gaussian quadrature formula (28) delivers the weights as well as the function values if the discretization is known by $t_k = \psi(kh)$ with $k = -M, \ldots, N$ and $h = \pi/\sqrt{N}$. Note since the conformal map ϕ depends on the structure of the arc Γ; i.e., finite, semi-infinite or infinite, the approximation is defined for domains $[a, b]$, $(0, \infty)$, or $(-\infty, \infty)$, respectively [11]. The following Theorem summarizes these results.

Theorem 2. *Definite Integrals.*

If ϕ denotes a one−to−one transformation of the interval (a, b) onto the real line $\mathbb{R}$, let h denote a fixed positive number, and let the Sinc points be defined on (a, b) by $z_k = \phi^{-1}(kh)$, $k \in \mathbb{Z}$, where $\phi^{-1} = \psi$ denotes the inverse function of the conformal map ϕ. Let M and N be positive integers, set $m = M + N + 1$, and for a given function f defined on (a, b), define the vector $\boldsymbol{V}_m(f) = (f(z_{-M}), \ldots, f(z_N))$, and a vector $\boldsymbol{V}_m(1/\phi') = (1/\phi'(z_{-M}), \ldots, 1/\phi'(z_N))$, then the definite integral is approximated by

$$J(f) \approx h\boldsymbol{V}_m(f).\boldsymbol{V}_m(1/\phi') = J_{h,M,N}[f](z), \tag{29}$$

and the error of this approximation was estimated in [11] as

$$\epsilon_N = \|J(f) - J_{h,M,N}[f](z)\| \sim K_2 N^{1/2} \exp\left(-k_2 N^{1/2}\right), \tag{30}$$

where K_2 and k_2 are constants independent of N.

2.3. Sinc Approximation of Mellin-Barnes Integrals

The Sinc approximation of the Fox H functions needs two discretization steps. Foremost the Sinc discretization of the arc Γ on which the function should be represented finite or semi-infinite and second the Sinc quadrature of the Mellin-Barnes integral at these Sinc points on the arc. The second discretization is a Sinc quadrature on an infinite interval corresponding to the line at γ parallel to the imaginary axis in $s \in \mathbb{C}$. In formulas this means

$$\begin{aligned}H_{p,q}^{m,n}\left(z_k \Big| \begin{array}{c}(a_i, \alpha_i)_{1,p} \\ (b_j, \beta_j)_{1,q}\end{array}\right) &= \frac{1}{2\pi} \int_{-\infty}^{\infty} \mathcal{H}_{p,q}^{m,n}(\gamma + i\sigma) z_k^{-\gamma - i\sigma} d\sigma \\ &\approx \frac{h}{2\pi} \boldsymbol{V}_m(\mathcal{H}_{p,q}^{m,n}(\gamma + i\sigma_l) z_k^{-\gamma - i\sigma_l}).\boldsymbol{V}_m(1/\phi'(\sigma_l)),\end{aligned} \tag{31}$$

where $\sigma_l = \psi(lh)$, $l = -M, \ldots, N$, and $z_k = \psi(kh)$, $k = -M, \ldots, N$, generating a vector $\boldsymbol{V}_m(H_{p,q}^{m,n})$ which approximates the Fox H function pointwise at $z_k = \psi(kh)$ on an arc Γ. γ is selected according to the pole structure of the Γ functions of the numerator in the Mellin representation. Using the basis functions w_k (22) on the arc Γ, we shall approximate the Fox H function by

$$H_{p,q}^{m,n}(z) \approx \boldsymbol{V}_m(S).\boldsymbol{V}_m\left(H_{p,q}^{m,n}\right) = \sum_{k=-M}^{N} H_{p,q}^{m,n}(z_k) w_k(z). \tag{32}$$

This approach guarantees that the error ϵ_N will decay as given by (21). Note that a Sinc point based interpolation is able to deal with singularities at the end points of the arc Γ.

Since the ℵ function and the Saxena I functions are similarly defined by Mellin-Barnes integrals as the Fox H function, the procedure for the approximation follows the same line delivering for the ℵ function

$$\aleph^{m,n}_{p_k,q_k,\tau_k;r}(z) \approx V_m(S) \cdot \boldsymbol{V}_m\left(\aleph^{m,n}_{p_k,q_k,\tau_k;r}\right) = \sum_{k=-M}^{N} \aleph^{m,n}_{p_k,q_k,\tau_k;r}(z_k) w_k(z), \qquad (33)$$

and the Saxena I function

$$I^{m,n}_{p_k,q_k,1;r}(z) \approx V_m(S) \cdot \boldsymbol{V}_m\left(I^{m,n}_{p_k,q_k,1;r}\right) = \sum_{k=-M}^{N} I^{m,n}_{p_k,q_k,1;r}(z_k) w_k(z). \qquad (34)$$

All three approximations will satisfy the *a priory* error formula (21) and converge exponentially to their exact value.

The following section shall demonstrate by a few examples the numerical representation of the three generalized functions.

3. Numerical Examples

This section collects some examples demonstrating the efficient and accurate numerical evaluation of Sinc-based methods applied to Mellin-Barnes integrals, Fox H-, Saxena I-, and ℵ functions. We selected the examples concerning their analytic representation applied to specific physical or engineering problems. Allowing us to compare our results with exact expressions and thus delivering an *a priori* estimation of the numerical errors. For every comparison in which we calculated local errors, the analytical solution was employed. The following graphics display the analytical answer as a solid line. Over the solid line, the equivalent numerical approximation is displayed as a dashed curve. We may depend on the previously mentioned exponential convergence of the Sinc quadrature and Sinc approximation if no local errors are calculated in the graphs. The analytic Sinc approximations, however, are typically not represented because of their large symbolic representation since we are utilizing a computer algebra system.

3.1. Fox H Functions

In this subsection, we present some examples which are taken from the literature where the symbolic representation was given [1,2,4]. In most of these cases a numerical evaluation of the functions is not offered or discussed. For the first time we will show the numerical evaluation and the *a priori* error estimation using Sinc methods.

Example 1. *Exponential function*

It is well-known that the exponential function is connected with the Mellin transform via the Euler Γ function. The relations between the two functions are as follows

$$e^{-x} = \frac{1}{2\pi i}\int_{\gamma-i\infty}^{\gamma+i\infty} \Gamma(s) x^{-s} ds, \ \gamma > 0, \qquad (35)$$

and

$$\Gamma(s) = \int_0^\infty e^{-x} x^{s-1} dx, \qquad (36)$$

where the later of these two expressions is the Mellin transform of the exponential function and the first its inverse given by a Bromwich integral over the vertical line $\gamma = const$, of the complex s-plane. Whereas the last formula (36) is due to L. Euler who communicated it in two letters of 13 October 1729, and 8 January 1730, to Goldbach. The first formula (35) in a somewhat different form goes back to Pincherle [9,26] as Mellin reported in his paper [27]; but it was Mellin who first realized its great importance.

Let us first numerically examine the representation of the exponential function using the Fox H representation. The exponential function is defined in terms of a Fox H function by

$$e^{-x} = H_{0,2}^{2,0}\left(\frac{x}{2}\bigg| \left(0,\tfrac{1}{2}\right)\ \left(\tfrac{1}{2},\tfrac{1}{2}\right)\right), \text{ with } \mathcal{H}_{0,2}^{2,0}(s) = \frac{\Gamma\left(\tfrac{s}{2}+\tfrac{1}{2}\right)\Gamma\left(\tfrac{s}{2}\right)}{2\sqrt{\pi}}. \tag{37}$$

Using the duplication formula for the Γ function in the right most term of (37), we end up with the Mellin representation in (35). The line integral is then calculated by the Mellin-Barnes integral via

$$\begin{aligned} e^{-z} &= \frac{1}{2\pi i}\int_{\mathcal{C}}\mathcal{H}_{0,2}^{2,0}(s)\,z^{-s}ds = \frac{1}{2\pi i}\int_{\gamma-i\infty}^{\gamma+i\infty}\mathcal{H}_{0,2}^{2,0}(s)\,z^{-s}ds \\ &= \frac{1}{2\pi}\int_{-\infty}^{\infty}\mathcal{H}_{0,2}^{2,0}(\gamma-i\sigma)\,z^{-\gamma+i\sigma}d\sigma, \end{aligned} \tag{38}$$

where the path $\mathcal{C}$ is chosen according to the pole structure of the Γ functions so that γ is a fixed real number. For different z values selected as Sinc points, we compute the numerical values of the integral in the domain for $\sigma \in (-\infty,\infty)$. The set of values $\{z_k, I_k\}_{k=-N}^{N}$ is used in a Sinc approximation delivering an analytic representation of the function $f(z) = e^{-z}$ in terms of the Sinc basis. Results of such an approximation are illustrated in the following Figure 1. Figure 1 shows the exact function (solid line), the Sinc approximation (dashed), and the discrete set of Sinc points (dots). The right panel shows the local error of the approximation. In Figure 2, we depict the error decay of the Sinc approximation as a function of the used number of Sinc points N. A least square fit was used to get the two parameters K_2 and k_2 which determine the error formula. The example demonstrates that the approximation of the Fox H function is accurate and the precision of the approximation can be a priori estimated using the error decay Formula (30).

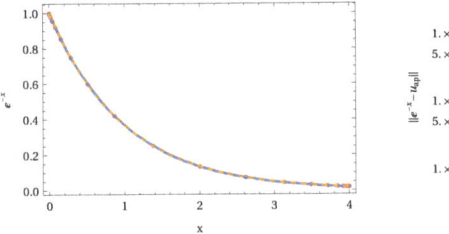
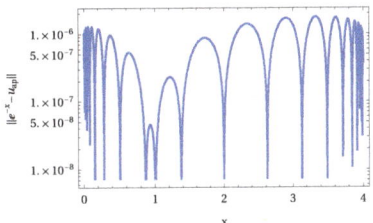

Figure 1. Numerical representation of the Fox H function $H_{0,2}^{2,0}(x) = e^{-x}$ as a Sinc approximation based on (35) using $N = 24$ Sinc points for x. The L^2 norm over the local error delivers a value of $1.784\,10^{-6}$.

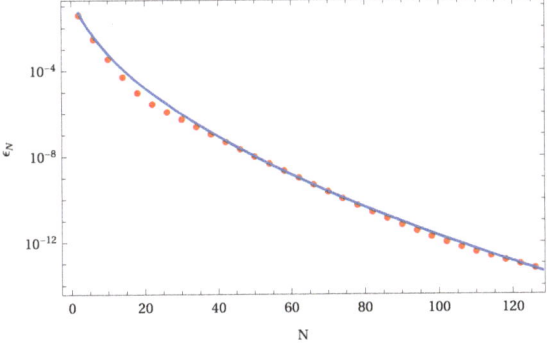

Figure 2. Error decay $\epsilon_N = \|u - u_{ex}\| \sim K_2 N^{1/2}\exp\left(-k_2 N^{1/2}\right)$ with $K_2 = 2.623$ and $k_2 = 3.017$. The two parameters K_2 and k_2 are the result of a least square fit.

Example 2. *Mittag-Leffler functions*

Over the years it turned out that Mittag-Leffler (ML) functions are of central importance in fractional calculus [5,8,14,28]. This kind of functions are used in many applications and in theoretical work [2]. However, these functions need a special approach when it comes to their numerical representation. Quite recently, we presented an approach to tackle the numerical representation by an inverse Laplace transform [7]. It was shown that a Sinc based approach has some advantages over the standard Talbot or Weideman approach used by Garrappa et al. [6,29,30]. A second approach to numerically represent Mittag-Leffler functions is now available with high accuracy and precision using Fox H functions in connection with Sinc quadrature. We will restrict our discussions to the main three types of Mittag-Leffler functions which are classified as single-, two-, and three-parameter ML functions. The three-parameter ML function is also known as Prabhakar's function. There are in fact higher parameter ML functions in use which are defined via Fox H functions [28]. We note that these functions are also numerically available with high accuracy. However, due to lack of space, we will not present them here.

The three ML functions we have in mind are defined by the following relations:

$$E_\alpha(z) = H_{1,2}^{1,1}\left(-z \middle| \begin{array}{cc} (0,1) & \\ (0,1) & (0,\alpha) \end{array}\right), \text{ with } \mathcal{H}_{1,2}^{1,1}(s) = \frac{\Gamma(1-s)\Gamma(s)}{\Gamma(1-s\alpha)}, \quad (39)$$

$$E_{\alpha,\beta}(z) = H_{1,2}^{1,1}\left(-z \middle| \begin{array}{cc} (0,1) & \\ (0,1) & (1-\beta,\alpha) \end{array}\right), \text{ with } \mathcal{H}_{1,2}^{1,1}(s) = \frac{\Gamma(1-s)\Gamma(s)}{\Gamma(\beta-s\alpha)}, \quad (40)$$

and

$$E_{\alpha,\beta}^\mu(z) = H_{1,2}^{1,1}\left(-z \middle| \begin{array}{cc} (1-\mu,1) & \\ (0,1) & (1-\beta,\alpha) \end{array}\right), \text{ with } \mathcal{H}_{1,2}^{1,1}(s) = \frac{\Gamma(\mu-s)\Gamma(s)}{\Gamma(\beta-s\alpha)}. \quad (41)$$

The line integral is computed by the Mellin-Barnes integral via

$$\begin{aligned} I &= \frac{1}{2\pi i} \int_\mathcal{C} \mathcal{H}_{1,2}^{1,1}(s)\, z^{-s} ds = \frac{1}{2\pi i} \int_{\gamma-i\infty}^{\gamma+i\infty} \mathcal{H}_{1,2}^{1,1}(s)\, z^{-s} ds \\ &= \frac{1}{2\pi} \int_{-\infty}^{\infty} \mathcal{H}_{1,2}^{1,1}(\gamma-i\sigma)\, z^{-\gamma+i\sigma} d\sigma, \end{aligned} \quad (42)$$

where the path $\mathcal{C}$ is selected according to the pole structure of the Γ functions so that γ is a fixed real number. For different z values selected as Sinc points, we compute the numerical values of the integral in the domain for $\sigma \in (-\infty, \infty)$. The set of values $\{z_k, I_k\}_{k=-N}^{N}$ is used in a Sinc approximation.

In Figure 3 we graph the solution for the one-, two-, and three-parameter ML function for a specific selection of parameters (left column of Figure 3). The dashed lines correspond to the Sinc approximation while the solid line represents the Mathematica approximation for the first two ML functions and a higher order Sinc approximation with $N = 128$ for the Prabhakar ML function. Obviously there is no visible difference for all three types of ML functions. This becomes obvious if we examine the right column of Figure 3. Here the absolute value of the local error is shown for the two first ML functions and a relative error for Prabhakar's function. The magnitude in all cases is less than 10^{-10}. Figure 4 collects the error decay as a function of the number of Sinc points N used in the approximations. It is obvious that for all three types of ML functions nearly the same functional error decay results. This indicates that the upper bound estimation of Equation (30) is satisfied and allows an a priori estimation of the expected error.

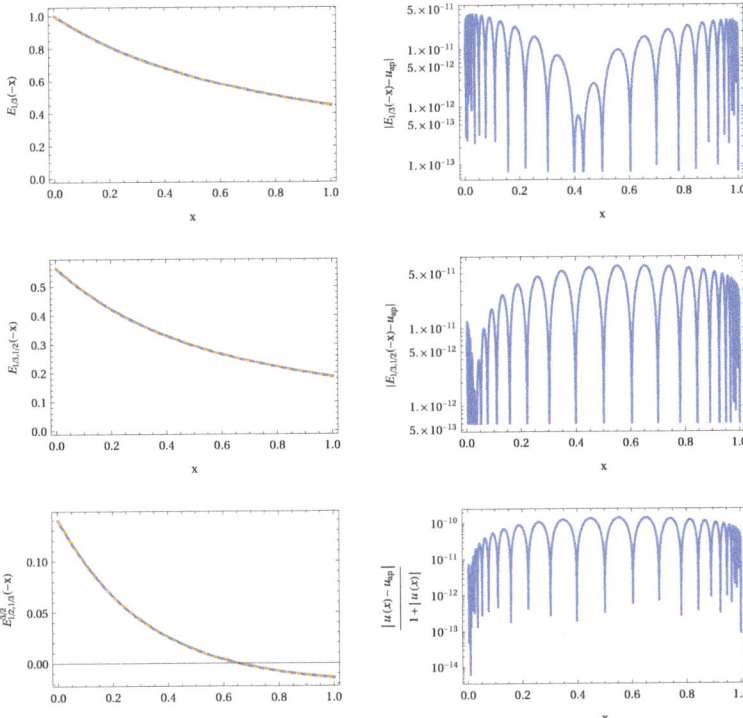

Figure 3. Function representation for $E_\alpha(x)$, $E_{\alpha,\beta}(x)$, and $E^\mu_{\alpha,\beta}(x)$ from top to bottom, left column with $N = 56$ Sinc points. The parameters α, β, and μ are indicated in the axis labels, respectively. The local errors are shown in the right column accordingly. For Prabhakar's function we have to use a relative error because the exact representation is not available. The reference solution $u(x)$ was computed with $N = 128$ Sinc points.

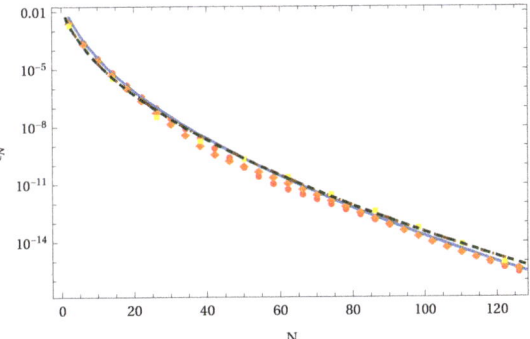

Figure 4. Error decay $\epsilon_N = \|u - u_{\text{ex}}\| \sim K_2 N^{1/2} \exp\left(-k_2 N^{1/2}\right)$ for the three ML functions E_α, $E_{\alpha,\beta}$, and $E^\mu_{\alpha,\beta}$ (dots, solid), (diamond, dot dashed), and (square, dashed), respectively. The least square fit for each function delivered the values $(K_2, k_2) = (0.421, 3.288)$, $(K_2, k_2) = (0.347, 3.292)$, and $(K_2, k_2) = (0.126, 3.123)$.

The least square parameters of the three error decays also indicates that all three functions belong to the same function space introduced in Definition 2.

Example 3. *Krätzel Function*

The Krätzel integral $Z_\rho^\nu(z)$ was defined by Krätzel [31] as the kernel of an integral transform as follows:
$$Z_\rho^\nu(z) = \int_0^\infty y^{\nu-1} e^{-y^\rho - x/y} dy. \tag{43}$$

Today we know that the Krätzel function occurs in many fields of applications, such as the study of astrophysical thermonuclear reactions, reaction rate probability integrals in the theory of nuclear reaction rates, in applied analysis, inverse Gaussian distribution, generalized families of distributions in statistical distribution theory, and in statistical mechanics as well as the general pathway model are all shown to be connected to the integral (43) [4]. The generalized Krätzel function was examined by Kilbas and Kumar [32]. Solar radiation data were examined recently in connection with probability distribution functions by Princy [33]. Due to the versatile applications of the Krätzel function, we demonstrate the numerical representation as a density function.

The normalized probability density can be represented as Fox H function by
$$f(z) = cz^{\alpha-1} Z_\rho^\nu(z) = \frac{1}{\Gamma(\alpha)\Gamma\left(\frac{\alpha+\nu}{\rho}\right)} H_{0,2}^{2,0}\left(z \bigg| (\alpha-1,1)\ \left(\frac{\alpha+\nu-1}{\rho}, \frac{1}{\rho}\right)\right), \text{with}$$
$$\mathcal{H}_{0,2}^{2,0}(s) = \Gamma(s + \alpha - 1)\Gamma\left(\frac{s}{\rho} + \frac{\alpha+\nu-1}{\rho}\right) \tag{44}$$

here $x \geq 0$, $\alpha > 0$, $\rho > 0$, and $\nu > 0$. The corresponding line integral representation is computed by the Mellin-Barnes integral via
$$I = \frac{1}{2\pi i} \int_\mathcal{C} \mathcal{H}_{0,2}^{2,0}(s)\, z^{-s} ds = \frac{1}{2\pi i} \int_{\gamma - i\infty}^{\gamma + i\infty} \mathcal{H}_{0,2}^{2,0}(s)\, z^{-s} ds$$
$$= \frac{1}{2\pi} \int_{-\infty}^\infty \mathcal{H}_{0,2}^{2,0}(\gamma - i\sigma)\, z^{-\gamma + i\sigma} d\sigma, \tag{45}$$

where the path $\mathcal{C}$ is selected according to the pole structure of the Γ functions, so that γ is a fixed real number. For different discrete z values using Sinc points, we compute the numerical values of the integral in the real domain $\sigma \in (-\infty, \infty)$. The set of values $\{z_k, I_k\}_{k=-N}^N$ is used in a Sinc approximation. An example using specific parameters $\alpha = 2$ and $\rho = \nu = 3$ is shown in Figure 5. The left panel of Figure 5 represents the probability density based on $N = 128$ and $N = 56$ (dashed) Sinc points. The right panel of Figure 5 shows the relative local error of these two versions of the approximation. It is obvious that the local error is small and nearly homogenous on the domain $[0, 10]$. In Figure 6, we present the error decay of computations with different number of Sinc points z_k used in the approximation. The solid line represents the least square approximation of the two parameter error formula (30). Note that for small numbers of Sinc points we already reach an acceptable small error. If we double the number of Sinc points, we gain more than one decade of accuracy. Figure 6 clearly demonstrates that we have an exponential decay of the error.

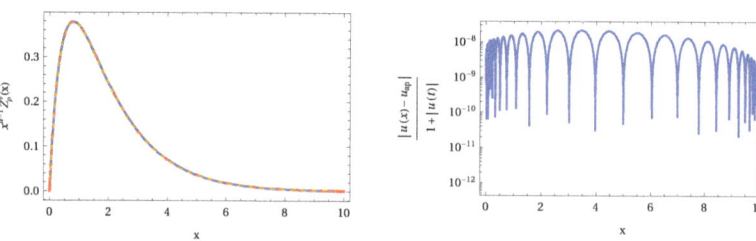

Figure 5. The Krätzel function used as a probability density function for $\rho = 3$, $\nu = 2$, and $\alpha = 2$ (left panel). The relative local error of the distribution $f(x) = x^{\alpha-1} Z_\rho^\nu(x)$ (right panel). Number of Sinc points $N = 56$.

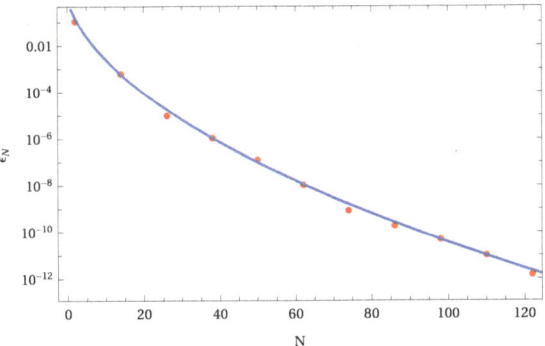

Figure 6. Error decay $\epsilon_N = \|u - u_{\text{ex}}\| \sim K_2 N^{1/2} \exp\left(-k_2 N^{1/2}\right)$ for the Krätzel function with $\rho = \nu = 3$, $\alpha = 2$. The least square fit delivered the values $(K_2, k_2) = (5.713, 2.807)$.

In Figure 7 we demonstrate the variation of the Krätzel function if we change one of the parameters α or ν, respectively.

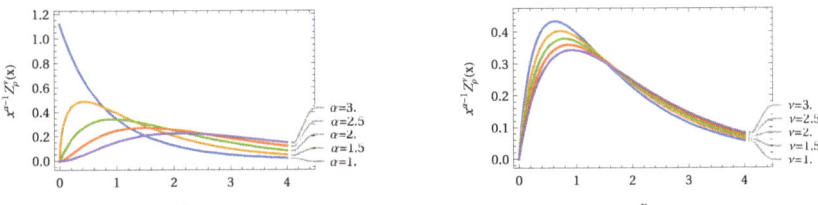

Figure 7. The Krätzel function for $\rho = \nu = 3$ with α variation (left graph) and ν variation (right graph).

For the special choice $\rho = 1$, the Krätzel density is reduced to the modified Bessel function $K_\nu(x)$ with the specific representation

$$f(z) = cz^{\alpha-1} Z_\rho^\nu(z) = \frac{2}{\Gamma(\alpha)\Gamma(\alpha+\nu)} x^{\alpha+\nu/2-1} K_\nu(2\sqrt{x}), \text{ with } x \geq 0, \alpha > 0, \nu > 0. \quad (46)$$

This relation can be used to check the accuracy of our numerical computations shown in Figure 8. For a few number of approximation points $N = 56$, we are able to reach a low level of local errors.

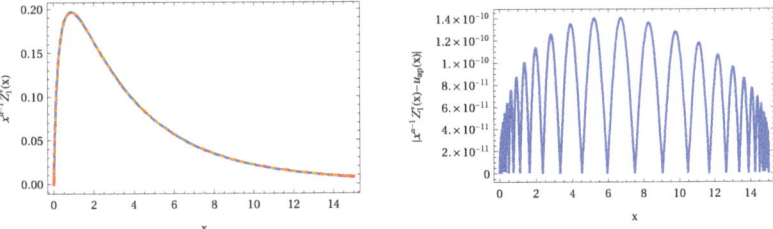

Figure 8. The Krätzel function for $\rho = 1$, $\nu = 1/3$ and $\alpha = 2$ (left graph). Right panel local error between the approximation and the Bessel representation. Number of Sinc points $N = 56$.

Example 4. *Abel Equation*

In the current example, we will examine the following Abel integral equation

$$u(x) = f(x) + \frac{\lambda}{\Gamma(\alpha)} \int_0^x (x-\xi)^{\alpha-1} u(\xi) d\xi, \qquad (47)$$

where λ and $0 < \alpha < 1$ are real parameters [8,34]. The integral can also be identified as a Riemann-Liouville fractional integral so that (47) can be written as

$$u(x) = f(x) + \lambda \mathcal{D}_{0,x}^{-\alpha} u(x). \qquad (48)$$

This in turn opens the connection to the fractional kinetic equation for astrophysical systems examined by Haubold and Mathai [35] using a constant function $f(x) = N_0$ and $\lambda = -c^\alpha$. However, such kind of equation was already examined in 1991 by Glöckle and Nonnemacher in connection with viscoelastic materials [36]. We will numerically demonstrate that the use of Fox H functions in connection with a Sinc convolution integral allows a general solution as long as the Laplace transform of $f(x)$ exists. In their work on Mittag-Leffler functions, Gorenflow et al. [8] state in Theorem 4.2 the problem based on [37] in which the solution of (47) using convolution integrals are examined. The solution of (47) using two parameter Mittag-Leffler functions [35] reads

$$u(x) = f(x) + \lambda \int_0^x (x-\xi)^{\alpha-1} E_{\alpha,\alpha}(\lambda(x-\xi)^\alpha) f(\xi) d\xi. \qquad (49)$$

This result goes back to the pioneering work of Hille and Tamarkin in 1930 [37]. Introducing new variables in (49) by $\eta = x - \xi$ and using the Fox H representation of the ML function allows us to rewrite the convolution integral as

$$u(x) = f(x) + \lambda \int_0^x \eta^{\alpha-1} H_{1,2}^{1,1}\left[-\lambda\eta^\alpha \,\middle|\, \begin{matrix}(0,1)\\(0,1) \quad (1-\beta,\alpha)\end{matrix}\right]_{\alpha,\beta=\alpha} (\lambda\eta^\alpha) f(x-\eta) d\eta, \qquad (50)$$

which can be rewritten by using properties of the Fox H function [4] as

$$u(x) = f(x) + \lambda \int_0^x H_{1,2}^{1,1}\left[-\lambda\eta^\alpha \,\middle|\, \begin{matrix}(\alpha-1,1)\\(\alpha-1,1) \quad (1-\beta+\alpha(\alpha-1),\alpha)\end{matrix}\right]_{\alpha,\beta=\alpha} f(x-\eta) d\eta. \qquad (51)$$

This representation of the solution is suitable for Sinc convolution computations because we already know how to get the discrete Sinc representation of the Fox H function. This data at hand, we only need the Stenger Laplace representation of f to perform the convolution. For details of the numerical approach and implementation see [7,13].

Applying the numerical Sinc methods, we can generate solution approximations for different fractional orders $\alpha = \beta$ (see Figure 9). The results in Figure 9 demonstrate that the solution starts at $x = 0$ like the function f (dashed line). A single peak is observed with varying maximum value and location when $\alpha = \beta$ is changed. The location of the maximum shifts to the right if the values for $\alpha = \beta$ become smaller.

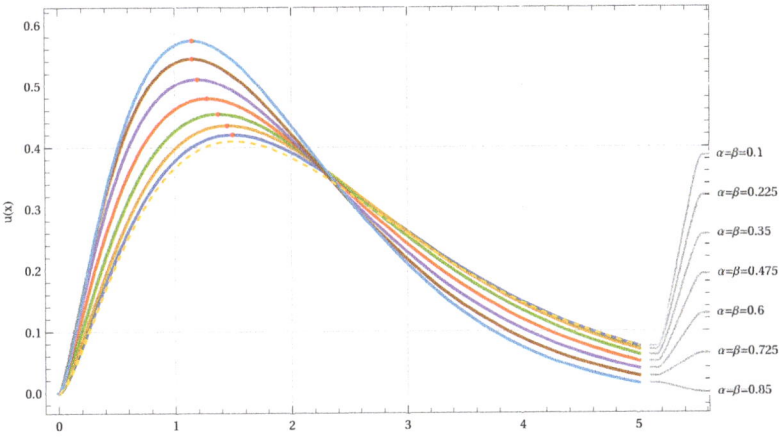

Figure 9. Solutions of Equation (47) represented by (51) for varying $\alpha = \beta$ (see inset) using an inhomogeneity $f(x) = x^{3/2} \exp(-x)$ (dashed line). The parameter value for $\lambda = 1$. Number of Sinc points $N = 48$.

In astrophysical applications, the Maxwell-Boltzmann distribution is used as a standard model for idealized gases. Abel's Equation (47) can be solved by using a Maxwell-Boltzmann distribution as inhomogeneity. Convolution with the Fox H kernel delivers a shifted distribution as shown in Figure 10 (top graph). The double logarithmic graph (bottom) of Figure 10 for the same computation indicates a similarity observed for the solar neutrino spectrum [38] with a sharp decline on the right side of the function and a linear relation on the left end (in scaled figures).

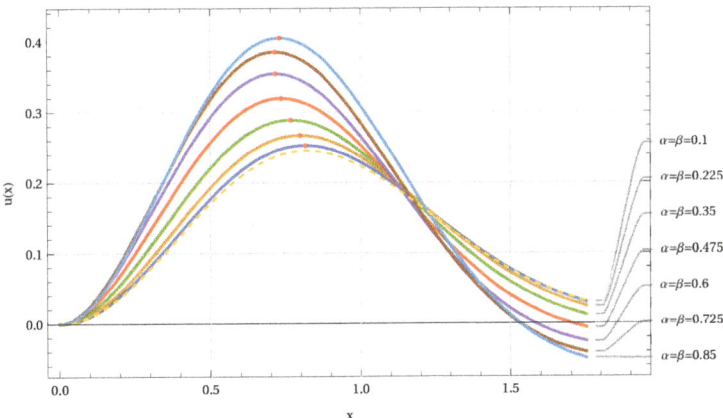

Figure 10. *Cont.*

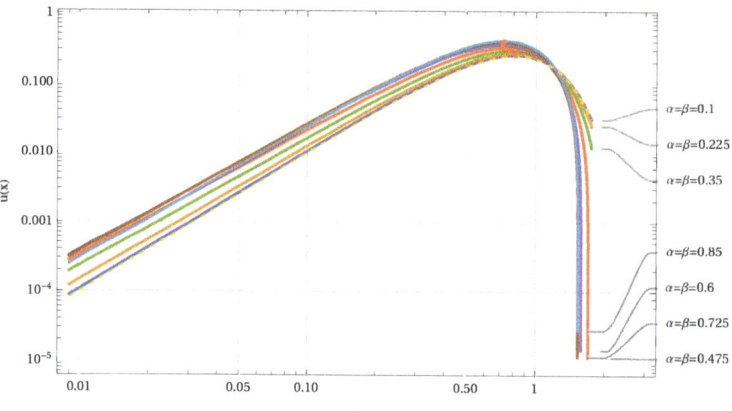

Figure 10. Solutions of Equation (47) represented by (51) for varying $\alpha = \beta$ (see inset) using an inhomogeneity of Maxwell-Boltzmann type $f(x) = x^2 \exp(-3x^2/2)$ (dashed line). The parameter value for $\lambda = 1$. Number of Sinc points $N = 32$.

The examples demonstrate that our approach to represent numerically Fox H functions is highly efficient.

3.2. ℵ Functions

This subsection is discussing numerical representations of different ℵ functions as "simple" functions and advanced applications, as introduced in Equation (8). One characteristic of the ℵ function is the weighted sum of Γ functions in the denominator in Mellin space. We will present different simple and advanced rational expressions of Γ functions to represent functions for which their analytic expressions are unknown. In general, we do not know the specific names of the resulting functions, but we are able to generate analytic representations based on Sinc approximations. The Sinc representation in turn allows generalizations of the Fox H and Saxena I functions. In turn, the Sinc representation allows a numeric computation of function values. Since we do not know what kind of analytic function is represented by the fractions in Mellin space, we shall use a reference representation generated by numerous Sinc points ($N = 128$) to estimate a relative error. This approach to estimate the error of the approximation can be used because we know from (21) and (30) that the Sinc approximation converges exponentially. Due to this fact, the error given in the following examples is always a relative error with respect to this large Sinc point approximation.

Recently some applications of ℵ functions to engineering and biomedical applications were discussed in the literature [39–41] while applications are discussed in [42,43]. However, the authors stop at the analytical representation of their results and do not generate a numerical verification. We will extend their approaches by going one step further to show that a numerical representation of ℵ functions is possible. Thus, the discussed models can be numerically verified. Due to lack of space, we will restrict ourselves to the function representation only.

Example 5. *Characteristic simple ratio*

This example uses a rational expression of Γ functions in such a way that it cannot be reduced to a Fox H or a Saxena I function. The ratio keeps the characteristic of the ℵ function, with a sum of weighted Γ functions in the denominator. We examine the following ratio numerically

$$\mathcal{A}^{m,n}_{p_k,q_k,\tau_k;r}(s) = \frac{\Gamma(2s+1)}{2\Gamma(s)+1}, \tag{52}$$

by evaluating the following Mellin-Barnes integral on a line parallel to the imaginary axis

$$\begin{aligned} I &= \frac{1}{2\pi i}\int_{\mathcal{C}} \mathcal{A}^{m,n}_{p_k,q_k,\tau_k;r}(s)\, z^{-s}ds = \frac{1}{2\pi i}\int_{\gamma-i\infty}^{\gamma+i\infty} \mathcal{A}^{m,n}_{p_k,q_k,\tau_k;r}(s)\, z^{-s}ds \\ &= \frac{1}{2\pi}\int_{-\infty}^{\infty} \mathcal{A}^{m,n}_{p_k,q_k,\tau_k;r}(\gamma - i\sigma)\, z^{-\gamma+i\sigma} d\sigma. \end{aligned} \tag{53}$$

A reference approximation using $N = 128$ Sinc points is plotted in the same graph as solid line. Obviously there is no visual difference between the low and high approximation. The used Sinc points $m = 49$ for approximation are shown as dots in the graph. The right panel of Figure 11 shows the local relative error of the approximation. The reference in this graph is the Sinc approximation with the large number of Sinc points. The right panel reflects a mean error of approximately 10^{-8} which is acceptable for applications.

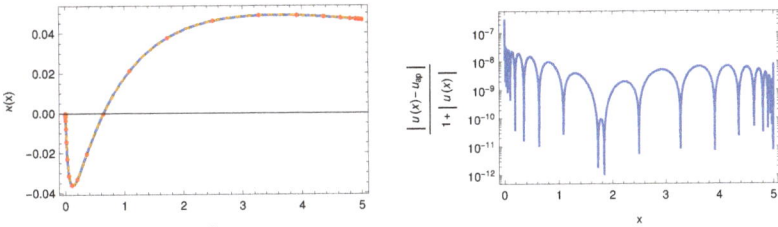

Figure 11. A true ℵ function using a Mellin representation $\Gamma(1+2s)/(1+2\Gamma(s))$ approximated with $N = 24$ Sinc points (left panel). The right panel shows the local relative error where $u(x)$ is given by a Sinc approximation with $N = 128$.

First, we verify the accurate representation of the approximation shown in Figure 11. The left panel shows the function approximation using $N = 24$. In Figure 12 we examine the error based on the L_2 norm of the relative local error. The error ϵ_N shows an exponential decay if the number of approximation points N is increased. The upper bound of this decay follows the relation (30) which is indicated by the solid line.

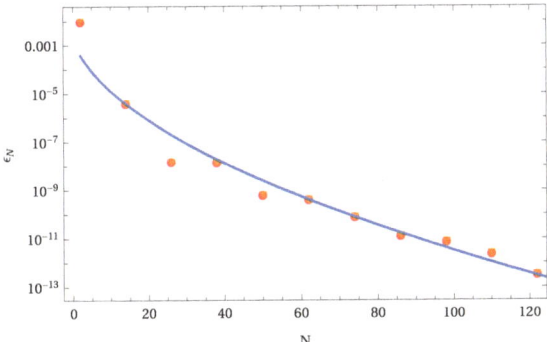

Figure 12. Error decay $\epsilon_N = \|u - u_{\text{ex}}\| \sim K_2 N^{1/2} \exp\left(-k_2 N^{1/2}\right)$. The least square fit delivered the values $(K_2, k_2) = (0.007, 2.391)$. The ● and the ▼ indicate the error estimation based on the relative L_2 norm error and the L_2 norm, respectively. In the L_2 norms, the exact function is replaced by the Sinc approximation using $N = 128$ Sinc points. It is obvious that the two error estimations deliver nearly the same numerical values.

We were also curious to see how the ℵ function changes when some Mellin representation elements are changed. As a result, we included four factors at various points in (53). Because the current form in (53) is so straightforward, we modified it to a single parameter representation as follows:

$$\mathcal{A}_\alpha(s) = \frac{\Gamma(2s+1)}{\alpha\Gamma(s)+1}, \quad \mathcal{A}_\beta(s) = \frac{\Gamma(\beta s+1)}{\Gamma(s)/2+1}, \tag{54}$$

and

$$\mathcal{A}_\delta(s) = \frac{\Gamma(s+1)}{\Gamma(s)/2+\delta}, \quad \mathcal{A}_\eta(s) = \frac{\Gamma(s+1)}{\Gamma(\eta s)/2+1}. \tag{55}$$

The Mellin-Barnes integral yields the equivalent function

$$\begin{aligned} I &= \frac{1}{2\pi i}\int_\mathcal{C} \mathcal{A}^{m,n}_{p_k,q_k,\tau_k;r}(s)\, z^{-s}ds = \frac{1}{2\pi i}\int_{\gamma-i\infty}^{\gamma+i\infty}\mathcal{A}^{m,n}_{p_k,q_k,\tau_k;r}(s)\, z^{-s}ds \\ &= \frac{1}{2\pi}\int_{-\infty}^{\infty}\mathcal{A}^{m,n}_{p_k,q_k,\tau_k;r}(\gamma-i\sigma)\, z^{-\gamma+i\sigma}d\sigma, \end{aligned} \tag{56}$$

where α, β, δ, and η are all derived from $\mathbb{R}^+$. Variation of the parameters α, β, δ, and η result in distinct variations of the function according to the definition of the $\aleph$ function in (54) and (55). Figure 13 depicts the variation results. We can see that the function behavior varies continuously within a defined region of parameters.

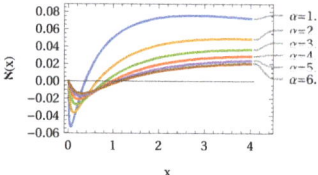
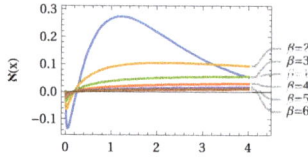
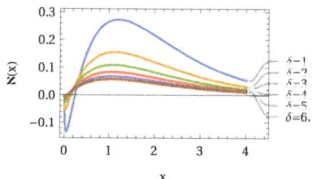
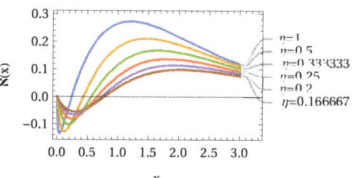

Figure 13. Variation of parameters (indicated in the panels) for $\mathcal{A}_\alpha(s)$, $\mathcal{A}_\beta(s)$, $\mathcal{A}_\delta(s)$, and $\mathcal{A}_\eta(s)$.

Example 6. *Two parameter weighted Mittag-Leffler (wML) function*

It is simple to generalize some types of functions when a tool like the $\aleph$ function is available. In the next example, we will demonstrate this. A Fox H function defines the two-parameter Mittag-Leffler (ML) function, as shown in (40). We may introduce the following representation by following the same line of representation as an $\aleph$ function.

$$E^{\delta,\gamma}_{\alpha,\beta}(s) = \frac{\Gamma(1-s)\Gamma(s)}{\delta\Gamma(\beta-s\alpha)+\gamma\Gamma(1-s)} = \mathcal{A}(s). \tag{57}$$

$$\begin{aligned} I &= \frac{1}{2\pi i}\int_\mathcal{C} \mathcal{A}^{m,n}_{p_k,q_k,\tau_k;r}(s)\, z^{-s}ds = \frac{1}{2\pi i}\int_{\gamma-i\infty}^{\gamma+i\infty}\mathcal{A}^{m,n}_{p_k,q_k,\tau_k;r}(s)\, z^{-s}ds \\ &= \frac{1}{2\pi}\int_{-\infty}^{\infty}\mathcal{A}^{m,n}_{p_k,q_k,\tau_k;r}(\gamma-i\sigma)\, z^{-\gamma+i\sigma}d\sigma, \end{aligned} \tag{58}$$

The Mellin representation of the extended Mittag-Leffler function is similar to the two parameter Mittag-Leffler function represented as Fox H function with three Γ terms. The numerator is exactly the same as the Equation (40). The denominator term is weighted by the coefficients δ

and γ. The term containing the weight of δ is the same as (40). The difference exists only in the γ weighted term. If we select $\gamma = 0$ and $\delta = 1$, we reproduce the two parameter Mittag-Leffler function $E_{\alpha,\beta}(-x)$. To examine the influence of the two weight parameters $\delta, \gamma \in \mathbb{R}^+$, we vary them and represent the results in Figure 14. The Figure indicates that a variation of either of δ or γ in a fractional or integer way will approach the two parameter Mittag-Leffler function from above or below, respectively. In Figure 14 we represent in each row the variation of the parameter δ and γ. The left column of the Figure show changes approaching values larger than one, while the right column shows an approach to smaller values than one. Larger values than one separate the graph of the wML function from the two parameter ML function. Smaller values than one move the graphs of the wML function towards the unweighted ML function, or transpass the ML function in case of δ variation. In addition, we observe that the asymptotic values for larger x values approach a different asymptotic behavior of the ML function. While for $\gamma = 1$ (top row) the asymptotic slope is nearly the same for $\delta = 1$ (bottom row) we observe a fanning out of the asymptotic behavior. In general, we can state that the asymptotic behavior of the wML function assumes a different slope than the ML function, which is typically larger than the slope of the ML function.

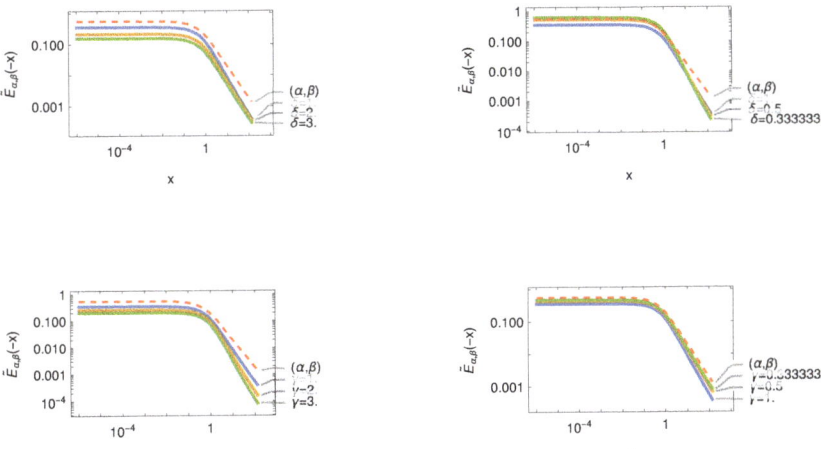

Figure 14. Variation of parameters (indicated in the panels) for the weighted Mittag-Leffler function $\tilde{E}_{\alpha,\beta}^{\delta,\gamma}(-x) = \tilde{E}_{\alpha,\beta}(-x)$ using $\alpha = 1/3$ and $\beta = 1/2$. The top row uses $\gamma = 1$ and the bottom row $\delta = 1$. The Mittag-Leffler function $E_{\alpha,\beta}(-x)$ is shown as reference (dashed line). The number of Sinc points in all approximations is $N = 72$.

This example demonstrates that well-known functions can be modified straightforwardly if we introduce weights in an $\aleph$ representation in Mellin space. This bears the potential that we can adapt specific functions which do not fit to practical data properly within a well-defined function environment. Such a tool is of utmost practical importance if the data set is of experimental origin.

Example 7. *Solution of Abel's Integral Equation (47) Generalized*

The present example deals with Abel's equation's solution (51). We assume that (51) is a function $(u(x))$ produced by a convolution based on a known function $f(x)$. If we view (51) as a convolution integral, we may alter the restrictions $\alpha = \beta$ to $\alpha \neq \beta$ and/or substitute the ML function with a wML function based on $\aleph$ functions. These modifications will produce a convolution integral representation of the type:

$$u(x) = f(x) + \lambda \int_0^x \aleph_{1,2,\tau_k;2}^{1,1}\left[-\lambda \eta^\alpha \,\middle|\, \begin{matrix}(\alpha-1,1) \\ (\alpha-1,1)\end{matrix} \quad (1-\beta+\alpha(\alpha-1),\alpha)\right] f(x-\eta)d\eta; \quad (59)$$

i.e., in the convolution, we replace the Fox H function with an ℵ function. This is a simple assignment in terms of basic arithmetic. The related integral equation, on the other hand, will convert to an unknown equation. We will employ Sinc convolution techniques to produce the function $u(x)$ once more, [7,13]. Consider first the case when $\alpha < \beta$ with $\alpha = 1/3$ and $\beta = 1/2$. As previously stated, the weights γ and δ allow for the adaptation of the function $u(x)$ to a desired structure, which is more adaptable to a specific instance than the Fox H example. This trait is depicted in Figure 15. The weights allow the curves in the double logarithmic representations to be spread out by approximately four decades in amplitude.

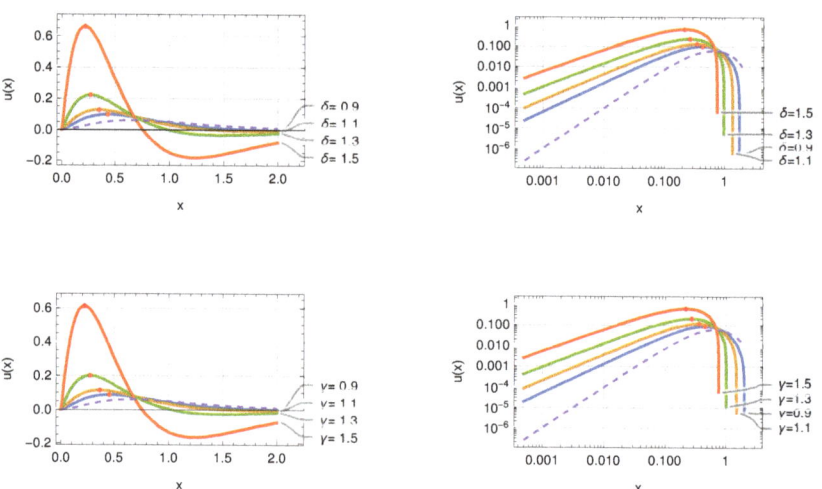

Figure 15. Variation of parameters (indicated in the panels) for the convolution integral (56) using a weighted Mittag-Leffler function $E_{\alpha,\beta}^{\delta,\gamma}(-x) = \tilde{E}_{\alpha,\beta}(-x)$ based on ℵ functions. The parameters are $\alpha = 1/3$ and $\beta = 1/2$. The top row uses $\gamma = 2$ and the bottom row $\delta = 2$. The number of Sinc points in all approximations is $N = 48$. The inhomogeneity used is $f(x) = x^2 \exp(-3x)$ (dashed line).

The second situation considered is given by $\alpha > \beta$ with $\alpha = 1/2$ and $\beta = 1/3$. We also modified the weights δ and γ for this set of parameters, resulting in Figure 16. A comparison of Figures 15 and 16 illustrates that changing the relationship between α and β modifies the original function $f(x) = x^2 \exp(-3x)$. If $\alpha < \beta$ pronounced peaks and minima appear, while just a prominent maximum and shallow minima appear in the opposite case. The position of maxima is marked by dots in both Figures.

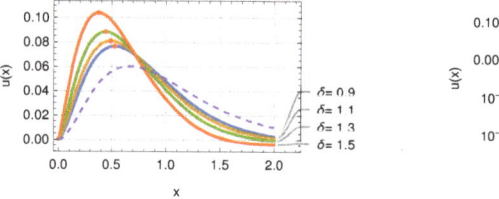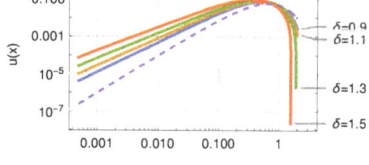

Figure 16. Cont.

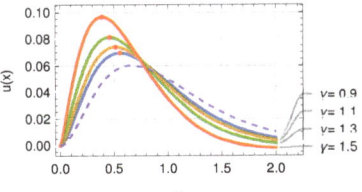
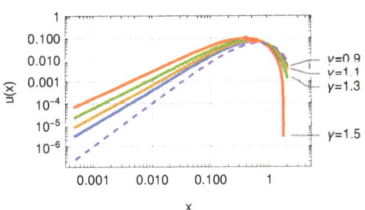

Figure 16. Variation of parameters (indicated in the panels) for the convolution integral (56) using a weighted Mittag-Leffler function $E_{\alpha,\beta}^{\delta,\gamma}(-x) = \tilde{E}_{\alpha,\beta}(-x)$ based on $\aleph$ functions. The parameters are $\alpha = 1/2$ and $\beta = 1/3$. The top row uses $\gamma = 2$ and the bottom row $\delta = 2$. The number of Sinc points in all approximations is $N = 48$. The inhomogeneity used is $f(x) = x^2 \exp(-3x)$ (dashed line).

The examples revealed that we can get numerical values for unknown functions with a few discretization points. The parameter variation allows for a continual modification in the functions, resulting in the desired representation.

3.3. Saxena I Functions

Rather of examining the Saxena I function, we compare the three special functions in this section. As a result, we utilize the case of stable distributions, which Schneider initially looked at in conjunction with Fox H functions [44]. Later, Mainardi and Pagnini used Mellin-Barnes integrals to investigate the Schneider technique [45]. This representation of Fox H functions in Mellin space will be extended to $\aleph$- and Saxena I functions. We already know that this change in the Mellin model of "stable distributions" leads to various distributions. However, it is fascinating how close some of these functions are to one another. We can use the restrictions on the weights to go back to the Fox H function for the $\aleph$ function. The purpose of this section is to compare these classes of functions graphically by graphing their numerical representations.

Example 8. *Stable Distributions*

Schneider established stable one-sided Lévy distributions using a Fourier-Stieltjes transform in conjunction with the Mellin transform [44]. As a result, the density representation in Mellin space is as follows:

$$\hat{f}_{\alpha,\beta}(s) = \epsilon \frac{\Gamma(s)\Gamma(\epsilon - \epsilon s)}{\Gamma(\eta - \eta s)\Gamma(1 - \eta + \eta s)}, \text{ with } \epsilon = \alpha^{-1} \text{ and } \eta = \frac{\alpha - \beta}{2\alpha}, \tag{60}$$

where $0 < \alpha < 2$ and $\beta = \max(\alpha, \alpha - 2)$. In Mellin space, however, relation (60) is nothing more than a Fox H representation. As a result, we may write

$$\hat{\mathcal{H}}_{2,2}^{1,1}(s) = \epsilon \mathcal{H}_{2,2}^{1,1}\left(s \left| \begin{array}{cc} (1-\epsilon,\epsilon) & (1-\eta,\eta) \\ (0,1) & (1-\eta,\eta) \end{array}\right.\right) = \hat{f}_{\alpha,\beta}(s), \tag{61}$$

which will deliver using the Mellin-Barnes integral the probability density $f_{\alpha,\beta}$

$$\begin{aligned} f_{\alpha,\beta}(z) &= \frac{1}{2\pi i}\int_{\mathcal{C}} \hat{\mathcal{H}}_{2,2}^{1,1}(s) z^{-s} ds = \frac{1}{2\pi i}\int_{\gamma-i\infty}^{\gamma+i\infty} \hat{\mathcal{H}}_{2,2}^{1,1}(s) z^{-s} ds \\ &= \frac{1}{2\pi}\int_{-\infty}^{\infty} \hat{\mathcal{H}}_{2,2}^{1,1}(\gamma - i\sigma) z^{-\gamma+i\sigma} d\sigma, \end{aligned} \tag{62}$$

with $0 < \gamma < 1$. Now we may ask what happens if we replace H with either the $\aleph$ or the Saxena I function in (62); i.e., we set

$$\hat{\mathcal{A}}_{p_k,q_k,\tau_k;2}^{m,n}(s) = \epsilon \mathcal{A}_{p_k,q_k,\tau_k;2}^{m,n}\left(s \left| \begin{array}{cc} (1-\epsilon,\epsilon) & (1-\eta,\eta) \\ (0,1) & (1-\eta,\eta) \end{array}\right.\right) = \hat{a}_{\alpha,\beta}(s), \tag{63}$$

or

$$\hat{\mathcal{I}}_{p_k,q_k,1;2}^{m,n}(s) = \epsilon \mathcal{I}_{p_k,q_k,1;2}^{m,n}\left(s \left| \begin{array}{cc} (1-\epsilon,\epsilon) & (1-\eta,\eta) \\ (0,1) & (1-\eta,\eta) \end{array}\right.\right) = \hat{i}_{\alpha,\beta}(s), \quad (64)$$

as integrand in (62) and get $a_{\alpha,\beta}(z)$ or $i_{\alpha,\beta}(z)$, respectively. The results are quite interesting and have some similarities with the original definition of the one-sided stable distribution function. The results are collected for a view examples in Figure 17. We depict the Cauchy-Lorentz case with $(\alpha,\beta) = (1,0)$, the Lévy case using $(\alpha,\beta) = (1/2,-1/2)$, and one of the Whittaker cases using $(\alpha,\beta) = (2/3,-2/3)$ shown in each row, respectively. The Fox column in Figure 17 shows the one-sided stable distribution. The Aleph- and the Saxena columns represent the graphs based on the respective function representation. As a reference, we graph in each row the analytic representation of the function as a dashed line. For Cauchy-Lorentz we have $f_{1,0}(z) = 1/(z^2+1)$, the Lévy distribution is $f_{1/2,-1/2}(z) = \frac{x^{-3/2}e^{-\frac{1}{4x}}}{2\sqrt{\pi}}$, and the Whittaker distribution is $f_{2/3,-2/3}(z) = \sqrt{3/\pi}\exp\left(-\frac{4}{2(27z^2)}\right)z^{-1}W_{1/2,1/6}\left(\frac{4}{27z^2}\right)$, where $W_{\alpha,\beta}(z)$ is Whittaker's W function. The "distributions" based on Aleph or Saxena are graphed as solid lines. We also included an inset to each graph that shows the approximation's local absolute error. The Aleph and Saxena-based approximations clearly resemble the original distribution in various ways. If the weights are experiencing some limiting process like $\tau_1 \to 0$ and $\tau_2 \to 1$, the original distribution can be restored using the Aleph approximation. We don't have the freedom to adjust the numerical approximation in the Saxena approximation; the numerical approximation is set. The local absolute and relative error ϵ_N is a minor number, as seen in the insets. Furthermore, we may infer from Figure 17 that the asymptotic behavior of the Aleph and Saxena approximations take the values of the Fox H function.

The example shows that, in addition to the Fox and Aleph approximations, the Mellin-Barnes representation technique also works for the Saxena I function.

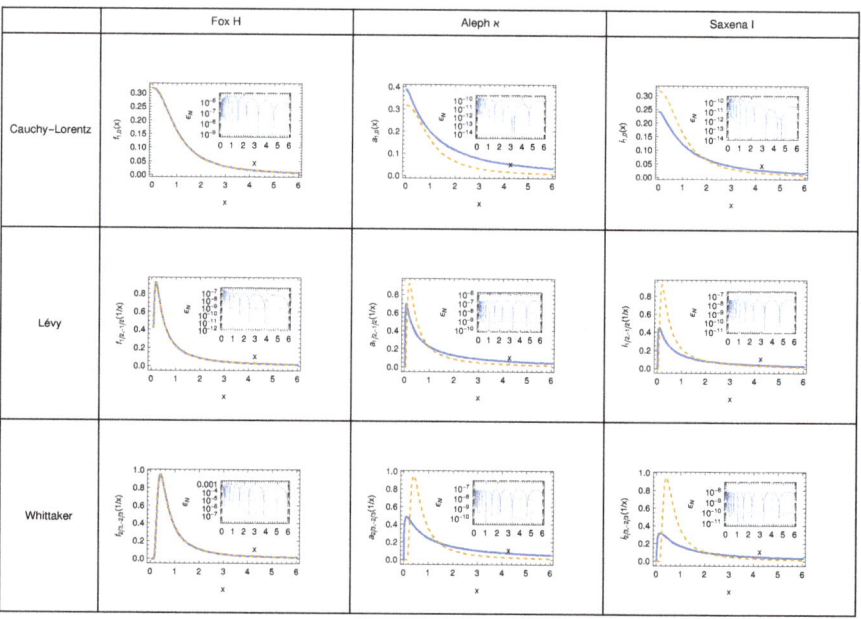

Figure 17. Three one sided stable distributions and their Aleph and Saxena variants. The number of Sinc points in all approximations is $N = 48$.

4. Conclusions

We showed that a Sinc approximation of the Mellin-Barnes integral produces acceptable numerical results for three classes of special functions. We were able to construct numerical representations of the Aleph- and Saxena *I* functions for the first time. The above example demonstrates how simple it is to deal numerically with new and unknown functions. It was observed that the Sinc approximation works effectively with an exponential convergence rate. The calculation benefits greatly from the very small number of discretization points. Furthermore, the approximation approach can handle singularities at the approximation interval's endpoints. This is only foreseeable by an asymptotic analysis for a certain choice of parameters in the Mellin representation of the functions. In this work, we looked at standard integration pathways parallel to the imaginary axis. However, the Mellin-Barnes contour $\mathcal{C}$ is not limited to this particular example. In future studies, we are going to investigate alternative contours that may be useful in numerically representing special functions.

Author Contributions: Conceptualization, G.B. and N.S.; methodology, G.B.; software, G.B.; validation, G.B. and N.S.; formal analysis, G.B.; investigation, G.B.; writing—original draft preparation, G.B.; writing—review and editing, G.B. and N.S.; visualization, G.B.; supervision, G.B.; project administration, G.B.; All authors have read and agreed to the published version of the manuscript.

Funding: This research received no external funding.

Acknowledgments: The authors acknowledge the inspiring discussions and valuable ideas by Frank Stenger.

Conflicts of Interest: The authors declare no conflict of interest.

References

1. Kochubei, A.N.; Luchko, Y.F.; Karniadakis, G.; Tarasov, V.E.; Petráš, I.; Baleanu, D.; Lopes, A.M. (Eds.) *Handbook of Fractional Calculus with Applications*; De Gruyter Reference; De Gruyter: Berlin, Germany; Boston, MA, USA, 2019; Volumes 1–8. ISBN 978-3-11-057081-6.
2. Beghin, L.; Mainardi, F.; Garrappa, R. (Eds.) *Workshop on Nonlocal and Fractional Operators*; Nonlocal and Fractional Operators; Springer: Cham, Switzerland, 2021; ISBN 978-3-030-69236-0.
3. Kilbas, A.A.; Saigo, M. *H-Transforms: Theory and Applications; Analytical Methods and Special Functions*; Chapman & Hall/CRC: Boca Raton, FL, USA, 2004; ISBN 978-0-415-29916-9.
4. Mathai, A.M.; Saxena, R.K.; Haubold, H.J. *The H-Function: Theory and Applications*; Springer: New York, NY, USA, 2010; ISBN 978-1-4419-0915-2.
5. Garrappa, R. Numerical Evaluation of Two and Three Parameter Mittag-Leffler Functions. *SIAM J. Numer. Anal.* **2015**, *53*, 1350–1369. [CrossRef]
6. Weideman, J.A.C.; Trefethen, L.N. Parabolic and Hyperbolic Contours for Computing the Bromwich Integral. *Math. Comp.* **2007**, *76*, 1341–1357. [CrossRef]
7. Baumann, G. Sinc Based Inverse Laplace Transforms, Mittag-Leffler Functions and Their Approximation for Fractional Calculus. *Fractal Fract.* **2021**, *5*, 43. [CrossRef]
8. Gorenflo, R.; Kilbas, A.A.; Mainardi, F.; Rogosin, S.V. *Mittag-Leffler Functions, Related Topics and Applications*; Springer Monographs in Mathematics; Springer: Berlin/Heidelberg, Germany, 2014; ISBN 978-3-662-43929-6.
9. Mainardi, F.; Pagnini, G. Salvatore Pincherle: The Pioneer of the Mellin—Barnes Integrals. *J. Comput. Appl. Math.* **2003**, *153*, 331–342. [CrossRef]
10. Saxena, V.P. Formal Solution of Certain New Pair of Dual Integral Equations Involving H-Functions. *Proc. Nat. Acad. Sci. India Sect. A* **1982**, *52*, 366–375.
11. Stenger, F. *Numerical Methods Based on Sinc and Analytic Functions*; Springer Series in Computational Mathematics; Springer: New York, NY, USA, 1993; Volume 20; ISBN 978-1-4612-7637-1.
12. Baumann, G.; Stenger, F. Fractional Calculus and Sinc Methods. *Fract. Calc. Appl. Anal.* **2011**, *14*, 568. s13540-011-0035-3. [CrossRef]
13. Stenger, F. *Handbook of Sinc Numerical Methods*; Chapman & Hall/CRC Numerical Analysis and Scientific Computing; CRC Press: Boca Raton, FL, USA, 2011; ISBN 978-1-4398-2158-9.
14. Baumann, G. *New Sinc Methods of Numerical Analysis: Festschrift in Honor of Frank Stenger's 80th Birthday*; Trends in Mathematics; Springer International Publishing: Cham, Switzerland, 2021; ISBN 978-3-030-49715-6.
15. Fox, C. A Formal Solution of Certain Dual Integral Equations. *Trans. Am. Math. Soc.* **1965**, *119*, 389–398. S0002-9947-1965-0180817-5. [CrossRef]

16. Mathai, A.M.; Saxena, R.K. *Generalized Hypergeometric Functions with Applications in Statistics and Physical Sciences*; Lecture Notes in Mathematics; Springer: Berlin/Heidelberg, Germany; New York, NY, USA, 1973; ISBN 978-3-540-06482-4.
17. Südland, N.; Baumann, G.; Nonnenmacher, T.F. Open problem: Who knows about the Aleph-functions. *Fract. Calc. Appl. Anal.* **1998**, *1*, 401–402.
18. Südland, N.; Baumann, G.; Nonnenmacher, T.F. Fractional driftless Fokker-Planck equation with power law diffusion coefficients. In Proceedings of the Computer Algebra in Scientific Computing CASC 2001: Proceedings of the Fourth International Workshop on Computer Algebra in Scientific Computing, Konstanz, Germany, 22–26 September 2001; Ganzha, V.G., Mayr, E.W., Vorozhtsov, E.V., Eds.; Springer: Berlin/Heidelberg, Germany, 2001; pp. 513–528; ISBN 978-3-642-56666-0.
19. Saxena, R.K.; Pogány, T.K. On Fractional Integration Formulae for Aleph Functions. *Appl. Math. Comput.* **2011**, *218*, 985–990. [CrossRef]
20. Südland, N.; Volkmann, J.; Kumar, D. Applications to Give an Analytical Solution to the Black Scholes Equation. *Integral Transform. Spec.* **2019**, *30*, 205–230. [CrossRef]
21. Gupta, P.; Shekhawat, A.S. Fractional Calculus Associated with General Polynomials and Aleph Functions. *Glob. J. Pure Appl. Math.* **2017**, *13*, 957–966.
22. Chaurasia, V.B.L.; Singh, Y. Lambert's Law and Aleph Function. *Int. J. Modern Math. Sci.* **2012**, *4*, 84–88.
23. Khan, Y.; Sharma, P. Some Integral Properties of Aleph Function, General Class of Polynomials Associated with Feynman Integrals. *Int. J. Math. Stat. Invent.* **2014**, *2*, 21–27.
24. Stenger, F.; El-Sharkawy, H.A.M.; Baumann, G. The Lebesgue Constant for Sinc Approximations. In *New Perspectives on Approximation and Sampling Theory*; Zayed, A.I., Schmeisser, G., Eds.; Applied and Numerical Harmonic Analysis; Springer International Publishing: Cham, Switzerland, 2014; pp. 319–335. ISBN 978-3-319-08800-6.
25. Stenger, F. Collocating Convolutions. *Math. Comp.* **1995**, *64*, 211. [CrossRef]
26. Pincherle, S. Sulle funzioni ipergeometriche generallizate. *Rend. Accad. Naz. Lincei* **1888**, *4*, 792–799.
27. Mellin, H. *Über die fundamentale Wichtigkeit des Satzes von Cauchy für die Theorien der Gamma- und hypergeometrischen Funktionen*; Acta Societatis Scientiarum Fennicae: Helsinki, Finland, 1896; Volume 21, pp. 1–115.
28. Haubold, H.J.; Mathai, A.M.; Saxena, R.K. Mittag-Leffler Functions and Their Applications. *J. Appl. Math.* **2011**, *2011*, 1–51. [CrossRef]
29. Talbot, A. The Accurate Numerical Inversion of Laplace Transforms. *IMA J. Appl. Math.* **1979**, *23*, 97–120. imamat/23.1.97. [CrossRef]
30. Garrappa, R.; Popolizio, M. Fast methods for the computation of the Mittag-Leffler function. In *Handbook of Fractional Calculus with Applications*; Kochubei, A.N., Luchko, Y.F., Karniadakis, G., Tarasov, V.E., Petráš, I., Baleanu, D., Lopes, A.M., Eds.; De Gruyter: Berlin, 2019; pp. 329–346.
31. Krätzel, E. Integral Transformations of Bessel-Type. In Proceedings of the International Conference on Generalized Functions and Operational Calculus, Varna, Bulgaria, 29 September–6 October 1975; pp. 148–155.
32. Kilbas, A.A.; Kumar, D. On Generalized Krätzel Function. *Integral Transform. Spec. Funct.* **2009**, *20*, 835–846. 1080/10652460902819024. [CrossRef]
33. Princy, T. Krätzel Function and Related Statistical Distributions. *Commun. Math. Stat.* **2014**, *2*, 413–429. s40304-015-0048-z. [CrossRef]
34. Gorenflo, R.; Vessella, S. *Abel Integral Equations: Analysis and Applications*; Lecture notes in mathematics; Springer: Berlin, Germany; New York, NY, USA, 1991; ISBN 978-3-540-53668-0.
35. Haubold, H.J.; Mathai, A.M. The Fractional Kinetic Equation and Thermonuclear Functions. *Astrophys. Space Sci.* **2000**, *273*, 53–63. [CrossRef]
36. Glöckle, W.G.; Nonnenmacher, T.F. Fractional Integral Operators and Fox Functions in the Theory of Viscoelasticity. *Macromolecules* **1991**, *24*, 6426–6434. [CrossRef]
37. Hille, E.; Tamarkin, J.D. On the Theory of Linear Integral Equations. *Ann. Math.* **1930**, *31*, 479. [CrossRef]
38. Coraddu, M.; Kaniadakis, G.; Lavagno, A.; Lissia, M.; Mezzorani, G.; Quarati, P. Thermal Distributions in Stellar Plasmas, Nuclear Reactions and Solar Neutrinos. *Braz. J. Phys.* **1999**, *29*, 153–168. [CrossRef]
39. Dubey, R.S. An Application of the Aleph (ℵ)-Function for Detecting Glucose Supply in Human Blood. *Int. J. Modern Math. Sci.* **2016**, *14*, 221–226.
40. Suthar, D.L.; Habenom, H.; Tadesse, H. Certain integrals involving aleph function and wright's generalized hypergeometric function. *Acta Univ. Apulensis Math. Inform.* **2017**, *52*, 1–10. [CrossRef]
41. Tyagi, S.; Jain, M.; Singh, J. Application of S-Function and the Aleph Function in the Electric Circuit Theory. *Int. J. Appl. Comput. Math.* **2021**, *7*, 193. [CrossRef]
42. Singh, Y.; Gill, V.; Singh, J.; Kumar, D.; Khan, I. Computable Generalization of Fractional Kinetic Equation with Special Functions. *J. King Saud Univ.-Sci.* **2021**, *33*, 101221. [CrossRef]
43. Saxena, R.K.; Daiya, J. Integral Transforms of the S-Functions. *Le Mat.* **2015**, *70*, 147–159. [CrossRef]
44. Schneider, W.R. Stable Distributions: Fox Function Representation and Generalization. In *Stochastic Processes in Classical and Quantum Systems*; Springer: Berlin/Heidelberg, Germany, 1986; pp. 497–511.
45. Mainardi, F.; Pagnini, G. Mellin-Barnes Integrals for Stable Distributions and Their Convolutions. *Fract. Calc. Appl. Anal.* **2008**, *11*, 443–456.

Review

Stability Properties of Multi-Term Fractional-Differential Equations

Oana Brandibur [1,†] and Éva Kaslik [1,2,*,†]

1. Department of Mathematics and Computer Science, West University of Timişoara, 300223 Timişoara, Romania
2. Institute for Advanced Environmental Research, West University of Timişoara, 300223 Timişoara, Romania
* Correspondence: eva.kaslik@e-uvt.ro
† These authors contributed equally to this work.

Abstract: Necessary and sufficient stability and instability conditions are reviewed and extended for multi-term homogeneous linear fractional differential equations with Caputo derivatives and constant coefficients. A comprehensive review of the state of the art regarding the stability analysis of two-term and three-term fractional-order differential equations is provided, which is then extended to the case of four-term fractional-order differential equations. The stability and instability properties are characterized with respect to the coefficients of the multi-term fractional differential equations, leading to both fractional-order-dependent and fractional-order-independent characterizations. In the general case, fractional-order-independent stability and instability properties are described for fractional-order differential equations with an arbitrary number of fractional derivatives.

Keywords: multi-order fractional differential equation; stability; instability; Caputo derivative

1. Introduction

Fractional-order differential equations have been extensively used in modelling real-world phenomena from a wide range of domains [1–5], considering the memory and hereditary properties that the fractional derivatives are provided with [1,5]. Two-term fractional differential equations describe the modelling of the motion of a rigid plate that is immersed in a viscous liquid, also known as the Bagley–Torvik equation [6], whereas the Basset equation [7] is also described using linear two-term fractional differential equation. Other examples worth mentioning are the equation of the inextensible pendulum [8] and the fractional harmonic oscillator [9,10], which are both described by multi-term fractional-order differential equations with three fractional derivatives of Caputo type.

The most well-known types of fractional derivatives, which are typically not equivalent, are the Grünwald–Letnikov derivative, the Riemann–Liouville derivative, and the Caputo derivative. Given that it only requires initial conditions defined in terms of integer-order derivatives, which represent well-understood characteristics of physical phenomena, the Caputo derivative seems to be more applicable to real-world problems.

The existence and uniqueness of solutions for multi-term fractional differential equations have been explored the past years [11–13]. Stability theory has been broadly explored as well. Two-term fractional-order differential equations have been investigated in terms of their stability properties. Refs. [14–18] studied the boundary-value problems for multi-term fractional-differential equations. The asymptotic behaviour of solutions of linear multi-order fractional differential systems are determined in Ref. [19], whereas Ref. [20] summarize the recent stability results of fractional differential equations, most of them in comparison to their classical integer-order counterparts.

The stability of linear systems of fractional-order differential equations is also considered in Ref. [21], where the fractional orders are proportional and transformations form the physical plane to the fractional-domain is discussed. Moreover, recent results [22]

Citation: Brandibur, O.; Kaslik, E. Stability Properties of Multi-Term Fractional-Differential Equations. *Fractal Fract.* **2023**, *7*, 117. https://doi.org/10.3390/fractalfract7020117

Academic Editors: Angelo B. Mingarelli, Leila Gholizadeh Zivlaei and Mohammad Dehghan

Received: 20 December 2022
Revised: 22 January 2023
Accepted: 24 January 2023
Published: 26 January 2023

Copyright: © 2023 by the authors. Licensee MDPI, Basel, Switzerland. This article is an open access article distributed under the terms and conditions of the Creative Commons Attribution (CC BY) license (https://creativecommons.org/licenses/by/4.0/).

generalize the formulation, the existence of the solution, and provide stability properties for multi-term systems of fractional-order differential equations. Some stability theorems are also obtained in Ref. [23] for both systems of fractional differential equations with multi-order and for multi-term fractional differential equations.

The purpose of this paper is to investigate multi-term fractional-order equations in terms of their stability and instability properties, both with respect to the roots of the corresponding characteristic equations and with respect to the coefficients of the considered equations. Moreover, we obtain sufficient conditions for the asymptotic stability and instability of the fractional-order differential equation, independent of the choice of the considered fractional orders. Furthermore, we also determine the stability and instability conditions for multi-term fractional differential equations with four fractional-order derivatives of Caputo type, by extending the recent results obtained for multi-term fractional-order equations with three derivatives [24], considering the analogy of the corresponding characteristic equations.

The structure of this paper is as follows. The preliminaries regarding basic definitions in fractional calculus are included in Section 2. The main results obtained for fractional-order differential equations with an arbitrary number of derivatives, as well as fractional-order-independent stability and instability results, are provided in Section 3. As a particular case, we recall the main stability and instability conditions for two-term fractional differential equations described in Section 4. These are followed by an overview of the main results recently obtained in the case of three-term fractional-order differential equations, which are listed in Section 5. The next section aims to present and prove the main novel results of this work, by extending the stability and instability conditions to the case of multi-term fractional differential equations with four derivatives of Caputo type, in Section 6. Both fractional-order dependent and independent stability and instability conditions are obtained. The conclusions are drawn in Section 7.

2. Preliminaries

Definition 1. *The Caputo fractional differential operator of order $q > 0$ is defined as*

$$^c D^q x(t) := \begin{cases} \dfrac{1}{\Gamma(n-q)} \displaystyle\int_0^t \dfrac{x^{(n)}(\tau)}{(t-\tau)^{q+1-n}} d\tau, & \text{if } n-1 < q < n \\ \dfrac{d^n x(t)}{dt^n}, & \text{if } q = n \end{cases},$$

where $n \in \mathbb{N}$ and the Gamma function is $\Gamma(z) = \displaystyle\int_0^\infty y^{z-1} e^{-y} dy$, for $\Re(z) > 0$.

The Laplace transform of the Caputo derivative or an arbitrary fractional order q is given as in Ref. [12]:

Proposition 1. *The Laplace transform for the fractional-order Caputo derivative of order $q \in (n-1, n]$, $n \in \mathbb{N}^*$, of a function x is:*

$$\mathcal{L}(^c D^q x)(s) = s^q X(s) - \sum_{k=0}^{n-1} s^{q-k-1} x^{(k)}(0),$$

where $X(s)$ represents the Laplace transform of the function x.

Consider the following general linear multi-term fractional differential equation

$$^c D^q x(t) + \sum_{i=1}^{n-1} \alpha_i \, ^c D^{q_i} x(t) + \beta x(t) = 0 \qquad (1)$$

where α_i, β are real coefficients, for any $i \in \{1, 2, \ldots, n-1\}$, and $q, q_1, q_2, \ldots, q_{n-1}$ are the fractional orders of the Caputo derivatives, such that $0 < q_1 < q_2 < \ldots < q_{n-1} < q \leq 2$.

The linear homogeneous fractional-order differential Equation (1) can be seen as the linearization at the trivial equilibrium of a nonlinear autonomous fractional-order differential equation of the following form

$$^cD^q x(t) = f(x(t), {}^cD^{q_1}x(t), {}^cD^{q_2}x(t), \ldots, {}^cD^{q_{n-1}}x(t)) \qquad (2)$$

where $f : \mathbb{R}^n \to \mathbb{R}$ is a continuously differentiable function such that $f(0, 0, \ldots, 0) = 0$.

The initial condition associated to Equation (1) is either

i. $x_i = x(0) = x_0 \in \mathbb{R}$, if $q \in (0, 1]$, or
ii. $x_i = (x(0), x'(0)) = (x_0, x_1) \in \mathbb{R}^2$ if $q \in (1, 2]$.

In what follows, $\varphi(t, x_i)$ represents the unique solution of (1), which satisfies one of the initial considered above. One can prove the existence and uniqueness of the solution of the initial value problem associated to the equation (1) in a similar way to the case of fractional-order systems of differential equations [8,11]. As a matter of fact, we can express the solution of the linear constant coefficient fractional differential Equation (1) using the fractional Green's function as presented in Ref. [12], or by employing the fractional meta-trigonometric approach in the commensurate case [25].

Henceforward, we consider a non-exponential asymptotic stability concept, named Mittag–Leffler stability [26], in particular $\mathcal{O}(t^{-q})$-asymptotic stability, as it reflects the algebraic decay of the solution. This is justified by the fact that fractional derivatives have a memory effect and hereditary properties and therefore the asymptotic stability of the trivial solution of equation (1) is not of exponential type [15,27].

Definition 2.

i. *The trivial solution of (1) is called* **stable** *if for any* $\varepsilon > 0$ *there exists* $\delta = \delta(\varepsilon) > 0$ *such that for every* $\mathbf{x}_0 \in \mathbb{R}^n$ *satisfying* $\|\mathbf{x}_0\| < \delta$ *we have* $\|\varphi(t, \mathbf{x}_0)\| \leq \varepsilon$ *for any* $t \geq 0$;
ii. *The trivial solution of (1) is called* **asymptotically stable** *if it is stable and there exists* $\rho > 0$ *such that* $\lim_{t \to \infty} \varphi(t, \mathbf{x}_0) = 0$ *whenever* $\|\mathbf{x}_0\| < \rho$;
iii. *Let* $q > 0$. *The trivial solution of (1) is called* $\mathcal{O}(t^{-q})$-**asymptotically stable** *if it is stable and there exists* $\rho > 0$ *such that for any* $\|\mathbf{x}_0\| < \rho$ *one has:*

$$\|\varphi(t, \mathbf{x}_0)\| = \mathcal{O}(t^{-q}) \quad as\ t \to \infty.$$

3. General Fractional-Order-Independent Stability and Instability Results

In what follows, we determine the characteristic equation associated to the multi-term fractional-order differential Equation (1), which we will analyse in order to obtain fractional-order-independent stability and instability results.

Applying the Laplace transform, Equation (1) becomes

$$\left(s^q + \sum_{i=1}^{n-1} \alpha_i s^{q_i} + \beta \right) X(s) = F(s),$$

where $X(s)$ represents the Laplace transform of the function x, s^{q^*} represents the first branch of the complex power function [28], with $q^* \in \{q, q_1, q_2, \ldots, q_{n-1}\}$ and $F(s)$ incorporates the initial conditions.

Thus, we obtain the characteristic equation

$$s^q + \sum_{i=1}^{n-1} \alpha_i s^{q_i} + \beta = 0. \qquad (3)$$

Our aim is to analyse the distribution of the roots of Equation (3). Therefore, we consider the complex valued function

$$\Delta(s; \alpha_1, \ldots, \alpha_{n-1}, \beta, q_1, \ldots, q_{n-1}, q) = s^q + \sum_{i=1}^{n-1} \alpha_i s^{q_i} + \beta.$$

The next result gives us the necessary and sufficient conditions regarding the asymptotic stability and instability of the trivial solution of Equation (1) with respect to the sign of the real parts of the roots of its associated characteristic in Equation (3). A similar result has been formulated for the case of three-term linear fractional-order differential equations [24].

Theorem 1.
i. Equation (1) is $\mathcal{O}(t^{-q'})$-asymptotically stable if and only if all the roots of the characteristic function $\Delta(s; \alpha_1, \ldots, \alpha_{n-1}, \beta, q_1, \ldots, q_{n-1}, q)$ are in the open left half-plane ($\Re(s) < 0$), where $q' = \min\{\{q_1\}, \{q_2\}, \ldots, \{q_{n-1}\}, \{q\}\}$, with $\{q^*\} = q^* - \lfloor q^* \rfloor$, $q^* \in \{q_1, q_2, \ldots, q_{n-1}, q\}$;
ii. If $\beta \neq 0$ and the characteristic function $\Delta(s; \alpha_1, \ldots, \alpha_{n-1}, \beta, q_1, \ldots, q_{n-1}, q)$ has at least one root in the open right half-plane ($\Re(s) > 0$), and Equation (1) is unstable.

In what follows, let us consider the set

$$D = \{(q_1, q_2, \ldots, q_{n-1}, q) \in \mathbb{R}^n : 0 < q_1 < q_2 < \ldots < q_{n-1} < q \leq 2\}.$$

The following lemma provides a sufficient condition for the instability of the Equation (1) with respect to its coefficients, regardless of the fractional orders $(q_1, q_2, \ldots, q_{n-1}, q) \in D$.

Lemma 1. *If $\beta < 0$ or $\alpha_1 + \alpha_2 + \ldots + \alpha_{n-1} + \beta + 1 \leq 0$, the trivial solution of Equation (1) is unstable, regardless of the fractional orders $q_1, q_2, \ldots, q_{n-1}$ and q.*

Proof. If $\alpha_1 + \alpha_2 + \ldots + \alpha_{n-1} + \beta + 1 \leq 0$ we have that

$$\Delta(1; \alpha_1, \ldots, \alpha_{n-1}, \beta, q_1, \ldots, q_{n-1}, q) = 1 + \alpha_1 + \alpha_2 + \ldots + \alpha_{n-1} + \beta \leq 0.$$

For $\beta < 0$, it is obvious that

$$\Delta(0; \alpha_1, \ldots, \alpha_{n-1}, \beta, q_1, \ldots, q_{n-1}, q) = \beta < 0.$$

On the other hand, we notice that

$$\Delta(s; \alpha_1, \ldots, \alpha_{n-1}, \beta, q_1, \ldots, q_{n-1}, q) \to \infty \quad \text{for } s \to \infty.$$

Hence, for both cases the function $s \mapsto \Delta(s; \alpha_1, \ldots, \alpha_{n-1}, \beta, q_1, \ldots, q_{n-1}, q)$ has at least one strictly positive real root. Therefore, Equation (1) is unstable, regardless of the fractional orders $q_1, q_2, \ldots, q_{n-1}$ and q. □

In what follows, we only consider the case $\beta > 0$, as we have previously seen in Lemma 1 that if $\beta < 0$, the Equation (1) is unstable, regardless of the fractional orders $(q_1, q_2, \ldots, q_{n-1}, q) \in D$. Therefore, we can state the following result, which provides a sufficient condition for the asymptotic stability of the trivial solution of Equation (1), regardless of its fractional orders.

Lemma 2. *If $\alpha_i > 0$, $i \in \{1, 2, \ldots, n-1\}$ and $\beta > 0$, the trivial solution of Equation (1) is asymptotically stable, for any fractional orders $q_1, q_2, \ldots, q_{n-1}$ and q.*

Proof. Let $\alpha_i > 0$, $i \in \{1, 2, \ldots, n-1\}$ and $\beta > 0$. Assuming the contrary, that there exists $s_0 \neq 0$ a root of the characteristic function $\Delta(s; \alpha_1, \ldots, \alpha_{n-1}, \beta, q_1, \ldots, q_{n-1}, q)$ such that $\Re(s_0) \geq 0$, we have

$$s_0^q + \alpha_1 s_0^{q_1} + \alpha_2 s_0^{q_2} + \ldots + \alpha_{n-1} s_0^{q_{n-1}} + \beta = 0.$$

Multiplying this previous relation by $s_0^{-\frac{q}{2}}$, it follows that

$$s_0^{\frac{q}{2}} + \alpha_1 s_0^{q_1 - \frac{q}{2}} + \alpha_2 s_0^{q_2 - \frac{q}{2}} + \ldots + \alpha_{n-1} s_0^{q_{n-1} - \frac{q}{2}} + \beta s_0^{-\frac{q}{2}} = 0.$$

Since $\pm \frac{q}{2} \in [-1, 1]$ and $q_1 - \frac{q}{2}, q_2 - \frac{q}{2}, \ldots, q_{n-1} - \frac{q}{2} \in (-1, 1)$, we have that the real parts of each term from the left-hand side of the equality from above are positive. Therefore,

$$\Re\left(s_0^{\frac{q}{2}} + \alpha_1 s_0^{q_1 - \frac{q}{2}} + \alpha_2 s_0^{q_2 - \frac{q}{2}} + \ldots + \alpha_{n-1} s_0^{q_{n-1} - \frac{q}{2}} + \beta s_0^{-\frac{q}{2}}\right) > 0,$$

which is a contradiction.

Thus, $\Re(s) < 0$, for any s being a root of the characteristic function Δ, which shows that the trivial solution of Equation (1) is asymptotically stable, regardless of the fractional orders $q_1, q_2, \ldots, q_{n-1}$ and q. □

It is important to emphasize that Lemmas 1 and 2 generalize the recent results from Ref. [24], which strictly refer to three-term fractional differential equations. The techniques employed in the proofs presented above allow for a simple generalization to the multi-term case, leading to easily verifiable inequalities involving the constant coefficients, which guarantee the instability/stability of the trivial solution of Equation (1), for any choice of the fractional orders of the Caputo derivatives.

In the following sections, we explore fractional-order-dependent stability and instability conditions for particular cases of multi-term fractional-order differential equations. We will first review some results from the literature for the cases of two-term and three-term fractional-order differential equations, followed by an extension of the results to four-term fractional differential equations

4. Two-Term Fractional-Order Differential Equations

In this section, we review some stability properties of two-term fractional differential equations similar to those obtained by Čermák and Kisela [15], as a particular case of the multi-term fractional differential Equation (1).

Consider the following two-term fractional differential equation

$$^cD^q x(t) + \alpha\, ^cD^{q_1} x(t) + \beta x(t) = 0, \tag{4}$$

where the coefficients α and β are the real numbers and q_1 and q are the fractional orders of the Caputo derivatives, with $0 < q_1 < q \leq 2$.

The associated characteristic equation for the two-term fractional differential Equation (4) is

$$s^q + \alpha s^{q_1} + \beta = 0. \tag{5}$$

In what follows, we give a characterisation of the stability properties of Equation (4), which may be obtained as a particular case of Theorem 2. For the proof of this theorem we refer to Ref. [24].

Proposition 2. *Let $0 < q_1 < q \leq 2$. For $\beta > 0$, let*

$$\alpha^* = -\frac{\beta^{1-\frac{q_1}{q}} \sin \frac{q\pi}{2}}{\left(\sin \frac{q_1 \pi}{2}\right)^{\frac{q_1}{q}} \left(\sin \frac{(q-q_1)\pi}{2}\right)^{1-\frac{q_1}{q}}}.$$

Then

i. If $\beta < 0$ or $\alpha + \beta + 1 \leq 0$ the trivial solution of Equation (4) is unstable, regardless of the fractional orders q_1 and q;
ii. If $\beta > 0$ and $\alpha > \alpha^*$, the trivial solution of Equation (4) is asymptotically stable;
iii. If $\beta > 0$ and $\alpha < \alpha^*$, the trivial solution of Equation (4) is unstable.

Remark 1. *The previous proposition gives us sufficient conditions of instability of the considered equation regardless of the fractional orders q_1 and q and sufficient conditions of both asymptotic stability and instability dependent of the fractional orders of Equation (4). We notice that the results obtained are in accordance to the conditions of stability and instability determined by Cermak and Kisela in Ref. [15], where particular rational fractional orders were considered.*

In what follows, we will recall some well-known examples of two-term fractional-order differential equations, which were comprehensively described in Ref. [24].

Example 1. *The Basset equation is described by the following linear fractional-order differential equation*

$$\dot{x}(t) + \alpha^c D^{q_1} x(t) + \beta x(t) = 0, \quad 0 < q_1 < 1, \tag{6}$$

which originates in the study of the generalised Basset force ensuing when a spherical object is submerged in an incompressible viscous fluid [7].

It is clear that the characteristic equation associated to (6) is

$$s + \alpha s^{q_1} + \beta = 0.$$

Based on the theoretical results previously mentioned we notice that:

- If $\beta < 0$, the trivial solution of (6) is unstable, regardless of the fractional order q_1;
- If $\alpha > 0$ and $\beta > 0$, the trivial solution of Equation (6) is asymptotically stable, for any fractional order q_1;
- If $\alpha \leq 0$ and $\beta > 0$, the stability of the linear Equation (6) depends on the fractional order $q_1 \in (0,1)$; more precisely, the trivial solution of Equation (6) is $\mathcal{O}(t^{-q_1})$-asymptotically stable if and only if

$$\alpha > \alpha^*(\beta, q_1) = -\beta^{1-q_1}\left(\cot\frac{q_1\pi}{2}\right)^{q_1}\sec\frac{q_1\pi}{2}.$$

Example 2. *The Bagley–Torvik equation is described by following fractional-order differential equation:*

$$x''(t) + \alpha^c D^{q_1} x(t) + \beta x(t) = 0, \quad 0 < q_1 < 2 \tag{7}$$

which arises when modelling the motion of a rigid plate that immerses in a viscous liquid [6].

The characteristic equation associated to Equation (7) is

$$s^2 + \alpha s^{q_1} + \beta = 0.$$

The critical value for the parameter α is $\alpha^*(\beta, q_1) = 0$, for any fractional order q_1 and any $\beta > 0$. The trivial solution of Equation (7) will then be asymptotically stable of order $\mathcal{O}(t^{-\{q_1\}})$ if and only if $\alpha > 0$ and $\beta > 0$, which is in accordance to the results obtained in Ref. [29].

5. Three-Term Fractional-Differential Equations

The results presented in this section were rigorously investigated in Ref. [24] and will be enumerated in the following.

We consider the following multi-term fractional differential equation

$$^c D^q x(t) + \alpha_1^c D^{q_1} x(t) + \alpha_2^c D^{q_2} x(t) + \beta x(t) = 0 \tag{8}$$

where $\alpha_1, \alpha_2, \beta$ are the real numbers and q, q_1, q_2 are the fractional orders of the Caputo derivatives, with $0 < q_1 < q_2 < q \leq 2$.

The characteristic equations becomes

$$\Delta(s; \alpha_1, \alpha_2, \beta, q_1, q_2, q) := s^q + \alpha_1 s^{q_1} + \alpha_2 s^{q_2} + \beta = 0. \tag{9}$$

Let $D = \{(q_1, q_2, q) \in \mathbb{R}^3 : 0 < q_1 < q_2 < q \leq 2\}$ and let $\beta > 0$.

Lemma 3. *Let $(q_1, q_2, q) \in D$ and $\beta > 0$ be arbitrarily fixed. We consider the smooth parametric curve in the (α_1, α_2)-plane defined by*

$$\Gamma(\beta, q_1, q_2, q) : \begin{cases} \alpha_1 = \beta^{1-\frac{q_1}{q}} h(\omega, q_1, q_2, q) \\ \alpha_2 = \beta^{1-\frac{q_2}{q}} h(\omega, q_2, q_1, q) \end{cases}, \quad \omega > 0,$$

where $h : (0, \infty) \times D \to (0, \infty)$ is given by:

$$h(\omega, q_1, q_2, q) = \omega^{-\frac{q_1}{q}} [\omega \rho(q - q_2, q_2 - q_1) - \rho(q_2, q_2 - q_1)]$$

with the function ρ defined as $\rho(a,b) = \dfrac{\sin \frac{a\pi}{2}}{\sin \frac{b\pi}{2}}$, for any $a \in [0,2]$, $b \in [-1,0) \cup (0,1]$.

The following statements hold:

i. *The curve $\Gamma(\beta, q_1, q_2, q)$ is the graph of a smooth, decreasing, convex bijective function $\phi_{\beta, q_1, q_2, q} : \mathbb{R} \to \mathbb{R}$ in the (α_1, α_2)-plane;*

ii. *The curve $\Gamma(\beta, q_1, q_2, q)$ lies outside the first quadrant of the (α_1, α_2)-plane.*

Theorem 2 (Fractional-order-dependent results).

Let $\beta > 0$, $0 < q_1 < q_2 < q \leq 2$ be arbitrarily fixed. Consider the curve $\Gamma(\beta, q_1, q_2, q)$ and the function $\phi_{\beta, q_1, q_2, q} : \mathbb{R} \to \mathbb{R}$ previously defined.

i. *The characteristic Equation (9) has a pair of complex conjugated roots on the imaginary axis of the complex plane if and only if $(\alpha_1, \alpha_2) \in \Gamma(\beta; q_1, q_2, q)$;*

ii. *The trivial solution of equation (8) is $\mathcal{O}(t^{-q'})$-asymptotically stable (where $q' = \min\{\{q\}, \{q_1\}, \{q_2\}\}$) if and only if*

$$\alpha_2 > \phi_{\beta, q_1, q_2, q}(\alpha_1).$$

iii. *If $\alpha_2 < \phi_{\beta, q_1, q_2, q}(\alpha_1)$, the trivial solution of equation (8) is unstable.*

Remark 2. *If $q_1 = q_2 =: q^*$, $\Gamma(\beta, q_1, q_2, q)$ becomes the line*

$$\alpha_1 + \alpha + 2 = -\frac{\beta^{1-\frac{q^*}{q}} \sin \frac{q\pi}{2}}{\left(\sin \frac{q^*\pi}{2}\right)^{\frac{q^*}{q}} \left(\sin \frac{(q-q^*)\pi}{2}\right)^{1-\frac{q^*}{q}}},$$

which is in accordance with the results from Proposition 2.

Remark 3. *We emphasize that in the particular case of multi-term fractional-order differential equations with three derivatives, the fractional-order independent asymptotic stability and instability conditions described by Lemmas 1 and 2 become necessary and sufficient conditions, compared to the general case of fractional-order differential equations of n fractional derivatives.*

Remark 4. *In Figure 1, we have plotted three parametric curves $\Gamma(\beta, q_1, q_2, q)$ for $\beta = 3$ and different values of the fractional orders q_1, q_2, q such that $0 < q_1 < q_2 < q \leq 2$ in the (α_1, α_2)-plane, along with the fractional-order-independent stability and instability regions, respectively (plotted with red and blue). In fact, we have proved in Ref. [24] that the reunion of all the parametric* curves $\Gamma(\beta, q_1, q_2, q)$ fill the space between the fractional-order-independent stability and instability regions and will not intersect neither of them.

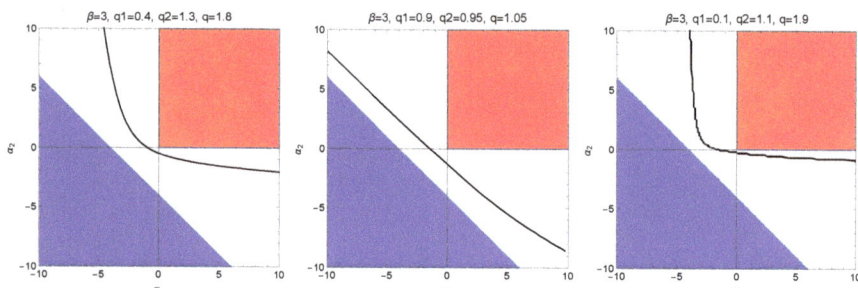

Figure 1. Parametric curves $\Gamma(\beta, q_1, q_2, q)$ (black) for $\beta = 3$ and several values of the fractional orders q_1, q_2 and q. The blue and red regions represent the *fractional-order-independent* instability and asymptotic stability regions, given by Lemma 1 and Lemma 2, respectively.

Similar to the case of two-term fractional-order differential equations described in Section 3, we will next enumerate some examples of practical applications described by three-term fractional-order differential equations, which were presented in detail in [24].

Example 3. *The equation of motion of the inextendible pendulum [8] is described by the following three term fractional-differential equation*

$$\phi'' + \mu \tau^{q_1} \cdot {}^C D^{q_1} \phi + \nu \tau^{q_2} \cdot {}^C D^{q_2} \phi + \frac{g}{L} \sin \phi = 0. \qquad (10)$$

The trivial equilibrium of the equation is asymptotically stable, for any fractional orders q_1 and q_2. Moreover, Theorem 1 gives us that

$$\phi(t) = \mathcal{O}(t^{-q'}) \quad \text{as } t \to \infty, \quad \text{where } q' = \min\{\{q_1\}, \{q_2\}\}.$$

Example 4. *The fractional harmonic oscillator is modelled by the following fractional differential equation:*

$$x'' + \alpha_1^c D^{q_1} x + \alpha_2 x' + \beta x = 0, \quad \text{with } q_1 \in (0,1) \qquad (11)$$

where α_1 and α_2 represent the friction coefficient and viscous damping coefficient [9,10], and $\beta > 0$.
- If $\alpha_1 > 0$, $\alpha_2 > 0$ and $\beta > 0$, then Equation (11) is asymptotically stable, regardless of the fractional order q_1;
- If $\alpha_2 < 0$ (negative damping), the stability properties of Equation (11) depend on the fractional order q_1 and on the magnitude of the parameters.

6. Four-Term Fractional-Differential Equations

In this section, our main objective is to generalize the previously presented results of Theorem 2, by considering a linear fractional differential equations with four Caputo derivatives:

$$^c D^q x(t) + \alpha_1^c D^{q_1} x(t) + \alpha_2^c D^{q_2} x(t) + \alpha_3^c D^{q_3} x(t) + \beta x(t) = 0, \qquad (12)$$

where $\alpha_1, \alpha_2, \alpha_3, \beta$ are the real numbers and q, q_1, q_2, q_3 are the fractional orders of the Caputo derivatives, with $0 < q_1 < q_2 < q_3 < q \leq 2$.

By means of the Laplace transform technique, we obtain the characteristic equation

$$\Delta(s; \alpha_1, \alpha_2, \alpha_3, \beta, q_1, q_2, q_3, q) = s^q + \alpha_1 s^{q_1} + \alpha_2 s^{q_2} + \alpha_3 s^{q_3} + \beta = 0. \qquad (13)$$

Next, we will assume that the fractional orders q_1, q_2, q_3, q are arbitrarily fixed inside the domain
$$D = \{(q_1, q_2, q_3, q) \in \mathbb{R}^4 : 0 < q_1 < q_2 < q_3 < q \leq 2\}.$$

Moreover, as $\beta < 0$ implies that the Equation (12) is unstable (according to Lemma 1), for any choice of the fractional orders q_1, q_2, q_3, q, we will further assume that $\beta > 0$.

Lemma 4. *Let $(q_1, q_2, q_3, q) \in D$ and $\beta > 0$ be arbitrarily fixed. Consider the parametric surface in the $(\alpha_1, \alpha_2, \alpha_3)$-space defined by*

$$S(\beta, q_1, q_2, q_3, q) : \begin{cases} \alpha_1 = \beta^{1-\frac{q_1}{q}} h(\omega, \eta, q_1, q_2, q_3, q) \\ \alpha_2 = \beta^{1-\frac{q_2}{q}} h(\omega, \eta, q_2, q_1, q_3, q) \\ \alpha_3 = \beta^{1-\frac{q_3}{q}} \eta \omega^{-\frac{q_3}{q}} \end{cases}, \quad \omega > 0, \eta \in \mathbb{R}$$

where $h : (0, \infty) \times \mathbb{R} \times D \to (0, \infty)$ is given by:

$$h(\omega, \eta, q_1, q_2, q_3, q) = \omega^{-\frac{q_1}{q}} [\eta \rho(q_3 - q_2, q_2 - q_1) + \omega \rho(q - q_2, q_2 - q_1) - \rho(q_2, q_2 - q_1)]$$

with the function ρ defined as

$$\rho(a, b) = \frac{\sin \frac{a\pi}{2}}{\sin \frac{b\pi}{2}}, \quad \forall a \in [0, 2], b \in [-1, 0) \cup (0, 1].$$

The surface $S(\beta, q_1, q_2, q_3, q)$ lies outside the first octant ($\alpha_1 > 0, \alpha_2 > 0, \alpha_3 > 0$) of the $(\alpha_1, \alpha_2, \alpha_3)$-space.

Proof. Assuming the contrary, that there exist $\omega > 0$ and $\eta \in \mathbb{R}$ such that $\alpha_1 > 0$, $\alpha_2 > 0$ and $\alpha_3 > 0$, it follows that $\eta > 0$ and

$$\begin{cases} \eta \rho(q_3 - q_2, q_2 - q_1) + \omega \rho(q - q_2, q_2 - q_1) - \rho(q_2, q_2 - q_1) > 0 \\ \eta \rho(q_3 - q_1, q_1 - q_2) + \omega \rho(q - q_1, q_1 - q_2) - \rho(q_1, q_1 - q_2) > 0 \end{cases}$$

which is equivalent to

$$\begin{cases} \eta \cdot \sin(q_3 - q_2) \frac{\pi}{2} + \omega \cdot \sin(q - q_2) \frac{\pi}{2} - \sin \frac{q_2 \pi}{2} > 0 \\ -\eta \cdot \sin(q_3 - q_1) \frac{\pi}{2} - \omega \cdot \sin(q - q_1) \frac{\pi}{2} + \sin \frac{q_1 \pi}{2} > 0 \end{cases}$$

Eliminating ω, it leads to the following inequality:

$$\eta \left(\sin(q_3 - q_2) \frac{\pi}{2} \sin(q - q_1) \frac{\pi}{2} - \sin(q_3 - q_1) \frac{\pi}{2} \sin(q - q_2) \frac{\pi}{2} \right) >$$
$$> \sin \frac{q_2 \pi}{2} \sin(q - q_1) \frac{\pi}{2} - \sin \frac{q_1 \pi}{2} \sin(q - q_2) \frac{\pi}{2}.$$

By applying elementary trigonometric identities, the previous relation is equivalent to the inequality:

$$\eta \sin(q_3 - q) \frac{\pi}{2} > \sin \frac{q \pi}{2},$$

which is absurd, as $\eta > 0$, $\sin(q_3 - q) \frac{\pi}{2} < 0$ and $\sin \frac{q \pi}{2} > 0$.

Thus, the surface $S(\beta, q_1, q_2, q_3, q)$ does not intersect the first octant of the $(\alpha_1, \alpha_2, \alpha_3)$-space. □

Remark 5. If $q_1 = q_2 = q_3 =: q^*$, $S(\beta, q_1, q_2, q_3, q)$ represents the plane

$$\alpha_1 + \alpha_2 + \alpha_3 = -\frac{\beta^{1-\frac{q^*}{q}} \sin\frac{q\pi}{2}}{\left(\sin\frac{q^*\pi}{2}\right)^{\frac{q^*}{q}} \left(\sin\frac{(q-q^*)\pi}{2}\right)^{1-\frac{q^*}{q}}}.$$

Lemma 5. *Let $\beta > 0$, $(q_1, q_2, q_3, q) \in D$ be arbitrarily fixed. Consider the surface $S(\beta, q_1, q_2, q_3, q)$ defined in Lemma 4. The characteristic Equation (13) has a pair of complex conjugated roots on the imaginary axis of the complex plane if and only if $(\alpha_1, \alpha_2, \alpha_3) \in S(\beta, q_1, q_2, q_3, q)$.*

Proof. The characteristic Equation (13) has a pair of pure imaginary roots if and only if there exists $\omega > 0$ such that

$$\Delta(s; \alpha_1, \alpha_2, \alpha_3, \beta, q_1, q_2, q_3, q) = 0, \quad \text{where } s = i(\beta\omega)^{\frac{1}{q}},$$

which is equivalent to

$$i^q \beta\omega + \alpha_1 i^{q_1} (\beta\omega)^{\frac{q_1}{q}} + \alpha_2 i^{q_2} (\beta\omega)^{\frac{q_2}{q}} + \alpha_3 i^{q_3} (\beta\omega)^{\frac{q_3}{q}} + \delta = 0.$$

Dividing the previous relation by β, we have:

$$i^q \omega + \alpha_1 \beta^{\frac{q_1}{q}-1} \omega^{\frac{q_1}{q}} i^{q_1} + \alpha_2 \beta^{\frac{q_2}{q}-1} \omega^{\frac{q_2}{q}} i^{q_2} + \alpha_3 \beta^{\frac{q_3}{q}-1} \omega^{\frac{q_3}{q}} i^{q_3} + 1 = 0.$$

Taking the real and imaginary part from the relation from above, we obtain the following system:

$$\begin{cases} \omega \cos\frac{q\pi}{2} + \alpha_1 \beta^{\frac{q_1}{q}-1} \omega^{\frac{q_1}{q}} \cos\frac{q_1\pi}{2} + \alpha_2 \beta^{\frac{q_2}{q}-1} \omega^{\frac{q_2}{q}} \cos\frac{q_2\pi}{2} + \alpha_3 \beta^{\frac{q_3}{q}-1} \omega^{\frac{q_3}{q}} \cos\frac{q_3\pi}{2} + 1 = 0 \\ \omega \sin\frac{q\pi}{2} + \alpha_1 \beta^{\frac{q_1}{q}-1} \omega^{\frac{q_1}{q}} \sin\frac{q_1\pi}{2} + \alpha_2 \beta^{\frac{q_2}{q}-1} \omega^{\frac{q_2}{q}} \sin\frac{q_2\pi}{2} + \alpha_3 \beta^{\frac{q_3}{q}-1} \omega^{\frac{q_3}{q}} \sin\frac{q_3\pi}{2} = 0 \end{cases}$$

We solve the previous system for α_1 and α_2 and, denoting $\eta = \alpha_3 \omega^{\frac{q_3}{q}} \delta^{\frac{q_3}{q}-1}$, it follows that the characteristic Equation (13) has a pair of complex conjugated roots on the imaginary axis if and only if the triplet $(\alpha_1, \alpha_2, \alpha_3)$ belongs to the parametric surface $S(\beta, q_1, q_2, q_3, q)$ defined in Lemma 4. □

Theorem 3 (Fractional-order-dependent results).

Let $\beta > 0$, $0 < q_1 < q_2 < q_3 < q \leq 2$ be arbitrarily fixed. Consider the surface $S(\beta, q_1, q_2, q_3, q)$ previously defined. The trivial solution of Equation (12) is $\mathcal{O}(t^{-q'})$-asymptotically stable (where $q' = \min\{\{q\}, \{q_1\}, \{q_2\}, \{q_3\}\}$) if and only if $(\alpha_1, \alpha_2, \alpha_3)$ belongs to the connected component of the three-dimensional space bounded by the surface $S(\beta, q_1, q_2, q_3, q)$, which contains the positive octant.

Proof. If $\alpha_i > 0$, for $i = \overline{1,3}$, it follows from Lemma 2 that the trivial solution of Equation (12) is asymptotically stable. As the parameters α_i, $i = \overline{1,3}$ are varied, the qualitative behaviour may change if and only if $(\alpha_1, \alpha_2, \alpha_3) \in S(\beta, q_1, q_2, q_3, q)$, which follows from Lemma 5. Therefore, it is clear that if $(\alpha_1, \alpha_2, \alpha_3)$ belongs to the open connected region, which contains the positive octant, then the trivial solution of Equation (12) is asymptotically stable.

In what follows, we verify the transversality condition.

Let $\beta > 0$, $(q_1, q_2, q_3, q) \in D$ be arbitrarily fixed. Consider the surface $S(\beta, q_1, q_2, q_3, q)$ defined in Lemma 4. For simplicity, denote $Q_j = \frac{q_j}{q}$, with $j \in \{1, 2, 3\}$.

We first compute the cross product of the vectors $\left(\frac{\partial \alpha_1}{\partial \omega}, \frac{\partial \alpha_2}{\partial \omega}, \frac{\partial \alpha_3}{\partial \omega}\right)$ and $\left(\frac{\partial \alpha_1}{\partial \eta}, \frac{\partial \alpha_2}{\partial \eta}, \frac{\partial \alpha_3}{\partial \eta}\right)$, which is the normal vector to the surface $S(\beta, q_1, q_2, q_3, q)$.

$$\vec{N} = \left(\frac{\partial \alpha_1}{\partial \omega}, \frac{\partial \alpha_2}{\partial \omega}, \frac{\partial \alpha_3}{\partial \omega}\right) \times \left(\frac{\partial \alpha_1}{\partial \eta}, \frac{\partial \alpha_2}{\partial \eta}, \frac{\partial \alpha_3}{\partial \eta}\right) =$$

$$= \left(\frac{\partial \alpha_2}{\partial \omega} \cdot \frac{\partial \alpha_3}{\partial \eta} - \frac{\partial \alpha_2}{\partial \eta} \cdot \frac{\partial \alpha_3}{\partial \omega}, \frac{\partial \alpha_1}{\partial \eta} \cdot \frac{\partial \alpha_3}{\partial \omega} - \frac{\partial \alpha_1}{\partial \omega} \cdot \frac{\partial \alpha_3}{\partial \eta}, \frac{\partial \alpha_1}{\partial \omega} \cdot \frac{\partial \alpha_2}{\partial \eta} - \frac{\partial \alpha_1}{\partial \eta} \cdot \frac{\partial \alpha_2}{\partial \omega}\right)$$

where

$$\frac{\partial \alpha_1}{\partial \omega} = \beta^{1-Q_1} \omega^{-Q_1-1}[-Q_1 \eta \rho(q_3-q_2, q_2-q_1) - Q_1 \omega \rho(q-q_2, q_2-q_1) +$$
$$+ Q_1 \rho(q_2, q_2-q_1) + \omega \rho(q-q_2, q_2-q_1)]$$

$$\frac{\partial \alpha_2}{\partial \omega} = \beta^{1-Q_2} \omega^{-Q_2-1}[-Q_2 \eta \rho(q_3-q_1, q_1-q_2) - Q_2 \omega \rho(q-q_1, q_1-q_2) +$$
$$+ Q_2 \rho(q_1, q_1-q_2) + \omega \rho(q-q_1, q_1-q_2)]$$

$$\frac{\partial \alpha_3}{\partial \omega} = -Q_3 \eta \beta^{1-Q_3} \omega^{-Q_3-1}$$

$$\frac{\partial \alpha_1}{\partial \eta} = \beta^{1-Q_1} \omega^{-Q_1} \rho(q_3-q_2, q_2-q_1)$$

$$\frac{\partial \alpha_2}{\partial \eta} = \beta^{1-Q_2} \omega^{-Q_2} \rho(q_3-q_1, q_1-q_2)$$

$$\frac{\partial \alpha_3}{\partial \eta} = \beta^{1-Q_3} \omega^{-Q_3}$$

Let $s(\alpha_1, \alpha_2, \alpha_3, \beta, q_1, q_2, q_3, q)$ denote the root of the characteristic function $\Delta(s; \alpha_1, \alpha_2, \alpha_3, \beta, q_1, q_2, q_3, q)$ which satisfies $s(\alpha_1^*, \alpha_2^*, \alpha_3^*, \beta, q_1, q_2, q_3, q) = i(\beta\omega)^{\frac{1}{q}}$, with $(\alpha_1^*, \alpha_2^*, \alpha_3^*) \in S(\beta, q_1, q_2, q_3, q)$.

Taking the derivative with respect to α_1 in the characteristic equation

$$s^q + \alpha_1 s^{q_1} + \alpha_2 s^{q_2} + \alpha_3 s^{q_3} + \beta = 0,$$

we obtain

$$q s^{q-1} \frac{\partial s}{\partial \alpha_1} + s^{q_1} + \alpha_1 q_1 s^{q_1-1} \frac{\partial s}{\partial \alpha_1} + \alpha_2 q_2 s^{q_2-1} \frac{\partial s}{\partial \alpha_1} + \alpha_3 q_3 s^{q_3-1} \frac{\partial s}{\partial \alpha_1} = 0,$$

which is equivalent to

$$\frac{\partial s}{\partial \alpha_1} = \frac{-s^{q_1}}{q s^{q-1} + \alpha_1 q_1 s^{q_1-1} + \alpha_2 q_2 s^{q_2-1} + \alpha_3 q_3 s^{q_3-1}}.$$

Taking the real part of the previous relation, it follows that:

$$\frac{\partial \Re(s)}{\partial \alpha_1} = \Re\left(\frac{\partial s}{\partial \alpha_1}\right) = \Re\left(\frac{-s^{q_1}}{q s^{q-1} + \alpha_1 q_1 s^{q_1-1} + \alpha_2 q_2 s^{q_2-1} + \alpha_3 q_3 s^{q_3-1}}\right).$$

We have:

$$\left.\frac{\partial \Re(s)}{\partial \alpha_1}\right|_{(\alpha_1^*,\alpha_2^*,\alpha_3^*)} = \Re\left(\frac{-(i(\beta\omega)^{\frac{1}{q}})^{q_1}}{P(i(\beta\omega)^{\frac{1}{q}})}\right) = -(\beta\omega)^{\frac{q_1}{q}}\Re\left(\frac{i^{q_1}\overline{P(i(\beta\omega)^{\frac{1}{q}})}}{|P(i(\beta\omega)^{\frac{1}{q}})|^2}\right) =$$

$$= \frac{-(\beta\omega)^{\frac{q_1}{q}}}{|P(i(\beta\omega)^{\frac{1}{q}})|^2}\Re\left(i^{q_1}\overline{P(i(\beta\omega)^{\frac{1}{q}})}\right).$$

Computing $\Re\left(i^{q_1}\overline{P(i(\beta\omega)^{\frac{1}{q}})}\right)$ we obtain:

$$\Re\left(i^{q_1}\overline{P(i(\beta\omega)^{\frac{1}{q}})}\right) = \Re\left(\overline{i^{q_1}}P(i(\beta\omega)^{\frac{1}{q}})\right) =$$

$$= \Re\left(i^{-q_1}(\beta\omega)^{-\frac{1}{q}}\left[qi^{q-1}\beta\omega + \alpha_1^* q_1 i^{q_1-1}(\beta\omega)^{Q_1} + \alpha_2^* q_2 i^{q_2-1}(\beta\omega)^{Q_2} + \alpha_3^* q_3 i^{q_3-1}(\beta\omega)^{Q_3}\right]\right)$$

$$= \Re(q\beta^{1-\frac{1}{q}}\omega^{-\frac{1}{q}}[i^{q-q_1-1}\omega + Q_1 i^{-1}\omega^{Q_1} h(\omega,\eta,q_1,q_2,q_3,q) +$$

$$+ Q_2 i^{q_2-q-1}\omega^{Q_2} h(\omega,\eta,q_2,q_1,q_3,q) + Q_3 i^{q_3-q_1-1}\eta])$$

As the second term from the precious relation is purely imaginary and

$$\Re(i^{q-q_1-1}) = \sin\frac{(q-q_1)\pi}{2}, \quad \Re(i^{q_2-q_1-1}) = \sin\frac{(q_2-q_1)\pi}{2}, \quad \Re(i^{q_3-q_1-1}) = \sin\frac{(q_3-q_1)\pi}{2},$$

it follows that

$$\Re\left(\overline{i^{q_1}}P(i(\beta\omega)^{\frac{1}{q}})\right) = q\beta^{1-\frac{1}{q}}\omega^{-\frac{1}{q}}\left(\omega\sin(q-q_1)\frac{\pi}{2} + Q_2\sin(q_2-q_1)\frac{\pi}{2}\left[\eta\rho(q_3-q_1,q_1-q_2) + \right.\right.$$

$$\left.\left.+ \omega\rho(q-q_1,q_1-q_2) - \rho(q_1,q_1-q_2)\right] + Q_3\eta\sin(q_3-q_1)\frac{\pi}{2}\right)$$

A simple computation leads to

$$\left.\frac{\partial \Re(s)}{\partial \alpha_1}\right|_{(\alpha_1^*,\alpha_2^*,\alpha_3^*)} = \frac{q\beta^{Q_1+Q_2+Q_3-\frac{1}{q}-1}\omega^{Q_1+Q_2+Q_3-\frac{1}{q}+1}}{|P(i(\beta\omega)^{\frac{1}{q}})|^2\sin(q_2-q_1)\frac{\pi}{2}}\cdot\left(\frac{\partial \alpha_2}{\partial \omega}\cdot\frac{\partial \alpha_3}{\partial \eta} - \frac{\partial \alpha_2}{\partial \eta}\cdot\frac{\partial \alpha_3}{\partial \omega}\right).$$

Following similar steps, we can deduce that

$$\left.\frac{\partial \Re(s)}{\partial \alpha_2}\right|_{(\alpha_1^*,\alpha_2^*,\alpha_3^*)} = \frac{q\beta^{Q_1+Q_2+Q_3-\frac{1}{q}-1}\omega^{Q_1+Q_2+Q_3-\frac{1}{q}+1}}{|P(i(\beta\omega)^{\frac{1}{q}})|^2\sin(q_2-q_1)\frac{\pi}{2}}\cdot\left(\frac{\partial \alpha_1}{\partial \eta}\cdot\frac{\partial \alpha_3}{\partial \omega} - \frac{\partial \alpha_1}{\partial \omega}\cdot\frac{\partial \alpha_3}{\partial \eta}\right)$$

and

$$\left.\frac{\partial \Re(s)}{\partial \alpha_3}\right|_{(\alpha_1^*,\alpha_2^*,\alpha_3^*)} = \frac{q\beta^{Q_1+Q_2+Q_3-\frac{1}{q}-1}\omega^{Q_1+Q_2+Q_3-\frac{1}{q}+1}}{|P(i(\beta\omega)^{\frac{1}{q}})|^2\sin(q_2-q_1)\frac{\pi}{2}}\cdot\left(\frac{\partial \alpha_1}{\partial \omega}\cdot\frac{\partial \alpha_2}{\partial \eta} - \frac{\partial \alpha_1}{\partial \eta}\cdot\frac{\partial \alpha_2}{\partial \omega}\right).$$

Therefore, we obtain that

$$\nabla \Re(s)(\alpha_1^*,\alpha_2^*,\alpha_3^*) = \left.\left(\frac{\partial \Re(s)}{\partial \alpha_1},\frac{\partial \Re(s)}{\partial \alpha_2},\frac{\partial \Re(s)}{\partial \alpha_3}\right)\right|_{(\alpha_1^*,\alpha_2^*,\alpha_3^*)} =$$

$$= \frac{q\beta^{Q_1+Q_2+Q_3-\frac{1}{q}-1}\omega^{Q_1+Q_2+Q_3-\frac{1}{q}+1}}{|P(i(\beta\omega)^{\frac{1}{q}})|^2\sin(q_2-q_1)\frac{\pi}{2}}\left(\frac{\partial \alpha_1}{\partial \omega},\frac{\partial \alpha_2}{\partial \omega},\frac{\partial \alpha_3}{\partial \omega}\right)\times\left(\frac{\partial \alpha_1}{\partial \eta},\frac{\partial \alpha_2}{\partial \eta},\frac{\partial \alpha_3}{\partial \eta}\right)$$

Thus, the vector $\nabla \Re(s)(\alpha_1^*, \alpha_2^*, \alpha_3^*)$ is a normal vector to the surface $S(\beta, q_1, q_2, q_3, q)$. Moreover, the vector $\nabla \Re(s)(\alpha_1^*, \alpha_2^*, \alpha_3^*)$ points away from the open connected region which contains the positive octant and is bounded by the surface $S(\beta, q_1, q_2, q_3, q)$, as it is perpendicular to the tangent vector $\left(\dfrac{\partial \alpha_1}{\partial \eta}, \dfrac{\partial \alpha_2}{\partial \eta}, \dfrac{\partial \alpha_3}{\partial \eta} \right)$, where $\dfrac{\partial \alpha_i}{\partial \eta} > 0, i = \overline{1,3}$. □

Remark 6. *In Figure 2, we have plotted three parametric surfaces $S(\beta, q_1, q_2, q_3, q)$ for $\beta = 5$ and different values of the fractional orders q_1, q_2, q_3, q such that $0 < q_1 < q_2 < q_3 < q \leq 2$ in the $(\alpha_1, \alpha_2, \alpha_3)$-space, along with the fractional-order-independent stability and instability regions, respectively (plotted red and blue). We theorize that the reunion of all the parametric surfaces $S(\beta, q_1, q_2, q_3, q)$ will fill the space between the fractional-order-independent stability and instability regions and will not intersect neither of them.*

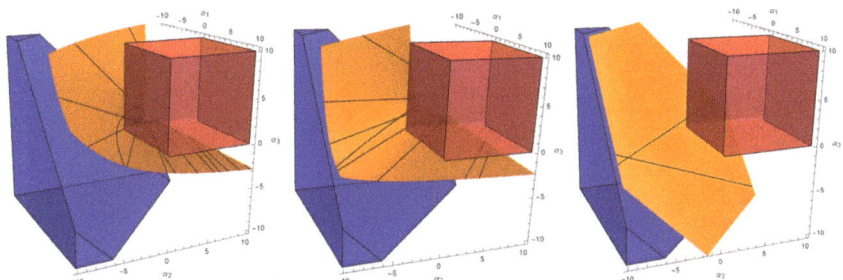

Figure 2. Parametric surfaces $S(\beta, q_1, q_2, q_3, q)$ (yellow) for $\beta = 5$ and several values of the fractional orders: $q_1 = 0.4, q_2 = 0.8, q_3 = 1.5, q = 1.8$ (left), $q_1 = 0.2, q_2 = 0.3, q_3 = 1.2, q = 1.5$ (centre) and $q_1 = 0.7, q_2 = 0.71, q_3 = 0.72, q = 1.5$ (right). The blue and red regions represent the *fractional-order-independent* instability and asymptotic stability regions, given by Lemma 1 and Lemma 2, respectively.

Example 5. *To exemplify the previous theoretical results, we consider a mathematical model of a damped unforced Duffing-type oscillator expressed as the following multi-term fractional differential equation:*

$$mx'' + c_1 {}^C D^{q_1} x + c_2 {}^C D^{q_2} x + cx' + k_1 x + k_2 x^3 = 0, \quad \text{with } q_1, q_2 \in (0,1) \quad (14)$$

where $m > 0$ is the mass, k_1 and k_2 are the linear and non-linear stiffness coefficients, respectively, while c_1, c_2 and c are linear viscous damping coefficients [30]. The linearization of this equation at the trivial equilibrium represents a particular case of Equation (12) with $q = 2$ and $q_3 = 1$.

By Lemma 2 it follows that if $c_1 > 0$, $c_2 > 0$, $c > 0$ and $k_1 > 0$, then the trivial equilibrium of (14) is asymptotically stable, regardless of the choice of the fractional order q_1. Nevertheless, if a negative damping coefficient c is chosen, the stability of the trivial solution depends on the fractional orders q_1 and q_2.

For example, if $m = 1, c_1 = 1, c_2 = 0.1, c_3 = -1, k_1 = 4$ and $k_2 = 1$, for $q_2 = 0.95$, then the corresponding critical value of the fractional order q_1 is found numerically by solving the parametric equations of the surface defined in Lemma 4 for ω, η and q_1, leading to $q_1^* = 0.885052$. The trivial equilibrium of Equation (14) is asymptotically stable if and only if $q_1 > q_1^*$. The numerical solutions [31,32] of Equation (14) with respect to several values of q_1 are plotted in Figure 3, showing that when $q_1 < q_1^*$, the trivial solution of (14) becomes unstable and persistent oscillations appear.

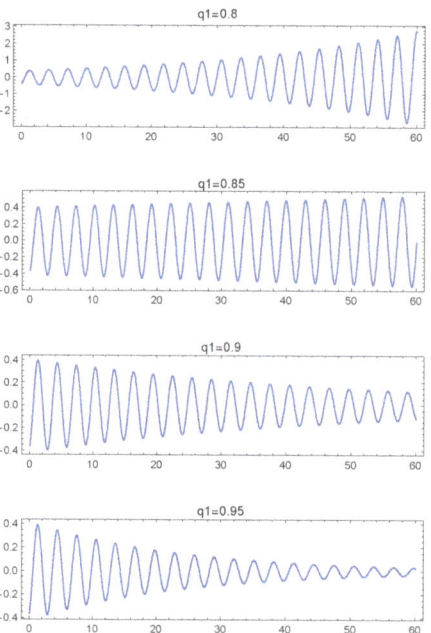

Figure 3. Numerical solutions of (14) for $m = 1$, $c_1 = 1$, $c_2 = 0.1$, $c_3 = -1$, $k_1 = 4$ and $k_2 = 1$, for $q_2 = 0.95$ and several values of the fractional order q_1.

7. Conclusions

In this paper, on the one hand, we have focused our attention on determining general **fractional-order-independent** stability and instability conditions for multi-term fractional-order differential equations of an arbitrary number of terms. In fact, the obtained conditions are formulated as easily verifiable inequalities involving the constant coefficients of the linear fractional differential equations.

On the other hand, we also presented a brief overview of **fractional-order-dependent** stability and instability conditions for two-term and three-term fractional-order differential equations, previously reported in the literature. As a generalisation, we provided an investigation of fractional-order dependent stability and instability conditions for four-term fractional-differential equations.

Employing similar techniques as in the proof of Theorem 3, these results can further be generalized to the case of fractional differential equations with multiple Caputo derivatives, leading to a characterisation of the hypersurface, which represents the boundary of the stability region in the hyperspace of coefficients. However, it becomes clear that fractional-order-dependent stability and instability conditions for multi-term fractional differential equations cannot be expressed in a simple way, and as expected, the complexity of the problem increases along with the number of Caputo derivatives included in the fractional differential equation. As a possible direction for future research, our aim is to find a way to overcome this limitation, possibly by finding a different parametrization of the hypersurface at the boundary of the stability region.

Moreover, at this stage, the results presented in this paper represent a timely review of the main contributions related to qualitatively characterizing the stability and instability properties of multi-term fractional-order differential equations with Caputo derivatives. Fractional-order dependent stability and instability properties for multi-order fractional differential equations having an arbitrary number of Caputo derivatives are still yet to be determined. Moreover, we foresee that this investigation shall become more arduous as we increase the number of fractional derivatives, or if we consider different types of fractional derivatives, such as the more general Prabhakar derivatives or derivatives with Sonine kernels.

Author Contributions: Conceptualization, O.B. and É.K.; methodology, O.B. and É.K.; software, O.B. and É.K.; validation, O.B. and É.K.; formal analysis, O.B. and É.K.; investigation, O.B. and É.K.; resources, O.B. and É.K.; data curation, O.B. and É.K.; writing—original draft preparation, O.B. and É.K.; writing—review and editing, O.B. and É.K.; visualization, O.B. and É.K.; supervision, O.B. and É.K.; project administration, O.B. and É.K.; funding acquisition, O.B. and É.K. All authors have read and agreed to the published version of the manuscript.

Funding: This research received no external funding.

Data Availability Statement: Not applicable.

Conflicts of Interest: The authors declare no conflict of interest.

References

1. Cottone, G.; Paola, M.D.; Santoro, R. A novel exact representation of stationary colored Gaussian processes (fractional differential approach). *J. Phys. A Math. Theor.* **2010**, *43*, 085002. [CrossRef]
2. Engheia, N. On the role of fractional calculus in electromagnetic theory. *IEEE Antennas Propag. Mag.* **1997**, *39*, 35–46. [CrossRef]
3. Henry, B.; Wearne, S. Existence of Turing instabilities in a two-species fractional reaction-diffusion system. *SIAM J. Appl. Math.* **2002**, *62*, 870–887. [CrossRef]
4. Heymans, N.; Bauwens, J.C. Fractal rheological models and fractional differential equations for viscoelastic behavior. *Rheol. Acta* **1994**, *33*, 210–219. [CrossRef]
5. Mainardi, F. Fractional Relaxation-Oscillation and Fractional Phenomena. *Chaos Solitons Fractals* **1996**, *7*, 1461–1477. [CrossRef]
6. Torvik, P.; Bagley, R. On the appearance of the fractional derivative in the behavior of real materials. *J. Appl. Mech.* **1984**, *51*, 294–298. [CrossRef]
7. Mainardi, F. Fractional calculus. Some basic problems in continuum and statistical mechanics. In *Fractals and Fractional Calculus in Continuum Mechanics*; Carpinteri, A., Mainardi, F., Eds.; Springer: Vienna, Austria, 1997.
8. Seredyńska, M.; Hanyga, A. Nonlinear differential equations with fractional damping with applications to the 1dof and 2dof pendulum. *Acta Mech.* **2005**, *176*, 169–183. [CrossRef]
9. Chen, L.; Wang, W.; Li, Z.; Zhu, W. Stationary response of Duffing oscillator with hardening stiffness and fractional derivative. *Int. J. Non-Linear Mech.* **2013**, *48*, 44–50. [CrossRef]
10. Guo, F.; Zhu, C.; Cheng, X.; Li, H. Stochastic resonance in a fractional harmonic oscillator subject to random mass and signal-modulated noise. *Phys. Stat. Mech. Its Appl.* **2016**, *459*, 86–91. [CrossRef]
11. Diethelm, K. *The Analysis of Fractional Differential Equations*; Springer: Berlin/Heidelberg, Germany, 2004.
12. Podlubny, I. *Fractional Differential Equations*; Academic Press: Cambridge, MA, USA, 1999.
13. Kilbas, A.; Srivastava, H.; Trujillo, J. *Theory and Applications of Fractional Differential Equations*; Elsevier: Amsterdam, The Netherlands, 2006.
14. Čermák, J.; Kisela, T. Asymptotic stability of dynamic equations with two fractional terms: continuous versus discrete case. *Fract. Calc. Appl. Anal.* **2015**, *18*, 437. [CrossRef]
15. Čermák, J.; Kisela, T. Stability properties of two-term fractional differential equations. *Nonlinear Dyn.* **2015**, *80*, 1673–1684. [CrossRef]
16. Jiao, Z.; Chen, Y.Q. Stability of fractional-order linear time-invariant systems with multiple noncommensurate orders. *Comput. Math. Appl.* **2012**, *64*, 3053–3058. [CrossRef]
17. Daftardar-Gejji, V.; Bhalekar, S. Boundary value problems for multi-term fractional differential equations. *J. Math. Anal. Appl.* **2008**, *345*, 754–765. [CrossRef]
18. Luchko, Y. Initial-boundary-value problems for the generalized multi-term time-fractional diffusion equation. *J. Math. Anal. Appl.* **2011**, *374*, 538–548. [CrossRef]
19. Diethelm, K.; Siegmund, S.; Tuan, H. Asymptotic behavior of solutions of linear multi-order fractional differential systems. *Fract. Calc. Appl. Anal.* **2017**, *20*, 1165–1195. [CrossRef]
20. Li, C.; Zhang, F. A survey on the stability of fractional differential equations. *Eur. Phys. J.-Spec. Top.* **2011**, *193*, 27–47. [CrossRef]
21. Radwan, A.; Soliman, A.; Elwakil, A.; Sedeek, A. On the stability of linear systems with fractional-order elements. *Chaos Solitons Fractals* **2009**, *40*, 2317–2328. [CrossRef]
22. Ahmad, D.; Agarwal, R.P.; ur Rahman, G. Formulation, Solution's Existence, and Stability Analysis for Multi-Term System of Fractional-Order Differential Equations. *Symmetry* **2022**, *14*, 1342. [CrossRef]
23. Deng, W.; Li, C.; Guo, Q. Analysis of fractional differential equations with multi-orders. *Fractals* **2007**, *15*, 173–182. [CrossRef]
24. Brandibur, O.; Kaslik, E. Stability analysis of multi-term fractional-differential equations with three fractional derivatives. *J. Math. Anal. Appl.* **2021**, *495*, 124751. [CrossRef]
25. Lorenzo, C.; Hartley, T.; Malti, R. Application of the principal fractional meta-trigonometric functions for the solution of linear commensurate-order time-invariant fractional differential equations. *Philos. Trans. R. Soc. A Math. Phys. Eng. Sci.* **2013**, *371*, 20120151. [CrossRef] [PubMed]

26. Li, Y.; Chen, Y.; Podlubny, I. Mittag-Leffler stability of fractional order nonlinear dynamic systems. *Automatica* **2009**, *45*, 1965–1969. [CrossRef]
27. Gorenflo, R.; Mainardi, F. Fractional calculus, integral and differential equations of fractional order. In *Fractals and Fractional Calculus in Continuum Mechanics*; Carpinteri, A., Mainardi, F., Eds.; CISM Courses and Lecture Notes; Springer: Vienna, Austria, 1997; Volume 378, pp. 223–276.
28. Doetsch, G. *Introduction to the Theory and Application of the Laplace Transformation*; Springer: Berlin/Heidelberg, Germany, 1974.
29. Čermák, J.; Kisela, T. Exact and discretized stability of the Bagley–Torvik equation. *J. Comput. Appl. Math.* **2014**, *269*, 53–67. [CrossRef]
30. Mani, A.K.; Narayanan, M. Analytical and numerical solution of an n-term fractional nonlinear dynamic oscillator. *Nonlinear Dyn.* **2020**, *100*, 999–1012. [CrossRef]
31. Diethelm, K.; Luchko, Y. Numerical solution of linear multi-term initial value problems of fractional order. *J. Comput. Anal. Appl* **2004**, *6*, 243–263.
32. Garrappa, R. Numerical solution of fractional differential equations: A survey and a software tutorial. *Mathematics* **2018**, *6*, 16. [CrossRef]

Disclaimer/Publisher's Note: The statements, opinions and data contained in all publications are solely those of the individual author(s) and contributor(s) and not of MDPI and/or the editor(s). MDPI and/or the editor(s) disclaim responsibility for any injury to people or property resulting from any ideas, methods, instructions or products referred to in the content.

Article

Constructing Analytical Solutions of the Fractional Riccati Differential Equations Using Laplace Residual Power Series Method

Aliaa Burqan *, Aref Sarhan and Rania Saadeh

Department of Mathematics, Zarqa University, Zarqa 13132, Jordan
* Correspondence: aliaaburqan@zu.edu.jo

Abstract: In this article, a hybrid numerical technique combining the Laplace transform and residual power series method is used to construct a series solution of the nonlinear fractional Riccati differential equation in the sense of Caputo fractional derivative. The proposed method is implemented to construct analytical series solutions of the target equation. The method is tested for eminent examples and the obtained results demonstrate the accuracy and efficiency of this technique by comparing it with other numerical methods.

Keywords: fractional Riccati differential equation; Laplace transform; approximate solution; residual power series

1. Introduction

The Riccati equation was named after Count Jacopo Francesco Riccati (1676–1754), an Italian nobleman [1]. This sort of equation has a long history of use in random processes, optimal control and other fields [2–9]. In many research studies, the fractional Riccati differential equation has emerged as a more complete form with a different value of fractional derivative order.

Numerous methods, including Laplace transforms, the Chebyshev wavelet operational matrix approach, the homotopy method, the Pade–variational iteration method, the finite difference method, the Adomian decomposition method and others [10–24] are devoted to solving fractional differential equations. The fractional Riccati equation has been successfully solved using the residual power series method (RPSM) [25]. It is a model and simple technique for generating approximate series solutions to differential equations. The Laplace residual power series method (LRPSM), on the other hand, was created in [26] to solve both linear and nonlinear fractional differential equations.

The LRPSM recommends using an approach that replicates the RPSM, but with a novel mechanism that is simpler than the RPSM, in which it uses the concept of the limit in determining the expansion coefficients, which speeds up the work of the MATHEMATICA software in performing symbolic and numerical calculations of the problem.

The motivation of this paper is to apply the LRPSM to solve the quadratic fractional Riccati differential equation. The accuracy and effectiveness of the method is clarified by displaying numerical examples and comparing the solutions with the results of some approved approaches.

The novelty of this work is illustrated in presenting the solution of the Ricatti equation in a form of rapidly convergent series using the LRPSM. The proposed method is simpler and faster than other numerical methods in establishing series solutions without needing linearization, discretization or differentiations. As a result, it could generate many terms of the series solutions with fewer efforts in comparison to other numerical methods and it could also be programed easily using computer software such as Mathematica.

2. Basic Concepts and Theorems

The definition of the Caputo fractional derivative and its properties are introduced in this section. In addition, we present some essential theories related to fractional Taylor expansion that will be used to create a series solution of the nonlinear fractional Riccati differential equation.

Definition 1. *The Caputo fractional derivative of order $\beta > 0$ is given by*

$$\mathfrak{D}^\beta u(t) = \begin{cases} \frac{1}{\Gamma(\beta)} \int_0^t (t-\omega)^{\beta-1} u^{(n)}(\omega)\, d\omega, & n-1 < \beta < n,\ t > \omega \geq 0 \\ u^{(n)}(t), & \beta = n. \end{cases}$$

In the following, we mention some popular properties of $\mathfrak{D}^\beta$ that are useful in our work.

$$\mathfrak{D}^\beta c = 0$$

$$\mathfrak{D}^\beta t^\alpha = \frac{\Gamma(\alpha+1)}{\Gamma(\alpha+1-\beta)} t^{\alpha-\beta}$$

where $\alpha > -1, c \in \mathbb{R}, n-1 < \beta < n$ and $t \geq 0$. For more properties about the operator $\mathfrak{D}^\beta$, see Ref. [27].

Definition 2. *Let $u(t)$ be a piecewise continuous function on the interval $[0, \infty]$ of exponential order δ, the Laplace transform of $u(t)$, $U(s)$ is given by*

$$U(s) = \mathcal{L}[u(t)] = \int_0^\infty e^{-st} u(t)\, dt,\ s > \delta,$$

and the inverse Laplace transform of $U(s)$ is given by

$$u(t) = \mathcal{L}^{-1}[U(s)] = \int_{z-i\infty}^{z+i\infty} e^{st} U(s)\, ds,\ z = \text{Re}(s) > z_0.$$

We summarize the necessary properties of the Laplace transform and its inverse in the following lemma.

Lemma 1 ([26]). *Let $u(t), v(t)$ be a piecewise continuous function on the interval $[0, \infty]$. If $U(s) = \mathcal{L}[u(t)]$, $V(s) = \mathcal{L}[v(t)]$ and $a, b \in \mathbb{R}$, then*

i. $\mathcal{L}[au(t) + bv(t)] = aU(s) + bV(s)$.
ii. $\mathcal{L}^{-1}[aU(s) + bV(s)] = au(t) + bv(t)$.
iii. $\lim_{s \to \infty} sU(s) = u(0)$
iv. $\mathcal{L}[t^\beta] = \frac{\Gamma(\beta+1)}{s^{\beta+1}}, n-1 < \beta < n.$
v. $\mathcal{L}[\mathfrak{D}^\beta u(t)] = s^\beta U(s) - \sum_{k=0}^{n-1} s^{\beta-k-1} u^{(k)}(0),\ n-1 < \beta < n.$

Theorem 1 ([26]). *Assume that $u(t)$ has the following fractional power series representation at about $t = 0$*

$$u(t) = \sum_{n=0}^\infty h_n t^{n\beta},\ 0 < \beta \leq 1,\ 0 \leq t < R, \tag{1}$$

where R is the radius of convergence of the series. If $\mathfrak{D}^{n\beta}u(t)$ is continuous on $(0, R)$, $n = 0, 1, 2, \ldots$, then the coefficients h_n's are given by

$$h_n = \frac{\mathfrak{D}^{n\beta}y(0)}{\Gamma(n\beta + 1)}, \; n = 0, 1, 2, \ldots. \tag{2}$$

Moreover, researchers in [26] have presented the basic theories and results that they used in the LRPSM as follows:

Theorem 2. *Assume that the fractional power series representation of the function $U(s) = \mathcal{L}[u(t)]$ is*

$$U(s) = \sum_{n=0}^{\infty} \frac{h_n}{s^{n\beta+1}}, 0 < \beta \leq 1, \; s > 0, \tag{3}$$

then $h_n = \mathfrak{D}^{n\beta}u(0)$, where $\mathfrak{D}^{n\beta} = \mathfrak{D}^{\beta}\mathfrak{D}^{\beta}\ldots\mathfrak{D}^{\beta}$ (n-times).

The next theorem provides the conditions of convergence of the series expansion in the previous equation.

Theorem 3. *Assume that $U(s) = \mathcal{L}[u(t)]$ has the fractional Taylor expansion in Equation (4). If $\left|s\,\mathcal{L}\left[\mathfrak{D}^{(n+1)\beta}u(t)\right]\right| \leq \mathcal{K}$ on (δ_1, δ_2), where $0 < \beta \leq 1$, then the remainder $\mathcal{R}_n(s)$ will satisfy the inequality*

$$|\mathcal{R}_n(s)| \leq \frac{\mathcal{K}}{s^{(n+1)\beta+1}}, \; \delta_1 < s \leq \delta_2. \tag{4}$$

3. Constructing the Laplace Residual Power Series Solution for the Nonlinear Fractional Riccati Differential Equation

This section explains how to use the LRPSM to solve the nonlinear fractional Riccati differential equation. The basic idea behind the offered approach is to apply the RPSM to the Laplace transform, which may be achieved by applying the Laplace transform to the stated equation before taking into consideration the suggested fractional Taylor series to describe the resulting equation's solution. We quickly calculate the unknown coefficients using justifications similar to those found in the typical RPSM. In order to obtain the solution in the original space, we then perform the inverse Laplace transform on the series expansion.

Now, we explain the algorithm of the LRPSM to construct a solution of the nonlinear fractional Riccati differential equation:

$$\mathfrak{D}^{\beta}u(t) + au(t) + bu^2(t) = c, \tag{5}$$

with initial condition

$$u(0) = d, \tag{6}$$

where $0 < \beta \leq 1$, $t \geq 0$ and a, b, c, d are constants.

Firstly, operate the Laplace transform on both sides of Equation (5) to get

$$\mathcal{L}\left[\mathfrak{D}^{\beta}u(t)\right] + a\mathcal{L}[u(t)] + b\mathcal{L}[u^2(t)] = \mathcal{L}[c] \tag{7}$$

Applying Lemma 1 and using the initial condition in Equation (6), Equation (7) can be written as

$$U(s) + \frac{a}{s^{\beta}}U(s) + \frac{b}{s^{\beta}}\mathcal{L}\left[\left(\mathcal{L}^{-1}[U(s)]\right)^2\right] - \frac{d}{s} - \frac{c}{s^{\beta+1}} = 0, \; s > \delta \geq 0. \tag{8}$$

Now, we construct a series solution for the nonlinear ordinary differential Equation (8); let the solution of Equation (8) have the representation form

$$U(s) = \sum_{n=0}^{\infty} \frac{h_n}{s^{n\beta+1}}, \quad s > \delta \geq 0 \qquad (9)$$

and the kth truncated series of $U(s)$ have the form

$$U_k(s) = \sum_{n=0}^{k} \frac{h_n}{s^{n\beta+1}}, \quad s > \delta \geq 0, \qquad (10)$$

where h_n are the to-be-determined constant coefficients.

The initial condition in Equation (6) with Lemma 1 part (iii) yielded that $h_0 = d$. So, the kth truncated series of $U(s)$ can be written as

$$U_k(s) = \frac{d}{s} + \sum_{n=1}^{k} \frac{h_n}{s^{n\beta+1}}, \quad s > \delta \geq 0 \qquad (11)$$

In the next step, to obtain the series' coefficients in Equation (11), we define the Laplace–residual function of Equation (8):

$$LRes(s) = U(s) + \frac{a}{s^\beta} U(s) + \frac{b}{s^\beta} \mathcal{L}\left[\left(\mathcal{L}^{-1}[U(s)]\right)^2\right] - \frac{d}{s} - \frac{c}{s^{\beta+1}}, \quad s > \delta \geq 0 \qquad (12)$$

The kth Laplace–residual function is as follows:

$$LRes_k(s) = U_k(s) + \frac{a}{s^\beta} U_k(s) + \frac{b}{s^\beta} \mathcal{L}\left[\left(\mathcal{L}^{-1}[U_k(s)]\right)^2\right] - \frac{d}{s} - \frac{c}{s^{\beta+1}}, \quad s > \delta \geq 0. \qquad (13)$$

It is clear that $LRes(s) = 0$, $s > 0$, and thus $s^{k\beta+1} LRes(s) = 0, k = 0,1,2,\ldots$. Therefore,

$$\lim_{s\to\infty}\left(s^{k\beta+1} LRes(x,s)\right) = 0, \; k = 0,1,2,\ldots. \qquad (14)$$

With a view to finding the first unknown coefficient h_1 in Equation (11), we substitute $U_1(s) = \frac{d}{s} + \frac{h_1}{s^{\beta+1}}$ in the first Laplace–residual function $LRes_1(s)$ to get

$$\begin{aligned}
LRes_1(s) &= \frac{h_1}{s^{\beta+1}} + \frac{a}{s^\beta}\left(\frac{d}{s} + \frac{h_1}{s^{\beta+1}}\right) + \frac{b}{s^\beta}\mathcal{L}\left[\left(\mathcal{L}^{-1}\left[\frac{d}{s} + \frac{h_1}{s^{\beta+1}}\right]\right)^2\right] - \frac{c}{s^{\beta+1}} \\
&= \frac{h_1}{s^{\beta+1}} + \frac{ad}{s^{\beta+1}} + \frac{a h_1}{s^{2\beta+1}} + \frac{b}{s^\beta}\mathcal{L}\left[\left(d + \frac{h_1 t^\beta}{\Gamma(\beta+1)}\right)^2\right] - \frac{c}{s^{\beta+1}} \\
&= \frac{1}{s^{\beta+1}}(h_1 + ad + bd^2 - c) + \frac{1}{s^{2\beta+1}}(a h_1 + 2bd h_1) + \frac{1}{s^{3\beta+1}}\left(\frac{b h_1^2 \, \Gamma(2\beta+1)}{\Gamma^2(\beta+1)}\right).
\end{aligned} \qquad (15)$$

Now, multiply both sides of the previous equation by $s^{\beta+1}$ to get

$$s^{\beta+1} LRes_1(r,s) = \left(h_1 + ad + bd^2 - c\right) + \frac{1}{s^\beta}(ah_1 + 2bd h_1) + \frac{1}{s^{2\beta}}\left(\frac{b h_1^2 \, \Gamma(2\beta+1)}{\Gamma^2(\beta+1)}\right). \qquad (16)$$

Finding the limit of Equation (16) as $s \to \infty$ and using the fact in Equation (14), we can calculate

$$h_1 = c - ad - bd^2. \qquad (17)$$

Now, we substitute $U_2(r,s) = \frac{d}{s} + \frac{h_1}{s^{\beta+1}} + \frac{h_2}{s^{2\beta+1}}$ into the second Laplace–residual function $LRes_2(s)$ to find the second unknown coefficient h_2 as follows

$$LRes_2(s) = \frac{1}{s^{\beta+1}}\left(h_1 + ad + bd^2 - c\right) + \frac{1}{s^{2\beta+1}}\left(h_2 + ah_1 + 2bd\, h_1\right)$$
$$+ \frac{1}{s^{3\beta+1}}\left(ah_2 + 2bd\, h_2 + \frac{bh_1^2\,\Gamma(2\beta+1)}{\Gamma^2(\beta+1)}\right) + \frac{1}{s^{4\beta+1}}\left(\frac{2bh_1\, h_2\Gamma(3\beta+1)}{\Gamma(\beta+1)\Gamma(2\beta+1)}\right) \quad (18)$$
$$+ \frac{1}{s^{5\beta+1}}\left(\frac{bh_2^2\,\Gamma(4\beta+1)}{\Gamma^2(2\beta+1)}\right).$$

Thus, h_2 is obtained by inserting the value of h_1 into Equation (18), then multiplying the resulting equation by $s^{2\beta+1}$ and valuating the limit as $s \to \infty$:

$$h_2 = -(a+2bd)h_1. \quad (19)$$

Again, to find h_3, we substitute $U_3(r,s) = \frac{d}{s} + \frac{h_1}{s^{\beta+1}} + \frac{h_2}{s^{2\beta+1}} + \frac{h_3}{s^{3\beta+1}}$ into the third Laplace–residual function $LRes_3(s)$ to get

$$LRes_3(s) = \frac{1}{s^{\beta+1}}\left(h_1 + ad + bd^2 - c\right) + \frac{1}{s^{2\beta+1}}\left(h_2 + ah_1 + 2bdh_1\right)$$
$$+ \frac{1}{s^{3\beta+1}}\left(h_3 + ah_2 + 2bdh_2 + \frac{bh_1^2\Gamma(2\beta+1)}{\Gamma^2(\beta+1)}\right)$$
$$+ \frac{1}{s^{4\beta+1}}\left(ah_3 + 2bdh_3 + \frac{2bh_1h_2\Gamma(3\beta+1)}{\Gamma(\beta+1)\Gamma(2\beta+1)}\right) \quad (20)$$
$$+ \frac{1}{s^{5\beta+1}}\left(\frac{bh_2^2\Gamma(4\beta+1)}{\Gamma^2(2\beta+1)} + \frac{2bh_1h_3\Gamma(4\beta+1)}{\Gamma(\beta+1)\Gamma(3\beta+1)}\right) + \frac{1}{s^{6\beta+1}}\left(\frac{2bh_2h_3\Gamma(5\beta+1)}{\Gamma(2\beta+1)\Gamma(3\beta+1)}\right)$$
$$+ \frac{1}{s^{7\beta+1}}\left(\frac{bh_3^2\Gamma(6\beta+1)}{\Gamma^2(3\beta+1)}\right).$$

Thus, h_3 is obtained by inserting the values of h_1, h_2 into Equation (20), then multiplying the resulting equation by $s^{3\beta+1}$ and evaluating the limit as $s \to \infty$:

$$h_3 = -\left((a+2bd)h_2 + \frac{bh_1^2\Gamma(2\beta+1)}{\Gamma^2(\beta+1)}\right). \quad (21)$$

To find h_4, substitute $U_3(r,s) = \frac{d}{s} + \frac{h_1}{s^{\beta+1}} + \frac{h_2}{s^{2\beta+1}} + \frac{h_3}{s^{3\beta+1}} + \frac{h_4}{s^{4\beta+1}}$ into the fourth Laplace–residual function $LRes_4(s)$ to get

$$LRes_4(s) = \frac{1}{s^{\beta+1}}\left(h_1 + ad + bd^2 - c\right) + \frac{1}{s^{2\beta+1}}\left(h_2 + ah_1 + 2bd\, h_1\right)$$
$$+ \frac{1}{s^{3\beta+1}}\left(h_3 + ah_2 + 2bd\, h_2 + \frac{bh_1^2\Gamma(2\beta+1)}{\Gamma^2(\beta+1)}\right)$$
$$+ \frac{1}{s^{4\beta+1}}\left(h_4 + ah_3 + 2bdh_3 + \frac{2bh_1h_2\,\Gamma(3\beta+1)}{\Gamma(\beta+1)\Gamma(2\beta+1)}\right)$$
$$+ \frac{1}{s^{5\beta+1}}\left(ah_4 + 2bdh_4 + \frac{bh_2^2\Gamma(4\beta+1)}{\Gamma^2(2\beta+1)} + \frac{2bh_1h_3\Gamma(4\beta+1)}{\Gamma(\beta+1)\Gamma(3\beta+1)}\right) \quad (22)$$
$$+ \frac{1}{s^{6\beta+1}}\left(\frac{2bh_2h_3\Gamma(5\beta+1)}{\Gamma(2\beta+1)\Gamma(3\beta+1)} + \frac{2bh_1h_4\Gamma(5\beta+1)}{\Gamma(\beta+1)\Gamma(4\beta+1)}\right)$$
$$+ \frac{1}{s^{7\beta+1}}\left(\frac{bh_3^2\Gamma(6\beta+1)}{\Gamma^2(3\beta+1)} + \frac{2bh_2h_4\Gamma(6\beta+1)}{\Gamma(2\beta+1)\Gamma(4\beta+1)}\right) + \frac{1}{s^{8\beta+1}}\left(\frac{2bh_3h_4\Gamma(7\beta+1)}{\Gamma(3\beta+1)\Gamma(4\beta+1)}\right)$$
$$+ \frac{1}{s^{9\beta+1}}\left(\frac{bh_4^2\Gamma(8\beta+1)}{\Gamma^2(4\beta+1)}\right).$$

With steps similar to the above, we have

$$h_4 = -\left((a+2bd)h_3 + \frac{2bh_1h_2\Gamma(3\beta+1)}{\Gamma(\beta+1)\Gamma(2\beta+1)}\right). \quad (23)$$

If we proceed in the same way by substituting the kth truncated series $U_k(s)$ into $LRes_k(s)$, multiplying the result by $s^{k\beta+1}$ and evaluating the limit as $s \to \infty$, h_{k+1} for $k \geq 2$ can be obtained by the following recurrence relation

$$h_{k+1} = -\left((a+2bd)h_k + \sum_{\substack{i+j=k \\ i,j \in \mathbb{Z}^+}}^{\infty} \frac{rbh_ih_j \Gamma(k\beta+1)}{\Gamma(i\beta+1)\Gamma(j\beta+1)} \right), \qquad (24)$$

where $= \begin{cases} 2, & |i-j| \neq 0 \\ 1, & |i-j| = 0 \end{cases}$, for $k = 2,3,4,\ldots$, $i+j = k$.

According to what was introduced, the series solution of Equation (8) is

$$U(s) = \frac{d}{s} + \frac{(c-ad-bd^2)}{s^{\beta+1}} - \frac{(a+2bd)(c-ad-bd^2)}{s^{2\beta+1}} + \sum_{k=3}^{\infty} \frac{h_k}{s^{k\beta+1}}, \quad s > \delta \geq 0. \qquad (25)$$

So, the series solution of the nonlinear fractional Riccati differential Equation (5) can be obtained by applying the inverse Laplace transform in the solution in Equation (25). Therefore, the Laplace residual power series solution of Equation (5) is given by

$$u(t) = d + \frac{(c-ad-bd^2)t^\beta}{\Gamma(\beta+1)} - \frac{(a+2bd)(c-ad-bd^2)t^{2\beta}}{\Gamma(2\beta+1)} + \sum_{k=3}^{\infty} \frac{h_k\, t^{k\beta}}{\Gamma(k\beta+1)}, t \geq 0. \qquad (26)$$

To test the accuracy of the proposed method, we introduce two kinds of error: absolute error and relative error, that are defined as follows:

$$\text{Absolute error} = |Exact\ value - Approximate\ value|,$$

$$\text{Relative error} = \left| \frac{Exact\ value - Approximate\ value}{Exact\ value} \right|$$

4. Illustrative Example

Example 1. *Consider the nonlinear fractional Riccati differential equation*

$$\mathfrak{D}^\beta u(t) - 2u(t) + u^2(t) = 1, \ 0 < \beta \leq 1, \qquad (27)$$

with the initial condition

$$u(0) = 0 \qquad (28)$$

Comparing Equations (27) and (28) with Equations (5) and (6), we find that $a = -2, b = 1$, $c = 1$ and $d = 0$. Therefore, the Laplace residual power series solution of Equation (27), according to the construction in Section 3, is as follows:

$$u(t) = \frac{t^\beta}{\Gamma(1+\beta)} + \frac{2t^{2\beta}}{\Gamma(1+2\beta)} + \frac{t^{3\beta}\left(4 - \frac{\Gamma(1+2\beta)}{\Gamma^2(1+\beta)}\right)}{\Gamma(1+3\beta)} + \frac{t^{4\beta}\left(2\left(4 - \frac{\Gamma(1+2\beta)}{\Gamma^2(1+\beta)}\right) - \frac{4\Gamma(1+3\beta)}{\Gamma(1+\beta)\Gamma(1+2\beta)}\right)}{\Gamma(1+4\beta)}$$

$$+ \frac{t^{5\beta}\left(2\left(2\left(4 - \frac{\Gamma(1+2\beta)}{\Gamma^2(1+\beta)}\right) - \frac{4\Gamma(1+3\beta)}{\Gamma(1+\beta)\Gamma(1+2\beta)}\right) - \frac{4\Gamma(1+4\beta)}{\Gamma^2(1+2\beta)} - \frac{2\left(4 - \frac{\Gamma(1+2\beta)}{\Gamma^2(1+\beta)}\right)\Gamma(1+4\beta)}{\Gamma(1+\beta)\Gamma(1+3\beta)}\right)}{\Gamma(1+5\beta)} \qquad (29)$$

$$+ \ldots$$

It should be noted here that the series solutions of Equations (27) and (28) obtained by the LRPSM are identical to those obtained by the RPSM [25].

In a particular case, when $\beta = 1$, the Laplace residual power series solution of the problem (27) is

$$u(t) = t + t^2 + \frac{t^3}{3} - \frac{t^4}{3} - \frac{7t^5}{15} - \frac{7t^6}{45} + \frac{53t^7}{315} + \frac{71t^8}{315} + \frac{197t^9}{2835} - \frac{1213t^{10}}{14175} + \dots \quad (30)$$

which matches with the identical terms of the series expansions of the exact solution

$$u(t) = 1 + \sqrt{2}\tanh\left(\sqrt{2}t + \frac{1}{2}Log\left(\frac{\sqrt{2}-1}{\sqrt{2}+1}\right)\right). \quad (31)$$

Figure 1 depicts the behavior of the approximate solutions $u(t)$, $t \in I = [0, 0.5]$ of problem (27), (28) for various values of $0 < \beta \leq 1$.

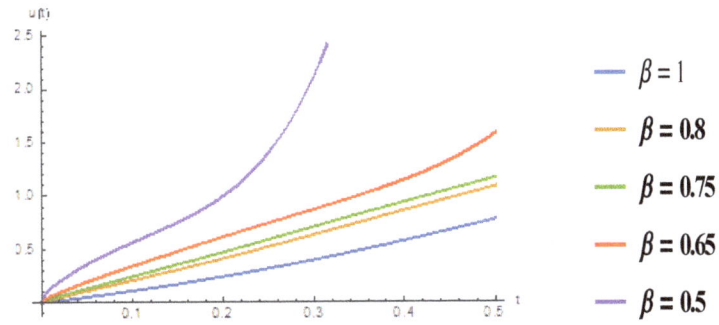

Figure 1. The behavior of the approximate solutions $u(t)$, $t \in I = [0, 0.5]$ of problem (27) and (28).

Table 1 presents comparison between our approach of problems (27) and (28) and other existing numerical methods, the Laplace–Adomian–Pade method (LAPM) [28] and the modified homotopy perturbation method (HPM) [29] for $\beta = 0.5$ and $\beta = 0.75$, respectively. As shown in the table, the results produced by the 10-term LRPS approximate solution compare favorably with those of other techniques, especially when the result is close to 1 while having components that are simple to calculate. As a result, by adding more terms, higher precision may be gained for varied values of β.

Table 1. Comparison for the solution of problems (27) and (28) with different methods for $\beta = 0.5, \beta = 0.75$.

$\beta = 0.5$	LRPS	LAPM	HPM	$\beta = 0.75$	LRPS	LAPM	HPM
t = 0.1	0.593178	0.356803	0.321730	t = 0.1	0.245431	0.193401	0.216866
t = 0.2	0.955952	0.922865	0.629666	t = 0.2	0.475107	0.454602	0.428892
t = 0.3	1.389321	1.634139	0.940941	t = 0.3	0.710342	0.784032	0.654614
t = 0.4	2.351819	2.204441	1.250737	t = 0.4	0.941954	1.161985	0.891404
t = 0.5	4.693042	2.400447	1.549439	t = 0.5	1.169808	1.543881	1.132763

Example 2. *Consider the nonlinear fractional Riccati differential equation*

$$\mathfrak{D}^\beta u(t) + u^2(t) = 1, \quad 0 < \beta \leq 1, \quad t \geq 0, \quad (32)$$

with the initial condition

$$u(0) = 0 \quad (33)$$

Comparing Equations (32) and (33) with Equations (5) and (6), we find that $a=0$, $b=1$, $c=1$ and $d=0$. Therefore, the Laplace residual power series solution of Equation (27), according to the construction in the previous section, is

$$u(t) = \frac{t^\beta}{\Gamma[1+\beta]} - \frac{t^{3\beta}\Gamma[1+2\beta]}{\Gamma[1+\beta]^2\Gamma[1+3\beta]} + \frac{2t^{5\beta}\Gamma[1+2\beta]\Gamma[1+4\beta]}{\Gamma[1+\beta]^3\Gamma[1+3\beta]\Gamma[1+5\beta]} + \frac{t^{7\beta}\left(-\frac{\Gamma[1+2\beta]^2\Gamma[1+6\beta]}{\Gamma[1+\beta]^4\Gamma[1+3\beta]^2} - \frac{4\Gamma[1+2\beta]\Gamma[1+4\beta]\Gamma[1+6\beta]}{\Gamma[1+\beta]^4\Gamma[1+3\beta]\Gamma[1+5\beta]}\right)}{\Gamma[1+7\beta]} +$$
$$t^{9\beta}\left(\frac{4\Gamma[1+2\beta]^2\Gamma[1+4\beta]\Gamma[1+8\beta]}{\Gamma[1+\beta]^5\Gamma[1+3\beta]^2\Gamma[1+5\beta]\Gamma[1+9\beta]} - \frac{2\left(-\frac{\Gamma[1+2\beta]^2\Gamma[1+6\beta]}{\Gamma[1+\beta]^4\Gamma[1+3\beta]^2} - \frac{4\Gamma[1+2\beta]\Gamma[1+4\beta]\Gamma[1+6\beta]}{\Gamma[1+\beta]^4\Gamma[1+3\beta]\Gamma[1+5\beta]}\right)\Gamma[1+8\beta]}{\Gamma[1+\beta]\Gamma[1+7\beta]\Gamma[1+9\beta]}\right) + \cdots \quad (34)$$

It should be noted here that the series solution of Equations (32) and (33) obtained by the LRPSM is identical to that obtained by the RPSM [25].

In a particular case, when $\beta = 1$, the Laplace residual power series solution of the problem (32) is

$$u_{11}(t) = t - \frac{t^3}{3} + \frac{2t^5}{15} - \frac{17t^7}{315} + \frac{62t^9}{2835} - \frac{1382t^{11}}{155925} + \ldots \quad (35)$$

which matches with the identical terms of the series expansions of the exact solution

$$u(t) = \left(e^{2t} - 1\right)\left(e^{2t} + 1\right)^{-1}.$$

Figure 2 depicts the behavior of the approximate solutions $u(t)$, $t \in I = [0, 0.5]$ of problems (32) and (33) for various values of $0 < \beta \leq 1$.

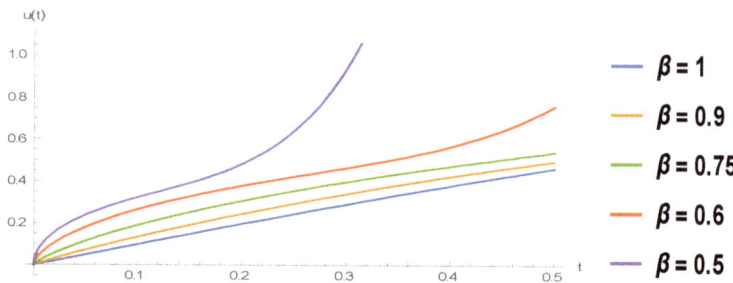

Figure 2. The behavior of the approximate solutions $u(t)$, $t \in I = [0, 0.5]$ of problems (32) and (33).

To test the accuracy of the approximate solution in Equation (35), we calculate in Table 2 two types of error, the absolute error and the relative error, that are defined, respectively, as follows:

Table 2. The absolute and relative errors of the 11th approximate LRPS solution of problems (32) and (33) at $\beta = 1$.

	Exact Solution	Approximate Solution	Absolute Error	Relative Error
$t = 0.1$	0.099667	0.099667	1.68079×10^{-11}	1.686388×10^{-10}
$t = 0.2$	0.197375	0.197375	2.11082×10^{-10}	1.069444×10^{-9}
$t = 0.3$	0.291312	0.291312	1.51948×10^{-8}	5.215977×10^{-8}
$t = 0.4$	0.379949	0.379949	3.4917×10^{-7}	9.189918×10^{-7}
$t = 0.5$	0.462121	0.462121	3.92967×10^{-6}	8.503622×10^{-6}

$E_{u,11} = |u - u_{11}|$, $RE_{u,11} = \left|\frac{u - u_{11}}{u}\right|$, where u is the exact value and u_{11} is the 11th approximate value obtained by the LRPSM.

5. Conclusions

Despite the fact that there are several numerical and analytical methods for solving a fractional differential equation, certain methods have benefits over others. Some are precise and efficient, but they need mathematical operations that can be time-consuming, complex or even fail. Others are quick and easy, yet they may not provide precise results. It should be noted that one of the most significant advantages of the LRPSM is that the MATHEMATICA program works faster while performing numerical and symbolic computations of the problem, since we do not need to calculate fractional derivatives during the steps of executing mathematical operations to extract results. It should be emphasized at the conclusion of this paper that this approach may be used to generate precise and approximate solutions for various kinds of integral and differential equations of fractional or nonfractional orders that fit the method's requirements.

Author Contributions: Conceptualization, A.B., A.S. and R.S.; methodology, A.B. and R.S.; software, A.S.; validation, A.B., A.S. and R.S.; formal analysis, A.B. and R.S.; investigation A.B., A.S. and R.S.; data curation, A.B., A.S. and R.S.; writing—original draft preparation, A.B.; writing—review and editing, A.S. and R.S.; visualization, A.B., A.S. and R.S.; supervision, A.B.; project administration, A.B.; funding acquisition, A.B. and R.S. All authors have read and agreed to the published version of the manuscript.

Funding: This research received no external funding.

Data Availability Statement: Not applicable.

Conflicts of Interest: The authors declare no conflict of interest.

References

1. Reid, T. *Riccati Differential Equations*; Elsevier: Amsterdam, The Netherlands, 1972.
2. Lasiecka, I.; Triggiani, R. (Eds.) *Differential and Algebraic Riccati Equations with Application to Boundary Point Control Problems: Continuous Theory and Approximation Theory*; Springer: Berlin/Heidelberg, Germany, 1991.
3. Khalil, I.S.; Doyle, J.C.; Glover, K. *Robust and Optimal Control*; Prentice Hall: Hoboken, NJ, USA, 1996.
4. Benner, P.; Li, J.-R.; Penzl, T. Numerical solution of large-scale Lyapunov equations, Riccati equations, and linear-quadratic optimal control problems. *Numer. Linear Algebra Appl.* **2008**, *15*, 755–777. [CrossRef]
5. Yong, J. Linear-quadratic optimal control problems for mean-field stochastic differential equations. *SIAM J. Control. Optim.* **2013**, *51*, 2809–2838. [CrossRef]
6. El Karoui, N.; Peng, S.; Quenez, M.C. Backward stochastic differential equations in finance. *Math. Financ.* **1997**, *7*, 1–71. [CrossRef]
7. Bittanti, S.; Laub, A.J.; Willems, J.C. (Eds.) *The Riccati Equation*; Springer Science & Business Media: Berlin/Heidelberg, Germany, 2012.
8. Raja, M.A.Z.; Khan, J.A.; Qureshi, I.M. A new stochastic approach for solution of Riccati differential equation of fractional order. *Ann. Math. Artif. Intell.* **2010**, *60*, 229–250. [CrossRef]
9. Suazo, E.; Sergei, K.S.; José, M.V. The Riccati differential equation and a diffusion-type equation. *N. Y. J. Math* **2011**, *17*, 225–244.
10. Kazem, S. Exact solution of some linear fractional differential equations by Laplace transform. *Int. J. Nonlinear Sci.* **2013**, *16*, 3–11.
11. Yavuz, M.; Ozdemir, N. Numerical inverse Laplace homotopy technique for fractional heat equations. *Therm. Sci.* **2018**, *22*, 185–194. [CrossRef]
12. Jafari, H.; Tajadodi, H. He's variational iteration method for solving fractional Riccati differential equation. *Int. J. Diff. Equ.* **2010**, *2010*, 764738. [CrossRef]
13. El-Ajou, A.; Odibat, Z.; Momani, S.; Alawneh, A. Construction of analytical solutions to fractional differential equations using homotopy analysis method. *Int. J. Appl. Math.* **2010**, *40*, 43–51.
14. Dehghan, M.; Manafian, J.; Saadatmandi, A. Solving nonlinear fractional partial differential equations using the homotopy analysis method. *Numer. Methods Partial. Differ. Equ.* **2009**, *26*, 448–479. [CrossRef]
15. Sweilam, N.H.; Khader, M.M.; S Mahdy, A.M. Numerical studies for solving fractional Riccati differential equation. *Appl. Appl. Math. Int. J. (AAM)* **2012**, *7*, 8.
16. Liu, J.; Li, X.; Wu, L. An operational matrix of fractional differentiation of the second kind of Chebyshev polynomial for solving multiterm variable order fractional differential equation. *Math. Probl. Eng.* **2016**, *2016*, 7126380. [CrossRef]
17. Wang, Q. Numerical solutions for fractional KdV–Burgers equation by Adomian decomposition method. *Appl. Math. Comput.* **2006**, *182*, 1048–1055. [CrossRef]
18. Saadeh, R.; Qazza, A.; Burqan, A. A new integral transform: ARA transform and its properties and applications. *Symmetry* **2020**, *12*, 925. [CrossRef]

19. Neamaty, A.; Agheli, B.; Darzi, R. The shifted Jacobi polynomial integral operational matrix for solving Riccati differential equation of fractional order. *Appl. Appl. Math. Int. J. (AAM)* **2015**, *10*, 16.
20. Qazza, A.; Burqan, A.; Saadeh, R. A new attractive method in solving families of fractional differential equations by a new transform. *Mathematics* **2021**, *9*, 3039. [CrossRef]
21. Burqan, A.; Saadeh, R.; Qazza, A. A novel numerical approach in solving fractional neutral pantograph equations via the ara integral transform. *Symmetry* **2021**, *14*, 50. [CrossRef]
22. Burqan, A.; El-Ajou, A.; Saadeh, R.; Al-Smadi, M. A new efficient technique using Laplace transforms and smooth expansions to construct a series solution to the time-fractional Navier-Stokes equations. *Alex. Eng. J.* **2021**, *61*, 1069–1077. [CrossRef]
23. Khandaqji, M.; Burqan, A. Results on sequential conformable fractional derivatives with applications. *J. Comput. Anal. Appl.* **2021**, *29*, 1115–1125.
24. Qiang, X.; Mahboob, A.; Chu, Y.M. Numerical approximation of fractional-order Volterra integrodifferential equation. *J. Funct. Spaces* **2020**, *2020*, 8875792. [CrossRef]
25. Ali, M.; Jaradat, I.; Alquran, M. New computational method for solving fractional Riccati equation. *J. Math. Comput. Sci.* **2017**, *17*, 106–114. [CrossRef]
26. Eriqat, T.; El-Ajou, A.; Oqielat, M.N.; Al-Zhour, Z.; Momani, S. A new attractive analytic approach for solutions of linear and nonlinear neutral fractional pantograph equations. *Chaos Solitons Fractals* **2020**, *138*, 109957. [CrossRef]
27. Oldham, K.; Spanier, J. *The Fractional Calculus Theory and Applications of Differentiation and Integration to Arbitrary Order*; Elsevier: Amsterdam, The Netherlands, 1974.
28. Khan, N.A.; Ara, A.; Khan, N.A. Fractional-order Riccati differential equation: Analytical approximation and numerical results. *Adv. Differ. Equ.* **2013**, *2013*, 185. [CrossRef]
29. Odibat, Z.; Momani, S. Modified homotopy perturbation method: Application to quadratic Riccati differential equation of fractional order. *Chaos Solitons Fractals* **2008**, *36*, 167–174. [CrossRef]

Disclaimer/Publisher's Note: The statements, opinions and data contained in all publications are solely those of the individual author(s) and contributor(s) and not of MDPI and/or the editor(s). MDPI and/or the editor(s) disclaim responsibility for any injury to people or property resulting from any ideas, methods, instructions or products referred to in the content.

Article

Fractional Sturm–Liouville Eigenvalue Problems, II

Mohammad Dehghan * and Angelo B. Mingarelli

School of Mathematics and Statistics, Carleton University, Ottawa, ON K1S 5B6, Canada
* Correspondence: dehghan@math.carleton.ca

Abstract: We continue the study of a non-self-adjoint fractional three-term Sturm–Liouville boundary value problem (with a potential term) formed by the composition of a left Caputo and left Riemann–Liouville fractional integral under *Dirichlet type* boundary conditions. We study the existence and asymptotic behavior of the real eigenvalues and show that for certain values of the fractional differentiation parameter α, $0 < \alpha < 1$, there is a finite set of real eigenvalues and that, for α near $1/2$, there may be none at all. As $\alpha \to 1^-$ we show that their number becomes infinite and that the problem then approaches a standard Dirichlet Sturm–Liouville problem with the composition of the operators becoming the operator of second order differentiation.

Keywords: Fractional Sturm–Liouville; fractional calculus; Laplace transform; Mittag-Leffler function; eigenvalues; asymptotics

1. Introduction

This is a continuation of [1] where the results therein are extended to three-term Fractional Sturm–Liouville operators (with a potential term) formed by the composition of a left Caputo and left-Riemann–Liouville fractional integral. Similar kinds of spectral problems have been considered in [2–11]. Specifically, the boundary value problem considered here is of the form,

$$-{}^c\mathcal{D}^\alpha_{0^+} \circ \mathcal{D}^\alpha_{0^+} y(t) + q(t)y(t) = \lambda y(t), \quad 1/2 < \alpha < 1, \quad 0 \leq t \leq 1, \tag{1}$$

with boundary conditions

$$\mathcal{I}^{1-\alpha}_{0^+}y(t)|_{t=0} = c_1, \quad \text{and} \quad \mathcal{I}^{1-\alpha}_{0^+}y(t)|_{t=1} = c_2, \tag{2}$$

where c_1, c_2 are real constants and the real valued unspecified potential function, $q \in L^\infty[0,1]$. We note that these are not self-adjoint problems and so there may be a non-real spectrum, in general. A well-known property of the Riemann–Liouville integral gives that if the solutions are continuous on $[0,1]$ then the boundary conditions (2) reduce to the usual fixed-end boundary conditions, $y(0) = y(1) = 0$, as $\alpha \to 1$.

For the analogue of the Dirichlet problem described above we study the existence and asymptotic behaviour of the real eigenvalues and show that for each α, $0 < \alpha < 1$, there is a finite set of real eigenvalues and that, for α near $1/2$, there may be none at all. As $\alpha \to 1^-$ we show that their number becomes infinite and that the problem then approaches a standard Dirichlet Sturm–Liouville problem with the composition of the operators becoming the operator of second order differentiation acting on a suitable function space.

Our approach is different from most in this area. Specifically, we start with the existence and uniqueness of solutions of the Equation (1) along with the initial conditions (2), then we formulate the boundary value problem as an integral equation, after which we show that the solution of this integral equation as a function of λ is an entire function of λ of order of at most $1/2\alpha$. Since α is between $1/2$ and 1, this entire function is of fractional order and therefore must have an infinite number of zeros, some of which may be complex. These zeros are the eigenvalues of our problem and therefore we get their existence. Using

Citation: Dehghan, M.; Mingarelli, A.B. Fractional Sturm–Liouville Eigenvalue Problems, II. *Fractal Fract.* **2022**, *6*, 487. https://doi.org/10.3390/fractalfract6090487

Academic Editor: António Lopes

Received: 29 July 2022
Accepted: 25 August 2022
Published: 30 August 2022

Publisher's Note: MDPI stays neutral with regard to jurisdictional claims in published maps and institutional affiliations.

Copyright: © 2022 by the authors. Licensee MDPI, Basel, Switzerland. This article is an open access article distributed under the terms and conditions of the Creative Commons Attribution (CC BY) license (https://creativecommons.org/licenses/by/4.0/).

asymptotic methods and hard analysis, we proved our bounds on the real eigenvalues of which there must be a finite number for each α. Finally, we show that as α tends to 1, the number of real eigenvalues becomes infinite and the original problem approaches the standard Sturm–Liouville eigenvalue problem.

2. Preliminaries

We recall some definitions from fractional calculus and refer the reader to our previous paper [1] for further details.

Definition 1. *The left and the right Riemann–Liouville fractional integrals $\mathcal{I}_{a+}^\alpha$ and $\mathcal{I}_{b-}^\alpha$ of order $\alpha \in \mathbb{R}^+$ are defined by*

$$\mathcal{I}_{a+}^\alpha f(t) := \frac{1}{\Gamma(\alpha)} \int_a^t \frac{f(s)}{(t-s)^{1-\alpha}} ds, \quad t \in (a,b], \tag{3}$$

and

$$\mathcal{I}_{b-}^\alpha f(t) := \frac{1}{\Gamma(\alpha)} \int_t^b \frac{f(s)}{(s-t)^{1-\alpha}} ds, \quad t \in [a,b), \tag{4}$$

respectively. Here $\Gamma(\alpha)$ denotes Euler's Gamma function. The following property is easily verified.

Property 1. *For a constant C, we have $\mathcal{I}_{a+}^\alpha C = \frac{(t-a)^\alpha}{\Gamma(\alpha+1)} \cdot C$.*

The proof is by direct calculation.

Definition 2. *The left and the right Caputo fractional derivatives ${}^c\mathcal{D}_{a+}^\alpha$ and ${}^c\mathcal{D}_{b-}^\alpha$ are defined by*

$${}^c\mathcal{D}_{a+}^\alpha f(t) := \mathcal{I}_{a+}^{n-\alpha} \circ \mathcal{D}^n f(t) = \frac{1}{\Gamma(n-\alpha)} \int_a^t \frac{f^{(n)}(s)}{(t-s)^{\alpha-n+1}} ds, \quad t > a, \tag{5}$$

and

$${}^c\mathcal{D}_{b-}^\alpha f(t) := (-1)^n \mathcal{I}_{b-}^{n-\alpha} \circ \mathcal{D}^n f(t) = \frac{(-1)^n}{\Gamma(n-\alpha)} \int_t^b \frac{f^{(n)}(s)}{(s-t)^{\alpha-n+1}} ds, \quad t < b, \tag{6}$$

respectively, where f is sufficiently differentiable and $n-1 \leq \alpha < n$.

Definition 3. *Similarly, the left and the right Riemann–Liouville fractional derivatives $\mathcal{D}_{a+}^\alpha$ and $\mathcal{D}_{b-}^\alpha$ are defined by*

$$\mathcal{D}_{a+}^\alpha f(t) := \mathcal{D}^n \circ \mathcal{I}_{a+}^{n-\alpha} f(t) = \frac{1}{\Gamma(n-\alpha)} \frac{d^n}{dt^n} \int_a^t \frac{f(s)}{(t-s)^{\alpha-n+1}} ds, \quad t > a, \tag{7}$$

and

$$\mathcal{D}_{b-}^\alpha f(t) := (-1)^n \mathcal{D}^n \circ \mathcal{I}_{b-}^{n-\alpha} f(t) = \frac{(-1)^n}{\Gamma(n-\alpha)} \frac{d^n}{dt^n} \int_t^b \frac{f(s)}{(s-t)^{\alpha-n+1}} ds, \quad t < b, \tag{8}$$

respectively, where f is sufficiently differentiable and $n-1 \leq \alpha < n$.

Property 2. *For $\Re(\nu) > -1$, $0 < \alpha < 1$, and $t > 0$, we have*

$$\mathcal{D}_{0+}^\alpha (t^\nu) = \frac{\Gamma(1+\nu)}{\Gamma(1+\nu-\alpha)} t^{\nu-\alpha}$$

Property 3. *For $\Re(\nu) > 0$, $0 < \alpha < 1$, and $t > 0$, we have*

$${}^c\mathcal{D}_{0+}^\alpha (t^\nu) = \frac{\Gamma(1+\nu)}{\Gamma(1+\nu-\alpha)} t^{\nu-\alpha}$$

Property 4. *If $y(t) \in L^1(a,b)$ and $\mathcal{I}_{a+}^{1-\alpha}y, \mathcal{I}_{b-}^{1-\alpha}y \in AC[a,b]$, then*

$$\mathcal{I}_{a+}^{\alpha}\mathcal{D}_{a+}^{\alpha}y(t) = y(t) - \frac{(t-a)^{\alpha-1}}{\Gamma(\alpha)}\mathcal{I}_{a+}^{1-\alpha}y(a),$$

$$\mathcal{I}_{b-}^{\alpha}\mathcal{D}_{b-}^{\alpha}y(t) = y(t) - \frac{(b-t)^{\alpha-1}}{\Gamma(\alpha)}\mathcal{I}_{b-}^{1-\alpha}y(b).$$

Property 5. *If $y(t) \in AC[a,b]$ and $0 < \alpha \leq 1$, then*

$$\mathcal{I}_{a+}^{\alpha}\,{}^c\mathcal{D}_{a+}^{\alpha}y(t) = y(t) - y(a),$$
$$\mathcal{I}_{b-}^{\alpha}\,{}^c\mathcal{D}_{b-}^{\alpha}y(t) = y(t) - y(b).$$

Property 6. *For $0 < \alpha < 1$ we have*

$$\mathcal{D}_{a+}^{\alpha}f(t) = \frac{f(a)}{\Gamma(1-\alpha)}(t-a)^{-\alpha} + {}^c\mathcal{D}_{a+}^{\alpha}f(t).$$

The Mittag-Leffler Function

The function $E_\delta(z)$ defined by

$$E_\delta(z) := \sum_{k=0}^{\infty} \frac{z^\delta}{\Gamma(\delta k + 1)}, \quad (z \in \mathbb{C}, \Re(\delta) > 0), \tag{9}$$

was introduced by Mittag-Leffler [12]. In particular, when $\delta = 1$ and $\delta = 2$, we have

$$E_1(z) = e^z, \quad E_2(z) = \cosh(\sqrt{z}). \tag{10}$$

The generalized Mittag-Leffler function $E_{\delta,\theta}(z)$ is defined by

$$E_{\delta,\theta}(z) = \sum_{k=0}^{\infty} \frac{z^k}{\Gamma(\delta k + \theta)}, \tag{11}$$

where $z, \theta \in \mathbb{C}$ and $\mathrm{Re}(\delta) > 0$. When $\theta = 1$, $E_{\delta,\theta}(z)$ coincides with the Mittag-Leffler function (9):

$$E_{\delta,1}(z) = E_\delta(z). \tag{12}$$

Two other particular cases of (11) are as follows:

$$E_{1,2}(z) = \frac{e^z - 1}{z}, \quad E_{2,2}(z) = \frac{\sinh(\sqrt{z})}{\sqrt{z}}. \tag{13}$$

Property 7. *For any δ with $\Re(\delta) > 0$ and for any $z \neq 0$ we have*

$$E_{\delta,\delta}(z) = \frac{1}{z}E_{\delta,0}(z)$$

Further properties of this special function may be found in [13].

Property 8 (See [14], p. 43). *If $0 < \delta < 2$ and $\mu \in (\frac{\delta\pi}{2}, \min(\pi, \delta\pi))$, then the function $E_{\delta,\theta}(z)$ has the following exponential expansion as $|z| \to \infty$*

$$E_{\delta,\theta}(z) = \begin{cases} \frac{1}{\delta}z^{\frac{1-\theta}{\delta}}\exp(z^{\frac{1}{\delta}}) - \sum_{k=1}^{N}\frac{1}{\Gamma(\theta-\delta k)}\frac{1}{z^k} + O(\frac{1}{z^{N+1}}), & |\arg(z)| \leq \mu, \\ -\sum_{k=1}^{N}\frac{1}{\Gamma(\theta-\delta k)}\frac{1}{z^k} + O(\frac{1}{z^{N+1}}), & \mu \leq |\arg(z)| \leq \pi. \end{cases} \tag{14}$$

3. Existence and Uniqueness of the Solution of SLPs

In this section we convert (1) and (2) to an integral equation and prove that it has a solution that satisfies the relevant equations and initial conditions. First, we proceed formally. Separating terms in (1), we get

$$^c\mathcal{D}_{0+}^\alpha \circ \mathcal{D}_{0+}^\alpha y(t) = (q(t) - \lambda)y(t), \quad 1/2 < \alpha < 1, \quad 0 \le t \le 1.$$

Taking the left Riemann–Liouville fractional integrals $\mathcal{I}_{a+}^\alpha$ on both sides of the above equation and using Property 5, we have

$$\mathcal{D}_{0+}^\alpha y(t) - \mathcal{D}_{0+}^\alpha y(t)|_{t=0} = \mathcal{I}_{0+}^\alpha((q(t) - \lambda)y(t)).$$

Taking the left Riemann–Liouville fractional integrals $\mathcal{I}_{a+}^\alpha$ from both sides of the above equation once again and using Property 4, we get

$$y(t) - \frac{t^{\alpha-1}}{\Gamma(\alpha)}\mathcal{I}_{0+}^{1-\alpha}y(t)|_{t=0} - \mathcal{I}_{0+}^\alpha(\mathcal{D}_{0+}^\alpha y(t)|_{t=0}) = \mathcal{I}_{0+}^\alpha(\mathcal{I}_{0+}^\alpha((q(t) - \lambda)y(t))).$$

Using Property 1, we can write

$$y(t) = c_1\frac{t^{\alpha-1}}{\Gamma(\alpha)} + c_2\frac{t^\alpha}{\Gamma(\alpha+1)} + \mathcal{I}_{0+}^\alpha(\mathcal{I}_{0+}^\alpha((q(t) - \lambda)y(t)))$$

in which

$$c_1 = \mathcal{I}_{0+}^{1-\alpha}y(t)|_{t=0}, \quad c_2 = \mathcal{D}_{0+}^\alpha y(t)|_{t=0}.$$

We obtain, through the double fractional integral in the above equation, the following:

$$y(t) = c_1\frac{t^{\alpha-1}}{\Gamma(\alpha)} + c_2\frac{t^\alpha}{\Gamma(\alpha+1)} + \frac{1}{\Gamma^2(\alpha)}\int_0^t (t-s)^{\alpha-1}\left(\int_0^s \frac{(q(r) - \lambda)y(r)}{(s-r)^{1-\alpha}}dr\right)ds.$$

By changing the order of integrals in the above equation we get

$$y(t) = c_1\frac{t^{\alpha-1}}{\Gamma(\alpha)} + c_2\frac{t^\alpha}{\Gamma(\alpha+1)} + \frac{1}{\Gamma^2(\alpha)}\int_0^t (q(r) - \lambda)y(r)\left(\int_r^t (t-s)^{\alpha-1}(s-r)^{\alpha-1}ds\right)dr$$

Solving the inner integral gives us

$$y(t,\lambda) = c_1\frac{t^{\alpha-1}}{\Gamma(\alpha)} + c_2\frac{t^\alpha}{\Gamma(\alpha+1)} + \frac{1}{\Gamma(2\alpha)}\int_0^t (q(s) - \lambda)y(s,\lambda)(t-s)^{2\alpha-1}ds. \quad (15)$$

We will now show that (15) has a solution that exists in a neighbourhood of $t = 0$ and is unique there. Working backwards will then provide us with a unique solution to (1) and (2). Although this result already appears in [15], we give a shorter proof part of which will be required later.

To this end, let $t > 0$. Define

$$y_n(t,\lambda) = y_0(t,\lambda) + \frac{1}{\Gamma(2\alpha)}\int_0^t (t-s)^{2\alpha-1}(q(s) - \lambda)y_{n-1}(s,\lambda)ds, \quad (16)$$

where

$$y_0(t,\lambda) = c_1\frac{t^{\alpha-1}}{\Gamma(\alpha)} + c_2\frac{t^\alpha}{\Gamma(\alpha+1)}. \quad (17)$$

Let $\lambda \in \mathbf{C}$, $|\lambda| < \Lambda$, where $\Lambda > 0$ is arbitrary but fixed. Then,

$$|y_1(t,\lambda) - y_0(t,\lambda)| \leq \frac{1}{\Gamma(2\alpha)} \int_0^t (t-s)^{2\alpha-1} |q(s) - \lambda| |y_0(s,\lambda)| ds \\ \leq \frac{||q||_\infty + \Lambda}{\Gamma(2\alpha)} \int_0^t (t-s)^{2\alpha-1} |y_0(s,\lambda)| ds, \quad (18)$$

in which $||q||_\infty = \sup_{t \in [0,1]} |q(t)|$. Substituting (17) in (18) and using the fact that,

$$\int_a^t (t-s)^{\alpha-1}(s-a)^{\beta-1} ds = \frac{(t-a)^{\alpha+\beta-1}\Gamma(\alpha)\Gamma(\beta)}{\Gamma(\alpha+\beta)},$$

we have

$$|y_1(t,\lambda) - y_0(t,\lambda)| \leq (||q||_\infty + \Lambda)\left(\frac{c_1}{\Gamma(3\alpha)} t^{3\alpha-1} + c_2 \frac{t^{3\alpha}}{\Gamma(3\alpha+1)}\right),$$

Now, for $n = 2$ in (16) we get

$$|y_2(t,\lambda) - y_1(t,\lambda)| \leq \frac{1}{\Gamma(2\alpha)} \int_0^t (t-s)^{2\alpha-1} |q(s) - \lambda| |y_1(s,\lambda) - y_0(s,\lambda)| ds \\ \leq \frac{1}{\Gamma(2\alpha)} \int_0^t (t-s)^{2\alpha-1} |q(s) - \lambda| \left((||q||_\infty + \Lambda)(\frac{c_1}{\Gamma(3\alpha)} s^{3\alpha-1} + c_2 \frac{s^{3\alpha}}{\Gamma(3\alpha+1)})\right) ds \\ \leq (||q||_\infty + \Lambda)^2 \left(\frac{c_1}{\Gamma(5\alpha)} t^{5\alpha-1} + \frac{c_2}{\Gamma(5\alpha+1)} t^{5\alpha}\right). \quad (19)$$

Continuing in this way we get that the series

$$y(t,\lambda) := y_0(t,\lambda) + \sum_{n=1}^\infty (y_n(t,\lambda) - y_{n-1}(t,\lambda)) \quad (20)$$

where

$$\sum_{n=1}^\infty |y_n(t,\lambda) - y_{n-1}(t,\lambda)| \leq c_1 t^{-1} \sum_{n=1}^\infty \frac{(||q||_\infty + \Lambda)^n}{\Gamma(2n\alpha + \alpha)} t^{2n\alpha+\alpha} + c_2 \sum_{n=1}^\infty \frac{(||q||_\infty + \Lambda)^n}{\Gamma(2n\alpha + \alpha + 1)} t^{2n\alpha+\alpha} \quad (21)$$

converges uniformly on compact subsets of $(0, 1]$. Denote the sum of the infinite series in (20) by $y(t,\lambda)$. So, by virtue of (17) and (21), (20) gives us,

$$|y(t,\lambda)| \leq |y_0(t,\lambda)| + \sum_{n=1}^\infty |y_n(t,\lambda) - y_{n-1}(t,\lambda)| \\ \leq \frac{c_1}{\Gamma(\alpha)} t^{\alpha-1} + \frac{c_2}{\Gamma(\alpha+1)} t^\alpha + c_1 t^{-1} \sum_{n=1}^\infty \frac{(||q||_\infty + \Lambda)^n}{\Gamma(2n\alpha + \alpha)} t^{2n\alpha+\alpha} + c_2 \sum_{n=1}^\infty \frac{(||q||_\infty + \Lambda)^n}{\Gamma(2n\alpha + \alpha + 1)} t^{2n\alpha+\alpha} \\ = c_1 t^{-1} \sum_{n=0}^\infty \frac{(||q||_\infty + \Lambda)^n}{\Gamma(2n\alpha + \alpha)} t^{2n\alpha+\alpha} + c_2 \sum_{n=0}^\infty \frac{(||q||_\infty + \Lambda)^n}{\Gamma(2n\alpha + \alpha + 1)} t^{2n\alpha+\alpha} \\ = c_1 t^{\alpha-1} E_{2\alpha,\alpha}((||q||_\infty + \Lambda) t^{2\alpha}) + c_2 t^\alpha E_{2\alpha,\alpha+1}((||q||_\infty + \Lambda) t^{2\alpha}).$$

Note that for a solution $y(t,\lambda)$ of (15) to be $C([0,1])$, it is necessary and sufficient that $c_1 = 0$, i.e., $\mathcal{I}_{0^+}^{1-\alpha} y(t)|_{t=0} = 0$. This then proves the global existence of a solution of (15) on $[\delta, 1]$, $\delta > 0$, since $q \in L^\infty[0,1]$ for given c_1 and c_2, as defined in (2).

From the proof comes the following a priori estimate when $c_1 = 0$, that is,

$$|y(t,\lambda)| \leq c_2 t^\alpha \left(\frac{1}{\Gamma(\alpha+1)} + \left|E_{2\alpha,\alpha+1}((\|q\|_\infty + \Lambda)t^{2\alpha})\right| \right)$$

$$\leq c_2 \left(\frac{1}{\Gamma(\alpha+1)} + \left|E_{2\alpha,\alpha+1}((\|q\|_\infty + \Lambda)t^{2\alpha})\right| \right)$$

valid for each $t \in [0,1]$ and all $|\lambda| < \Lambda$.

The previous bound can be made into an absolute constant by taking the sup over all t and $|\lambda| < \Lambda$. Of course, the bound goes to infinity as $|\lambda| \to \infty$ over non-real values, as it must. Thus,

$$|y(t,\lambda)| \leq c_2 \left(\frac{1}{\Gamma(\alpha+1)} + \sup_{|\lambda|<\Lambda, t\in[0,1]} \left|E_{2\alpha,\alpha+1}((\|q\|_\infty + \Lambda)t^{2\alpha})\right| \right)$$

$$= c_2 \left(\frac{1}{\Gamma(\alpha+1)} + |E_{2\alpha,\alpha+1}((\|q\|_\infty + \Lambda))| \right) := c_3. \quad (22)$$

for all $|\lambda| < \Lambda, t \in [0,1]$. Uniqueness follows easily by means of Gronwall's inequality, as usual. Let $\varepsilon > 0$. Assume that (15) has two solutions $y(t,\lambda), z(t,\lambda)$. Since $q \in L^\infty[0,1]$ and $|\lambda| < \Lambda$ we can derive that,

$$|y(t,\lambda) - z(t,\lambda)| \leq \varepsilon e^{\frac{1}{\Gamma(2\alpha)}(\|q\|_\infty + \Lambda)\frac{t^{2\alpha}}{2\alpha}}.$$

and since $t \in [0,1]$, we get

$$|y(t,\lambda) - z(t,\lambda)| \leq O(\varepsilon)$$

where the O-term can be made independent of both t, λ. Letting $\varepsilon \to 0$ yields uniqueness for $t \in [0,1]$ and $|\lambda| < \Lambda$.

4. Another Integral Equation

In the previous section we showed that (15) has a solution that, for each $\lambda \in \mathbb{C}$, exists on $[0,1]$, is unique, and is continuous there if and only if $c_1 = 0$. On the other hand, if $c_1 \neq 0$ then the solution is merely continuous on all compact subsets of $(0,1]$. In this section we find another expression for the integral equation which is equivalent to both (15) and the problem (1) with boundary conditions (2).

Lemma 1. *For $0 < \alpha < 1$ and $0 < t < 1$, we have*

$$-{}^c\mathcal{D}_{0+}^\alpha \mathcal{D}_{0+}^\alpha \left(t^{\alpha-1} E_{2\alpha,\alpha}(-\lambda t^{2\alpha}) \right) = \lambda t^{\alpha-1} E_{2\alpha,\alpha}(-\lambda t^{2\alpha})$$

Proof. Using properties of the Mittag-Leffler function we can write

$$\mathcal{D}_{0+}^\alpha \left(t^{\alpha-1} E_{2\alpha,\alpha}(-\lambda t^{2\alpha}) \right) = \mathcal{D}_{0+}^\alpha \left(\sum_{k=0}^\infty \frac{(-\lambda)^k t^{2\alpha k + \alpha - 1}}{\Gamma(2\alpha k + \alpha)} \right)$$

$$= \sum_{k=0}^\infty \frac{(-\lambda)^k \mathcal{D}_{0+}^\alpha \left(t^{2\alpha k + \alpha - 1} \right)}{\Gamma(2\alpha k + \alpha)}$$

$$= \sum_{k=0}^\infty \frac{(-\lambda)^k t^{2\alpha k - 1}}{\Gamma(2\alpha k)} \quad (23)$$

$$= t^{-1} E_{2\alpha,0}(\lambda t^{2\alpha})$$

$$= -\lambda t^{2\alpha-1} E_{2\alpha,2\alpha}(-\lambda t^{2\alpha}),$$

in which the third and the last equalities come from Property 2 and Property 7, respectively. Now, taking the left Caputo fractional derivative of both sides of (23) we get

$$-{}^c\mathcal{D}_{0+}^\alpha \mathcal{D}_{0+}^\alpha \left(t^{\alpha-1}E_{2\alpha,\alpha}(-\lambda t^{2\alpha})\right) = {}^c\mathcal{D}_{0+}^\alpha \left(\lambda t^{2\alpha-1}E_{2\alpha,2\alpha}(-\lambda t^{2\alpha})\right)$$

$$= \lambda\, {}^c\mathcal{D}_{0+}^\alpha \left(\sum_{k=0}^\infty \frac{(-\lambda)^k t^{2\alpha k+2\alpha-1}}{\Gamma(2\alpha k+2\alpha)}\right)$$

$$= \lambda \left(\sum_{k=0}^\infty \frac{(-\lambda)^k\, {}^c\mathcal{D}_{0+}^\alpha \left(t^{2\alpha k+2\alpha-1}\right)}{\Gamma(2\alpha k+2\alpha)}\right)$$

$$= \lambda t^{\alpha-1} \sum_{k=0}^\infty \frac{(-\lambda)^k t^{2\alpha k}}{\Gamma(2\alpha k+\alpha)}$$

$$= \lambda t^{\alpha-1} E_{2\alpha,\alpha}(-\lambda t^{2\alpha})$$

as required. □

Lemma 2. *For $0 < \alpha < 1$ and $0 < t < 1$, we have*

$$-{}^c\mathcal{D}_{0+}^\alpha \mathcal{D}_{0+}^\alpha \left(t^\alpha E_{2\alpha,\alpha+1}(-\lambda t^{2\alpha})\right) = \lambda t^\alpha E_{2\alpha,\alpha+1}(-\lambda t^{2\alpha})$$

Proof. Once again, using the properties of the Mittag-Leffler function we can write

$$\mathcal{D}_{0+}^\alpha \left(t^\alpha E_{2\alpha,\alpha+1}(-\lambda t^{2\alpha})\right) = \mathcal{D}_{0+}^\alpha \left(\sum_{k=0}^\infty \frac{(-\lambda)^k t^{2\alpha k+\alpha}}{\Gamma(2\alpha k+\alpha+1)}\right)$$

$$= \sum_{k=0}^\infty \frac{(-\lambda)^k \mathcal{D}_{0+}^\alpha \left(t^{2\alpha k+\alpha}\right)}{\Gamma(2\alpha k+\alpha+1)} \qquad (24)$$

$$= \sum_{k=0}^\infty \frac{(-\lambda)^k t^{2\alpha k}}{\Gamma(2\alpha k+1)}$$

$$= E_{2\alpha,1}(-\lambda t^{2\alpha}).$$

in which the third equality comes from Property 3. Now, taking the left Caputo fractional derivative of both sides of (24) we get

$$^c\mathcal{D}_{0+}^\alpha \mathcal{D}_{0+}^\alpha \left(t^\alpha E_{2\alpha,\alpha+1}(-\lambda t^{2\alpha})\right) = {}^c\mathcal{D}_{0+}^\alpha \left(E_{2\alpha,1}(\lambda t^{2\alpha})\right)$$

$$= {}^c\mathcal{D}_{0+}^\alpha \left(\sum_{k=0}^\infty \frac{(-\lambda)^k t^{2\alpha k}}{\Gamma(2\alpha k+1)}\right)$$

$$= \sum_{k=0}^\infty \frac{(-\lambda)^k\, {}^c\mathcal{D}_{0+}^\alpha \left(t^{2\alpha k}\right)}{\Gamma(2\alpha k+1)}$$

$$= \sum_{k=1}^\infty \frac{(-\lambda)^k t^{\alpha(2k-1)}}{\Gamma(1+\alpha(2k-1))}$$

$$= \sum_{k=0}^\infty \frac{(-\lambda)^{k+1} t^{\alpha(2k+1)}}{\Gamma(1+\alpha(2k+1))}$$

$$= -\lambda t^\alpha \sum_{k=0}^\infty \frac{(-\lambda)^k t^{2\alpha k}}{\Gamma(2k\alpha+\alpha+1)}$$

$$= -\lambda t^\alpha E_{2\alpha,\alpha+1}(-\lambda t^{2\alpha})$$

as desired. □

Lemma 3. *For $0 < \alpha < 1$ and $0 < t < 1$, we have*

$$-{}^c\mathcal{D}_{0+}^\alpha \mathcal{D}_{0+}^\alpha \left(\int_0^t (t-s)^{2\alpha-1} E_{2\alpha,2\alpha}(-\lambda(t-s)^{2\alpha})q(s)y(s)ds \right) = -q(t)y(t) + \lambda \int_0^t (t-s)^{2\alpha-1} E_{2\alpha,2\alpha}(-\lambda(t-s)^{2\alpha})q(s)y(s)ds$$

Proof. Let $c_4 = 1/\Gamma(1-\alpha)$. Observe that,

$$\mathcal{I}_{0+}^{1-\alpha} \int_0^t (t-s)^{2\alpha-1} E_{2\alpha,2\alpha}(-\lambda(t-s)^{2\alpha})q(s)y(s)ds = c_4 \int_0^t \frac{\int_0^r (r-s)^{2\alpha-1} E_{2\alpha,2\alpha}(-\lambda(r-s)^{2\alpha})q(s)y(s)ds}{(t-r)^\alpha} dr$$

$$= c_4 \int_0^t q(s)y(s) \left(\int_s^t \frac{(r-s)^{2\alpha-1}}{(t-r)^\alpha} E_{2\alpha,2\alpha}(-\lambda(r-s)^{2\alpha}) dr \right) ds$$

$$= c_4 \int_0^t q(s)y(s) \left(\sum_{k=0}^\infty \frac{(-\lambda)^k}{\Gamma(2\alpha k + 2\alpha)} \int_s^t \frac{(r-s)^{2\alpha-1+2\alpha k}}{(t-r)^\alpha} dr \right) ds \quad (25)$$

$$= \int_0^t q(s)y(s) \left(\sum_{k=0}^\infty \frac{(-\lambda)^k (t-s)^{2\alpha k + \alpha}}{\Gamma(2\alpha k + \alpha + 1)} \right) ds$$

$$= \int_0^t q(s)y(s)(t-s)^\alpha E_{2\alpha,\alpha+1}(-\lambda(t-s)^{2\alpha})ds.$$

Next, differentiating both sides of (25) with respect to t and noting that $\mathcal{D}_{0+}^\alpha = D(\mathcal{I}_{0+}^{1-\alpha})$ we find,

$$\mathcal{D}_{0+}^\alpha \left(\int_0^t (t-s)^{2\alpha-1} E_{2\alpha,2\alpha}(-\lambda(t-s)^{2\alpha})q(s)y(s)ds \right) = \int_0^t (t-s)^{\alpha-1} E_{2\alpha,\alpha}(-\lambda(t-s)^{2\alpha})q(s)y(s)ds. \quad (26)$$

as $\frac{d}{dt}(t^\alpha E_{2\alpha,\alpha+1}(-\lambda t^{2\alpha})) = t^{\alpha-1} E_{2\alpha,\alpha}(-\lambda t^{2\alpha})$. Next, we are going to take the left Caputo fractional derivative of both sides of (26). However, since the right hand side of (26) as a function of t is zero at $t = 0$, we can use Property 6 and replace the Caputo fractional derivative ${}^c\mathcal{D}_{0+}^\alpha$ by the Riemann–Liouville one $\mathcal{D}_{0+}^\alpha$. In order to do so, first we need to apply $\mathcal{I}_{0+}^{1-\alpha}$ followed by the classical derivative of the right hand side of (26) as follows,

$$\mathcal{I}_{0+}^{1-\alpha} \int_0^t (t-s)^{\alpha-1} E_{2\alpha,\alpha}(-\lambda(t-s)^{2\alpha})q(s)y(s)ds = c_4 \int_0^t \frac{\int_0^r (r-s)^{\alpha-1} E_{2\alpha,\alpha}(-\lambda(r-s)^{2\alpha})q(s)y(s)ds}{(t-r)^\alpha} dr$$

$$= c_4 \int_0^t q(s)y(s) \left(\int_s^t \frac{(r-s)^{\alpha-1}}{(t-r)^\alpha} E_{2\alpha,\alpha}(-\lambda(r-s)^{2\alpha}) dr \right) ds$$

$$= c_4 \int_0^t q(s)y(s) \left(\sum_{k=0}^\infty \frac{(-\lambda)^k}{\Gamma(2\alpha k + \alpha)} \int_s^t \frac{(r-s)^{\alpha-1+2\alpha k}}{(t-r)^\alpha} dr \right) ds$$

$$= \int_0^t q(s)y(s) \left(\sum_{k=0}^\infty \frac{(-\lambda)^k (t-s)^{2\alpha k}}{\Gamma(2\alpha k + 1)} \right) ds$$

$$= \int_0^t q(s)y(s) E_{2\alpha,1}(-\lambda(t-s)^{2\alpha})ds.$$

Taking the derivative of the previous equation and using the fact stated in the previous paragraph, we get

$${}^c\mathcal{D}_{0+}^\alpha \int_0^t (t-s)^{\alpha-1} E_{2\alpha,\alpha}(-\lambda(t-s)^{2\alpha})q(s)y(s)ds = q(t)y(t) + \int_0^t q(s)y(s)(t-s)^{-1} E_{2\alpha,0}(-\lambda(t-s)^{2\alpha})ds$$

$$= q(t)y(t) - \lambda \int_0^t (t-s)^{2\alpha-1} E_{2\alpha,2\alpha}(-\lambda(t-s)^{2\alpha})q(s)y(s)ds. \quad (27)$$

where we used Property 7 to arrive at the second equality above. Combining (26) and (27) completes the proof. $\square$

Theorem 1. *For $1/2 < \alpha < 1$, the integral equation*

$$y(t,\lambda) = c_1 t^{\alpha-1} E_{2\alpha,\alpha}(-\lambda t^{2\alpha}) + c_2 t^\alpha E_{2\alpha,\alpha+1}(-\lambda t^{2\alpha}) + \int_0^t (t-s)^{2\alpha-1} E_{2\alpha,2\alpha}(-\lambda(t-s)^{2\alpha}) q(s) y(s,\lambda) \, ds \qquad (28)$$

satisfies (1) *with initial conditions* $\mathcal{I}_{0^+}^{1-\alpha} y(t)|_{t=0} = c_1$ *and* $\mathcal{D}_{0^+}^\alpha y(t)|_{t=0} = c_2$ *in which c_1 and c_2 are given constants, and that this solution is unique.*

Proof. We apply $-{}^c\mathcal{D}_{0^+}^\alpha \mathcal{D}_{0^+}^\alpha$ on both sides of (28) to find,

$$-{}^c\mathcal{D}_{0^+}^\alpha \mathcal{D}_{0^+}^\alpha (y(t,\lambda)) = -{}^c\mathcal{D}_{0^+}^\alpha \mathcal{D}_{0^+}^\alpha \left(c_1 t^{\alpha-1} E_{2\alpha,\alpha}(-\lambda t^{2\alpha}) + c_2 t^\alpha E_{2\alpha,\alpha+1}(-\lambda t^{2\alpha}) \right) +$$

$$- {}^c\mathcal{D}_{0^+}^\alpha \mathcal{D}_{0^+}^\alpha \left(\int_0^t (t-s)^{2\alpha-1} E_{2\alpha,2\alpha}(-\lambda(t-s)^{2\alpha}) q(s) y(s,\lambda) \, ds \right)$$

$$= \lambda c_1 t^{\alpha-1} E_{2\alpha,\alpha}(-\lambda t^{2\alpha}) + \lambda c_2 t^\alpha E_{2\alpha,\alpha+1}(-\lambda t^{2\alpha}) - q(t) y(t) +$$

$$\lambda \int_0^t (t-s)^{2\alpha-1} E_{2\alpha,2\alpha}(-\lambda(t-s)^{2\alpha}) q(s) y(s,\lambda) \, ds \qquad (29)$$

$$= -q(t) y(t) + \lambda \left(c_1 t^{\alpha-1} E_{2\alpha,\alpha}(-\lambda t^{2\alpha}) + c_2 t^\alpha E_{2\alpha,\alpha+1}(-\lambda t^{2\alpha}) \right) +$$

$$\lambda \left(\int_0^t (t-s)^{2\alpha-1} E_{2\alpha,2\alpha}(-\lambda(t-s)^{2\alpha}) q(s) y(s,\lambda) \, ds \right)$$

$$= -q(t) y(t) + \lambda (y(t,\lambda)),$$

in which second equality come from Lemmas 1–3. We verify the initial conditions. Taking $\mathcal{I}_{0^+}^{1-\alpha}$ of both sides (28), we get,

$$\mathcal{I}_{0^+}^{1-\alpha}(y(t,\lambda)) = \mathcal{I}_{0^+}^{1-\alpha}\left(c_1 t^{\alpha-1} E_{2\alpha,\alpha}(-\lambda t^{2\alpha}) + c_2 t^\alpha E_{2\alpha,\alpha+1}(-\lambda t^{2\alpha}) \right) +$$

$$\mathcal{I}_{0^+}^{1-\alpha}\left(\int_0^t (t-s)^{2\alpha-1} E_{2\alpha,2\alpha}(-\lambda(t-s)^{2\alpha}) q(s) y(s,\lambda) \, ds \right) \qquad (30)$$

$$= c_1 E_{2\alpha,1}(-\lambda t^{2\alpha}) + c_2 t E_{2\alpha,2}(-\lambda t^{2\alpha}) + \int_0^t (t-s)^\alpha E_{2\alpha,2\alpha+1}(-\lambda(t-s)^{2\alpha}) q(s) y(s,\lambda) \, ds,$$

where the third term of the second equality comes from (25). Since $E_{2\alpha,1}(-\lambda t^{2\alpha})|_{t=0} = 1$ and the other two terms of the above equality vanish when $t = 0$, we have verified the first initial condition. Again Taking $\mathcal{D}_{0^+}^\alpha$ on both sides (28), we can find,

$$\mathcal{D}_{0^+}^\alpha(y(t,\lambda)) = \mathcal{D}_{0^+}^\alpha \left(c_1 t^{\alpha-1} E_{2\alpha,\alpha}(-\lambda t^{2\alpha}) + c_2 t^\alpha E_{2\alpha,\alpha+1}(-\lambda t^{2\alpha}) \right) +$$

$$\mathcal{D}_{0^+}^\alpha \left(\int_0^t (t-s)^{2\alpha-1} E_{2\alpha,2\alpha}(-\lambda(t-s)^{2\alpha}) q(s) y(s,\lambda) \, ds \right) \qquad (31)$$

$$= -c_1 \lambda t^{2\alpha-1} E_{2\alpha,2\alpha}(-\lambda t^{2\alpha}) + c_2 E_{2\alpha,1}(-\lambda t^{2\alpha}) + \int_0^t (t-s)^{\alpha-1} E_{2\alpha,\alpha}(-\lambda(t-s)^{2\alpha}) q(s) y(s,\lambda) \, ds,$$

where the second equality above comes from (23), (24) and (26). The second initial condition can readily be obtained by substituting $t = 0$ in (31). □

5. Analyticity of Solutions with Respect to the Parameter λ

In this section we show that the solutions (15) or (28) are, generally speaking, entire functions of the parameter λ for each t under consideration and $\lambda \in \mathbb{C}$. First, we show continuity with respect to said parameter. Consider the case where $c_1 = 0$, i.e., $y \in C[0,1]$.

Lemma 4. *Let $y \in C[0,1]$, $\lambda \in \mathbb{C}$. Then, for each fixed $t \in [0,1]$, $y(t,\lambda)$ is continuous with respect to λ.*

Proof. Let $\Lambda > 0$ be arbitrary but fixed, and let $|\lambda|, |\lambda_0| < \Lambda$. Using (28),

$$y(t,\lambda) - y(t,\lambda_0) = \frac{1}{\Gamma(2\alpha)} \int_0^t (t-s)^{2\alpha-1}((q(s)-\lambda)y(s,\lambda) - (q(s)-\lambda_0)y(s,\lambda_0))ds$$
$$= \frac{1}{\Gamma(2\alpha)} \int_0^t (t-s)^{2\alpha-1}((\lambda_0-\lambda)y(s,\lambda) + (q(s)-\lambda_0)(y(s,\lambda)-y(s,\lambda_0)))ds.$$

So,

$$y(t,\lambda) - y(t,\lambda_0) = -(\lambda-\lambda_0)\frac{1}{\Gamma(2\alpha)}\int_0^t (t-s)^{2\alpha-1}y(s,\lambda)ds + \frac{1}{\Gamma(2\alpha)}\int_0^t (t-s)^{2\alpha-1}(q(s)-\lambda_0)(y(s,\lambda)-y(s,\lambda_0))ds. \quad (32)$$

Now, let $\epsilon > 0$ and $|\lambda - \lambda_0| < \delta$ where $\delta > 0$ is to be chosen later. Then,

$$|y(t,\lambda)-y(t,\lambda_0)| \le \delta\frac{1}{\Gamma(2\alpha)}\int_0^t (t-s)^{2\alpha-1}|y(s,\lambda)|ds + \frac{1}{\Gamma(2\alpha)}\int_0^t (t-s)^{2\alpha-1}|q(s)-\lambda_0||y(s,\lambda)-y(s,\lambda_0)|ds.$$

Using (22) and Gronwall's inequality, we get

$$|y(t,\lambda) - y(t,\lambda_0)| \le \frac{\delta c_3 t^{2\alpha}}{2\alpha\,\Gamma(2\alpha)} + \frac{1}{\Gamma(2\alpha)}\int_0^t (t-s)^{2\alpha-1}|q(s)-\lambda_0||y(s,\lambda)-y(s,\lambda_0)|ds$$
$$\le \frac{\delta c_3}{\Gamma(2\alpha+1)} e^{\frac{1}{\Gamma(2\alpha)}\int_0^1 (t-s)^{2\alpha-1}|q(s)-\lambda_0|\,ds}$$
$$\le \frac{\delta c_3}{\Gamma(2\alpha+1)} e^{\frac{1}{\Gamma(2\alpha)}\int_0^1 (1-s)^{2\alpha-1}|q(s)-\lambda_0|\,ds} := C\delta$$

where

$$C = \frac{c_3}{\Gamma(2\alpha+1)} e^{\frac{1}{\Gamma(2\alpha)}\int_0^1 (1-s)^{2\alpha-1}|q(s)-\lambda_0|\,ds}$$

is a function of α and λ_0 only as $q \in L^\infty(0,1)$. Thus, for any $t \in [0,1]$, the continuity of $y(t,\lambda)$ follows by choosing $\delta < \frac{\epsilon}{C}$. It also follows from this that,

$$\sup_{t\in[0,1]} |y(t,\lambda)-y(t,\lambda_0)| < \epsilon, \quad |\lambda-\lambda_0| < \delta. \quad (33)$$

□

Next, we consider the differentiability of $y(t,\lambda)$ with respect to λ.

Lemma 5. *Let $y \in C[0,1]$, $\lambda \in \mathbb{C}$. Then, for each fixed $t \in [0,1]$, $y(t,\lambda)$ is differentiable with respect to λ.*

Proof. As before let $|\lambda| < \Lambda$, $t \in [0,1]$. Equation (32) can be rewritten as

$$\frac{y(t,\lambda)-y(t,\lambda_0)}{\lambda-\lambda_0} = -\frac{1}{\Gamma(2\alpha)}\int_0^t (t-s)^{2\alpha-1}y(s,\lambda)\,ds + \frac{1}{\Gamma(2\alpha)}\int_0^t (t-s)^{2\alpha-1}(q(s)-\lambda_0)\frac{y(s,\lambda)-y(s,\lambda_0)}{\lambda-\lambda_0}ds.$$

As $y(t,\lambda_0)$ is given, we define $h(t,\lambda_0)$ to be the unique solution of the Volterra integral equation of the second kind,

$$h(t,\lambda_0) = -\frac{1}{\Gamma(2\alpha)}\int_0^t (t-s)^{2\alpha-1}y(s,\lambda_0)\,ds + \frac{1}{\Gamma(2\alpha)}\int_0^t (t-s)^{2\alpha-1}(q(s)-\lambda_0)h(s,\lambda_0)\,ds.$$

So,

$$\left|\frac{y(t,\lambda)-y(t,\lambda_0)}{\lambda-\lambda_0}-h(t,\lambda_0)\right| \leq \frac{1}{\Gamma(2\alpha)}\int_0^t (t-s)^{2\alpha-1}|y(s,\lambda)-y(s,\lambda_0)|\,ds$$
$$+\frac{1}{\Gamma(2\alpha)}\int_0^t (t-s)^{2\alpha-1}|q(s)-\lambda_0|\left|\frac{y(s,\lambda)-y(s,\lambda_0)}{\lambda-\lambda_0}-h(s,\lambda_0)\right|ds.$$

Let $\varepsilon > 0$ and choose $\delta > 0$ as in (33). Using Gronwall's inequality and (33) we get, for $t \in [0,1]$,

$$\left|\frac{y(t,\lambda)-y(t,\lambda_0)}{\lambda-\lambda_0}-h(t,\lambda_0)\right| \leq \frac{\varepsilon}{2\alpha\Gamma(2\alpha)}+\frac{1}{\Gamma(2\alpha)}\int_0^t (t-s)^{2\alpha-1}|q(s)-\lambda_0|\left|\frac{y(s,\lambda)-y(s,\lambda_0)}{\lambda-\lambda_0}-h(s,\lambda_0)\right|ds,$$
$$\leq \frac{\varepsilon}{\Gamma(2\alpha+1)}e^{\frac{1}{\Gamma(2\alpha)}\int_0^1 (t-s)^{2\alpha-1}|q(s)-\lambda_0|\,ds} = O(\varepsilon). \tag{34}$$

for λ near λ_0 since, for $t \in [0,1]$, $\int_0^1 (t-s)^{2\alpha-1}|q(s)-\lambda_0|\,ds = O(1)$. Thus,

$$\frac{\partial y(t,\lambda)}{\partial \lambda}\bigg|_{\lambda=\lambda_0} := \lim_{\lambda \to \lambda_0}\frac{y(t,\lambda)-y(t,\lambda_0)}{\lambda-\lambda_0} = h(t,\lambda_0),$$

exists at λ_0. Since λ_0 is arbitrary $y_\lambda(t,\lambda)$ exists for all λ with $|\lambda| < \Lambda$, real or complex and the result follows. $\square$

Theorem 2. *For each $t \in [0,1]$, $y(t,\lambda)$ is an entire function of λ.*

Proof. This follows from Lemma 5 since $\lambda \in \mathbf{C}$ and $|\lambda| < \Lambda$ where $\Lambda > 0$ is arbitrary. $\square$

6. A Dirichlet-Type Problem

Let $y \in C[0,1]$, $\lambda \in \mathbf{C}$ be fixed. In this case we note that the first of the boundary conditions (2) is equivalent to the usual fixed end (Dirichlet) boundary conditions, that is,

$$y \in C[0,1] \iff \mathcal{I}_{0+}^{1-\alpha}y(t,\lambda)|_{t=0} = 0 \iff y(0,\lambda) = 0.$$

The continuity assumption implies that there is a number M such that $|y(t,\lambda)| \leq M$, for all $t \in [0,1]$. Thus,

$$|\mathcal{I}_{0+}^{1-\alpha}y(t,\lambda)| \leq \frac{M}{\Gamma(\alpha)}\int_0^t (t-s)^{-\alpha}\,ds = \frac{Mt^{1-\alpha}}{(1-\alpha)\Gamma(\alpha)},$$

and so $\mathcal{I}_{0+}^{1-\alpha}y(t,\lambda)|_{t=0} = 0$. On the other hand (15) now implies that $c_1 = 0$, i.e., $y(0,\lambda) = 0$, so that $y \in C[0,1]$. However, the condition $y(1,\lambda) = 0$ is independent of the statement that $\mathcal{I}_{0+}^{1-\alpha}y(t,\lambda)|_{t=1} = 0$.

Since, for any $z \neq 0$, the Mittag-Leffler functions satisfy

$$E_{\delta,\delta}(z) = \frac{1}{z}E_{\delta,0}(z),$$

we get

$$t^{2\alpha-1}E_{2\alpha,2\alpha}(-\lambda t^{2\alpha}) = -\frac{1}{\lambda t}E_{2\alpha,0}(-\lambda t^{2\alpha}). \tag{35}$$

Hence, using (28) and (35) we get

$$y(t,\lambda) = c_1 t^{\alpha-1}E_{2\alpha,\alpha}(-\lambda t^{2\alpha}) + c_2 t^\alpha E_{2\alpha,\alpha+1}(-\lambda t^{2\alpha}) - \int_0^t \frac{E_{2\alpha,0}(-\lambda(t-s)^{2\alpha})}{\lambda(t-s)}q(s)y(s,\lambda)\,ds. \tag{36}$$

Remark 1. When $\alpha \to 1$, the integral Equation (36) becomes

$$y(t,\lambda) = y(0,\lambda)\cos(\sqrt{\lambda}t) + y'(0,\lambda)\frac{\sin(\sqrt{\lambda}t)}{\sqrt{\lambda}} + \int_0^t \frac{\sin(\sqrt{\lambda}(t-s))}{\sqrt{\lambda}}q(s)y(s,\lambda)ds, \quad (37)$$

which is exactly the integral equation equivalent of the classical Sturm–Liouville equation $-y'' + q(t)y = \lambda y$ for $\lambda > 0$.

Remark 2. Observe that, for each α,

$$\lim_{s \to t^-} -\frac{E_{2\alpha,0}(-\lambda(t-s)^{2\alpha})}{\lambda(t-s)} = \begin{cases} 0, & \text{if } \alpha \in (1/2,1], \\ 1, & \text{if } \alpha = 1/2. \end{cases}$$

and so, for each $1/2 < \alpha < 1$, the kernel appearing in (36) is uniformly bounded on $[0,1]$. This agrees with the equivalent result for the classical case (37).

7. Existence and Asymptotic Distribution of the Eigenvalues

Without loss of generality we may assume that $c_2 = 1$ in (36) and $y(t,\lambda)$ is the corresponding solution. In the sequel we always assume that $1/2 < \alpha < 1$.

Lemma 6. *For each* $t \in [0,1]$, $1/2 < \alpha < 1$, *and* $|\arg(-\lambda)| \leq \mu$ *where* $\mu \in (\alpha\pi, \pi)$, *we have* $|t^\alpha E_{2\alpha,\alpha+1}(-\lambda t^{2\alpha})| \to 0$ *as* $|\lambda| \to \infty$.

Proof. By (14) we can write

$$t^\alpha E_{2\alpha,\alpha+1}(-\lambda t^{2\alpha}) = t^\alpha \left(\frac{1}{2\alpha}(-\lambda t^{2\alpha})^{\frac{1-(\alpha+1)}{2\alpha}}\right)\exp\left\{(-\lambda t^{2\alpha})^{\frac{1}{2\alpha}}\right\} + O\left(\frac{1}{\lambda}\right)$$

$$= -\frac{i}{2\alpha\sqrt{\lambda}}\exp\left\{(-\lambda)^{\frac{1}{2\alpha}}t\right\} + O\left(\frac{1}{\lambda}\right)$$

$$= -\frac{i}{2\alpha\sqrt{\lambda}}\exp\left\{|\lambda|^{\frac{1}{2\alpha}}\left(\cos(\frac{\arg(-\lambda)}{2\alpha}) + i\sin(\frac{\arg(-\lambda)}{2\alpha})\right)t\right\} + O\left(\frac{1}{\lambda}\right).$$

Therefore,

$$\left|t^\alpha E_{2\alpha,\alpha+1}(-\lambda t^{2\alpha})\right| = \frac{1}{2\alpha\sqrt{\lambda}}\exp\left\{|\lambda|^{\frac{1}{2\alpha}}\cos(\frac{\arg(-\lambda)}{2\alpha})t\right\}.$$

Regarding the assumption on $\arg(-\lambda)$, we have $\cos(\frac{\arg(-\lambda)}{2\alpha}) < 0$ and it completes the proof. □

Lemma 7. *For each* $t \in [0,1]$, $s \in [0,t]$, $1/2 < \alpha < 1$, *and* $|\arg(-\lambda)| \leq \mu$ *where* $\mu \in (\alpha\pi, \pi)$, *we have* $\left|\frac{E_{2\alpha,0}(-\lambda(t-s)^{2\alpha})}{\lambda(t-s)}\right| \to 0$ *as* $|\lambda| \to \infty$.

Proof. By (14) we can write

$$\frac{E_{2\alpha,0}(-\lambda(t-s)^{2\alpha})}{\lambda(t-s)} = \frac{\left(\frac{1}{2\alpha}(-\lambda(t-s)^{2\alpha})^{\frac{1}{2\alpha}}\right)\exp\left\{(-\lambda(t-s)^{2\alpha})^{\frac{1}{2\alpha}}\right\} + O\left(\frac{1}{\lambda}\right)}{\lambda(t-s)}$$

$$= \frac{1}{2\alpha}\frac{(-\lambda)^{\frac{1}{2\alpha}}}{\lambda}\exp\left\{(-\lambda)^{\frac{1}{2\alpha}}(t-s)\right\} + O\left(\frac{1}{\lambda^2}\right).$$

Then,

$$\left|\frac{E_{2\alpha,0}(-\lambda(t-s)^{2\alpha})}{\lambda(t-s)}\right| = \frac{1}{2\alpha|\lambda|^{(2\alpha-1)/2\alpha}}\exp\left\{(t-s)|\lambda|^{1/2\alpha}\cos\left(\frac{\arg(-\lambda)}{2\alpha}\right)\right\} + o\left(\frac{1}{|\lambda|^2}\right).$$

Arguing as in the previous lemma we reach the desired conclusion. □

Lemma 8. *For each $t \in [0,1]$, $s \in [0,t]$, $1/2 < \alpha < 1$, and $|\arg(-\lambda)| \leq \mu$ where $\mu \in (\alpha\pi, \pi)$, we have $\left| \frac{E_{2\alpha, 1-\alpha}(-\lambda(t-s)^{2\alpha})}{\lambda(t-s)^{\alpha}} \right| \to 0$ as $|\lambda| \to \infty$.*

Proof. By (14) we can write

$$\frac{E_{2\alpha,1-\alpha}(-\lambda(t-s)^{2\alpha})}{\lambda(t-s)^{\alpha}} = \frac{\left(\frac{1}{2\alpha}(-\lambda(t-s)^{2\alpha})^{\frac{1-(1-\alpha)}{2\alpha}}\right) \exp\left\{(-\lambda(t-s)^{2\alpha})^{\frac{1}{2\alpha}}\right\} + O\left(\frac{1}{\lambda}\right)}{\lambda(t-s)^{\alpha}}$$

$$= \frac{i}{\sqrt{\lambda}2\alpha} \exp\left\{(-\lambda)^{\frac{1}{2\alpha}}(t-s)\right\} + O\left(\frac{1}{\lambda^2}\right).$$

Then,

$$\left| \frac{E_{2\alpha,1-\alpha}(-\lambda(t-s)^{2\alpha})}{\lambda(t-s)^{\alpha}} \right| = \frac{1}{2\alpha\sqrt{|\lambda|}} \exp\left\{(t-s)|\lambda|^{1/2\alpha} \cos\left(\frac{\arg(-\lambda)}{2\alpha}\right)\right\}. \quad (38)$$

The result follows since the exponential term is uniformly bounded. □

Lemma 9. *For each $t \in [0,1]$, and $1/2 < \alpha < 1$, the solution $y(t, \lambda)$ is an entire function of λ of order at most $1/2\alpha$.*

Proof. Let $\lambda \in \mathbf{C}$. Define f by

$$y(t, \lambda) = \exp\left\{t|\lambda|^{1/2\alpha} \cos\left(\frac{\arg(-\lambda)}{2\alpha}\right)\right\} f(t). \quad (39)$$

Then, using (36),

$$f(t) = t^{\alpha} E_{2\alpha, \alpha+1}(-\lambda t^{2\alpha}) \exp\left\{-t|\lambda|^{1/2\alpha} \cos\left(\frac{\arg(-\lambda)}{2\alpha}\right)\right\}$$

$$- \int_0^t \frac{E_{2\alpha,0}(-\lambda(t-s)^{2\alpha})}{\lambda(t-s)} \exp\left\{-(t-s)|\lambda|^{1/2\alpha} \cos\left(\frac{\arg(-\lambda)}{2\alpha}\right)\right\} q(s) f(s) \, ds$$

Applying Lemma 6 there exists $\Lambda \in \mathbf{R}^+$ such that for all $|\lambda| > \Lambda$ we have

$$|f(t)| \leq 1 + \frac{1}{2\alpha|\lambda|^{(2\alpha-1)/2\alpha}} \int_0^t |q(s)||f(s)| \, ds$$

which, on account of Gronwall's inequality, gives us

$$|f(t)| \leq \exp\left\{\frac{1}{2\alpha|\lambda|^{(2\alpha-1)/2\alpha}} \int_0^1 |q(s)| \, ds\right\} \quad (40)$$

for all sufficiently large $|\lambda|$. Thus, $f \in L^{\infty}[0,1]$ so that (39) yields, for some M,

$$|y(t, \lambda)| \leq M \exp\left(|\lambda|^{1/2\alpha}\right)$$

and the order claim is verified. □

Lemma 10. *For each $t \in [0,1]$, $\mathcal{I}_{0^+}^{1-\alpha} y(t, \lambda)$ is an entire function of λ of order at most 2α.*

Proof. This is clear from the definition, the possible values of α, and since $y(t, \lambda)$ is itself entire and of order at most $1/2\alpha$, from Lemma 9. □

Lemma 11. *The boundary value problem* (1) *and* (2) *has infinitely many complex eigenvalues (real eigenvalues are not to be excluded here).*

Proof. By Lemma 10, we know that $\mathcal{I}_{0^+}^{1-\alpha} y(t, \lambda)$ is entire for each $t \in [0, 1]$, and $1/2 < \alpha < 1$ as well. So, the eigenvalues of our problem are given by the zeros of $\mathcal{I}_{0^+}^{1-\alpha} y(1, \lambda)$, which must be countably infinite in number since the latter function is of fractional order $1/2\alpha$ (on account of the restriction on α). This gives us the existence of infinitely many eigenvalues, generally in **C**. □

Next, we give the asymptotic distribution of these eigenvalues when α is either very close to $1/2$ from the right or very close to 1 from the left. Recall (36) with $c_2 = 1$, so that

$$y(t, \lambda) = t^\alpha E_{2\alpha, \alpha+1}(-\lambda t^{2\alpha}) - \int_0^t \frac{E_{2\alpha, 0}(-\lambda(t-s)^{2\alpha})}{\lambda(t-s)} q(s) y(s, \lambda) \, ds. \quad (41)$$

An iterative method for solving for approximate solutions of (41) maybe found in [16]. Keeping in mind the boundary condition (2) at $t = 1$, we calculate $\mathcal{I}_{0^+}^{1-\alpha} y(t, \lambda)$ and then evaluate this at $t = 1$ in order to find the dispersion relation for the eigenvalues. However, our derivation is theoretical in nature. A straightforward though lengthy calculation using (41) and the definition of the Mittag-Leffler functions show that

$$\mathcal{I}_{0^+}^{1-\alpha} y(t, \lambda) = \mathcal{I}_{0^+}^{1-\alpha}\{t^\alpha E_{2\alpha, \alpha+1}(-\lambda t^{2\alpha})\} + \mathcal{I}_{0^+}^{1-\alpha}\left(\int_0^t \frac{E_{2\alpha, 0}(-\lambda(t-s)^{2\alpha})}{\lambda(t-s)} q(s) y(s, \lambda) \, ds\right)$$

$$= t E_{2\alpha, 2}(-\lambda t^{2\alpha}) + \frac{1}{\lambda} \int_0^t \frac{E_{2\alpha, 1-\alpha}(-\lambda(t-s)^{2\alpha})}{(t-s)^\alpha} q(s) y(s, \lambda) \, ds \quad (42)$$

so that the eigenvalues of (1) and (2) are given by those $\lambda \in \mathbf{C}$ such that

$$E_{2\alpha, 2}(-\lambda) + \frac{1}{\lambda} \int_0^1 \frac{E_{2\alpha, 1-\alpha}(-\lambda(1-s)^{2\alpha})}{(1-s)^\alpha} q(s) y(s, \lambda) \, ds = 0. \quad (43)$$

Let us consider first the case where $\lambda \in \mathbf{R}$. Lemma 8 implies that the right side of (38) tends to 0 as $\lambda \to \infty$. Indeed this, combined with (39), implies that

$$\left| \frac{E_{2\alpha, 1-\alpha}(-\lambda(t-s)^{2\alpha})}{\lambda(t-s)^\alpha} y(s, \lambda) \right| = O\left(\frac{1}{\sqrt{|\lambda|}}\right)$$

for all sufficiently large λ.

Thus, the real eigenvalues of the problem (1) and (2) become the zeros of a transcendental equation of the form,

$$E_{2\alpha, 2}(-\lambda) + O\left(\frac{1}{\sqrt{\lambda}}\right) = 0.$$

We are concerned with the asymptotic behaviour of these real zeros. Recall the distribution of the real zeros of $E_{2\alpha, 2}(-\lambda)$ in [1]. There we showed that, for each $n = 0, 1, 2, \ldots, N^* - 1$, where N^* depends on α, the interval

$$I_n(\alpha) := \left(\left(\frac{(2n + \frac{1}{2} + \frac{1}{2\alpha})\pi}{\sin(\frac{\pi}{2\alpha})} \right)^{2\alpha}, \left(\frac{(2n + \frac{3}{2} + \frac{1}{2\alpha})\pi}{\sin(\frac{\pi}{2\alpha})} \right)^{2\alpha} \right), \quad (44)$$

always contains at least two real zeros of $E_{2\alpha,2}(-\lambda)$. For $\alpha \to 1$, these intervals approach the intervals

$$\left((2n+1)^2\pi^2, (2n+2)^2\pi^2\right),$$

whose end-points are each eigenvalues of the Dirichlet problem for the classical equation $-y'' = \lambda y$ on $[0,1]$. Since each interval I_n contains two zeros we can denote the first of these two zeros by $\lambda_{2n}(\alpha)$. Equation (44) now gives the a-priori estimate

$$\left(\frac{(2n+\frac{1}{2}+\frac{1}{2\alpha})\pi}{\sin(\frac{\pi}{2\alpha})}\right)^{2\alpha} \le \lambda_{2n}(\alpha) \le \left(\frac{(2n+\frac{3}{2}+\frac{1}{2\alpha})\pi}{\sin(\frac{\pi}{2\alpha})}\right)^{2\alpha}. \tag{45}$$

For each $\alpha < 1$, and close to 1, and for large λ, the real zeros of the preceding equation approach those of $E_{2\alpha,2}(-\lambda)$ and spread out towards the end-points of intervals of the form (44). For α close to $1/2$ there are no zeros, the first two zeros appearing only when $\alpha \approx 0.7325$. For α larger than this critical value, the zeros appear in pairs and in intervals of the form (44).

Next, recall that for $\alpha < 1$ there are only *finitely many* such real zeros, (see [1]) their number growing without bound as $\alpha \to 1$. It also follows from Lemma 11 that, for each α, the remaining infinitely many eigenvalues must be non-real. As $\alpha \to 1^-$ these non-real eigenvalues tend to the real axis thereby forming more and more real eigenvalues until the spectrum is totally real when $\alpha = 1$ and the problem then reduces to a (classical) regular Sturm–Liouville problem.

Finally, for α close to 1, (45) leads to the approximation,

$$\lambda_{2n}(\alpha) \approx \left(\frac{(2n+2)\pi}{\sin(\frac{\pi}{2\alpha})}\right)^{2\alpha},$$

from which this, in conjunction with (44) and $\alpha \to 1$, we can derive the classical eigenvalue asymptotics, $\lambda_n \sim n^2\pi^2$ as $n \to \infty$.

8. Conclusions

We consider the fractional eigenvalue problem,

$$-{}^c\mathcal{D}^\alpha_{0+} \circ \mathcal{D}^\alpha_{0+} y(t) + q(t)y(t) = \lambda y(t), \quad 0 \le t \le 1,$$

where α is a real parameter, $1/2 < \alpha < 1$, λ is a generally unspecified complex parameter, with mixed Caputo and Riemann–Liouville derivatives and q an essentially bounded function, subject to the following boundary conditions involving the Riemann–Liouville integrals,

$$\mathcal{I}^{1-\alpha}_{0+}y(t)|_{t=0} = 0, \quad \text{and} \quad \mathcal{I}^{1-\alpha}_{0+}y(t)|_{t=1} = 0.$$

We show that this problem admits, for each α under consideration, and for eigenfunctions that are in $C[0,1]$, a finite number of real eigenvalues and an infinite number of non-real eigenvalues. The real eigenvalues, though finite in number for each α, are approximated by (44) and (45), which as $\alpha \to 1$ gives the classical asymptotic relation $\lambda_n \sim n^2\pi^2$ as $n \to \infty$.

As $\alpha \to 1^-$ we observe that the spectrum obtained approaches the Sturm–Liouville spectrum of the classical problem

$$-y'' + q(t)y = \lambda y, \quad y(0) = y(1) = 0.$$

The same results hold if the eigenfunctions are merely $C(0,1]$ (i.e., $c_1 \ne 0$) except that now the latter have an infinite discontinuity at $t = 0$ for each α. The proofs are identical and are therefore omitted.

Author Contributions: Conceptualization, M.D. and A.B.M.; methodology, M.D. and A.B.M.; software, M.D. and A.B.M.; validation, M.D. and A.B.M.; formal analysis, M.D. and A.B.M.; investigation, M.D. and A.B.M.; resources, M.D. and A.B.M.; data curation, Not applicable; writing—original draft preparation, M.D. and A.B.M.; writing—review and editing, M.D. and A.B.M.; visualization, Not applicable; supervision, M.D. and A.B.M.; project administration, M.D. and A.B.M.; funding acquisition, M.D. and A.B.M. All authors have read and agreed to the published version of the manuscript.

Funding: This research was partially supported by a grant from the Office of the Dean of Science, Carleton University.

Institutional Review Board Statement: Not applicable.

Informed Consent Statement: Not applicable.

Data Availability Statement: No data were used to support this study.

Conflicts of Interest: The authors declare no conflict of interest.

References

1. Dehghan, M.; Mingarelli, A.B. Fractional Sturm-Liouville eigenvalue problems, I. *Rev. Real Acad. Cienc. Exactas Fis. Nat. Ser. A Mat.* **2020**, *114*, 46.
2. Aleroev, T.S.; Aleroeva, H.T. Problems of Sturm-Liouville type for differential equations with fractional derivatives. In *Volume 2 Fractional Differential Equations*; Kochubei, A., Luchko, Y., Eds.; De Gruyter: Berlin, Germany; Boston, MA, USA, 2019; pp. 21–46. [CrossRef]
3. Al-Mdallal, Q.M. An efficient method for solving fractional Sturm-Liouville problems. *Chaos Solitons Fractals* **2009**, *40*, 183–189.
4. Blaszczyk, T.; Ciesielski, M. Numerical solution of fractional Sturm-Liouville equation in integral form. *Fract. Calculus Appl. Anal.* **2014**, *17*, 307–320.
5. Heydarpour, Z.; Izadi J.; George, R.; Ghaderi, M.; Rezapour, S. On a Partial Fractional Hybrid Version of Generalized Sturm-Liouville-Langevin Equation. *Fractal Fract.* **2022**, *6*, 269.
6. Klimek, M.; Agrawal, O.P. On a regular fractional Sturm-Liouville problem with derivatives of order $(0,1)$. In Proceedings of the 13th International Carpathian Control Conference, High Tatras, Slovakia, 28–31 May 2012. [CrossRef]
7. Klimek, M.; Agrawal, O.P. Fractional Sturm-Liouville problem. *Comput. Math. Appl.* **2013**, *66*, 795–812.
8. Klimek, M.; Odzijewicz, T.; Malinowska, A.B. Variational methods for the fractional Sturm-Liouville problem. *J. Math. Anal. Appl.* **2014**, *416*, 402–426. [CrossRef]
9. Klimek, M.; Ciesielski, M.; Blaszczyk, T. Exact and Numerical Solution of the Fractional Sturm-Liouville Problem with Neumann Boundary Conditions. *Entropy* **2022**, *24*, 143. [CrossRef] [PubMed]
10. Min, D.; Chen, F. Variational methods to the p-Laplacian type nonlinear fractional order impulsive differential equations with Sturm-Liouville boundary-value problem. *Fract. Calc. Appl. Anal.* **2021** *24*, 1069–1093. [CrossRef]
11. Zayernouri, M.; Karniadakis, G.E. Fractional Sturm-Liouville eigen-problems: theory and numerical approximation. *J. Comput. Phys.* **2013**, *252*, 495–517.
12. Mittag-Leffler, G. Sur la nouvelle function $E_\alpha(x)$. *C. R. Acad. Sci. Paris* **1903**, *137*, 554–558.
13. Erdélyi, A.; Bateman, H. *Higher Transcendental Functions*; McGraw-Hill Book Company, Inc.: New York, NY, USA, 1953; Volume 3.
14. Kilbas, A.A.; Srivastava, H.M.; Trujillo, J.J. *Theory and Application of Fractional Differential Equations*; Elsevier: Amsterdam, The Netherlands, 2006.
15. Maralani, E.M.; Saei, F.D.; Akbarfam, A.J.; Ghanbari, K. Eigenvalues of fractional Sturm-Liouville problems by successive method. *Comput. Methods Differ. Equ.* **2021**, *9*, 1163–1175.
16. Ma, H.J.; Wang, Y. Full Information Control of Borel-Measurable Markov Jump. *Mathematics* **2022**, *10*, 37. [CrossRef]

 *fractal and fractional*

Article

On the Basic Theory of Some Generalized and Fractional Derivatives

Leila Gholizadeh Zivlaei and Angelo B. Mingarelli *

School of Mathematics and Statistics, Carleton University, Ottawa, ON K1S 5B6, Canada
* Correspondence: angelo@math.carleton.ca

Abstract: We continue the development of the basic theory of generalized derivatives as introduced and give some of their applications. In particular, we formulate necessary conditions for extrema, Rolle's theorem, the mean value theorem, the fundamental theorem of calculus, integration by parts, along with an existence and uniqueness theorem for a generalized Riccati equation, each of which provides simple proofs of the corresponding version for the so-called conformable fractional derivatives considered by many. Finally, we show that for each $\alpha > 1$ there is a fractional derivative and a corresponding function whose fractional derivative fails to exist everywhere on the real line.

Keywords: fractional differential equation; p-derivative

MSC: Primary 34B24, 34C10; Secondary 47B50

Citation: Gholizadeh Zivlaei, L.; Mingarelli, A.B. On the Basic Theory of Some Generalized and Fractional Derivatives. *Fractal Fract.* **2022**, *6*, 672. https://doi.org/10.3390/fractalfract6110672

Academic Editor: Carlo Cattani

Received: 8 October 2022
Accepted: 9 November 2022
Published: 14 November 2022

Publisher's Note: MDPI stays neutral with regard to jurisdictional claims in published maps and institutional affiliations.

Copyright: © 2022 by the authors. Licensee MDPI, Basel, Switzerland. This article is an open access article distributed under the terms and conditions of the Creative Commons Attribution (CC BY) license (https://creativecommons.org/licenses/by/4.0/).

1. Introduction

In a previous paper [1] generalized derivatives of the form

$$D_p f(t) = \lim_{h \to 0} \frac{f(p(t,h)) - f(t)}{h} \quad (1)$$

were introduced whenever the limit exists and is finite. Here p is a real valued function of the two real variables (t, h) where t is defined on some interval $I \subseteq \mathbf{R}$. Recently, two special cases of fractional derivatives of order α (with $0 < \alpha < 1$) were defined by means of the limit definition,

$$D^\alpha f(t) = \lim_{h \to 0} \frac{f(p(t,h,\alpha)) - f(t)}{h} \quad (2)$$

where $p(t, h, \alpha) = t + ht^{1-\alpha}$ see Katugampola [2], and where $p(t, h, \alpha) = t \exp(ht^{-\alpha})$, see Khalil [3]. Under mild conditions on p it can be shown (see [1]) that such p-derivatives satisfy all the basic rules of differentiation (Product rule, etc.) and that indeed, the derivatives defined in [2,3] are special cases of these where, however, $p_h(t, 0) \neq 0$ ($p_h(t, h)$ is the partial derivative of p with respect to its second variable). We note that these generalized derivatives, that are not of themselves fractional derivatives, may include some recently considered fractional derivatives. For example, criteria for considering a derivative as fractional can be found in [4] where it was noticed that, according to that criteria, the conformable fractional derivative defined in [3] would not, per se, be a fractional derivative. However, the notion of generalized derivatives defined herein should not be made to adhere to the strict assumptions outlined in [4] as these p-derivatives are not, strictly speaking, fractional and thus we take as basic the properties accepted in [5] and other books in analysis as our starting point.

We will show below that the fractional derivatives considered in [2,3] among others specified later are essentially integer valued ordinary derivatives except possibly in at most one point. This is another reason, in addition to [4], to suggest that they should not be considered "fractional".

We now know (see [1]) that whenever f is a differentiable function (in the ordinary sense, i.e., when $p(t,h) = t + h$) and $p_h(t,0) \neq 0$, then the generalized derivative (1) exists at t and

$$D_p f(t) = p_h(t,0) \, f'(t). \tag{3}$$

where the prime is the ordinary derivative of f at t. This shows that the existence of a derivative implies the existence of a p-derivative so long as $p_h(t,0) \neq 0$. Indeed, (3) shows that generalized or even the so-called fractional derivatives defined by either (1) and (2), or by [2,3], are simply multiplication operators on the space of derivatives of differentiable functions, or just *weighted* first order differential operators where the weight, represented by $p_h(t,0)$, may itself be sign-indefinite on I.

Possible physical applications of the foregoing theory can be found in [1], where it is shown that in non-relativistic celestial mechanics elliptical orbits prevail independently of the fractional derivative chosen. The resulting theory can then be included within the framework of weighted operator theory of ordinary differential operators, not without its own difficulties especially when the indicated partial derivative changes sign on intervals or, more generally, on sets of positive measure.

One may think of these generalized derivatives as momentum operators where the p_h-term in (3) can serve both as a classical positive mass or hypothetically as a negative mass. We note that such negative mass particles are a subject of current interest; see, for example, [6] and the references therein. Negative masses can be interpreted as the negative mass density, which belongs to a kind of exotic hypothetical matter distribution like dark matter or dark energy. This could happen conceptually, for example, due to a region of space where the stress component of the Einstein energy-momentum tensor is larger in magnitude than the mass density or due to the Casimir effect. More importantly, from the physical point of view, a negative mass violates energy conditions in general relativity and has its own consequence [7–9]. However, positive energy is not a required condition for the mathematical consistency of the theory, and this concept can be built up only mathematically.

By way of examples, there has been a flurry of activity of late in the area of locally defined fractional differential operators and corresponding equations. Among these we cite [2,3,10–18]. We cannot begin to cite all the references related to these as, for example, Google Scholar refers to more than 2000 references to paper [3] alone! Clearly, our bibliography cannot be exhaustive. In the sequel, unless otherwise specified, α, β will denote real parameters with $0 < \alpha < 1$, $\beta \neq 0$, and $\beta \notin \mathbf{Z}^-$.

Khalil, et al. [3] define a function f to be **α-differentiable** at $t > 0$ if the limit,

$$T_0^\alpha f(t) = \lim_{h \to 0} \frac{f(t + h t^{1-\alpha}) - f(t)}{h}. \tag{4}$$

exists and is finite. Katugampola [2] presented another (locally defined) derivative by requiring that, for $t > 0$,

$$T_0^\alpha f(t) = \lim_{h \to 0} \frac{f(t e^{h t^{-\alpha}}) - f(t)}{h}. \tag{5}$$

exist and be finite. Recently, other authors, e.g., [10], considered minor variations in the definition (4) by assuming that, for $t > 0$,

$$D^{GFD} f(t) = \lim_{h \to 0} \frac{f(t + \frac{\Gamma(\beta) h t^{1-\alpha}}{\Gamma(\beta - \alpha + 1)}) - f(t)}{h}. \tag{6}$$

exist and be finite. Note that in each of the three definitions, the case $\alpha = 1$ (and $\beta = 1$ in (6)) leads to the usual definition of a derivative (see Section 2 in the case of (5)).

Observe that, in each case, (4)–(6), the derivatives are defined for $t > 0$. As many authors have noticed one merely needs to replace $t^{1-\alpha}$ by $(t-a)^{1-\alpha}$ in each of these definitions to allow for a derivative to be defined on an a given interval (a,b), whether finite or infinite. In the case of (5) the point $t = 0$ must be excluded as it is not in the domain of definition of the exponential.

More recently, Gúzman et al. [19], considered a fractional derivative called the *N-derivative* defined for $t > 0$ by

$$N_F^\alpha f(t) = \lim_{h \to 0} \frac{f(t + he^{t^{-\alpha}}) - f(t)}{h}. \tag{7}$$

The function f is said to be N-differentiable if (7) exists and is finite. In a later paper [20], the authors stated slight extensions of the previous definition to another $N_F^\alpha(t)$ derivative defined by the existence and finiteness of the limit,

$$N_F^\alpha f(t) = \lim_{h \to 0} \frac{f(t + hF(t, \alpha)) - f(t)}{h}. \tag{8}$$

Here F seems to have been left generally unspecified, yet the authors obtain the relation (see [20], Equation (2))

$$N_F^\alpha f(t) = F(t, \alpha) f'(t), \tag{9}$$

also a consequence of Theorem 3 below and the results in [1] but whose validity is sensitive to the behaviour of the function F. We will show below that the fractional derivatives defined by anyone of (4)–(8) are, in fact, integer ordered differential operators multiplied by a weight function.

By way of another example, we show that the definition of the generalized derivative,

$$D^\alpha f(t) = \lim_{h \to 0} \frac{f(t + \sin(h) (\cos t)^{1-\alpha}) - f(t)}{h}, \tag{10}$$

where $0 < \alpha < 1$ and the limit exists and is finite for $t \in [0, b]$, $b < \pi/2$, can also be handled by our methods and will lead to results that are a consequence of the definition in [1]. Observe, in passing, that the case where $\alpha = 1$ in (10), i.e., $D^\alpha f(t) = f'(t)$ whenever f is differentiable in the ordinary sense.

These definitions of a generalized derivative function (sometimes called a fractional derivative) on the real line will be referred to occasionally as *locally defined* derivatives as, in each case, knowledge of f is required merely in a neighborhood of the point t under consideration. In contrast, in the case of the more traditional Riemann-Liouville or Caputo fractional derivatives, knowledge of the function f is required on a much larger interval including the point t, see e.g., [21]. The previous, though very popular, derivatives defined in terms of singular integral operators will not be considered here.

In this paper we continue the study of the generalized derivatives introduced in [1] and show that a large number of definitions such as (4)–(8) and (10) can be included in the more general framework of [1]. Thus, the results obtained in papers using either of the above definitions are actually a corollary of our results. We also find versions of Rolle's theorem, the mean value theorem, and the fundamental theorem of calculus, a result on the nowhere fractional differentiability of a class of fractional derivatives and corresponding functions, as well as an existence and uniqueness theorem for a generalized Riccati differential equation, all of which generalize many results in the literature.

In Section 2 we show that a large class of known *fractional* derivatives are actually integer order derivatives at all points except at most one. In Section 3 we summarize briefly the notion of p-derivatives as introduced in [1] and show that these derivatives all satisfy the usual properties (such as linearity, the product rule, the quotient rule, and the chain rule). We then formulate general versions of the mean value theorem (see Theorem 5) and study the cases where $p_h(t, 0) \neq 0$ and $p_h(t, 0) = 0$, separately as each leads to widely differing results. Thus, in Section 4 we formulate a fundamental theorem of calculus and an integration by parts formula in the former case where $p_h(t, 0) \neq 0$ while in Section 5 we consider the same results in the anomalous case where $p_h(t, 0) = 0$ and show that, generally speaking, such fundamental results are not possible. In the same section we consider the problem of determining classes of functions that are p-differentiable everywhere and nowhere p-differentiable everywhere. In Section 6 we apply the preceding theory to the formulation of an existence and uniqueness theorem for a p-differential equation of Riccati-type on a finite interval whose solutions can be approximated arbitrarily closely and uniformly by the method of successive approximations. We conclude by asking a question to which the answer evades us, namely, whether there is a function p, satisfying (20), and a function f such that f is p-differentiable and such that $D_p f(t) \neq 0$ for all t in some interval.

2. Preliminary Observations

The authors in each of [2,3,10] point out that the notion of differentiability represented by either one of the definitions (4)–(6), is more general than the usual one by showing that there are examples whereby α-differentiability does not imply differentiability in the usual sense, although the converse holds. However, note that for $t > 0$ the change of variable $s = t + ht^{1-\alpha}$ shows that

$$\lim_{h \to 0} \frac{f(t + ht^{1-\alpha}) - f(t)}{h} = \frac{1}{t^{\alpha-1}} \lim_{s \to t} \frac{f(s) - f(t)}{s - t}.$$

Consequently, the left hand limit exists if and only if the right hand limit exists. Thus, for $t > 0$, p-differentiability is equivalent to ordinary differentiability and the only possible exception is at $t = 0$ (which is excluded anyway, by definition). A similar argument applies in the case of (6).

Insofar as (5) is concerned, observe that solving for h after the change of variable $s = te^{ht^{-\alpha}}$ is performed, and $t > 0$, leads one to

$$\lim_{h \to 0} \frac{f(te^{ht^{-\alpha}}) - f(t)}{h} = \frac{1}{t^\alpha}\left(\lim_{s \to t} \frac{f(s) - f(t)}{s - t}\right)\left(\lim_{s \to t} \frac{s - t}{\ln s - \ln t}\right) = \frac{1}{t^{\alpha-1}} \lim_{s \to t} \frac{f(s) - f(t)}{s - t}.$$

It follows that both definitions, (4) and (5), coincide for $t > 0$ (see also [1]). Definition (6) is simply a re-scaling of (4) by a constant as can be verified by replacing h in (4) by hc where $c = \Gamma(\beta)/\Gamma(\beta - \alpha + 1)$. Thus, strictly speaking, although it appears to be more general than (4), it isn't really so.

Next, observe that, for $t > 0$, the N-derivative defined by (7),

$$\lim_{h \to 0} \frac{f(t + he^{t^{-\alpha}}) - f(t)}{h} = \frac{1}{e^{-t^\alpha}}\left(\lim_{s \to t} \frac{f(s) - f(t)}{s - t}\right) = e^{t^\alpha} f'(t)$$

if either limit exists. Thus, for $t > 0$, f is N-differentiable if and only if f is differentiable in the ordinary sense. This means that in [19] (and Theorem 2.3 (f) therein), N-differentiability is equivalent to ordinary differentiability (see the Remark in [19], p.91).

For definition (10), note that, for $t \in [0, b]$, $b < \pi/2$,

$$\lim_{h \to 0} \frac{f(t + \sin(h)\cos(t)^{1-\alpha}) - f(t)}{h} = \lim_{s \to t} \frac{f(s) - f(t)}{s - t} \lim_{s \to t} \frac{s - t}{\arcsin((s - t)\sec^{1-\alpha}(t))} = \cos^{1-\alpha}(t) f'(t),$$

if either limit on the left or right exists.

Definition (10) gives something new that hasn't been studied before but falls within the framework of the theory developed in [1]. These observations lead to the following theorem (see also Theorem 2.4 in [1]).

Finally, for the generalized derivative defined by (8), it can be shown that this and the previous results are consequences of Proposition 3 below.

Theorem 1. *For $t > 0$ (resp. $t \geq 0$) a function is differentiable in the sense of either (4), (5), or (6), (8), (9) (resp. (10)) if and only if it is differentiable in the usual sense.*

Remark 1. *It follows that the conformable fractional derivatives defined above (except for (10)) are actually differentiable in the ordinary sense whenever $t > 0$, the only possible point of non-differentiability being at $t = 0$.*

3. Generalized Derivatives

Let $f : I \to \mathbb{R}$, $I \subseteq \mathbb{R}$ and $p : U_\delta \to \mathbb{R}$ where $U_\delta = \{(t,h) : t \in I, |h| < \delta\}$ for some $\delta > 0$ is some generally unspecified neighborhood of $(t,0)$. Unless δ is needed in a calculation we shall simply assume that this condition is always met. Of course, we always assume that the range of p is contained in I. In the sequel, $L(I) \equiv L_1(I)$ is the usual space of Lebesgue integrable functions on I.

For a given α, the **generalized derivative** or **p-derivative** in [1] is defined by

$$D_p f(t) = \lim_{h \to 0} \frac{f(p(t,h)) - f(t)}{h}. \tag{11}$$

whenever the limit exists and is finite. Occasionally, we'll introduce the parameter α mentioned above into the definition so that the limit

$$D_p^\alpha f(t) = \lim_{h \to 0} \frac{f(p(t,h,\alpha)) - f(t)}{h}. \tag{12}$$

will then be called the **p-derivative of order α**. Since α is a parameter (12) is actually a special case of (11).

The main hypotheses on the function p are labeled $H1^\pm$ and $H2$ in [1] and can be summarized together as follows:

Hypothesis 1. *Given an interval $I \subset \mathbb{R}$, in addition to requiring that for $t \in I$, the function $p(t,h)$, $p_h(t,h)$ are continuous in a neighborhood of $h = 0$, we ask that for $t \in I$ and for all sufficiently small $\varepsilon > 0$, $p(t,h) = t \pm \varepsilon$ has a solution $h = h(t,\varepsilon)$ such that $h \to 0$ as $\varepsilon \to 0$.*

Occasionally, we will assume, in addition, that $\frac{1}{p_h(\cdot,0)} \in L(I)$.

NOTATION: The notations $D, D^\alpha, D_p, D_p^\alpha$ will be used interchangeably, occasionally for emphasis.

It is easy to see that the notion of p-differentiability as defined in (11) is very general in that it includes all the above definitions. To this end, it suffices to show that hypothesis (H) is satisfied and this is a simple matter, see also [1].

Theorem 2. *Each of the derivatives defined by (4)–(8), and (10) above are p-derivatives for an appropriate function p satisfying (H).*

The following basic property is expected of a generalized derivative and indeed holds for the class considered here and in [1].

Theorem 3. *(See Theorem 2.1 in [1]). Let p satisfy (H). If f is p-differentiable at a then f is continuous at a.*

Corollary 1. *Let f be α-differentiable where the α-derivative is defined in either (4)–(8) or (10). Then f is continuous there.*

Remark 2. *We note that Corollary 1 includes Theorem 2.1 in [3]; Theorem 2.2 in [2], and Theorem 2.2 in [19]).*

The usual rules for differentiation are also valid in this more general scenario. In the sequel for a given function p satisfying (H) we will write $D_p := D$ or, if there is a parameter dependence, $D_p^\alpha := D$, for simplicity.

Proposition 1. *(See Theorem 2.2 in [1] for proofs.)*

(a) *(Linearity) If f, g are both p-differentiable at $t \in I$ and α is a constant, then then so is their sum, $f + \alpha g$, and*
$$D(f + \alpha g)(t) = Df(t) + \alpha Dg(t).$$

(b) *(The product rule) Assume that p satisfies (H) and that for $t \in I$, $p(t, h)$ is continuous at $h = 0$. If f, g are both p-differentiable at $t \in I$ then so is their product, $f \cdot g$, and*
$$D(f \cdot g)(t) = f(t) \cdot Dg(t) + g(t) \cdot Df(t).$$

(c) *(The quotient rule) Assume that p satisfies (H). If f, g are both p-differentiable at $t \in I$ and $g(t) \neq 0$ then so is their quotient, f/g, and*
$$D\left(\frac{f}{g}\right)(t) = \frac{g(t) \cdot Df(t) - f(t) \cdot Dg(t)}{g(t)^2}.$$

As a result we obtain,

Corollary 2. *(See Theorem 2.2 in [3]; Theorem 2.3 in [2]; Theorem 4 in [10], and Theorem 2.3 in [19].) For each of the definitions (4)–(8) and (10) there holds an analog of the sum/product/and quotient rule for differentiation of corresponding p-derivatives.*

Proposition 2. *(See [1], Theorem 2.4) Assume (H). Let f be continuous and non-constant on I, and let f be p-differentiable at $t \in I$. Let g be defined on the range of f and let g be differentiable at $f(t)$. Then the composition $g \circ f$ is p-differentiable at t and*
$$D(g \circ f)(t) = g'(f(t)) Df(t).$$

Corollary 3. *(See [3], p.66 (iv), although the chain rule is not stated correctly there, and Theorem 2.3 in [2].) For each of the definitions (4)–(8) and (10) there holds an analog of the chain rule for differentiation of corresponding p-derivatives in the form*
$$D(g \circ f)(t) = g'(f(t)) Df(t),$$
where $D := D^\alpha$ (resp. $D := D_p^\alpha$) is the corresponding p-derivative in question defined in (11) (resp. (12)).

We now proceed to formulating fundamental theorems of a calculus for generalized derivatives. We begin by stating a necessary condition for extrema in terms of generalized derivatives.

Theorem 4. *Let $f : [a, b] \to \mathbb{R}$ be such that $D_p f(t)$ exists for every $t \in (a, b)$. If f has a local maximum (resp. minimum) at $c \in (a, b)$ and for each $t \in (a, b)$, and for all sufficiently small $|h|$ we have,*

$$p(t, h) < t, \quad h < 0 \quad (\text{resp. } p(t, h) > t, \quad h > 0), \tag{13}$$

$$p(t, h) > t, \quad h > 0 \quad (\text{resp. } p(t, h) < t, \quad h < 0), \tag{14}$$

then $D_p f(c) = 0$.

Proof. We give the proof in the case where $f(c)$ is a local maximum. By hypothesis (14), there exists δ_0 such that
$$p(t, h) > t, \quad 0 < h < \delta_0.$$

Since
$$p(c,h) > c, \quad 0 < h < \delta_0,$$
and $f(c)$ is a maximum, we can conclude that
$$f(p(c,h)) \leq f(c).$$
Therefore
$$\lim_{h \to 0^+} \frac{f(p(c,h)) - f(c)}{h} \leq 0.$$
Hence, $D_p f(c) \leq 0$. Next, by hypothesis (13), there exists δ_1 such that
$$p(c,h) < c, \quad -\delta_1 < h < 0.$$
As before, since $f(c)$ is a maximum,
$$\lim_{h \to 0^-} \frac{f(p(c,h)) - f(c)}{h} \geq 0.$$
So, $D_p f(c) \geq 0$. However, since $D_p f(c)$ exists, it follows that $D_p f(c) = 0$. The proof in the case where $f(c)$ is a minimum is similar, and therefore omitted. □

Next, we present a weak form of a general mean value theorem.

Theorem 5. A generalized mean value theorem. *Let p satisfy the conditions of Theorem 4 and let f be continuous on $[a,b]$. As an additional condition on p, assume that the p-derivative of the function whose values are $t - a$ exists for all $t \in (a,b)$. Then there is a constant $c \in (a,b)$ such that*

$$D_p f(c) = \frac{f(b) - f(a)}{b - a} k, \tag{15}$$

where the constant k is the p-derivative of the function whose values are $t - a$ evaluated at $t = c$, i.e., $k = D_p(t - a)\big|_{t=c}$.

Proof. Define
$$h(t) = f(t) - f(a) - \frac{f(b) - f(a)}{b - a}(t - a).$$
Then, by hypothesis, h is p-differentiable on (a,b), continuous on $[a,b]$ and
$$D_p h(t) = D_p f(t) - \frac{f(b) - f(a)}{b - a} D_p(t - a).$$
In the event that $D_p h(t) = 0$ for all $t \in (a,b)$, c can be chosen to be any point in (a,b). If $D_p h(t) \neq 0$ for all such t we may assume, without loss of generality, that $h(t) > 0$ somewhere. Since $h(a) = h(b) = 0$, and h is continuous, it must achieve its maximum at, say, $t = c \in (a,b)$. By Theorem 4, $D_p h(c) = 0$. The result follows. □

Theorem 6. *If, in addition to the hypotheses in Theorem 5, we have $p(t,0) = t$, for every t, and $p_h(t,0)$ exists, then*
$$D_p f(c) = \frac{f(b) - f(a)}{b - a} p_h(c, 0).$$

Proof. Since
$$D_p(t - a)\big|_{t=c} = \lim_{h \to 0} \frac{p(t,h) - a - (t - a)}{h} = \lim_{h \to 0} \frac{p(t,h) - p(t,0)}{h} = p_h(t,0),$$

the result follows. □

In the next two sections we can formulate more precise results by considering the two cases, $p_h(t,0) \neq 0$ and $p_h(t,0) = 0$.

4. The Case where $p_h(t,0) \neq 0$

We'll see below that this restriction on p is the most common one and all fractional derivatives presented (i.e., (4)–(8), and (10)) satisfy this condition. The next result, when combined with Theorem 1, allows us to transform p-derivatives into ordinary derivatives.

Proposition 3. (See Theorem 2.4 in [1]) *Let p satisfy hypothesis (H). In addition, for $t \in I$, let*

$$\lim_{\varepsilon \to 0} \frac{\varepsilon}{h(t,\varepsilon)} \neq 0. \tag{16}$$

Then f is differentiable at t iff and only if f is p-differentiable at t. In addition,

$$Df(t) = p_h(t,0)\, f'(t). \tag{17}$$

Remark 3. *Violation of either (16) or the tacit assumption, $p_h(t,0) \neq 0$, can void (17), see Remark 2.4 in [1] and the example therein. In other words, if (16) is not satisfied there may exist p-derivatives that are not necessarily representable as multiplication operators of the form (17) on the space of derivatives of differentiable functions. In fact, the function $p(t,h) = t + h^3$ on $(-1,1)$ is such an example with $f(t) = |t|$. It is easily seen that (16) does not hold and yet f is p-differentiable at $t = 0$ but not differentiable there.*

Corollary 4. (See Theorem 2.2 in [3]; Theorem 2.3 in [2]; and Theorem 1 in [10].) *Let the α-derivative be defined as in either (4) or (5) and let f be α-differentiable at t. Then,*

$$T_0^\alpha f(t) = t^{1-\alpha}\, f'(t).$$

If f is α-differentiable in the sense of (6) then,

$$D^{GFD} f(t) = \frac{\Gamma(\beta)}{\Gamma(\beta - \alpha + 1)} t^{1-\alpha}\, f'(t). \tag{18}$$

If f is α-differentiable in the sense of (10) then, for $t \in [0,b]$, $b < \pi/2$,

$$Df(t) = (\cos t)^{1-\alpha}\, f'(t). \tag{19}$$

Similar results hold for derivatives defined by either (7) or (8) (if $F(t,\alpha) \neq 0$.)

Corollary 5. *Let $t > 0$ (resp. $t \geq 0$). Then f is α-differentiable at t in the sense of anyone of (4), (5), or (6), (resp. (10)) if and only if f is differentiable at t.*

Stronger versions of a generalized mean value theorem follow in which we do not require the assumptions in Theorem 4 above but do require that $p_h(t,0) \neq 0$.

Theorem 7. *A generalized mean value theorem. Let p satisfy the conditions of Proposition 3 and let f be p-differentiable on (a,b) and continuous on $[a,b]$. Then there exists $c \in (a,b)$ such that*

$$D_p f(c) = \left[\frac{f(b) - f(a)}{b - a}\right] p_h(c,0).$$

Proof. The proof is clear on account of the usual mean value theorem applied to f on (a,b) since f is necessarily differentiable there by Proposition 3. Since there exists $c \in (a,b)$ such that $f(b) - f(a) = (b-a) f'(c)$ we get $D_p f(c) = p_h(c,0) f'(c)$ and the result follows. □

Theorem 8. *[Another generalized mean value theorem] Let p satisfy the conditions of Proposition 3 and let f, g be p-differentiable on (a, b), continuous on $[a, b]$, and $D_p(g(t)) \neq 0$ there. Then there exists $c \in (a, b)$ such that*

$$\frac{f(b) - f(a)}{g(b) - g(a)} = \frac{D_p f(c)}{D_p g(c)}.$$

Proof. Write

$$h(t) = f(t) - f(a) - \left[\frac{f(b) - f(a)}{g(b) - g(a)}\right](g(t) - g(a)).$$

then $h(a) = h(b) = 0$ and h satisfies the conditions of Theorem 7. So, there exists $c \in (a, b)$ such that $D_p h(c) = 0$. However,

$$D_p h(c) = D_p f(c) - \left[\frac{f(b) - f(a)}{g(b) - g(a)}\right] D_p g(c).$$

The result follows. □

Remark 4. *Specializing to the case where*

$$p(t, h) = t + \frac{\Gamma(\beta) h t^{1-\alpha}}{\Gamma(\beta - \alpha + 1)}$$

and $g(t) = t^\alpha / \Gamma(\alpha)$ with $\alpha \in (0, 1)$ we get [[10], Theorem 6]. The choice $g(t) = t^\alpha / \alpha$ gives [[2], Theorem 2.9].

Next, if $p_h(t, 0)$ exists everywhere on (a, b) and $p(t, 0) = 0$, then Theorem 6 gives us that k in (15) is given by $k = p_h(c, 0)$. In this case, we note that the function f need not be differentiable in the usual sense here (see Theorem 3) and $p_h(c, 0)$ may or may not be zero.

Example 1. *Given $I = [a, b]$, $f(t) = |t|$ and $p(t, h) = t + th + t^3 h^3$. Then p satisfies the conditions of Theorem 5. Furthermore, $p_h(t, 0) \neq 0$ for $t \neq 0$. A simple calculation shows that $D_p f(t) = |t| = f(t)$, for all $t \in (a, b)$. By Theorem 5, there exists $c \in (a, b)$ that*

$$D_p f(c) = \left[\frac{f(b) - f(a)}{b - a}\right] p_h(c, 0),$$

i.e.,

$$|c| = \left[\frac{f(b) - f(a)}{b - a}\right] c.$$

The existence of c can be calculated directly as follows. Let $a < b < 0$. Then,

$$|c| = \left[\frac{-b + a}{b - a}\right] c,$$

so that $|c| = -c$. So, we may choose any c such that $a < c < b$. Let $0 < a < b$. In this case,

$$|c| = \left[\frac{b - a}{b - a}\right] c.$$

It suffices to choose c such that $a < c < b$ again. Finally, let $a < 0 < b$. As

$$|c| = \left[\frac{b + a}{b - a}\right] c,$$

it suffices to choose $c = 0$.

Remark 5. In this example, $p_h(0,0) = 0$ and consequently $D_p f(0) = 0$ even though $f'(0)$ does not exist.

Of course, Rolle's theorem is obtained by setting $f(a) = f(b) = 0$ in Theorem 8. The latter then includes [[2], Theorem 2.8].

Definition 1. Let p satisfy (H), and let $f : [a,b] \to \mathbb{R}$ be continuous. Then

$$I_p(f)(t) = \int_a^t \frac{f(x)}{p_h(x,0)} \, dx.$$

This definition includes the fractional integral considered in [2] (and Definition 3.1 therein). Observe that, since $1/p_h \in L(a,b)$ and f is bounded, this integral always exists (absolutely). It follows that $I_p(f) \in AC[a,b]$ and consequently $I_p'(f)$ exists a.e. In this case, the continuity of p_h guarantees that $I_p(f) \in C^1(a,b)$.

Next we state and prove a version of the generalized fundamental theorem of calculus for such p-derivatives. The first part is clear, i.e.,

Theorem 9. Let p satisfy (H), and let $f : [a,b] \to \mathbb{R}$ be continuous. Then $D_p(I_p(f)(t)) = f(t)$.

Proof. By Proposition 3, since $I_p(f)$ is differentiable, we have,

$$D_p(I_p(f)(t)) = p_h(t,0) I_p'(f)(t) = f(t).$$

□

NOTE: The preceding includes [2] (and Theorem 3.2 therein) as a special case.

Theorem 10. Let p satisfy (H) and let $F : [a,b] \to \mathbb{R}$ be continuous. If F is p-differentiable on (a,b) and $D_p F$ is continuous on $[a,b]$, then $I_p(D_p F)(b) = F(b) - F(a)$.

Proof. Let $a = x_0 < x_1 < x_2 < \ldots < x_n = b$ be a partition of $[a,b]$. Applying Corollary 7 to each $[x_{i-1}, x_i]$ we get, for some t_i,

$$D_p F(t_i) = \frac{F(x_i) - F(x_{i-1})}{x_i - x_{i-1}} p_h(t_i, 0)$$

or

$$F(x_i) - F(x_{i-1}) = (x_i - x_{i-1}) \frac{D_p F(t_i)}{p_h(t_i, 0)}.$$

Thus,

$$F(b) - F(a) = \sum_{i=1}^n F(x_i) - F(x_{i-1}) = \sum_{i=1}^n \frac{D_p F(t_i)}{p_h(t_i, 0)} \Delta x_i.$$

Now since f is continuous on every subinterval $[x_{i-1}, x_i]$ of $[a,b]$, we can pass to the limit as $\Delta x_i \to 0$. This gives,

$$F(b) - F(a) = \int_a^b \frac{D_p F(t)}{p_h(t,0)} \, dt.$$

This shows that $I_p(D_p F)(b) = F(b) - F(a)$ and we are done. □

Combining Theorems 9 and 10 we get the generalized fundamental theorem of calculus. In addition, using the above relation, we can get a generalized integration by parts formula, i.e.,

Corollary 6. *If f, g are both p-differentiable on (a, b) and continuous on $[a, b]$, then,*

$$I_p(fD_p(g)) = [fg] - I_p(D_p(f)g).$$

This is clear on account of the product rule in Proposition 1(b) and Theorem 10, above.

5. The Case where $p_h(t, 0) = 0$

In this section we consider the exceptional case

$$p_h(t, 0) = 0. \tag{20}$$

The effect of (20) is that it tends to smooth out discontinuities in the ordinary derivative of functions. A glance at (3) would lead one to guess that whenever (20) holds we have $D_p f(t) = 0$ but that is not the case, in general.

Example 2. *Consider the special case $p(t, h) = t + h^2$ which satisfies (20). Then the function $f(x) = \sqrt{x}$, $x > 0$, although not differentiable at $x = 0$, is clearly right-p-differentiable at $x = 0$ with $D_p^+ f(0) = 1$.*

Theorem 11. *Let (20) hold, $p(t, 0) = t$, and assume that (13), (14) are satisfied for each t, as well. If f is continuous on $[a, b]$ and $D_p f(t)$ exists, then $D_p f(t) = 0$.*

Proof. Note that f is continuous on (a, b) on account of the hypothesis and Theorem 3. Using the proofs of Theorems 5 and 6 we observe that the function h defined there is continuous on $[a, b]$, as f is continuous there, and therefore its maximum value is attained at $x = c$. Thus $k = p_h(c, 0) = 0$ by (15). □

Of course, the previous example had an ordinary derivative with an infinite discontinuity at $x = 0$ but still simple discontinuities in the ordinary derivative can lead to the existence of their *p*-derivative for certain *p*.

Remark 6. *Incidentally, Example 2 also shows that (13) cannot be waived in the statement of Theorem 11.*

Example 3. *As before we let $p(t, h) = t + h^2$. Then the function f, defined by $f(x) = |x|$, although not differentiable at $x = 0$ it is clearly p-differentiable at $x = 0$ with $D_p f(0) = 0$.*

Below we study the consequences of this extraordinary assumption (20) and its impact on the study of such *p*-derivatives.

5.1. Consequences of $p_h(t, 0) = 0$

We have seen that the notion of *p*-differentiability can be used to turn non-differentiable functions into *p*-differentiable ones, for some exceptional *p*'s and these can have a *p*-derivative equal to zero, as well. We first look at some simple special cases of *p* satisfying (20).

As is usual we define a polygonal function as a function whose planar graph is composed of line segments only, i.e., it is piecewise linear.

Theorem 12. *Let $p(t, h) = t + h^2$. Then every polygonal function f on $\mathbf{R}$ is p-differentiable everywhere and $D_p f(x) = 0$ for all $x \in \mathbf{R}$.*

Proof. Since the graph of every polygonal function consists of an at most countable and discrete set of simple discontinuities in its ordinary derivative, it is easy to show that its *p*-derivative at the cusp points must be zero (just like the absolute value function above).

The curve being linear elsewhere it is easy to see that at all such points its p-derivative exists and must be equal to zero (see Example 3.1 in [1]). □

Remark 7. *In contrast with the case where $p_h(t,0) \neq 0$ where an integral can be defined via Definition 1, in this case such an inverse cannot be constructed, in general, as the preceding example shows.*

There must be limitations to this theory of generalized or p-derivatives. Thus, we investigate the non-existence of p-derivatives under condition (20) for a class of power functions defining the derivative. Our main result is Theorem 1 below which states that for power-like p-functions there are functions that are nowhere p-differentiable on the real line. In the event that $p_h(t,0) \neq 0$, Proposition 3 makes it easy to construct functions that are nowhere p-differentiable on the whole real axis simply by choosing, in particular, any function with $p_h(t,0) = 1$. For a fascinating historical survey of classical nowhere differentiable functions, the reader is encouraged to look at [22]

At this point one may think that p-differentiability is normal and that most functions have a zero p-derivative if $p_h(t,0) = 0$. This motivates the next question: Does there exist a function p satisfying (20) such that it is continuous and nowhere p-differentiable on **R**? The answer is yes and is in the next theorem.

5.2. Weierstrass' Continuous, Nowhere Differentiable Function

In this subsection we show that the series (21), first considered by Weierstrass, and one that led to a continuous nowhere differentiable function, [5], can also serve as the basis for a continuous nowhere p-differentiable function for a large class of functions p satisfying (20), namely power functions. Below we show that for each $\alpha > 1$ there is a function p satisfying (20) and a function f that is nowhere p-differentiable on the whole line.

Theorem 13. *Let $p(t,h) = t + h^\alpha$ where $\alpha > 1$. Then Weierstrass' continuous and nowhere differentiable function*

$$f(x) = \sum_{n=0}^{\infty} b^n \cos(a^n \pi x) \qquad (21)$$

where $0 < b < 1$, a is a positive integer, and

$$\sqrt[\alpha]{a}\, b > 1 + \frac{3}{2}\pi, \qquad (22)$$

*is also nowhere p-differentiable on **R**.*

Proof. Observe that the cases where $\alpha \leq 1$ are excluded by (20), so we let $\alpha > 1$. We will show, as usual, that there exists a sequence of $h \to 0$ along which $|(f(x+h^\alpha) - f(x))/h| \to \infty$. Now, for fixed $x \in \mathbf{R}$,

$$\begin{aligned}
\frac{f(x+h^\alpha) - f(x)}{h} &= \sum_{n=0}^{\infty} b^n \frac{\cos(a^n \pi (x+h^\alpha)) - \cos(a^n \pi x)}{h} \\
&= \sum_{n=0}^{m-1} b^n \frac{\cos(a^n \pi (x+h^\alpha)) - \cos(a^n \pi x)}{h} + \sum_{n=m}^{\infty} b^n \frac{\cos(a^n \pi (x+h^\alpha)) - \cos(a^n \pi x)}{h} \\
&:= S_m + R_m.
\end{aligned}$$

Estimating S_m by the mean value theorem shows that for some $0 < \theta < 1$,

$$|\cos(a^n \pi (x+h^\alpha)) - \cos(a^n \pi x)| = |h^\alpha a^n \pi \sin(a^n \pi (x+\theta h^\alpha))| \leq a^n \pi |h|^\alpha, \qquad (23)$$

so that

$$|S_m| \leq \pi |h|^{\alpha-1} \sum_{n=0}^{m-1} (ab)^n < \frac{\pi |h|^{\alpha-1}(ab)^m}{ab-1}. \tag{24}$$

Recall that x is fixed at the outset. Now, for any positive integer m, we can write $a^m x$ in the form $a^m x = \alpha_m + t_m$ where α_m is an integer and $|t_m| \leq 1/2$. Define a sequence $h_m > 0$ by

$$h_m = \sqrt[\alpha]{\frac{1-t_m}{a^m}}.$$

Then $0 < h_m^\alpha \leq 3/(2a^m)$. From this choice of a sequence and (24) we get the estimate,

$$|S_m| < \pi \left(\frac{1-t_m}{a^m}\right)^{\frac{\alpha-1}{\alpha}} \frac{(ab)^m}{ab-1} \leq \pi \left(\frac{3}{2a^m}\right)^{\frac{\alpha-1}{\alpha}} \frac{(ab)^m}{ab-1} = \pi \left(\frac{3}{2}\right)^{\frac{\alpha-1}{\alpha}} \frac{a^{\frac{m}{\alpha}} b^m}{ab-1}. \tag{25}$$

The next step is to show that the remainder term, R_m, remains bounded away from 0. To this end note that $a^n \pi (x + h_m^\alpha) = a^{n-m} a^m \pi (x + h_m^\alpha) = a^{n-m} \pi (\alpha_m + 1)$. It follows that since a is odd, then for $n \geq m$, we have

$$\cos(a^n \pi (x + h_m^\alpha)) = (-1)^{\alpha_m + 1}. \tag{26}$$

A similar calculation shows that

$$\cos(a^n \pi x) = \cos(a^{n-m} \pi (\alpha_m + t_m)) = (-1)^{\alpha_m} \cos(a^{n-m} \pi t_m). \tag{27}$$

Combining (26) and (27) we see that

$$R_m = \sum_{n=m}^{\infty} b^n \frac{(-1)^{\alpha_m+1} - (-1)^{\alpha_m} \cos(a^{n-m} \pi t_m)}{h_m}$$

$$= \frac{(-1)^{\alpha_m+1}}{h_m} \sum_{n=m}^{\infty} b^n (1 + \cos(a^{n-m} \pi t_m))$$

i.e., $|R_m| = \frac{1}{|h_m|} \sum_{n=m}^{\infty} b^n (1 + \cos(a^{n-m} \pi t_m))$.

Since the previous series is a series of non-negative terms we can drop all terms except the first. In this case note that $\cos(\pi t_m) \geq 0$ since $|t_m| \leq 1/2$. So,

$$|R_m| > \frac{b^m}{|h_m|} > \sqrt[\alpha]{\frac{2}{3}} a^{m/\alpha} b^m. \tag{28}$$

Finally, using (28) and (25) we get

$$\left|\frac{f(x+h_m^\alpha) - f(x)}{h_m}\right| \geq |R_m| - |S_m| > \sqrt[\alpha]{\frac{2}{3}} a^{\frac{m}{\alpha}} b^m - \pi \left(\frac{3}{2}\right)^{\frac{\alpha-1}{\alpha}} \frac{a^{\frac{m}{\alpha}} b^m}{ab-1} = \left(\sqrt[\alpha]{\frac{2}{3}} - \frac{\pi}{ab-1}\left(\frac{3}{2}\right)^{\frac{\alpha-1}{\alpha}}\right) a^{\frac{m}{\alpha}} b^m \tag{29}$$

Since $b < 1$ we must have $a \geq 3$ so that $ab > \sqrt[\alpha]{ab}$. The stronger hypothesis (22) forces both $\sqrt[\alpha]{ab} > 1$ and the term in the parentheses in (29) to be positive. Since $h_m \to 0$ as $m \to \infty$, the left hand side of (29) tends to infinity, so that the resulting p-derivative cannot exist at x. Since x is arbitrary, the conclusion follows. □

6. An Existence and Uniqueness Theorem

In the final section we give conditions under which an initial value problem for a generalized Riccati equation with p-derivatives has a solution that exists and is unique.

Theorem 14. Let p satisfy (H) and $q : [0, T] \to \mathbb{R}, T < \infty$ be continuous. Assume that for some $b > 0$, we have

$$\left\|\frac{1}{p_h}\right\|_{L^1[0,T]} < \min\left\{\frac{b}{\|q\|_\infty + b^2}, \frac{1}{2b}\right\}. \tag{30}$$

Then the initial value problem for the (generalized) Riccati differential equation

$$D_p u(t) + u^2(t) = q(t), \quad u(0) = u_0, \tag{31}$$

has a unique continuous solution $u(t)$ on $[0, T]$.

Proof. Let $B = \{u \in C[0, T], \|u\|_\infty \leq b\}$. Then B is a complete metric space. Define an operator F on B by $F(u) = I_p(q(t) - u^2(t)) + u_0$. Then for every $u, v \in B$.

$$\begin{aligned}
|Fu - Fv| &= |I_p(q(t) - u^2(t)) - I_p(q(t) - v^2(t))| \\
&= \left|\int_0^t \frac{q(s) - u^2(s)}{p_h(s,0)} - \frac{q(s) - v^2(s)}{p_h(s,0)} ds\right| \\
&= \left|\int_0^t \frac{(v(s) - u(s))(v(s) + u(s))}{p_h(s,0)} ds\right| \\
&\leq 2b\|u - v\|_\infty \int_0^t \left|\frac{1}{p_h(s,0)}\right| ds
\end{aligned}$$

It follows that $\|Fu - Fv\|_\infty < k\|u - v\|$ is a contraction on B, with $k = 2b\|\frac{1}{p_h}\|_{L^1[0,T]} < 1$, by hypothesis.

Next, we show that $F : B \to B$. Clearly, for $u \in B$, Fu is continuous on $[0, T]$. Next, observe that

$$\|Fu\|_\infty \leq \int_0^T \frac{\|q(s) - u^2(s)\|_\infty}{|p_h(s,0)|} ds \leq (\|q\|_\infty + b^2)\left\|\frac{1}{p_h}\right\|_{L^1[0,T]} \leq b,$$

by hypothesis. Hence F maps B into itself. Applying the contraction principle we get that F has a unique fixed point $u \in C[0, T]$ such that $Fu = u$. Theorem 9 gives us the final result. □

Remark 8. Observe that there are no sign restrictions on $p_h(t,0)$. Note that D_p may in fact depend on a parameter α, subject only to the L^1-condition on $1/p_h$ at the outset. For example, if we choose $p(t,h) = t + ht^{1-\alpha}$ as in [3], the hypothesis (30) above becomes,

$$\frac{T^\alpha}{\alpha} \leq \min\left\{\frac{b}{\|q\|_\infty + b^2}, \frac{1}{2b}\right\},$$

so we can see that the assumption that $\alpha \in (0,1)$ is not necessary, just that $\alpha > 0$. Of course, T will generally decrease as α grows. Finally, this solution can always be found using the method of successive approximations as implied by the contraction principle.

Similarly, if $p(t,h) = t + \frac{\Gamma(\beta)}{\Gamma(\beta - \alpha + 1)} h t^{1-\alpha}$ with $\beta > -1, \beta \in \mathbb{R}^+$ and $0 < \alpha \leq 1$ as in [10], the generalized Rolle's theorem, mean value theorem and Riccati differential equation studied here include the corresponding theorems in [10]. In addition, this existence theorem clarifies the purely numerical results obtained in [10] when solving a special Riccati equation of the form (31) using the fractional derivative (6), which, as we have shown, is contained in our theory.

7. Open Question

1. Is there a function p, satisfying (20), and a function f such that f is p-differentiable and such that $D_p f(t) \neq 0$ for all t in some interval (or, more generally, some set of positive measure)?

8. Conclusions

In this paper we have extended the theory of p-derivatives in [1] to include results such as the mean-value theorem, Rolle's theorem and integration by parts. In so doing we showed that the so-called *conformable fractional derivative* of a given function, as considered by [2,3], is actually an ordinary (integer-valued) derivative of the first order except in at most one point. We expanded on the cases where the partial derivative $p_h(t,0)$ either vanishes or doesn't and in so doing showed that in the former case there exists, for each $\alpha > 1$, a fractional derivative and a function whose fractional derivative exists nowhere on the real line. In the case where $p_h(t,0) = 0$ many of the previous results have no analogues and an inverse of the p-derivative generally does not exist. We also presented an existence and uniqueness theorem for a Riccati-type equation involving a p-derivative whose solution may always be found using successive approximations. The results presented here extend many of the results found in the literature as referred to in the text.

Author Contributions: Conceptualization, L.G.Z. and A.B.M.; methodology, L.G.Z. and A.B.M.; software, L.G.Z. and A.B.M.; validation, L.G.Z. and A.B.M.; formal analysis, L.G.Z. and A.B.M.; investigation, L.G.Z. and A.B.M.; resources, L.G.Z. and A.B.M.; data curation, Not applicable; writing?original draft preparation, L.G.Z. and A.B.M.; writing?review and editing, L.G.Z. and A.B.M.; visualization, Not applicable; supervision, L.G.Z. and A.B.M.; project administration, L.G.Z. and A.B.M.; funding acquisition, L.G.Z. and A.B.M. All authors have read and agreed to the published version of the manuscript.

Funding: This research was partially supported by a grant from the Office of the Dean of Science, Carleton University.

Acknowledgments: We thank the many referees for comments that have led to an improved presentation of the results herein.

Conflicts of Interest: The authors declare no conflict of interest.

Abbreviations

The following abbreviations are used in this manuscript:

MDPI   Multidisciplinary Digital Publishing Institute
DOAJ   Directory of open access journals
TLA   Three letter acronym
LD   Linear dichroism

References

1. Mingarelli, A.B. On generalized and fractional derivatives and their applications to classical mechanics. *J. Phys. A Math. Theor.* **2018**, *51*, 365204. [CrossRef]
2. Katugampola, U.N. A new fractional derivative with classical properties. *arXiv* **2014**, arXiv:1410.6535.
3. Khalil, R.; Horani, M.A.; Yousef, A.; Sababheh, M. A new definition of fractional derivative. *J. Comp. Appl. Math.* **2014**, *264*, 65–70. [CrossRef]
4. Ortigueira, M.D.; Machado, J.T. What is a fractional derivative? *J. Comp. Phys.* **2015**, *293*, 4–13. [CrossRef]
5. Rudin, W. *Principles of Mathematical Analysis*; Mc Graw-Hill: New York, NY, USA, 1953.
6. Farnes, J.S. A Unifying Theory of Dark Energy and Dark Matter: Negative Masses and Matter Creation within a Modified? CDM Framework. *Astron. Astrophys.* **2018**, *620*, A92. [CrossRef]
7. Bondi, H. Negative mass in General Relativity. In *The Role of Gravitation in Physics: Report from the 1957 Chapel Hill Conference*; DeWitt-Morette, C., Ed.; ASTIA document; Edition Open Access: Washington, DC, USA, 2017; p. 159. Available online: https://books.google.ca/books?id=i5vJzQEACAAJ (accessed on 11 November 2022).
8. Bonnor, W.B. Negative mass in General relativity. *Gen. Relat. Grav.* **1989**, *21*, 1143–1157 [CrossRef]
9. Nieto, M.M.; Goldman, T. The arguments against "antigravity" and the gravitational acceleration of antimatter. *Phys. Rep.* **1991**, *205*, 221–281. [CrossRef]
10. Abu-Shady, M.; Kaabar, M.K. A Generalized Definition of the Fractional Derivative with Applications. *Math. Probl. Eng.* **2021**, *2021*, 9444803. [CrossRef]
11. Abdeljawad, T. On conformable fractional calculus. *J. Comput. Appl. Math.* **2015**, *279*, 57–66. [CrossRef]

12. Anderson, D.R.; Ulness, D.J. Properties of the Katugampola fractional derivative with potential application in quantum mechanics. *J. Math. Phys.* **2015**, *56*, 063502. [CrossRef]
13. Anderson, D.R.; Ulness, D.J. Newly Defined Conformable Derivatives. *Adv. Dyn. Syst. Appl.* **2015**, *10*, 109–137.
14. Atangana, A.; Baleanu, D.; Alsaedi, A. New properties of conformable derivative. *Open Math.* **2015**, *13*, 889–898. [CrossRef]
15. Baleanu, D.; Fernandez, A.; Akgül, A. On a Fractional Operator Combining Proportional and Classical Differintegrals. *Mathematics* **2020**, *8*, 360. [CrossRef]
16. Chu, Y.M.; Adil, Khan, M.; Ali, T.; Silvestru, Dragomir, S. Inequalities for α-fractional differentiable functions. *J. Inequalities Appl.* **2017**, *2017*, 93. [CrossRef] [PubMed]
17. Ekici, M.; Mirzazadeh, M.; Eslami, M.; Zhou, Q.; Moshokoa, S.P.; Biswas, A.; Belic, M. Optical soliton perturbation with fractional-temporal evolution by first integral method with conformable fractional derivatives. *Optik* **2016**, *127*, 10659–10669. [CrossRef]
18. Teodoro, G.S.; Machado, J.T.; De Oliveira, E.C. A review of definitions of fractional derivatives and other operators. *J. Comput. Phys.* **2019**, *388*, 195–208. [CrossRef]
19. Gúzman, P.M.; Langton, G.; Bittencurt, L.M.L.M.; Medina, J.; Valdes, J.E.N. A new definition of a fractional derivative of local type. *J. Math. Anal.* **2018**, *9*, 88–98.
20. Vivas-Cortez, M.; Imbert, A.F.; Gúzman, P.M.; Napoles, J. Newton's Law of Cooling with generalized conformable derivatives. *Symmetry* **2021**, *13*, 1093. [CrossRef]
21. Jin, B. *Fractional Differential Equations—An Approach via Fractional Derivatives*; Applied Mathematical Sciences; Springer: Cham, Switzerland, 2021; Volume 206.
22. Thim, J. Continuous Nowhere Differentiable Functions. Master's Thesis, Luleå University of Technology, Luleå, Sweden, 2003; 94p.

Article

A Cubic Spline Collocation Method to Solve a Nonlinear Space-Fractional Fisher's Equation and Its Stability Examination

Adel R. Hadhoud [1], Faisal E. Abd Alaal [2], Ayman A. Abdelaziz [2] and Taha Radwan [3,4,*]

1 Department of Mathematics and Computer Science, Faculty of Science, Menoufia University, Shebin El-Kom 13829, Egypt
2 Department of Mathematics, Faculty of Science, Damanhour University, Damanhour 22511, Egypt
3 Department of Mathematics, College of Science and Arts in Ar-Rass, Qassim University, Ar Rass 51452, Saudi Arabia
4 Department of Mathematics and Statistics, Faculty of Management Technology and Information Systems, Port Said University, Port Said 42511, Egypt
* Correspondence: t.radwan@qu.edu.sa

Abstract: This article seeks to show a general framework of the cubic polynomial spline functions for developing a computational technique to solve the space-fractional Fisher's equation. The presented approach is demonstrated to be conditionally stable using the von Neumann technique. A numerical illustration is given to demonstrate the proposed algorithm's effectiveness. The novelty of the present work lies in the fact that the results suggest that the presented technique is accurate and convenient in solving such problems.

Keywords: Caputo sense; space-fractional Fisher's equation; cubic polynomial spline; von Neumann stability

1. Introduction

Fractional calculus is a generalization of classical calculus that deals with fractional order differentiation and integration operations. Everyone who has studied elementary calculus is familiar with the differentiation operator, $D = d/dx$. Additionally, the n th derivative of a suitable function, $D^n f(x) = d^n f(x)/d^n x$, is properly defined as long as n is a positive integer. In 1695, L'Hopital enquired to Leibniz about the meaning of $D^n f$ if n was fractional. Many prominent mathematicians, including Euler, Laplace, Fourier, Abel, Liouville, Riemann, and Laurent, have since studied time-fractional calculus. However, it was not until 1884 that the theory of generalized operators progressed to the point where it could be used as a starting point for modern mathematicians. Fractional calculus has been utilized in thermodynamics, viscoelasticity, bioengineering, aerodynamics, control theory, electromagnetics, finance, chemistry, and signal processing in recent decades [1–3]. Fractional calculus theory dates back to Leibniz in the sixteenth century, and many different types of fractional operators have been created and developed virtually as far as the classical theory has evolved. The Riemann–Liouville, Caputo, conformable, and Riesz operator approaches are among these [4–9]. Fractional differential equations (FDEs) appear in engineering processes, a number of physical phenomena, financial products, and biological systems, such as non-exponential relaxation patterns and anomalous diffusion [10]. Several numerical methods have been developed to obtain an approximate solution of FDEs. These methods include the Adomian decomposition method [11], finite difference method [12], variational iteration method [13], spectral methods [14], and homotopy perturbation method [15,16].

Fisher [17] introduced the nonlinear fractional Fisher equation as a mathematical model to describe the kinetic advancing rate of an advantageous gene. The fractional

Fisher's equation is also used in autocatalytic chemical reactions, nuclear reactor theory, neurophysiology, flame propagation, and branching Brownian motion processes [18–20]. In the open literature, many works describe solving the nonlinear fractional Fisher equation, see [20–23]. In our article, we propose a cubic polynomial spline-based technique for obtaining approximation solutions for the space-fractional Fisher's equation in the following form [24]:

$$\frac{\partial^\alpha u(x,t)}{\partial x^\alpha} = \frac{\partial u(x,t)}{\partial t} - u(x,t)(1-u(x,t)) + f(x,t), x > 0, \quad (1)$$

subject to the conditions:

$$u(a,t) = \varnothing_1(t), u(b,t) = \varnothing_2(t), 0 < t \leq T, \quad (2)$$

and

$$u(x,0) = g(x), a \leq x \leq b, \quad (3)$$

where α is a parameter in the Caputo sense that describes the fractional order of the space derivative, and $1 < \alpha \leq 2$; if we take $\alpha = 2$, Equation (1) reduces to the classical nonlinear Fisher's equation. Several scholars have studied and solved the space-fractional nonlinear Fisher's equation using various numerical techniques, for example, the generalized differential transform method (GDTM) and the variational iteration method (VIM) [25], the radial basis functions method [26], the quadratic polynomial spline-based method (QPSM) [24], and the Legendre spectral collocation method [27]. The above-mentioned articles show how to solve the space-fractional Fisher's equation in which the exact solution is unknown, but, as far as we are aware, no papers are using cubic polynomial spline for space-fractional Fisher's equation; hence, that is the motivation for our study.

Definition 1. *The Caputo space-fractional derivative operator of order $\alpha > 0$ is given by [25]*:

$${}_a^C D_x^\alpha u(x,t) = \frac{\partial^\alpha u(x,t)}{\partial x^\alpha} = \begin{cases} \frac{1}{\Gamma(n-\alpha)} \int_a^x \frac{\partial^n u(\tau,t)}{\partial \tau^n} (x-\tau)^{n-\alpha-1} d\tau, & n-1 < \alpha < n, \\ \frac{\partial^n u(x,t)}{\partial x^n}, & \alpha = n \in \mathbb{N}, \end{cases}$$

where $\Gamma(\ )$ is the gamma function. The right and left Caputo fractional derivatives of order α are given, respectively, by [28]:

$${}_x^C D_b^\alpha u(x,t) = \frac{1}{\Gamma(n-\alpha)} \int_x^b (-1)^n \frac{\partial^n u(\tau,t)}{\partial \tau^n} (\tau-x)^{n-\alpha-1} d\tau, n-1 < \alpha \leq n,$$

$${}_a^C D_x^\alpha u(x,t) = \frac{1}{\Gamma(n-\alpha)} \int_a^x \frac{\partial^n u(\tau,t)}{\partial \tau^n} (x-\tau)^{n-\alpha-1} d\tau, n-1 < \alpha \leq n.$$

The numerical solutions of fractional differential equations using numerical methods with spline functions and their use is an important area of research in numerical analysis, see [29–34]. Such problems appear very often in physics, engineering, medicine, biology, and other sciences. Spline functions can be integrated and differentiated due to being piecewise polynomials and, since they have a basis with small support, many of the integrals that occur in numerical methods are zero. Numerical methods with spline functions in obtaining the numerical solution of the differential equations lead to band matrices with a low computational cost. Cubic splines were used instead of using linear or quadratic splines, because they produce smooth approximations while maintaining a low computational cost.

Definition 2. *Polynomial Spline Function [35,36]*:

Let $a = x_0 < \cdots < x_{n-1} < x_n = b$ be a subdivision of the interval $[a,b]$ and $m \in \mathbb{N}$. A function $P : [a,b] \to R$ is called a spline of degree m for this subdivision if P is $(m-1)$ times continuously differentiable on $[a, b]$ and if the restriction of P to each subinterval $[x_i, x_{i+1}]$ for $i = 0, 1, \cdots, n-1$ reduces to a polynomial of degree at most m. Thus, the polynomial spline function has the form:

$$P(x) = \begin{cases} P_0(x), & \text{if } x \in [x_0, x_1], \\ P_1(x), & \text{if } x \in [x_1, x_2], \\ \vdots & \vdots \\ \vdots & \vdots \\ P_{n-1}(x), & \text{if } x \in [x_{n-1}, x_n]. \end{cases}$$

such that each polynomial spline segment is given by:

$$P_i(x) = \sum_{r=0}^{m} a_{ir}(x - x_r)^r, i = 0, 1, \cdots, n-1, x \in [x_i, x_{i+1}].$$

The remainder of this article is structured as follows. In Section 2, a method is proposed that is based on the cubic spline polynomial method. In Section 3, the von Neumann method is used to discuss stability theoretically. In Section 4, we use a numerical example to demonstrate the suggested method's efficiency and accuracy. The conclusion is presented in Section 5.

2. Derivation of the Method

To approximate $u(x, t)$ by a cubic polynomial spline-based method over finite elements, let the region $M = [a, b] \times [0, T]$ be discretized by a set of points M_{ij}, which are the vertices of a grid of points (x_i, t_j) where $x_i = a + ih$, with $h = \Delta x = \frac{b-a}{N}$ for each $i = 0, 1, \ldots, N$ and $t_j = jk$, $k = \Delta t$ for $j = 0, 1, \ldots, R$.

Let W_i^j be an approximation to $u(x_i, t_j)$ obtained by the segment $P_i(x_i, t_j)$ of the spline function passing through the points $\left(x_i, W_i^j\right)$ and $\left(x_{i+1}, W_{i+1}^j\right)$. Each segment has the form [37,38]:

$$P_i(x, t_j) = a_i(t_j)(x - x_i)^3 + b_i(t_j)(x - x_i)^2 + c_i(t_j)(x - x_i) + d_i(t_j), \quad (4)$$

for each $i = 0, 1, \ldots, N-1$. To obtain expressions for the coefficients of Equation (4) in terms of W_i^j, W_{i+1}^j, S_i^j, and S_{i+1}^j, we first define:

$$P_i(x_i, t_j) = W_i^j, \quad (5)$$

$$P_i(x_{i+1}, t_j) = W_{i+1}^j, \quad (6)$$

$$P_i^{(\alpha)}(x_i, t_j) = \frac{\partial^\alpha}{\partial x^\alpha} P_i(x_i, t_j) = S_i^j, \quad (7)$$

$$P_i^{(\alpha)}(x_{i+1}, t_j) = \frac{\partial^\alpha}{\partial x^\alpha} P_i(x_{i+1}, t_j) = S_{i+1}^j, \quad (8)$$

where $1 < \alpha \leq 2$. By using (4), (5), and (6), we have:

$$d_i = W_i^j, \quad (9)$$

$$h^3 a_i + h^2 b_i + h c_i + d_i = W_{i+1}^j, \quad (10)$$

where $a_i \equiv a_i(t_j)$, $b_i \equiv b_i(t_j)$, $c_i \equiv c_i(t_j)$, and $d_i \equiv d_i(t_j)$. Using the right Caputo fractional derivative and (4) in (7), we obtain:

$$\frac{\partial^\alpha}{\partial x^\alpha} P_i(x_i, t_j) = \frac{1}{\Gamma(2-\alpha)} \int_{x_i}^{x_{i+1}} (\tau - x_i)^{1-\alpha} P_i^{(2)}(\tau, t_j) d\tau$$
$$= \frac{6(2-\alpha)h^{3-\alpha}}{\Gamma(4-\alpha)} a_i + \frac{2h^{2-\alpha}}{\Gamma(3-\alpha)} b_i = S_i^j, \quad (11)$$

and from using the left Caputo fractional derivative and (4) in (8), we obtain:

$$\frac{\partial^\alpha}{\partial x^\alpha} P_i(x_{i+1}, t_j) = \frac{1}{\Gamma(2-\alpha)} \int_{x_i}^{x_{i+1}} (x_{i+1} - \tau)^{1-\alpha} P_i^{(2)}(\tau, t_j) d\tau$$
$$= \frac{6h^{3-\alpha}}{\Gamma(4-\alpha)} a_i + \frac{2h^{2-\alpha}}{\Gamma(3-\alpha)} b_i = S_{i+1}^j, \quad (12)$$

We obtain the following expressions by solving (9)–(12):

$$a_i = \frac{\Gamma(4-\alpha)}{6(1-\alpha)h^{3-\alpha}} \left(S_i^j - S_{i+1}^j \right),$$

$$b_i = \frac{\Gamma(3-\alpha)}{2(1-\alpha)h^{2-\alpha}} \left((2-\alpha) S_{i+1}^j - S_i^j \right),$$

$$c_i = \frac{1}{h}\left(W_{i+1}^j - W_i^j\right) + \frac{\Gamma(4-\alpha)}{6(1-\alpha)h^{1-\alpha}} \left(S_{i+1}^j - S_i^j\right) + \frac{\Gamma(3-\alpha)}{2(1-\alpha)h^{1-\alpha}} \left(S_i^j - (2-\alpha)S_{i+1}^j\right),$$

$$d_i = W_i^j. \quad (13)$$

Using the first derivative's continuity condition at $x = x_i$, that is $P_i^{(1)}(x_i, t_j) = P_{i-1}^{(1)}(x_i, t_j)$, we obtain:

$$c_i - c_{i-1} = 3h^2 a_{i-1} + 2h b_{i-1} \quad (14)$$

Substituting the expressions a_i, b_i, and c_i from Equation (13) into Equation (14), we obtain:

$$W_{i+1}^j - 2W_i^j + W_{i-1}^j + \frac{\Gamma(4-\alpha)}{6(1-\alpha)h^{-\alpha}} \left(S_{i+1}^j - S_i^j\right) + \frac{\Gamma(3-\alpha)}{2(1-\alpha)h^{-\alpha}} \left(S_i^j - (2-\alpha)S_{i+1}^j\right)$$
$$+ \frac{\Gamma(4-\alpha)}{6(1-\alpha)h^{-\alpha}} \left(S_{i-1}^j - S_i^j\right) + \frac{\Gamma(3-\alpha)}{2(1-\alpha)h^{-\alpha}} \left((2-\alpha)S_i^j - S_{i-1}^j\right) \quad (15)$$
$$= \frac{\Gamma(4-\alpha)}{2(1-\alpha)h^{-\alpha}} \left(S_{i-1}^j - S_i^j\right) + \frac{\Gamma(3-\alpha)}{(1-\alpha)h^{-\alpha}} \left((2-\alpha)S_i^j - S_{i-1}^j\right).$$

Equation (15) can be rewritten in the form:

$$W_{i+1}^j - 2W_i^j + W_{i-1}^j$$
$$= \left(\frac{\Gamma(4-\alpha)}{2(1-\alpha)h^{-\alpha}} - \frac{\Gamma(3-\alpha)}{(1-\alpha)h^{-\alpha}} - \frac{\Gamma(4-\alpha)}{6(1-\alpha)h^{-\alpha}} + \frac{\Gamma(3-\alpha)}{2(1-\alpha)h^{-\alpha}} \right) S_{i-1}^j$$
$$+ \left(\frac{2\Gamma(4-\alpha)}{6(1-\alpha)h^{-\alpha}} - \frac{\Gamma(3-\alpha)}{2(1-\alpha)h^{-\alpha}} - \frac{(2-\alpha)\Gamma(3-\alpha)}{2(1-\alpha)h^{-\alpha}} \right. \quad (16)$$
$$\left. - \frac{\Gamma(4-\alpha)}{2(1-\alpha)h^{-\alpha}} + \frac{(2-\alpha)\Gamma(3-\alpha)}{(1-\alpha)h^{-\alpha}} \right) S_i^j$$
$$+ \left(\frac{(2-\alpha)\Gamma(3-\alpha)}{2(1-\alpha)h^{-\alpha}} - \frac{\Gamma(4-\alpha)}{6(1-\alpha)h^{-\alpha}} \right) S_{i+1}^j$$

After slight rearrangements, Equation (16) becomes:

$$W_{i-1}^j - 2W_i^j + W_{i+1}^j = \beta S_{i-1}^j + \gamma S_i^j + \beta S_{i+1}^j, \quad i = 1, \ldots, N-1, \quad (17)$$

where $\beta = \frac{(2\alpha-3)h^\alpha \Gamma(3-\alpha)}{6(\alpha-1)}$ and $\gamma = \frac{\alpha h^\alpha \Gamma(3-\alpha)}{3(\alpha-1)}$. As $\alpha \to 2$, system (17) reduces to:

$$W_{i-1}^j - 2W_i^j + W_{i+1}^j = \frac{1}{6}\left(S_{i-1}^j + 4S_i^j + S_{i+1}^j\right), \quad i = 1, \ldots, N-1. \quad (18)$$

Remark 1: *For Equation (17), the local truncation error is:*

$$T_i^{*j} = \beta\left(u_{i-1}^j + u_{i+1}^j\right) - 2\gamma u_i^j - \beta\left(D_x^2 u_{i-1}^j + D_x^2 u_{i+1}^j\right) - \gamma D_x^2 u_i^j, \tag{19}$$

and can be obtained by expanding this equation in terms of $u(x_i, t_j)$ and its derivatives in the Taylor series, as follows:

$$T_i^{*j} = \left(h^2 - (\gamma + 2\beta)\right)D_x^2 u_i^j + \left(\frac{h^4}{12} - \beta h^2\right)D_x^4 u_i^j + \left(\frac{h^6}{360} - \frac{\beta h^4}{12}\right)D_x^6 u_i^j + \ldots. \tag{20}$$

Then, the last expression T_i^{*j} can be written as:

$$T_i^{*j} = h^\alpha\left(h^{2-\alpha} - \theta\right)D_x^2 u_i^j + h^{2+\alpha}\left(\frac{h^{2-\alpha}}{12} - \delta\right)D_x^4 u_i^j + h^{4+\alpha}\left(\frac{h^{2-\alpha}}{360} - \frac{\delta}{12}\right)D_x^6 u_i^j + \ldots. \tag{21}$$

where $\theta = \Gamma(3-\alpha)$ and $\delta = \frac{(2\alpha-3)\Gamma(3-\alpha)}{6(\alpha-1)}$. From the expression (21) of the local truncation error, our scheme (17) is reduced to $O(h^\alpha)$, $1 < \alpha \leq 2$.

The fractional Fisher's Equation (1) can now be defined as follows in terms of S_i^j:

$$S_i^j = \frac{\partial^\alpha W_i^j}{\partial x^\alpha} = \frac{\partial W_i^j}{\partial t} - W_i^j\left(1 - W_i^j\right) + f(x_i, t_j).$$

Using the finite difference method, we obtain:

$$\frac{\partial W_i^j}{\partial t} \approx \frac{W_i^j - W_i^{j-1}}{k}.$$

This allows us to express S_{i-1}^j, S_i^j, and S_{i+1}^j as follows:

$$\begin{aligned}
S_{i-1}^j &= \frac{W_{i-1}^j - W_{i-1}^{j-1}}{k} - \sigma_{i-1}^j W_{i-1}^j + f_{i-1}^j, \\
S_i^j &= \frac{W_i^j - W_i^{j-1}}{k} - \sigma_i^j W_i^j + f_i^j, \\
S_{i+1}^j &= \frac{W_{i+1}^j - W_{i+1}^{j-1}}{k} - \sigma_{i+1}^j W_{i+1}^j + f_{i+1}^j,
\end{aligned} \tag{22}$$

where $\sigma_i^j = \left(1 - W_i^j\right)$. Substituting (22) into (17) gives us the following system:

$$A_i W_{i-1}^j + B_i W_i^j + C_i W_{i+1}^j = A_i^* W_{i-1}^{j-1} + B_i^* W_i^{j-1} + C_i^* W_{i+1}^{j-1} + \rho_i^j, \tag{23}$$
$$i = 1, \ldots, N-1, j = 1, \ldots, R,$$

where:

$$A_i = k - \beta + \beta k \sigma_{i-1}^j, \ A_i^* = -\beta,$$
$$B_i = -2k - \gamma + \gamma k \sigma_i^j, \ B_i^* = -\gamma,$$
$$C_i = k - \beta + \beta k \sigma_{i+1}^j, \ C_i^* = -\beta,$$

and:

$$\rho_i^j = \beta k f_{i-1}^j + \gamma k f_i^j + \beta k f_{i+1}^j.$$

System (23) consists of $N-1$ equations in the unknowns W_i, $i = 0, 1, \ldots, N$. Two additional equations are required to solve this system. The boundary conditions in (2) are used to derive these equations, which can be represented as:

$$W_0^j = \varnothing_1(t_j), \ W_N^j = \varnothing_2(t_j), j = 0, 1, \ldots, R. \tag{24}$$

Writing (23) and (24) in matrix form gives:

$$\Phi W^j = \Phi^* W^{j-1} + r^j, \qquad (25)$$

where:

$$W^j = \left(W_0^j, W_1^j, W_2^j, \ldots\ldots\ldots, W_{N-1}^j, W_N^j\right)^T,$$

$$\Phi = \begin{bmatrix} 1 & 0 & 0 & 0 & \cdots & 0 & 0 & 0 \\ A_1 & B_1 & C_1 & 0 & \cdots & 0 & 0 & 0 \\ 0 & A_2 & B_2 & C_2 & \cdots & 0 & 0 & 0 \\ \vdots & \vdots & \vdots & \vdots & \ddots & \vdots & \vdots & \vdots \\ 0 & 0 & 0 & 0 & \cdots & A_{N-1} & B_{N-1} & C_{N-1} \\ 0 & 0 & 0 & 0 & \cdots & 0 & 0 & 1 \end{bmatrix},$$

$$\Phi^* = \begin{bmatrix} 0 & 0 & 0 & 0 & \cdots & 0 & 0 & 0 \\ A_1^* & B_1^* & C_1^* & 0 & \cdots & 0 & 0 & 0 \\ 0 & A_2^* & B_2^* & C_2^* & \cdots & 0 & 0 & 0 \\ \vdots & \vdots & \vdots & \vdots & \ddots & \vdots & \vdots & \vdots \\ 0 & 0 & 0 & 0 & \cdots & A_{N-1}^* & B_{N-1}^* & C_{N-1}^* \\ 0 & 0 & 0 & 0 & \cdots & 0 & 0 & 0 \end{bmatrix},$$

and,

$$r^j = \left(\varnothing_1(t_j), \rho_1^j, \rho_2^j, \ldots\ldots\ldots, \rho_{N-1}^j, \varnothing_2(t_j)\right)^T$$

where Φ^* and Φ are $(N+1) \times (N+1)$ matrices and W^j and r^j are $(N+1)$ vectors.

Now, the initial condition, $u(x, t_0) = g(x)$ for $a \leq x \leq b$, implies that W_i^0 for $i = 0, 1, \ldots, N$. These values can be utilized in (25) to obtain the value of W_i^1 for $i = 0, 1, \ldots, N$. If the technique is reapplied once all the approximations W_i^1 are determined, the values of $W_i^2, W_i^3, \ldots, W_i^R$ can be derived in the same way.

The nonlinear term in the system is linearized using the technique in (25). For example, if $j = 1$, we approximate σ_i^1 by σ_i^{1*} computed from w_i^0, which obtains an approximation to w_i^1. For $j = m$, we approximate σ_i^m by σ_i^{m*} computed from w_i^{m-1} and obtain an approximation to w_i^m.

3. Stability Analysis

The von Neumann technique will be used to investigate our system's stability (23). To do this, we must linearize the nonlinear term $u(x, t)(1 - u(x, t))$ of Fisher's Equation (1), by assuming that the corresponding quantities $\sigma_{i-1}^j, \sigma_i^j$, and σ_{i+1}^j are equal to a local constant λ^* in (23). The key part of the von Neumann analysis is to assume a solution of the form [39]:

$$W_i^j = \xi^j \exp(\varphi q i h), \qquad (26)$$

where $q = \sqrt{-1}$, h is the element size, φ is the mode number, and ξ^j is the amplification factor at time level j. As j increases (more time steps are computed), adding the latter W_i^j expression to the system (23) gives the following characteristic equation:

$$\xi^j(A_i \exp(\varphi q(i-1)h) + B_i \exp(\varphi q i h) + C_i \exp(\varphi q(i+1)h)) \\ = \xi^{j-1}(A_i^* \exp(\varphi q(i-1)h) + B_i^* \exp(\varphi q i h) + C_i^* \exp(\varphi q(i+1)h)), \qquad (27)$$

where:

$$A_i = k - \beta + \beta k \lambda^*, A_i^* = -\beta,$$
$$B_i = -2k - \gamma + \gamma k \lambda^*, B_i^* = -\gamma,$$
$$C_i = k - \beta + \beta k \lambda^*, C_i^* = -\beta,$$

After simple basic calculations, (27) becomes:

$$\zeta = \frac{A_i^* \exp(-q\phi) + B_i^* + C_i^* \exp(q\phi)}{A_i \exp(-q\phi) + B_i + C_i \exp(q\phi)}, \qquad (28)$$

where $\phi = \varphi h$. After using Euler's formula $\exp(q\phi) = \cos\phi + q\sin\phi$, the last equation (28) can be simplified as:

$$\zeta = \frac{(A_i^* + C_i^*)\cos\phi + B_i^* + q(C_i^* - A_i^*)\sin\phi}{(A_i + C_i)\cos\phi + B_i + q(C_i - A_i)\sin\phi}. \qquad (29)$$

Equation (29) can be rewritten in the forms:

$$\zeta = \frac{-2\beta\cos\phi - \gamma}{(2k - 2\beta + 2\beta k\lambda^*)\cos\phi + (-2k - \gamma + \gamma k\lambda^*)}. \qquad (30)$$

or

$$\zeta = \frac{(2\beta\cos\phi + \gamma)}{(2\beta\cos\phi + \gamma) + 2k(1 - \cos\phi) - \lambda^*(2\beta k\cos\phi + \gamma k)}. \qquad (31)$$

The quantity $(1 - \cos\phi)$ is positive or equal to zero but $2\beta\cos\phi + \gamma$ is surely positive if we choose $\gamma > 0$ and $\beta > 0$ such that $\gamma > 2\beta$. If we choose k, β, and γ small enough to make $\lambda^*(2\beta k\cos(\phi) + \gamma k) \to 0$, then last (31) is close to:

$$\zeta = \frac{(2\beta\cos\phi + \gamma)}{(2\beta\cos\phi + \gamma) + 2k(1 - \cos\phi)}. \qquad (32)$$

For stability, we must have $|\zeta| \leq 1$ (otherwise ζ_j in (26) would expand in an unbounded manner). This condition is satisfied for $\gamma > 0$ and $\beta > 0$ such that $\gamma > 2\beta$. Finally, we can say that our numerical scheme is conditionally stable for $\gamma > 0$, $\beta > 0$, and $\gamma > 2\beta$, if k, β, and γ values chosen are small enough.

4. Numerical Results

In this part, we employ the suggested method for solving the nonlinear space-fractional Fisher's equation [17,18] with $\alpha = 1.5$, $f(x,t) = -x^2$, and $u(x,0) = x$ and subject to conditions:

$$u(0.0125, t) \approx 0.0125(1 + t) + 0.00609375t^2 - 0.082176t^3 - 0.0210541t^4 - 7.16634 \times 10^{-6} t^5,$$

$$u(1.0125, t) \approx 1.0125(1 + t) - 0.518906t^2 - 0.921366\, t^3 + 0.310529t^4 + 0.0845434\, t^5.$$

The solution of the space-fractional Fisher's equation, like that of most fractional partial differential equations, is unknown, so we will compare it with the known computational approaches such as GDTM and VIM. We used $k = 0.0005$ and $N = 80$ in all our numerical results. Tables 1–3 compare our method, which was improved in Section 2, to other existing methods.

Table 1. The comparison between the proposed method and other existing methods for $t = 0.1$ and various x values.

x	Present Method	VIM [18]	GDTM [18]	QPSM [17]
0.0	0.000000	0.000000	0.000000	0.000000
0.2	0.220600	0.220589	0.220348	0.210917
0.4	0.440452	0.440329	0.439957	0.425837
0.6	0.659483	0.659214	0.658707	0.645538
0.8	0.877676	0.877185	0.876585	0.869671
1.0	1.094273	1.094096	1.093587	1.093920

Table 2. The comparison between the proposed method and other existing methods for $t = 0.2$ and various x values.

x	Present Method	VIM [18]	GDTM [18]	QPSM [17]
0.0	0.000000	0.000000	0.000000	0.000000
0.2	0.241796	0.242240	0.240212	0.223360
0.4	0.480839	0.480928	0.477796	0.453229
0.6	0.716555	0.716018	0.711692	0.691755
0.8	0.948791	0.947058	0.941796	0.936764
1.0	1.173899	1.172904	1.168067	1.173100

Table 3. The comparison between the proposed method and other existing methods for $t = 0.4$ and various x values.

x	Present Method	VIM [18]	GDTM [18]	QPSM [17]
0.0	0.000000	0.000000	0.000000	0.000000
0.2	0.283243	0.287146	0.269327	0.275929
0.4	0.557963	0.559433	0.531749	0.542191
0.6	0.819056	0.816392	0.777297	0.798553
0.8	1.064467	1.054714	1.004978	1.044459
1.0	1.273878	1.265508	1.214400	1.277563

Tables 1–3 show that for all values of x and t, our approximate solutions are in good agreement with the approximate solutions using other existing methods. This is also shown in Figures 1 and 2.

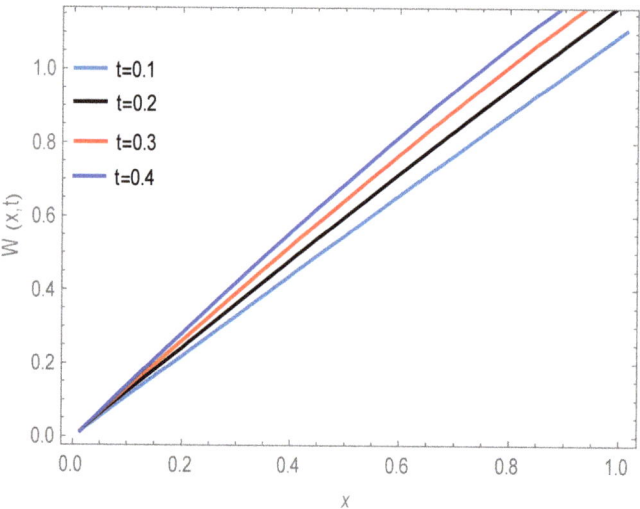

Figure 1. The behaviors of the numerical solution $W(x, t)$ for various time levels.

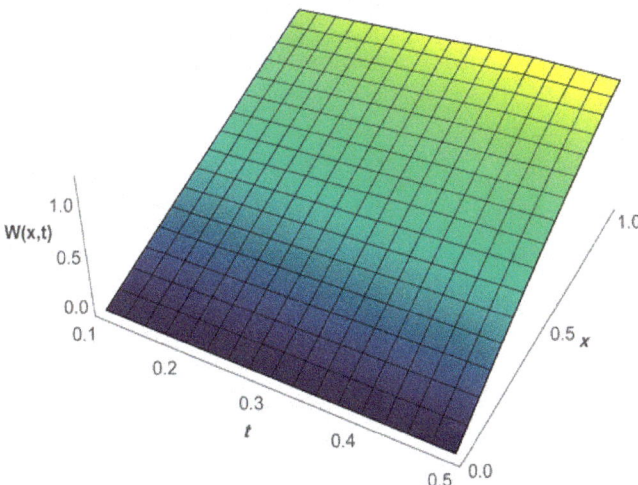

Figure 2. Graphs of the approximate solutions $W(x, t)$ for $t \leq 0.5$ ($h = 0.0125$, $k = 0.0005$).

5. Conclusions

The nonlinear space-fractional Fisher's equation is numerically treated in this article using a collocation method with cubic polynomial spline functions. The proposed method is demonstrated to be conditionally stable using the von Neumann stability technique. Compared to other useful techniques, such as VIM, GDTM, and QPSM, the numerical results illustrate that our proposed method retains efficiency, capability, and good versatility. The findings of our study are hoped to pique the attention of academics interested in using the cubic polynomial spline to numerically solve nonlinear fractional partial differential equations of the same type. It is proven that our scheme's local truncation error is to $O(h^\alpha)$, $1 < \alpha \leq 2$. Furthermore, the novelty of the present work lies in the fact that the results illustrate that the proposed technique is convenient, accurate, and very efficient in solving such problems.

Author Contributions: A.R.H., F.E.A.A., A.A.A. and T.R.; methodology, A.R.H., F.E.A.A., A.A.A. and T.R.; software, A.R.H., F.E.A.A., A.A.A. and T.R.; validation, A.R.H., F.E.A.A., A.A.A. and T.R.; formal analysis, A.R.H., F.E.A.A., A.A.A. and T.R.; investigation, A.R.H., F.E.A.A., A.A.A. and T.R.; resources, A.R.H., F.E.A.A., A.A.A. and T.R.; data curation, A.R.H., F.E.A.A., A.A.A. and T.R.; writing—original draft preparation, A.R.H., F.E.A.A., A.A.A. and T.R.; writing—review and editing, A.R.H., F.E.A.A., A.A.A. and T.R.; visualization, A.R.H., F.E.A.A., A.A.A. and T.R.; supervision, A.R.H.; project administration, T.R.; funding acquisition, All authors have read and agreed to the published version of the manuscript.

Funding: This research has received no external funding.

Institutional Review Board Statement: Not applicable.

Informed Consent Statement: Not applicable.

Data Availability Statement: No new data were created or analyzed in this study. Data sharing is not applicable to this article.

Acknowledgments: The researchers would like to thank the Deanship of Scientific Research, Qassim University, for funding the publication of this project.

Conflicts of Interest: All the authors declare that they have no conflict of interest.

References

1. Bagley, R.L.; Torvik, P.J. Fractional calculus in the transient analysis of viscoelasticity damped structures. *AIAA J.* **1985**, *23*, 918–925. [CrossRef]
2. Podlubny, I. Fractional Differential Equations. In *Mathematics in Science and Engineering*; Academic Press: San Diego, CA, USA, 1999.
3. Kilbas, A.A.; Srivastava, H.M.; Trujillo, J.J. *Theory and Applications of Fractional Differential Equations*; Elsevier: New York, NY, USA, 2006.
4. Cheng, X.; Duan, J.; Li, D. A novel compact ADI scheme for two-dimensional Riesz space fractional nonlinear reaction–diffusion equations. *Appl. Math. Comput.* **2019**, *346*, 452–464. [CrossRef]
5. Hadhoud, A.R.; Rageh, A.A.M.; Radwan, T. Computational solution of the time-fractional Schrödinger equation by using trigonometric B-spline collocation method. *Fractal Fract.* **2022**, *6*, 127. [CrossRef]
6. Xie, J.; Zhang, Z. The high-order multistep ADI solver for two-dimensional nonlinear delayed reaction–diffusion equations with variable coefficients. *Comput. Math. Appl.* **2018**, *75*, 3558–3570. [CrossRef]
7. Kumar, D.; Nisar, K.S. A novel linearized Galerkin finite element scheme with fractional Crank–Nicolson method for the nonlinear coupled delay subdiffusion system with smooth solutions. *Math. Methods Appl. Sci.* **2022**, *45*, 1377–1401. [CrossRef]
8. Hadhoud, A.R.; Alaal, F.E.; Abdelaziz, A.A.; Radwan, T. Numerical treatment of the generalized time—fractional Huxley—Burgers' equation and its stability examination. *Demonstr. Math.* **2021**, *54*, 436–451. [CrossRef]
9. Hadhoud, A.R.; Abd Alaal, F.E.; Abdelaziz, A.A. On the numerical investigations of the time-fractional modified Burgers' equation with conformable derivative, and its stability analysis. *J. Math. Comput. Sci.* **2021**, *12*, 36.
10. Metzler, R.; Klafter, J. The random walk's guide to anomalous diffusion: A fractional dynamics approach. *Phys. Rep.* **2000**, *339*, 1–77. [CrossRef]
11. Ray, S.S.; Bera, R.K. An approximate solution of a nonlinear fractional differential equation by Adomian decomposition method. *Appl. Math. Comput.* **2005**, *167*, 561–571.
12. Zhang, Y.; Sun, Z.Z.; Liao, H.L. Finite difference methods for the time-fractional diffusion equation on non-uniform meshes. *J. Comput. Phys.* **2014**, *265*, 195–210. [CrossRef]
13. Elsaid, A. The variational iteration method for solving Riesz fractional partial differential equations. *Comput. Math. Appl.* **2010**, *60*, 1940–1947. [CrossRef]
14. Bhrawy, A.H.; Zaky, M.A.; Baleanu, D. New numerical approximations for space-time fractional Burgers' equations via a Legendre spectral-collocation method. *Rom. Rep. Phys.* **2015**, *67*, 340–349.
15. Javeed, S.; Baleanu, D.; Waheed, A.; Khan, M.S.; Affan, H. Analysis of homotopy perturbation method for solving fractional order differential equations. *Mathematics* **2019**, *7*, 40. [CrossRef]
16. Yavuz, M.; Ozdemir, N. Numerical inverse Laplace homotopy technique for fractional heat equations. *Therm. Sci.* **2018**, *22*, S185–S194. [CrossRef]
17. Fisher, R.A. The wave of advance of advantageous genes. *Ann. Eugen.* **1937**, *7*, 355–369. [CrossRef]
18. Malfliet, W. Solitary wave solutions of nonlinear wave equations. *Am. J. Phys.* **1992**, *60*, 650–654. [CrossRef]
19. Canosa, J. Diffusion in nonlinear multiplicative media. *J. Math. Phys.* **1969**, *10*, 1862–1868. [CrossRef]
20. Majeed, A.; Kamran, M.; Iqbal, M.K.; Baleanu, D. Solving time fractional Burgers' and Fisher's equations using cubic B-spline approximation method. *Adv. Differ. Equ.* **2020**, *2020*, 175. [CrossRef]
21. Khader, M.M.; Saad, K.M. A numerical approach for solving the fractional Fisher equation using Chebyshev spectral collocation method. *Chaos Solitons Fractals* **2018**, *110*, 169–177. [CrossRef]
22. Wang, X.Y. Exact and explicit solitary wave solutions for the generalised Fisher equation. *Phys. Lett. A* **1988**, *131*, 277–279. [CrossRef]
23. Tyson, J.J.; Brazhnik, P.K. On traveling wave solutions of Fisher's equation in two spatial dimensions. *SIAM J. Appl. Math.* **2000**, *60*, 371–391. [CrossRef]
24. El-Danaf, T.S.; Hadhoud, A.R. Computational method for solving space fractional Fisher's nonlinear equation. *Math. Methods Appl. Sci.* **2014**, *37*, 657–662. [CrossRef]
25. Momani, S.; Odibat, Z. A novel method for nonlinear fractional partial differential equations: Combination of DTM and generalized Taylor's formula. *J. Comput. Appl. Math.* **2008**, *220*, 85–95. [CrossRef]
26. Vanani, S.K.; Aminataei, A. On the numerical solution of fractional partial differential equations. *Math. Comput. Appl.* **2012**, *17*, 140–151. [CrossRef]
27. Liu, Z.; Lv, S.; Li, X. Legendre collocation spectral method for solving space fractional nonlinear fisher's equation. *Commun. Comput. Inf. Sci.* **2016**, *643*, 245–252.
28. Caputo, M.C.; Torres, D.F.M. Duality for the left and right fractional derivatives. *Signal Processing* **2015**, *107*, 265–271. [CrossRef]
29. Zahra, W.K.; Elkholy, S.M. Quadratic spline solution for boundary value problem of fractional order. *Numer. Algorithms* **2012**, *59*, 373–391. [CrossRef]
30. Liu, J.; Fu, H.; Chai, X.; Sun, Y.; Guo, H. Stability and convergence analysis of the quadratic spline collocation method for time-dependent fractional diffusion equations. *Appl. Math. Comput.* **2019**, *346*, 633–648. [CrossRef]
31. Pitolli, F.; Sorgentone, C.; Pellegrino, E. Approximation of the Riesz–Caputo Derivative by Cubic Splines. *Algorithms* **2022**, *15*, 69. [CrossRef]
32. Shui-Ping, Y.; Ai-Guo, X. Cubic Spline Collocation Method for Fractional Differential Equations. *J. Appl. Math.* **2013**, *2013*, 20.

33. Akram, T.; Abbas, M.; Ismail, A.I.; Ali, N.H.M.; Baleanu, D. Extended cubic B-splines in the numericalsolution of time fractional telegraph equation. *Adv. Differ. Equ.* **2019**, *2019*, 1–20. [CrossRef]
34. Madiha, S.; Muhammad, A.; Farah, A.A.; Abdul, M.; Thabet, A.; Manar, A.A. Numerical solutions of time fractional Burgers' equation involving Atangana–Baleanu derivative via cubic B-spline functions. *Results Phys.* **2022**, *34*, 105244.
35. Schumaker, L. *Spline Functions, Basic Theory.*; John Wiley & Sons, Inc.: Hoboken, NJ, USA, 1981.
36. Ahlberg, J.H.; Nilson, E.N.; Walsh, J.L. The Theory of Splines and their Applications. In *Mathematics in Science and Engineering*; Academic Press: Cambridge, MA, USA, 1967; Available online: https://www.sciencedirect.com/bookseries/mathematics-in-science-and-engineering/vol/38/suppl/C (accessed on 19 July 2022).
37. El-Danaf, T.S.; Ramadan, M.A.; Abd Alaal, F.E.I. Numerical studies of the cubic non-linear Schrodinger equation. *Nonlinear Dyn.* **2012**, *67*, 619–627. [CrossRef]
38. Ramadan, M.A.; Lashien, I.F.; Zahra, W.K. Polynomial and nonpolynomial spline approaches to the numerical solution of second order boundary value problems. *Appl. Math. Comput.* **2007**, *184*, 476–484. [CrossRef]
39. Ramadan, M.A.; El-Danaf, T.S.; Abd Alaal, F.E.I. A numerical solution of the Burgers' equation using septic B-splines. *Chaos Solitons Fractals* **2005**, *26*, 1249–1258. [CrossRef]

Article

Fractional-Order Nonlinear Multi-Agent Systems: A Resilience-Based Approach to Consensus Analysis with Distributed and Input Delays

Asad Khan [1,*], Azmat Ullah Khan Niazi [2,*], Waseem Abbasi [3], Faryal Awan [2] and Anam Khan [4]

1 School of Computer Science and Cyber Engineering, Guangzhou University, Guangzhou 510006, China
2 Department of Mathematics and Statistics, The University of Lahore, Sargodha 40100, Pakistan
3 Department of Computer Science and IT, Superior University, Lahore 54000, Pakistan
4 Department of Mathematics, Superior University, Lahore 54000, Pakistan
* Correspondence: asad@gzhu.edu.cn (A.K.); azmatullah.khan@math.uol.edu.pk (A.U.K.N.)

Abstract: In this article, a resilient consensus analysis of fractional-order nonlinear leader and follower systems with input and distributed delays is assumed. To make controller design more practical, it is considered that the controller is not implemented as it is, and a disturbance term is incorporated into the controller part. A multi-agent system's topology ahead to a weighted graph which may be directed or undirected is used. The article examines a scenario of leader–follower consensus through the application of algebraic graph theory and the fractional-order Razumikhin method. Numerical simulations are also provided to show the effectiveness of the proposed design for the leader–follower consensus.

Keywords: fractional-order nonlinear system; Razumikhin approach; input delay; distributed delay; leader–following consensus

MSC: 34K37; 34B15

1. Introduction

There are different fields where cooperative control has achieved rising importance for its vast application, for example satellite formation flying [1], -multi-vehicle cooperative control [2], etc. Multi-agent system consensus has attained great attention. Great investigation is made on leader–follower consensus [3–7] and nonleader–follower consensus [8–15]. Some researchers give importance to dynamical standards of integer order [16–18]. Therefore, fractional derivatives are convenient for describing many complicated phenomena and processes in comparing with classical derivatives of integer order [19]. By using graph theory and the Lyapunov function method, Yu et al. suppose a group of fractional-order leader–follower consensus [20]. Bai et al. investigated a multi-agent system's consensus by designing a useful controller [21]. By using the proposed lemma and by constructing a suitable Lyapunov function, Xu et al. analyse the replica of complicated systems of fractional-order [22,23].

In a real dynamical system, a delay in time is a common phenomenon which influences the behavioural system of dynamical standards, and due to it, the system can become ambiguous.

An investigation of the fractional-order-delayed system's consensus can be conducted by an analysis method of frequency-domain, such as in [24,25], considering the system's delay in input. Directed multi-agent systems with delays in nonuniform input and communication were studied by Shen et al. [26]. With a delay in heterogeneous input, an undirected multi-agent system is considered in [27]. In time domain analysis, the most suitable access was given by the theory of Lyapunov stability for finding adherence and a complicated dynamical system's consensus.

Citation: Khan, A.; Niazi, A.U.K.; Abbasi, W.; Awan, F.; Khan, A. Fractional-Order Nonlinear Multi-Agent Systems: A Resilience-Based Approach to Consensus Analysis with Distributed and Input Delays. *Fractal Fract.* **2023**, *7*, 322. https://doi.org/10.3390/fractalfract7040322

Academic Editors: Riccardo Caponetto, Angelo B. Mingarelli, Leila Gholizadeh Zivlaei and Mohammad Dehghan

Received: 5 March 2023
Revised: 28 March 2023
Accepted: 10 April 2023
Published: 11 April 2023

Copyright: © 2023 by the authors. Licensee MDPI, Basel, Switzerland. This article is an open access article distributed under the terms and conditions of the Creative Commons Attribution (CC BY) license (https://creativecommons.org/licenses/by/4.0/).

For dealing with the adherence of differential equations of fractional-order, the most suitable approach was presented by Liu et al. in inequality on Riemann–Liouville derivatives of quadratic function [28]. In many systems of fractional-order, certain stability criteria are obtained by using a proposed lemma [29,30]. By using Caputo sense, a little progress is made in systems of fractional-order through stability analysis. Since the fractional-order operational composition property does not hold, some problems may occur while studying a Caputo fractional-order delayed system's consensus. The main reason for using the Lyapunov direct method is convenience. Xu et al. investigated a fractional-order nonautonomous system's global asymptotical stability by selecting the convenient Lyapunov function [31]. It is still a challenging problem involving which Lyapunov function to select and how to show certain conditions for a fractional-order nonlinear delayed system consensus. Wang et al. compared a fractional-order delayed system's exponential consensus with heterogeneous impulsive controllers, where an undirected graph was drawn with the topology of coupling [32]. Zhu et al. studied systems of fractional-order with delay in input by finding states of error where the topology of coupling headed a directed graph[33]. Generally, the topology of coupling leads to a weighted graph (directed).

The objective of this paper is to analyze the resilient consensus of a nonlinear multi-agent system with distributed and input delays. To achieve this goal, the authors employ the fractional Razumikhin approach and algebraic graph theory to derive algebraic conditions for leader–follower consensus. This paper also includes examples to demonstrate the applicability of the presented cases for consensus checking.

The main contributions can be described as follows.

(1) The parameters of controllers and multi-agent systems are co-designed based on the model of nonlinear MASs. Compared with published results, the obtained fractional-order controller is resilient to uncertainties.

(2) The majority of the results mentioned in previous related references [24–28] deals with the assumptions that the nonlinear part $f(\tau, u(\tau)) = 0$ as $u(\tau) = 0$. However, the remainder of the nonlinear term $f(\tau, u(\tau))$ in the system dynamics model is not negligible and cannot be completely canceled. Since $f(\tau, u(\tau)) \neq 0$ and $u(\tau) = 0$ in many cases, it should be well addressed in the design of the controller. Furthermore, in the abovementioned references, it is assumed that the controllers derived by these techniques are precise, accurate and exactly implemented, but this is not always appropriate as it is difficult to have exact dynamics of the system. Therefore, in this paper, we consider both the effect of uncertainty in the controller and the nonvanishing nonlinearity in multi-agent dynamic systems to enhance the implementation of the controller.

2. Preliminaries

First, we offer some definitions and some important lemmas which will be subsequently used. Consider a directed weighted graph $A = (\mu, \epsilon)$, which contains a set of vertices $B = \{\varsigma_1, \varsigma_2, \varsigma_3, ..., \varsigma_M\}$ and a directed edge's set $\epsilon \subset \{\{\varsigma_j, \varsigma_k\} : \varsigma_j, \varsigma_k \in B\}$, where every directed edge ϵ_{jk} is an ordered pair of vertices $(\varsigma_j, \varsigma_k)$ which shows an edge which originates at vertices ς_k and ends at vertices ς_j. ς_j is called the tail, and ς_k is the head. $M_j = \{\varsigma_k | (\varsigma_k, \varsigma_j) : \varsigma_j, \varsigma_k \in \epsilon\}$ shows the neighbor's set of the vertices ς_j. Consider $C = (c_{jk})_{M \times M}$ as a weighted adjacency matrix, where $c_{jk} > 0$ for $(\varsigma_j, \varsigma_k) \in \epsilon$. Otherwise, $c_{jk} = 0$. Let A be a digraph. Then, its directed spanning tree is a subgraph of A, where by following the directed edge, the root vertices can approach every other vertex [34].

Let $D = (I_{jk})_{M \times M}$ be the Laplacian matrix of graph A

$$\begin{cases} I_{jk} = -c_{jk}, \ j \neq k \\ I_{jj} = \sum_{k=1, k \neq j}^{M} c_{jk} \ j = k. \end{cases}$$

It is obvious that $\sum_{k=1}^{M} I_{jk} = 0$ for $j = 1, 2, ..., M$.

Lemma 1 ([34]). *The directed graph A has a directed spanning tree if and only if the eigenvalue of the Laplacian matrix D is zero, and all other eigenvalue's real components are non-negative.*

Definition 1 ([19]). *Let $f(\tau)$ be a function. Then, the annotation of Caputo derivative with order α is*

$$_{\tau_0}^{C}D_\tau^\alpha f(\tau) = \frac{1}{\Gamma(n-\alpha)} \int_{\tau_0}^\tau \frac{f^n(s)}{(\tau-s)^{\alpha-n+1}} ds. \tag{1}$$

$0 \leq n-1 < \alpha \leq n$, $n \in Z^+$.

Definition 2 ([35]). *Let $f : R^m \times R \to R^m$ be a function. Then, it is $QUAD(\Delta, e)$ if there exists a diagonal matrix $\Delta \in R^{m \times m}$ and a constant $e > 0$ satisfy*

$$(x-y)^T[f(\tau, x) - f(\tau, y)] - (x-y)^T \Delta(x-y) \leq -e(x-y)^T(x-y), \text{ for any } x, y \in R^m. \tag{2}$$

Lemma 2 ([36]). *Let E, F, G be three matrices. Then, the inequality*

$$\begin{pmatrix} E & F \\ E^T & G \end{pmatrix} < 0 \tag{3}$$

is equivalent to these inequalities

$$E < 0 \text{ and } G - F^T E^{-1} F < 0. \tag{4}$$

Lemma 3 ([37]). *Let $x(t) \in R^m$ be a continuously differentiable function, $H > 0$. The following relationship holds*

$$\frac{1}{2} {}_{\tau_0}^{C}D_\tau^\alpha(x^T(\tau) H x(\tau)) \leq x^T(\tau) H \, {}_{\tau_0}^{C}D_\tau^\alpha x(\tau), \forall \alpha \in (0,1). \tag{5}$$

Consider $G = \{\theta | \theta : [-r_1, 0] \to R^m \text{ is continous}\}$ denotes the Banach space containing a supremum norm. Suppose a general fractional nonlinear equation with delay in time

$$_{\tau_0}^{C}D_\tau^\alpha u(\tau) = f(\tau, u_\tau), \tau \geq \tau_0 \tag{6}$$

for $0 < \alpha \leq 1$ and $u_\tau(\varpi) = u(\tau + \varpi)$, $\varpi \in [-r_1, 0]$, f maps $R \times$ (bounded sets of G) into bounded sets of R^m which satisfy $f(\tau, 0) = 0$.

Lemma 4 ([38]). *Suppose $\gamma_1, \gamma_2, \gamma_3 : R \to R$ are continuous increasing functions, $\gamma_1(s)$ and $\gamma_2(s)$ are positive if s is positive, and $\gamma_1(0) = \gamma_2(0) = 0$, $\dot{\gamma}_2 > 0$ if differential function $J : R \times R^m \to R$ and continuous increasing function $\eta(s)$ greater than s for $s > 0$ exists such that for $\theta \in G$ and $u \in R^m$*

$$\gamma_1(||u||) \leq J(\tau, u) \leq \gamma_2(||u||), \tag{7}$$

if

$$J(\tau + \phi, \theta(\phi)) \leq \eta(J(\tau, \theta(0))).$$

$$_{\tau_0}^{C}D_\tau^\alpha J(\tau, \theta(0)) \leq -\gamma_3(||\theta(0)||), \tau \geq \tau_0. \tag{8}$$

Zero solution $u = 0$ of equation (6) is asymptotically stable for $\phi \in [-\varpi, 0]$. $u = 0$ is globally stable if $\gamma_1(s) \to \infty$ as $s \to \infty$.

Lemma 5 ([39]). *If $\lambda_1, \lambda_2, ..., \lambda_n$ are the eigenvalues of matrix $E \in R^{n \times n}$ and $\mu_1, \mu_2, ..., \mu_m$, are eigenvalues of matrix $F \in R^{m \times m}$, then $\lambda_j \mu_k (j = 1, 2, ..., n, k = 1, 2, ..., m)$ are the eigenvalues of $E \otimes F$.*

3. Leader-Following Consensus

Here, with distributed and input delay, resilient-based consensus analysis of a fractional-order nonlinear multi-agent system is discussed. On the basis of a fractional-order Razumikhin approach, many convenient conditions are shown.

Consider the jth agent is

$$ {}_{\tau_0}^C D_\tau^\alpha u_j(\tau) = F u_j(\tau) + f(\tau, u_j(\tau)) + G \int_{-r_1}^{0} u_j(\tau+\phi) d\phi + \hat{x}_j(\tau) + \Delta x_j(\tau). \tag{9}$$

$j = 1, 2, ..., M$, where $u_j(\tau) = (u_{j1}(\tau), u_{j2}(\tau), ..., u_{jm}(\tau))^T$ and F is a constant matrix, and $\Delta x_j(\tau)$ is a disturbance in the controller and $\Delta x_j(\tau) = \sin t$, which is assumed to be bounded here. The leader satisfies

$$ {}_{\tau_0}^C D_\tau^\alpha u_0(\tau) = F u_0(\tau) + f(\tau, u_0(\tau)) + G \int_{-r_1}^{0} u_0(\tau+\phi) d\phi. \tag{10}$$

The controller will be designed as follows:

$$ x_j(\tau) = K \sum_{k=1}^{M} c_{jk}(u_k(\tau-r_2) - u_j(\tau-r_2)) + K c_{j0}(u_0(\tau-r_2) - u_j(\tau-r_2)) + \Delta x_j(\tau), j = 1, 2, ..., M \tag{11}$$

where r_2 is the input delay, r_1 is the distributed delay, and K is the constant matrix whose eigenvalues are positive. If a directed connection is present from $u_k(\tau)$ to $u_j(\tau)$, $j = 1, 2, ..., M$, $k = 0, 1, ..., M$. Then, $E = (c_{jk})_{M \times M}$, and $c_{jk} = 0$ otherwise.

Definition 3 ([6]). *Under the control law (11), leader–follower consensus of the multi-agent system (9) and (10) is attained if for any $j = 1, 2, ..., M$.*

$$ \lim_{\tau \to \infty} ||u_j(\tau) - u_0(\tau)|| = 0. \tag{12}$$

We need some lemmas and assumptions for obtaining results.

(H1). f is $QUAD(\Delta, e)$.

(H2). With the leader rooted, the multi-agent system's corresponding diagraph has a spanning tree.

Lemma 6 ([33]). *Consider $L = D + A_0$, $A_0 = diag(c_{10}, ..., c_{M0})$. (H2) holds if and only if all eigenvalues of matrix L have positive real parts.*

Lemma 7. *According to Lemma 5, if (H2) is satisfied, then eigenvalues of matrix of $L \otimes K$ have non-negative real parts.*

Lemma 8. *If there are a scalar $\beta > 0$ and a scalar $\sigma > 0$ and a positive definite matrix $R > 0$ and if (H1) and (H2) hold, then under the control law (11) the leader and follower consensus of system (9) and (10) can be obtained.*

$$ I_M \otimes (F + F^T + 2\Delta - 2e I_m + \beta I_m + R + \frac{4\Delta x(\tau)}{\sigma}) + \frac{1}{\beta}(L^T \otimes K^T)(L \otimes K) < 0. \tag{13}$$

$$ I_M \otimes (\beta I_m - \frac{1}{r_1} R) + \frac{1}{\beta}(I_M \otimes G^T)(I_M \otimes G) < 0. \tag{14}$$

Proof. Putting Equation (11) in Equation (9)

$$ {}_{\tau_0}^C D_\tau^\alpha u_j(\tau) = F u_j(\tau) + f(\tau, u_j(\tau)) + G \int_{-r_1}^{0} u_j(\tau+\phi) d\phi + K \sum_{k=1}^{M} c_{jk}(u_k(\tau-r_2) - u_j(\tau-r_2)) $$
$$ + K c_{j0}(u_0(\tau-r_2) - u_j(\tau-r_2)) + \Delta xj(\tau) + \Delta x_j(\tau)). \tag{15}$$

Subtracting Equation (10) from Equation (15)

$$\begin{aligned}
{}_{\tau_0}^{C}D_\tau^\alpha u_j(\tau) - {}_{\tau_0}^{C}D_\tau^\alpha u_0(\tau) &= Fu_j(\tau) + f(\tau, u_j(\tau)) + G\int_{-r_1}^{0} u_j(\tau+\phi)d\phi + K\sum_{k=1}^{M} c_{jk}(u_k(\tau-r_2) \\
&\quad -u_j(\tau-r_2)) + Kc_{j0}(u_0(\tau-r_2) - u_j(\tau-r_2)) + 2\Delta x_j(\tau) - Fu_0(\tau) \\
&\quad -f(\tau, u_0(\tau)) - G\int_{-r_1}^{0} u_0(\tau+\phi)d\phi \\
{}_{\tau_0}^{C}D_\tau^\alpha[u_j(\tau) - u_0(\tau)] &= F[u_j(\tau) - u_0(\tau)] + f(\tau, u_j(\tau)) - f(\tau, u_0(\tau)) + G\int_{-r_1}^{0}[u_j(t+\phi) \\
&\quad -u_0(\tau+\phi)]d\phi + K\sum_{k=1}^{M} c_{jk}[u_k(\tau-r_2) - u_0(\tau-r_2) + u_0(\tau-r_2) \\
&\quad -u_j(\tau-r_2)] - Kc_{j0}[u_j(\tau-r_2) - u_0(\tau-r_2)] + 2\Delta x_j(\tau).\\
{}_{\tau_0}^{C}D_\tau^\alpha[u_j(\tau) - u_0(\tau)] &= F[u_j(\tau) - u_0(\tau)] + f(\tau, u_j(\tau)) - f(\tau, u_0(\tau)) + G\int_{-r_1}^{0}[u_j(t+\phi) - u_0(\tau+\phi)]d\phi \\
&\quad +K\sum_{k=1}^{M} c_{jk}[u_k(\tau-r_2) - u_0(\tau-r_2)] - K\sum_{k=1}^{M} c_{jk}[u_j(\tau-r_2) - u_0(\tau-r_2)] \\
&\quad -Kc_{j0}[u_j(\tau-r_2) - u_0(\tau-r_2)] + 2\Delta x_j(\tau). \quad (16)
\end{aligned}$$

Suppose
$$\omega_j(\tau) = u_j(\tau) - u_0(\tau), j = 1, 2, ..., M. \quad (17)$$

Then, Equation (13) becomes

$$\begin{aligned}
{}_{\tau_0}^{C}D_\tau^\alpha \omega_j(\tau) &= F\omega_j(\tau) + f(\tau, u_j(\tau)) - f(\tau, u_0(\tau)) + G\int_{-r_1}^{0} \omega_j(\tau+\phi)d\phi + K\sum_{k=1}^{M} c_{jk}(\omega_k(\tau-r_2) \\
&\quad -\omega_j(\tau-r_2)) - Kc_{j0}\omega_j(\tau-r_2) + 2\Delta x_j(\tau). \quad (18)
\end{aligned}$$

Choose a quadratic Lyapunov function

$$J(\tau) = \sum_{j=1}^{M} \omega_j^T(\tau)\omega_j(\tau). \quad (19)$$

From Lemma 3 and along the solutions of (18), find the α-order derivative of $J(\tau)$.

$${}_{\tau_0}^{C}D_\tau^\alpha J(\tau) \leq 2\sum_{j=1}^{M} \omega_j^T(\tau){}_{\tau_0}^{C}D_\tau^\alpha \omega_j(\tau). \quad (20)$$

Putting Equation (18) in Equation (20).

$$\begin{aligned}
{}_{\tau_0}^{C}D_\tau^\alpha J(\tau) &\leq 2\sum_{j=1}^{M} \omega_j^T(\tau)[F\omega_j(\tau) + f(\tau, u_j(\tau)) - f(\tau, u_0(\tau)) + G\int_{-r_1}^{0} \omega_j(\tau+\phi)d\phi \\
&\quad +K\sum_{k=1}^{M} c_{jk}(\omega_k(\tau-r_2) - \omega_j(\tau-r_2)) - Kc_{j0}\omega_j(\tau-r_2) + 2\Delta x_j(\tau)]. \quad (21)
\end{aligned}$$

From (H1), we have

$$\omega_j^T(\tau)[f(\tau, u_j(\tau)) - f(\tau, u_0(\tau))] - \omega_j^T(\tau)\Delta\omega_j(\tau) \leq -e\omega_j^T(\tau)\omega_j(\tau).$$

Then,

$$\omega_j^T(\tau)[f(\tau,u_j(\tau))-f(\tau,u_0(\tau))] \leq \omega_j^T(\tau)\Delta\omega_j(\tau) - eI_m\omega_j^T(\tau)\omega_j(\tau).$$

which implies that

$$\omega_j^T(\tau)[f(\tau,u_j(\tau))-f(\tau,u_0(\tau)] \leq \omega_j^T(\tau)(\Delta - eI_m)\omega_j(\tau). \tag{22}$$

Notice that

$$I_{jk} = -c_{jk}, j \neq k \text{ and } I_{jj} = \sum_{k=1,k\neq j}^{M} c_{jk},$$

We obtain

$$\sum_{k=1}^{M} c_{jk}(\omega_k(\tau)-\omega_j(\tau)) = \sum_{k=1,k\neq j}^{M} c_{jk}(\omega_k(\tau)-\omega_j(\tau)) = \sum_{k=1,k\neq j}^{M} c_{jk}\omega_k(\tau) - \sum_{k=1,k\neq j}^{M} c_{jk}\omega_j(\tau)$$

$$= -\sum_{k=1,k\neq j}^{M} I_{jk}\omega_k(\tau) - I_{jj}\omega_j(\tau).$$

Then, we obtain

$$\sum_{k=1}^{M} c_{jk}(\omega_k(\tau)-\omega_j(\tau)) = -\sum_{k=1}^{M} I_{jk}\omega_k(\tau). \tag{23}$$

Now, putting values in Equation (21)

$$\begin{aligned}{}_{\tau_0}^{C}D_\tau^\alpha J(\tau) &\leq 2\omega_j^T(\tau)\sum_{j=1}^{M}[F\omega_j(\tau)+f(\tau,u_j(\tau))-f(\tau,u_0(\tau))+G\int_{-r_1}^{0}\omega_j(\tau+\phi)d\phi\\
&+K\sum_{k=1}^{M} c_{jk}(\omega_k(\tau-r_2)-\omega_j(\tau-r_2))-Kc_{j0}\omega_j(\tau-r_2)+2\Delta x_j(\tau)]\\
&\leq 2\sum_{j=1}^{M}[\omega_j^T(\tau)F\omega_j(\tau)+\omega_j^T(\tau)(f(\tau,u_j(\tau))-f(\tau,u_0(\tau)))\\
&+2\int_{-r_1}^{0}\sum_{j=1}^{M}\omega_j^T(\tau)G\omega_j(\tau+\phi)d\phi+2\sum_{j=1}^{M}\omega_j^T(\tau)K\sum_{k=1}^{M}c_{jk}(\omega_k(\tau-r_2)-\omega_j(\tau-r_2))\\
&-2\sum_{j=1}^{M}\omega_j^T(\tau)Kc_{j0}\omega_j(\tau-r_2)+2\sum_{j=1}^{M}\omega_j^T(\tau)[2\Delta x_j(\tau)]].\end{aligned}$$

By using Equation (22),

$$\begin{aligned}{}_{\tau_0}^{C}D_\tau^\alpha J(\tau) &\leq 2\sum_{j=1}^{M}[\omega_j^T(\tau)F\omega_j(\tau)+\omega_j^T(\tau)(\Delta-2eI_m)\omega_j(\tau)]\\
&+2\int_{-r_1}^{0}\sum_{j=1}^{M}\omega_j^T(\tau)G\omega_j(\tau+\phi)d\phi+2\sum_{j=1}^{M}\omega_j^T(\tau)K\sum_{k=1}^{M}c_{jk}(\omega_k(\tau-r_2)-\omega_j(\tau-r_2))\\
&-2\sum_{j=1}^{M}\omega_j^T(\tau)Kc_{j0}\omega_j(\tau-r_2)+4\Delta x(\tau)\omega^T(\tau).\end{aligned}$$

$$\begin{aligned}
{}_{\tau_0}^C D_\tau^\alpha J(\tau) &\leq 2\sum_{j=1}^M \omega_j^T(\tau)(F+\Delta-eI_m)\omega_j(\tau)+2\int_{-r_1}^0 \sum_{j=1}^M \omega_j^T(\tau)G\omega_j(\tau+\phi)d\phi \\
&\quad +2\sum_{j=1}^M \omega_j^T(\tau)K(-\sum_{k=1}^M I_{jk}\omega_k(\tau-r_2))-2\sum_{j=1}^M \omega_j^T(\tau)Kc_{j0}\omega_j(\tau-r_2) \\
&\quad +\Delta x_j(\tau)\omega_j(\tau-r_2)+4\Delta x(\tau)\omega^T(\tau) \\
&\leq 2\sum_{j=1}^M \omega_j^T(\tau)(F+\Delta-eI_m)\omega_j(\tau)+2\int_{-r_1}^0 \sum_{j=1}^M \omega_j^T(\tau)\omega_j(\tau+\phi)d\phi \\
&\quad -2\sum_{j=1}^M \omega_j^T(\tau)K\sum_{k=1}^M I_{jk}e_k(\tau-r_2)-2\sum_{j=1}^M \omega_j^T(\tau)Kc_{j0}\omega_j(\tau-r_2)+4\Delta x\omega^T(\tau). \\
&\leq 2\omega^T(\tau)(I_M\otimes(F+\Delta-eI_m)\omega(\tau)+2\int_{-r_1}^0 \omega^T(\tau)(I_M\otimes G)\omega(\tau+\phi)d\phi \\
&\quad -2\omega^T(\tau)(D\otimes K)\omega(\tau-r_2)-2\omega^T(\tau)(A_0\otimes K)\omega(\tau-r_2)+4\Delta x(\tau)\omega^T(\tau) \\
&\leq 2\omega^T(\tau)(I_M\otimes(F+\Delta-eI_m)\omega(\tau)+2\int_{-r_1}^0 \omega^T(\tau)(I_M\otimes G)\omega(\tau+\phi)d\phi \\
&\quad -2\omega^T(\tau)(D+A_0)\otimes K\omega(\tau-r_2)+4\Delta x(\tau)\omega^T(\tau).
\end{aligned}$$

By using Lemma 6,

$$\begin{aligned}
{}_{\tau_0}^C D_\tau^\alpha J(\tau) &\leq 2\omega^T(\tau)(I_M\otimes(F+\Delta-eI_m)\omega(\tau)+2\int_{-r_1}^0 \omega^T(\tau)(I_M\otimes G)\omega(\tau+\phi)d\phi \\
&\quad -\omega^T(\tau)(L\otimes K)\omega(\tau-r_2)+4\Delta x(\tau)\omega^T(\tau) \\
&\leq \omega^T(\tau)(I_M\otimes(2F+2\Delta-2eI_m)\omega(\tau)+2\int_{-r_1}^0 \omega^T(\tau)(I_M\otimes G)\omega(\tau+\phi)d\phi \\
&\quad -2\omega^T(\tau)(L\otimes K)\omega(\tau-r_2)+4\Delta x(\tau)\omega^T(\tau) \\
&\leq \omega^T(\tau)(I_M\otimes(F+F^T+2\Delta-2eI_m)\omega(\tau)+2\int_{-r_1}^0 \omega^T(\tau)(I_M\otimes G)\omega(\tau+\phi)d\phi \\
&\quad -2\omega^T(\tau)(L\otimes K)\omega(\tau-r_2)+4\Delta x(\tau)\omega^T(\tau).
\end{aligned}$$

where
$$\omega^T(\tau)=(\omega_1^T(\tau),...,\omega_M^T(\tau))^T.$$

Whenever
$$J(\tau+\varpi,u(\tau+\varpi))<\eta J(\tau,u(\tau)), for\ all\ -r\leq\varpi<0$$
here $r=\max\{r_1,r_2\}$, for any $\beta>0$ and for some $\eta>1$

$$\begin{aligned}
{}_{\tau_0}^C D_\tau^\alpha J(\tau) &\leq \omega^T(\tau)(I_M\otimes(F+F^T+2\Delta-2eI_m)\omega(\tau)+2\int_{-r_1}^0 \omega^T(\tau)(I_M\otimes G)\omega(\tau+\phi)d\phi \\
&\quad -2\omega^T(\tau)(L\otimes K)\omega(\tau-r_2)+4\Delta x(\tau)\omega^T(\tau)+\beta[\eta\omega^T(\tau)(I_M\otimes I_m)\omega(\tau) \\
&\quad -\omega^T(\tau-r_2)(I_M\otimes I_m)\omega(\tau-r_2)]+\int_{-r_1}^0 \beta[\eta\omega^T(\tau)(I_M\otimes I_m)\omega(\tau) \\
&\quad -\omega^T(\tau+\phi)(I_M\otimes I_m)\omega\omega(\tau+\phi)]d\phi.
\end{aligned}$$

Which implies that

$$\begin{aligned}
{}^C_{\tau_0}D^\alpha_\tau J(\tau) &\leq \omega^T(\tau)[I_M \otimes (F + F^T + 2\Delta - 2eI_m + \beta\eta I_m + R)]\omega(\tau) - 2\omega^T(\tau)(L \otimes K)\omega(\tau - r_2) \\
&- \beta\omega^T(\tau - r_2)(I_M \otimes I_m)\omega(\tau - r_2) + \int_{-r_1}^0 [\omega^T(\tau)(I_M \otimes (\beta\eta I_m - \frac{1}{r_1}R)\omega(\tau))] + 2\omega^T(\tau)(I_M \otimes G) \\
&\omega(\tau + \phi) - \beta\omega^T(\tau + \phi)(I_M \otimes I_m)\omega(\tau + \phi)]d\phi + \frac{4\Delta x(\tau)\omega^T(\tau)\omega(\tau)}{\omega(\tau)}.
\end{aligned}$$

$$_{\tau_0}^C D_\tau^\alpha J(\tau) \leq \chi_{r2}^T$$

$$\begin{pmatrix} I_M \otimes (F + F^T + 2\Delta - 2eI_m + \beta\eta I_m + R + \frac{4\Delta x(\tau)}{\omega(\tau)}) & -L \otimes K \\ -L^T \otimes K^T & -\beta I_M \otimes I_m \end{pmatrix} \chi_{r2}$$

$$+ \int_{-r_1}^0 \chi_\phi^T \begin{pmatrix} I_M \otimes (\beta\eta I_m - \frac{1}{r_1}R) & I_M \otimes G \\ I_M \otimes G^T & \beta I_M \otimes I_m \end{pmatrix} \chi_\phi d\phi. \tag{24}$$

where $\chi_{r2} = (\omega^T(\tau), \omega^T(\tau - r_2))^T$, $\chi_\phi = (\omega^T(\tau), \omega^T(\tau + \phi))^T$, $\sigma = \frac{1}{\omega(\tau)}$ and $\phi \in [-r_1, 0]$.
Suppose $\eta \to +1$

$$_{\tau_0}^C D_\tau^\alpha J(\tau) \leq \chi_{r2}^T$$

$$\begin{pmatrix} I_M \otimes (F + F^T + 2\Delta - 2eI_m + \beta I_m + R + \frac{4\Delta x(\tau)}{\sigma}) & -L \otimes K \\ -L^T \otimes K^T & -\beta I_M \otimes I_m \end{pmatrix} \chi_{r2} + \int_{-r_1}^0 \chi_\phi^T$$

$$\begin{pmatrix} I_M \otimes (\beta I_m - \frac{1}{r_1}R) & I_M \otimes G \\ I_M \otimes G^T & -\beta I_M \otimes I_m \end{pmatrix} \chi_\phi d\phi.$$

By using inequalities (13) and (14) and Lemma 2

$$\begin{pmatrix} I_M \otimes (F + F^T + 2\Delta - 2eI_m + \beta I_m + R + \frac{4\Delta x(\tau)}{\sigma}) & -L \otimes K \\ -L^T \otimes K^T & -\beta I_M \otimes I_m \end{pmatrix} < 0, \tag{25}$$

and

$$\begin{pmatrix} I_m \otimes (\beta I_m - \frac{1}{r_1}R) & I_M \otimes G \\ I_M \otimes G^T & -\beta I_M \otimes I_m \end{pmatrix} < 0. \tag{26}$$

Systems (13) and (14) are satisfied in the sense of Lemma 2. It shows that if $J(\tau + \varpi, u(\tau + \varpi)) < \eta J(\tau, u(\tau))$, then ${}^C_{\tau_0}D^\alpha_\tau J(\tau) < 0$, for some $\varpi \in [-r, 0]$ and $\eta > 1$. Hence, according to Lemma 4, the system (15) is asymptotically stable. Under the control law (11), for systems (9) and (10), leader–follower consensus is obtained. □

Corollary 1. *If (H1) and (H2) are satisfied, and there are a scalar $\beta > 0$, a scalar $\sigma > 0$ and a non-negative definite matrix $R > 0$, then under control law (11), leader–follower consensus of (9) and (10) can be obtained.*

$$\lambda_{max}[I_M \otimes (F + F^T + 2\Delta - 2eI_m + \beta I_m + R + \frac{4\Delta x(\tau)}{\sigma}) + \frac{1}{\beta}(L^T \otimes K^T)(L \otimes K)] < 0, \tag{27}$$

and

$$\lambda_{max}(\beta I_m - \frac{1}{r_1}R + \frac{1}{\beta}G^T G) < 0. \tag{28}$$

Lemma 9. *By using our criteria, it is more suitable to calculate a multi-agent system's consensus, in spite of criteria used in [33]. In this paper, the system which is being considered not only contains* input and distributed delay, but it leads to a weighted directed graph too. Our criteria can be used for more general multi-agent systems because criteria used in [33] lead to a directed graph only. If "$\omega^T(\tau)(I_M \otimes R)\omega(\tau)$" is replaced with $r_1\omega^T(\tau)(I_M \otimes R)\omega(\tau)'$ in the first equation of Formula (24), then we obtain the following theorem.

Lemma 10. *If (H1) and (H2) are satisfied and if there are scalars σ and $\beta > 0$ and a non-negative definite matrix $R > 0$, then under the control law (11), we can obtain leader–follower consensus of (9) and (10).*

$$I_M \otimes (F + F^T + 2\Delta - 2eI_m + \beta I_m + r_1 R + \frac{4\Delta x(\tau)}{\sigma}) + \frac{1}{\beta}(L^T \otimes K^T)(L \otimes K) < 0, \quad (29)$$

and

$$I_M \otimes (\beta I_m - R) + \frac{1}{\beta}(I_M \otimes G^T)(I_M \otimes G) < 0. \quad (30)$$

The results that are obtained must be suitable for FOMAS having undirected topology.

Lemma 11 ([34]). *A graph A is considered connected if and only if its corresponding Laplacian matrix D is a non-negative semi-definite matrix in an undirected graph A. The Laplacian matrix D has a single, nonrepeated eigenvalue of zero, and all other eigenvalues are non-negative.*

Lemma 12. *The system leads to a directed weighted graph in Lemmas 8 and 11. If the system's topology is a connected undirected graph, then only Lemma 1 is replaced, and the proof is continued in the same way.*

4. Numerical Examples

Consider some examples for determining the convenience of results.

Example 1. *Under the control law (11), consider nonlinear system (9) and (10) with four followers and one leader, as shown in Figure 1. Consider the matrices F and G.*

$$F = \begin{pmatrix} -5.3 & 0 & 1.1 \\ 0 & -3.2 & 0 \\ 0 & 0 & -2.5 \end{pmatrix},$$

and

$$G = \begin{pmatrix} 0.19 & 0 & 0 \\ 0.12 & 0.35 & 0 \\ 0 & 0 & 0.17 \end{pmatrix}$$

From Figure 1

$$E = \begin{pmatrix} 0 & 0 & 0 & 0.5 \\ 0.2 & 0 & 0 & 0 \\ 0 & 0 & 0 & 1.4 \\ 0 & 0 & 0.6 & 0 \end{pmatrix}$$

$$A_0 = \begin{pmatrix} 0.5 & 0 & 0 & 0 \\ 0 & 0 & 0 & 0 \\ 0 & 0 & 0 & 0 \\ 0 & 0 & 0 & 0.9 \end{pmatrix}$$

$$D = \begin{pmatrix} 0.5 & 0 & 0 & -0.5 \\ -0.2 & 0.2 & 0 & 0 \\ 0 & 0 & 1.4 & -1.4 \\ 0 & 0 & -0.6 & 0.6 \end{pmatrix}$$

$$L = \begin{pmatrix} 0.5 & 0 & 0 & -0.5 \\ -0.2 & 0.2 & 0 & 0 \\ 0 & 0 & 1.4 & -1.4 \\ 0 & 0 & -0.6 & 0.6 \end{pmatrix} + \begin{pmatrix} 0.5 & 0 & 0 & 0 \\ 0 & 0 & 0 & 0 \\ 0 & 0 & 0 & 0 \\ 0 & 0 & 0 & 0.9 \end{pmatrix}$$

which implies that

$$L = \begin{pmatrix} 1 & 0 & 0 & -0.5 \\ -0.2 & 0.2 & 0 & 0 \\ 0 & 0 & 1.4 & -1.4 \\ 0 & 0 & -0.6 & 0.75 \end{pmatrix}$$

here $f(\tau, u_j(\tau)) = \cos(u_j(\tau))$, $j = 0, 1, ..., 4$, $\alpha = 0.6$, $r_1 = 0.7$.

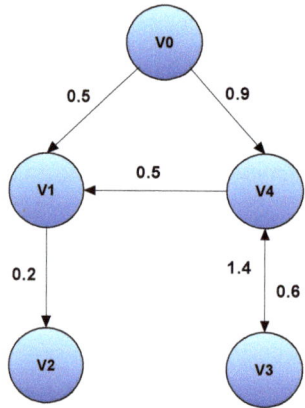

Figure 1. Directed spanning tree shown by nonlinear multi-agent system topology.

Consider $e = 0.3$ by using assumption (H1).

$$\Delta = \begin{pmatrix} 0.7 & 0 & 0 \\ 0 & 0.7 & 0 \\ 0 & 0 & 0.7 \end{pmatrix}$$

Take $\beta = 0.4$, we have according to (14)
$I_M \otimes (\beta I_m - \frac{1}{r_1}R) + \frac{1}{\beta}(I_M \otimes G^T)(I_M \otimes G)$.
$= I_M \otimes (\beta I_m - \frac{1}{r_1}R) + I_M \otimes \frac{1}{\beta}G^TG$.
$= I_M \otimes (\beta I_m + \frac{1}{\beta}G^TG - \frac{1}{r_1}R) < 0$. That is,

$$\beta r_1 I_m + \frac{r_1}{\beta}G^TG - R < 0. \tag{31}$$

Therefore,

$$R = \begin{pmatrix} 0.72 & 0 & 0.08 \\ 0 & 0.56 & 0 \\ 0.08 & 0 & 0.64 \end{pmatrix}$$

for satisfying (30) can be chosen.
Similarly, (13) implies

$$\beta I_M \otimes (F + F^T + 2\Delta - 2eI_m + R + \frac{4\Delta x(\tau)}{\sigma}) + L^TL \otimes K^TK < 0. \tag{32}$$

Here $\Delta x(\tau) = 20\cos(0.2)$, and $\sigma = 0.1$. Hence,

$$K = \begin{pmatrix} 0.2 & 0 & 0 \\ 0.3 & 0.5 & 0 \\ 0 & 0 & 0.1 \end{pmatrix}$$

for satisfying (31) can be chosen. According to Lemma 8, systems' (9) and (10) leader–follower consensuses under the control law (11) are obtained, and in Figures 2–5 the error states $\omega_j(\tau)$ are discussed.

Example 2. *Let nonlinear systems (9) and (10) under control law (11) with a leader and four followers be as shown in Figure 3. Consider matrices F and G*

$$F = \begin{pmatrix} -3.8 & 0.4 & 0.9 \\ 0 & -4.5 & 0 \\ 1 & 0.3 & -3.7 \end{pmatrix}, G = \begin{pmatrix} 0.19 & 0 & 0.1 \\ 0.16 & 0.3 & 0.1 \\ 0 & 0.2 & 0.1 \end{pmatrix} \quad (33)$$

From Figure 6,

$$E = \begin{pmatrix} 0 & 0.4 & 0 & 0 \\ 0 & 0 & 1.1 & 0.3 \\ 0 & 1.1 & 0 & 0 \\ 0 & 0.3 & 0 & 0 \end{pmatrix}.$$

and

$$A_0 = \begin{pmatrix} 0.2 & 0 & 0 & 0 \\ 0 & 0.7 & 0 & 0 \\ 0 & 0 & 0 & 0 \\ 0 & 0 & 0 & 0 \end{pmatrix}$$

$$D = \begin{pmatrix} 0.4 & -0.4 & 0 & 0 \\ -0.4 & 1.8 & -1.1 & -0.3 \\ 0 & -1.1 & 1.1 & 0 \\ 0 & -0.3 & 0 & 0.3 \end{pmatrix}$$

and

$$L = \begin{pmatrix} 0.4 & -0.4 & 0 & 0 \\ -0.4 & 1.8 & -1.1 & -0.3 \\ 0 & -1.1 & 1.1 & 0 \\ 0 & -0.3 & 0 & 0.3 \end{pmatrix} + \begin{pmatrix} 0 & 0.4 & 0 & 0 \\ 0 & 0 & 1.1 & 0.3 \\ 0 & 1.1 & 0 & 0 \\ 0 & 0.3 & 0 & 0 \end{pmatrix}$$

which implies that

$$L = \begin{pmatrix} 0.4 & 0 & 0 & 0 \\ -0.4 & 1.8 & 0 & 0 \\ 0 & 0 & 1.1 & 0 \\ 0 & 0 & 0 & 0.3 \end{pmatrix}$$

here $f(\tau, u_j(\tau)) = \frac{1}{4}\tanh u_j(\tau)$, $j = 0, 1, \ldots, 4$, $\alpha = 0.5$, $r_1 = 0.3$.
Let $e = 0.3$, $\Delta x(\tau) = 20\sin(0.3)$ and

$$\Delta = \begin{pmatrix} 0.6 & 0 & 0 \\ 0 & 0.6 & 0 \\ 0 & 0 & 0.6 \end{pmatrix}$$

Take $\alpha = 0.9$. For fulfilling the consensus's conditions

$$R = \begin{pmatrix} 0.48 & 0 & 0.04 \\ 0.2 & 0.52 & 0 \\ 0.04 & 0 & 0.56 \end{pmatrix}$$

and
$$K = \begin{pmatrix} 0.3 & 0 & 0 \\ 0.2 & 0.5 & 0 \\ 0 & 0 & 0.4 \end{pmatrix}$$

can be taken. According to Lemma 8 under control law (11), the leader–follower consensus of systems (9) and (10) with undirected topology is obtained. In Figures 7–10, the error states $\omega_j(\tau)$ are explained.

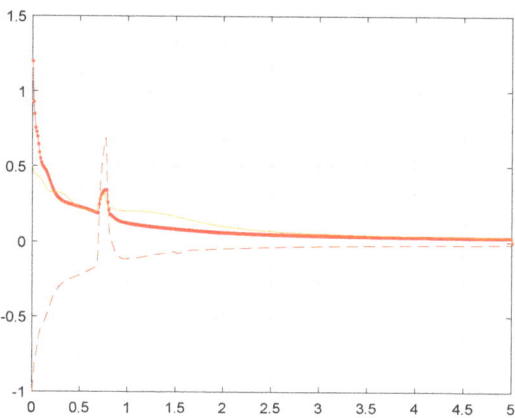

Figure 2. The graph represents the error state $\omega_j(\tau)$ of a multi-agent system following leader.

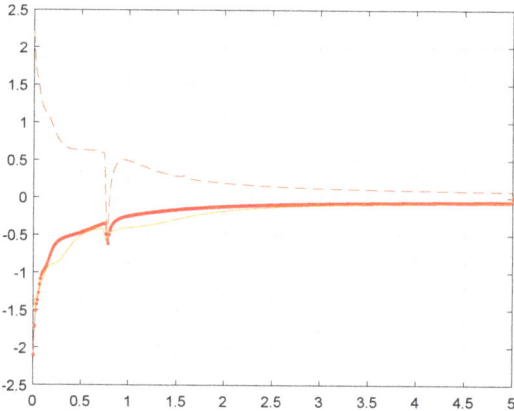

Figure 3. Leader–follower multi-agent system's error state $\omega_j(\tau)$.

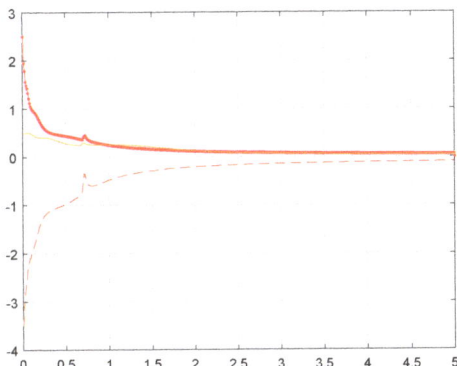

Figure 4. The leader–follower multi-agent system error states $\omega_j(\tau)$.

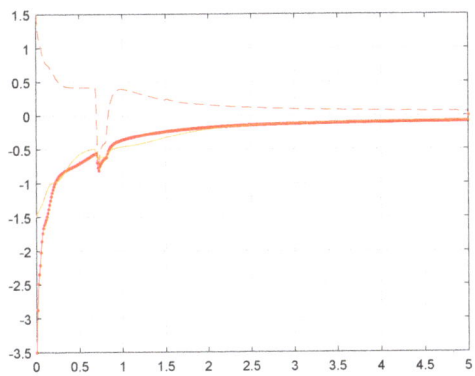

Figure 5. The leader–follower multi-agent system error states $\omega_j(\tau)$.

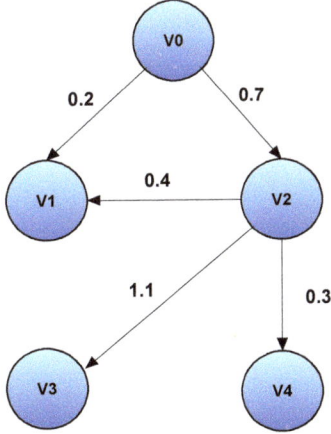

Figure 6. Undirected connected graph shown by topology of a nonlinear multi-agent system.

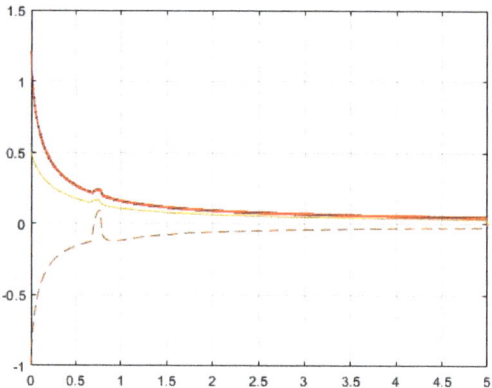

Figure 7. Graph represents error state $\omega_j(\tau)$ of a multi-agent system following leader.

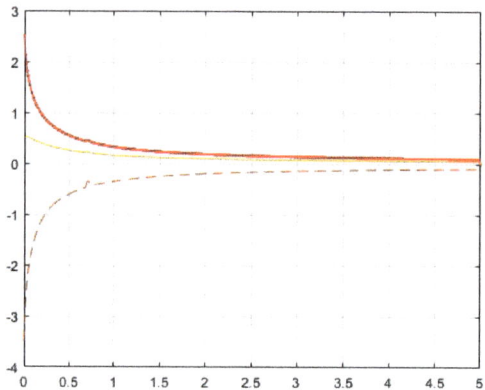

Figure 8. Leader–follower multi-agent system's error state $\omega_j(\tau)$.

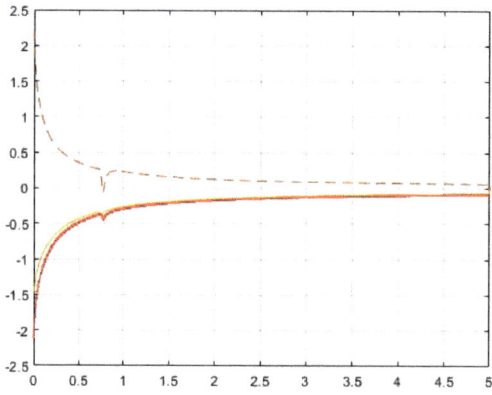

Figure 9. The leader–follower multi-agent system error states $\omega_j(\tau)$.

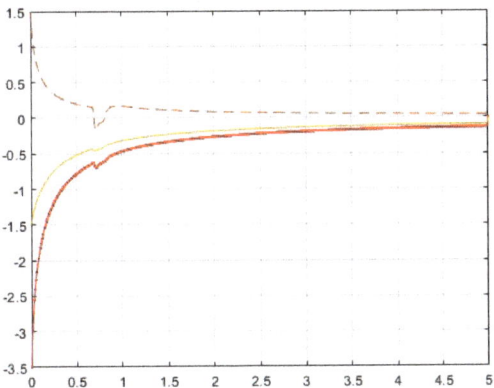

Figure 10. The leader–follower multi-agent system error states $\omega_j(\tau)$.

5. Conclusions

Fractional-order nonlinear leader and follower systems with input and distributed delay-resilient-based consensus were studied. By using the Razumikhin approach, some suitable conditions were achieved. The criteria were expressed as linear matrix inequalities, providing a suitable way to calculate consensus. This multi-agent system leads to a weighted directed graph, and the results obtained are convenient for an undirected graph. This shows that our criteria is more convenient for vast leader and follower systems. Our upcoming research focuses on fractional-order singular multi-agent systems with delayed consensus.

Author Contributions: Conceptualization, W.A.; Software, W.A.; Validation, A.K. (Asad Khan); Formal analysis, A.K. (Anam Khan); Resources, A.K. (Asad Khan); Data curation, A.K. Anum Khan; Writing—original draft, F.A.; Writing—review & editing, A.U.K.N.; Supervision, A.U.K.N.; Project administration, A.K. (Asad Khan). All authors have read and agreed to the published version of the manuscript.

Funding: This research was sponsored by the Guangzhou Government Project under Grant No. 62216235, and the National Natural Science Foundation of China (Grant No. 622260-1).

Conflicts of Interest: The authors declare that they have no known competing financial interests or personal relationships that could have appeared to influence the work reported in this paper.

References

1. Wei, R.; Beard, R. *Distributed Consensus in Multi-Vehicle Cooperative Control: Theory and Applications*; Springer: London, UK, 2008.
2. Carpenter, J. Decentralized control of sattellite formations. *Int. J. Robust Non linear Control* **2002**, *12*, 141–161. [CrossRef]
3. Zhu, W.; Jiang, Z.P. Event-based-following consensus of multi-agent systems with input time delay. *IEEE Trans. Autom. Control* **2015**, *60*, 1362–1367. [CrossRef]
4. Liu, L.; Shan, J. Event-triggered consensus of nonlinear multi-agent systems with stochastic switching topology. *J. Frankl. Inst.* **2017**, *354*, 5350–5373. [CrossRef]
5. Wu, J.; Li, H.; Chen, X. Leader-following consensus of nonlinear discrete-time multi-agent systems with limited communication channel capacity. *J. Frankl. Inst.* **2017**, *354*, 4179–4195. [CrossRef]
6. Ni, W.; Cheng, D. Leader-following consensus of multi-agent systems under fixed and switching topologies. *Syst. Control Lett.* **2010**, *59*, 209–217. [CrossRef]
7. Yang, R.; Liu, S.; Tan, Y.; Zhang, Y.; Jiang, W. Consensus analysis of fractional-order nonlinear multi-agent systems with distributed and input delays. *Neurocomputing* **2019**, *329*, 46–52. [CrossRef]
8. Gong, P. Distributed consensus of nonlinear fractional-order multi-agent systems with directed topologies. *IET Control Theory Appl.* **2016**, *10*, 2515–2525. [CrossRef]
9. Zhu, W.; Li, W.; Zhou, P.; Yang, C. Consensus of fractional-order multi-agent systems with linear models via oberver-type protocol. *Neurocomputing* **2017**, *230*, 60–65. [CrossRef]

10. Ren, G.; Yu, Y. Robust consensus of fractional multi-agent systems with external disturbances. *Neurocomputing* **2016**, *218*, 339–345. [CrossRef]
11. Yu, H.; Xia, X. Adaptive leaderless consensus of agents in jointly connected networks. *Neurocomputing* **2017**, *241*, 64–70. [CrossRef]
12. Bai, J.; Wen, G.; Rahmani, A.; Yu, Y. Consensus problem with a reference state for fractional-order multi-agent systems. *Asian J. Control* **2017**, *19*, 1009–1018. [CrossRef]
13. Ma, X.; Sun, F.; Li, H.; He, B. The consensus region design and analysis of fractional-order multi-agent systems. *Int. J. Syst. Sci.* **2017**, *48*, 629–636. [CrossRef]
14. Zhang, X.; Wu, R. Modified projective synchronization of fractional-order chaotic systems with different dimensions. *Acta Math. Appl. Sin. Engl. Ser.* **2020**, *36*, 527–538. [CrossRef]
15. Tian, Y.; Xia, Q.; Chai, Y.; L.Chen; Lopes, A.; Chen, Y. Guaranteed cost leaderless consensus protocol design for fractional-order uncertain multi-agent systems with state and input delays. *Fractal Fract.* **2021**, *5*, 141. [CrossRef]
16. Qin, J.; Gao, H.; W.X. Zheng, Second-order consensus for multi-agent systems with switching topology and communication delay. *Syst. Control Lett.* **2011**, *60*, 390–397. [CrossRef]
17. Liu, H.; Karimi, H.; Du, S.; Xia, W.; Zhong, C. Leader-following consensus of discrete-time multi-agent systems with time-varying delay based on large delay theory. *Inf. Sci.* **2017**, *417*, 236–246. [CrossRef]
18. Wang, Z.; Zhang, H.; Song, X.; Zhang, H. Consensus problems for discrete-time agents with communication delay. *Int. J. Control Autom. Syst.* **2017**, *15*, 1515–1523. [CrossRef]
19. Podlubny, I. *Fractional Differential Equations*; Academic Press: New York, NY, USA, 1999.
20. Yu, Z.; Jiang, H.; Hu, C. Leader-following consensus of fractional-order multi-agent systems under fixed topology. *Neurocomputing* **2015**, *149*, 613–620. [CrossRef]
21. Bia, J.; Wen, G.; Rahmani, A.; Yu, Y. Distributed consensus tracking for the fractional-order multi-agent systems based on the sliding mode control method. *Neurocomputing* **2017**, *235*, 210–216.
22. Xu, Q.; Zhuang, S.; Che, C.; Xia, Y. stabalization of a class of fractional-order nonautonomous systems using quadratic Lyapunov functions. *Adv. Differ. Equ.* **2018**, *2018*, 1–15. [CrossRef]
23. Xu, Q.; Xu, X.; Zhuang, S.; Xiao, J.; Che, C. New complex projective synchronization strategies for derive -response networks with fractional-complex variable dynamics. *Appl. Math. Comput.* **2018**, *338*, 552–566.
24. Liu, X.; Zhang, Z.; Li, X. Consensus control of fractional-order systems based on delayed state fractional order derivative. *Asian J. Control* **2017**, *19*, 2199–2210. [CrossRef]
25. Liu, J.; Qin, K.; Chen, W.; Li, P.; Shi, M. Consensus of fractional-order multi-agent systems with nonuniform time delays. *Math. Probl. Eng.* **2018**, *2018*, 2850757.
26. Shen, J.; Cao, J.; Lu, J. Consensus of fractional-order systems with non-nuniform input and communication delays. *Proc. Inst. Mech. Eng. Part I-J. Syst. Control Eng.* **2012**, *226*, 271–283. [CrossRef]
27. Shen, J.; Cao, J. Necessary and sufficient conditions for consensus of delayed fractional-order systems. *Asian J. Control* **2012**, *14*, 1690–1697. [CrossRef]
28. Liu, S.; Wu, X.; Zhou, X.; Jiang, W. Asymptotical stability of Riemann-Liouville fractional nonlinear systems. *Nonlinear Dyn.* **2016**, *86*, 65–71. [CrossRef]
29. Liu, S.; Zhou, X.; Li, X.; Jiang, W. Asymptotical stability of Riemann-Liouville fractional singular systems with multiple time-varying delays. *Appl. Math. Lett.* **2017**, *65*, 32–39. [CrossRef]
30. Liu, S.; Wu, X.; Zhang, Y.; Yang, R. Asymptotical stability of Riemann-Liouville fractional neutral systems. *Appl. Math. Lett.* **2017**, *69*, 168–173. [CrossRef]
31. Xu, Q.; Zhuang, S.; Liu, S.; Xiao, J. Decentralized adaptive coupling synchronization of fractional-order complex-variable dynamical networks. *Neurocomputing* **2016**, *186*, 119–216. [CrossRef]
32. Wang, F.; Yang, Y., Leader-following exponential consensus of fractional-order nonlinear multi-agents system with hybrid time-varying delay: A heterogenous impulsive method. *Phys. A* **2017**, *482*, 158–172. [CrossRef]
33. Zhu, W.; Chen, B.; Yang, J. Consensus of fractional-order multi-agent systems with input time delay. *Fract. Calc. Appl. Anal.* **2017**, *20*, 52–70. [CrossRef]
34. Yu, W.; Wen, G.; Chen, G.; Cao, J. *Distributed Cooperative Control of Multi-Agent Systems*; Higher Education Press: Beijing, China, 2016.
35. DeLellis, P.; di Bernardo, M.; Russo, G. On QUAD, Lipschitz, and contracting vector fields for consensus and synchronization of networks. *IEEE Trans. Circuits Syst. I* **2011**, *58*, 576–583. [CrossRef]
36. Gu, K.; Kharitonov, V.; Chen, J. *Stability of Time-Delay Systems*; Birkhauser: Boston, MA, USA, 2022.
37. Duarte-Mermoud, M.; Aguila-Camacho, N.; Gallegos, J. Castro-Linares, Using general quadratic Lyapunov functions to prove Lyapunov uniform stability for fractional order systems. *Commun. Nonlinear Sci. Numer. Simul.* **2015**, *22*, 650–659. [CrossRef]
38. Wen, Y.; Zhou, X.; Zhang, Z.; Liu, S. Lyapunov method for nonlinear fractional differential systems with delay. *Nonlinear Dyn* **2015**, *82*, 1015–1025. [CrossRef]
39. Xu, Z.; Zhang, K.; Lu, Q.; Leng, G. *Concise Tutorial of Matrix Theory*; Science Press: Beijing, China, 2001. (In Chinese)

Disclaimer/Publisher's Note: The statements, opinions and data contained in all publications are solely those of the individual author(s) and contributor(s) and not of MDPI and/or the editor(s). MDPI and/or the editor(s) disclaim responsibility for any injury to people or property resulting from any ideas, methods, instructions or products referred to in the content.

Article

Cauchy Problem for an Abstract Evolution Equation of Fractional Order

Maksim V. Kukushkin

Moscow State University of Civil Engineering, 129337 Moscow, Russia; kukushkinmv@rambler.ru

Abstract: In this paper, we define an operator function as a series of operators corresponding to the Taylor series representing the function of the complex variable. In previous papers, we considered the case when a function has a decomposition in the Laurent series with the infinite principal part and finite regular part. Our central challenge is to improve this result having considered as a regular part an entire function satisfying the special condition of the growth regularity. As an application, we consider an opportunity to broaden the conditions imposed upon the second term not containing the time variable of the evolution equation in the abstract Hilbert space.

Keywords: evolution equations; operator function; fractional differential equations; Abel–Lidskii basis property; Schatten–von Neumann class

MSC: 47B28; 47A10; 47B12; 47B10; 34K30; 58D25

1. Introduction

The urbanization of the sea coast and the active use of shelf resources have led to an increase in accidents of man-made origin and their negative impact on the environment. In these conditions, it becomes critically important to control natural catastrophic phenomena and assess their consequences in order to minimize possible human and material losses. This was the reason for the development in recent years of acoustic measurement methods and long-term monitoring of the parameters of the aquatic environment in shallow waters. Hydroacoustic complexes operating on the basis of the proposed methods provide remote measurement of the parameters of the aquatic environment in bays, straits and inland reservoirs, allowing the early detection of sources of natural and man-made threats. Ferroelectrics are a promising class of polar dielectrics and the study of their nonequilibrium dynamics, phase transitions and domain kinetics is of key importance in acoustics. In the paper [1], the description of the process of switching the polarization of ferroelectrics is implemented by modeling a fractal system. Since the polarization switching process is the result of the formation of self-similar structures, the domain configurations of many ferroelectrics are characterized by a self-similar structure, and electrical responses are characterized by fractal patterns. The manifestation of fractal properties is due to the complex mechanisms of domain boundary movement, the anisotropy properties of real crystals, the stochastic nature of the nucleation process, and the presence of memory effects. The field of application of the results of fractal system modeling is focused on the description of the process of switching the polarization of ferroelectrics. The main mathematical object of research is the Cauchy problem for the evolution equation with a fractional Riemann–Liouville derivative in the first term. The proposed methods are numerical, based on a finite difference method.

At the same time, the method invented in this paper allows us to solve such problems analytically, which is undoubtedly a great advantage. Having created a direction of the spectral theory of non-self-adjoint operators, we can consider abstract theoretical results as a base for further research studying such mathematical objects as a Cauchy problem

for the evolution equation of fractional order in the abstract Hilbert space. We consider in the second term an operator function defined on a special operator class covering a generator transform considered in [2], where a corresponding semigroup is supposed to be a C_0 semigroup of contractions. In its own turn, the transform reduces to a linear composition of differential operators of real order in various senses, such as the Riemann–Liouville fractional differential operator, the Kipriyanov operator, the Riesz potential, and the difference operator [2–5]. Moreover, in the paper [6], we broadened the class of differential operators having considered the artificially constructed normal operator that cannot be covered by the Lidskii results [7]. The application part of the theory appeals to the results and problems which can be considered particular cases of the abstract ones; the following papers are worth noting within this context [8–11]. At the same time, we should admit that abstract methods can be "clumsy", as some peculiarities can be considered only by a unique technique, which forms the main contribution of the specialists dealing with concrete differential equations. The significance of the problem for physics and engineering sciences is based upon the wide field of applications; here, we refer to the valuable example considered above [1], which gives us an opportunity to demonstrate the significance in a plain way. The main idea of the results connected with the basis property in a more refined sense—the Abel–Lidskii sense [12]—allows to consider many problems [6] in the theory of evolution equations and in this way obtain remarkable applications.

As a main objective of the paper, we consider a method by virtue of which we can principally weaken conditions imposed upon the second term of the abstract evolution equation. The concept of an operator function, realized in terms of the involved contour integral, is an effective technical tool giving an advantage in solving the applied problems let alone abstract generalizations. In this regard, it is rather reasonable to develop a theory analogous to the spectral theorem for self-adjoint operators having defined a family of projectors. At the same time, from an applied point of view, we intend to realize the idea considering a notion of operator function applicably to a Cauchy problem for an abstract fractional evolution equation with an operator function in the second term not containing the time variable, where the derivative in the first term is supposed to be of a fractional order. Here, we should note that regarding functional spaces, we have that an operator function generates a variety of operators acting in a corresponding space. In this regard, even a power function gives us an interesting result [6]. In the context of existence and uniqueness theorems, a significant refinement that is worth highlighting is the obtained formula for the solution represented by a series on the root vectors. In the absence of the norm convergence of the root vector series, we need to consider a notion of convergence in weaker Bari, Riesz, and Abel–Lidskii senses [7,13,14].

In spite of the claimed rather applied objectives, we admit that the problem of the root vectors expansion for a non-self-adjoint unbounded operator still remains relevant in the context of the paper. It is remarkable that the problem originates nearly from the first half of the last century [2,7,12,13,15–22]. However, we have a particular interest when an operator is represented by a linear combination of operators, where a so-called senior term is non-self-adjoint for a case corresponding to a self-adjoint operator; this was thoroughly studied in the papers [16,18–22]. Thus, the results [2,17] covering the very case corresponding to a non-self-adjoint senior term are worth highlighting; moreover, they have a natural mathematical origin that appears brightly while we are considering abstract constructions expressed in terms of the semigroup theory [2].

2. Preliminaries

2.1. Convergence Exponent

Below, for the reader's convenience, we introduce some basic notions and facts of the entire function theory. To characterize the growth of an entire function f, we introduce the functions

$$M_f(r) = \max_{|z|=r} |f(z)|,\ m_f(r) = \min_{|z|=r} |f(z)|.$$

An entire function $f(z)$ is said to be a function of finite order if there exists a positive constant k such that the inequality

$$M_f(r) < e^{r^k}$$

is valid for all sufficiently large values of r. The greatest lower bound of such numbers k is called the *order* of the entire function $f(z)$. We need the following obvious fact that follows from the definition. If ϱ is the order of the entire function $f(z)$, and if ε is an arbitrary positive number, then

$$e^{r^{\varrho-\varepsilon}} < M_f(r) < e^{r^{\varrho+\varepsilon}}, \tag{1}$$

where the inequality on the right-hand side is satisfied for all sufficiently large values of r, and the inequality on the left-hand side holds for some sequence $\{r_n\}$ of values of r, tending to infinity. Define a *type* σ of the entire function f having the order ϱ as the greatest lower bound of positive numbers C such that for a sufficiently large value r, the following relation holds:

$$M_f(r) < e^{Cr^\varrho}.$$

The following relation can be obtained easily by virtue of the definition given above:

$$\sigma = \varlimsup_{r \to \infty} \frac{\ln M_f(r)}{r^\varrho}.$$

We use the following notations:

$$G(z, p) := (1-z)e^{z + \frac{z^2}{2} + \dots + \frac{z^p}{p}}, \; p \in \mathbb{N}, \; G(z, 0) := (1-z).$$

Assume that an entire function has zeros for which the following relation holds:

$$\sum_{n=1}^{\infty} \frac{1}{|a_n|^\zeta} < \infty, \tag{2}$$

where $\zeta > 0$. In this case, we denote by p the smallest integer number for which the following condition holds:

$$\sum_{n=1}^{\infty} \frac{1}{|a_n|^{p+1}} < \infty. \tag{3}$$

It is clear that $0 \leq p < \zeta$. Note that in accordance with [23], relation (2) guarantees the uniform convergence of the following infinite product:

$$\prod_{n=1}^{\infty} G\left(\frac{z}{a_n}, p\right). \tag{4}$$

This infinite product is called a *canonical product*, and the value p is called the *genus* of the canonical product. Let us define a *convergence exponent* ρ of the sequence $\{a_n\}_1^\infty \subset \mathbb{C}$, $a_n \neq 0$, $a_n \to \infty$ as the greatest lower bound for such numbers ζ that the series (2) converges. However, a more precise characteristic of the sequence $\{a_n\}_1^\infty$ density than the convergence exponent can be considered (see [23]). For this purpose, let us define a counting function $n(r)$ as a function that equals a number of points of the sequence in the circle $|z| < r$. The upper density of the sequence is defined as follows:

$$\Delta = \varlimsup_{r \to \infty} n(r)/r^\rho.$$

Note that in the case when the limit exists in the ordinary sense, the upper density is called the density. The following fact is proved in Lemma 1 [23], where we have

$$\lim_{r \to \infty} n(r)/r^{\rho+\varepsilon} \to 0, \; \varepsilon > 0.$$

We need Theorem 13 [23] (Chapter I, § 10) presented below, which gives us a representation of the entire function of the finite order. To avoid any sort of inconvenient form of writing, we will also call a root a zero of the entire function.

Theorem 1. *The entire function f of the finite order ϱ has the following representation:*

$$f(z) = z^m e^{P(z)} \prod_{n=1}^{\omega} G\left(\frac{z}{a_n}; p\right), \ \omega \leq \infty,$$

where a_n are non-zero roots of the entire function, $p \leq \varrho$, $P(z)$ is a polynomial, and $\deg P(z) \leq \varrho$, m is a multiplicity of the zero root.

The infinite product represented in Theorem 1 is called a canonical product of the entire function.

2.2. Proximate Order and Angular Density of Zeros

The scale of the growth admits further clarifications. As a simplest generalization, E.L. Lindelöf made a comparison $M_f(r)$ with the functions of the type

$$r^\varrho \ln^{\alpha_1} r \ln_2^{\alpha_2} r \dots \ln_n^{\alpha_n} r,$$

where $\ln_j r = \ln \ln_{j-1} r$, $\alpha_j \in \mathbb{R}$, $j = 1, 2, \dots, n$. In order to make the further generalization, it is natural (see [23]) to define a class of the functions $L(r)$ having *low growth* and compare $\ln M_f(r)$ with $r^\varrho L(r)$. Following this idea, G. Valiron introduced a notion of proximate order of the growth of the entire function f, in accordance with which a function $\varrho(r)$, satisfying the following conditions

$$\lim_{r \to \infty} \varrho(r) = \varrho; \ \lim_{r \to \infty} r\varrho'(r) \ln r = 0,$$

is said to be of proximate order if the following relation holds:

$$\sigma_f = \overline{\lim_{r \to \infty}} \frac{\ln M_f(r)}{r^{\varrho(r)}}, \ 0 < \sigma_f < \infty.$$

In this case, the value σ_f is said to be a type of function f under the proximate order $\varrho(r)$.

To guarantee some technical results, we need to consider a class of entire functions whose zero distributions have a certain type of regularity. We follow the monograph [23], where the regularity of the distribution of the zeros is characterized by a certain type of density of the set of zeros.

We will say that the set Ω of the complex plane has an *angular density of index*

$$\xi(r) \to \xi, \ r \to \infty,$$

if for an arbitrary set of values ϕ and ψ ($0 < \phi < \psi \leq 2\pi$), maybe except for denumerable sets, there exists the limit

$$\Delta(\phi, \psi) = \lim_{r \to \infty} \frac{n(r, \phi, \psi)}{r^{\xi(r)}}, \quad (5)$$

where $n(r, \phi, \psi)$ is the number of points of the set Ω within the sector $|z| \leq r$, $\phi < \arg z < \psi$. The quantity $\Delta(\phi, \psi)$ will be called the angular density of the set Ω within the sector $\phi < \arg z < \psi$. For a fixed ϕ, the relation

$$\Delta(\psi) - \Delta(\phi) = \Delta(\phi, \psi)$$

determines, within the additive constant, a nondecreasing function $\Delta(\psi)$. This function is defined for all values of ψ, maybe except for a denumerable set of values. It is shown in the monograph [23] (p. 89), that the exceptional values of ϕ and ψ for which there does not exist an angular density must be the points of discontinuity of the function $\Delta(\psi)$. A set will be said to be *regularly distributed* relative to $\check{\varsigma}(r)$ if it has an angular density $\check{\varsigma}(r)$ with a $\check{\varsigma}$ non-integer.

The asymptotic equalities which we will establish are related to the order of growth. By the asymptotic equation
$$f(r) \approx \varphi(r)$$
we will mean the fulfillment of the following condition:
$$[f(r) - \varphi(r)]/r^{\varrho(r)} \to 0,\ r \to \infty.$$

Consider the following conditions allowing us to solve technical problems related to the estimation of contour integrals.

(I) There exists a value $d > 0$ such that circles of radii
$$r_n = d|a_n|^{1-\frac{\varrho(|a_n|)}{2}}$$
with the centers situated at the points a_n do not intersect each other, where a_n.

(II) The points a_n lie inside angles with a common vertex at the origin but with no other points in common, which are such that if one arranges the points of the set $\{a_n\}$ within any one of these angles in the order of increasing moduli, then for all points which lie inside the same angle, the following relation holds:
$$|a_{n+1}| - |a_n| > d|a_n|^{1-\varrho(|a_n|)},\ d > 0.$$

The circles $|z - a_n| \leq r_n$ in the first case, and $|z - a_n| \leq d|a_n|^{1-\varrho(|a_n|)}$ in the second case, will be called the exceptional circles.

The following theorem is a central point of the study. Below, for the reader's convenience, we present Theorem 5 [23] (Section II, § 1) in a slightly changed form.

Theorem 2. *Assume that the entire function f of the proximate order $\varrho(r)$, where ϱ is not an integer, is represented by its canonical product, i.e.,*
$$f(z) = \prod_{n=1}^{\infty} G\left(\frac{z}{a_n}; p\right),$$
the set of zeros is regularly distributed relative to the proximate order and satisfies one of the conditions (I) or (II). Then, outside of the exceptional set of circulus, the entire function satisfies the following asymptotical inequality:
$$\ln|f(re^{i\psi})| \approx H(\psi)r^{\varrho(r)},$$
where
$$H(\psi) := \frac{\pi}{\sin \pi \varrho} \int_{\psi - 2\pi}^{\psi} \cos \varrho(\psi - \varphi - \pi) d\Delta(\varphi).$$

The following lemma gives us a key for the technical part of being constructed theory. Although it does not contain implications of any subtle sort, it is worth being presented in the expanded form for the reader's convenience.

Lemma 1. *Assume that $\varrho \in (0, 1/2]$ then the function $H(\psi)$ is positive if $\psi \in (-\pi, \pi)$.*

Proof. Taking into account the facts $\cos \varrho(\psi - \varphi - \pi) = \cos \varrho(|\psi - \varphi| - \pi)$, $\psi - 2\pi < \varphi < \psi$, $\cos \varrho(|\psi - \varphi| - \pi) = \cos \varrho(|\psi - (\varphi + 2\pi)| - \pi)$, we obtain the following form:

$$H(\psi) := \frac{\pi}{\sin \pi \varrho} \int_0^{2\pi} \cos \varrho(|\psi - \varphi| - \pi) d\Delta(\varphi).$$

Having noticed the following correspondence between sets $\varphi \in [0, \psi] \Rightarrow \xi \in [\varrho(\psi - \pi), -\varrho\pi]$, $\varphi \in [\psi, \psi + \pi] \Rightarrow \xi \in [-\varrho\pi, 0]$, $\varphi \in [\psi + \pi, 2\pi] \Rightarrow \xi \in [0, \varrho(\pi - \psi)]$, where $\xi := \varrho(|\psi - \varphi| - \pi)$, we conclude that $\cos \varrho(|\psi - \varphi| - \pi) \geq 0$, $\varphi \in [0, 2\pi]$. Taking into account the fact that the function $\Delta(\varphi)$ is non-decreasing, we obtain the desired result. □

3. Main Results

This section is devoted to a method allowing us to consider an entire function as an operator function. In this regard, we involve a special technique providing a proof of convergence of contour integrals, a similar scheme of reasonings was implemented in the papers [6,24]. At the same time, the behavior of the entire function in the neighborhood of the point at infinity is the main obstacle to realize the scheme of reasonings. Thus, to overcome difficulties related to the evaluation of improper contour integrals, we need to study more comprehensive innate properties of the entire function. The property of the growth regularity is a key for the desired estimates for the involved integral constructions. However, the lack of the latter approach is that the condition of the growth regularity is supposed to be satisfied within the complex plane, except for the exceptional set of circles, the location of which in general cannot be described. On the other hand, we need not use the subtle estimates for the Fredholm determinant established in [7], as we can be completely satisfied by the application of the Wieman theorem in accordance with which we can obtain the required estimate on the boundary of circle. Finally, we represent a suitable algebraic reasoning, allowing to involve a fractional derivative in the first term. The idea gives an opportunity to reformulate in abstract form many results in the framework of the theory of fractional differential equations, to say nothing for previously unsolved problems.

3.1. Estimate of a Real Component from Below

In this subsection, we aim to produce estimates of the real component from below for the technical purposes formulated in the further paragraphs. We should admit that it is formulated in rather a rough manner, but its principal value is the discovered way of constructing entire functions fallen in the scope of the theory of fractional evolution equations with the operator function in the second term. Apparently, having put a base, we can weaken conditions imposed upon the entire functions class afterwards, and in this way, come to the natural theory. We need to involve some technicalities related to the estimates of the entire unction from below; we remind that this matter is very important in the constructed theory. Below, we consider a sector $\mathfrak{L}_0(\theta_0, \theta_1) := \{z \in \mathbb{C}, \theta_0 \leq \arg z \leq \theta_1\}$ and use a short-hand notation $\mathfrak{L}_0(\theta) := \mathfrak{L}_0(-\theta, \theta)$.

Lemma 2. *Assume that the entire function f is of the proximate order $\varrho(r)$, $\varrho \in (0, 1/2]$, maps the ray $\arg z = \theta_0$ within a sector $\mathfrak{L}_0(\zeta)$, $0 < \zeta < \pi/2$, the set of zeros is regularly distributed relative to the proximate order and satisfies one of the conditions (I) or (II), there exists $\varepsilon > 0$ such that the angle $\theta_0 - \varepsilon < \arg z < \theta_0 + \varepsilon$ does not contain the zeros with a sufficiently large absolute value. Then, for a sufficiently large value r, the following relation holds:*

$$\mathrm{Re} f(z) > Ce^{H(\theta_0)r^{\varrho(r)}}, \arg z = \theta_0.$$

Proof. Using Theorem 1, we obtain the following representation:

$$f(z) = Cz^m \prod_{n=1}^{\infty} G\left(\frac{z}{a_n}; p\right),$$

here, we should remark that $\deg P(z) = 0$. Let us show that the proximate order of the canonical product of the entire function is the same, and we have

$$M_f(r) = Cr^m M_F(r), \quad F(z) = \prod_{n=1}^{\infty} G\left(\frac{z}{a_n}; p\right).$$

Therefore, in accordance with the definition of proximate order, we have

$$\overline{\lim_{r \to \infty}} \left\{ \frac{m \ln r + \ln C}{r^{\varrho(r)}} + \frac{\ln M_F(r)}{r^{\varrho(r)}} \right\} = \sigma_f, \quad 0 < \sigma_f < \infty,$$

from which follows easily the fact that $0 < \sigma_F < \infty$, and further, $\sigma_F = \sigma_f$. Note that due to the condition that guarantees that the image of the ray $\arg z = \theta_0$ belongs to a sector in the right half-plane, we obtain

$$\operatorname{Re} f(z) \geq (1 + \tan \zeta)^{-1/2} |f(z)|, \quad r = |z|, \quad \arg z = \theta_0.$$

Applying Theorem 2, we conclude that excluding the intersection of the exceptional set of circulus with the ray $\arg z = \theta_0$, the following relation holds for sufficiently large values r:

$$|f(z)| = Cr^m \left| \prod_{n=1}^{\infty} G\left(\frac{z}{a_n}; p\right) \right| \geq Cr^m e^{H(\theta_0) r^{\varrho(r)}},$$

where $H(\theta_0) > 0$ in accordance with Lemma 1. It is clear that if we show that the intersection of the ray $\arg z = \theta_0$ with the exceptional set of circulus is empty, then we complete the proof. Note that the character of the zeros distribution allows us to claim that that is true. In accordance with the lemma conditions, it suffices to consider the neighborhoods of the zeros defined as follows $|z - a_n| < d|a_n|^{1-\varrho(|a_n|)}$, $|z - a_n| < d|a_n|^{1-\varrho(|a_n|)/2}$ and note that $0 < \varrho(|a_n|) < 1$ for a sufficiently large number $n \in \mathbb{N}$, since $\varrho(|a_n|) \to \varrho, n \to \infty$. Here, we ought to remind that the zeros are arranged in order with their absolute value growth. Thus, using simple properties of the power function with the positive exponent less than one, we obtain the fact that the intersection of the exceptional set of circulus with the ray $\arg z = \theta_0$ is empty for a sufficiently large $n \in \mathbb{N}$. □

3.2. Classical Lemmas in the Refined Form

Denote by $\mathfrak{H}$ the abstract separable Hilbert space and consider an invertible operator $B : \mathfrak{H} \to \mathfrak{H}$ with a dense range. We use notation $W := B^{-1}$. Note that such agreements are justified by the significance of the operator with a compact resolvent, of which the detailed information of spectral properties can be found in the papers cited in the introduction section. Consider an entire function φ; due to the Taylor series expansion, we can write formally

$$\varphi(W) := \sum_{j=0}^{\infty} c_j W^j. \tag{6}$$

The latter construction is called an operator function, where c_n are the Taylor coefficients. Below, we consider conditions that guarantee the convergence of series (6) on some elements of the Hilbert space $\mathfrak{H}$; here, we ought to note that in this case, the operator $\varphi(W)$ is defined.

Assume that a compact operator T acts in the Hilbert space $\mathfrak{H}$, $\overline{\Theta(T)} \subset \mathfrak{L}_0(\theta_0, \theta_1)$, here we used notations accepted in [25], define the following contour

$$\Upsilon(T) := \{\lambda : |\lambda| = r > 0, \theta_0 \leq \arg \lambda \leq \theta_1\} \cup \{\lambda : |\lambda| > r, \arg \lambda = \theta_0, \arg \lambda = \theta_1\},$$

where the number r is chosen so that the operator $(I - \lambda T)^{-1}$ is regular within the corresponding closed circle. Consider the following hypotheses separately written for the convenience of the reader.

(HI) The operator B is compact, $\overline{\Theta(B)} \subset \mathfrak{L}_0(\theta_0,\theta_1)$, the entire function φ of the order of less than a half maps the sector $\mathfrak{L}_0(\theta_0,\theta_1)$ into the sector $\mathfrak{L}_0(\omega)$, $\omega < \pi/2\alpha$, $\alpha > 0$, its zeros with a sufficiently large absolute value do not belong to the sector $\mathfrak{L}_0(\theta_0,\theta_1)$.

Lemma 3. *Assume that the condition* (HI) *holds, then we have the following relation:*

$$\int_{Y(B)} \varphi(\lambda)e^{-\varphi^\alpha(\lambda)t}B(I-\lambda B)^{-1}fd\lambda = \varphi(W)\int_{Y(B)} e^{-\varphi^\alpha(\lambda)t}B(I-\lambda B)^{-1}fd\lambda,\ f \in D(W^n),\ \forall n \in \mathbb{N},$$

and moreover,

$$\lim_{t\to+0} \frac{1}{2\pi i} \int_{Y(B)} e^{-\varphi^\alpha(\lambda)t}B(I-\lambda B)^{-1}fd\lambda = f,\ f \in D(W).$$

Proof. Firstly, we should note that the made assumptions regarding the order allow us to claim that the latter integral converges for a concrete value of the parameter t. Let us establish the formula

$$\int_{Y(B)} \varphi(\lambda)e^{-\varphi^\alpha(\lambda)t}B(I-\lambda B)^{-1}fd\lambda = \sum_{n=0}^{\infty} c_n \int_{Y(B)} e^{-\varphi^\alpha(\lambda)t}\lambda^n B(I-\lambda B)^{-1}fd\lambda. \tag{7}$$

To prove this fact, we should show that

$$\int_{Y_j(B)} \varphi(\lambda)e^{-\varphi^\alpha(\lambda)t}B(I-\lambda B)^{-1}fd\lambda = \sum_{n=0}^{\infty} c_n \int_{Y_j(B)} e^{-\varphi^\alpha(\lambda)t}\lambda^n B(I-\lambda B)^{-1}fd\lambda, \tag{8}$$

where

$$Y_j(B) := \{\lambda:\ |\lambda|=r>0,\ \theta_0 \leq \arg\lambda \leq \theta_1\} \cup \{\lambda:\ r<|\lambda|<r_j,\ \arg\lambda=\theta_0,\ \arg\lambda=\theta_1\},$$

$r_j \uparrow \infty$. Note that in accordance with Lemma 6 [12], we obtain

$$\|(I-\lambda B)^{-1}\| \leq C,\ r<|\lambda|<r_j,\ \arg\lambda=\theta_0,\ \arg\lambda=\theta_1.$$

Using this estimate, we can easily obtain the fact

$$\sum_{n=0}^{\infty} |c_n| |e^{-\varphi^\alpha(\lambda)t}| |\lambda^n| \cdot \|B(I-\lambda B)^{-1}f\| \leq C\|B\| \cdot \|f\| \sum_{n=0}^{\infty} |c_n| |\lambda|^n e^{-\operatorname{Re}\varphi^\alpha(\lambda)t},\ \lambda \in Y_j(B),$$

where the latter series is convergent. Therefore, reformulating the well-known theorem of calculus on the absolutely convergent series in terms of the norm, we obtain (8). Now, let us show that the series

$$\sum_{n=0}^{\infty} c_n \int_{Y_j(B)} e^{-\varphi^\alpha(\lambda)t}\lambda^n B(I-\lambda B)^{-1}fd\lambda \tag{9}$$

is uniformly convergent with respect to $j \in \mathbb{N}$. Using Lemma 1 [24], we obtain a trivial inequality

$$\left\| \int_{Y_j(B)} e^{-\varphi^\alpha(\lambda)t}\lambda^n B(I-\lambda B)^{-1}fd\lambda \right\|_{\mathfrak{H}} \leq C\|f\|_{\mathfrak{H}} \int_{Y_j(B)} e^{-\operatorname{Re}\varphi^\alpha(\lambda)t}|\lambda|^n |d\lambda| \leq$$

$$\leq C\|f\|_{\mathfrak{H}} \int_{Y_j(B)} e^{-C|\varphi(\lambda)|^\alpha t}|\lambda|^n |d\lambda|.$$

Here, we should note that to obtain the desired result, one is satisfied with a rather rough estimate dictated by the estimate obtained in Lemma 2. We obtain

$$\int_{Y_j(B)} e^{-|\varphi(\lambda)|^\alpha t}|\lambda|^n |d\lambda| \leq C \int_r^{r_j} e^{-xt}x^n dx \leq Ct^{-n}\Gamma(n+1).$$

Thus, we obtain

$$\left\| \int_{Y_j(B)} e^{-\varphi^\alpha(\lambda)t}\lambda^n B(I-\lambda B)^{-1} f d\lambda \right\|_{\mathfrak{H}} \leq Ct^{-n}n!.$$

Using the standard formula establishing the estimate for the Taylor coefficients of the entire function, then applying the Stirling formula, we obtain

$$|c_n| < (e\sigma\varrho)^{n/\varrho} n^{-n/\varrho} < (2\pi)^{1/2\varrho}(\sigma\varrho)^{n/\varrho}\left(\frac{\sqrt{n}}{n!}\right)^{1/\varrho},$$

where $0 < \sigma < \infty$ is a type of the function φ. Thus, we obtain

$$\sum_{n=1}^{\infty} |c_n| \left\| \int_{Y_j(B)} e^{-\varphi^\alpha(\lambda)t}\lambda^n B(I-\lambda B)^{-1} f d\lambda \right\| \leq C \sum_{n=1}^{\infty} (\sigma\varrho)^{n/\varrho} t^{-n}(n!)^{1-1/\varrho} n^{1/2\varrho}.$$

The latter series is convergent for an arbitrary fixed $t > 0$, which proves the uniform convergence of the series (9) with respect to j. Therefore, reformulating the well-known theorem of calculus applicably to the norm of the Hilbert space, taking into account the facts

$$\int_{Y_j(B)} \varphi(\lambda) e^{-\varphi^\alpha(\lambda)t} B(I-\lambda B)^{-1} f d\lambda \xrightarrow{\mathfrak{H}} \int_{Y(B)} \varphi(\lambda) e^{-\varphi^\alpha(\lambda)t} B(I-\lambda B)^{-1} f d\lambda,$$

$$\int_{Y_j(B)} e^{-\varphi^\alpha(\lambda)t}\lambda^n B(I-\lambda B)^{-1} f d\lambda \xrightarrow{\mathfrak{H}} \int_{Y(B)} e^{-\varphi^\alpha(\lambda)t}\lambda^n B(I-\lambda B)^{-1} f d\lambda, \ j \to \infty,$$

we obtain formula (7). Further, using the formula

$$\lambda^k B^k (I-\lambda B)^{-1} = (I-\lambda B)^{-1} - (I + \lambda B + \ldots + \lambda^{k-1} B^{k-1}), \ k \in \mathbb{N},$$

taking into account the facts that the operators B^k and $(I-\lambda B)^{-1}$ commute, we obtain

$$\int_{Y(B)} e^{-\varphi^\alpha(\lambda)t}\lambda^n B(I-\lambda B)^{-1} f d\lambda =$$

$$= \int_{Y(B)} e^{-\varphi^\alpha(\lambda)t} B(I-\lambda B)^{-1} W^n f d\lambda - \int_{Y(B)} e^{-\varphi^\alpha(\lambda)t} \sum_{k=0}^{n-1} \lambda^k B^{k+1} W^n f d\lambda = I_1(t) + I_2(t).$$

Since the operators W^n and $B(I-\lambda B)^{-1}$ commute, this fact can be obtained by direct calculation, and we obtain

$$I_1(t) = W^n \int_{Y(B)} e^{-\varphi^\alpha(\lambda)t} B(I-\lambda B)^{-1} f d\lambda.$$

Consider $I_2(t)$, using the technique applied in Lemma 5 [24]. It is rather reasonable to consider the following representation:

$$I_2(t) := -\sum_{k=0}^{n-1} \beta_k(t) B^{k-n+1} f, \quad \beta_k(t) := \int_{Y(B)} e^{-\varphi^\alpha(\lambda)t} \lambda^k d\lambda.$$

Analogous to the scheme of reasonings of Lemma 5 [24], we can show that $\beta_k(t) = 0$ under the imposed condition of the entire function growth regularity. Below, we produce a complete reasoning to avoid any kind of misunderstanding. Since the function under the integral is analytic inside the contour, then

$$\oint_{Y_R(B)} e^{-\varphi^\alpha(\lambda)t} \lambda^k d\lambda = 0,$$

where $Y_R(B) := \mathrm{Fr}\{\mathrm{int}\, Y(B) \cap \{\lambda : r < |\lambda| < R\}\}$. Hence, it suffices to show that there exists such a sequence $\{R_n\}_1^\infty$, $R_n \uparrow \infty$ that

$$\oint_{Y_{R_n}(B)} e^{-\varphi^\alpha(\lambda)t} \lambda^k d\lambda \to \beta_k(t), \quad n \to \infty. \tag{10}$$

Consider $\tilde{Y}_R := \{\lambda : |\lambda| = R, \theta_0 \leq \arg\lambda \leq \theta_1\}$, $\hat{Y}_R := \{\lambda : |\lambda| = r, \theta_0 \leq \arg\lambda \leq \theta_1\} \cup \{\lambda : r < |\lambda| < R, \arg\lambda = \theta_0, \arg\lambda = \theta_1\}$. We have obviously

$$\oint_{Y_R(B)} e^{-\varphi^\alpha(\lambda)t} \lambda^k d\lambda = \int_{\tilde{Y}_R} e^{-\varphi^\alpha(\lambda)t} \lambda^k d\lambda + \int_{\hat{Y}_R} e^{-\varphi^\alpha(\lambda)t} \lambda^k d\lambda.$$

Therefore, it suffices to prove that

$$\int_{\tilde{Y}_{R_n}} e^{-\varphi^\alpha(\lambda)t} \lambda^k d\lambda \to 0, \tag{11}$$

where $\{R_n\}_1^\infty$, $R_n \uparrow \infty$. Observe that the latter claim is not so trivial and requires to involve some subtle estimates on the boundary of a circle. However, the following approach gives us what we need, and we have

$$\left| \int_{\tilde{Y}_R} e^{-\varphi^\alpha(\lambda)t} \lambda^k d\lambda \right| \leq R^k \int_{\tilde{Y}_R} |e^{-\varphi^\alpha(\lambda)t}| |d\lambda| \leq R^{k+1} \int_{\theta_0}^{\theta_1} e^{-\mathrm{Re}\varphi^\alpha(\lambda)t} d\arg\lambda.$$

Using Theorem 30, §18, Chapter I [23], we can establish the fact that there exists a sequence $R_n \uparrow \infty$ such that for arbitrary positive ε the following estimate holds for sufficiently large numbers

$$e^{-C|\varphi(\lambda)|^\alpha t} \leq e^{-Cm_\varphi^\alpha(R_n)t} \leq e^{-Ct[M_\varphi(R_n)]^{(\cos \pi\varrho - \varepsilon)\alpha}}, \quad \lambda \in \tilde{Y}_{R_n},$$

where ϱ is the order. Applying this result, taking into account condition (HI), we obtain

$$\int_{\theta_0}^{\theta_1} e^{-\mathrm{Re}\varphi^\alpha(\lambda)t} d\arg\lambda \leq \int_{\theta_0}^{\theta_1} e^{-Ct|\varphi(\lambda)|^\alpha} d\arg\lambda \leq e^{-Ct[M_\varphi(R_n)]^{(\cos \pi\varrho - \varepsilon)\alpha}} \int_{\theta_0}^{\theta_1} d\arg\lambda,$$

which gives us (11). Having recollected the previously made implications, we obtain the fact $\beta_k(t) = 0$, hence $I_2(t) = 0$ and we get

$$\int_{Y(B)} e^{-\varphi^\alpha(\lambda)t} \lambda^n B(I - \lambda B)^{-1} f d\lambda = W^n \int_{Y(B)} e^{-\varphi^\alpha(\lambda)t} B(I - \lambda B)^{-1} f d\lambda.$$

Substituting the latter relation into the formula (7), we obtain the first statement of the lemma.

The scheme of the proof corresponding to the second statement is absolutely analogous to the one presented in Lemma 4 [24]. We should just use Lemma 2 providing the estimates along the sides of the contour. Thus, the completion of the reasonings is due to the technical repetition of the Lemma 4 [24] reasonings, which we leave to the reader. □

3.3. Series Expansion and Its Application to the Existence and Uniqueness Theorems

In this paragraph, we represent two theorems valuable from theoretical and applied points of view, respectively. The first one is a generalization of the Lidskii method, which is why following the classical approach, we divide it into two statements that can be claimed separately. The first statement establishes a character of the series convergence having a principal meaning within the whole concept. The second statement reflects the name of convergence, Abel–Lidskii; since the latter can be connected with the definition of the series convergence in the Abel sense, more detailed information can be found in the monograph by Hardy G.H. [26]. The second theorem is a valuable application of the first one, and it is based upon suitable algebraic reasonings noticed by the author, allowing us to involve a fractional derivative in the first term. We should note that previously, a concept of an operator function represented in the second term was realized in the paper [6], where a case corresponding to a function represented by a Laurent series with a polynomial regular part was considered. Below, we consider a comparatively more difficult case obviously related to the infinite regular part of the Laurent series and therefore requiring a principally different method of study.

It is a well-known fact that each eigenvalue μ_q, $q \in \mathbb{N}$ of the compact operator B generates a set of Jordan chains containing eigenvectors and root vectors. Denote by $m(q)$ a geometrical multiplicity of the corresponding eigenvalue and consider a Jordan chain corresponding to an eigenvector e_{q_ξ}, $\xi = 1, 2, ..., m(q)$. We have

$$e_{q_\xi}, e_{q_\xi+1}, ..., e_{q_\xi+k(q_\xi)}, \tag{12}$$

where $k(q_\xi)$ indicates a number of elements in the Jordan chain, the symbols except for the first one denote root vectors of the operator B. Note that combining the Jordan chains corresponding to an eigenvalue, we obtain a Jordan basis in the invariant subspace generated by the eigenvalue; moreover, we can arrange a so-called system of major vectors $\{e_i\}_1^\infty$ (see [7]) of the operator B having combined Jordan chains. It is remarkable that the eigenvalue $\bar{\mu}_q$ of the operator B^* generates the Jordan chains of the operator B^* corresponding to (12). In accordance with [12], we have

$$g_{q_\xi+k(q_\xi)}, g_{q_\xi+k(q_\xi)-1}, ..., g_{q_\xi},$$

where the symbols, except for the first one, denote root vectors of the operator B^*. Combining Jordan chains of the operator B^*, we can construct a biorthogonal system $\{g_n\}_1^\infty$ with respect to the system of the major vectors of the operator B. This fact is given in detail in the paper [12]. The following construction plays a significant role in the theory created in the papers [6,12,24] and therefore deserves to be considered separately. Denote

$$\mathcal{A}_\nu(\varphi, t) f := \sum_{q=N_\nu+1}^{N_{\nu+1}} \sum_{\xi=1}^{m(q)} \sum_{i=0}^{k(q_\xi)} e_{q_\xi+i} c_{q_\xi+i}(t), \tag{13}$$

where $\{N_\nu\}_1^\infty$ is a sequence of natural numbers,

$$c_{q_\xi+i}(t) = e^{-\varphi(\lambda_q)t} \sum_{j=0}^{k(q_\xi)-i} H_j(\varphi, \lambda_q, t) c_{q_\xi+i+j}, \ i = 0, 1, 2, \ldots, k(q_\xi), \quad (14)$$

$c_{q_\xi+i} = (f, g_{q_\xi+k-i})/(e_{q_\xi+i}, g_{q_\xi+k-i})$, $\lambda_q = 1/\mu_q$ is a characteristic number corresponding to e_{q_ξ},

$$H_j(\varphi, z, t) := \frac{e^{\varphi(z)t}}{j!} \cdot \lim_{\zeta \to 1/z} \frac{d^j}{d\zeta^j} \left\{ e^{-\varphi(\zeta^{-1})t} \right\}, \ j = 0, 1, 2, \ldots.$$

More detailed information on the considered above Jordan chains can be found in [12].

Theorem 3. *Assume that the condition* (HI) *holds,* $B \in \mathfrak{S}_s$, $0 < s < \infty$. *Then a sequence of natural numbers* $\{N_\nu\}_0^\infty$ *can be chosen so that*

$$\sum_{\nu=0}^\infty \|\mathcal{A}_\nu(\varphi^\alpha, t)f\|_{\mathfrak{H}} < \infty, f \in \mathfrak{H}; \ f = \lim_{t \to +0} \sum_{\nu=0}^\infty \mathcal{A}_\nu(\varphi^\alpha, t)f, f \in D(W). \quad (15)$$

Proof. Firstly, we will establish the fact of the series convergence. Let us choose $R > 0$, $0 < \kappa < 1$, so that $R(1-\kappa) = r$, thus we get a sequence $\{R_\nu\}_0^\infty$, $R_\nu = R(1-\kappa)^{-\nu+1}$. Applying Lemma 5 [12], we obtain

$$\|(I - \lambda B)^{-1}\|_{\mathfrak{H}} \leq e^{\gamma(\xi_\nu)\xi_\nu^\sigma} \xi_\nu^m, \ \sigma > s, \ m = [\sigma], \ R_\nu < \xi_\nu < R_{\nu+1},$$

where

$$\gamma(\tau) = \beta(\tau^{m+1}) + C_1\beta(C_2\tau^{m+1}), \ C_1, C_2 > 0,$$

$$\beta(\tau) = \tau^{-\frac{\sigma}{m+1}} \left(\int_0^\tau \frac{n_{B^{m+1}}(t)dt}{t} + \tau \int_\tau^\infty \frac{n_{B^{m+1}}(t)dt}{t^2} \right), \ \tau > 0.$$

Applying Lemma 3 [7], we can claim

$$\sum_{i=1}^\infty \lambda_i^{\frac{\sigma}{(m+1)}}(\tilde{B}) \leq \sum_{i=1}^\infty s_i^\sigma(B) < \infty, \quad (16)$$

where $\tilde{B} := (B^{*m+1}A^{m+1})^{1/2}$. Using (16), we obtain easily $\tilde{B} \in \mathfrak{S}_\phi$, $\phi < \sigma/(m+1)$. Consider a contour $Y_\nu := \mathrm{Fr}\{\mathrm{int}\, Y(B) \cap \{\lambda : \xi_\nu < |\lambda| < \xi_{\nu+1}\}\}$, denote by N_ν a number of poles of the resolvent contained in the set $\mathrm{int}\, Y(B) \cap \{\lambda : r < |\lambda| < \xi_\nu\}$. Applying Lemma 3 [24], we have

$$\frac{1}{2\pi i} \oint_{Y_\nu} e^{-\varphi^\alpha(\lambda)t} B(I - \lambda B)^{-1} f d\lambda = \sum_{q=N_\nu+1}^{N_{\nu+1}} \sum_{\xi=1}^{m(q)} \sum_{i=0}^{k(q_\xi)} e_{q_\xi+i} c_{q_\xi+i}(t), \ f \in \mathfrak{H}. \quad (17)$$

Further reasoning is devoted to estimating the above integral and based on the contour Y_ν decomposition on terms $\tilde{Y}_\nu := \{\lambda : |\lambda| = \xi_\nu, \theta_0 \leq \arg\lambda \leq \theta_1\}$, $\tilde{Y}_{\nu+1}$, $Y_{\nu-} := \{\lambda : \xi_\nu < |\lambda| < \xi_{\nu+1}, \arg\lambda = \theta_0\}$, $Y_{\nu+} := \{\lambda : \xi_\nu < |\lambda| < \xi_{\nu+1}, \arg\lambda = \theta_1\}$. In accordance with Theorem 30, §18, Chapter I [23] (Wieman theorem), we can choose such a sequence $\{x_n\}_1^\infty$, $x_n \uparrow \infty$, $\xi_\nu < x_\nu < \xi_{\nu+1}$ that for an arbitrary positive ε and sufficiently large numbers ν, we have

$$e^{-C|\varphi(\lambda)|^\alpha t} \leq e^{-Cm_\varphi^\alpha(x_\nu)t} \leq e^{-Ct[M_\varphi(x_\nu)]^{(\cos\pi\varrho-\varepsilon)\alpha}}, \ \lambda \in \tilde{Y}_\nu, \quad (18)$$

where ϱ is the order. We should note that the assumption $\xi_\nu < x_\nu < \xi_{\nu+1}$ is made without loss of generality of the reasonings, as in the context of the proof, we do not care about the accurate arrangement of the contours but need to prove the existence of an arbitrary one. This inconvenience is based upon the uncertainty in the way of choosing the contours in accordance with the Wieman theorem; at the same time at any rate, we can extract a subsequence of the sequence $\{\xi_\nu\}_1^\infty$ in the way we need. Thus, using the given reasonings, Applying Lemma 5 [12], relation (18), we obtain

$$J_\nu := \left\| \int_{\tilde{Y}_\nu} e^{-\varphi^\alpha(\lambda)t} B(I - \lambda B)^{-1} f d\lambda \right\|_{\mathfrak{H}} \leq \int_{\tilde{Y}_\nu} e^{-t\operatorname{Re}\varphi^\alpha(\lambda)} \left\| B(I - \lambda B)^{-1} f \right\|_{\mathfrak{H}} |d\lambda| \leq$$

$$\leq e^{\gamma(\xi_\nu)\xi_\nu^\sigma} \xi_\nu^{m+1} C e^{-Ct[M_\varphi(x_\nu)]^{(\cos \pi\varrho - \varepsilon)\alpha}} \int_{\theta_0}^{\theta_1} d\arg\lambda.$$

As a result, we obtain

$$J_\nu \leq e^{\gamma(\xi_\nu)\xi_\nu^\sigma} \xi_\nu^{m+1} C e^{-Ct[M_\varphi(x_\nu)]^{(\cos \pi\varrho - \varepsilon)\alpha}}, \; m = [\sigma].$$

Using Lemma 2 [12], we have $\gamma(|\lambda|) \to 0$, $|\lambda| \to \infty$. In accordance with the Formula (1) we can extract a subsequence from the sequence $\{x_\nu\}_1^\infty$ and as a result from the sequence $\{\xi_\nu\}_1^\infty$ so that for a fixed t and a sufficiently large ν, we have $\gamma(|\xi_\nu|)|\xi_\nu|^\sigma - Ct[M_\varphi(x_\nu)]^{(\cos \pi\varrho - \varepsilon)\alpha} < 0$. Here, we have not used a subsequence to simplify the form of writing. Therefore, we have

$$\sum_{\nu=0}^\infty J_\nu < \infty.$$

Applying Lemma 6 [12], Lemma 2, we obtain

$$J_\nu^+ := \left\| \int_{Y_{\nu+}} e^{-\varphi^\alpha(\lambda)t} B(I - \lambda B)^{-1} f d\lambda \right\|_{\mathfrak{H}} \leq C\|f\|_{\mathfrak{H}} \int_{R_\nu}^{R_{\nu+1}} e^{-Ct\operatorname{Re}\varphi^\alpha(\lambda)} |d\lambda| \leq$$

$$\leq C \int_{R_\nu}^{R_{\nu+1}} e^{-Ct|\varphi(\lambda)|^\alpha} |d\lambda| \leq C e^{-Ct e^{\alpha H(\theta_1)R_\nu^\varrho(R_\nu)}} \int_{R_\nu}^{R_{\nu+1}} |d\lambda| = C e^{-Ct e^{\alpha H(\theta_1)R_\nu^\varrho(R_\nu)}} \{R_{\nu+1} - R_\nu\}.$$

$$J_\nu^- := \left\| \int_{Y_{\nu-}} e^{-\varphi^\alpha(\lambda)t} B(I - \lambda B)^{-1} f d\lambda \right\|_{\mathfrak{H}} \leq C e^{-Ct e^{\alpha H(\theta_0)R_\nu^\varrho(R_\nu)}} \int_{R_\nu}^{R_{\nu+1}} |d\lambda| = C e^{-Ct e^{\alpha H(\theta_0)R_\nu^\varrho(R_\nu)}} \{R_{\nu+1} - R_\nu\}.$$

The obtained results allow us to claim (the proof is omitted) that

$$\sum_{\nu=0}^\infty J_\nu^+ < \infty, \; \sum_{\nu=0}^\infty J_\nu^- < \infty.$$

Therefore, applying Formula (17), we obtain the first relation (15). To prove the second relation (15), we should note that in accordance with (17), the properties of the contour integral, we have

$$\frac{1}{2\pi i} \oint_{Y_{\xi_n}(B)} e^{-\varphi^\alpha(\lambda)t} B(I - \lambda B)^{-1} f d\lambda = \sum_{\nu=0}^{n-1} \sum_{q=N_\nu+1}^{N_{\nu+1}} \sum_{\xi=1}^{m(q)} \sum_{i=0}^{k(q_\xi)} e_{q_\xi+i} c_{q_\xi+i}(t), \; f \in \mathfrak{H}, \; n \in \mathbb{N},$$

where $Y_{\zeta_n}(B) := \text{Fr}\{\text{int}\, Y(B) \cap \{\lambda : r < |\lambda| < \zeta_n\}\}$. Using the fact $J_\nu \to 0, \nu \to \infty$, we obtain

$$\frac{1}{2\pi i} \oint_{Y_{\zeta_n}(B)} e^{-\varphi^\alpha(\lambda)t} B(I - \lambda B)^{-1} f\, d\lambda \to \frac{1}{2\pi i} \oint_{Y(B)} e^{-\varphi^\alpha(\lambda)t} B(I - \lambda B)^{-1} f\, d\lambda, \; n \to \infty.$$

The latter relation allows to obtain the formula

$$\frac{1}{2\pi i} \oint_{Y(B)} e^{-\varphi^\alpha(\lambda)t} B(I - \lambda B)^{-1} f\, d\lambda = \sum_{\nu=0}^\infty \mathcal{A}_\nu(\varphi^\alpha, t) f, \; f \in \mathfrak{H}. \tag{19}$$

If $f \in D(W)$, then applying Lemma 3, we obtain the second relation (15). □

Consider element-functions $u : \mathbb{R}_+ \to \mathfrak{H}$, $u := u(t), t \geq 0$, belonging to the Hilbert space $\mathfrak{H}$; using the approach [6], we understand the differentiation and integration operations in the generalized sense, i.e., the derivative is defined as a limit in the sense of the norm (see [12,27]). Involving a superposition of the operations, we can define a generalized fractional derivative in the Riemann–Liouville sense (see [4,6]). In the formal sense, we have

$$\mathfrak{D}_-^{1/\alpha} f(t) := -\frac{1}{\Gamma(1 - 1/\alpha)} \frac{d}{dt} \int_0^\infty f(t+x) x^{-1/\alpha} dx, \; \alpha > 1.$$

Consider a Cauchy problem

$$\mathfrak{D}_-^{1/\alpha} u = \varphi(W) u, \; u(0) = f \in D(W^n), \; \forall n \in \mathbb{N}. \tag{20}$$

Theorem 4. *Assume that the conditions of Theorem 3 hold, then there exists a solution of the Cauchy problem (20) in the form*

$$u(t) = \sum_{\nu=0}^\infty \mathcal{A}_\nu(\varphi^\alpha, t) f. \tag{21}$$

Moreover, the existing solution is unique if the operator $\mathfrak{D}_-^{1-1/\alpha} \varphi(W)$ is accretive.

Proof. Firstly, we will show that $u(t)$ is a solution of the problem (20), we need prove the following formula

$$\frac{d}{dt} \int_{Y(B)} \varphi(\lambda)^{1-\alpha} e^{-\varphi^\alpha(\lambda)t} B(I - \lambda B)^{-1} f\, d\lambda = -\int_{Y(B)} \varphi(\lambda) e^{-\varphi(\lambda)^\alpha t} B(I - \lambda B)^{-1} f\, d\lambda, \; h \in \mathfrak{H}. \tag{22}$$

Using simple reasonings, we obtain the fact that that for an arbitrary

$$Y_j(B) := \{\lambda : |\lambda| = r > 0, \theta_0 \leq \arg\lambda \leq \theta_1\} \cup \{\lambda : r < |\lambda| < r_j, \arg\lambda = \theta_0, \arg\lambda = \theta_1\},$$

there exists a limit $(e^{-\varphi^\alpha(\lambda)\Delta t} - 1) e^{-\varphi^\alpha(\lambda)t} / \Delta t \longrightarrow -\varphi^\alpha(\lambda) e^{-\varphi^\alpha(\lambda)t}$, $\Delta t \to 0$, where convergence is uniform with respect to $\lambda \in Y_j(B)$. By virtue of the decomposition on the Taylor series, we get

$$\left| \frac{e^{-\varphi^\alpha(\lambda)\Delta t} - 1}{\Delta t} e^{-\varphi^\alpha(\lambda)t} \right| \leq |\varphi(\lambda)|^\alpha e^{|\varphi(\lambda)|^\alpha \Delta t} e^{-\text{Re}\,\varphi^\alpha(\lambda)t} \leq |\varphi(\lambda)|^\alpha e^{(\Delta t - Ct)|\varphi(\lambda)|^\alpha}, \; \lambda \in Y(B).$$

Thus, applying the latter estimate, Lemma 6 [12], for a sufficiently small value Δt, we obtain

$$\left\|\int_{Y(B)} \frac{e^{-\varphi^{\alpha}(\lambda)\Delta t} - 1}{\Delta t} \varphi^{1-\alpha}(\lambda) e^{-\varphi^{\alpha}(\lambda)t} B(I - \lambda B)^{-1} f d\lambda\right\|_{\mathfrak{H}} \leq C\|f\|_{\mathfrak{H}} \int_{Y(B)} e^{-Ct|\varphi(\lambda)|^{\alpha}} |\varphi(\lambda)||d\lambda|. \quad (23)$$

Let us establish the convergence of the last integral. Applying Theorem 2, we obtain

$$\int_{Y(B)} e^{-Ct|\varphi(\lambda)|^{\alpha}} |\varphi(\lambda)||d\lambda| \leq \int_{Y(B)} e^{-te^{C|\lambda|\varrho(|\lambda|)}} e^{C|\lambda|^{\varrho}} |d\lambda|.$$

It is clear that the latter integral is convergent for an arbitrary positive value t, which guarantees that the improper integral at the left-hand side of (23) is uniformly convergent with respect to Δt. These facts give us an opportunity to claim that relation (22) holds. Here, we should explain that this conclusion is based on the generalization of the well-known theorem of the calculus; we left a complete investigation of the matter to the reader, having noted that the reasonings are absolutely analogous to the ordinary calculus.

Applying the scheme of the proof corresponding to the ordinary integral calculus, using the contour $Y_j(B)$, applying Lemma 6 [12] respectively, we can establish a formula

$$\int_0^\infty x^{-\xi} dx \int_{Y(B)} e^{-\varphi^{\alpha}(\lambda)(t+x)} B(I - \lambda B)^{-1} f d\lambda = \int_{Y(B)} e^{-\varphi^{\alpha}(\lambda)t} B(I - \lambda B)^{-1} f d\lambda \int_0^\infty x^{-\xi} e^{-\varphi^{\alpha}(\lambda)x} dx, \quad (24)$$

where $\xi \in (0,1)$. Taking into account the obvious formula

$$\int_0^\infty x^{-1/\alpha} e^{-\varphi^{\alpha}(\lambda)x} dx = \Gamma(1 - 1/\alpha) \varphi^{1-\alpha}(\lambda),$$

we get

$$\mathfrak{D}_-^{1/\alpha} \int_{Y(B)} e^{-\varphi^{\alpha}(\lambda)t} B(I - \lambda B)^{-1} f = \int_{Y(B)} e^{-\varphi^{\alpha}(\lambda)t} \varphi(\lambda) B(I - \lambda B)^{-1} f d\lambda. \quad (25)$$

Applying Lemma 3, relation (19), we obtain the fact that u is a solution of the Equation (20). The fact that the initial condition holds, in the sense $u(t) \xrightarrow{\mathfrak{H}} f$, $t \to +0$, follows from the second relation (15) Theorem 3. The scheme of the proof corresponding to the uniqueness part is given in Theorem 6 [6]. We complete the proof. □

3.4. Applications to Concrete Operators and Physical Processes

Note that the method considered above allows to obtain a solution for the evolution equation with the operator function in the second term, where the operator argument belongs to a sufficiently wide class of operators. One can find a lot of examples in [6], where such well-known operators as the Riesz potential, the Riemann–Liouville fractional differential operator, the Kipriyanov operator, and the difference operator are studied. Some interesting examples that cannot be covered by the results established in [22] are represented in the paper [17]. The general approach, applied in the paper [2], creates a theoretical base to produce a more abstract example—a transform of the m-accretive operator. We should point out a significance of the last statement since the class contains the infinitesimal generator of a strongly continuous semigroup of contractions. Here, we recall that fractional differential operators of the real order can be expressed in terms of the infinitesimal generator of the corresponding semigroup [2]. Application of the obtained results appeals to electron-induced kinetics of ferroelectrics polarization switching as the self-similar memory physical systems. The whole point is that the mathematical model of the fractal dynamic system includes a Cauchy problem for the differential equation of the fractional order considered in the paper [1], where computational schemes for solving the problem were constructed using the Adams–Bashforth–Moulton-type predictor–corrector methods. The stochastic algorithm based on the Monte Carlo method was proposed to simulate the domain nucleation process during the restructuring domain structure in ferroelectrics.

At the same time, the results obtained in this paper allow us not only to solve the problem analytically, but consider a whole class of problems for evolution equations of fractional order. As for the mentioned concrete case [1], we just need consider a suitable functional Hilbert space and apply Theorem 4 directly. For instance, it can be the Lebesgue space of square-integrable functions. Here, we should note that in the case corresponding to a functional Hilbert space, we gain more freedom in constructing the theory, and thus, some modifications of the method can appear, but it is an issue for further more detailed study, which is not supposed in the framework of this paper. However, the following example may be of interest to the reader.

Goldstein et al. proved in [28] several new results having replaced the Laplacian by the Kolmogorov operator:

$$L = \Delta + \frac{\nabla \rho}{\rho} \cdot \nabla,$$

here, ρ is a probability density on $\mathbb{R}^N$ satisfying $\rho \in C_{lok}^{1+\alpha}(\mathbb{R}^N)$ for some $\alpha \in (0,1)$, $\rho(x) > 0$ for all $x \in \mathbb{R}^N$. A reasonable question can appear: are there possible connections between the developed theory and the operator L? Indeed, the mentioned operator gives us an opportunity to show brightly capacity of the spectral theory methods. First of all, let us note that the relation $L = \rho^{-1}W$ holds, where $W := \mathrm{div}\rho\nabla$. Thus, at first glance, the right direction of the issue investigation should be connected with the operator composition $\rho^{-1}W$ since the operator W is uniformly elliptic and satisfies the following hypotheses (see [2]).

(H1) There exists a Hilbert space $\mathfrak{H}_+ \subset\subset \mathfrak{H}$ and a linear manifold $\mathfrak{M}$ that is dense in $\mathfrak{H}_+$. The operator V is defined on $\mathfrak{M}$.

(H2) $|(Vf,g)_\mathfrak{H}| \leq C_1 \|f\|_{\mathfrak{H}_+} \|g\|_{\mathfrak{H}_+}$, $\mathrm{Re}(Vf,f)_\mathfrak{H} \geq C_2 \|f\|_{\mathfrak{H}_+}^2$, $f,g \in \mathfrak{M}$, $C_1, C_2 > 0$.

Apparently, the results [2,12,17] can be applied to the operator after an insignificant modification. A couple of words on the difficulties appear while we study the operator composition. Superficially, the problem looks good, but it is not so for the inverse operator (one needs to prove that it is a resolvent) which is a composition of an unbounded operator and a resolvent of the operator W, indeed since $R_W W = I$, then formally, we have $L^{-1} f = R_W \rho f$. Most likely, the general theory created in the papers [2,17] can be adopted to some operator composition, but it is a tremendous work. Instead of that, we may find a suitable pair of Hilbert spaces that is also not so easy. However, we shall see. Below, we consider a space $\mathbb{R}^N$ endowed with the norm

$$|x| = \sqrt{\sum_{k=1}^n |x_k|^2}, \ x = (x_1, x_2, ..., x_n) \in \mathbb{R}^N.$$

Assume that there exists a constant $\lambda > 2$ such that the following condition holds:

$$\left\| \rho^{1/\lambda - 1} \nabla \rho \right\|_{L_\infty(\mathbb{R}^N)} < \infty, \ \rho^{1/\lambda}(x) = O(1 + |x|).$$

One can verify easily that this condition is not unnatural, as it holds for a function $\rho(x) = (1 + |x|)^\lambda$, $x \in \mathbb{R}^N$, $\lambda \geq 1$. Let us define a Hilbert space $\mathfrak{H}_+$ as a completion of the set $C_0^\infty(\mathbb{R}^N)$ with the norm

$$\|f\|_{\mathfrak{H}_+}^2 = \|\nabla f\|_{L_2(\mathbb{R}^N)}^2 + \|f\|_{L_2(\mathbb{R}^N, \varphi^{-2})}^2, \ \varphi(x) = (1 + |x|),$$

here, one can easily see that it is generated by the corresponding inner product. The following result can be obtained as a consequence of the Adams theorem (see Theorem 1 [29]). Using the formula
$$\varphi^{\lambda/2}\nabla f = \nabla(f\varphi^{\lambda/2}) - f\nabla\varphi^{\lambda/2}, f = g\varphi^{-\lambda/2}, g \in C_0^\infty(\mathbb{R}^N),$$
we can easily obtain
$$\left(\int_{\mathbb{R}^N} |\nabla(g\varphi^{-\lambda/2})|^2 \varphi^\lambda dx\right)^{1/2} \leq C\|g\|_{\mathfrak{H}_+}.$$

It is clear that the latter relation can be expanded to the elements of the space $\mathfrak{H}_+$. Note that
$$\|g\|_{L_2(\mathbb{R}^N, \varphi^{-\lambda})} \leq \|g\|_{L_2(\mathbb{R}^N, \varphi^{-2})}, g \in L_2(\mathbb{R}^N, \varphi^{-2}), \lambda > 2.$$

This relation gives us the inclusion $\mathfrak{H}_+ \subset L_2(\mathbb{R}^N, \varphi^{-\lambda})$, thus we conclude that $g\varphi^{-\lambda/2} \in L_2(\mathbb{R}^N), g \in \mathfrak{H}_+$. In accordance with Theorem 1 [29], we conclude that if a set is bounded in the sense of the norm $\mathfrak{H}_+$, then it is compact in the sense of the norm $L_2(\mathbb{R}^N, \varphi^{-\lambda})$.

Thus, we have created a pair of Hilbert spaces $\mathfrak{H}_- := L_2(\mathbb{R}^N, \varphi^{-\lambda})$ and $\mathfrak{H}_+$, satisfying the condition of compact embedding, i.e., $\mathfrak{H}_+ \subset\subset \mathfrak{H}_-$. Let us see how can it help us in studying the operator L. Considering an operator $L' := -L + \eta\rho^{-2/\lambda}I, \eta > 0$, we ought to remark here that we need involve an additional summand to apply the methods [2]. The crucial point is related to how to estimate the second term of the operator $-L$ from below. Here, we should point out that some peculiar techniques of the theory of functions can be involved. However, along with this, we can consider a simplified case (since we have imposed additional conditions upon the function ρ) in order to show how the invented method works. The following reasonings are made under the assumption that the functions $f, g \in C_0^\infty(\mathbb{R}^N)$. Using simple reasonings based upon the Cauchy–Schwarz inequality, we obtain

$$\left|\int_{\mathbb{R}^N} \frac{\nabla\rho}{\rho}\cdot\nabla f\,\bar{g}dx\right| \leq \int_{\mathbb{R}^N}\left|\frac{\nabla\rho}{\rho}\right||\nabla f||g|dx \leq \left\|\rho^{1/\lambda-1}\nabla\rho\right\|_{L_\infty(\mathbb{R}^N)}\frac{1}{2}\left\{\varepsilon\|\nabla f\|_{L_2(\mathbb{R}^N)}^2 + \frac{1}{\varepsilon}\|g\|_{L_2(\mathbb{R}^N, \rho^{-2/\lambda})}^2\right\},$$

where $\varepsilon > 0$. Therefore,
$$-\mathrm{Re}\left(\frac{\nabla\rho}{\rho}\cdot\nabla f, f\right)_{L_2(\mathbb{R}^N)} \geq -\left\|\rho^{1/\lambda-1}\nabla\rho\right\|_{L_\infty(\mathbb{R}^N)}\frac{1}{2}\left\{\varepsilon\|\nabla f\|_{L_2(\mathbb{R}^N)}^2 + \frac{1}{\varepsilon}\|g\|_{L_2(\mathbb{R}^N, \rho^{-2/\lambda})}^2\right\}.$$

Choosing η, ε, we easily obtain
$$\mathrm{Re}(L'f, f)_{L_2(\mathbb{R}^N)} \geq C\|f\|_{\mathfrak{H}_+}^2, C > 0.$$

Using the above estimates, we obtain
$$\left|(L'f, g)_{L_2(\mathbb{R}^N)}\right| \leq \|\nabla f\|_{L_2(\mathbb{R}^N)}\|\nabla g\|_{L_2(\mathbb{R}^N)} + \left\|\rho^{1/\lambda-1}\nabla\rho\right\|_{L_\infty(\mathbb{R}^N)}\|\nabla f\|_{L_2(\mathbb{R}^N)}\|g\|_{L_2(\mathbb{R}^N, \rho^{-2/\lambda})}$$
$$+ \eta\|f\|_{L_2(\mathbb{R}^N, \rho^{-2/\lambda})}\|g\|_{L_2(\mathbb{R}^N, \rho^{-2/\lambda})} \leq C\|f\|_{\mathfrak{H}_+}\|g\|_{\mathfrak{H}_+}, C > 0.$$

Thus, we have a fulfillment of the hypothesis H2 [2]. Taking into account the fact that a negative space $L_2(\mathbb{R}^N, \varphi^{-\lambda})$ is involved, we are forced to involve a modification of the hypothesis H1 [2] expressed as follows. There exist pairs of Hilbert spaces $\mathfrak{H} \subset \mathfrak{H}_-$, $\mathfrak{H}_+ \subset\subset \mathfrak{H}_-, \mathfrak{H} := L_2(\mathbb{R}^N)$ and a linear manifold $\mathfrak{M} := C_0^\infty(\mathbb{R}^N)$ that is dense in $\mathfrak{H}_+$. The operator L' is defined on $\mathfrak{M}$. However, we can go further and modify a norm $\mathfrak{H}_+$ adding a summand; in this case, the considered operator can be changed, and we have

$$\|f\|^2_{\mathfrak{H}_+} := \|\nabla f\|^2_{L_2(\mathbb{R}^N)} + \|f\|^2_{L_2(\mathbb{R}^N,\psi)}, \ \psi(x) = (1+|x|)^{-2}+1, \ L':= L+\eta I, \ \eta > 0.$$

Implementing the same reasonings, one can prove that in this case, Hypothesis H2 [2] is fulfilled, and the modified analog of Hypothesis H1 [2] can be formulated as follows.

(H1*) There exists a chain of Hilbert spaces $\mathfrak{H}_+ \subset \mathfrak{H} \subset \mathfrak{H}_-, \mathfrak{H}_+ \subset\subset \mathfrak{H}_-$ and a linear manifold $\mathfrak{M}$ that is dense in $\mathfrak{H}_+$. The operator L' is defined on $\mathfrak{M}$.

However, we have $\mathfrak{H}_+ \subset\subset \mathfrak{H}_-$ instead of the required inclusion $\mathfrak{H}_+ \subset\subset \mathfrak{H}$. This inconvenience can stress a peculiarity of the chosen method; at the same time, the central point of the theory—Theorem 1 [2]—can be reformulated under newly obtained conditions corresponding to both variants of the operator L'. The further step is how to calculate order of the real component $\mathfrak{Re} L' := (L' + L'^*)/2$ (a more precise definition can be seen see in the paper [2]). Formally, we can avoid the appeared difficulties connected with the fact that the set $\mathbb{R}^N$ is not bounded since we can refer to the Fefferman concept presented in the monograph [30] (p. 47), in accordance with which we can choose such an unbounded subset of $\mathbb{R}^N$ that the relation $\lambda_j(\mathfrak{Re} L') \asymp j^{2/N}$ holds, where the symbol λ_j denotes an eigenvalue. It gives us $\mu(\mathfrak{Re} L') = 2/N$, where the symbol μ denotes the order of the real component of the operator L' (see [2]). Thus, we leave this question to the reader for a more detailed study and reasonably allow ourselves to assume that the operator L' has a finite non-zero order. Having obtained an analog of Theorem 1 [2] and order of the real component of the operator L', we have a key to the theory created in the papers [6,12,24]. Now, we can consider a Cauchy problem for the evolution equation with the operator L' in the second term as well as a function of the operator L' in the second term, which leads us to the integro-differential evolution equation—it corresponds to an operator function having finite principal and major parts of the Laurent series.

One more example of a non-self-adjoint operator that is not completely subordinated in the sense of forms (see [17,22]) is given below. Consider a differential operator acting in the complex Sobolev space

$$\mathcal{L}f := (c_k f^{(k)})^{(k)} + (c_{k-1} f^{(k-1)})^{(k-1)} + ... + c_0 f,$$

$$D(\mathcal{L}) = H^{2k}(I) \cap H_0^k(I), \ k \in \mathbb{N},$$

where $I := (a,b) \subset \mathbb{R}$, the complex-valued coefficients $c_j(x) \in C^{(j)}(\bar{I})$ satisfy the condition $\text{sign}(\text{Re}\, c_j) = (-1)^j, \ j = 1,2,...,k$. Consider a linear combination of the Riemann–Liouville fractional differential operators (see [4], (p. 44)) with the constant real-valued coefficients

$$\mathcal{D}f := p_n D_{a+}^{\alpha_n} + q_n D_{b-}^{\beta_n} + p_{n-1} D_{a+}^{\alpha_{n-1}} + q_{n-1} D_{b-}^{\beta_{n-1}} + ... + p_0 D_{a+}^{\alpha_0} + q_0 D_{b-}^{\beta_0},$$

$$D(\mathcal{D}) = H^{2k}(I) \cap H_0^k(I), \ n \in \mathbb{N},$$

where $\alpha_j, \beta_j \geq 0, \ 0 \leq [\alpha_j],[\beta_j] < k, \ j = 0,1,...,n.$,

$$q_j \geq 0, \ \text{sign}\, p_j = \begin{cases} (-1)^{\frac{[\alpha_j]+1}{2}}, & [\alpha_j] = 2m-1, \ m \in \mathbb{N}, \\ (-1)^{\frac{[\alpha_j]}{2}}, & [\alpha_j] = 2m, \ m \in \mathbb{N}_0. \end{cases}$$

The following result is represented in the paper [17]. Consider the operator

$$G = \mathcal{L} + \mathcal{D},$$

$$D(G) = H^{2k}(I) \cap H_0^k(I).$$

and suppose $\mathfrak{H} := L_2(I)$, $\mathfrak{H}^+ := H_0^k(I)$, $\mathfrak{M} := C_0^\infty(I)$, then we have that the operator G satisfies the conditions H1, H2. Using the minimax principle for estimating eigenvalues, we can easily see that the operator $\mathfrak{Re} G$ has a non-zero order. Hence, we can successfully apply Theorem 1 [2] to the operator G, in accordance with which the resolvent of the operator G belongs to the Schatten–von Neumann class $\mathfrak{S}_s$ with the value of the index $0 < s < \infty$ defined by the formula given in Theorem 1 [2]. Thus, it gives us an opportunity to apply Theorem 3 to the operator.

A couple of words on condition H1 in the context of operators generating semigroups. Assume that an operator $-A$ acting in a separable Hilbert space $\mathfrak{H}$ is the infinitesimal generator of a C_0 semigroup such that A^{-1} is compact. By virtue of Corollary 2.5 [31] (p. 5), we have that the operator A is densely defined and closed. Let us check the fulfillment of condition H1. Consider a separable Hilbert space $\mathfrak{H}_A := \{f, g \in D(A), (f, g)_{\mathfrak{H}_A} = (Af, Ag)_{\mathfrak{H}}\}$, where the fact that $\mathfrak{H}_A$ is separable follows from the properties of the energetic space. Note that since A^{-1} is compact, then we conclude that the following relation holds $\|f\|_{\mathfrak{H}} \leq \|A^{-1}\| \cdot \|Af\|_{\mathfrak{H}}$, $f \in D(A)$ and the embedding provided by this inequality is compact. Thus, we have obtained in the natural way a pair of Hilbert spaces such that $\mathfrak{H}_A \subset\subset \mathfrak{H}$. We may say that this general property of infinitesimal generators is not so valuable, as it requires a rather strong and unnatural condition of compactness of the inverse operator. However, if we additionally deal with the semigroup of contractions, then we can formulate a significant result (see Theorem 2 [2]), allowing us to study the spectral properties of the infinitesimal generator transform

$$T := A^* G A + F A^\alpha, \ \alpha \in [0, 1),$$

where the symbols G, F denote operators acting in $\mathfrak{H}$. Having analyzed the proof of Theorem 2 [2], one can easily see that the condition of contractions can be omitted in the case $\alpha = 0$.

4. Conclusions

In this paper, we invented a method to study a Cauchy problem for the abstract fractional evolution equation with the operator function in the second term. The considered class corresponding to the operator argument is rather wide and includes non-selfadjoint unbounded operators. As a main result, we represent a technique allowing to principally weaken conditions imposed upon the second term not containing the time variable. Obviously, the application section of the paper is devoted to the theory of fractional differential equations.

The invented method allows to solve the Cauchy problem for the abstract fractional evolution equation analytically, which is undoubtedly a great advantage. We used the results of the spectral theory of non-self-adjoint operators as a base for studying the mathematical objects. Characteristically, the operator function is defined on a special operator class covering the infinitesimal generator transform (see [2]), where a corresponding semigroup is assumed to be a strongly continuous semigroup of contractions. The corresponding particular cases lead us to a linear composition of differential operators of real order in various senses listed in the introduction section. In connection with this, various types of fractional integro-differential operators can be considered, which becomes clear if we involve an operator function represented by the Laurent series with finite principal and regular parts. Moreover, the artificially constructed normal operator [6] belonging to the special operator class indicates that the application part is beyond the class of differential operators of real order. Below, we represent a comparison analysis to show brightly the main contribution of the paper, particularly the newly invented method allowing us to consider an entire function as the operator function. First of all, the technique related to the proof of the contour integral convergence is similar to the papers [6,7,12,24]; one can italicize a similar scheme of reasonings, but the last one is nothing without the required properties of the considered entire function. Such theorems as the Wieman theorem, the theorem on the entire function growth regularity and their applications form the main author's creative contribution to the paper. To be honest, it was not so easy to find such a condition that makes the contour integral convergent on the entire function. We should note that the latter idea in its precise statement was not considered previously. The following fact is also worth noting—a suitable algebraic reasonings having noticed by the author and allowing us to involve a fractional derivative in the first term. This idea allows to cover many results in the framework of the theory of fractional differential equations. The latter which is a relevant result. As for other mathematicians, here, the Lidskii name ought to be sounded; however, the peculiarities of the author's own technique were shown and discussed in the papers [2,12,17] and one can study them properly. We may say that the main concept of the root vector series expansion jointly with the method analogous to the Abel's one belongs to Lidskii, which is reflected in the name: Abel–Lidskii sense of the series convergence. As for the author's contribution to this method, it is not so small, as one can observe in the paper [12] since the main result establishes clarification of the results by Lidskii. In the framework of the discussion, the following papers by Markus [20], Matsaev [19], Shkalikov [22] can undergo a comparison analysis. The latter represents in the paper [22] only an idea of the proof of Theorem 5.1 [22] even the statement of which differs from the statement of Theorem 4 [12], which is provided with a detailed proof and clarifies the Lidskii results represented in [12]. Particular attention can be paid to a special class of operators with which, due to the author's results [2], the reader can successfully deal. The latter benefit stresses the relevance of the results for initially the theoretical results in the framework of the developed direction of the spectral theory [2,17] originated from the ones [15] devoted to uniformly elliptic non-selfadjoint operators, which cannot be covered by the results by Markus [20], Matsaev [19], Shkalikov [22] due to the absence of a so-called complete subordination condition imposed upon the operator (a corresponding example is given in the paper [17]).

We hope that the general concept will have a more detailed study, as well as concrete applied problems being solved by virtue of the invented theoretical approach.

Funding: This research received no external funding.

Acknowledgments: I am sincerely grateful to my scientific colleagues and reviewers for discussions on related problems.

Conflicts of Interest: The author declares no conflict of interest.

References

1. Moroz, L.; Maslovskaya, A.G. Hybrid stochastic fractal-based approach to modeling the switching kinetics of ferroelectrics in the injection mode. *Math. Model. Comput. Simul.* **2020**, *12*, 348–356.
2. Kukushkin, M.V. Abstract fractional calculus for m-accretive operators. *Int. J. Appl. Math.* **2021**, *34*, 1–41. [CrossRef]
3. Kipriyanov, I.A. The operator of fractional differentiation and powers of the elliptic operators. *Proc. Acad. Sci.* **1960**, *131*, 238–241.
4. Samko, S.G.; Kilbas, A.A.; Marichev, O.I. *Fractional Integrals and Derivatives: Theory and Applications*; Gordon and Breach Science Publishers: Philadelphia, PA, USA, 1993.
5. Nakhushev, A.M. The Sturm-Liouville problem for an ordinary differential equation of the second order with fractional derivatives in lower terms. *Proc. Acad. Sci.* **1977**, *234*, 308–311.
6. Kukushkin, M.V. Evolution Equations in Hilbert Spaces via the Lacunae Method. *Fractal Fract.* **2022**, *6*, 229. [CrossRef]
7. Lidskii, V.B. Summability of series in terms of the principal vectors of non-selfadjoint operators. *Tr. Mosk. Mat. Obs.* **1962**, *11*, 3–35.
8. Andronova, O.A.; Voytitsky, V.I. On spectral properties of one boundary value problem with a surface energy dissipation. *Ufa Math. J.* **2017**, *9*, 3–16.
9. Mamchuev, M.O. Solutions of the main boundary value problems for the time-fractional telegraph equation by the Green function method. *Fract. Calc. Appl. Anal.* **2017**, *20*, 190–211. [CrossRef]
10. Mamchuev, M.O. Boundary value problem for the time-fractional telegraph equation with Caputo derivatives Mathematical Modelling of Natural Phenomena. *Spec. Funct. Anal. PDEs* **2017**, *12*, 82–94. [CrossRef]
11. Pskhu, A.V. The fundamental solution of a diffusion-wave equation of fractional order. *Mathematics* **2009**, *73*, 351–392.
12. Kukushkin, M.V. Natural lacunae method and Schatten-von Neumann classes of the convergence exponent. *Mathematics* **2022**, *10*, 2237. [CrossRef]
13. Agranovich, M.S. On series with respect to root vectors of operators associated with forms having symmetric principal part. *Funct. Anal. Its Appl.* **1994**, *28*, 151–167.

14. Gohberg, I.C.; Krein, M.G. *Introduction to the Theory of Linear Non-Selfadjoint Operators in a Hilbert Space*; Nauka, Fizmatlit: Moscow, Russia, 1965.
15. Kukushkin, M.V. Asymptotics of eigenvalues for differential operators of fractional order. *Fract. Calc. Appl. Anal.* **2019**, *22*, 658–681. [CrossRef]
16. Katsnelson, V.E. Conditions under which systems of eigenvectors of some classes of operators form a basis. *Funct. Anal. Appl.* **1967**, *1*, 122–132. [CrossRef]
17. Kukushkin, M.V. *On One Method of Studying Spectral Properties of Non-Selfadjoint Operators*; Abstract and Applied Analysis; Hindawi: London, UK, 2020. [CrossRef]
18. Krein, M.G. Criteria for completeness of the system of root vectors of a dissipative operator. *Am. Math. Soc. Transl. Ser.* **1963**, *26*, 221–229.
19. Markus, A.S.; Matsaev, V.I. Operators generated by sesquilinear forms and their spectral asymptotics. *Mat. Issled.* **1981**, *61*, 86–103.
20. Markus, A.S. Expansion in root vectors of a slightly perturbed selfadjoint operator. *Sov. Math. Dokl.* **1962**, *3*, 104–108.
21. Motovilov, A.K.; Shkalikov, A.A. Preserving of the unconditional basis property under non-self-adjoint perturbations of self-adjoint operators. *Funktsional. Anal. Prilozhen.* **2019**, *53*, 45–60.
22. Shkalikov, A.A. Perturbations of selfadjoint and normal operators with a discrete spectrum. *Russ. Math. Surv.* **2016**, *71*, 113–174.
23. Levin, B.J. *Distribution of Zeros of Entire Functions*; Translations of Mathematical Monographs: Providence, RI, USA, 1964.
24. Kukushkin, M.V. Abstract Evolution Equations with an Operator Function in the Second Term. *Axioms* **2022**, *11*, 434. [CrossRef]
25. Kato, T. *Perturbation Theory for Linear Operators*; Springer: Berlin/Heidelberg, Germany, 1980.
26. Hardy, G.H. *Divergent Series*; Oxford University Press: London, UK, 1949.
27. Krasnoselskii, M.A.; Zabreiko, P.P.; Pustylnik, E.I.; Sobolevskii, P.E. *Integral Operators in the Spaces of Summable Functions*; Science, FIZMATLIT: Moscow, Russia, 1966.
28. Goldstein, G.R.; Goldstein, J.A.; Rhandi, A. Weighted Hardys inequality and the Kolmogorov equation perturbed by an inverse-square potential. *Appl. Anal.* **2012**, *91*, 2057–2071. [CrossRef]
29. Adams, R.A. Compact lmbeddings of Weighted Sobolev Spaces on Unbounded Domains. *J. Differ. Equ.* **1971**, *9*, 325–334.
30. Rozenblyum, G.V.; Solomyak, M.Z.; Shubin, M.A. Spectral theory of differential operators. *Results Sci. Technol.* **1989**, *64*, 5–242.
31. Pazy, A. *Semigroups of Linear Operators and Applications to Partial Differential Equations*; Springer Applied Mathematical Sciences: Berlin/Heidelberg, Germany, 1983.

Disclaimer/Publisher's Note: The statements, opinions and data contained in all publications are solely those of the individual author(s) and contributor(s) and not of MDPI and/or the editor(s). MDPI and/or the editor(s) disclaim responsibility for any injury to people or property resulting from any ideas, methods, instructions or products referred to in the content.

 *fractal and fractional*

Article

Stability of Time Series Models Based on Fractional-Order Weakening Buffer Operators

Chong Li [1], Yingjie Yang [2] and Xinping Zhu [1,*]

1. School of Air Traffic Management, Civil Aviation Flight University of China, Guanghan 618307, China
2. School of Computer Science and Informatics, De Montfort University, Leicester LE1 9BH, UK
* Correspondence: fdskkj@126.com

Abstract: Different weakening buffer operators in a time-series model analysis usually result in different model sensitivities, which sometimes affect the effectiveness of relevant operator-based methods. In this paper, the stability of two classic fractional-order weakening buffer operator-based series models is studied; then, a new data preprocessing method based on a novel fractional-order bidirectional weakening buffer operator is provided, whose effect in improving the model's stability is tested and utilized in prediction problems. Practical examples are employed to demonstrate the efficiency of the proposed method in improving the model's stability in noise scenarios. The comparison indicates that the proposed method overcomes the disadvantage of many weakening buffer operators in the subjectively biased weighting of the new or old information in forecasting. These expand the application of the proposed method in time series analysis.

Keywords: time series; sequence operator; fractional-order operator; model stability; model perturbation analysis

1. Introduction

Time series prediction models play important roles in many real-world applications, including economic and social forecasting problems [1,2]. A literature survey reveals that fractional-order dynamical models sometimes provide more valuable insights to portray complex natural phenomena than their integer-order counterparts [3,4]. However, data noise and missing data are often encountered in model applications, and they affect the effectiveness of prediction results. The existence and stability of stationary solutions are basic problems for models subject to exogenous random perturbations [5,6]. Researchers have proposed ways and methods to improve the accuracy of model solutions [7–10].

Sequence operators play an important role in reducing the interference information in collected data and highlight the potential development process of analyzed objects. Among them are the widely used exponential smoothing operators [11], especially the seasonal exponential smoothing method in the application of forecasting [12,13]. The buffer operators in the grey systems theory also exhibit similar features [14]. They are based on the three axioms of the buffer operator and are suitable for small sample analyses. They greatly improve the performance of grey prediction models in real applications [15]. These operators can be further subdivided into weakening operators and strengthening operators [16,17]. When it comes to system development trend analysis or series prediction, weakening buffer operators (WBO) are preferred. These types of operators include the average weakening buffer operator (AWBO), the geometric averageweakening buffer operator (GAWBO), and the weighted WBOs (WAWBO, WGAWBO), etc., see [18,19]. The main disadvantage of these operators is their subjective determination of the weight coefficients of data [20]. This will undoubtedly miss some of the useful information under certain conditions and limit their applications.

Wu et al. first studied the essence of WBOs in grey prediction models [21–23]. Based on the perturbation theory, they found that series prediction models are more sensitive to earlier data than newer data in a given sequence. Their findings reveal that the classic integral accumulated generating operator, 1-AGO, and the extended fractional accumulated generating operator attach more importance to the earlier data than to recent data, and both operators donot satisfy the priority theory of new information in the grey systems theory. To solve this problem, they later proposed some reverse fractional-order operators in Wu et al. [23] and Wu et al. [21], which attach more importance to the morerecent data and thus are consistent with the priority theory of new information. Recent studies show that these new fractional-order accumulation and inverse accumulation operators could improve the prediction performance of time series models [24–26]. However, these new fractional-order operators emphasize either the new or old data and thus are only suitable for series analyses with special time preferences.

To solve the above problems, this paper applies a data preprocessing method based on a novel fractional-order bidirectional weakening buffer operator, which was first proposed by Li et al. [27]. Recent studies have demonstrated the good performance of this fractional-order weakening buffer operator in predictions against data noise interference [28]. The effect of this adopted operator, together with two other widely used fractional-order operators, on improving the stability of time series models is examined and compared. When applying the perturbation theory, this study shows that: (1) the disadvantage of the two classic fractional-order weakening buffer operators lies in the subjectively biased weighting of either the new or old information in forecasting; (2) the proposed data preprocessing method, based on a fractional bidirectional weakening buffer operator, improves the stability of time series models; (3) this newly adopted fractional-order weakening buffer operator-based method can more objectively deal with both the old and new data noise in samples and thereby improve the accuracy of model predictions. Both theoretical investigations and numerical experiments show favorable effects for the new fractional-order bidirectional weakening buffer operator in improving the performance of time series models. These enlarge the application of series prediction models.

This paper is structured as follows: Section 2 introduces three important fractional-order weakening buffer operators used in the series models. Section 3 analyzes the performance of the proposed operator-based data preprocessing method on the sensitivity of a fractional-order accumulate discrete grey model $DGM^p(1,1)$. Section 4 shows the model perturbation analysis result of the proposed method and its comparison operator on another model—the new information prior to the grey model $NIGM(p,1)$. The case studiesin Section 5 demonstrate the effect of the new method in improving the model's stability. Finally, conclusions are drawn in Section 6.

2. Fractional-Order Weakening Buffer Operators

Weakening buffer operators are commonly used in series prediction models for finding the implicit pattern in samples. In order to show the advantage of the adopted fractional-order bidirectional weakening buffer operator in the proposed data preprocessing method, two other widely used classic fractional-order weakening buffer operators are introduced in Definition 1 and Definition 2. They are chosen as the comparative objects of the proposed one.

Definition 1 [22]. *Let* $X^{(0)} = \left\{x^{(0)}(1), x^{(0)}(2), \ldots, x^{(0)}(n)\right\}$ *be the original sequence, and* $D^p X^{(0)} = X^p = \{x^p(1), x^p(2), \ldots, x^p(n)\}$ *be the fractional p-order* $(0 < p < 1)$ *accumulated generating operator sequence of non-negative* $X^{(0)}$, *with operator* D^p *satisfying:*

$$x^p(k) = \sum_{i=1}^{k} C_{k-i+p-1}^{k-i} x^{(0)}(i), \quad (k=1,2,\ldots n) \tag{1}$$

where $C_{p-1}^0 = 1$, $C_{k-1}^k = 0$, $C_{k-i+p-1}^{k-i} = \frac{(k-i+p-1)(k-i+p-2)\ldots(p+1)(p)}{(k-i)!}$.

Definition 2 [23]. Let $X^{(0)} = \left\{x^{(0)}(1), x^{(0)}(2), \ldots, x^{(0)}(n)\right\}$ be the original sequence, and $D^r X^{(0)} = X_{(r)} = \left\{x_{(r)}(1), x_{(r)}(2), \ldots, x_{(r)}(n)\right\}$ be defined as the reverse fractional r-order accumulated generating operator sequence of non-negative $X^{(0)}$, with operator D^r satisfying:

$$x_{(r)}(k) = \sum_{i=k}^{n} C_{i-k+r-1}^{i-k} x^{(0)}(i), \quad (k = 1, 2, \ldots n) \tag{2}$$

where $C_{r-1}^{0} = 1$, $C_{n-1}^{n} = 1$, $C_{i-k+r-1}^{i-k} = \frac{(i-k+r-1)(i-k+r-2)\cdots(r+1)r}{(i-k)!}$.

If order parameters p in Definition 1 and r in Definition 2 are limited to positive integers, the p-AGO and the r-IAGO are obtained. The important properties of these operators have been intensively studied [23,29]. In this study, the fractional-order bidirectional weakening buffer operator adopted in the proposed data preprocessing method of the time series prediction models is provided in the following definition:

Definition 3 [27]. For the original sequence $X^{(0)} = \left\{x^{(0)}(1), x^{(0)}(2), \ldots, x^{(0)}(n)\right\}$, an operator sequence $X_v = \{x_v(1), x_v(2), \ldots, x_v(n)\}$ is obtained by $D_v X^{(0)} = X_v$, where the time series operator $D_v(v \in R^+)$ is a fractional-order bidirectional weakening buffer operator, and elements in sequence X_v satisfy:

$$x_v(i) = \left(\sum_{j=i-\alpha(i)}^{i} w(i-j)x^{(0)}(j) + \sum_{j=i+1}^{i+\alpha(i)} w(j-i)x^{(0)}(j)\right) \Bigg/ \left(\sum_{j=i-\alpha(i)}^{i} w(i-j) + \sum_{j=i+1}^{i+\alpha(i)} w(j-i)\right), \tag{3}$$
$$i = 1, 2, \ldots n$$

where $\alpha(i) = \min(i-1, n-i)$, and

$$w(i) = \begin{cases} \left(n^v(v+1-n) + (n-1)^{v+1}\right)/\Gamma(v+2), & i = n \\ \left((i+1)^{v+1} - 2i^{v+1} + (i-1)^{v+1}\right)/\Gamma(v+2), & i = 1, 2, \ldots, (n-1) \\ 1/\Gamma(v+2), & i = 0 \end{cases} \tag{4}$$

It has been proved by Li et al. [27] that the fractional-order bidirectional weakening buffer operator D_v defined in (3) is a weakening buffer operator. According to Definition 3, the value adjustment of an element in a given series is determined by both the older and newer data, while it is exclusively determined by the old or new data if applying Definition 1 or Definition 2. In the following sections, we will test the performance of operator D_v in improving the stability of two grey prediction models, which are based on the operators presented in Definition 1 and Definition 2, respectively.

3. Perturbation Analysis of Model 1: The Fractional-Order Accumulate Discrete Grey Model in [22]

Whether a time series model is sensitive to the data samples plays different functions in different applications. In this section, the perturbation theory is employed to test the effect of the fractional-order bidirectional weakening buffer operator D_v on the sensitivity of the fractional-order accumulate discrete grey model $DGM^p(1,1)$ designed in [22]. In this paper, we denote the consistent matrix norm by $\|.\|$ and denote the spectral matrix norm by $\|.\|_2$.

Lemma 1 [30]. Let matrices $A \in C^{n \times n}$, $F \in C^{n \times n}$, and vectors $b \in C^n$, $c \in C^n$. Assume that the matrix or vector norm $\|.\|$ is consistent, $rank(A) = rank(A+F) = n$ and the matrix norm

$||A^{-1}||\,||F|| < 1$ is true, then the least squares estimation solution x of the linear system models $Ax = b$ and the least squares estimation solution $x + h$ of the model $(A + F)(x + h) = b + c$ satisfy:

$$||h|| \leq \frac{\kappa_+}{\gamma_+}\left(\frac{||F||_2||x||}{||A||} + \frac{||c||}{||A||} + \frac{\kappa_+}{\gamma_+}\frac{||F||_2||\gamma_x||}{||A||^2}\right) \tag{5}$$

where $\kappa_+ = ||A^{-1}||_2||A||$, $\gamma_+ = 1 - ||A^{-1}||_2||F||_2$, $\gamma_x = b - Ax$.

To keep the consistency of the parameters, the fractional-order parameter p/q used in [22] is replaced by parameter p in the rest of this paper.

Definition 4 [22]. *Let $X^{(0)} = \left\{x^{(0)}(1), x^{(0)}(2), \ldots, x^{(0)}(n)\right\}$ be the original sequence, and $X^p = \{x^p(1), x^p(2), \ldots, x^p(n)\}$ be its fractional p-order accumulated generating operator sequence based on Definition 1, then the following time series model is called a fractional-order accumulate discrete grey model $DGM^p(1,1)$:*

$$x^p(k+1) = \beta_1 x^p(k) + \beta_2, \quad k = 1, 2, \ldots, n-1 \tag{6}$$

The least squares estimation of model parameters β_1 and β_2 in model (6) are:

$$\begin{bmatrix}\beta_2 \\ \beta_1\end{bmatrix} = (B^T B)^{-1} B^T Y, \tag{7}$$

where

$$B = \begin{bmatrix} 1 & x^p(1) \\ 1 & x^p(2) \\ \vdots & \vdots \\ 1 & x^p(n-2) \\ 1 & x^p(n-1) \end{bmatrix}, \quad Y = \begin{bmatrix} x^p(2) \\ x^p(3) \\ \vdots \\ x^p(n-1) \\ x^p(n) \end{bmatrix}.$$

For simplicity, let $\beta = [\beta_2, \beta_1]^T$. The perturbation analysis result of model (6) in [22] is summarized in the following Theorems 1–3.

Theorem 1 [22]. *For the $DGM^p(1,1)$ model with original data $X^{(0)} = \left\{x^{(0)}(1), \ldots, x^{(0)}(n)\right\}$, let β be its least squares estimation. When the raw data is disturbed, $DGM^p(1,1)$ becomes $(B + \Delta B)\tilde{\beta} = (Y + \Delta Y)$, where ΔB and ΔY are determined by the disturbance item ε. Assume that the matrixnorm condition $||B^{-1}||_2||\Delta B||_2 < 1$ holds for $DGM^p(1,1)$. Let $\kappa_+ = ||B^{-1}||_2||B||$, $\gamma_+ = 1 - ||B^{-1}||_2||\Delta B||_2$, $\gamma_\beta = Y - B\beta$. If the disturbance occurs in the first data of the original sequence, that is $\tilde{x}^{(0)}(1) = x^{(0)}(1) + \varepsilon$, then the difference between solutions $\tilde{\beta}$ and β is denoted by $||\delta(x^{(0)}(1))||$ and it satisfies:*

$$||\delta(x^{(0)}(1))|| \leq |\varepsilon|\frac{\kappa_+}{\gamma_+}\left(\frac{\sqrt{\sum_{k=1}^{n-1}\left(C_{k+p-2}^{k-1}\right)^2}||\beta||}{||B||} + \frac{\sqrt{\sum_{k=2}^{n}\left(C_{k+p-2}^{k-1}\right)^2}}{||B||} + \frac{\kappa_+}{\gamma_+}\frac{\sqrt{\sum_{k=1}^{n-1}\left(C_{k+p-2}^{k-1}\right)^2}||\gamma_\beta||}{||B||^2}\right). \tag{8}$$

Theorem 2 [22]. *For the same model and parameters as those in Theorem 1, if the disturbance occurs in the non-boundary nodes, that is $\tilde{x}^{(0)}(k) = x^{(0)}(k) + \varepsilon$, $(k = 2, 3, \ldots, n-1)$, then the difference between solutions of model $DGM^p(1,1)$ is denoted by $||\delta(x^{(0)}(k))||$, and it satisfies:*

$$\|\delta(x^{(0)}(k))\| \le |\varepsilon|\frac{\kappa_+}{\gamma_+}\left(\frac{\sqrt{\sum_{i=1}^{n-k}\left(C_{i+p-2}^{i-1}\right)^2}\|\beta\|}{\|B\|} + \frac{\sqrt{\sum_{i=1}^{n-k+1}\left(C_{i+p-2}^{i-1}\right)^2}}{\|B\|} + \frac{\kappa_+}{\gamma_+}\frac{\sqrt{\sum_{i=1}^{n-k}\left(C_{i+p-2}^{i-1}\right)^2}\|\gamma_\beta\|}{\|B\|^2}\right). \tag{9}$$

Theorem 3 [22]. *For the same model and parameters as those in Theorem 1, if the disturbance occurs in the last data of the original sequence, that is $\tilde{x}^{(0)}(n) = x^{(0)}(n) + \varepsilon$, then the difference between solutions of model $DGM^p(1,1)$ is denoted by $\|\delta(x^{(0)}(n))\|$, and it satisfies:*

$$\|\delta(x^{(0)}(n))\| \le \frac{\kappa_+}{\gamma_+}\frac{|\varepsilon|}{\|B\|} \tag{10}$$

Based on the above theorems, Wu et al. [22] demonstrate that the proposed $DGM^p(1,1)$ has better solution stability than the classic $GM(1,1)$ model. Now, to test the advantage of the fractional-order bidirectional weakening buffer operator D_v in improving the model's stability, we first apply a preprocessing step to the original time series based on operator D_v and then carry out the $DGM^p(1,1)$ analysis. The perturbation theory is employed to test the effect of operator D_v on the solution stability of $DGM^p(1,1)$.

Let $X^{(0)} = \left\{x^{(0)}(1), x^{(0)}(2), \ldots, x^{(0)}(n)\right\}$ be the original sequence, $X_v = \{x_v(1), x_v(2), \ldots, x_v(n)\}$ be its weakening buffer operator sequence based on operator D_v. Apply the $DGM^p(1,1)$ model to sequence X_v and let β_v be the new model solution values of parameters $[\beta_2, \beta_1]^T$; then we have

$$\beta_v = (B_v^T B_v)^{-1} B_v^T Y_v, \tag{11}$$

where $x_v^p(k) = \sum_{i=1}^k C_{k-i+p-1}^{k-i} x_v(i)$, and

$$B_v = \begin{bmatrix} 1 & x_v^p(1) \\ 1 & x_v^p(2) \\ \vdots & \vdots \\ 1 & x_v^p(n-2) \\ 1 & x_v^p(n-1) \end{bmatrix}, \quad Y_v = \begin{bmatrix} x_v^p(2) \\ x_v^p(3) \\ \vdots \\ x_v^p(n-1) \\ x_v^p(n) \end{bmatrix}.$$

When the raw data is disturbed, let ΔB_v and ΔY_v be the disturbance items of B_v and Y_v, respectively, and $\tilde{\beta}_v$ be the new model solution. Assume that $\|B_v^{-1}\|_2\|\Delta B_v\|_2 < 1$ and set $\kappa_{v+} = \|B_v^{-1}\|_2\|B_v\|$, $\gamma_{v+} = 1-\|B_v^{-1}\|_2\|\Delta B_v\|_2$ and $\gamma_{v\beta} = Y_v - B_v\beta_v$. The parameters $\alpha(i)$ and $w(i)$ used in the remaining part of this section are the same as those defined in model (3). The main results are stated in the following theorems.

Theorem 4. *If a raw data disturbance occurs in the first data of the original sequence, that is $\tilde{x}^{(0)}(1) = x^{(0)}(1) + \varepsilon$, then the difference between $\tilde{\beta}_v$ and β_v satisfies:*

$$\|\delta(x^{(0)}(1))\| \le |\varepsilon|\frac{\kappa_{v+}}{\gamma_{v+}}\left(\frac{M_v\|\beta_v\|}{\|B_v\|} + \frac{N_v}{\|B_v\|} + \frac{\kappa_{v+}}{\gamma_{v+}}\frac{M_v\|\gamma_{v\beta}\|}{\|B_v\|^2}\right), \tag{12}$$

where: (i). If sequence size n is even, then:

$$M_v = \sqrt{\sum_{i=1}^{n/2}\left(\sum_{j=1}^{i} C_{j+p-2}^{j-1}\frac{w(i-j)}{w(0)+2\sum_{k=1}^{\alpha(i-j+1)}w(k)}\right)^2 + \sum_{i=n/2+1}^{n-1}\left(\sum_{j=1}^{n/2} C_{i+p-j-1}^{i-j}\frac{w(j-1)}{w(0)+2\sum_{k=1}^{\alpha(j)}w(k)}\right)^2},$$
$$N_v = \sqrt{\sum_{i=2}^{n/2}\left(\sum_{j=1}^{i} C_{j+p-2}^{j-1}\frac{w(i-j)}{w(0)+2\sum_{k=1}^{\alpha(i-j+1)}w(k)}\right)^2 + \sum_{i=n/2+1}^{n}\left(\sum_{j=1}^{n/2} C_{i+p-j-1}^{i-j}\frac{w(j-1)}{w(0)+2\sum_{k=1}^{\alpha(j)}w(k)}\right)^2}.$$
(13)

(ii). If sequence size n is odd, then:

$$M_v = \sqrt{\sum_{i=1}^{(n+1)/2}\left(\sum_{j=1}^{i} C_{j+p-2}^{j-1}\frac{w(i-j)}{w(0)+2\sum_{k=1}^{\alpha(i-j+1)}w(k)}\right)^2 + \sum_{i=(n+3)/2}^{n-1}\left(\sum_{j=1}^{(n+1)/2} C_{i+p-j-1}^{i-j}\frac{w(j-1)}{w(0)+2\sum_{k=1}^{\alpha(j)}w(k)}\right)^2},$$
$$N_v = \sqrt{\sum_{i=2}^{(n+1)/2}\left(\sum_{j=1}^{i} C_{j+p-2}^{j-1}\frac{w(i-j)}{w(0)+2\sum_{k=1}^{\alpha(i-j+1)}w(k)}\right)^2 + \sum_{i=(n+3)/2}^{n}\left(\sum_{j=1}^{(n+1)/2} C_{i+p-j-1}^{i-j}\frac{w(j-1)}{w(0)+2\sum_{k=1}^{\alpha(j)}w(k)}\right)^2}.$$
(14)

Proof of Theorem 4. (i). Sequence size n is even. When $\widetilde{x}^{(0)}(1) = x^{(0)}(1) + \varepsilon$, according to the logic of $DGM^p(1,1)$, we have

$$\Delta B_v = \begin{bmatrix} 0 & \varepsilon \\ 0 & C_p^1\varepsilon + \frac{w(1)\varepsilon}{w(0)+2w(1)} \\ \vdots & \vdots \\ 0 & C_{p+n/2-2}^{n/2-1}\varepsilon + C_{p+n/2-3}^{n/2-2}\frac{w(1)\varepsilon}{w(0)+2w(1)} + \cdots \frac{w(n/2-1)\varepsilon}{w(0)+2\sum_{k=1}^{\alpha(n/2)}w(k)} \\ 0 & C_{p+n/2-1}^{n/2}\varepsilon + C_{p+n/2-2}^{n/2-1}\frac{w(1)\varepsilon}{w(0)+2w(1)} + \cdots C_p^1\frac{w(n/2-1)\varepsilon}{w(0)+2\sum_{k=1}^{\alpha(n/2)}w(k)} \\ 0 & C_{p+n/2}^{n/2+1}\varepsilon + C_{p+n/2-1}^{n/2}\frac{w(1)\varepsilon}{w(0)+2w(1)} + \cdots C_{p+1}^2\frac{w(n/2-1)\varepsilon}{w(0)+2\sum_{k=1}^{\alpha(n/2)}w(k)} \\ \vdots & \vdots \\ 0 & C_{p+n-3}^{n-2}\varepsilon + C_{p+n-4}^{n-3}\frac{w(1)\varepsilon}{w(0)+2w(1)} + \cdots C_{p+n/2-2}^{n/2-1}\frac{w(n/2-1)\varepsilon}{w(0)+2\sum_{k=1}^{\alpha(n/2)}w(k)} \end{bmatrix},$$

$$\Delta Y_v = \begin{bmatrix} C_p^1\varepsilon + \frac{w(1)\varepsilon}{w(0)+2w(1)} \\ C_{p+1}^2\varepsilon + C_p^1\frac{w(1)\varepsilon}{w(0)+2w(1)} + \frac{w(2)\varepsilon}{w(0)+2(w(1)+w(2))} \\ \vdots \\ C_{p+n/2-1}^{n/2}\varepsilon + C_{p+n/2-2}^{n/2-1}\frac{w(1)\varepsilon}{w(0)+2w(1)} + \cdots C_p^1\frac{w(n/2-1)\varepsilon}{w(0)+2\sum_{k=1}^{\alpha(n/2)}w(k)} \\ C_{p+n/2}^{n/2+1}\varepsilon + C_{p+n/2-1}^{n/2}\frac{w(1)\varepsilon}{w(0)+2w(1)} + \cdots C_{p+1}^2\frac{w(n/2-1)\varepsilon}{w(0)+2\sum_{k=1}^{\alpha(n/2)}w(k)} \\ C_{p+n/2+1}^{n/2+2}\varepsilon + C_{p+n/2}^{n/2+1}\frac{w(1)\varepsilon}{w(0)+2w(1)} + \cdots C_{p+2}^3\frac{w(n/2-1)\varepsilon}{w(0)+2\sum_{k=1}^{\alpha(n/2)}w(k)} \\ \vdots \\ C_{p+n-2}^{n-1}\varepsilon + C_{p+n-3}^{n-2}\frac{w(1)\varepsilon}{w(0)+2w(1)} + \cdots C_{p+n/2-1}^{n/2}\frac{w(n/2-1)\varepsilon}{w(0)+2\sum_{k=1}^{\alpha(n/2)}w(k)} \end{bmatrix}.$$

Now, calculate the norms of the matrices ΔB_v and ΔY_v, extract parameter ε and apply Lemma 1; parameter expressions in Equation (13) are then obtained.

(ii). When sequence size n is odd, we have:

$$\Delta B_v = \begin{bmatrix} 0 & & & & \varepsilon \\ 0 & & & & C_p^1\varepsilon + \frac{w(1)\varepsilon}{w(0)+2w(1)} \\ \vdots & & & & \vdots \\ 0 & C_{p+(n-3)/2}^{(n-1)/2}\varepsilon + C_{p+(n-5)/2}^{(n-3)/2}\frac{w(1)\varepsilon}{w(0)+2w(1)} + \cdots & & & \frac{w((n-1)/2)\varepsilon}{w(0)+2\sum_{k=1}^{a((n+1)/2)}w(k)} \\ 0 & C_{p+(n-1)/2}^{(n+1)/2}\varepsilon + C_{p+(n-3)/2}^{(n-1)/2}\frac{w(1)\varepsilon}{w(0)+2w(1)} + \cdots & & C_p^1 & \frac{w((n-1)/2)\varepsilon}{w(0)+2\sum_{k=1}^{a((n+1)/2)}w(k)} \\ \vdots & & & & \vdots \\ 0 & C_{p+n-3}^{n-2}\varepsilon + C_{p+n-4}^{n-3}\frac{w(1)\varepsilon}{w(0)+2w(1)} + \cdots & & C_{p+(n-5)/2}^{(n-3)/2} & \frac{w((n-1)/2)\varepsilon}{w(0)+2\sum_{k=1}^{a((n+1)/2)}w(k)} \end{bmatrix},$$

$$\Delta Y_v = \begin{bmatrix} C_p^1\varepsilon + \frac{w(1)\varepsilon}{w(0)+2w(1)} \\ C_{p+1}^2\varepsilon + C_p^1\frac{w(1)\varepsilon}{w(0)+2w(1)} + \frac{w(2)\varepsilon}{w(0)+2w(1)+2w(2)} \\ \vdots \\ C_{p+(n-1)/2}^{(n+1)/2}\varepsilon + C_{p+(n-3)/2}^{(n-1)/2}\frac{w(1)\varepsilon}{w(0)+2w(1)} + \cdots C_p^1 \frac{w((n-1)/2)\varepsilon}{w(0)+2\sum_{k=1}^{a((n+1)/2)}w(k)} \\ C_{p+(n+1)/2}^{(n+3)/2}\varepsilon + C_{p+(n-1)/2}^{(n+1)/2}\frac{w(1)\varepsilon}{w(0)+2w(1)} + \cdots C_{p+1}^2 \frac{w((n-1)/2)\varepsilon}{w(0)+2\sum_{k=1}^{a((n+1)/2)}w(k)} \\ \vdots \\ C_{p+n-2}^{n-1}\varepsilon + C_{p+n-3}^{n-2}\frac{w(1)\varepsilon}{w(0)+2w(1)} + \cdots C_{p+(n-3)/2}^{(n-1)/2} \frac{w((n-1)/2)\varepsilon}{w(0)+2\sum_{k=1}^{a((n+1)/2)}w(k)} \end{bmatrix}.$$

Then, calculate the matrix norm $||\Delta B_v||_2$ and vector norm $||\Delta Y_v||$, extract parameter ε and apply Lemma 1; parameter expressions in Equation (14) are then obtained. □

Theorem 5. *If a raw data disturbance occurs in the non-boundary nodes of the first half of the original sequence, that is $\widetilde{x}^{(0)}(k) = x^{(0)}(k) + \varepsilon$, then the difference between $\widetilde{\beta}_v$ and β_v satisfies expression (12); however, the values of parameters M_v and N_v are determined by the following scenarios. Let φ_1 be the largest integer less than $k/2$, φ_2 be the largest integer less than $(k-1)/2$, then M_v and N_v are:*

(i). *If sequence size n is even, then $k = 2, 3, \ldots, n/2$ and*

$$M_v = \sqrt{\sum_{i=\varphi_1+1}^{n/2+\varphi_1}\left(\sum_{j=1}^{i-\varphi_1} C_{j+p-2}^{j-1} \frac{w(|k+j-i-1|)}{w(0)+2\sum_{h=1}^{a(i-j+1)}w(h)}\right)^2 + \sum_{i=n/2+\varphi_1+1}^{n-1}\left(\sum_{j=1}^{n/2} C_{p+i+j-\varphi_1-2-n/2}^{i+j-\varphi_1-1-n/2}\frac{w(|k+j-\varphi_1-1-n/2|)}{w(0)+2\sum_{h=1}^{a(n/2+\varphi_1+1-j)}w(h)}\right)^2},$$

$$N_v = \sqrt{\sum_{i=\varphi_1+1}^{n/2+\varphi_1}\left(\sum_{j=1}^{i-\varphi_1} C_{j+p-2}^{j-1} \frac{w(|k+j-i-1|)}{w(0)+2\sum_{h=1}^{a(i-j+1)}w(h)}\right)^2 + \sum_{i=n/2+\varphi_1+1}^{n}\left(\sum_{j=1}^{n/2} C_{p+i+j-\varphi_1-2-n/2}^{i+j-\varphi_1-1-n/2}\frac{w(|k+j-\varphi_1-1-n/2|)}{w(0)+2\sum_{h=1}^{a(n/2+\varphi_1+1-j)}w(h)}\right)^2}.$$

(15)

(ii). *If sequence size n is odd, then $k = 2, 3, \ldots, (n+1)/2$ and*

$$M_v = \sqrt{\sum_{i=\varphi_1+1}^{(n+1)/2+\varphi_2}\left(\sum_{j=1}^{i-\varphi_1} C_{j+p-2}^{j-1} \frac{w(|k+j-i-1|)}{w(0)+2\sum_{h=1}^{a(i-j+1)}w(h)}\right)^2 + \sum_{i=(n+1)/2+\varphi_2+1}^{n-1}\left(\sum_{j=1}^{(n+1)/2+\varphi_2-\varphi_1} C_{p+i+j-\varphi_2-2-(n+1)/2}^{i+j-\varphi_2-1-(n+1)/2}\frac{w(|k+j-\varphi_2-1-(n+1)/2|)}{w(0)+2\sum_{h=1}^{a((n+1)/2+\varphi_2+1-j)}w(h)}\right)^2},$$

$$N_v = \sqrt{\sum_{i=\varphi_1+1}^{(n+1)/2+\varphi_2}\left(\sum_{j=1}^{i-\varphi_1} C_{j+p-2}^{j-1} \frac{w(|k+j-i-1|)}{w(0)+2\sum_{h=1}^{a(i-j+1)}w(h)}\right)^2 + \sum_{i=(n+1)/2+\varphi_2+1}^{n}\left(\sum_{j=1}^{(n+1)/2+\varphi_2-\varphi_1} C_{p+i+j-\varphi_2-2-(n+1)/2}^{i+j-\varphi_2-1-(n+1)/2}\frac{w(|k+j-\varphi_2-1-(n+1)/2|)}{w(0)+2\sum_{h=1}^{a((n+1)/2+\varphi_2+1-j)}w(h)}\right)^2}.$$

(16)

Proof of Theorem 5. Please see Appendix A.1. □

Theorem 6. *If a raw data disturbance occurs in the second half of the original sequence, excluding the last data, then the difference between $\widetilde{\beta}_v$ and β_v satisfies expression (12). Let φ_3 be the largest integer less than $(n-k)/2$, φ_4 be the largest integer less than $(n-k+1)/2$, then M_v and N_v are:*
(i). If sequence size n is even, then $k = n/2+1, n/2+2, \ldots, n-1$ and

$$M_v = \sqrt{\sum_{i=n/2+1-\varphi_4}^{n-\varphi_4}\left(\sum_{j=1}^{i-n/2+\varphi_4}C_{j+p-2}^{j-1}\frac{w(|k+j-i-1|)}{w(0)+2\sum_{h=1}^{a(i-j+1)}w(h)}\right)^2 + \sum_{i=n+1-\varphi_4}^{n-1}\left(\sum_{j=1}^{n/2}C_{p+i+j+\varphi_4-2-n}^{i+j+\varphi_4-1-n}\frac{w(|k+j+\varphi_4-1-n|)}{w(0)+2\sum_{h=1}^{a(n+1-\varphi_4-j)}w(h)}\right)^2},$$

$$N_v = \sqrt{\sum_{i=n/2+1-\varphi_4}^{n-\varphi_4}\left(\sum_{j=1}^{i-n/2+\varphi_4}C_{j+p-2}^{j-1}\frac{w(|k+j-i-1|)}{w(0)+2\sum_{h=1}^{a(i-j+1)}w(h)}\right)^2 + \sum_{i=n+1-\varphi_4}^{n}\left(\sum_{j=1}^{n/2}C_{p+i+j+\varphi_4-2-n}^{i+j+\varphi_4-1-n}\frac{w(|k+j+\varphi_4-1-n|)}{w(0)+2\sum_{h=1}^{a(n+1-\varphi_4-j)}w(h)}\right)^2}.$$

(17)

(ii). If the sequence size n is odd, then $k = (n+1)/2+1, (n+1)/2+2, \ldots, n-1$ and

$$M_v = \sqrt{\sum_{i=(n+1)/2-\varphi_3}^{n-\varphi_4}\left(\sum_{j=1}^{i+\varphi_3-(n-1)/2}C_{j+p-2}^{j-1}\frac{w(|k+j-i-1|)}{w(0)+2\sum_{h=1}^{a(i+1-j)}w(h)}\right)^2 + \sum_{i=n-\varphi_4+1}^{n-1}\left(\sum_{j=1}^{(n+1)/2+\varphi_3-\varphi_4}C_{p+i+j+\varphi_4-2-n}^{i+j+\varphi_4-1-n}\frac{w(|k+j+\varphi_4-1-n|)}{w(0)+2\sum_{h=1}^{a(n+1-\varphi_4-j)}w(h)}\right)^2},$$

$$N_v = \sqrt{\sum_{i=(n+1)/2-\varphi_3}^{n-\varphi_4}\left(\sum_{j=1}^{i+\varphi_3-(n-1)/2}C_{j+p-2}^{j-1}\frac{w(|k+j-i-1|)}{w(0)+2\sum_{h=1}^{a(i-j+1)}w(h)}\right)^2 + \sum_{i=n-\varphi_4+1}^{n}\left(\sum_{j=1}^{(n+1)/2+\varphi_3-\varphi_4}C_{p+i+j+\varphi_4-2-n}^{i+j+\varphi_4-1-n}\frac{w(|k+j+\varphi_4-1-n|)}{w(0)+2\sum_{h=1}^{a(n+1-\varphi_4-j)}w(h)}\right)^2}.$$

(18)

Proof of Theorem 6. Please see Appendix A.2. □

Theorem 7. *If a raw data disturbance occurs in the last data of the original sequence, that is $\widetilde{x}^{(0)}(n) = x^{(0)}(n) + \varepsilon$, then the difference between $\widetilde{\beta}_v$ and β_v satisfies expression (12); however, the values of parameters M_v and N_v are determined by the size of samples.*
(i). If sequence size n is even, then

$$M_v = \sqrt{\sum_{i=1}^{n/2-1}\left(\sum_{j=1}^{i}C_{i+p-j-1}^{i-j}\frac{w(n/2-j)}{w(0)+2\sum_{h=1}^{a(n/2+j)}w(h)}\right)^2},$$

$$N_v = \sqrt{\sum_{i=1}^{n/2}\left(\sum_{j=1}^{i}C_{i+p-j-1}^{i-j}\frac{w(n/2-j)}{w(0)+2\sum_{h=1}^{a(n/2+j)}w(h)}\right)^2}.$$

(19)

(ii). If sequence size n is odd, then

$$M_v = \sqrt{\sum_{i=1}^{(n-1)/2}\left(\sum_{j=1}^{i}C_{i+p-j-1}^{i-j}\frac{w((n+1)/2-j)}{w(0)+2\sum_{h=1}^{a((n+1)/2+j-1)}w(h)}\right)^2},$$

$$N_v = \sqrt{\sum_{i=1}^{(n+1)/2}\left(\sum_{j=1}^{i}C_{i+p-j-1}^{i-j}\frac{w((n+1)/2-j)}{w(0)+2\sum_{h=1}^{a((n+1)/2+j-1)}w(h)}\right)^2}.$$

(20)

Proof of Theorem 7. Please see Appendix A.3. □

4. Perturbation Analysis of Model 2: The $NIGM(p,1)$ Model in [23]

The fractional-order accumulate discrete grey model in Section 3 emphasizes old data in the modeling samples. To provide more weight to the new information, Wu et al. [23] provide the following model.

Definition 5 [23]. *Let $X^{(0)} = \left\{x^{(0)}(1), x^{(0)}(2), \ldots, x^{(0)}(n)\right\}$ be the original sequence, and $X_{(1-p)} = \left\{x_{(1-p)}(1), x_{(1-p)}(2), \ldots, x_{(1-p)}(n)\right\}$ $(0 < p < 1)$ be the fractional $(1-p)$-order reverse accumulated generating operator sequence of $X^{(0)}$ (see Definition 2). Set mean formula*

$z^{(0)}(k) = \left(x^{(0)}(k) + x^{(0)}(k-1)\right)/2$ and formula $d_{(1)}x_{(1-p)}(k) = x_{(1-p)}(k) - x_{(1-p)}(k-1)$, then the new information prior grey model $NIGM(p,1)$ is defined by:

$$d_{(1)}x_{(1-p)}(k) + \tau_1 z^{(0)}(k) = \tau_2 \quad (21)$$

The least squares estimation of model parameters τ_1 and τ_2 in (21) can be obtained by:

$$\begin{bmatrix} \tau_1 \\ \tau_2 \end{bmatrix} = (E^T E)^{-1} E^T U \quad (22)$$

where

$$E = \begin{bmatrix} -z^{(0)}(2) & 1 \\ -z^{(0)}(3) & 1 \\ \vdots & \vdots \\ -z^{(0)}(n) & 1 \end{bmatrix}, \quad U = \begin{bmatrix} d_{(1)}x_{(1-p)}(2) \\ d_{(1)}x_{(1-p)}(3) \\ \vdots \\ d_{(1)}x_{(1-p)}(n) \end{bmatrix}$$

Let $\tau = [\tau_1, \tau_2]^T$, ΔE and ΔU be the disturbance items of model parameters E and U, respectively, and ε be the disturbance item on raw data. Assume that the matrix norm condition $||E^{-1}||_2 ||\Delta E||_2 < 1$ holds for model $NIGM(p,1)$. Let $\mu_+ = ||E^{-1}||_2 ||E||$, $\eta_+ = 1 - ||E^{-1}||_2 ||\Delta E||_2$, $\eta_\tau = U - E\tau$. Based on Lemma 1, the perturbation analysis results of $NIGM(p,1)$ are summarized in the following Theorems 8 to 10. Theorem 8 directly comes from Wu et al. [23], while Theorems 9 to 10 are derived from the corrected parameters.

Theorem 8 [23]. If the disturbance ε occurs in the first data of the original sequence, that is $\tilde{x}^{(0)}(1) = x^{(0)}(1) + \varepsilon$, then the difference between solutions $\tilde{\tau}$ and τ is denoted by $||\delta(x^{(0)}(1))||$ and it satisfies:

$$||\delta(x^{(0)}(1))|| \leq |\varepsilon| \frac{\mu_+}{\eta_+} \left(\frac{||\tau||}{2||E||} + \frac{1}{||E||} + \frac{\mu_+}{\eta_+} \frac{||\eta_\tau||}{2||E||^2} \right). \quad (23)$$

Theorem 9. If the disturbance occurs in the non-boundary nodes, that is $\tilde{x}^{(0)}(i) = x^{(0)}(i) + \varepsilon$, $(i = 2, 3, \ldots, n-1)$, then the difference between the solutions of model $NIGM(p,1)$ with and without data disturbance is denoted by $||\delta(x^{(0)}(i))||$, and it satisfies:

$$||\delta(x^{(0)}(i))|| \leq |\varepsilon| \frac{\mu_+}{\eta_+} \left(\frac{\sqrt{2}||\tau||}{2||E||} + \frac{\sqrt{\sum_{j=2}^{i}(C_{j-2-p}^{j-1})^2 + 1}}{||E||} + \frac{\mu_+}{\eta_+} \frac{\sqrt{2}||\eta_\tau||}{2||E||^2} \right). \quad (24)$$

Proof of Theorem 9. (i). When $\tilde{x}^{(0)}(2) = x^{(0)}(2) + \varepsilon$, the disturbance items of parameters ΔE and ΔU are:

$$\Delta E = \begin{bmatrix} -\varepsilon/2 & 0 \\ -\varepsilon/2 & 0 \\ 0 & 0 \\ \vdots & \vdots \\ 0 & 0 \end{bmatrix}, \quad \Delta U = \begin{bmatrix} p\varepsilon \\ -\varepsilon \\ 0 \\ \vdots \\ 0 \end{bmatrix}.$$

Then, $||\Delta E||_2 = \sqrt{2}|\varepsilon|/2$, $||\Delta U|| = |\varepsilon|\sqrt{p^2 + 1}$.

(ii). When $\tilde{x}^{(0)}(3) = x^{(0)}(3) + \varepsilon$, the disturbance items of model parameters ΔE and ΔU are:

$$\Delta E = \begin{bmatrix} 0 & 0 \\ -\varepsilon/2 & 0 \\ -\varepsilon/2 & 0 \\ 0 & 0 \\ \vdots & \vdots \\ 0 & 0 \end{bmatrix}, \quad \Delta U = \begin{bmatrix} -C_{1-p}^2 \varepsilon \\ p\varepsilon \\ -\varepsilon \\ 0 \\ \vdots \\ 0 \end{bmatrix}.$$

Then, $\|\Delta E\|_2 = \sqrt{2}|\varepsilon|/2$, $\|\Delta U\| = |\varepsilon|\sqrt{(p^4 - 2p^3 + 5p^2)/4 + 1}$.

Likewise, (iii) when $\tilde{x}^{(0)}(i) = x^{(0)}(i) + \varepsilon$, $(i = 4, \ldots n - 1)$, the disturbance items of model parameters ΔE and ΔU are:

$$\Delta E = \begin{bmatrix} 0 & 0 \\ \vdots & \vdots \\ 0 & 0 \\ -\varepsilon/2 & 0 \\ -\varepsilon/2 & 0 \\ 0 & 0 \\ \vdots & \vdots \\ 0 & 0 \end{bmatrix}, \quad \Delta U = \begin{bmatrix} -C_{i-p-2}^{i-1} \varepsilon \\ -C_{i-p-3}^{i-2} \varepsilon \\ \vdots \\ p\varepsilon \\ -\varepsilon \\ 0 \\ \vdots \\ 0 \end{bmatrix}.$$

Then, $\|\Delta E\|_2 = \sqrt{2}|\varepsilon|/2$, $\|\Delta U\| = |\varepsilon|\sqrt{\sum_{j=2}^{i} (C_{j-2-p}^{j-1})^2 + 1}$.

Summarizing the above three scenarios, the perturbation result (24) is obtained. □

Theorem 10. *If the disturbance occurs in the last sample point, that is $\tilde{x}^{(0)}(n) = x^{(0)}(n) + \varepsilon$, then the difference between the solutions of model $NIGM(p, 1)$ is denoted by $\|\delta(x^{(0)}(n))\|$, and it satisfies:*

$$\|\delta(x^{(0)}(n))\| \le |\varepsilon| \frac{\mu_+}{\eta_+} \left(\frac{\|\tau\|}{2\|E\|} + \frac{\sqrt{\sum_{j=2}^{n} (C_{j-2-p}^{j-1})^2}}{\|E\|} + \frac{\mu_+}{\eta_+} \frac{\|\eta_\tau\|}{2\|E\|^2} \right). \quad (25)$$

Proof of Theorem 10. When $\tilde{x}^{(0)}(n) = x^{(0)}(n) + \varepsilon$, the disturbance items of parameters ΔE and ΔU are:

$$\Delta E = \begin{bmatrix} 0 & 0 \\ 0 & 0 \\ \vdots & \vdots \\ 0 & 0 \\ -\varepsilon/2 & 0 \end{bmatrix}, \quad \Delta U = \begin{bmatrix} -C_{n-p-2}^{n-1} \varepsilon \\ -C_{n-p-3}^{n-2} \varepsilon \\ \vdots \\ -C_{1-p}^{2} \varepsilon \\ p\varepsilon \end{bmatrix}.$$

Then, $\|\Delta E\|_2 = |\varepsilon|/2$, $\|\Delta U\| = |\varepsilon|\sqrt{\sum_{j=2}^{n} (C_{j-2-p}^{j-1})^2}$. Apply these norms to Lemma 1; perturbation bound (25) is proved. □

Now, we consider the effect of operator D_v on the stability of model $NIGM(p, 1)$. $X^{(0)} = \{x^{(0)}(1), x^{(0)}(2), \ldots, x^{(0)}(n)\}$ and $X_v = \{x_v(1), x_v(2), \ldots, x_v(n)\}$ are the same as those defined in Section 3. Set $x_v^{(1-p)}(k) = \sum_{i=k}^{n} C_{i-k-p}^{i-k} x_v(i)$, $d_{(1)} x_v^{(1-p)}(k) = x_v^{(1-p)}(k) - $

$x_v^{(1-p)}(k-1)$ and $z_v^{(0)}(k) = (x_v(k) + x_v(k-1))/2$. Let τ_v be the least squares solution of model $NIGM(p,1)$ based on sequence X_v. Then we have

$$\tau_v = (E_v^T E_v)^{-1} E_v^T U_v \tag{26}$$

where

$$E_v = \begin{bmatrix} -z_v^{(0)}(2) & 1 \\ -z_v^{(0)}(3) & 1 \\ \vdots & \vdots \\ -z_v^{(0)}(n) & 1 \end{bmatrix}, \quad U_v = \begin{bmatrix} d_{(1)} x_v^{(1-p)}(2) \\ d_{(1)} x_v^{(1-p)}(3) \\ \vdots \\ d_{(1)} x_v^{(1-p)}(n) \end{bmatrix}.$$

Let ΔE_v and ΔU_v be the disturbance items of E_v and U_v, respectively, and $\widetilde{\tau}_v$ be the new model solution. Assume that $||E_v^{-1}||_2 ||\Delta E_v||_2 < 1$ holds and let $\eta_{v\dagger} = 1 - ||E_v^{-1}||_2 ||\Delta E_v||_2$, $\mu_{v\dagger} = ||E_v^{-1}||_2 ||E_v||$, $\eta_{v\tau} = U_v - E_v \tau_v$. The perturbation analysis results of model $NIGM(p,1)$ with operator D_v are stated in the following theorems.

Theorem 11. *If a raw data disturbance occurs in the first data of the original sequence, that is $\widetilde{x}^{(0)}(1) = x^{(0)}(1) + \varepsilon$, then the difference between $\widetilde{\tau}_v$ and τ_v satisfies:*

$$||\delta(x^{(0)}(1))|| \leq |\varepsilon| \frac{\mu_{v\dagger}}{\eta_{v\dagger}} \left(\frac{P_v ||\tau_v||}{||E_v||} + \frac{Q_v}{||E_v||} + \frac{\mu_{v\dagger}}{\eta_{v\dagger}} \frac{P_v ||\eta_{v\tau}||}{||E_v||^2} \right) \tag{27}$$

where (i). If sequence size n is even, then:

$$\begin{aligned} P_v &= \frac{1}{2} \sqrt{\sum_{i=1}^{n/2-1} \left(\frac{w(i-1)}{w(0) + 2\sum_{k=1}^{\alpha(i)} w(k)} + \frac{w(i)}{w(0) + 2\sum_{k=1}^{\alpha(i+1)} w(k)} \right)^2 + \left(\frac{w(n/2-1)}{w(0) + 2\sum_{k=1}^{\alpha(n/2)} w(k)} \right)^2}, \\ Q_v &= \sqrt{\sum_{i=1}^{n/2-1} \left(\frac{w(i-1)}{w(0) + 2\sum_{k=1}^{\alpha(i)} w(k)} + \sum_{j=1}^{n/2-i} C_{j-p-1}^{j} \frac{w(i+j-1)}{w(0) + 2\sum_{k=1}^{\alpha(i+j)} w(k)} \right)^2 + \left(\frac{w(n/2-1)}{w(0) + 2\sum_{k=1}^{\alpha(n/2)} w(k)} \right)^2}. \end{aligned} \tag{28}$$

(ii). If sequence size n is odd, then:

$$\begin{aligned} P_v &= \frac{1}{2} \sqrt{\sum_{i=1}^{(n-1)/2} \left(\frac{w(i-1)}{w(0) + 2\sum_{k=1}^{\alpha(i)} w(k)} + \frac{w(i)}{w(0) + 2\sum_{k=1}^{\alpha(i+1)} w(k)} \right)^2 + \left(\frac{w((n-1)/2)}{w(0) + 2\sum_{k=1}^{\alpha((n+1)/2)} w(k)} \right)^2}, \\ Q_v &= \sqrt{\sum_{i=1}^{(n-1)/2} \left(\frac{w(i-1)}{w(0) + 2\sum_{k=1}^{\alpha(i)} w(k)} + \sum_{j=1}^{(n+1)/2-i} C_{j-p-1}^{j} \frac{w(i+j-1)}{w(0) + 2\sum_{k=1}^{\alpha(i+j)} w(k)} \right)^2 + \left(\frac{w((n-1)/2)}{w(0) + 2\sum_{k=1}^{\alpha((n+1)/2)} w(k)} \right)^2}. \end{aligned} \tag{29}$$

Proof of Theorem 11. (i). The sequence size n is even. When $\widetilde{x}^{(0)}(1) = x^{(0)}(1) + \varepsilon$, according to the logic of $NIGM(p,1)$, we have

$$\Delta E_v = \begin{bmatrix} -\frac{\varepsilon}{2}\left(1+\frac{w(1)}{w(0)+2w(1)}\right) & 0 \\ -\frac{\varepsilon}{2}\left(\frac{w(1)}{w(0)+2w(1)}+\frac{w(2)}{w(0)+2\sum_{h=1}^{\alpha(3)}w(h)}\right) & 0 \\ \vdots & \vdots \\ -\frac{\varepsilon}{2}\left(\frac{w(n/2-2)}{w(0)+2\sum_{h=1}^{\alpha(n/2-1)}w(h)}+\frac{w(n/2-1)}{w(0)+2\sum_{h=1}^{\alpha(n/2)}w(h)}\right) & 0 \\ -\frac{\varepsilon}{2}\frac{w(n/2-1)}{w(0)+2\sum_{h=1}^{\alpha(n/2)}w(h)} & 0 \\ 0 & 0 \\ \vdots & \vdots \\ 0 & 0 \end{bmatrix}, \Delta U_v = \begin{bmatrix} -\varepsilon - \varepsilon \sum_{i=1}^{n/2-1}\left(C_{i-p-1}^i\right)\frac{w(i)}{w(0)+2\sum_{h=1}^{\alpha(i+1)}w(h)} \\ -\varepsilon\frac{w(1)}{w(0)+2w(1)} - \varepsilon \sum_{i=1}^{n/2-2}\left(C_{i-p-1}^i\right)\frac{w(i+1)}{w(0)+2\sum_{h=1}^{\alpha(i+2)}w(h)} \\ \vdots \\ -\varepsilon\frac{w(n/2-2)}{w(0)+2\sum_{h=1}^{\alpha(n/2-1)}w(h)}+\varepsilon p\frac{w(n/2-1)}{w(0)+2\sum_{h=1}^{\alpha(n/2)}w(h)} \\ -\varepsilon\frac{w(n/2-1)}{w(0)+2\sum_{h=1}^{\alpha(n/2)}w(h)} \\ 0 \\ \vdots \\ 0 \end{bmatrix}.$$

Then, calculate the matrix norm $||\Delta E_v||_2$ and vector norm $||\Delta U_v||$, extract parameter ε and apply Lemma 1; then, the parameter expressions in Equation (28) are obtained.

(ii). When sequence size n is odd, we obtain:

$$\Delta E_v = \begin{bmatrix} -\frac{\varepsilon}{2}\left(1+\frac{w(1)}{w(0)+2w(1)}\right) & 0 \\ -\frac{\varepsilon}{2}\left(\frac{w(1)}{w(0)+2w(1)}+\frac{w(2)}{w(0)+2\sum_{h=1}^{\alpha(3)}w(h)}\right) & 0 \\ \vdots & \vdots \\ -\frac{\varepsilon}{2}\left(\frac{w((n-3)/2)}{w(0)+2\sum_{h=1}^{\alpha((n-1)/2)}w(h)}+\frac{w((n-1)/2)}{w(0)+2\sum_{h=1}^{\alpha((n+1)/2)}w(h)}\right) & 0 \\ -\frac{\varepsilon}{2}\frac{w((n-1)/2)}{w(0)+2\sum_{h=1}^{\alpha((n+1)/2)}w(h)} & 0 \\ 0 & 0 \\ \vdots & \vdots \\ 0 & 0 \end{bmatrix}, U_v = \begin{bmatrix} -\varepsilon - \varepsilon \sum_{i=1}^{(n-1)/2}\left(C_{i-p-1}^i\right)\frac{w(i)}{w(0)+2\sum_{h=1}^{\alpha(i+1)}w(h)} \\ -\varepsilon\frac{w(1)}{w(0)+2w(1)} - \varepsilon \sum_{i=1}^{(n-3)/2}\left(C_{i-p-1}^i\right)\frac{w(i+1)}{w(0)+2\sum_{h=1}^{\alpha(i+2)}w(h)} \\ \vdots \\ -\varepsilon\frac{w((n-3)/2)}{w(0)+2\sum_{h=1}^{\alpha((n-1)/2)}w(h)}+\varepsilon p\frac{w((n-1)/2)}{w(0)+2\sum_{h=1}^{\alpha((n+1)/2)}w(h)} \\ -\varepsilon\frac{w((n-1)/2)}{w(0)+2\sum_{h=1}^{\alpha((n+1)/2)}w(h)} \\ 0 \\ \vdots \\ 0 \end{bmatrix}.$$

Then, calculate the matrix norm $||\Delta E_v||_2$ and vector norm $||\Delta U_v||$, extract parameter ε and apply Lemma 1; then, the parameter expressions in Equation (29) are obtained. □

Theorem 12. *If a raw data disturbance occurs in the non-boundary nodes of the first half of the original sequence, that is $\tilde{x}^{(0)}(k) = x^{(0)}(k) + \varepsilon$, then the difference between $\tilde{\tau}_v$ and τ_v satisfies expression (27); however, the values of parameters P_v and Q_v are determined by the following scenarios. Let parameters φ_1 and φ_2 be the same as those defined in Theorem 5, then P_v and Q_v are:*

(i). If sequence size n is even, then $k = 2, 3, \ldots, n/2$ and

$$P_v = \frac{1}{2}\sqrt{\left(\frac{w(|k-\varphi_1-1|)}{w(0)+2\sum_{h=1}^{a(\varphi_1+1)}w(h)}\right)^2 + \sum_{i=\varphi_1+1}^{n/2+\varphi_1-1}\left(\frac{w(|k-i-1|)}{w(0)+2\sum_{h=1}^{a(i+1)}w(h)} + \frac{w(|k-i|)}{w(0)+2\sum_{h=1}^{a(i)}w(h)}\right)^2 + \left(\frac{w(|k-n/2-\varphi_1|)}{w(0)+2\sum_{h=1}^{a(n/2+\varphi_1)}w(h)}\right)^2},$$

$$Q_v = \sqrt{\sum_{i=1}^{\varphi_1}\left(\sum_{j=\varphi_1+1}^{n/2+\varphi_1} C_{j-p-2}^{j-1}\frac{w(|k-j|)}{w(0)+2\sum_{h=1}^{a(j)}w(h)}\right)^2 + \sum_{i=\varphi_1+1}^{n/2+\varphi_1-1}\left(\sum_{j=i+1}^{n/2+\varphi_1} C_{j-p-2}^{j-1}\frac{w(|k-j|)}{w(0)+2\sum_{h=1}^{a(j)}w(h)} + \frac{w(|k-i|)}{w(0)+2\sum_{h=1}^{a(i)}w(h)}\right)^2} \qquad (30)$$
$$+ \left(\frac{w(|k-n/2-\varphi_1|)}{w(0)+2\sum_{h=1}^{a(n/2+\varphi_1)}w(h)}\right)^2.$$

(ii). If sequence size n is odd, then $k = 2, 3, \ldots, (n+1)/2$ and

$$P_v = \frac{1}{2}\sqrt{\left(\frac{w(|k-\varphi_1-1|)}{w(0)+2\sum_{h=1}^{a(\varphi_1+1)}w(h)}\right)^2 + \sum_{i=\varphi_1+1}^{(n+1)/2+\varphi_2-1}\left(\frac{w(|k-i-1|)}{w(0)+2\sum_{h=1}^{a(i+1)}w(h)} + \frac{w(|k-i|)}{w(0)+2\sum_{h=1}^{a(i)}w(h)}\right)^2 + \left(\frac{w(|k-(n+1)/2-\varphi_2|)}{w(0)+2\sum_{h=1}^{a((n+1)/2+\varphi_2)}w(h)}\right)^2},$$

$$Q_v = \sqrt{\sum_{i=1}^{\varphi_1}\left(\sum_{j=\varphi_1+1}^{(n+1)/2+\varphi_2} C_{j-p-2}^{j-1}\frac{w(|k-j|)}{w(0)+2\sum_{h=1}^{a(j)}w(h)}\right)^2 + \sum_{i=\varphi_1+1}^{(n+1)/2+\varphi_2-1}\left(\sum_{j=i+1}^{(n+1)/2+\varphi_2} C_{j-p-2}^{j-1}\frac{w(|k-j|)}{w(0)+2\sum_{h=1}^{a(j)}w(h)} + \frac{w(|k-i|)}{w(0)+2\sum_{h=1}^{a(i)}w(h)}\right)^2} \qquad (31)$$
$$+ \left(\frac{w(|k-(n+1)/2-\varphi_2|)}{w(0)+2\sum_{h=1}^{a((n+1)/2+\varphi_2)}w(h)}\right)^2.$$

Proof of Theorem 12. The proof is similar to that of Theorem 5, and we omit the details here. □

Theorem 13. *If a raw data disturbance occurs in the second half of the original sequence, excluding the last data, let φ_3 and φ_4 be the same as those defined in Theorem 6, then the difference between $\widetilde{\tau}_v$ and τ_v satisfies expression (27), where parameters P_v and Q_v are determined by:*
(i). *If sequence size n is even, then $k = n/2 + 1, n/2 + 2, \ldots, n - 1$ and*

$$P_v = \frac{1}{2}\sqrt{\left(\frac{w(|k+\varphi_4-n/2-1|)}{w(0)+2\sum_{h=1}^{a(n/2+1-\varphi_4)}w(h)}\right)^2 + \sum_{i=n/2+1-\varphi_4}^{n-\varphi_4-1}\left(\frac{w(|k-i-1|)}{w(0)+2\sum_{h=1}^{a(i+1)}w(h)} + \frac{w(|k-i|)}{w(0)+2\sum_{h=1}^{a(i)}w(h)}\right)^2 + \left(\frac{w(|k+\varphi_4-n|)}{w(0)+2\sum_{h=1}^{a(n-\varphi_4)}w(h)}\right)^2},$$

$$Q_v = \sqrt{\sum_{i=1}^{n/2-\varphi_4}\left(\sum_{j=n/2+1-\varphi_4}^{n-\varphi_4} C_{j-p-2}^{j-1}\frac{w(|k-j|)}{w(0)+2\sum_{h=1}^{a(j)}w(h)}\right)^2 + \sum_{i=n/2+1-\varphi_4}^{n-\varphi_4-1}\left(\sum_{j=i+1}^{n-\varphi_4} C_{j-p-2}^{j-1}\frac{w(|k-j|)}{w(0)+2\sum_{h=1}^{a(j)}w(h)} + \frac{w(|k-i|)}{w(0)+2\sum_{h=1}^{a(i)}w(h)}\right)^2} \qquad (32)$$
$$+ \left(\frac{w(|k+\varphi_4-n|)}{w(0)+2\sum_{h=1}^{a(n-\varphi_4)}w(h)}\right)^2.$$

(ii). *If sequence size n is odd, then $k = (n+1)/2 + 1, (n+1)/2 + 2, \ldots, n - 1$ and*

$$P_v = \frac{1}{2}\sqrt{\left(\frac{w(|k+\varphi_3-(n+1)/2|)}{w(0)+2\sum_{h=1}^{a((n+1)/2-\varphi_3)}w(h)}\right)^2 + \sum_{i=(n+1)/2-\varphi_3}^{n-\varphi_4-1}\left(\frac{w(|k-i-1|)}{w(0)+2\sum_{h=1}^{a(i+1)}w(h)} + \frac{w(|k-i|)}{w(0)+2\sum_{h=1}^{a(i)}w(h)}\right)^2 + \left(\frac{w(|k+\varphi_4-n|)}{w(0)+2\sum_{h=1}^{a(n-\varphi_4)}w(h)}\right)^2},$$

$$Q_v = \sqrt{\sum_{i=1}^{(n-1)/2-\varphi_3}\left(\sum_{j=(n+1)/2-\varphi_3}^{n-\varphi_4} C_{j-p-2}^{j-1}\frac{w(|k-j|)}{w(0)+2\sum_{h=1}^{a(j)}w(h)}\right)^2 + \sum_{i=(n+1)/2-\varphi_3}^{n-\varphi_4-1}\left(\sum_{j=i+1}^{n-\varphi_4} C_{j-p-2}^{j-1}\frac{w(|k-j|)}{w(0)+2\sum_{h=1}^{a(j)}w(h)} + \frac{w(|k-i|)}{w(0)+2\sum_{h=1}^{a(i)}w(h)}\right)^2}$$
$$+ \left(\frac{w(|k+\varphi_4-n|)}{w(0)+2\sum_{h=1}^{a(n-\varphi_4)}w(h)}\right)^2. \qquad (33)$$

Proof of Theorem 13. The proof is similar to that of Theorem 6, and we omit the details here. □

Theorem 14. *If a disturbance occurs in the last data of the original sequence: $\widetilde{x}^{(0)}(n) = x^{(0)}(n) + \varepsilon$, then the difference between $\widetilde{\tau}_v$ and τ_v satisfies expression (27) with the following values of parameters P_v and Q_v:*

(i). If sequence size n is even, then

$$P_v = \frac{1}{2}\sqrt{\left(\frac{w(n/2-1)}{w(0)+2\sum_{h=1}^{a(n/2+1)}w(h)}\right)^2 + \sum_{i=n/2+1}^{n-1}\left(\frac{w(n-i-1)}{w(0)+2\sum_{h=1}^{a(i+1)}w(h)} + \frac{w(n-i)}{w(0)+2\sum_{h=1}^{a(i)}w(h)}\right)^2},$$

$$Q_v = \sqrt{\sum_{i=1}^{n/2}\left(\sum_{j=n/2+1}^{n}C_{j-p-2}^{j-1}\frac{w(n-j)}{w(0)+2\sum_{h=1}^{a(j)}w(h)}\right)^2 + \sum_{i=n/2+1}^{n-1}\left(\frac{w(n-i)}{w(0)+2\sum_{h=1}^{a(i)}w(h)} + \sum_{j=i+1}^{n}C_{j-p-2}^{j-1}\frac{w(n-j)}{w(0)+2\sum_{h=1}^{a(j)}w(h)}\right)^2}.$$

(34)

(ii). If sequence size n is odd, then

$$P_v = \frac{1}{2}\sqrt{\left(\frac{w((n-1)/2)}{w(0)+2\sum_{h=1}^{a((n+1)/2)}w(h)}\right)^2 + \sum_{i=(n+1)/2}^{n-1}\left(\frac{w(n-i-1)}{w(0)+2\sum_{h=1}^{a(i+1)}w(h)} + \frac{w(n-i)}{w(0)+2\sum_{h=1}^{a(i)}w(h)}\right)^2},$$

$$Q_v = \sqrt{\sum_{i=1}^{(n-1)/2}\left(\sum_{j=(n+1)/2}^{n}C_{j-p-2}^{j-1}\frac{w(n-j)}{w(0)+2\sum_{h=1}^{a(j)}w(h)}\right)^2 + \sum_{i=(n+1)/2}^{n-1}\left(\frac{w(n-i)}{w(0)+2\sum_{h=1}^{a(i)}w(h)} + \sum_{j=i+1}^{n}C_{j-p-2}^{j-1}\frac{w(n-j)}{w(0)+2\sum_{h=1}^{a(j)}w(h)}\right)^2}.$$

(35)

Proof of Theorem 14. The proof is similar to that of Theorem 7, and we omit the details here. □

5. Numerical Performance of Operator D_v in Improving Model Stability

5.1. Numerical Study on Model $DGM^p(1,1)$

To evaluate the effect of the fractional-order bidirectional weakening buffer operator D_v in improving the stability of model $DGM^p(1,1)$, we consider a real case presented in [22]. This example predicts the annual cargo turnover in Jiangsu, a large coastal province in China. The original data are shown in Table 1, and the forecasting values of four compared models are presented in Table 2.

Table 1. The original data of the annual cargo turnover used in [22]. (Unit: 100 million ton-km).

	Modeling Period					Forecasting Period
	2003	2004	2005	2006	2007	2008	2009
Freight Ton-Kilometers	1817.44	2398.13	3068.3	3644.14	4098.42	4707.5	5154.46

Table 2. The forecasting results of four different models.

	$DGM^{1/2}(1,1)$	$D_v+DGM^{1/2}(1,1)$	$DGM^{2/3}(1,1)$	$D_v+DGM^{2/3}(1,1)$
Freight Ton-Kilometers (2009)	5236.45 *	5238.69	5303.33 *	5305.58
MAPE (%)	1.59 *	1.63	2.89 *	2.93

* values obtained from [22].

Table 2 reveals that the forecasting results of the $DGM^p(1,1)$ model with data preprocessing based on D_v ($v = 0.02$) are small, which means the validity of the predicted values is maintained.

Then, data noise interferences with different noise amplitudes (ranging from -10% to 10% of the original value) are studied. The effectiveness of operator D_v on the prediction model is evaluated from two aspects: model stability and model accuracy. The model stability is measured by the perturbation bounds of the model parameter values with and without noise interference. Based on the theorems in Section 3, the perturbation bounds of the prediction models are calculated and summarized in Table 3. The model accuracy is measured by the variations in the predicted values (VP). Let $y_0(i)$ $(i = 1, \ldots n)$ be the predicted value based on the original modeling data without noise interference and $y_1(i)$ $(i = 1, \ldots n)$ be the predicted value with data noise. We define $VP = (\sum_{i=1}^{n}|y_1(i) - y_0(i)|)/n$ and $\Delta VP = VP(DGM^p(1,1)) - VP(D_v + DGM^p(1,1))$. If ΔVP falls into the positive domain, it means D_v improves the stability of the model $DGM^p(1,1)$. The results are shown in Table 4.

Table 3. The perturbation bounds of four models in different noise scenarios.

Noise Position	Model Index *	Noise Amplitude									
		−10%	−8%	−6%	−4%	−2%	2%	4%	6%	8%	10%
2003	A	90.3	72.5	54.6	36.5	18.3	18.5	37.1	55.8	74.7	93.7
	B	87.2	70.1	52.7	35.3	17.7	17.8	35.8	54.0	72.2	90.6
2004	A	110.7	90.2	68.9	46.8	23.8	24.7	50.2	76.5	103.7	131.8
	B	109.3	89.0	67.8	46.0	23.4	24.1	49.0	74.6	100.9	128.1
2005	A	128.5	104.5	79.7	54.0	27.4	28.2	57.2	87.0	117.5	148.7
	B	127.0	103.0	78.3	52.9	26.8	27.5	55.6	84.3	113.6	143.6
2006	A	113.6	92.9	71.1	48.4	24.6	25.5	51.8	78.9	106.7	135.1
	B	112.3	91.4	69.7	47.2	24.0	24.6	49.9	75.7	102.2	129.1
2007	A	26.9	25.1	21.4	15.9	8.8	10.3	22.1	35.2	49.7	65.4
	B	33.5	29.9	24.6	17.9	9.6	10.9	23.1	36.5	51.0	66.6
2008	A	198.0	158.4	118.8	79.2	39.6	39.6	79.2	118.8	158.4	198.0
	B	195.3	156.2	117.2	78.1	39.0	39.0	78.1	117.1	156.1	195.2
2003	C	68.0	54.5	41.0	27.4	13.8	13.8	27.7	41.7	55.8	70.0
	D	64.8	52.0	39.1	26.2	13.1	13.2	26.5	39.8	53.2	66.7
2004	C	115.8	93.8	71.2	48.0	24.3	24.8	50.2	76.2	102.7	129.8
	D	113.8	92.0	69.8	47.0	23.8	24.3	49.0	74.3	100.0	126.2
2005	C	131.8	106.5	80.6	54.2	27.3	27.8	56.1	84.8	113.9	143.4
	D	129.7	104.5	79.0	53.1	26.7	27.1	54.6	82.4	110.6	139.1
2006	C	110.8	89.8	68.2	46.0	23.3	23.8	48.0	72.7	97.9	123.5
	D	108.8	87.9	66.6	44.8	22.6	23.0	46.4	70.2	94.2	118.7
2007	C	21.8	19.7	16.4	12.0	6.5	7.5	16.0	25.5	35.8	47.0
	D	27.4	23.9	19.3	13.8	7.4	8.2	17.3	27.2	37.8	49.2
2008	C	175.3	140.2	105.2	70.1	35.1	35.1	70.1	105.2	140.2	175.3
	D	173.0	138.4	103.8	69.2	34.6	34.6	69.2	103.7	138.3	172.9

* Model index: A—$DGM^{1/2}(1,1)$; B—$D_v + DGM^{1/2}(1,1)$; C—$DGM^{2/3}(1,1)$; D—$D_v + DGM^{2/3}(1,1)$.

Table 4. The ΔVP values of $DGM^p(1,1)$ in different noise scenarios.

Model Parameter	Noise Position	Noise Amplitude									
		−10%	−8%	−6%	−4%	−2%	2%	4%	6%	8%	10%
$p = 0.5$	2003	2.6628	2.1243	1.5884	1.0552	0.5247	0.5285	1.0513	1.5715	2.0892	2.6044
	2004	1.7216	1.5510	1.2953	0.9532	0.5230	0.6081	1.3126	2.1123	3.0087	4.0037
	2005	0.7736	0.9582	0.9699	0.8125	0.4891	0.6420	1.4430	2.3964	3.4982	4.7444
	2006	0.2291	0.6812	0.8729	0.8164	0.5230	0.7329	1.6756	2.8156	4.1435	5.6502
	2007	12.633	9.5106	6.7037	4.1937	1.9632	1.7191	3.1968	4.4470	5.4795	6.3032
	2008	−3.4280	−2.7186	−2.0199	−1.3334	−0.6607	−0.6377	−1.2610	−1.8653	−2.4499	−3.0140
$p = 2/3$	2003	2.8174	2.2531	1.6890	1.1250	0.5612	0.5660	1.1295	1.6928	2.2561	2.8194
	2004	2.7897	2.3443	1.8434	1.2866	0.6732	0.7262	1.5134	2.3598	3.2661	4.2327
	2005	1.5322	1.4354	1.2316	0.9234	0.5129	0.6054	1.3085	2.1042	2.9900	3.9635
	2006	0.6858	0.8631	0.8772	0.7345	0.4410	0.5755	1.2875	2.1284	3.0930	4.1764
	2007	12.560	9.6861	6.9995	4.4937	2.1617	2.0047	3.8503	5.5440	7.0902	8.4931
	2008	−4.5834	−3.6746	−2.7613	−1.8443	−0.9244	−0.9208	−1.8446	−2.7685	−3.6919	−4.6142

Table 3 shows that the $DGM^p(1,1)$ models with the fractional-order bidirectional weakening buffer operator D_v have smaller perturbation bounds in almost all the noise scenarios except for when the data noise occurred in 2007. The results indicate that the data preprocessing method based on the fractional-order bidirectional weakening buffer operator improves the stability of the $DGM^p(1,1)$ models. Table 4 shows that operator D_v improves the accuracy of prediction performance in most noise samples, except for the noises in the last modeling time point (in 2008). The variations in the predicted values increase with increasing noise amplitudes; however, the data preprocessing based on D_v effectively reduced the noise effect on the prediction results. Though D_v fails when the noise occurs in the last modeling time point, the data interference occurring in other time points is well controlled.

5.2. Numerical Study on Model $NIGM(p,1)$

We now consider the effect of operator $D_v(v = 0.06)$ in improving the stability of the model $NIGM(p, 1)$ in forecasting the annual electricity consumption in Russia [23]. The forecasting results of the four compared models without any data noise interference are shown in Table 5. It is clear that operator D_v improves the short-term (2004–2005) forecasting of $NIGM(p, 1)$. Though its long-term (2006–2007) prediction performance is worse than those from $NIGM(p, 1)$, its prediction accuracy is still acceptable and higher than the other two models ($DGM(1, 1)$ and $GM(0.98, 1)$).

Table 5. The forecasting results of $NIGM(p, 1)$ models with and without operator D_v.

	Modeling Period				Forecasting Period		
	2000	2001	2002	2003	2004	2005	2006	2007
Actual value	52333	53151	53168	54372	55516	55898	58600	60281
$DGM(1,1)$ *	52333	52953	53561	54176	54798	55428	56065	56709
$GM(0.98,1)$ *	52333	53704	54858	55849	56704	57445	58087	58645
$NIGM(0.997,1)$ *	52333	52627	53051	53666	54559	55855	57736	60464
$D_v + NIGM(0.997,1)$	52333	52701	53193	53854	54742	55934	57534	59684

* values obtained from [23].

Table 6 shows the perturbation bounds of the $NIGM(p, 1)$ models with and without operator D_v in different noise scenarios. It is clear that the operator D_v results in smaller perturbation values in all noise scenarios and thereby improves the stability of the $NIGM(p, 1)$ model in this numerical study. When applying the indicator VP defined in Section 5.1, the difference between $NIGM(p, 1)$ with and without D_v can be expressed by $\Delta VP = VP(NIGM(p, 1)) - VP(D_v + NIGM(p, 1))$. Table 7 shows the ΔVP results in different noise amplitude scenarios. We can see that when a data disturbance occurs in the early modeling period (2000 or 2001 in this case), operator D_v improves the accuracy of the prediction results in all thirty noise amplitude conditions. When noise occurs in the later modeling time point in 2002 (or 2003), the prediction without D_v outperforms that of with D_v in only four (or five) out of thirty noise perturbations. These confirm the effectiveness of operator D_v in improving the stability of the prediction model $NIGM(p, 1)$.

Table 6. The perturbation bounds of two models in different noise scenarios.

Noise Position	Model Index *	Noise Amplitude (%)													
		−0.03	−0.028	−0.026	−0.024	−0.022	−0.020	−0.018	−0.016	−0.014	−0.012	−0.010	−0.008	−0.006	−0.004	−0.002
2000	E	1183	1104	1026	947	869	790	711	633	554	475	396	317	238	159	79
	F	962	898	834	771	707	643	579	515	450	386	322	258	193	129	65
2001	E	680	635	591	546	501	456	411	366	320	275	229	184	138	92	46
	F	640	598	555	513	471	428	386	343	301	258	215	172	129	86	43
2002	E	1424	1328	1232	1136	1041	945	850	755	660	565	471	376	282	188	94
	F	1076	1003	931	859	787	715	643	571	499	428	356	285	214	142	71
2003	E	923	861	799	737	675	613	552	490	428	367	306	244	183	122	61
	F	757	706	655	604	554	503	452	402	351	301	251	201	150	100	50
		0.002	0.004	0.006	0.008	0.010	0.012	0.014	0.016	0.018	0.020	0.022	0.024	0.026	0.028	0.030
2000	E	79	159	238	318	397	477	557	637	716	796	876	956	1037	1117	1197
	F	65	129	194	259	323	388	453	518	583	648	713	778	844	909	974
2001	E	46	93	139	186	232	279	326	373	420	468	515	563	610	658	706
	F	43	87	130	174	217	261	304	348	392	436	480	524	568	613	657
2002	E	94	187	280	374	467	559	652	744	837	929	1021	1113	1204	1296	1387
	F	71	142	213	283	354	424	495	565	635	706	776	846	915	985	1055
2003	E	61	122	183	243	304	364	425	485	546	606	666	726	786	846	906
	F	50	100	150	200	249	299	349	398	448	497	547	596	645	694	744

* Model index: E—$NIGM(p,1)$; F—$D_v + NIGM(p,1)$.

Table 7. The ΔVP values of $NIGM(p,1)$ in different noise scenarios.

Noise Position	Noise Amplitude (%)													
	−0.03	−0.028	−0.026	−0.024	−0.022	−0.020	−0.018	−0.016	−0.014	−0.012	−0.010	−0.008	−0.006	−0.004	−0.002
2000	26.90	36.95	46.95	56.91	66.82	76.69	86.51	96.28	106.00	115.66	125.28	134.84	144.35	153.80	163.20
2001	162.80	163.51	164.21	164.91	165.59	166.27	166.94	167.60	168.25	168.89	169.52	170.14	170.75	171.35	171.95
2002	143.20	144.05	145.33	148.15	150.84	153.40	155.83	158.14	160.33	162.40	164.36	166.21	167.94	169.58	171.10
2003	−85.52	−68.22	−50.94	−33.66	−16.40	0.85	18.09	35.31	52.52	69.71	86.89	104.05	121.19	138.32	155.44
	0.002	0.004	0.006	0.008	0.010	0.012	0.014	0.016	0.018	0.020	0.022	0.024	0.026	0.028	0.030
2000	170.73	168.87	166.94	164.95	162.89	160.77	158.57	156.31	153.98	151.58	149.10	146.55	143.93	141.23	138.45
2001	162.74	152.94	143.13	133.30	123.47	113.62	103.76	93.89	84.01	74.12	64.21	54.29	44.37	34.42	24.47
2002	158.24	143.88	129.45	114.96	100.40	85.78	71.10	56.37	41.58	26.74	11.86	−3.07	−18.04	−33.06	−43.95
2003	172.27	171.98	171.66	171.31	170.94	170.53	170.10	169.64	169.15	168.63	168.08	167.50	166.89	166.24	165.57

The numerical cases in this section demonstrate that the fractional-order bidirectional weakening buffer operator D_v reduces the one-sided reaction to sample disturbances, and on the other hand, it can effectively improve the stability of time series prediction models by taking into account both the old and new information.

6. Conclusions

The performance of sequence operators in the stability of operator-based time series models has a direct impact on the validity of the model findings. Without a specific requirement for a particular part of the information in a series object, all data elements in this series should be treated equally. However, some widely used fractional-order weakening buffer operators are too subjectively biased in dealing with samples and sample disturbances. In contrast, the fractional-order bidirectional weakening buffer operator D_v presents a more objective approach to data processing. Both theoretical investigations and numerical experiments, based on real cases, show the favorable effects of operator D_v. This study reveals that the proposed fractional-order weakening buffer operator-based data preprocessing method reduces the perturbation bounds of models in data noise scenarios, thereby improving the stability and prediction accuracy of time series models. Other features of the various fractional-order operators and their effects in time series models are worth further studies.

Author Contributions: Conceptualization, C.L. and Y.Y.; methodology, C.L. and Y.Y.; formal analysis, C.L.; data curation, C.L. and X.Z.;writing—original draft preparation, C.L.; writing—review and editing, Y.Y.; supervision, Y.Y. and X.Z.; funding acquisition, C.L. and X.Z. All authors have read and agreed to the published version of the manuscript.

Funding: This research was funded by the National Key Research and Development Program of China (GrantNo. 2021YFB2601704), the Science and Technology Project of Sichuan Province (GrantNo. 2021YFS0319) and the Fundamental Research Funds for the Central Universitiesof China (GrantNo.ZHMH2022–008, J2022–062 and J2023–049).

Data Availability Statement: Not applicable.

Conflicts of Interest: The authors declare no conflict of interest.

Appendix A

Appendix A.1. Proof of Theorem 5

Proof. (i). Sequence size n is even and $k = 2, 3, \ldots, n/2$. According to the proposed fractional-order operator D_v, the sequences with and without disturbance applied to $DGM^p(1,1)$ satisfy

$$\tilde{x}_v(i) = \begin{cases} x_v(i), & \text{when } 1 \leq i \leq \varphi_1 \text{ or } n/2 + \varphi_1 < i \leq n \\ x_v(i) + \dfrac{\varepsilon w(|i-k|)}{\left(w(0) + 2\sum_{j=1}^{A(i)} w(j)\right)}, & \text{when } \varphi_1 < i \leq n/2 + \varphi_1 \end{cases} \quad (A1)$$

Then, we can obtain

$$\Delta B_v = \begin{bmatrix} 0 & 0 \\ \vdots & \vdots \\ 0 & 0 \\ 0 & 0 \\ 0 & \dfrac{w(|k-\varphi_1-1|)\varepsilon}{w(0)+2\sum\limits_{h=1}^{\alpha(\varphi_1+1)}w(h)} \\ 0 & C_p^1\dfrac{w(|k-\varphi_1-1|)\varepsilon}{w(0)+2\sum\limits_{h=1}^{\alpha(\varphi_1+1)}w(h)} + \dfrac{w(|k-\varphi_1-2|)\varepsilon}{w(0)+2\sum\limits_{h=1}^{\alpha(\varphi_1+2)}w(h)} \\ \vdots & \vdots \\ 0 & C_{p+n/2-2}^{n/2-1}\dfrac{w(|k-\varphi_1-1|)\varepsilon}{w(0)+2\sum\limits_{h=1}^{\alpha(\varphi_1+1)}w(h)} + C_{p+n/2-3}^{n/2-2}\dfrac{w(|k-\varphi_1-2|)\varepsilon}{w(0)+2\sum\limits_{h=1}^{\alpha(\varphi_1+2)}w(h)} + \cdots \dfrac{w(|k-\varphi_1-n/2|)\varepsilon}{w(0)+2\sum\limits_{h=1}^{\alpha(n/2+\varphi_1)}w(h)} \\ 0 & C_{p+n/2-1}^{n/2}\dfrac{w(|k-\varphi_1-1|)\varepsilon}{w(0)+2\sum\limits_{h=1}^{\alpha(\varphi_1+1)}w(h)} + C_{p+n/2-2}^{n/2-1}\dfrac{w(|k-\varphi_1-2|)\varepsilon}{w(0)+2\sum\limits_{h=1}^{\alpha(\varphi_1+2)}w(h)} + \cdots C_p^1\dfrac{w(|k-\varphi_1-n/2|)\varepsilon}{w(0)+2\sum\limits_{h=1}^{\alpha(n/2+\varphi_1)}w(h)} \\ \vdots & \vdots \\ 0 & C_{p+n-\varphi_1-3}^{n-\varphi_1-2}\dfrac{w(|k-\varphi_1-1|)\varepsilon}{w(0)+2\sum\limits_{h=1}^{\alpha(\varphi_1+1)}w(h)} + C_{p+n-\varphi_1-4}^{n-\varphi_1-3}\dfrac{w(|k-\varphi_1-2|)\varepsilon}{w(0)+2\sum\limits_{h=1}^{\alpha(\varphi_1+2)}w(h)} + \cdots C_{p+n/2-\varphi_1-2}^{n/2-\varphi_1-1}\dfrac{w(|k-\varphi_1-n/2|)\varepsilon}{w(0)+2\sum\limits_{h=1}^{\alpha(n/2+\varphi_1)}w(h)} \end{bmatrix},$$

$$\Delta Y_v = \begin{bmatrix} 0 \\ \vdots \\ 0 \\ \dfrac{w(|k-\varphi_1-1|)\varepsilon}{w(0)+2\sum\limits_{h=1}^{\alpha(\varphi_1+1)}w(h)} \\ C_p^1\dfrac{w(|k-\varphi_1-1|)\varepsilon}{w(0)+2\sum\limits_{h=1}^{\alpha(\varphi_1+1)}w(h)} + \dfrac{w(|k-\varphi_1-2|)\varepsilon}{w(0)+2\sum\limits_{h=1}^{\alpha(\varphi_1+2)}w(h)} \\ \vdots \\ C_{p+n/2-2}^{n/2-1}\dfrac{w(|k-\varphi_1-1|)\varepsilon}{w(0)+2\sum\limits_{h=1}^{\alpha(\varphi_1+1)}w(h)} + C_{p+n/2-3}^{n/2-2}\dfrac{w(|k-\varphi_1-2|)\varepsilon}{w(0)+2\sum\limits_{h=1}^{\alpha(\varphi_1+2)}w(h)} + \cdots \dfrac{w(|k-\varphi_1-n/2|)\varepsilon}{w(0)+2\sum\limits_{h=1}^{\alpha(n/2+\varphi_1)}w(h)} \\ C_{p+n/2-1}^{n/2}\dfrac{w(|k-\varphi_1-1|)\varepsilon}{w(0)+2\sum\limits_{h=1}^{\alpha(\varphi_1+1)}w(h)} + C_{p+n/2-2}^{n/2-1}\dfrac{w(|k-\varphi_1-2|)\varepsilon}{w(0)+2\sum\limits_{h=1}^{\alpha(\varphi_1+2)}w(h)} + \cdots C_p^1\dfrac{w(|k-\varphi_1-n/2|)\varepsilon}{w(0)+2\sum\limits_{h=1}^{\alpha(n/2+\varphi_1)}w(h)} \\ \vdots \\ C_{p+n-\varphi_1-2}^{n-\varphi_1-1}\dfrac{w(|k-\varphi_1-1|)\varepsilon}{w(0)+2\sum\limits_{h=1}^{\alpha(\varphi_1+1)}w(h)} + C_{p+n-\varphi_1-3}^{n-\varphi_1-2}\dfrac{w(|k-\varphi_1-2|)\varepsilon}{w(0)+2\sum\limits_{h=1}^{\alpha(\varphi_1+2)}w(h)} + \cdots C_{p+n/2-\varphi_1-1}^{n/2-\varphi_1}\dfrac{w(|k-\varphi_1-n/2|)\varepsilon}{w(0)+2\sum\limits_{h=1}^{\alpha(n/2+\varphi_1)}w(h)} \end{bmatrix}.$$

Then, calculate the matrix norm $||\Delta B_v||_2$ and vector norm $||\Delta Y_v||$, extract parameter ε and apply Lemma 1; then, the parameter expressions in Equation (15) are obtained.

(ii). Sequence size n is odd and $k = 2, 3, \ldots, (n+1)/2$. According to the fractional-order bidirectional weakening buffer operator D_v, the sequences with and without disturbance applied to $DGM^p(1,1)$ satisfy

$$\widetilde{x}_v(i) = \begin{cases} x_v(i), & \text{when } 1 \leq i \leq \varphi_1 \text{ or } (n+1)/2 + \varphi_2 < i \leq n \\ x_v(i) + \dfrac{\varepsilon w(|i-k|)}{\left(w(0)+2\sum_{j=1}^{\alpha(i)}w(j)\right)}, & \text{when } \varphi_1 < i \leq (n+1)/2 + \varphi_2 \end{cases} \quad (A2)$$

Then, we can obtain

$$\Delta B_v = \begin{bmatrix} 0 & 0 \\ \vdots & \vdots \\ 0 & 0 \\ 0 & \frac{w(|k-\varphi_1-1|)\varepsilon}{w(0)+2\sum_{h=1}^{\alpha(\varphi_1+1)}w(h)} \\ 0 & C_p^1 \frac{w(|k-\varphi_1-1|)\varepsilon}{w(0)+2\sum_{h=1}^{\alpha(\varphi_1+1)}w(h)} + \frac{w(|k-\varphi_1-2|)\varepsilon}{w(0)+2\sum_{h=1}^{\alpha(\varphi_1+2)}w(h)} \\ \vdots & \vdots \\ 0 & C_{p+(n+1)/2+\varphi_2-\varphi_1-2}^{(n+1)/2+\varphi_2-\varphi_1-1} \frac{w(|k-\varphi_1-1|)\varepsilon}{w(0)+2\sum_{h=1}^{\alpha(\varphi_1+1)}w(h)} + C_{p+(n+1)/2+\varphi_2-\varphi_1-3}^{(n+1)/2+\varphi_2-\varphi_1-2} \frac{w(|k-\varphi_1-2|)\varepsilon}{w(0)+2\sum_{h=1}^{\alpha(\varphi_1+2)}w(h)} + \cdots \frac{w(|k-\varphi_2-(n+1)/2|)\varepsilon}{w(0)+2\sum_{h=1}^{\alpha((n+1)/2+\varphi_2)}w(h)} \\ 0 & C_{p+(n+1)/2+\varphi_2-\varphi_1-1}^{(n+1)/2+\varphi_2-\varphi_1} \frac{w(|k-\varphi_1-1|)\varepsilon}{w(0)+2\sum_{h=1}^{\alpha(\varphi_1+1)}w(h)} + C_{p+(n+1)/2+\varphi_2-\varphi_1-2}^{(n+1)/2+\varphi_2-\varphi_1-1} \frac{w(|k-\varphi_1-2|)\varepsilon}{w(0)+2\sum_{h=1}^{\alpha(\varphi_1+2)}w(h)} + \cdots C_p^1 \frac{w(|k-\varphi_2-(n+1)/2|)\varepsilon}{w(0)+2\sum_{h=1}^{\alpha((n+1)/2+\varphi_2)}w(h)} \\ \vdots & \vdots \\ 0 & C_{p+n-\varphi_1-3}^{n-\varphi_1-2} \frac{w(|k-\varphi_1-1|)\varepsilon}{w(0)+2\sum_{h=1}^{\alpha(\varphi_1+1)}w(h)} + C_{p+n-\varphi_1-4}^{n-\varphi_1-3} \frac{w(|k-\varphi_1-2|)\varepsilon}{w(0)+2\sum_{h=1}^{\alpha(\varphi_1+2)}w(h)} + \cdots C_{p+(n-1)/2-\varphi_2-2}^{(n-1)/2-\varphi_2-1} \frac{w(|k-\varphi_2-(n+1)/2|)\varepsilon}{w(0)+2\sum_{h=1}^{\alpha((n+1)/2+\varphi_2)}w(h)} \end{bmatrix},$$

$$\Delta Y_v = \begin{bmatrix} 0 \\ \vdots \\ 0 \\ \frac{w(|k-\varphi_1-1|)\varepsilon}{w(0)+2\sum_{h=1}^{\alpha(\varphi_1+1)}w(h)} \\ C_p^1 \frac{w(|k-\varphi_1-1|)\varepsilon}{w(0)+2\sum_{h=1}^{\alpha(\varphi_1+1)}w(h)} + \frac{w(|k-\varphi_1-2|)\varepsilon}{w(0)+2\sum_{h=1}^{\alpha(\varphi_1+2)}w(h)} \\ \vdots \\ C_{p+(n+1)/2+\varphi_2-\varphi_1-2}^{(n+1)/2+\varphi_2-\varphi_1-1} \frac{w(|k-\varphi_1-1|)\varepsilon}{w(0)+2\sum_{h=1}^{\alpha(\varphi_1+1)}w(h)} + C_{p+(n+1)/2+\varphi_2-\varphi_1-3}^{(n+1)/2+\varphi_2-\varphi_1-2} \frac{w(|k-\varphi_1-2|)\varepsilon}{w(0)+2\sum_{h=1}^{\alpha(\varphi_1+2)}w(h)} + \cdots \frac{w(|k-\varphi_2-(n+1)/2|)\varepsilon}{w(0)+2\sum_{h=1}^{\alpha((n+1)/2+\varphi_2)}w(h)} \\ C_{p+(n+1)/2+\varphi_2-\varphi_1-1}^{(n+1)/2+\varphi_2-\varphi_1} \frac{w(|k-\varphi_1-1|)\varepsilon}{w(0)+2\sum_{h=1}^{\alpha(\varphi_1+1)}w(h)} + C_{p+(n+1)/2+\varphi_2-\varphi_1-2}^{(n+1)/2+\varphi_2-\varphi_1-1} \frac{w(|k-\varphi_1-2|)\varepsilon}{w(0)+2\sum_{h=1}^{\alpha(\varphi_1+2)}w(h)} + \cdots C_p^1 \frac{w(|k-\varphi_2-(n+1)/2|)\varepsilon}{w(0)+2\sum_{h=1}^{\alpha((n+1)/2+\varphi_2)}w(h)} \\ \vdots \\ C_{p+n-\varphi_1-2}^{n-\varphi_1-1} \frac{w(|k-\varphi_1-1|)\varepsilon}{w(0)+2\sum_{h=1}^{\alpha(\varphi_1+1)}w(h)} + C_{p+n-\varphi_1-3}^{n-\varphi_1-2} \frac{w(|k-\varphi_1-2|)\varepsilon}{w(0)+2\sum_{h=1}^{\alpha(\varphi_1+2)}w(h)} + \cdots C_{p+(n-1)/2-\varphi_2-1}^{(n-1)/2-\varphi_2} \frac{w(|k-\varphi_2-(n+1)/2|)\varepsilon}{w(0)+2\sum_{h=1}^{\alpha((n+1)/2+\varphi_2)}w(h)} \end{bmatrix}.$$

Then, calculate the matrix norm $||\Delta B_v||_2$ and vector norm $||\Delta Y_v||$, extract parameter ε and apply Lemma 1; then the parameter expressions in Equation (16) are obtained.

The proof of Theorem 5 is now complete. □

Appendix A.2. Proof of Theorem 6

Proof. (i). Sequence size n is even and $k = n/2 + 1, n/2 + 2, \ldots, n - 1$. According to the fractional-order bidirectional weakening buffer operator D_v, the sequences with and without disturbance applied to $DGM^p(1,1)$ satisfy

$$\widetilde{x}_v(i) = \begin{cases} x_v(i), & \text{when } 1 \leq i < n/2 + 1 - \varphi_4 \text{ or } n + 1 - \varphi_4 \leq i \leq n \\ x_v(i) + \frac{\varepsilon w(|i-k|)}{\left(w(0)+2\sum_{j=1}^{\alpha(i)}w(j)\right)}, & \text{when } n/2 + 1 - \varphi_4 \leq i < n + 1 - \varphi_4 \end{cases} \quad \text{(A3)}$$

Then, we can obtain

$$\Delta B_v = \begin{bmatrix} 0 & & & & & 0 \\ \vdots & & & & & \vdots \\ 0 & & & & & 0 \\ 0 & & & & & \frac{w(|k+\varphi_4-n/2-1|)\varepsilon}{\alpha(n/2+1-\varphi_4)\left(w(0)+2\sum_{h=1}w(h)\right)} \\ 0 & & C_p^1\frac{w(|k+\varphi_4-n/2-1|)\varepsilon}{\alpha(n/2+1-\varphi_4)\left(w(0)+2\sum_{h=1}w(h)\right)} + \frac{w(|k+\varphi_4-n/2-2|)\varepsilon}{\alpha(n/2+2-\varphi_4)\left(w(0)+2\sum_{h=1}w(h)\right)} \\ \vdots & & & & & \vdots \\ 0 & C_{p+n/2-2}^{n/2-1}\frac{w(|k+\varphi_4-n/2-1|)\varepsilon}{\alpha(n/2+1-\varphi_4)\left(w(0)+2\sum w(h)\right)} + C_{p+n/2-3}^{n/2-2}\frac{w(|k+\varphi_4-n/2-2|)\varepsilon}{\alpha(n/2+2-\varphi_4)\left(w(0)+2\sum w(h)\right)} + \cdots & \frac{w(|k+\varphi_4-n|)\varepsilon}{\alpha(n-\varphi_4)\left(w(0)+2\sum w(h)\right)} \\ 0 & C_{p+n/2-1}^{n/2}\frac{w(|k+\varphi_4-n/2-1|)\varepsilon}{\alpha(n/2+1-\varphi_4)\left(w(0)+2\sum w(h)\right)} + C_{p+n/2-2}^{n/2-1}\frac{w(|k+\varphi_4-n/2-2|)\varepsilon}{\alpha(n/2+2-\varphi_4)\left(w(0)+2\sum w(h)\right)} + \cdots C_p^1 \frac{w(|k+\varphi_4-n|)\varepsilon}{\alpha(n-\varphi_4)\left(w(0)+2\sum w(h)\right)} \\ \vdots & & & & & \vdots \\ 0 & C_{p+n/2+\varphi_4-3}^{n/2+\varphi_4-2}\frac{w(|k+\varphi_4-n/2-1|)\varepsilon}{\alpha(n/2+1-\varphi_4)\left(w(0)+2\sum w(h)\right)} + C_{p+n/2+\varphi_4-4}^{n/2+\varphi_4-3}\frac{w(|k+\varphi_4-n/2-2|)\varepsilon}{\alpha(n/2+2-\varphi_4)\left(w(0)+2\sum w(h)\right)} + \cdots C_{p+\varphi_4-2}^{\varphi_4-1} \frac{w(|k+\varphi_4-n|)\varepsilon}{\alpha(n-\varphi_4)\left(w(0)+2\sum w(h)\right)} \end{bmatrix},$$

$$\Delta Y_v = \begin{bmatrix} 0 \\ \vdots \\ 0 \\ \frac{w(|k+\varphi_4-n/2-1|)\varepsilon}{\alpha(n/2+1-\varphi_4)\left(w(0)+2\sum_{h=1}w(h)\right)} \\ C_p^1\frac{w(|k+\varphi_4-n/2-1|)\varepsilon}{\alpha(n/2+1-\varphi_4)\left(w(0)+2\sum w(h)\right)} + \frac{w(|k+\varphi_4-n/2-2|)\varepsilon}{\alpha(n/2+2-\varphi_4)\left(w(0)+2\sum w(h)\right)} \\ \vdots \\ C_{p+n/2-2}^{n/2-1}\frac{w(|k+\varphi_4-n/2-1|)\varepsilon}{\alpha(n/2+1-\varphi_4)\left(w(0)+2\sum w(h)\right)} + C_{p+n/2-3}^{n/2-2}\frac{w(|k+\varphi_4-n/2-2|)\varepsilon}{\alpha(n/2+2-\varphi_4)\left(w(0)+2\sum w(h)\right)} + \cdots \frac{w(|k+\varphi_4-n|)\varepsilon}{\alpha(n-\varphi_4)\left(w(0)+2\sum w(h)\right)} \\ C_{p+n/2-1}^{n/2}\frac{w(|k+\varphi_4-n/2-1|)\varepsilon}{\alpha(n/2+1-\varphi_4)\left(w(0)+2\sum w(h)\right)} + C_{p+n/2-2}^{n/2-1}\frac{w(|k+\varphi_4-n/2-2|)\varepsilon}{\alpha(n/2+2-\varphi_4)\left(w(0)+2\sum w(h)\right)} + \cdots C_p^1 \frac{w(|k+\varphi_4-n|)\varepsilon}{\alpha(n-\varphi_4)\left(w(0)+2\sum w(h)\right)} \\ \vdots \\ C_{p+n/2+\varphi_4-2}^{n/2+\varphi_4-1}\frac{w(|k+\varphi_4-n/2-1|)\varepsilon}{\alpha(n/2+1-\varphi_4)\left(w(0)+2\sum w(h)\right)} + C_{p+n/2+\varphi_4-3}^{n/2+\varphi_4-2}\frac{w(|k+\varphi_4-n/2-2|)\varepsilon}{\alpha(n/2+2-\varphi_4)\left(w(0)+2\sum w(h)\right)} + \cdots C_{p+\varphi_4-1}^{\varphi_4} \frac{w(|k+\varphi_4-n|)\varepsilon}{\alpha(n-\varphi_4)\left(w(0)+2\sum w(h)\right)} \end{bmatrix}.$$

Then, calculate the matrix norm $||\Delta B_v||_2$ and vector norm $||\Delta Y_v||$, extract parameter ε and apply Lemma 1; then, the parameter expressions in Equation (17) are obtained.

(ii). Sequence size n is odd and $k = (n+1)/2+1$, $(n+1)/2+2, \ldots, n-1$. Based on operator D_v, the sequences with and without disturbance applied to $DGM^p(1,1)$ satisfy

$$\widetilde{x}_v(i) = \begin{cases} x_v(i), & \text{when } 1 \leq i < (n+1)/2 - \varphi_3 \text{ or } n+1-\varphi_4 \leq i \leq n \\ x_v(i) + \dfrac{\varepsilon w(|i-k|)}{\left(w(0)+2\sum_{j=1}^{\frac{-\alpha(i)}{2}} w(j)\right)}, & \text{when } (n+1)/2 - \varphi_3 \leq i < n+1-\varphi_4 \end{cases} \quad (A4)$$

Then, we can obtain

$$\Delta B_v = \begin{bmatrix} 0 \\ \vdots \\ 0 \\ 0 \\ 0 \\ \vdots \\ 0 \\ 0 \\ \vdots \\ 0 \end{bmatrix} \begin{matrix} \\ \\ \\ \\ \frac{w(|k+\varphi_3-(n+1)/2|)\varepsilon}{w(0)+2\sum_{h=1}^{\alpha((n+1)/2-\varphi_3)} w(h)} \\ C_p^1 \frac{w(|k+\varphi_3-(n+1)/2|)\varepsilon}{w(0)+2\sum_{h=1}^{\alpha((n+1)/2-\varphi_3)} w(h)} + \frac{w(|k+\varphi_3-(n+3)/2|)\varepsilon}{w(0)+2\sum_{h=1}^{\alpha((n+3)/2-\varphi_3)} w(h)} \\ \vdots \\ C_{p+(n-3)/2+\varphi_3-\varphi_4}^{(n-1)/2+\varphi_3-\varphi_4} \frac{w(|k+\varphi_3-(n+1)/2|)\varepsilon}{w(0)+2\sum_{h=1}^{\alpha((n+1)/2-\varphi_3)} w(h)} + C_{p+(n-5)/2+\varphi_3-\varphi_4}^{(n-3)/2+\varphi_3-\varphi_4} \frac{w(|k+\varphi_3-(n+3)/2|)\varepsilon}{w(0)+2\sum_{h=1}^{\alpha((n+3)/2-\varphi_3)} w(h)} + \cdots + \frac{w(|k+\varphi_4-n|)\varepsilon}{w(0)+2\sum_{h=1}^{\alpha(n-\varphi_4)} w(h)} \\ C_{p+(n-1)/2+\varphi_3-\varphi_4}^{(n+1)/2+\varphi_3-\varphi_4} \frac{w(|k+\varphi_3-(n+1)/2|)\varepsilon}{w(0)+2\sum_{h=1}^{\alpha((n+1)/2-\varphi_3)} w(h)} + C_{p+(n-3)/2+\varphi_3-\varphi_4}^{(n-1)/2+\varphi_3-\varphi_4} \frac{w(|k+\varphi_3-(n+3)/2|)\varepsilon}{w(0)+2\sum_{h=1}^{\alpha((n+3)/2-\varphi_3)} w(h)} + \cdots C_p^1 \frac{w(|k+\varphi_4-n|)\varepsilon}{w(0)+2\sum_{h=1}^{\alpha(n-\varphi_4)} w(h)} \\ \vdots \\ C_{p+(n-5)/2+\varphi_3}^{(n-3)/2+\varphi_3} \frac{w(|k+\varphi_3-(n+1)/2|)\varepsilon}{w(0)+2\sum_{h=1}^{\alpha((n+1)/2-\varphi_3)} w(h)} + C_{p+(n-7)/2+\varphi_3}^{(n-5)/2+\varphi_3} \frac{w(|k+\varphi_3-(n+3)/2|)\varepsilon}{w(0)+2\sum_{h=1}^{\alpha((n+3)/2-\varphi_3)} w(h)} + \cdots C_{p+\varphi_4-2}^{\varphi_4-1} \frac{w(|k+\varphi_4-n|)\varepsilon}{w(0)+2\sum_{h=1}^{\alpha(n-\varphi_4)} w(h)} \end{matrix},$$

$$\Delta Y_v = \begin{bmatrix} 0 \\ \vdots \\ 0 \\ \frac{w(|k+\varphi_3-(n+1)/2|)\varepsilon}{w(0)+2\sum_{h=1}^{\alpha((n+1)/2-\varphi_3)} w(h)} \\ C_p^1 \frac{w(|k+\varphi_3-(n+1)/2|)\varepsilon}{w(0)+2\sum_{h=1}^{\alpha((n+1)/2-\varphi_3)} w(h)} + \frac{w(|k+\varphi_3-(n+3)/2|)\varepsilon}{w(0)+2\sum_{h=1}^{\alpha((n+3)/2-\varphi_3)} w(h)} \\ \vdots \\ C_{p+(n-3)/2+\varphi_3-\varphi_4}^{(n-1)/2+\varphi_3-\varphi_4} \frac{w(|k+\varphi_3-(n+1)/2|)\varepsilon}{w(0)+2\sum_{h=1}^{\alpha((n+1)/2-\varphi_3)} w(h)} + C_{p+(n-5)/2+\varphi_3-\varphi_4}^{(n-3)/2+\varphi_3-\varphi_4} \frac{w(|k+\varphi_3-(n+3)/2|)\varepsilon}{w(0)+2\sum_{h=1}^{\alpha((n+3)/2-\varphi_3)} w(h)} + \cdots \frac{w(|k+\varphi_4-n|)\varepsilon}{w(0)+2\sum_{h=1}^{\alpha(n-\varphi_4)} w(h)} \\ C_{p+(n-1)/2+\varphi_3-\varphi_4}^{(n+1)/2+\varphi_3-\varphi_4} \frac{w(|k+\varphi_3-(n+1)/2|)\varepsilon}{w(0)+2\sum_{h=1}^{\alpha((n+1)/2-\varphi_3)} w(h)} + C_{p+(n-3)/2+\varphi_3-\varphi_4}^{(n-1)/2+\varphi_3-\varphi_4} \frac{w(|k+\varphi_3-(n+3)/2|)\varepsilon}{w(0)+2\sum_{h=1}^{\alpha((n+3)/2-\varphi_3)} w(h)} + \cdots C_p^1 \frac{w(|k+\varphi_4-n|)\varepsilon}{w(0)+2\sum_{h=1}^{\alpha(n-\varphi_4)} w(h)} \\ \vdots \\ C_{p+(n-3)/2+\varphi_3}^{(n-1)/2+\varphi_3} \frac{w(|k+\varphi_3-(n+1)/2|)\varepsilon}{w(0)+2\sum_{h=1}^{\alpha((n+1)/2-\varphi_3)} w(h)} + C_{p+(n-5)/2+\varphi_3}^{(n-3)/2+\varphi_3} \frac{w(|k+\varphi_3-(n+3)/2|)\varepsilon}{w(0)+2\sum_{h=1}^{\alpha((n+3)/2-\varphi_3)} w(h)} + \cdots C_{p+\varphi_4-1}^{\varphi_4} \frac{w(|k+\varphi_4-n|)\varepsilon}{w(0)+2\sum_{h=1}^{\alpha(n-\varphi_4)} w(h)} \end{bmatrix}.$$

Then, calculate the matrix norm $||\Delta B_v||_2$ and vector norm $||\Delta Y_v||$, extract parameter ε and apply Lemma 1; then, the parameter expressions in Equation (18) are obtained. The proof of Theorem 6 is now complete. □

Appendix A.3. Proof of Theorem 7

Proof. (i). When sequence size n is even, according to the logic of $DGM^p(1,1)$, we have

$$\Delta B_v = \begin{bmatrix} 0 & 0 \\ \vdots & \vdots \\ 0 & 0 \\ 0 & \dfrac{w(n/2-1)\varepsilon}{w(0)+2\sum\limits_{h=1}^{\alpha(n/2+1)} w(h)} \\ 0 & C_p^1 \dfrac{w(n/2-1)\varepsilon}{w(0)+2\sum\limits_{h=1}^{\alpha(n/2+1)} w(h)} + \dfrac{w(n/2-2)\varepsilon}{w(0)+2\sum\limits_{h=1}^{\alpha(n/2+2)} w(h)} \\ \vdots & \vdots \\ 0 & C_{p+n/2-3}^{n/2-2} \dfrac{w(n/2-1)\varepsilon}{w(0)+2\sum\limits_{h=1}^{\alpha(n/2+1)} w(h)} + C_{p+n/2-4}^{n/2-3} \dfrac{w(n/2-2)\varepsilon}{w(0)+2\sum\limits_{h=1}^{\alpha(n/2+2)} w(h)} + \cdots \dfrac{w(1)\varepsilon}{w(0)+2\sum\limits_{h=1}^{\alpha(n-1)} w(h)} \end{bmatrix},$$

$$\Delta Y_v = \begin{bmatrix} 0 \\ \vdots \\ 0 \\ \dfrac{w(n/2-1)\varepsilon}{w(0)+2\sum\limits_{h=1}^{\alpha(n/2+1)} w(h)} \\ C_p^1 \dfrac{w(n/2-1)\varepsilon}{w(0)+2\sum\limits_{h=1}^{\alpha(n/2+1)} w(h)} + \dfrac{w(n/2-2)\varepsilon}{w(0)+2\sum\limits_{h=1}^{\alpha(n/2+2)} w(h)} \\ \vdots \\ C_{p+n/2-2}^{n/2-1} \dfrac{w(n/2-1)\varepsilon}{w(0)+2\sum\limits_{h=1}^{\alpha(n/2+1)} w(h)} + C_{p+n/2-3}^{n/2-2} \dfrac{w(n/2-2)\varepsilon}{w(0)+2\sum\limits_{h=1}^{\alpha(n/2+2)} w(h)} + \cdots \dfrac{w(0)\varepsilon}{w(0)+2\sum\limits_{h=1}^{\alpha(n)} w(h)} \end{bmatrix}.$$

Then, calculate the matrix norm $||\Delta B_v||_2$ and vector norm $||\Delta Y_v||$, extract parameter ε and apply Lemma 1; then, the parameter expressions in Equation (19) are obtained.

(ii). When sequence size n is odd, we can obtain:

$$\Delta B_v = \begin{bmatrix} 0 & 0 \\ \vdots & \vdots \\ 0 & 0 \\ 0 & \dfrac{w((n-1)/2)\varepsilon}{w(0)+2\sum\limits_{h=1}^{\alpha((n+1)/2)} w(h)} \\ 0 & C_p^1 \dfrac{w((n-1)/2)\varepsilon}{w(0)+2\sum\limits_{h=1}^{\alpha((n+1)/2)} w(h)} + \dfrac{w((n-3)/2)\varepsilon}{w(0)+2\sum\limits_{h=1}^{\alpha((n+3)/2)} w(h)} \\ \vdots & \vdots \\ 0 & C_{p+(n-5)/2}^{(n-3)/2} \dfrac{w((n-1)/2)\varepsilon}{w(0)+2\sum\limits_{h=1}^{\alpha((n+1)/2)} w(h)} + C_{p+(n-7)/2}^{(n-5)/2} \dfrac{w((n-3)/2)\varepsilon}{w(0)+2\sum\limits_{h=1}^{\alpha((n+3)/2)} w(h)} + \cdots \dfrac{w(1)\varepsilon}{w(0)+2\sum\limits_{h=1}^{\alpha(n-1)} w(h)} \end{bmatrix},$$

$$\Delta Y_v = \begin{bmatrix} 0 \\ \vdots \\ 0 \\ C_p^1 \dfrac{w((n-1)/2)\varepsilon}{w(0)+2\sum_{h=1}^{\alpha((n+1)/2)} w(h)} + \dfrac{w((n-3)/2)\varepsilon}{w(0)+2\sum_{h=1}^{\alpha((n+3)/2)} w(h)} \\ \vdots \\ C_{p+(n-3)/2}^{(n-1)/2} \dfrac{w((n-1)/2)\varepsilon}{w(0)+2\sum_{h=1}^{\alpha((n+1)/2)} w(h)} + C_{p+(n-5)/2}^{(n-3)/2} \dfrac{w((n-3)/2)\varepsilon}{w(0)+2\sum_{h=1}^{\alpha((n+3)/2)} w(h)} + \cdots + \dfrac{w(0)\varepsilon}{w(0)+2\sum_{h=1}^{\alpha(n)} w(h)} \end{bmatrix}.$$

Then, calculate the matrix norm $||\Delta B_v||_2$ and vector norm $||\Delta Y_v||$, extract parameter ε and apply Lemma 1; then, the parameter expressions in Equation (20) are obtained.
The proof of Theorem 7 is now complete. □

References

1. Yu, L.; Wang, S.; Lai, K.K.; Nakamori, Y. Time series forecasting with multiple candidate models: Selecting or combining? *J. Syst. Sci. Complex.* **2005**, *18*, 1–18.
2. Shahin, A.I.; Almotairi, S. A deep learning BiLSTM encoding-decoding model for COVID-19 pandemic spread forecasting. *Fractal Fract.* **2021**, *5*, 175. [CrossRef]
3. Xu, C.; Mu, D.; Liu, Z.; Pang, Y.; Liao, M.; Aouiti, C. New insight into bifurcation of fractional-order 4D neural networks incorporating two different time delays. *Commun. Nonlinear Sci.* **2023**, *118*, 107043. [CrossRef]
4. Xu, C.; Mu, D.; Liu, Z.; Pang, Y.; Liao, M.; Li, P.; Yao, L.; Qin, Q. Comparative exploration on bifurcation behavior for integer-order and fractional-order delayed BAM neural networks. *Nonlinear Anal. Model. Control* **2022**, *27*, 1030–1053. [CrossRef]
5. Braverman, E.; Rodkina, A. On convergence of solutions to difference equations with additive perturbations. *J. Differ. Equ. Appl.* **2016**, *22*, 878–903. [CrossRef]
6. Zhu, M.; Wang, D.; Guo, M. Existence and stability of stationary solutions of nonlinear difference equations under random perturbations. *J. Differ. Equ. Appl.* **2011**, *17*, 587–602. [CrossRef]
7. Xu, C.; Mu, D.; Pan, Y.; Aouiti, C.; Yao, L. Exploring bifurcation in a fractional-order predator-prey system with mixed delays. *J. Appl. Anal. Comput.* **2023**, *13*, 1119–1136. [CrossRef]
8. Ou, W.; Xu, C.; Cui, Q.; Liu, Z.; Pang, Y.; Farman, M.; Ahmad, S.; Zeb, A. Mathematical study on bifurcation dynamics and control mechanism of tri-neuron bidirectional associative memory neural networks including delay. *Math. Methods Appl. Sci.* **2023**, 1–25. [CrossRef]
9. Lin, Z.; Wang, H. Modeling and application of fractional-order economic growth model with time delay. *Fractal Fract.* **2021**, *5*, 74. [CrossRef]
10. Chandra, R.; Zhang, M. Cooperative coevolution of Elman recurrent neural networks for chaotic time series prediction. *Neurocomputing* **2012**, *86*, 116–123. [CrossRef]
11. Yager, R.R. Exponential smoothing with credibility weighted observations. *Inf. Sci.* **2013**, *252*, 96–105. [CrossRef]
12. Rasmussen, R. On time series data and optimal parameters. *Omega* **2004**, *32*, 111–120. [CrossRef]
13. Taylor, J.W.; Snyder, R.D. Forecasting intraday time series with multiple seasonal cycles using parsimonious seasonal exponential smoothing. *Omega* **2012**, *40*, 748–757. [CrossRef]
14. Liu, S.F.; Forrest, J.Y.L. *Grey Systems: Theory and Applications*; Springer: Berlin/Heidelberg, Germany, 2010.
15. Hu, Y.C. Grey prediction with residual modification using functional-link net and its application to energy demand forecasting. *Kybernetes* **2017**, *46*, 349–363. [CrossRef]
16. Lin, Y.; Chen, M.; Liu, S. Theory of grey systems: Capturing uncertainties of grey information. *Kybernetes* **2004**, *33*, 196–218. [CrossRef]
17. Liu, S.F.; Yang, Y.J.; Forrest, J. *Grey Data Analysis: Methods, Models and Applications*; Springer: Singapore, 2016.
18. Dang, Y.G.; Liu, S.F.; Liu, B.; Tang, X.W. Study on the buffer weakening operator. *Chin. J. Manag. Sci.* **2004**, *12*, 108–111.
19. Xie, N.M.; Liu, S.F. A new applicative weakening buffer operator. *Chin. J. Manag. Sci.* **2003**, *11*, 46–48.
20. Mao, S.; Gao, M.; Xiao, X.; Zhu, M. A novel fractional grey system model and its application. *Appl. Math. Model.* **2016**, *40*, 5063–5076. [CrossRef]
21. Wu, L.; Liu, S.; Yang, Y.; Ma, L.; Liu, H. Multi-variable weakening buffer operator and its application. *Inf. Sci.* **2016**, *339*, 98–107. [CrossRef]

22. Wu, L.F.; Liu, S.F.; Yao, L.G. Discrete grey model based on fractional order accumulate. *Syst. Eng. Theor. Pract.* **2014**, *34*, 1822–1827.
23. Wu, L.F.; Liu, S.F.; Yao, L.G. Grey model with Caputo fractional order derivative. *Syst. Eng. Theor. Pract.* **2015**, *35*, 1311–1316.
24. Ma, L.; Li, J.; Zhao, Y. Population forecast of China's rural community based on CFANGBM and improved Aquila optimizer algorithm. *Fractal Fract.* **2021**, *5*, 190. [CrossRef]
25. Tang, X.; Xie, N.; Hu, A. Forecasting annual foreign tourist arrivals to China by incorporating firefly algorithm into fractional non-homogenous discrete Grey model. *Kybernetes* **2022**, *51*, 676–693. [CrossRef]
26. Yuan, Y.; Zhao, H.; Yuan, X.; Chen, L.; Lei, X. Application of fractional order-based grey power model in water consumption prediction. *Environ. Earth Sci.* **2019**, *78*, 266. [CrossRef]
27. Li, C.; Yang, Y.; Liu, S. Comparative analysis of properties of weakening buffer operators in time series prediction models. *Commun. Nonlinear Sci.* **2019**, *68*, 257–285. [CrossRef]
28. Li, C.; Yang, Y.; Liu, S. A new method to mitigate data fluctuations for time series prediction. *Appl. Math. Model.* **2019**, *65*, 390–407. [CrossRef]
29. Xiao, X.; Guo, H.; Mao, S. The modeling mechanism, extension and optimization of grey GM (1, 1) model. *Appl. Math. Model.* **2014**, *38*, 1896–1910. [CrossRef]
30. Stewart, G.W.; Sun, J. *Matrix Perturbation Theory*; Academic Press: New York, NY, USA, 1990.

Disclaimer/Publisher's Note: The statements, opinions and data contained in all publications are solely those of the individual author(s) and contributor(s) and not of MDPI and/or the editor(s). MDPI and/or the editor(s) disclaim responsibility for any injury to people or property resulting from any ideas, methods, instructions or products referred to in the content.

 *fractal and fractional*

Article

Solutions of a Nonlinear Diffusion Equation with a Regularized Hyper-Bessel Operator

Nguyen Hoang Luc [1], Donal O'Regan [2] and Anh Tuan Nguyen [1,*]

[1] Division of Applied Mathematics, Thu Dau Mot University, Thu Dau Mot City 75000, Vietnam
[2] School of Mathematical and Statistical Sciences, National University of Ireland, H91 TK33 Galway, Ireland
* Correspondence: nguyenanhtuan@tdmu.edu.vn

Abstract: We investigate the Cauchy problem for a nonlinear fractional diffusion equation, which is modified using the time-fractional hyper-Bessel derivative. The source function is a gradient source of Hamilton–Jacobi type. The main objective of our current work is to show the existence and uniqueness of mild solutions. Our desired goal is achieved using the Picard iteration method, and our analysis is based on properties of Mittag–Leffler functions and embeddings between Hilbert scales spaces and Lebesgue spaces.

Keywords: gradient nonlinearity; fractional diffusion equation; hyper-Bessel; fractional partial differential equations

MSC: 35K20; 35K58

1. Introduction

Fractional partial differential equations (FPDEs) arise naturally in modeling since fractional derivatives help to describe phenomena efficiently [1], and FPDEs arise in many fields of applied science [2–8]; see also [9–29].

In this study, we consider a Cauchy problem for a time-space fractional hyper-Bessel differential equation as follows:

$$\begin{cases} {_C}\mathbb{D}_t^{\alpha,\beta}\varphi(t,x) + (-\Delta)^\sigma \varphi(t,x) = \big|\nabla \varphi(t,x)\big|^p, & \text{in } (0,T] \times \Omega, \\ \varphi(t,x) = 0 & \text{on } (0,T] \times \partial\Omega, \\ \varphi(0,x) = g(x) & \text{in } \Omega, \end{cases} \quad (1)$$

where Ω is a bounded domain in $\mathbb{R}^N$ ($N \geqslant 1$) with sufficiently smooth boundary $\partial\Omega$, and g is the initial function. Recall from [30] the fractional operator

$$\left(t^\alpha \frac{d}{dt}\right)^\beta \varphi(t) := (1-\alpha)^\beta t^{(\alpha-1)\beta} \frac{1-\alpha}{\Gamma(-\beta)} t^{(\alpha-1)\beta} \int_0^t (t^{1-\alpha} - s^{1-\alpha})^{\beta-1} s^{-\alpha} \varphi(s) ds, \quad (2)$$

where $\alpha < 1, \beta \in (0,1)$, Γ is the Gamma function and ∇ is the usual gradient operator. The notation ${_C}\mathbb{D}_t^{\alpha,\beta}$ stands for the Caputo-like counterpart of the hyper-Bessel operator with parameters $\alpha < 1$ of order $\beta \in (0,1)$ and can be defined as follows:

$$_C\mathbb{D}_t^{\alpha,\beta}\varphi(t) := \left(t^\alpha \frac{d}{dt}\right)^\beta \varphi(t) - \varphi(0)(1-\alpha)^\beta \frac{t^{(\alpha-1)\beta}}{\Gamma(1-\alpha)}, \quad (3)$$

provided that the right-hand side of the above equality makes sense. Since first introduced in [31] by Dimovski, the fractional hyper-Bessel operator has been shown to have applications in Brownian motion, fractional relaxation, and fractional diffusion models [30,32,33]. The regularized Caputo-like counterpart operator ${}_c\mathbb{D}_t^{\alpha,\beta}$ was introduced in [34] by Al-Musalhi et al., where the authors considered a direct problem and a inverse problem for a linear diffusion equation with the Caputo-like counterpart of the hyper-Bessel derivative. To provide an overview of topics related to Problem (1), we mention [35], where Au et al. investigated the Cauchy problem for the following equation:

$$ {}_c\mathbb{D}_t^{\alpha,\beta} u + \mathbb{L} u(t,x) = F(u), \qquad (4)$$

where $\mathbb{L}$ is a generalization of $-\Delta$ and F is a nonlinearity of logarithm type, and the authors established the existence and uniqueness of a mild solution. In addition, they studied the blowing-up behavior of this solution. Tuan et al. [29] considered a terminal value problem for (4) where F is given in a linear form, and they showed that the backward problem is ill-posed and then applied a regularized Tikhonov regularization method to construct an approximating solution. In [36], Baleanu et al. investigated mild solutions to Equation (4) where F satisfies an exponential growth, and they showed the local well-posedness of mild solutions.

The first equation of Problem (1) is a modification of the classical diffusion equation. In the classical problem, Newton's derivative describes the velocity of a particle or slope of a tangent, whereas the general conformable derivative in (1) can be regarded as a special velocity and its direction and strength rely on a particular function [37]. The main goal of this work is to study the theory of existence and uniqueness of mild solutions, by which we can find an efficient numerical approach to investigate (1). In comparison with the above studies, our work possesses some new features. First, our source function is a gradient nonlinearity of Hamilton–Jacobi type. The presence of this function requires us to use different methods and, motivated by Souplet [38], we use the Picard iteration method to establish the existence and uniqueness of mild solutions. However, to deduce our results, we balance the linear and nonlinear parts of Problem (1), and to do this, we apply properties of Mittag–Leffler functions in an efficient way. Additionally, some Sobolev embeddings between Hilbert scales spaces and Lebesgue space are required to find an appropriate estimate to deal with the gradient source.

The outline of the work is as follows. Section 2 provides some preliminaries, and the main result concerning Problem (1) is given in Section 3.

2. Basic Settings

We begin this section with a convention that $a \lesssim b$ means a positive constant C exists such that $a \leqslant Cb$. Let $(B, \|\cdot\|_B)$ be a Banach space. We define the following space:

$$ L^\infty(0,T;B) := \left\{ u : (0,T) \to B \,\big|\, u \text{ is bounded almost everywhere on } (0,T) \right\}. \qquad (5)$$

Next, we recall that in $L^2(\Omega)$, the negative Laplace operator subject to Dirichlet conditions satisfies the following spectral problem:

$$ \begin{cases} -\Delta \Theta_l(x) = \lambda_l \Theta_l(x), & x \in \Omega, \\ \Theta_l(x) = 0, & x \in \partial\Omega, \end{cases} \qquad (6)$$

where $\{\Theta_l\}_{l \in \mathbb{N}}$ is a set of eigenvectors which is also a orthonormal basic of $L^2(\Omega)$ and $\{\lambda_l\}_{l \in \mathbb{N}}$ is the corresponding increasing set of positive eigenvalues such that $\lambda_l \to \infty$ as $l \to \infty$. Then, for any $\sigma \geqslant 0$, we define the fractional Laplacian $(-\Delta)^\sigma$ by

$$ (-\Delta)^\sigma u := \sum_{l \in \mathbb{N}} \lambda_l^\sigma u_l \Theta_l, \qquad (7)$$

where $u_l := \int_\Omega u(x)\Theta_l(x)\mathrm{d}x$ and u belongs to the following space

$$\mathbb{D}^\sigma(\Omega) := \left\{ u \in L^2(\Omega) \ \Big| \ \sum_{l \in \mathbb{N}} \lambda_l^{2\sigma} u_l^2 < \infty \right\}. \tag{8}$$

We note that $\mathbb{D}^\sigma(\Omega)$ is a Hilbert space and possesses the following norm:

$$\|u\|_{\mathbb{D}^\sigma(\Omega)} := \left\|(-\Delta)^\sigma u\right\|_{L^2(\Omega)} = \left(\sum_{l \in \mathbb{N}} \lambda_l^{2\sigma} u_l^2\right)^{\frac{1}{2}}. \tag{9}$$

We define the Hilbert scale space with negative orders $\mathbb{D}^{-\sigma}(\Omega)$ as the dual space of $\mathbb{D}^\sigma(\Omega)$. Denote by $\langle \cdot, \cdot \rangle_*$ the dual product between $\mathbb{D}^{-\sigma}(\Omega)$ and $\mathbb{D}^\sigma(\Omega)$, and $\mathbb{D}^{-\sigma}(\Omega)$ is a Hilbert space equipped with the norm

$$\|u\|_{\mathbb{D}^{-\sigma}(\Omega)} := \left(\sum_{l \in \mathbb{N}} \lambda_l^{-2\sigma} \langle u, \Theta_l \rangle_*^2 \right)^{\frac{1}{2}}, \quad u \in \mathbb{D}^{-\sigma}(\Omega). \tag{10}$$

Remark 1 (Chapter 5 [39]). *For any $u \in L^2(\Omega)$ and $v \in \mathbb{D}^\sigma(\Omega)$, we have the following equality:*

$$\langle u, v \rangle_* = \int_\Omega u(x) v(x) \mathrm{d}x. \tag{11}$$

Proposition 1 (Lemma 4.7 [35]). *Let Ω be a smooth bounded domain of $\mathbb{R}^N$. The following embeddings are satisfied:*

$$L^q(\Omega) \hookrightarrow \mathbb{D}^\nu(\Omega) \quad \text{if} \quad \frac{-N}{4} < \nu \leqslant 0, \text{ and } q \geqslant \frac{2N}{N-4\nu}, \tag{12}$$

$$L^q(\Omega) \hookleftarrow \mathbb{D}^\nu(\Omega) \quad \text{if} \quad 0 \leqslant \nu < \frac{N}{4}, \text{ and } q \leqslant \frac{2N}{N-4\nu}. \tag{13}$$

Next, we derive the mild formula for solutions of Problem (1). First, we introduce the definition of Mittag–Leffler functions, which play an important role in investigating time-fractional differential equations.

Definition 1. *For $\beta_1 \in \mathbb{R}^+, \beta_2 \in \mathbb{R}$ and $z \in \mathbb{C}$, the Mittag-Leffler function is defined as follows*

$$E_{\beta_1,\beta_2}(z) := \sum_{n \in \mathbb{N}} \frac{z^n}{\Gamma(n\beta_1 + \beta_2)}. \tag{14}$$

Suppose that $\varphi \in L^\infty(0, \infty; L^2(\Omega))$, and we find from the first equation of Problem (1) that

$$_c\mathbb{D}_t^{\alpha,\beta} \varphi_l(t) + \lambda_l^\sigma \varphi_l(t) = \left| \nabla \varphi(t) \right|_l^p, \quad t > 0, \tag{15}$$

here, we recall that $\varphi_l = \int_\Omega \varphi(x)\Theta_l(x)\mathrm{d}x$, $|\nabla \varphi|$ is the module of the gradient of φ and $|\nabla \varphi(t)|_l^p = \int_\Omega |\nabla \varphi(t,x)|^p \Theta_l(x) \mathrm{d}x$.

In order to solve this equation, we recall the following theorem from ([34]) (Section 2):

Theorem 1. *Let $\alpha < (-\infty, 1)$, $\lambda > 0$ and $\beta \in (0,1)$. For any $t > 0$, solutions of the following fractional differential equation*

$$_c\mathbb{D}_t^{\alpha,\beta} u(t) + \lambda u(t) = f(t) \tag{16}$$

are represented by the formula below:

$$u(t) = E_{\beta,1}\left(\frac{-\lambda t^{(1-\alpha)\beta}}{(1-\alpha)^{\beta}}\right) u(0)$$
$$+ \frac{1}{(1-\alpha)^{\beta}\Gamma(\beta)} \int_{0}^{t} \left(t^{1-\alpha} - s^{1-\alpha}\right)^{\beta-1} f(s) d(s^{1-\alpha}) \qquad (17)$$
$$- \frac{\lambda}{(1-\alpha)^{2\beta}} \int_{0}^{t} \left(t^{1-\alpha} - s^{1-\alpha}\right)^{2\beta-1} E_{\beta,2\beta}\left(-\frac{\lambda\left(t^{1-\alpha}-s^{1-\alpha}\right)^{\beta}}{(1-\alpha)^{\beta}}\right) f(s) d(s^{1-\alpha}).$$

Based on the above theorem and some calculations, we derive the following equivalent equation of the (15):

$$\varphi_l(t) = E_{\beta,1}\left(\frac{-\lambda_l^{\sigma} t^{(1-\alpha)\beta}}{(1-\alpha)^{\beta}}\right) g_l$$
$$+ \int_{0}^{t} \frac{\left(t^{1-\alpha} - s^{1-\alpha}\right)^{\beta-1}}{(1-\alpha)^{\beta}} E_{\beta,\beta}\left(-\frac{\lambda_l^{\sigma}\left(t^{1-\alpha}-s^{1-\alpha}\right)^{\beta}}{(1-\alpha)^{\beta}}\right) \left|\nabla\varphi(s)\right|_l^p d(s^{1-\alpha}). \qquad (18)$$

Recall that, for any $u \in L^2(\Omega)$, we have the Fourier expansion $u(x) = \sum_{l\in\mathbb{N}} u_l \Theta_l(x)$. Based on (18), we obtain the formula of the Fourier coefficient $\varphi_l(t)$ at $t \in (0, T)$ of a mild solution $\varphi \in L^{\infty}(0, T; \mathbb{D}^{\nu}(\Omega))$ of Problem (1). In summary, the solution $\varphi \in L^{\infty}(0, T; \mathbb{D}^{\nu}(\Omega))$ can be studied via the following equivalent integral equation:

$$\varphi(t,x) = R_{1,\sigma}(t^{1-\alpha}) g(x) + \int_{0}^{t} R_{2,\sigma}(t^{1-\alpha} - s^{1-\alpha}) \left|\nabla\varphi(s,x)\right|^p d(s^{1-\alpha}), \qquad (19)$$

where

$$R_{1,\sigma}(t) u(x) := \sum_{l\in\mathbb{N}} E_{\beta,1}\left(\frac{-\lambda_l^{\sigma} t^{\beta}}{(1-\alpha)^{\beta}}\right) u_l \Theta_l(x), \qquad (20)$$

$$R_{2,\sigma}(t) u(x) := \sum_{l\in\mathbb{N}} \frac{t^{\beta-1}}{(1-\alpha)^{\beta}} E_{\beta,\beta}\left(-\frac{\lambda_l^{\sigma} t^{\beta}}{(1-\alpha)^{\beta}}\right) u_l \Theta_l(x). \qquad (21)$$

Remark 2. *The function φ in (19) is actually described by the limit (in $L^{\infty}(0, T; \mathbb{D}^{\nu}(\Omega))$) of the sequence $\{\varphi_j\}_{j\in\mathbb{N}}$, which is defined by*

$$\varphi_1(t,x) := R_{1,\sigma}(t^{1-\alpha}) g(x) \qquad (22)$$

and

$$\varphi_{j+1}(t,x) := \varphi_1(t,x) + \int_{0}^{t} R_{2,\sigma}(t^{1-\alpha} - s^{1-\alpha}) \left|\nabla\varphi_j(s,x)\right|^p d(s^{1-\alpha}). \qquad (23)$$

3. Existence and Uniqueness

This section begins with some linear estimates for $R_{1,\sigma}$ and $R_{2,\sigma}$, which are derived via the Fourier series of L^2 functions and Parseval's equality.

Lemma 1 ([8] Theorem 1.6). *Let $\beta_1 \in (0,1)$ and $\beta_2 \in \mathbb{R}$ and $\varsigma \in (\frac{\pi\beta_1}{2}, \pi)$. Then, for any $z \in \mathbb{C}$ such that*

$$\varsigma \leqslant |\arg z| \leqslant \pi, \qquad (24)$$

the following estimate is satisfied:

$$\left|E_{\beta_1,\beta_2}(z)\right| \lesssim \frac{1}{1+|z|}. \tag{25}$$

Lemma 2 (Linear estimates). *Let $\nu \geqslant 0$ and $0 < \sigma \leqslant 1$. The following estimates hold:*
1. *For any $u \in \mathbb{D}^\nu(\Omega)$,*

$$\left\|R_{1,\sigma}(t)u\right\|_{\mathbb{D}^\nu(\Omega)} \lesssim \|u\|_{\mathbb{D}^\nu(\Omega)}, \quad t > 0. \tag{26}$$

2. *For any $\theta \in [0,1]$ and $u \in \mathbb{D}^\nu(\Omega)$,*

$$\left\|R_{2,\sigma}(t)u\right\|_{\mathbb{D}^\nu(\Omega)} \lesssim t^{\beta-\theta\beta-1}\|u\|_{\mathbb{D}^{\nu-\theta\sigma}(\Omega)}, \quad t > 0. \tag{27}$$

Proof.
1. Suppose that $u \in \mathbb{D}^\nu(\Omega)$. The definition of $\mathbb{D}^\nu(\Omega)$ and Parseval's equality show that

$$\begin{aligned}\left\|R_{1,\sigma}(t)u\right\|_{\mathbb{D}^\nu(\Omega)}^2 &= \left\|(-\Delta)^\nu R_{1,\sigma}(t)u\right\|_{L^2(\Omega)} \\ &= \sum_{l\in\mathbb{N}} \lambda_l^{2\nu}\left[E_{\beta,1}\left(\frac{-\lambda_l^\sigma t^\beta}{(1-\alpha)^\beta}\right)\right]^2 u_l^2.\end{aligned} \tag{28}$$

Applying Lemma 1, we find that

$$\left|E_{\beta,1}\left(\frac{-\lambda_l^\sigma t^\beta}{(1-\alpha)^\beta}\right)\right| \lesssim \frac{(1-\alpha)^\beta}{(1-\alpha)^\beta + \lambda_l^\sigma t^\beta}. \tag{29}$$

Combining (28) and (29) yields

$$\left\|R_{1,\sigma}(t)u\right\|_{\mathbb{D}^\nu(\Omega)} \lesssim \|u\|_{\mathbb{D}^\nu(\Omega)}. \tag{30}$$

2. Similarly, Lemma 1 implies

$$\begin{aligned}\left|E_{\beta,\beta}\left(-\frac{\lambda_l^\sigma t^\beta}{(1-\alpha)^\beta}\right)\right| &\lesssim \left[\frac{(1-\alpha)^\beta}{(1-\alpha)^\beta + \lambda_l^\sigma t^\beta}\right]^{1-\theta}\left[\frac{(1-\alpha)^\beta}{(1-\alpha)^\beta + \lambda_l^\sigma t^\beta}\right]^\theta \\ &\lesssim \lambda_l^{-\sigma\theta}t^{-\theta\beta},\end{aligned} \tag{31}$$

for any $\theta \in [0,1]$. For any $u \in \mathbb{D}^{\nu-\theta\sigma}(\Omega)$, one has

$$\left\|R_{2,\sigma}(t)u\right\|_{\mathbb{D}^\nu(\Omega)}^2 = \sum_{l\in\mathbb{N}} \lambda_l^{2\nu}\left[\frac{t^{\beta-1}}{(1-\alpha)^\beta}E_{\beta,\beta}\left(\frac{-\lambda_l^\sigma t^\beta}{(1-\alpha)^\beta}\right)\right]^2 u_l^2. \tag{32}$$

Based on estimate (31), we deduce

$$\begin{aligned}\left\|R_{2,\sigma}(t)u\right\|_{\mathbb{D}^\nu(\Omega)} &\lesssim t^{\beta-\theta\beta-1}\left(\sum_{l\in\mathbb{N}} \lambda_l^{2\nu-2\theta\sigma}u_l^2\right)^{\frac{1}{2}} \\ &= t^{\beta-\theta\beta-1}\|u\|_{\mathbb{D}^{\nu-\theta\sigma}(\Omega)}.\end{aligned} \tag{33}$$

The proof is completed. □

Next, we provide a lemma about the nonlinear estimate that helps us to completely define the source function $|\nabla u|^p$ and find an appropriate way to deal with it.

Lemma 3 (Nonlinear estimates). *Let $N \geqslant 1$ and ν, γ, p be constants such that*

$$\nu < \gamma \leqslant \frac{N}{4} + \nu, \tag{34}$$

$$\frac{1}{2} \leqslant \nu < \frac{N}{4} + \frac{1}{2}, \tag{35}$$

$$\max\left\{1, \frac{2N}{N - 4(\nu - \gamma)}\right\} p \leqslant \frac{2N}{N - 4(\nu - \frac{1}{2})}. \tag{36}$$

Then, for any $u, v \in \mathbb{D}^\nu(\Omega)$, we have the following nonlinear estimate:

$$\left\| |\nabla u|^p - |\nabla v|^p \right\|_{\mathbb{D}^{\nu-\gamma}(\Omega)} \lesssim \left(\|u\|_{\mathbb{D}^\nu(\Omega)}^{p-1} + \|u\|_{\mathbb{D}^\nu(\Omega)}^{p-1} \right) \|u - v\|_{\mathbb{D}^\nu(\Omega)}. \tag{37}$$

Proof. We first note that there exists a positive constant q such that

$$\max\left\{1, \frac{2N}{N - 4(\nu - \gamma)}\right\} p \leqslant q \leqslant \frac{2N}{N - 4(\nu - \frac{1}{2})}. \tag{38}$$

Hölder's inequality thus helps us to derive

$$\left\| |\nabla u|^p - |\nabla v|^p \right\|_{L^{q/p}(\Omega)} \lesssim \left(\|\nabla u\|_{L^q(\Omega)}^{p-1} + \|\nabla u\|_{L^q(\Omega)}^{p-1} \right) \|\nabla u - \nabla v\|_{L^q(\Omega)}. \tag{39}$$

Then, we apply the inclusion $\mathbb{D}^{\nu - \frac{1}{2}}(\Omega) \hookrightarrow L^q(\Omega)$ and deduce

$$\left\| |\nabla u|^p - |\nabla v|^p \right\|_{L^{q/p}(\Omega)} \lesssim \left(\|\nabla u\|_{\mathbb{D}^{\nu-\frac{1}{2}}(\Omega)}^{p-1} + \|\nabla u\|_{\mathbb{D}^{\nu-\frac{1}{2}}(\Omega)}^{p-1} \right) \|\nabla u - \nabla v\|_{\mathbb{D}^{\nu-\frac{1}{2}}(\Omega)}. \tag{40}$$

It immediately follows that

$$\left\| |\nabla u|^p - |\nabla v|^p \right\|_{L^{q/p}(\Omega)} \lesssim \left(\|u\|_{\mathbb{D}^\nu(\Omega)}^{p-1} + \|u\|_{\mathbb{D}^\nu(\Omega)}^{p-1} \right) \|u - v\|_{\mathbb{D}^\nu(\Omega)}. \tag{41}$$

This result together with the embedding $L^{q/p}(\Omega) \hookrightarrow \mathbb{D}^{\nu-\gamma}(\Omega)$ yield the desired estimate, provided that $q/p \geqslant \frac{2N}{N-4(\nu-\gamma)}$. The proof is completed. □

Theorem 2. *Suppose that $N \geqslant 1$ and ν, σ, θ, p satisfy the following assumptions:*

$$0 < \theta < 1, 0 < \sigma \leqslant 1 \tag{42}$$

$$\frac{1}{2} \leqslant \nu < \frac{N}{4} + \frac{1}{2}, \tag{43}$$

$$\nu < \theta\sigma \leqslant \frac{N}{4} + \nu, \tag{44}$$

$$\max\left\{1, \frac{2N}{N - 4(\nu - \theta\sigma)}\right\} p \leqslant \frac{2N}{N - 4(\nu - \frac{1}{2})}. \tag{45}$$

In addition, assume that $g \in \mathbb{D}^\nu(\Omega)$. Then, there exists a positive constant $T > 0$ such that Problem (1) has a unique mild solution $\varphi \in L^\infty(0, T; \mathbb{D}^\nu(\Omega))$.

Proof. First, for any $T > 0$, we denote by $\mathbb{B}_R(0, T; \mathbb{D}^\nu(\Omega))$ a closed ball in $L^\infty(0, T; \mathbb{D}^\nu(\Omega))$ centered at zero with radius $R > 0$. Next, we consider a sequence of functions $\{\varphi_j\}_{j \in \mathbb{N}}$ defined in Remark 2. By induction, we show that if $g \in \mathbb{D}^\nu(\Omega)$, $\{\varphi_j\}_{j \in \mathbb{N}}$ is a subset of $\mathbb{B}_R(0, T; \mathbb{D}^\nu(\Omega))$ for some appropriate constants $R > 0$ and $T > 0$. Indeed, for $g \in \mathbb{D}^\nu(\Omega)$, we can apply Lemma 2 and deduce

$$\begin{aligned}\|\varphi_1(t)\|_{\mathbb{D}^\nu(\Omega)} &= \left\|R_{1,\sigma}(t^{1-\alpha})g\right\|_{\mathbb{D}^\nu(\Omega)} \\ &\lesssim \|g\|_{\mathbb{D}^\nu(\Omega)} \\ &< \frac{1}{2}R, \quad t > 0.\end{aligned} \tag{46}$$

Thus, $\varphi_1 \in \mathbb{B}_R(0, T; \mathbb{D}^\nu(\Omega))$. Next, for $j \geqslant 2$, we suppose that $\varphi_j \in \mathbb{B}_R(0, T; \mathbb{D}^\nu(\Omega))$. For $t > 0$, the triangle inequality yields

$$\|\varphi_{j+1}(t)\|_{\mathbb{D}^\nu(\Omega)} \leqslant \|\varphi_1(t)\|_{\mathbb{D}^\nu(\Omega)} + \int_0^t \left\|R_{2,\sigma}(t^{1-\alpha} - s^{1-\alpha})\left|\nabla \varphi_j(s,x)\right|^p\right\|_{\mathbb{D}^\nu(\Omega)} d(s^{1-\alpha}). \tag{47}$$

According to Lemma 2, the following estimate holds:

$$\left\|R_{2,\sigma}(t^{1-\alpha} - s^{1-\alpha})\left|\nabla \varphi_j(s,x)\right|^p\right\|_{\mathbb{D}^\nu(\Omega)} \lesssim (t^{1-\alpha} - s^{1-\alpha})^{\beta-\theta\beta-1}\left\||\nabla \varphi_j(s)|^p\right\|_{\mathbb{D}^{\nu-\theta\sigma}(\Omega)}. \tag{48}$$

Assumptions of ν, σ, θ enable us to use Lemma 3 and derive

$$\left\|R_{2,\sigma}(t^{1-\alpha} - s^{1-\alpha})\left|\nabla \varphi_j(s,x)\right|^p\right\|_{\mathbb{D}^\nu(\Omega)} \lesssim (t^{1-\alpha} - s^{1-\alpha})^{\beta-\theta\beta-1}\|\varphi_j(s)\|^p_{\mathbb{D}^\nu(\Omega)}, \tag{49}$$

where we chose $u = \varphi_j$ and $v = 0$. Therefore, for any $t > 0$, we find that

$$\begin{aligned}&\int_0^t \left\|R_{2,\sigma}(t^{1-\alpha} - s^{1-\alpha})\left|\nabla \varphi_j(s,x)\right|^p\right\|_{\mathbb{D}^\nu(\Omega)} d(s^{1-\alpha}) \\ &\lesssim \int_0^t (t^{1-\alpha} - s^{1-\alpha})^{\beta-\theta\beta-1}\|\varphi_j(s)\|^p_{\mathbb{D}^\nu(\Omega)} d(s^{1-\alpha}).\end{aligned} \tag{50}$$

Since $\varphi_j \in \mathbb{B}_R(0, T; \mathbb{D}^\nu(\Omega))$, one has

$$\|\varphi_j(t)\|_{\mathbb{D}^\nu(\Omega)} \leqslant R, \quad \text{for almost } t \in (0, T). \tag{51}$$

Thus, (50) is equivalent to

$$\begin{aligned}&\int_0^t \left\|R_{2,\sigma}(t^{1-\alpha} - s^{1-\alpha})\left|\nabla \varphi_j(s,x)\right|^p\right\|_{\mathbb{D}^\nu(\Omega)} d(s^{1-\alpha}) \\ &\lesssim \int_0^t (t^{1-\alpha} - s^{1-\alpha})^{\beta-\theta\beta-1}\left[\operatorname*{ess\,sup}_{t \in (0,T)} \|\varphi_j(s)\|_{\mathbb{D}^\nu(\Omega)}\right]^p d(s^{1-\alpha}) \\ &\lesssim M^p \int_0^t (t^{1-\alpha} - s^{1-\alpha})^{\beta-\theta\beta-1} d(s^{1-\alpha}).\end{aligned} \tag{52}$$

Since $\theta < 1$, the last integral is convergent. We thus can find a sufficiently small constant T such that $T^{(1-\alpha)\beta-\theta\beta}R^{p-1} \leqslant \frac{1}{2}$. Therefore, one has

$$\int_0^t \left\|R_{2,\sigma}(t^{1-\alpha} - s^{1-\alpha})\left|\nabla \varphi_j(s,x)\right|^p\right\|_{\mathbb{D}^\nu(\Omega)} d(s^{1-\alpha}) \leqslant \frac{1}{2}R. \tag{53}$$

Combining (46), (47) and (53) gives us

$$\|\varphi_{j+1}(t)\|_{\mathbb{D}^\nu(\Omega)} \leqslant R. \tag{54}$$

We can now conclude that $\varphi_{j+1} \in \mathbb{B}_R(0,T;\mathbb{D}^\nu(\Omega))$. Thus, $\{\varphi_j\}_{j\in\mathbb{N}}$ is a subset of $\mathbb{B}_R(0,T;\mathbb{D}^\nu(\Omega))$.

Next, we prove that $\{\varphi_j\}_{j\in\mathbb{N}}$ is a Cauchy sequence in $\mathbb{B}_R(0,T;\mathbb{D}^\nu(\Omega))$. Let φ_{j-1} and φ_j be two elements of $\{\varphi_j\}_{j\in\mathbb{N}} \subset \mathbb{B}_R(0,T;\mathbb{D}^\nu(\Omega))$. We have

$$\|\varphi_{j+1}(t) - \varphi_j(t)\|_{\mathbb{D}^\nu(\Omega)} \leqslant \int_0^t \left\|R_{2,\sigma}(t^{1-\alpha} - s^{1-\alpha})\left[|\nabla\varphi_j(s)|^p - |\nabla\varphi_{j-1}(s)|^p\right]\right\|_{\mathbb{D}^\nu(\Omega)} \mathrm{d}(s^{1-\alpha}). \tag{55}$$

Repeated application of Lemma 2 enables us to write

$$\|\varphi_{j+1}(t) - \varphi_j(t)\|_{\mathbb{D}^\nu(\Omega)} \lesssim \int_0^t (t^{1-\alpha} - s^{1-\alpha})^{\beta-\theta\beta-1}\left\||\nabla\varphi_j(s)|^p - |\nabla\varphi_{j-1}(s)|^p\right\|_{\mathbb{D}^{\nu-\theta\sigma}(\Omega)} \mathrm{d}(s^{1-\alpha}). \tag{56}$$

It follows that

$$\|\varphi_{j+1}(t) - \varphi_j(t)\|_{\mathbb{D}^\nu(\Omega)}$$
$$\lesssim \int_0^t (t^{1-\alpha} - s^{1-\alpha})^{\beta-\theta\beta-1}\left(\|\varphi_j(s)\|_{\mathbb{D}^\nu(\Omega)}^{p-1}(s) + \|\varphi_{j-1}\|_{\mathbb{D}^\nu(\Omega)}^{p-1}(s)\right)\|\varphi_j(s) - \varphi_{j-1}(s)\|_{\mathbb{D}^\nu(\Omega)} \mathrm{d}(s^{1-\alpha}). \tag{57}$$

Similar to the above arguments, since $\varphi_{j-1}, \varphi_j \in \mathbb{B}_R(0,T;\mathbb{D}^\nu(\Omega))$, we have

$$\begin{cases} \mathop{\mathrm{ess\,sup}}\limits_{t\in(0,T)} \|\varphi_{j-1}(t)\|_{\mathbb{D}^\nu(\Omega)} \leqslant R, \\ \mathop{\mathrm{ess\,sup}}\limits_{t\in(0,T)} \|\varphi_j(t)\|_{\mathbb{D}^\nu(\Omega)} \leqslant R. \end{cases} \tag{58}$$

Therefore, we obtain the following estimate:

$$\|\varphi_{j+1}(t) - \varphi_j(t)\|_{\mathbb{D}^\nu(\Omega)} \tag{59}$$
$$\lesssim \int_0^t (t^{1-\alpha} - s^{1-\alpha})^{\beta-\theta\beta-1}\left[\mathop{\mathrm{ess\,sup}}\limits_{s\in(0,T)} \|\varphi_j(s)\|_{\mathbb{D}^\nu(\Omega)}(s)\right]^{p-1} \|\varphi_j(s) - \varphi_{j-1}(s)\|_{\mathbb{D}^\nu(\Omega)} \mathrm{d}(s^{1-\alpha})$$
$$+ \int_0^t (t^{1-\alpha} - s^{1-\alpha})^{\beta-\theta\beta-1}\left[\mathop{\mathrm{ess\,sup}}\limits_{s\in(0,T)} \|\varphi_{j-1}(s)\|_{\mathbb{D}^\nu(\Omega)}(s)\right]^{p-1} \|\varphi_j(s) - \varphi_{j-1}(s)\|_{\mathbb{D}^\nu(\Omega)} \mathrm{d}(s^{1-\alpha})$$
$$\lesssim R^{p-1}\left[\int_0^t (t^{1-\alpha} - s^{1-\alpha})^{\beta-\theta\beta-1}\mathrm{d}(s^{1-\alpha})\right]\mathop{\mathrm{ess\,sup}}\limits_{t\in(0,T)} \|\varphi_j(t) - \varphi_{j-1}(t)\|_{\mathbb{D}^\nu(\Omega)}. \tag{60}$$

From the fact that

$$\int_0^t (t^{1-\alpha} - s^{1-\alpha})^{\beta-\theta\beta-1}\mathrm{d}(s^{1-\alpha}) \lesssim T^{(1-\alpha)\beta-\theta\beta}, \tag{61}$$

by a a suitable choice of T, we have

$$\|\varphi_{j+1}(t) - \varphi_j(t)\|_{\mathbb{D}^\nu(\Omega)} \leqslant \frac{1}{2}\mathop{\mathrm{ess\,sup}}\limits_{t\in(0,T)} \|\varphi_j(t) - \varphi_{j-1}(t)\|_{\mathbb{D}^\nu(\Omega)}, \quad t > 0. \tag{62}$$

This is equivalent to the following result:

$$\mathop{\mathrm{ess\,sup}}\limits_{t\in(0,T)} \|\varphi_{j+1}(t) - \varphi_j(t)\|_{\mathbb{D}^\nu(\Omega)} \leqslant \frac{1}{2}\mathop{\mathrm{ess\,sup}}\limits_{t\in(0,T)} \|\varphi_j(t) - \varphi_{j-1}(t)\|_{\mathbb{D}^\nu(\Omega)}. \tag{63}$$

From the above estimate, we easily deduce that $\{\varphi_j\}_{j \in \mathbb{N}}$ is a Cauchy sequence in $\mathbb{B}_R(0, T; \mathbb{D}^\nu(\Omega))$. The completeness of $L^\infty(0, T; \mathbb{D}^\nu(\Omega))$ ensures the unique existence of a function φ such that

$$\lim_{j \to \infty} \operatorname*{ess\,sup}_{t \in (0,T)} \left\| \varphi_j(t) - \varphi(t) \right\|_{\mathbb{D}^\nu(\Omega)} = 0. \tag{64}$$

Therefore, we find that

$$\varphi(t, x) = \lim_{j \to \infty} \varphi_j(t, x) = R_{1,\sigma}(t^{1-\alpha}) g(x) + \int_0^t R_{2,\sigma}(t^{1-\alpha} - s^{1-\alpha}) \left| \nabla \varphi(s, x) \right|^p \mathrm{d}(s^{1-\alpha}). \tag{65}$$

We can now conclude that Problem (1) possesses a unique mild solution $\varphi \in L^\infty(0, T; \mathbb{D}^\nu(\Omega))$. The theorem is thus proven. □

4. Conclusions

In this study, we prove the existence and uniqueness of a mild solution to an initial value problem for a fractional diffusion equation with the Caputo-like counterpart of the hyper-Bessel derivative and a gradient source function. The result hopefully can be extended in future works to global results, and indeed the blowing-up behavior of mild solutions is also an interesting open problem.

Author Contributions: Conceptualization: N.H.L., D.O. and A.T.N.; formal analysis: N.H.L., D.O. and A.T.N.; writing original draft preparation: N.H.L., D.O. and A.T.N.; writing review and editing: N.H.L., D.O. and A.T.N.; funding acquisition: N.H.L., D.O. and A.T.N. All authors have read and agreed to the published version of the manuscript.

Funding: This research received no external funding.

Data Availability Statement: Not applicable.

Acknowledgments: The authors thank to the anonymous reviewers for their help with this work.

Conflicts of Interest: The authors thank anonymous reviewers for helping with this work.

References

1. Chen, Z.Q.; Kim, K.H.; Kim, P. Fractional time stochastic partial differential equations. *Stoch. Process. Their Appl.* **2015**, *125*, 1470–1499. [CrossRef]
2. Akdemir, O.A.; Dutta, H.; Atangana, A. *Fractional Order Analysis: Theory, Methods and Applications*; John Wiley & Sons: Hoboken, NJ, USA, 2020.
3. Herrmann, R. *Fractional Calculus: An Introduction for Physicists*; World Scientific: Singapore, 2011.
4. Meerschaert, M.M.; Sikorskii, A. *Stochastic Models for Fractional Calculus*; De Gruyter Studies in Mathematics; Walter de Gruyter: Berlin/Heidelber, Germany; Boston, MA, USA, 2012; Volume 43.
5. Metzler, R.; Klafter, J. The random walk's guide to anomalous diffusion: A fractional dynamics approach. *Phys. Rep.* **2000**, *339*, 1–77. [CrossRef]
6. Saichev, A.I.; Zaslavsky, G.M. Fractional kinetic equations: Solutions and applications. *Chaos Interdiscip. J. Nonlinear Sci.* **1997**, *7*, 753–764. [CrossRef]
7. De Carvalho-Neto, P.M.; Planas, G. Mild solutions to the time fractional Navier-Stokes equations in R^N. *J. Differ. Equ.* **2015**, *259*, 2948–2980. [CrossRef]
8. Podlubny, I. Fractional Differential Equations. In *Mathematics in Sciene and Engineering*; Academic Press: San Diego, CA, USA, 1999; Volume 198.
9. Adiguzel, R.S.; Aksoy, U.; Karapinar, E.; Erhan, I.M. On the solution of a boundary value problem associated with a fractional differential equation. *Math. Methods Appl. Sci.* **2020**, 1–12. [CrossRef]
10. Adiguzel, R.S.; Aksoy, U.; Karapinar, E.; Erhan, I.M. Uniqueness of solution for higher-order nonlinear fractional differential equations with multi-point and integral boundary conditions. *RACSAM* **2021**, *115*, 1–16. [CrossRef]
11. Adiguzel, R.S.; Aksoy, U.; Karapinar, E.; Erhan, I.M. On The Solutions Of Fractional Differential Equations Via Geraghty Type Hybrid Contractions. *Appl. Comput. Math.* **2021**, *20*, 313–333.
12. Akdemir, A.O.; Karaoğlan, A.; Ragusa, M.A.; Set, E. Fractional integral inequalities via Atangana-Baleanu operators for convex and concave functions. *J. Funct. Spaces.* **2021**, *2021*, 1055434. [CrossRef]

13. Bao, T.N.; Caraballo, T.; Tuan, N.H. Existence and regularity results for terminal value problem for nonlinear fractional wave equations. *Nonlinearity* **2021**, *34*, 1448–1503. [CrossRef]
14. Caraballo, T.; Guo, B.; Tuan, N.H.; Wang, R. Asymptotically autonomous robustness of random attractors for a class of weakly dissipative stochastic wave equations on unbounded domains. *Proc. R. Soc. Edinb. Sect. Math.* **2021**, *151*, 1700–1730. [CrossRef]
15. Chen, P.; Wang, B.; Wang, R.; Zhang, X. Multivalued random dynamics of Benjamin-Bona-Mahony equations driven by nonlinear colored noise on unbounded domains. *Math. Ann.* **2022**, 1–31. [CrossRef]
16. Caraballo, T.; Ngoc, T.B.; Tuan, N.H.; Wang, R. On a nonlinear Volterra integrodifferential equation involving fractional derivative with Mittag-Leffler kernel. *Proc. Am. Math. Soc.* **2021**, *149*, 3317–3334. [CrossRef]
17. Karapinar, E.; Binh, H.D.; Luc, N.H.; Can, N.H. On continuity of the fractional derivative of the time-fractional semilinear pseudo-parabolic systems. *Adv. Differ. Equ.* **2021**, *2021*, 1–24. [CrossRef]
18. Önalan, H.K.; Akdemir, A.O.; Ardıç, M.A.; Baleanu, D. On new general versions of Hermite–Hadamard type integral inequalities via fractional integral operators with Mittag-Leffler kernel. *J. Inequalities Appl.* **2021**, *2021*, 1–16.
19. Nghia, B.; Luc, N.; Binh, H.; Long, L. Regularization method for the problem of determining the source function using integral conditions. *Adv. Theory Nonlinear Anal. Appl.* **2021**, *5*, 351–361. [CrossRef]
20. Nass, A.; Mpungu, K. Symmetry Analysis of Time Fractional Convection-reaction-diffusion Equation with a Delay. *Results Nonlinear Anal.* **2019**, *2*, 113–124.
21. Nguyen, A.T.; Caraballo, T.; Tuan, N.H. On the initial value problem for a class of nonlinear biharmonic equation with time-fractional derivative. *Proc. R. Soc. Edinb. Sect. A* **2021**, *26*, 1–43. [CrossRef]
22. Nguyen, H.T.; Tuan, N.A.; Yang, C. Global well-posedness for fractional Sobolev-Galpern type equations. *Discrete Contin. Dyn. Syst.* **2022**, *42*, 2637–2665. [CrossRef]
23. Wang, R.; Shi, L.; Wang, B. Asymptotic behavior of fractional nonclassical diffusion equations driven by nonlinear colored noise on $\mathbb{R}^N$. *Nonlinearity* **2019**, *32*, 4524. [CrossRef]
24. Wang, R.; Wang, B. Random dynamics of p-Laplacian lattice systems driven by infinite-dimensional nonlinear noise. *Stoch. Process. Appl.* **2020**, *130*, 7431–7462. [CrossRef]
25. Wang, R. Long-time dynamics of stochastic lattice plate equations with nonlinear noise and damping. *J. Dyn. Differ. Equ.* **2021**, *33*, 767–803. [CrossRef]
26. Tuan, N.H.; Debbouche, A.; Ngoc, T.B. Existence and regularity of final value problems for time fractional wave equations. *Comput. Math. Appl.* **2019**, *78*, 1396–1414. [CrossRef]
27. Tuan, N.H.; Zhou, Y.; Thach, T.N.; Can, N.H. Initial inverse problem for the nonlinear fractional Rayleigh-Stokes equation with random discrete data. *Commun. Nonlinear Sci. Numer. Simul.* **2019**, *78*, 104873. [CrossRef]
28. Tuan, N.H.; Nane, E. Inverse source problem for time-fractional diffusion with discrete random noise. *Stat. Probab. Lett.* **2017**, *120*, 126–134. [CrossRef]
29. Tuan, N.H.; Huynh, L.N.; Baleanu, D.; Can, N.H. On a terminal value problem for a generalization of the fractional diffusion equation with hyper-Bessel operator. *Math. Methods Appl. Sci.* **2020**, *43*, 2858–2882. [CrossRef]
30. Garra, R.; Giusti, A.; Mainardi, F.; Pagnini, G. Fractional relaxation with time-varying coefficient. *Fract. Calc. Appl. Anal.* **1999**, *2*, 383–414. [CrossRef]
31. Dimovski, I. Operational calculus for a class of differential operators. *C. R. Acad. Bulg. Sci.* **1966**, *19*, 1111–1114.
32. Orsingher, E.; Polito, F. Randomly stopped nonlinear fractional birth processes. *Stoch. Anal. Appl.* **2013**, *31*, 262–292. [CrossRef]
33. Pagnini, G. Erdélyi–Kober fractional diffusion. *Fract. Calc. Appl. Anal.* **2012**, *15*, 117–127. [CrossRef]
34. Al-Musalhi, F.; Al-Salti, N.; Karimov, E. Initial boundary value problems for a fractional differential equation with hyper-Bessel operator. *Fract. Calc. Appl. Anal.* **2018**, *21*, 200–219. [CrossRef]
35. Au, V.V.; Singh, J.; Anh, T.N. Well-posedness results and blow-up for a semi-linear time fractional diffusion equation with variable coefficients. *Electron. Res. Arch.* **2021**, *29*, 3581–3607. [CrossRef]
36. Baleanu, D.; Binh, H.D.; Nguyen, A.T. On a Fractional Parabolic Equation with Regularized hyper-Bessel Operator and Exponential Nonlinearities. *Symmetry* **2022**, *14*, 1419. [CrossRef]
37. Zhao, D.; Luo, M. General conformable fractional derivative and its physical interpretation. *Calcolo* **2017**, *54*, 903–917. [CrossRef]
38. Souplet, P. Recent results and open problems on parabolic equations with gradient nonlinearities. *Electron. J. Differ. Equ.* **2001**, *10*, 19.
39. Brezis, H. *Functional Analysis, Sobolev Spaces and Partial Differential Equations*; Springer: New York, NY, USA, 2011.

Article

Well-Posedness and Global Attractors for Viscous Fractional Cahn–Hilliard Equations with Memory

Eylem Öztürk [1] and Joseph L. Shomberg [2,*]

[1] Department of Mathematics, Hacettepe University, Beytepe, Ankara 06800, Turkey
[2] Department of Mathematics and Computer Science, Providence College, Providence, RI 02918, USA
* Correspondence: jshomber@providence.edu

Abstract: We examine a viscous Cahn–Hilliard phase-separation model with memory and where the chemical potential possesses a nonlocal fractional Laplacian operator. The existence of global weak solutions is proven using a Galerkin approximation scheme. A continuous dependence estimate provides uniqueness of the weak solutions and also serves to define a precompact pseudometric. This, in addition to the existence of a bounded absorbing set, shows that the associated semigroup of solution operators admits a compact connected global attractor in the weak energy phase space. The minimal assumptions on the nonlinear potential allow for arbitrary polynomial growth.

Keywords: Cahn–Hilliard equation; fractional Laplacian; memory

1. Introduction

Let Ω be a smooth (at least Lipschitz) bounded domain in $\mathbb{R}^N$, $N = 3, 2, 1$, with boundary $\partial \Omega$ and let $T > 0$. We consider the following viscous fractional Cahn–Hilliard equation in the unknown (order parameter) u satisfying

$$\partial_t u(t,x) = \int_0^\infty k(s) \Delta \mu(t-s, x) ds \quad \text{in} \quad \Omega \times (0,T), \tag{1}$$

k is a so-called relaxation kernel, with a chemical potential μ given by

$$\mu(t,x) = \alpha \partial_t u(t,x) + (-\Delta)^\beta u(t,x) + F'(u(t,x)) \quad \text{in} \quad \Omega \times \mathbb{R}, \tag{2}$$

$\alpha > 0$, $\beta \in (0,1)$, and typically, F is a double-well potential (the precise assumptions on F are stated in (N1)–(N3) below), subject to the boundary conditions

$$u = 0 \quad \text{on} \quad \mathbb{R}^N \setminus \Omega \times (0,T) \quad \text{and} \quad \partial_{\mathbf{n}} \mu = 0 \quad \text{on} \quad \partial \Omega \times (0,T), \tag{3}$$

with the given initial and past conditions

$$u(0) = u_0(0) \quad \text{in} \quad \Omega \quad \text{and} \quad u(-t) = u_0(-t) \quad \text{in} \quad \Omega \times [0,T), \tag{4}$$

for

$$u_0 : \Omega \times (-\infty, 0) \to \mathbb{R}.$$

Here, we define $(-\Delta)^\beta$ with $0 < \beta < 1$ as the (nonlocal) fractional Laplace operator. In other words, let $\Omega \subset \mathbb{R}^N$ be an arbitrary open set and fix

$$\mathcal{L}^1(\Omega) := \left\{ u : \Omega \to \mathbb{R} \text{ measurable}, \int_\Omega \frac{|u(x)|}{(1+|x|)^{N+2\beta}} dx < \infty \right\}.$$

For $u \in \mathcal{L}^1(\mathbb{R}^N)$, $x \in \mathbb{R}^N$, and $\varepsilon > 0$, we write

$$(-\Delta)^\beta_\varepsilon u(x) = C_{N,\beta} \int_{\{y \in \mathbb{R}^N, |y-x| > \varepsilon\}} \frac{u(x) - u(y)}{|x-y|^{N+2\beta}} dy$$

with the normalized constant $C_{N,\beta}$ given by

$$C_{N,\beta} = \frac{\beta 2^{2\beta}\Gamma\left(\frac{N+2\beta}{2}\right)}{\pi^{\frac{N}{2}}\Gamma(1-\beta)}, \tag{5}$$

where Γ denotes the usual gamma function. The (restricted) fractional Laplacian $(-\Delta)^\beta u$ of the function u is defined by the formula

$$(-\Delta)^\beta u(x) = C_{N,\beta}\text{P.V.}\int_{\mathbb{R}^N}\frac{u(x)-u(y)}{|x-y|^{N+2\beta}}dy = \lim_{\varepsilon\downarrow 0}(-\Delta)^\beta_\varepsilon u(x), \quad x\in\mathbb{R}^N, \tag{6}$$

provided that the limit exists. We call A^β the self-adjoint realization of the fractional Laplacian $(-\Delta)^\beta$ with Dirichlet boundary condition (3)$_1$, see, e.g., [1] (Section 2.2) (see also [2]).

Some remarks: First, observe the chemical potential (2) involves the Neumann (no-flux) condition described by (3). Hence, when the memory function k is *close* to the Dirac delta function, we recover the usual parabolic equation associated with the Cahn–Hilliard equation with the flux-free chemical potential.

Naturally, we are also interested in the closely related problem to (1)–(4) whereby the fractional Laplace operator $(-\Delta)^\beta$ is replaced with the *regional* fractional Laplacian, A^β_Ω, defined by first setting

$$A^\beta_{\Omega,\varepsilon}u(x) = C_{N,\beta}\int_{\{y\in\Omega,|y-x|>\varepsilon\}}\frac{u(x)-u(y)}{|x-y|^{N+2\beta}}dy,$$

where $C_{N,\beta}$ is given by (5), then

$$A^\beta_\Omega u(x) = C_{N,\beta}\text{P.V.}\int_\Omega \frac{u(x)-u(y)}{|x-y|^{N+2\beta}}dy = \lim_{\varepsilon\downarrow 0}A^\beta_{\Omega,\varepsilon}u(x), \quad x\in\Omega, \tag{7}$$

provided that the limit exists. Assuming $u\in\mathcal{D}(\Omega)$ (see [1] (page 1280)) then the two fractional Laplacian operators are related by

$$(-\Delta)^\beta u(x) = A^\beta_\Omega u(x) + V_\Omega(x)u(x), \quad \forall u\in\mathcal{D}(\Omega) \tag{8}$$

with the following potential

$$V_\Omega(x) := C_{N,\beta}\int_{\mathbb{R}^N\setminus\Omega}\frac{dy}{|x-y|^{N+2\beta}}, \quad x\in\Omega. \tag{9}$$

The comparable Cahn–Hilliard problem with the regional fractional Laplacian is then (1) with the chemical potential

$$\mu = \alpha\partial_t u + A^\beta_\Omega u + F'(u) \quad \text{in} \quad \Omega\times(0,T), \tag{10}$$

now subject to the boundary conditions

$$u = 0 \quad \text{on} \quad \partial\Omega\times(0,T) \quad \text{and} \quad \partial_n\mu = 0 \quad \text{on} \quad \partial\Omega\times(0,T), \tag{11}$$

with the above initial and past conditions in (4). Our focus here is on obtaining results for the restricted fractional Laplacian, of which the regional counterpart can be view as a perturbation thanks to (8). The restricted fractional Laplacian appears in the context of nonlocal phase transitions with Dirichlet boundary conditions in [3,4]. On the other hand, the regional fractional Laplacian is generally better suited to treat problems with nonhomogeneous boundary data and even dynamic boundary conditions (see [1,5] and the references therein).

It should also be noted that we only consider the viscous case, where $\alpha > 0$, since the nonviscous counterpart $\alpha = 0$ inherits no added regularity for $\alpha \partial_t \phi$.

Inside a bounded container $\Omega \subset \mathbb{R}^3$, the Cahn–Hilliard equation (see [6]) is a phase separation model for a binary solution (e.g., a cooling alloy, glass, or polymer),

$$\partial_t u = \nabla \cdot [\kappa(u) \nabla \mu],$$

where u is the *order-parameter* (the relative difference of the two phases), κ is the *mobility function* (we set $\kappa \equiv 1$ throughout this article), and μ is the *chemical potential* (the first variation of the free-energy E with respect to u). In the classical model,

$$\mu = -\Delta u + F'(u) \quad \text{and} \quad E(u) = \int_\Omega \left(\frac{1}{2}|\nabla u|^2 + F(u)\right) dx,$$

where F describes the density of potential energy in Ω (e.g., the double-well potential $F(s) = (1 - s^2)^2$).

Recently the nonlocal free-energy functional has appeared in the literature [7],

$$E(\phi) = \int_\Omega \int_\Omega \frac{1}{4} J(x - y)(\phi(x) - \phi(y))^2 dx dy + \int_\Omega F(\phi) dx,$$

hence, the *chemical potential* is,

$$\mu = a\phi - J * \phi + F'(\phi), \tag{12}$$

where

$$a(x) = \int_\Omega J(x - y) dy \quad \text{and} \quad (J * \phi)(x) = \int_\Omega J(x - y)\phi(y) dy. \tag{13}$$

In view of [8,9], the nonlocality expressed in (12)–(13) (see also [10–19]) is termed *weak* while the type under consideration here in (2) and (6) is called *strong*. Under certain conditions the strong type reduces to the weak (see [8], and also see [7]). Recently there has been much interest in the nonlocal Cahn–Hilliard equation with strong interactions of the restricted fractional Laplacian type (6) and the regional fractional Laplacian type (7) (see [3,5,8,9,20]). The results in these references concern global well-posedness, and when available, the existence of finite dimensional global attractors and regularity.

Additionally, there has been exceptional growth concerning dissipative infinite-dimensional systems with *memory* including models arising in the theory of heat conduction in special materials (see, e.g., [21–25]) and the theory of phase-transitions (see, e.g., [26–34]). One feature of equations that undergo "memory relaxation" is the admissibility of a so-called *inertia* term. For example, (see, e.g., [35]) the first-order equation with memory

$$u_t(t) + \int_0^\infty k_\varepsilon(s) f(u(t - s)) ds = 0$$

for

$$k_\varepsilon(s) = \frac{1}{\varepsilon} e^{-s/\varepsilon}$$

leads us (formally) to the "hyperbolic relaxation" equation

$$\varepsilon u_{tt}(t) + u_t(t) + f(u(t)) = 0.$$

In this way, our model also includes the viscous Cahn–Hilliard equation with inertial term (see [36]). Hence, the novelty in the present work is a relaxation of a phase-field model with a strongly interacting nonlocal diffusion mechanism.

In this article, our aims were:

- To provide a framework to establish the global (in time) well-posedness of the model problems (1)–(4) and (1), (4), (10), and (11).
- To prove the semigroup of solution operators admits a compact global attractor.

In order to reach these aims, we require sufficient growth conditions on F (given below) in order to employ a Galerkin scheme with suitable a priori estimates. With a finite energy phase space identified, a one-parameter family of solution operators is defined, hence generating a semidynamical system. This semigroup is dissipative on the energy phase space and also defines an α-contraction on the phase space. The existence of a compact global attractor follows.

2. Past History Formulation and Functional Setup

We now introduce the well-established past history approach from [37] (see also [27,29]) by defining the past history variable, for all $s > 0$ and $t > 0$,

$$\eta^t(x,s) = \int_0^s -\Delta\mu(x,t-\sigma)d\sigma. \tag{14}$$

Observe that η satisfies the boundary condition

$$\eta^t(x,0) = 0 \quad \text{on} \quad \Omega \times (0,\infty). \tag{15}$$

When k is sufficiently smooth and vanishes at $+\infty$ (these assumptions will be made more precise below), then integration by parts yields

$$\int_0^\infty k(s)\Delta\mu(x,t-s)ds = -\int_0^\infty \nu(s)\eta^t(x,s)ds$$

where $\nu(s) = -k'(s)$.

We may now formulate the model problem (1)–(4) as:

Problem P. Find $(u,\eta) = (u(x,t),\eta^t(x,s))$ on $(0,\infty)$ such that

$$\partial_t u(x,t) + \int_0^\infty \nu(s)\eta^t(x,s)ds = 0 \quad \text{in} \quad \Omega \times (0,\infty) \tag{16}$$

$$\mu(x,t) = \alpha\partial_t u(x,t) + (-\Delta)^\beta u(x,t) + F'(u(x,t)) \quad \text{in} \quad \Omega \times (0,\infty) \tag{17}$$

$$\partial_t \eta^t(x,s) + \partial_s \eta^t(x,s) = -\Delta\mu(x,t) \quad \text{in} \quad \Omega \times (0,\infty) \times (0,\infty) \tag{18}$$

held subject to (3) and (15), and satisfying the initial conditions (4)$_1$ and

$$\eta^0(x,s) = \eta_0(x,s) \quad \text{in} \quad \Omega \times (0,\infty), \tag{19}$$

whereby with (14),

$$\eta_0(x,s) = \int_0^s -\Delta\mu_0(x,-y)dy \quad \text{in} \quad \Omega \times (0,\infty), \tag{20}$$

where in light of (4)$_2$,

$$\mu_0(x,t) = \alpha\partial_t u_0(x,t) + (-\Delta)^\beta u_0(x,t) + F'(u_0(x,t)) \quad \text{for} \quad t \le 0. \tag{21}$$

Additionally, we are also interested in treating the related problem where the above fractional Laplace operator $(-\Delta)^\beta$ is replaced with the regional counterpart A_Ω^β. Hence, the formulation of the related *regional* Problem **P** is based on (1), (4), (10), and (11).

Here, we introduce some notation. From now on, we denote by $\|\cdot\|_X$ the norm in the specified (real) Banach space X, and $(\cdot,\cdot)_Y$ denotes the product on the specified (real) Hilbert space Y. The dual pairing between Y and the dual Y^* is denoted by $\langle u,v\rangle_{Y^*\times Y}$. The set Ω is omitted from the space when we indicate the norm. We denote the measure of the domain Ω by $|\Omega|$. In many calculations, functional notation indicating dependence on the variable t is dropped; for example, we write u in place of $u(t)$ or η^t in place of $\eta^t(s)$. Throughout the paper, C denotes a *generic* positive constant, while $Q: \mathbb{R}_+ \to \mathbb{R}_+$ denotes a *generic* increasing function. Such generic terms may or may not indicate dependencies on the (physical) parameters of the model problem, and may even change from line to line.

Let us define the linear operator $A_N := -\Delta$ on $D(A_N) = \{\psi \in H^2(\Omega) : \partial_n \psi = 0 \text{ on } \partial\Omega\}$, as the realization in $L^2(\Omega)$ of the Laplace operator endowed with Neumann boundary conditions. Here, $-\Delta$ denotes the usual (local) Laplace operator. It is well-known that A_N is the generator of a bounded analytic semigroup $e^{-A_N t}$ on $L^2(\Omega)$. Additionally, A_N is nonnegative and self-adjoint on $L^2(\Omega)$. With $H^{-r}(\Omega) := (H^r(\Omega))^*$, $r \in \mathbb{N}_+$, denote by $\langle \cdot \rangle$ the spatial average over Ω, i.e.,

$$\langle \psi \rangle := \frac{1}{|\Omega|} \langle \psi, 1 \rangle_{H^{-r} \times H^r}.$$

We set $H^r_{(0)}(\Omega) = \{\psi \in H^r(\Omega) : \langle \psi \rangle = 0\}$, $H^0(\Omega) = L^2(\Omega)$, and we know that $A_N^{-1} : H^0_{(0)}(\Omega) \to H^0_{(0)}(\Omega)$ is a well-defined mapping. We refer to the following norms in $H^{-r}(\Omega)$ (which are equivalent to the usual norms)

$$\|\psi\|^2_{H^{-r}} = \|A_N^{-r/2}(\psi - \langle \psi \rangle)\|^2 + |\langle \psi \rangle|^2. \tag{22}$$

The Sobolev space $H^1(\Omega)$ is endowed with the norm,

$$\|\psi\|^2_{H^1} := \|\nabla \psi\|^2 + \langle \psi \rangle^2. \tag{23}$$

Denote by $\lambda_\Omega > 0$ the constant in the Poincaré–Wirtinger inequality,

$$\|\psi - \langle \psi \rangle\| \leq \sqrt{\lambda_\Omega} \|\nabla \psi\|. \tag{24}$$

Whence, for $\lambda^*_\Omega := \max\{\lambda_\Omega, 1\}$, there holds, for all $\psi \in H^1(\Omega)$,

$$\begin{aligned}\|\psi\|^2 &\leq \lambda_\Omega \|\nabla \psi\|^2 + \langle \psi \rangle^2 \\ &\leq \lambda^*_\Omega \|\psi\|^2_{H^1}.\end{aligned} \tag{25}$$

We now more rigorously describe the fractional Laplacian with Dirichlet boundary conditions. For an arbitrary bounded domain $\Omega \subset \mathbb{R}^N$ and for $\beta \in (0,1)$, denote the fractional-order Sobolev space by,

$$W^{\beta,2}(\Omega) := \left\{ u \in L^2(\Omega) : \int_\Omega \int_\Omega \frac{|u(x) - u(y)|^2}{|x-y|^{N+2\beta}} dx dy < \infty \right\},$$

to be equipped with the norm

$$\|u\|_{W^{\beta,2}} := \left(\int_\Omega |u(x)|^2 dx + \frac{C_{N,\beta}}{2} \int_\Omega \int_\Omega \frac{|u(x) - u(y)|^2}{|x-y|^{N+2\beta}} dx dy \right)^{1/2},$$

where $C_{N,\beta}$ is given by (5). Let

$$W^{\beta,2}_0(\Omega) = \overline{\mathcal{D}(\Omega)}^{W^{\beta,2}(\Omega)}.$$

Hence, $W^{\beta,2}_0(\Omega)$ is a closed subspace of $W^{\beta,2}(\Omega)$ containing $\mathcal{D}(\Omega)$. Moreover, thanks to [38] (Theorem 10.1.1),

$$W^{\beta,2}_0(\Omega) = \{u \in W^{\beta,2}(\mathbb{R}^N) : \tilde{u} = 0 \text{ on } \mathbb{R}^N \setminus \Omega\},$$

where $\tilde{u}$ is the quasi-continuous version (with respect to the capacity defined with the space $W^{\beta,2}(\Omega)$) of u. One may easily show that the following defines an equivalent norm on the space $W_0^{\beta,2}(\Omega)$,

$$\begin{aligned}|||u|||_{W_0^{\beta,2}}^2 &= \frac{C_{N,\beta}}{2}\int_\Omega\int_\Omega \frac{|u(x)-u(y)|^2}{|x-y|^{N+2\beta}}dxdy + \int_\Omega V_\Omega(x)|u(x)|^2 dx \\ &= \frac{C_{N,\beta}}{2}\int_{\mathbb{R}^N}\int_{\mathbb{R}^N} \frac{|u(x)-u(y)|^2}{|x-y|^{N+2\beta}}dxdy.\end{aligned} \quad (26)$$

Here, V_Ω is the potential (9).

Remark 1. *Either definition of the space $W_0^{\beta,2}(\Omega)$ makes sense for any arbitrary open set $\Omega \subset \mathbb{R}^3$ (not necessarily bounded). Furthermore, if Ω has a Lipschitz boundary, then by [39], $W_0^{\beta,2}(\Omega) = W^{\beta,2}(\Omega)$ for every $0 < \beta \leq \frac{1}{2}$.*

From now on, we write $u \in W_0^{\beta,2}(\Omega)$ to mean $u \in W^{\beta,2}(\mathbb{R}^N)$ and $u = 0$ on $\mathbb{R}^N \setminus \Omega$. Let $a_{E,\beta}$ be the bilinear symmetric closed form with domain $D(a_{E,\beta}) = W_0^{\beta,2}(\Omega)$ and defined for $u, v \in W_0^{\beta,2}(\Omega)$ by

$$\begin{aligned}a_{E,\beta}(u,v) &= \frac{C_{N,\beta}}{2}\int_\Omega\int_\Omega \frac{(u(x)-u(y))(v(x)-v(y))}{|x-y|^{N+2\beta}}dxdy + \int_\Omega V_\Omega(x)u(x)v(x)dx \\ &= \frac{C_{N,\beta}}{2}\int_{\mathbb{R}^N}\int_{\mathbb{R}^N} \frac{(u(x)-u(y))(v(x)-v(y))}{|x-y|^{N+2\beta}}dxdy.\end{aligned} \quad (27)$$

Let $A_{E,\beta}$ be the closed linear self-adjoint operator on $L^2(\Omega)$ associated with $a_{E,\beta}$ by

$$\begin{cases} D(A_{E,\beta}) := \{u \in W_0^{\beta,2}(\Omega) : \exists v \in L^2(\Omega), a_{E,\beta}(u,\varphi) = (v,\varphi) \, \forall \varphi \in W_0^{\beta,2}(\Omega)\} \\ A_{E,\beta}u = v. \end{cases} \quad (28)$$

According to [1] (Proposition 2.2), the operator $A_{E,\beta}$ on $L^2(\Omega)$ associated with the bilinear form $a_{E,\beta}$ is given by

$$D(A_{E,\beta}) := \{u \in W_0^{\beta,2}(\Omega) : (-\Delta)_E^\beta u \in L^2(\Omega)\} \quad \text{and} \quad \forall u \in D(A_{E,\beta}), \quad A_{E,\beta}u := (-\Delta)_E^\beta u. \quad (29)$$

Observe that comparing (6) and (26)–(29) shows, for all $u \in D(A_{E,\beta})$,

$$((-\Delta)_E^\beta u, u) = a_{E,\beta}(u,u) = |||u|||_{W_0^{\beta,2}}^2. \quad (30)$$

Concerning the related regional problem discussed above, we let $a_{D,\beta}$ be the bilinear symmetric closed form with domain $D(a_{D,\beta}) = W_0^{\beta,2}(\Omega)$ and defined for $u, v \in W_0^{\beta,2}(\Omega)$ by

$$a_{D,\beta}(u,v) = \frac{C_{N,\beta}}{2}\int_\Omega\int_\Omega \frac{(u(x)-u(y))(v(x)-v(y))}{|x-y|^{N+2\beta}}dxdy. \quad (31)$$

Let $A_{D,\beta}$ be the closed linear self-adjoint operator on $L^2(\Omega)$ associated with $a_{D,\beta}$ by

$$\begin{cases} D(A_{D,\beta}) := \{u \in W_0^{\beta,2}(\Omega) : \exists v \in L^2(\Omega), a_{D,\beta}(u,\varphi) = (v,\varphi) \, \forall \varphi \in W_0^{\beta,2}(\Omega)\} \\ A_{D,\beta}u = v. \end{cases} \quad (32)$$

Then, by [1] (Proposition 2.3), the operator $A_{D,\beta}$ on $L^2(\Omega)$ associated with the bilinear form $a_{D,\beta}$ is given by

$$D(A_{D,\beta}) := \{u \in W_0^{\beta,2}(\Omega) : A_\Omega^\beta u \in L^2(\Omega)\} \quad \text{and} \quad \forall u \in D(A_{D,\beta}), \quad A_{D,\beta} u := A_\Omega^\beta u. \tag{33}$$

We introduce the spaces for the memory variable η. First, the product in $H^\sigma(\Omega)$ for $\sigma \in \mathbb{R}$ and $u_1, u_2 \in H^\sigma(\Omega)$ is defined by

$$(u_1, u_2)_{H^\sigma} = (A_N^{\sigma/2} u_1, A_N^{\sigma/2} u_2). \tag{34}$$

For a nonnegative measurable function θ defined on $\mathbb{R}_+$ and for a Hilbert space W (with inner-product $(\cdot, \cdot)_W$), let $L_\theta^2(\mathbb{R}_+; W)$ be the Hilbert space of W-valued functions on $\mathbb{R}_+$ equipped with the following product,

$$(\phi_1, \phi_2)_{L_\theta^2(\mathbb{R}_+; W)} = \int_0^\infty \theta(s)(\phi_1(s), \phi_2(s))_W ds.$$

Thus, we set

$$\mathcal{M}_\sigma = L_\nu^2(\mathbb{R}_+; H^\sigma(\Omega)) \quad \text{and} \quad \mathcal{M}_\sigma^{(0)} = L_\nu^2(\mathbb{R}_+; H_{(0)}^\sigma(\Omega)) \quad \text{for } \sigma \in \mathbb{R},$$

where $\nu = \nu(s)$ is the kernel from (16). Hence, for $\sigma \in \mathbb{R}$ and $\phi_1, \phi_2 \in \mathcal{M}_\sigma$, using (34) the product in $\mathcal{M}_\sigma$ (and $\mathcal{M}_\sigma^{(0)}$) can be expressed as

$$(\phi_1, \phi_2)_{\mathcal{M}_\sigma} = \int_0^\infty \nu(s)(A_N^{\sigma/2} \phi_1(s), A_N^{\sigma/2} \phi_2(s)) ds.$$

Naturally, we may also consider spaces of the form $H_\nu^k(\mathbb{R}_+; H^\sigma(\Omega))$ for $k \in \mathbb{N}$.

We mention that solutions of Problem **P** must also satisfy the mass conservation constraints,

$$\langle u(t) \rangle = \langle u_0(0) \rangle \quad \text{and} \quad \langle \eta^t(s) \rangle = 0 \quad \forall t > 0, \forall s > 0. \tag{35}$$

With this, it is important to realize that the norm of η^t in the space $\mathcal{M}_{-1}^{(0)}$ may be expressed *without* writing the average value of η_0 in (22) by virtue of the second constraint of (35). Indeed, for $\eta^t \in \mathcal{M}_{-1}^{(0)}$,

$$\|\eta^t\|_{\mathcal{M}_{-1}} = \left(\int_0^\infty \nu(s) \|\eta^t(s)\|_{H^{-1}}^2 ds \right)^{1/2}$$
$$= \left(\int_0^\infty \nu(s) \|A_N^{-1/2} \eta^t(s)\|^2 ds \right)^{1/2}.$$

We now state the basic function spaces we intend to study Problem **P** in. For each $\beta \in (0,1)$ and $\sigma \in \mathbb{R}$, define the following (weak) energy Hilbertian phase-space $\mathcal{H}_{\beta,\sigma} := W_0^{\beta,2}(\Omega) \times \mathcal{M}_{\sigma-1}^{(0)}$, equipped with the norm on $W_0^{\beta,2}(\Omega) \times \mathcal{M}_{\sigma-1}^{(0)}$ whose square is given by, for all $\phi = (u, \eta)^{tr} \in \mathcal{H}_{\beta,\sigma}$,

$$\|\phi\|_{\mathcal{H}_{\beta,\sigma}}^2 := \|u\|_{W_0^{\beta,2}}^2 + \|\eta^t\|_{\mathcal{M}_{\sigma-1}}^2.$$

Then, for each $M \geq 0$, define the closed subset

$$\mathcal{H}_{\beta,\sigma}^M = \{\phi = (u,\eta)^{tr} \in \mathcal{H}_{\beta,\sigma} : |\langle u \rangle| \leq M\}. \tag{36}$$

When we are concerned with the dynamical system associated with the model Problem **P**, we utilize the following metric space,

$$\mathcal{X}_{\beta,\sigma}^M := \left\{ \phi = (u,\eta)^{tr} \in \mathcal{H}_{\beta,\sigma}^M : F(u) \in L^1(\Omega) \right\},$$

endowed with the metric

$$d_{\mathcal{X}^M_{\beta,\sigma}}(\phi_1, \phi_2) := \|\phi_1 - \phi_2\|_{\mathcal{H}^M_{\beta,\sigma}} + \left|\int_\Omega F(u_1)dx - \int_\Omega F(u_2)dx\right|^{1/2}.$$

Remark 2. *The embedding $\mathcal{H}^M_{\beta,1} \hookrightarrow \mathcal{H}^M_{\beta,0}$ is continuous but not compact, due to the presence of the second component $\mathcal{M}^{(0)}_{\sigma-1}$. Indeed, see [40] for a counterexample.*

It is appropriate for us to state the various assumptions that may be used on the kernel ν.

(K1) $\nu \in C^1(\mathbb{R}_+) \cap L^1(\mathbb{R}_+)$ and $\nu(s) \geq 0$ for all $s \in \mathbb{R}_+$.
(K2) $\nu'(s) \leq 0$ for all $s \in \mathbb{R}_+$.
(K3) $k_0 = \int_0^\infty \nu(s)ds > 0$. (For the sake of simplicity, we now assume $k_0 = 1$ throughout the rest of the paper.)
(K4) $\nu_0 = \lim_{s\to 0^+} \nu(s) < \infty$.
(K5) $\nu'(s) + \lambda\nu(s) \leq 0$ for a.e. $s \in \mathbb{R}_+$, for some $\lambda > 0$.

Some remarks for these assumptions: By assumption (K2), the inequality holds for all $\eta^t \in D(T_r)$

$$(T_r\eta^t, \eta^t)_{\mathcal{M}_{-1}} \leq 0. \tag{37}$$

We remind the reader that the assumption (K5) is only required when we examine the asymptotic behavior of the solutions (and in that case, (K2) is redundant).

In order to formulate a suitable (abstract) evolution equation for η^t, we define the linear operator $T_r = -\partial_s$ with the domain

$$D(T_r) = \{\eta^t \in \mathcal{M}^{(0)}_{-1} : \partial_s\eta^t \in \mathcal{M}^{(0)}_{-1}, \eta^t(0) = 0\}.$$

It is well-known that T_r is the infinitesimal generator of the right-translation semigroup on $\mathcal{M}_{-1}$; indeed, the following result comes from [37] (Theorem 3.1).

Proposition 1. *The operator T_r with domain $D(T_r)$ is an infinitesimal generator of a strongly continuous semigroup of contractions on $\mathcal{M}_{-1}$, denoted $e^{T_r t}$.*

As a consequence, we also have (see, e.g., [41] (Corollary IV.2.2)).

Corollary 1. *Let $T > 0$ and assume $g \in L^1(0,T;H^{-1}(\Omega))$. Then, for every $\eta_0 \in \mathcal{M}_{-1}$, the Cauchy problem for η^t,*

$$\begin{cases} \partial_t \eta^t = T_r \eta^t + g(t), & \text{for } t > 0, \\ \eta^0 = \eta_0, \end{cases} \tag{38}$$

has a unique (mild) solution $\eta \in C([0,T]; \mathcal{M}_{-1})$ which can be explicitly given as

$$\eta^t(s) = \begin{cases} \int_0^s g(t-y)dy, & \text{for } 0 < s \leq t, \\ \eta_0(s-t) + \int_0^t g(t-y)dy, & \text{for } s > t, \end{cases} \tag{39}$$

see also [21] (Section 3.2) and [37] (Section 3).

3. Variational Formulation and Well-Posedness

To begin this section, we state the assumptions on the nonlinear term F and report some important consequences of these assumptions. These assumptions on F are based on [13,15] and can be found in [5] (Section 3).

(N1) $F \in C^2_{loc}(\mathbb{R})$ and there exists $c_F > 0$ such that, for all $r \in \mathbb{R}$,

$$F''(r) \geq -c_F.$$

(N2) There exist $c_F > 0$ and $p \in (1, 2]$ such that, for all $r \in \mathbb{R}$,

$$|F'(r)|^p \leq c_F(|F(r)| + 1).$$

(N3) There exist C_1, $C_2 > 0$ such that, for all $r \in \mathbb{R}$,

$$F(r) \geq C_1 |r|^{p/(p-1)} - C_2.$$

The last assumption is not needed to obtain the existence of weak solutions, but it is relied upon later when we seek the existence of strong/regular solutions and uniqueness of these solutions.

(N4) There exist $\rho \geq 2$ and $C_3 > 0$ such that, for all $r \in \mathbb{R}$,

$$|F''(r)| \leq C_3(1 + |r|^{\rho-2}). \tag{40}$$

The following remarks are from [5]. Assumption (N1) implies that the potential F is a quadratic perturbation of some strictly convex function; i.e., there holds,

$$F(r) = G(r) - \frac{c_F}{2}r^2, \tag{41}$$

with $G \in C^2(\mathbb{R})$ strictly convex as $G'' \geq 0$ in Ω. Furthermore, with (N1), for each $M \geq 0$ there are constants $C_i > 0$, $i = 3, \ldots, 6$, (with C_4 and C_5 depending on M and F) such that, for all $r \in \mathbb{R}$,

$$F(r) - C_3 \leq C_4(r - M)^2 + F'(r)(r - M), \tag{42}$$

$$\frac{1}{2}|F'(s)|(1 + |r|) \leq F'(r)(r - M) + C_5, \tag{43}$$

(see [26] (Equations (4.7) and (4.8))) and

$$|F(r)| - C_6 \leq |F'(r)|(1 + |r|). \tag{44}$$

The last inequality appears in [42] (page 8). With the positivity condition (N3), it follows that, for all $r \in \mathbb{R}$,

$$|F'(r)| \leq c_F(|F(r)| + 1). \tag{45}$$

Assumption (N2) allows for *arbitrary* polynomial growth $\bar{p} = p/(p-1)$ in the potential F. Significantly, the double-well potential $F(r) = (r^2 - 1)^2$ satisfies (N2) with $p = 4/3$ and (N4) with $p = 2$.

We are now ready to introduce the variational/weak formulation of Problem **P**.

Definition 1. Let $T > 0$ and $\phi_0 = (u_0, \eta_0)^{tr} \in \mathcal{H}_{\beta,0}^M = W_0^{\beta,2}(\Omega) \times \mathcal{M}_{-1}^{(0)}$ be such that $F(u_0) \in L^1(\Omega)$. A pair $\phi = (u, \eta)$ satisfying

$$\phi = (u, \eta) \in L^\infty(0, T; \mathcal{H}_{\beta,0}^M), \tag{46}$$

$$\partial_t u \in L^2(0, T; H^{-1}(\Omega)), \tag{47}$$

$$\partial_t \eta \in L^2(0, T; H_\nu^{-1}(\mathbb{R}_+; H_{(0)}^{-1}(\Omega))), \tag{48}$$

$$\mu \in L^2(0, T; W^{-\beta,2}(\Omega)), \tag{49}$$

$$F'(u) \in L^\infty(0, T; L^p(\Omega)) \tag{50}$$

is called a WEAK SOLUTION to Problem **P** on $[0, T]$ with initial data $\phi_0 = (u_0, \eta_0) \in \mathcal{H}_{\beta,0}^M$ if the following identities hold almost everywhere in $(0, T)$, and for all $v \in H^1(\Omega)$, $\xi \in W_0^{\beta,2}(\Omega) \cap L^p(\Omega)$, and $\zeta \in \mathcal{M}_1$:

$$\langle \partial_t u, v \rangle_{H^{-1} \times H^1} + \int_0^\infty \nu(s) \langle \eta^t(s), v \rangle_{H^{-1} \times H^1} ds = 0, \tag{51}$$

$$a_{E,\beta}(u, \xi) + \langle F'(u), \xi \rangle_{W^{-\beta,2} \times W_0^{\beta,2}} + \alpha \langle \partial_t u, \xi \rangle_{W^{-\beta,2} \times W_0^{\beta,2}} = \langle \mu, \xi \rangle_{W^{-\beta,2} \times W_0^{\beta,2}}, \tag{52}$$

$$(\partial_t \eta^t, \zeta)_{\mathcal{M}_{-1}} - (T_r \eta^t, \zeta)_{\mathcal{M}_{-1}} = (\mu, \zeta)_{\mathcal{M}_0}. \tag{53}$$

Furthermore, the initial conditions hold in the L^2-sense

$$u(0) = u_0 \quad \text{and} \quad \eta^0 = \eta_0. \tag{54}$$

Finally, we say that $\phi = (u, \eta)^{tr}$ is a GLOBAL WEAK SOLUTION of Problem **P** if it is a weak solution on $[0, T]$, for any $T > 0$.

Remark 3. It is important to note that although η_0 is defined by (14) and (21), η_0 may be taken to be initial data independent of u. Henceforth we consider a more general problem with respect to the original one.

Remark 4. Concerning Equation (53) and the representation Formula (39), we have

$$T_r \eta^t(s) = -\partial_s \eta^t(s) = \begin{cases} \Delta \mu(t - s) & \text{for } 0 < s \leq t, \\ -\partial_s \eta_0(s - t) & \text{for } s > t. \end{cases}$$

Thus, when given $\eta_0 \in \mathcal{M}_{-1}^{(0)}$, then $T_r \eta^t \in H_\nu^{-1}(\mathbb{R}_+; H^{-1}(\Omega))$, for each $t \in (0, T)$, by virtue of (49). Moreover, taking $\zeta = 1$ in the variational equation

$$(\partial_t \eta^t, \zeta)_{\mathcal{M}_{-1}} - (T_r \eta^t, \zeta)_{\mathcal{M}_{-1}} = -\int_0^\infty \nu(s) \langle -\Delta \mu, \zeta \rangle_{H^{-1} \times H^1} ds,$$

we find, for all $s > t$,

$$\frac{\partial}{\partial t} \langle \eta^t(s) \rangle + \frac{\partial}{\partial s} \langle \eta_0(s - t) \rangle = k_0 \langle \Delta \mu(t - s) \rangle.$$

We know that $\eta_0 \in \mathcal{M}_{-1}^{(0)}$ and $k_0 = 1$, hence

$$\frac{\partial}{\partial t} \langle \eta^t(s) \rangle = 0,$$

and it follows that

$$\langle \eta^t(s) \rangle = 0 \quad \forall t \geq 0.$$

Remark 5. *In the Cahn–Hilliard model, it is well-known that the average value of u is conserved (see, e.g., [43] (Section III.4.2)). A similar property holds here for our problem. Indeed, we may choose the test function $v = 1$ in (51) which yields*

$$\frac{\partial}{\partial t}\langle u(t)\rangle + \int_0^\infty \nu(s)\langle \eta^t(s)\rangle ds = 0.$$

By (4), there holds $\langle \eta^t(s)\rangle = 0$ for all $t > 0$ and for all $s > 0$. Hence, we recover the conservation of mass

$$\langle u(t)\rangle = \langle u_0\rangle \quad \text{and} \quad \langle \partial_t u(t)\rangle = 0, \quad \forall t \geq 0. \tag{55}$$

Remark 6. *Before we continue to the existence statement, it is worthwhile to recall Theorem A1 (d) in Appendix A for which the following embedding holds*

$$D(A_{E,\beta}) \hookrightarrow L^\infty(\Omega), \quad \forall \beta \in (\frac{N}{4}, 1), \quad \text{for } N = 1, 2, 3. \tag{56}$$

Theorem 1. *Let $T > 0$ and $\phi_0 = (u_0, \eta_0)^{tr} \in \mathcal{H}_{\beta,0}^M = W_0^{\beta,2}(\Omega) \times \mathcal{M}_{-1}^{(0)}$ for $\beta \in (\frac{N}{4}, 1)$, $N = 1, 2, 3$, be such that $F(u_0) \in L^1(\Omega)$. Assume $\alpha > 0$ and that (K1)–(K4) and (N1)–(N3) hold. Problem **P** admits at least one weak solution $\phi = (u, \eta)$ on $(0, T)$ according to Definition 1 with the additional regularity*

$$u \in L^\infty(0, T; L^{p/(p-1)}(\Omega)), \tag{57}$$

$$\sqrt{\alpha}\partial_t u \in L^2(\Omega \times (0, T)), \tag{58}$$

$$\eta \in L^2(0, T; L^2_{-\nu'}(\mathbb{R}_+; H^{-1}_{(0)}(\Omega))), \tag{59}$$

$$F(u) \in L^\infty(0, T; L^1(\Omega)), \quad F'(u) \in L^\infty(0, T; L^1(\Omega)). \tag{60}$$

for any $T > 0$. Furthermore, setting

$$\mathcal{E}(t) := |||u(t)|||^2_{W_0^{\beta,2}} + 2(F(u(t)), 1) + \|\eta^t\|^2_{\mathcal{M}_{-1}} + C \tag{61}$$

for some $C > 0$ sufficiently large, the following energy equality holds for every such weak solution,

$$\mathcal{E}(t) + 2\int_0^t \left(\alpha\|\partial_t u(\tau)\|^2 d\tau - \int_0^\infty \nu'(s)\|\eta^\tau(s)\|^2_{H^{-1}} ds\right) d\tau = \mathcal{E}(0). \tag{62}$$

Proof. The proof proceeds in several steps. The existence proof begins with a Faedo–Galerkin approximation procedure in which we later pass to the limit. We first assume that $u_0 \in D(A_{E,\beta})$. (This assumption will be used to show that there is a sequence $\{u_{0n}\}_{n=1}^\infty$ such that $u_{0n} \to u_0$ in $D(A_{E,\beta})$ as well as $L^\infty(\Omega)$ per (56), which will be important in light of the fact that $F(u_{0n})$ is of arbitrary polynomial growth per assumptions (N1)–(N3).) The existence of a weak solution for $u_0 \in W_0^{\beta,2}(\Omega)$ with $F(u_0) \in L^1(\Omega)$ follows from a density argument. To establish the equality in the energy identity, we exploit the fact that the potential F is a quadratic perturbation of some strictly convex function.

Step 1: The Galerkin approximation. To begin, we introduce the family $\{v_j\}_{j\geq 1}$ of eigenvectors of the fractional Laplacian $A_{E,\beta}$, which exist thanks to Theorem A1 in Appendix A. Moreover, there is a family $\{w_j\}_{j\geq 1}$ consisting of the eigenvectors of the Neumann–Laplacian A_N, and with this, we define the smooth sequence of $\{z_j\}_{j\geq 1} \subset D(T_r) \cap W_\nu^{1,2}(\mathbb{R}_+; H^1_{(0)}(\Omega))$ by $z_j = b_j w_j$ such that $\{b_j\}_{j\geq 1} \subset C_c^\infty(\mathbb{R}_+)$ is an orthonormal basis for $L^2_\nu(\mathbb{R}_+)$. Using these, we define the following finite-dimensional spaces:

$$V^n = \text{span}\{v_1, v_2, \ldots, v_n\}, \quad W^n = \text{span}\{w_1, w_2, \ldots, w_n\}, \quad \mathcal{M}^n = \text{span}\{z_1, z_2, \ldots, z_n\}, \tag{63}$$

and set
$$V^\infty = \bigcup_{n=1}^\infty V^n, \quad W^\infty = \bigcup_{n=1}^\infty W^n, \quad \mathcal{M}^\infty = \bigcup_{n=1}^\infty \mathcal{M}^n.$$

Clearly, V^∞ is a dense subspace of $W_0^{\beta,2}(\Omega)$ and W^∞ is a dense subspace of $H^1(\Omega)$. In addition, $\mathcal{M}^\infty$ is a dense subspace of $\mathcal{M}_{-1}^{(0)}$. For $T > 0$ fixed, we look for two functions of the form on $(0, T)$,

$$u_n(t) = \sum_{k=1}^n a_k^{(n)}(t) v_k \quad \text{and} \quad \eta_n^t(s) = \sum_{k=1}^n c_k^{(n)}(t) z_k, \tag{64}$$

where $a_j^{(n)}$ and $c_j^{(n)}$ are assumed to be (at least) $C^2([0, T])$ for each $j = 1, 2, \ldots$ an for each $n = 1, 2, \ldots$, which solve the following approximating Problem $\mathbf{P}_n$:

$$(\partial_t u_n, v) + \int_0^\infty \nu(s)(\eta_n^t(s), v) ds = 0 \tag{65}$$

$$a_{E,\beta}(u_n, \xi) + (F'(u_n), \xi) + \alpha(\partial_t u_n, \xi) = (\mu_n, \xi) \tag{66}$$

$$(\partial_t \eta_n^t, \zeta)_{\mathcal{M}_{-1}} - (T_r \eta_n^t, \zeta)_{\mathcal{M}_{-1}} = (\mu_n, \zeta)_{\mathcal{M}_0} \tag{67}$$

$$u_n(0) = u_{0n}, \quad \eta_n^0 = \eta_{0n} \tag{68}$$

for every $v \in V^n$, $\xi \in W^n$ and $\zeta \in \mathcal{M}^n$, and where u_{0n} and η_{0n} denote the finite-dimensional projections of u_0 and η_0 onto V^n and $\mathcal{M}^n$, respectively. This approximating problem is equivalent to solving a Cauchy problem for a system of ordinary differential equations (indeed, see, e.g., [26] (page 131)). Hence, the Cauchy–Lipschitz theorem ensures that there exists a $T_n \in (0, \infty]$ such that this approximating system has a unique maximal solution.

Step 2: A priori estimates. We now derive some a priori estimates in order to show that $T_n = \infty$ for every $n \geq 1$ and that the sequences of u_n, η_n^t, μ_n are bounded in suitable functional spaces. By using $v = \mu_n$ as a test function in (65) and $\xi = \partial_t u_n$ as a test function in (66) we obtain

$$(\partial_t u_n, \mu_n) + \int_0^\infty \nu(s)(\eta_n^t(s), \mu_n) ds = 0 \tag{69}$$

$$(\mu_n, \partial_t u_n) = ((-\Delta)_E^\beta u_n, \partial_t u_n) + (F'(u_n), \partial_t u_n) + \alpha \|\partial_t u_n\|^2, \tag{70}$$

and taking $\zeta = \eta_n^t$ as a test function in (67) yields (for the products in $\mathcal{M}_{-1}$, this is a multiplication by $(-\Delta)^{-1} \eta_n^t$ in $\mathcal{M}_0$)

$$\int_0^\infty \nu(s) \left(\int_\Omega \partial_t \eta_n^t(x,s)(-\Delta)^{-1} \eta_n^t(x,s) dx \right) ds + \int_0^\infty \nu(s) \left(\int_\Omega \partial_s \eta_n^t(x,s)(-\Delta)^{-1} \eta_n^t(x,s) dx \right) ds$$
$$= \int_0^\infty \nu(s) \left(\int_\Omega (-\Delta) \mu_n(x,t)(-\Delta)^{-1} \eta_n^t(x,s) dx \right) ds,$$

which is, after an integration by parts,

$$(\partial_t \eta_n^t, \eta_n^t)_{\mathcal{M}_{-1}} + (\partial_s \eta_n^t, \eta_n^t)_{\mathcal{M}_{-1}} = (\mu_n, \eta_n^t)_{\mathcal{M}_0}. \tag{71}$$

Then, combining the results produces the differential identity, which holds for almost all $t \in (0, T)$,

$$\frac{1}{2} \frac{d}{dt} \left\{ \|\|u_n\|\|_{W_0^{\beta,2}}^2 + 2(F(u_n), 1) + \|\eta^t\|_{\mathcal{M}_{-1}}^2 \right\} + \alpha \|\partial_t u_n\|^2 - (T_r \eta_n^t, \eta_n^t)_{\mathcal{M}_{-1}} = 0. \tag{72}$$

For all $t \in (0, T_n)$, set

$$\mathcal{E}_n(t) := |||u_n(t)|||^2_{W^{\beta,2}_0} + 2(F(u_n(t)), 1) + \|\eta^t_n\|^2_{\mathcal{M}_{-1}} + C \tag{73}$$

where in light of (N3), the functional $\mathcal{E}_n(t)$ is nonnegative for all $t \in (0, T_n)$. We have

$$\frac{d}{dt}\mathcal{E}_n + 2\alpha\|\partial_t u_n\|^2 - 2\int_0^\infty \nu'(s)\|\eta^t_n(s)\|^2_{H^{-1}} ds = 0 \tag{74}$$

for almost all $t \in (0, T_n)$. Hence, integrating the equation above with respect to time in $(0, t)$, we are led to the following integral equality (which does hold for the approximate solutions)

$$\mathcal{E}_n(t) + 2\int_0^t \left(\alpha\|\partial_t u_n(\tau)\|^2 - \int_0^\infty \nu'(s)\|\eta^\tau_n(s)\|^2_{H^{-1}} ds \right) d\tau = \mathcal{E}_n(0). \tag{75}$$

Furthermore, from (73) and assumption (N3), we find the lower bound

$$|||u_n(t)|||^2_{W^{\beta,2}_0} + 2C_1\|u_n(t)\|^{p/(p-1)}_{L^{p/(p-1)}} + \|\eta^t_n\|^2_{\mathcal{M}_{-1}} \leq \mathcal{E}_n(t). \tag{76}$$

Using the fact that $F(u_0) \in L^1(\Omega)$, we also obtain the upper bound

$$\mathcal{E}_n(t) \leq \mathcal{E}_n(0) \leq |||u_n(0)|||^2_{W^{\beta,2}_0} + (F(u_n(0)), 1) + \|\eta^0_n\|^2_{\mathcal{M}_{-1}}$$
$$\leq Q(\|\phi_n(0)\|_{\mathcal{H}^M_{\beta,0}}) + C. \tag{77}$$

In particular, the uniform bound derived from (75)–(77) implies that the local solution to Problem $\mathbf{P_n}$ can be extended up to time T, that is $T_n = T$, for every n. Moreover, from (75) and (76) we deduce the following bounds for the approximate solution

$$\|u_n\|_{L^\infty(0,T;W^{\beta,2}_0)} \leq C \tag{78}$$

$$\|\eta_n\|_{L^\infty(0,T;\mathcal{M}_{-1})} \leq C \tag{79}$$

$$\|F(u_n)\|_{L^\infty(0,T;L^1)} \leq C \tag{80}$$

$$\sqrt{\alpha}\|\partial_t u_n\|_{L^2(\Omega \times (0,T))} \leq C \tag{81}$$

$$\|\eta_n\|_{L^2(0,T;L^2_{-\nu'}(\mathbb{R}_+;H^{-1}))} \leq C \tag{82}$$

$$\|u_n\|_{L^\infty(0,T;L^{p/(p-1)})} \leq C. \tag{83}$$

Obviously, (45) and (80) immediately show us

$$\|F'(u_n)\|_{L^\infty(0,T;L^1)} \leq C. \tag{84}$$

Next, since $\langle A_N^{-1}\partial_t u_n \rangle = 0$ (recall (55)), we may (and do) take $v = A_N^{-1}\partial_t u_n$ in (65) which leads us to the estimate,

$$\|A_N^{-\frac{1}{2}}\partial_t u_n\|^2 \leq \int_0^\infty \nu(s)\|A_N^{-\frac{1}{2}}\eta^t_n(s)\|\|A_N^{-\frac{1}{2}}\partial_t u_n(t)\|ds, \tag{85}$$

that is,

$$\|\partial_t u_n\|^2_{H^{-1}} \leq \int_0^\infty \nu(s)\|\eta^t_n(s)\|_{H^{-1}}\|\partial_t u_n\|_{H^{-1}} ds. \tag{86}$$

Using the Cauchy–Schwartz inequality and assumption (K3), we can write

$$\|\partial_t u_n\|_{H^{-1}} \leq \|\eta^t_n\|_{\mathcal{M}_{-1}}. \tag{87}$$

Thus, (79) and (87) yield

$$\|\partial_t u_n\|_{L^\infty(0,T;H^{-1})} \leq C. \tag{88}$$

We need to bound $F'(u_n)$, then μ_n. In light of (66), we apply (84), (88), and the fact that operator $A_{E,\beta}$ is bounded from $W_0^{\beta,2}(\Omega)$ into $W^{-\beta,2}(\Omega)$ (in particular, $\|A_{E,\beta} u_n\|_{L^2(0,T;W^{-\beta,2}(\Omega))} \leq C$), to obtain the following uniform bounds for μ_n

$$|\langle \mu_n \rangle| \leq C, \tag{89}$$

and

$$\|\mu_n\|_{L^2(0,T;W^{-\beta,2}(\Omega))} \leq C. \tag{90}$$

This completes Step 2.

Step 3: Passage to the limit. On account of the above uniform inequalities, we can argue that there are functions u, η, μ, such that, up to subsequences,

$$u_n \rightharpoonup u \quad \text{weakly-* in} \quad L^\infty(0,T;W_0^{\beta,2}(\Omega)), \tag{91}$$

$$u_n \rightharpoonup u \quad \text{weakly-* in} \quad L^\infty(0,T;L^{p/(p-1)}(\Omega)), \tag{92}$$

$$\partial_t u_n \rightharpoonup \partial_t u \quad \text{weakly-* in} \quad L^\infty(0,T;H^{-1}(\Omega)), \tag{93}$$

$$\sqrt{\alpha}\partial_t u_n \rightharpoonup \sqrt{\alpha}\partial_t u \quad \text{weakly in} \quad L^2(\Omega \times (0,T)), \tag{94}$$

$$\eta_n \rightharpoonup \eta \quad \text{weakly-* in} \quad L^\infty(0,T;\mathcal{M}_{-1}), \tag{95}$$

$$\eta_n \rightharpoonup \eta \quad \text{weakly in} \quad L^2(0,T;L^2_{-\nu'}(\mathbb{R}_+;H^{-1}(\Omega))), \tag{96}$$

$$\partial_t \eta_n \rightharpoonup \partial_t \eta \quad \text{weakly in} \quad L^2(0,T;H_\nu^{-1}(\mathbb{R}_+;H^{-1}(\Omega))), \tag{97}$$

$$\mu_n \rightharpoonup \mu \quad \text{weakly in} \quad L^2(0,T;W^{-\beta,2}(\Omega)). \tag{98}$$

(Note that (97) is due to (67) and the definition of the operator T_r.) Using the above convergences (91) and (93), as well as the fact that the injection $W_0^{\beta,2}(\Omega) \hookrightarrow L^2(\Omega)$ is compact for any $\beta \in (0,1)$, we draw upon the conclusion of the Aubin–Lions Lemma (see Lemma A1 in Appendix A) to deduce the following embedding is compact

$$W := \{\chi \in L^2(0,T;W_0^{\beta,2}(\Omega)) : \partial_t \chi \in L^2(0,T;H^{-1}(\Omega))\} \hookrightarrow L^2(\Omega \times (0,T)). \tag{99}$$

Hence,

$$u_n \to u \quad \text{strongly in} \quad L^2(\Omega \times (0,T)), \tag{100}$$

and we deduce that u_n converges to u, almost everywhere in $\Omega \times (0,T)$. Using assumption (N1) with (100), we deduce

$$F'(u_n) \to F'(u) \quad \text{strongly in} \quad L^2(0,T;L^1(\Omega)). \tag{101}$$

Thus, we now have all the sufficient convergence results to pass to the limit in Equations (65) and (66) in order to recover (16) and (17), respectively. It remains to recover Equation (67) after we pass to the limit. An integration by parts on the first term in (67) and then an application of (95) yields, for any $\zeta \in C_0^\infty((0,T);C_0^\infty((0,T);H^1(\Omega)))$

$$\int_0^T (\partial_\tau \eta_n^\tau, \zeta)_{\mathcal{M}_{-1}} d\tau = -\int_0^T (\eta_n^\tau, \partial_\tau \zeta)_{\mathcal{M}_{-1}} d\tau \to -\int_0^T (\eta^\tau, \partial_\tau \zeta)_{\mathcal{M}_{-1}} d\tau. \tag{102}$$

With this, we have

$$\partial_t \eta_n^t \rightharpoonup \partial_t \eta^t \quad \text{weakly in} \quad L^2(0,T;H_\nu^{-1}(\mathbb{R}_+;H^{-1}(\Omega))) \tag{103}$$

and that $\eta^t \in L^\infty(0,T; H_\nu^{-1}(\mathbb{R}_+; H^{-1}(\Omega)))$. Furthermore, with the help of (96), we have

$$-\int_0^T (T_r \eta_n^\tau, \zeta)_{\mathcal{M}_{-1}} d\tau = -\int_0^T \nu'(s)(\eta_n^\tau, \zeta)_{H^{-1}} d\tau \to -\int_0^T \nu'(s)(\eta^\tau, \zeta)_{H^{-1}} d\tau. \quad (104)$$

By using a density argument (see [37]) and the following distributional equality

$$-\int_0^T (\eta_n^\tau, \partial_t \zeta)_{\mathcal{M}_{-1}} d\tau - \int_0^T \nu'(s)(\eta^\tau, \zeta)_{H^{-1}(\Omega)} d\tau = \int_0^T (\partial_t \eta^\tau - T_r \eta^\tau, \zeta)_{\mathcal{M}_{-1}} d\tau, \quad (105)$$

we also get (67) on account of (95) and (98). This completes Step 3 of the proof.

Step 4: Energy equality. To begin, let $u_0 \in D(A_{E,\beta})$, $\eta_0 \in \mathcal{M}_{-1}^{(0)}$ and let $\phi = (u, \eta)^{tr}$ be the corresponding weak solution. Recall from (100), we have, for almost all $t \in (0, T)$,

$$u_n(t) \to u(t) \quad \text{strongly in } L^2(\Omega) \text{ and a.e. in } \Omega. \quad (106)$$

Since F is measurable and positive (see (N1) and (N3), respectively), Fatou's lemma implies

$$\int_\Omega F(u(t)) dx \leq \liminf_{n \to +\infty} \int_\Omega F(u_n(t)) dx. \quad (107)$$

Passing to the limit in (75), and while keeping in mind (91), (94), (95), (97), (98), and (101), as well as the weak lower-semicontinuity of the norm, we arrive at the integral inequality which holds for any weak solution

$$\mathcal{E}(t) + 2\int_0^t \left(\alpha \|\partial_t u(\tau)\|^2 d\tau - \int_0^\infty \nu'(s) \|\eta^\tau(s)\|_{H^{-1}}^2 ds \right) d\tau \leq \mathcal{E}(0).$$

We argue as in the proof of [12] (Corollary 2) to establish the energy equality. Indeed, take $\xi = \mu$ in (51). By (17), we need to treat the dual pairing $\langle F'(u), \partial_t u \rangle_{W^{-\beta,2} \times W_0^{\beta,2}}$. It is here where we employ (41), where $F'(u) = G'(u) - c_F u$ and $G' \in C^1(\mathbb{R})$ is monotone increasing. Define the functional $\mathcal{G} : L^2(\Omega) \to \mathbb{R}$ by

$$\mathcal{G}(\phi) := \begin{cases} \int_\Omega G(u) dx & \text{if } G(u) \in L^1(\Omega), \\ +\infty & \text{otherwise.} \end{cases}$$

Now, by [44] (Proposition 2.8, Chapter II), it follows that $\mathcal{G}$ is convex, lower-semi-continuous on $L^2(\Omega)$, and $\chi \in \partial \mathcal{G}(u)$ if and only if $\chi = G'(u)$ almost everywhere in Ω. Since we have (47), we apply [45] (Proposition 4.2) to find that there holds, for almost all $t \in (0, T)$,

$$\langle \partial_t u, F'(u) \rangle_{W^{-\beta,2} \times W_0^{\beta,2}} = \langle \partial_t u, G'(u) \rangle_{W^{-\beta,2} \times W_0^{\beta,2}} - c_F \langle \partial_t u, u \rangle_{W^{-\beta,2} \times W_0^{\beta,2}}$$

$$= \frac{d}{dt} \left\{ \mathcal{G}(u) - \frac{c_F}{2} \|u\|^2 \right\}$$

$$= \frac{d}{dt} \int_\Omega F(u) dx.$$

Similar to Step 2 above, take $v = \mu$, $\xi = \partial_t u$, and $\zeta = \eta^t$ (now without the index n) in (51)–(53), respectively. Using the above result on the dual product with $F'(u)$ and (47), we are led to the differential identity (74) with E, u, and η in place of $\mathcal{E}_n$, u_n, and η_n, respectively. Integrating the resulting differential identity on $(0, t)$ produces (62) as claimed. This completes Step 4.

Step 5: (u, η) weak solution to Problem P. Now let us take $\phi_0 = (u_0, \eta_0)^{tr} \in \mathcal{H}_{\beta,0}^M$ where $F(u_0) \in L^1(\Omega)$. Proceeding exactly as in [12] (page 440) the bounds (78)–(84) and (88)–(90) hold. Moreover, with the aid of the Aubin–Lions compact embedding (again see Lemma A1 in Appendix A below) we deduce the existence of functions u, η, and μ that satisfy (46), (49),

(57), and (59). Thus, passing to the limit in the variational formulation for $\phi_k = (u_k, \eta_k)^{tr}$, we find $\phi = (u, \eta)^{tr}$ is a solution corresponding to the initial data $\phi_0 = (u_0, \eta_0)^{tr} \in \mathcal{H}_{\beta,0}^M$ for which $F(u_0) \in L^1(\Omega)$. This finishes the proof of the theorem. □

Before we continue, we make some important remarks.

Remark 7. *The continuity property*

$$u \in C([0, T]; W_0^{\beta-\iota,2}(\Omega)),$$

for any $\iota > 0$ sufficiently small follows from the conditions in Definition 1 after an application of the Aubin–Lions Lemma (see Lemma A1 in Appendix A). In addition, the property

$$\eta \in C([0, T]; \mathcal{M}_{-1}^{(0)})$$

follows from the density argument in [37]. Thus, we deduce the continuity properties

$$\phi = (u, \eta) \in C([0, T]; \mathcal{H}_{\beta,0}^M).$$

Remark 8. *From (62), we see that if there is a $t^* > 0$ in which*

$$\mathcal{E}(t^*) = \mathcal{E}(0),$$

then, for all $t \in (0, t^*)$,

$$\int_0^t \left(\alpha \|\partial_t u(\tau)\|^2 + \|\eta^\tau\|_{L^2_{-\nu'}(\mathbb{R}_+;H^{-1})}^2 \right) d\tau = 0. \tag{108}$$

We deduce $\partial_t u(t) = 0$ for all $t \in (0, t^*)$. Additionally, since $u(t) = u_0$ for all $t \in (0, t^*)$, Equation (17) shows

$$\mu(t) = A_{E,\beta} u_0 + F'(u_0) \quad \forall t \in (0, t^*),$$

i.e., $\mu(t) = \mu^*$ is also stationary. Thus, by the definition of η^t given in (14), we find here that, for each $t \in (0, t^*)$

$$\eta^t(s) = s A_N \mu^* \quad \forall s \geq 0.$$

Therefore, $\phi = (u, \eta)^{tr}$ is a fixed point of the trajectory $\phi(t) = \mathcal{S}(t)\phi_0$, where $\mathcal{S}$ is the solution operator defined below in Corollary 2.

The following result (see [26] (Theorem 3.4)) concerns the existence of strong/regular solutions which is utilized in the proof of the continuous dependence estimate. Note that we now employ the added assumption on the nonlinear term.

Theorem 2. *Let $T > 0$, $\beta \in (0, 1)$, and $\phi_0 = (u_0, \eta_0)^{tr} \in \mathcal{H}_{\beta+1,\beta+1}^M := W_0^{\beta+1,2}(\Omega) \times L_\nu^2(\mathbb{R}_+; W_0^{\beta,2}(\Omega))$ be such that $F(u_0) \in L^1(\Omega)$ and $\eta_0 \in D(T_r)$. Assume $\alpha > 0$ and that (K1)–(K4) and (N1)–(N3) hold. Additionally, assume that (N4) holds. Problem **P** admits at least one weak solution $\phi = (u, \eta)$ on $(0, T)$ according to Definition (1) with the additional regularity, for any $T > 0$,*

$$\phi = (u, \eta) \in L^\infty(0, T; \mathcal{H}_{\beta+1,\beta+1}^M) \cap W^{1,\infty}(0, T; \mathcal{H}_{\beta,0}^M), \tag{109}$$

$$\sqrt{\alpha} \partial_t u \in L^2(0, T; H^1(\Omega)) \tag{110}$$

$$\partial_{tt} u \in L^\infty(0, T; H^{-1}(\Omega)), \tag{111}$$

$$\sqrt{\alpha} \partial_{tt} u \in L^2(\Omega \times (0, T)), \tag{112}$$

$$\mu \in L^\infty(0, T; H^1(\Omega)), \tag{113}$$

$$\eta \in L^\infty(0, T; D(T_r)). \tag{114}$$

Proof. The proof relies on the Galerkin approximation scheme developed in the proof of Theorem 1. We seek $\phi_n = (u_n, \eta_n)$ of the form (64) satisfying Problem $\mathbf{P}_n$:

$$(\partial_{tt} u_n, v) + \int_0^\infty \nu(s)(\partial_t \eta_n^t(s), v)ds = 0 \tag{115}$$

$$a_{E,\beta}(\partial_t u_n, \xi) + (F''(u_n)\partial_t u, \xi) + \alpha(\partial_{tt} u_n, \xi) = (\partial_t \mu_n, \xi) \tag{116}$$

$$(\partial_{tt} \eta_n^t, \zeta)_{\mathcal{M}_{-1}} - (T_r \partial_t \eta_n^t, \zeta)_{\mathcal{M}_{-1}} = (\partial_t \mu_n, \zeta)_{\mathcal{M}_0} \tag{117}$$

for every $t \in (0, T)$, $v \in V^n$, $\xi \in W^n$, and $\zeta \in \mathcal{M}^n$, and which satisfy the initial conditions

$$u_n(0) = \tilde{u}_{0n} \quad \text{and} \quad \eta_n^0 = \tilde{\eta}_{0n}, \tag{118}$$

where we set

$$\tilde{u}_{0n} := -\int_0^\infty \nu(s) \eta_{0n}(s) ds, \tag{119}$$

and

$$\tilde{\eta}_{0n} := T_r \eta_{0n} + A_N \mu_{0n}, \tag{120}$$

and also

$$\mu_{0n} = -\alpha \int_0^\infty \nu(s) \eta_{0n}(s) ds + A_{E,\beta} u_{0n} + F'(u_{0n}). \tag{121}$$

It is important to note that when $\phi_0 = (u_0, \eta_0)$ satisfies the assumptions of Theorem 2, then it is guaranteed that $(\tilde{u}_0, \tilde{\eta}_0) \in \mathcal{H}_{1,0}^M$. Indeed, relying on the fact that $\|(u_{0n}, \eta_{0n})\|_{\mathcal{H}_{\beta,0}^M} \le \|(u_0, \eta_0)\|_{\mathcal{H}_{\beta,0}^M}$, we easily obtain the estimate $\|(\partial_t u_n(0), \partial_t \eta_n^0)\|_{\mathcal{H}_{\beta,0}^M} \le Q(\|(u_0, \eta_0)\|_{\mathcal{H}_{\beta+1,\beta+1}^M})$. Now, for any fixed $n \in \mathbb{N}$, we find a unique local maximal solution $\phi_n = (u_n, \eta_n) \in C^2([0, T_n]; \mathcal{H}_{\beta+1,2}^M)$. Next, we integrate (115) and (116) with respect to time on $(0, t)$ and argue as in the proof of Theorem 1 to find the uniform bounds (78)–(84), (88), and (90). In order to obtain the required higher-order estimates, let us begin by labeling

$$\tilde{u}(t) = \partial_t u(t), \quad \tilde{\eta}^t = \partial_t \eta^t, \quad \tilde{\mu}(t) = \partial_t \mu(t),$$

where we are also dropping the index n for the sake of simplicity. Then, $(\tilde{u}, \tilde{\eta})$ solves the system

$$\langle \partial_t \tilde{u}, v \rangle_{H^{-1} \times H^1} + \int_0^\infty \nu(s) \langle \tilde{\eta}^t(s), v \rangle_{H^{-1} \times H^1} ds = 0, \tag{122}$$

$$a_{E,\beta}(\tilde{u}, \xi) + (F''(u)\tilde{u}, \xi) + \alpha(\partial_t \tilde{u}, \xi) = \langle \tilde{\mu}, \xi \rangle_{W^{-\beta,2} \times W_0^{\beta,2}}, \tag{123}$$

$$(\partial_t \tilde{\eta}^t, \zeta)_{\mathcal{M}_{-1}} - (T_r \tilde{\eta}^t, \zeta)_{\mathcal{M}_{-1}} = (\tilde{\mu}, \zeta)_{\mathcal{M}_0}, \tag{124}$$

for all $v \in H^1(\Omega)$, $\xi \in W_0^{\beta,2}(\Omega)$, and $\zeta \in \mathcal{M}_1$, with the initial conditions

$$\tilde{u}(0) = \tilde{u}_0 \quad \text{and} \quad \tilde{\eta}^0 = \tilde{\eta}_0.$$

Let us now take $v = \tilde{\mu}$, $\xi = \partial_t \tilde{u}$, and $\zeta = \tilde{\eta}^t$ in (122)–(124), respectively. Summing the resulting identities together, we obtain, for all $t \in (0, T)$,

$$\frac{1}{2} \frac{d}{dt} \left\{ \|\tilde{u}\|_{W_0^{\beta,2}}^2 + \|\tilde{\eta}^t\|_{\mathcal{M}_{-1}}^2 \right\} - \int_0^\infty \nu'(s) \|\tilde{\eta}^t(s)\|_{H^{-1}}^2 ds + \alpha \|\partial_t \tilde{u}\|^2 = -(F''(u)\tilde{u}, \partial_t \tilde{u}).$$

Here, we apply (K5) as well as (N4) with (83) and the embedding $W_0^{\beta,2}(\Omega) \hookrightarrow L^2(\Omega)$ to find

$$\frac{1}{2}\frac{d}{dt}\left\{\|\tilde{u}\|^2_{W_0^{\beta,2}} + \|\tilde{\eta}^t\|^2_{\mathcal{M}_{-1}}\right\} + \lambda\|\tilde{\eta}^t\|^2_{\mathcal{M}_{-1}} + \alpha\|\partial_t\tilde{u}\|^2 \leq C_\alpha\|\tilde{u}\|^2 + \frac{\alpha}{2}\|\partial_t\tilde{u}\|$$

$$\leq C_\alpha\|\tilde{u}\|^2_{W_0^{\beta,2}} + \frac{\alpha}{2}\|\partial_t\tilde{u}\|, \qquad (125)$$

where $C_\alpha \sim \alpha^{-1}$ is a positive constant. Integrating (125) over $(0,t)$ produces

$$\|\tilde{u}(t)\|^2_{W_0^{\beta,2}} + \|\tilde{\eta}^t\|^2_{\mathcal{M}_{-1}} + \int_0^t \left(2\lambda\|\tilde{\eta}^\tau\|^2_{\mathcal{M}_{-1}} + \alpha\|\partial_t\tilde{u}(\tau)\|^2\right)d\tau$$

$$\leq \|\tilde{u}(0)\|^2_{W_0^{\beta,2}} + \|\tilde{\eta}^0\|^2_{\mathcal{M}_{-1}} + C_\alpha \int_0^t \|\tilde{u}(\tau)\|^2_{W_0^{\beta,2}}d\tau, \qquad (126)$$

and an application of Grönwall's (integral) inequality shows, for all $t \geq 0$,

$$\|(\tilde{u}(t), \tilde{\eta}^t)\|_{\mathcal{H}^M_{\beta,0}} \leq Q(\|(\tilde{u}_0, \tilde{\eta}_0)\|_{\mathcal{H}^M_{\beta,0}}) \qquad (127)$$

and

$$\sqrt{\alpha}\|\partial_t\tilde{u}(t)\|_{L^2(\Omega \times (0,T))} \leq Q(\|(\tilde{u}_0, \tilde{\eta}_0)\|_{\mathcal{H}^M_{\beta,0}}). \qquad (128)$$

Through (119)–(121), we find $\|(\tilde{u}_0, \tilde{\eta}_0)\|_{\mathcal{H}^M_{\beta,0}}$ depends on

$$\int_0^\infty \nu(s)\|\eta_0(s)\|^2_{W_0^{\beta,2}}ds, \quad \|A_N\mu_0\|_{\mathcal{M}_{-1}} \quad \text{and} \quad \|T_r\eta_0\|_{\mathcal{M}_{-1}},$$

hence the assumption on the initial data is justified.

Furthermore, we now consider (67) and take $\zeta = A_N\bar{\mu}(t)$ where $\bar{\mu} = \mu - \langle\mu\rangle$, so that, with (79), (82), and (127), we obtain, for all $t \geq 0$ and for every $\varepsilon > 0$,

$$\|\nabla\mu\|^2 = (\partial_t\eta^t, \mu)_{\mathcal{M}_0} - (T_r\eta^t, \mu)_{\mathcal{M}_0} \qquad (129)$$

$$= \int_0^\infty \nu(s)(\partial_t\eta^t(s), \mu(t))ds - \int_0^\infty \nu'(s)(\eta^t(s), \mu(t))ds \qquad (130)$$

$$\leq C_\varepsilon\left(\|\partial_t\eta^t\|^2_{\mathcal{M}_{-1}} - \int_0^\infty \nu'(s)\|\eta^t(s)\|^2_{H^{-1}}ds\right) + \varepsilon\|\nabla\mu\|^2 \qquad (131)$$

$$\leq C_\varepsilon\left(1 - \int_0^\infty \nu'(s)\|\eta^t(s)\|^2_{H^{-1}}ds\right) + \varepsilon\|\nabla\mu\|^2 \qquad (132)$$

$$\leq C_\varepsilon + \varepsilon\|\nabla\mu\|^2 \qquad (133)$$

where $C_\varepsilon \sim \varepsilon^{-1}$. Together (89) and (133) show us, for all $t \geq 0$,

$$\|\mu(t)\|_{H^1} \leq C. \qquad (134)$$

At this point we can reason as is in the proof of Theorem 1 to find that there is a solution $\phi = (u, \eta) \in W^{1,\infty}(0, T; \mathcal{H}^M_{\beta,0})$ to Problem **P** satisfying (111) and (112). Additionally, thanks to (134), the condition (113) holds. It remains to show that

$$\phi = (u, \eta) \in L^\infty\left(0, T; \left[W_0^{\beta+1,2}(\Omega) \times L^2_\nu(\mathbb{R}_+; W_0^{\beta,2}(\Omega))\right]\right).$$

First, in light of (127), we multiply (16) by $A_{E,\beta}\eta^t$ in $L^2(\Omega)$ which yields

$$\|\eta^t\|^2_{L^2_\nu(\mathbb{R}_+; W_0^{\beta,2}(\Omega))} = -\int_0^\infty \nu(s)(A_{E,\beta}^{\frac{1}{2}}\partial_t u(t), A_{E,\beta}^{\frac{1}{2}}\eta^t(s))ds.$$

Hence, $\eta \in L^\infty(0, T; L^2_\nu(\mathbb{R}_+; W_0^{\beta,2}(\Omega)))$. Next, we consider the identity (52) whereby we may now rely on the regularity properties of $\partial_t u$ and μ. We take $\xi = A_N \partial_t u$ to produce

$$\frac{1}{2}\frac{d}{dt}|||u|||^2_{W_0^{\beta+1,2}} + \langle F''(u)\nabla u, \nabla u\rangle + \alpha\|\partial_t u\|^2_{H^1} = \langle \nabla \mu, \nabla u\rangle.$$

After applying (N1) and integrating the resulting differential inequality with respect to t over $(0, t)$, we obtain for all $t \geq 0$,

$$|||u(t)|||^2_{W_0^{\beta+1,2}} + 2\int_0^\infty \alpha\|\partial_t u(\tau)\|^2_{H^1} d\tau \leq |||u(0)|||^2_{W_0^{\beta+1,2}} + Q(\|(u_0, \eta_0)\|_{\mathcal{H}^M_{\beta,0}}).$$

We now deduce

$$u \in L^\infty(0, T; W_0^{\beta+1,2}(\Omega)) \quad \text{and} \quad \sqrt{\alpha}\partial_t u \in L^2(0, T; H^1(\Omega)).$$

This completes the proof. $\square$

The following proposition provides continuous dependence and uniqueness for the solutions constructed above.

Proposition 2. *Let the assumptions of Theorem 1 hold. Additionally, assume (N4) holds. Let $T > 0$ and let $\phi_i = (u_i, \eta_i)^{tr}$, $i = 1, 2$, be two solutions to Problem P on $(0, T)$ corresponding to the initial data $\phi_{0i} = (u_{0i}, \eta_{0i})^{tr} \in \mathcal{H}^M_{\beta,0} = W_0^{\beta,2}(\Omega) \times \mathcal{M}_{-1}^{(0)}$, such that $F(u_{0i}) \in L^1(\Omega)$, $i = 1, 2$. Then, for each $\alpha > 0$, there is a positive constant $C_\alpha \sim \alpha^{-1}$ such that the following estimate holds, for any $t \in (0, T)$,*

$$\|\phi_1(t) - \phi_2(t)\|^2_{\mathcal{H}^M_{\beta,0}} + \int_0^t \left(\alpha\|\partial_t u_1(\tau) - \partial_t u_2(\tau)\|^2 + \|\eta_1^\tau - \eta_2^\tau\|^2_{L^2_{-\nu'}(\mathbb{R}_+; H^{-1})} \right) d\tau$$
$$\leq e^{C_\alpha t}\|\phi_{01} - \phi_{02}\|^2_{\mathcal{H}^M_{\beta,0}}. \quad (135)$$

Proof. To begin, we assume (u_{0i}, η_{0i}), $i = 1, 2$, satisfy the assumptions of Theorem 2 (recall, above we are assuming (N4) holds), and we work with the more regular solutions to obtain (135). For all $t \in [0, T]$, we then set

$$\phi(t) := \phi_1(t) - \phi_2(t), \quad u(t) := u_1(t) - u_2(t), \quad \eta^t := \eta_1^t - \eta_2^t \quad \text{and} \quad \mu := \mu_1 - \mu_2$$

where $\phi_i(t) = (u_i(t), \eta_i^t)$ is a solution corresponding to (u_{0i}, η_{0i}), $i = 1, 2$. Then, formally, $\phi = (u, \eta)$ solves the equations for all $v \in H^1(\Omega)$, $\xi \in W_0^{\beta,2}(\Omega) \cap L^p(\Omega)$, and $\zeta \in \mathcal{M}_1$:

$$\langle \partial_t u, v\rangle_{H^{-1} \times H^1} + \int_0^\infty \nu(s)\langle \eta^t(s), v\rangle_{H^{-1} \times H^1} ds = 0, \quad (136)$$

$$a_{E,\beta}(u, \xi) + \langle F'(u_1) - F'(u_2), \xi\rangle_{W^{-\beta,2} \times W_0^{\beta,2}} + \alpha\langle \partial_t u, \xi\rangle_{W^{-\beta,2} \times W_0^{\beta,2}} = \langle \mu, \xi\rangle_{W^{-\beta,2} \times W_0^{\beta,2}}, \quad (137)$$

$$(\partial_t \eta^t, \zeta)_{\mathcal{M}_{-1}} - (T_r \eta^t, \zeta)_{\mathcal{M}_{-1}} = (\mu, \zeta)_{\mathcal{M}_0} \quad (138)$$

with the initial data

$$u(0) = u_{01} - u_{02}, \quad \eta^0 = \eta_{01} - \eta_{02}.$$

In (136), we choose $v = \mu$ and in (137), we choose $\xi = \partial_t u$. Owing to Theorem 2, for each $t \in [0, T]$, these elements are in $H^1(\Omega)$ and $W_0^{\beta,2}(\Omega)$, respectively, then we sum the results to obtain

$$(A_{E,\beta} u, \partial_t u) + (F'(u_1) - F'(u_2), \partial_t u) + \alpha\|\partial_t u\|^2 + \int_0^\infty \nu(s)(\mu, \eta^t(s)) ds = 0. \quad (139)$$

243

Further, multiplying (138) by $A_N^{-1}\eta^t$ in $\mathcal{M}_0$, then adding the obtained relation to (139), we have

$$\frac{1}{2}\frac{d}{dt}\{\|\|u\|\|_{W_0^{\beta,2}}^2 + \|\eta^t\|_{\mathcal{M}_{-1}}^2\} + \alpha\|\partial_t u\|^2 - \int_0^\infty \nu'(s)\|\eta^t(s)\|_{H^{-1}}^2 ds + (F'(u_1) - F'(u_2), \partial_t u) = 0. \qquad (140)$$

Using Hölder's inequality, (N4), Young's inequality, and the embedding $L^\infty(\Omega) \hookrightarrow W_0^{\beta,2}(\Omega)$, we estimate the remaining product as

$$|(F'(u_1) - F'(u_2), \partial_t u)| \le \|F'(u_1) - F'(u_2)\|\|\partial_t u\|$$
$$\le C\|(1 + |u_1|^{\rho-2} + |u_2|^{\rho-2})u\|\|\partial_t u\|$$
$$\le C(1 + \|u_1\|_{L^{2(\rho-2)}}^{\rho-2} + \|u_2\|_{L^{2(\rho-2)}}^{\rho-2})\|u\|_{L^\infty}\|\partial_t u\|$$
$$\le Q_\alpha(\|(u_{0i}, \eta_{0i})\|_{\mathcal{H}_{\beta,0}^M})\|\|u\|\|_{W_0^{\beta,2}}^2 + \frac{\alpha}{2}\|\partial_t u\|^2, \qquad (141)$$

where the positive monotone increasing function $Q_\alpha(\cdot) \sim \alpha^{-1}$ (we remind the reader $\|(u_{0i}, \eta_{0i})\|_{\mathcal{H}_{\beta+1,\beta+1}^M} \le Q\|(u_{0i}, \eta_{0i})\|_{\mathcal{H}_{\beta,0}^M}$, for $i = 1, 2$ and the bounds on u_1 and u_2 follow from (61) and (62)). With (140) and (141), we obtain the following differential inequality which holds for almost all $t \in [0, T]$

$$\frac{d}{dt}\{\|\|u\|\|_{W_0^{\beta,2}}^2 + \|\eta^t\|_{\mathcal{M}_{-1}}^2\} + \alpha\|\partial_t u\|^2 + \|\eta^t\|_{L^2_{-\nu'}(\mathbb{R}_+; H^{-1})}^2 \le Q_\alpha(\|(u_{0i}, \eta_{0i})\|_{\mathcal{H}_{\beta,0}^M})\|\|u\|\|_{W_0^{\beta,2}}^2$$
$$\le Q_\alpha(\|(u_{0i}, \eta_{0i})\|_{\mathcal{H}_{\beta,0}^M})\left(\|\|u\|\|_{W_0^{\beta,2}}^2 + \|\eta^t\|_{\mathcal{M}_{-1}}^2\right). \qquad (142)$$

Applying a Grönwall inequality to (142), we obtain, for all $t \in [0, T]$,

$$\|\|u(t)\|\|_{W_0^{\beta,2}}^2 + \|\eta^t\|_{\mathcal{M}_{-1}}^2 + \int_0^t \left(\alpha\|\partial_t u(\tau)\|^2 + \|\eta^\tau\|_{L^2_{-\nu'}(\mathbb{R}_+; H^{-1})}^2\right) d\tau$$
$$\le e^{C_\alpha}\left(\|\|u(0)\|\|_{W_0^{\beta,2}}^2 + \|\eta^0\|_{\mathcal{M}_{-1}}^2\right). \qquad (143)$$

This shows the claim (135) holds for the regular solutions. Since none of the above constants due to the above estimate actually depend on the assumptions of Theorem 2, then standard approximation arguments can be employed to obtain (135) for the weak solutions as well. □

Remark 9. *It is quite important to remark that when $N = 3$, the uniqueness for the nonviscous problem (where $\alpha = 0$) remains an open problem (indeed, see [36,46,47]).*

We now formalize the semidynamical system generated by Problem **P**.

Corollary 2. *Let the assumptions of Theorem 1 be satisfied. Additionally, assume (N4) holds. We can define a strongly continuous semigroup of solution operators $\mathcal{S} = (\mathcal{S}(t))_{t \ge 0}$, for each $\alpha > 0$ and $\beta \in (0, 1)$,*

$$\mathcal{S}(t) : \mathcal{X}_{\beta,0}^M \to \mathcal{X}_{\beta,0}^M$$

by setting, for all $t \ge 0$,

$$\mathcal{S}(t)\phi_0 := \phi(t)$$

*where $\phi(t) = (u(t), \eta^t)$ is the unique global weak solution to Problem **P**. Furthermore, as a consequence of (135), the semigroup $\mathcal{S}(t) : \mathcal{X}_{\beta,0}^M \to \mathcal{X}_{\beta,0}^M$ is Lipschitz continuous on $\mathcal{X}_{\beta,0}^M$, uniformly in t on compact intervals.*

4. Absorbing Sets and Global Attractors

We now give a dissipation estimate for Problem **P** from which we deduce the existence of a bounded absorbing set and an important uniform bound on the solutions of Problem **P**. The existence of an absorbing set is also used later to show that the semigroup of solution operators $\mathcal{S}$ admits a compact global attractor in the metric space $\mathcal{X}_{\beta,0}^M$.

Lemma 1. *Let $\phi_0 = (u_0, \eta_0)^{tr} \in \mathcal{H}_{\beta,0}^M = W_0^{\beta,2}(\Omega) \times \mathcal{M}_{-1}^{(0)}$ for $\beta \in (\frac{N}{4}, 1)$, $N = 1, 2, 3$, be such that $F(u_0) \in L^1(\Omega)$. Assume (K1), (K3)–(K5), and (N1)–(N3) hold. Assume $\phi = (u, \eta)^{tr}$ is a weak solution to Problem **P**. There are positive constants κ_1 and C, each depending on Ω but independent of t, α, and ϕ_0, such that, for all $t \geq 0$, the following holds*

$$\|\phi(t)\|_{\mathcal{H}_{\beta,0}^M}^2 + \int_t^{t+1} \alpha \|\partial_t u(\tau)\|^2 d\tau \leq Q(\|\phi_0\|_{\mathcal{H}_{\beta,0}^M}) e^{-\kappa_1 t} + C, \tag{144}$$

for some monotonically increasing function Q independent of t and α.

Proof. The idea of the proof is from [26]. We give a formal calculation that can be justified by a suitable Faedo–Galerkin approximation based on the proof of Theorem 1 above. To begin, define the functional, for all $t \geq 0$,

$$\mathcal{Y}(t) := \mathcal{E}(t) + \varepsilon\alpha\|u(t)\|^2 - 2\varepsilon \int_0^\infty \nu(s)\left(u(t), A_N^{-1}\eta^t(s)\right)ds, \tag{145}$$

where $\varepsilon \in (0, \lambda)$ will be chosen sufficiently small later. From (16)–(18), we find

$$-\frac{d}{dt}\int_0^\infty \nu(s)(u, A_N^{-1}\eta^t(s))ds$$
$$= \|\partial_t u\|_{H^{-1}}^2 - \int_0^\infty \nu(s)(u, A_N^{-1}\partial_t\eta^t(s))ds$$
$$= \|\partial_t u\|_{H^{-1}}^2 - \int_0^\infty \nu'(s)(u, A_N^{-1}\eta^t(s))ds - \int_0^\infty \nu(s)(u,\mu)ds$$
$$= \|\partial_t u\|_{H^{-1}}^2 - \int_0^\infty \nu'(s)(u, A_N^{-1}\eta^t(s))ds - \frac{\alpha}{2}\frac{d}{dt}\|u\|^2 - \|\|u\|\|_{W_0^{\beta,2}}^2 - (F'(u), u). \tag{146}$$

Differentiating $\mathcal{Y}$ with respect to t while keeping in mind (73), (74) (without the index n), and (146), we find

$$\frac{d}{dt}\mathcal{Y} + \varepsilon_0 \mathcal{Y} - 2\int_0^\infty \nu'(s)\|\eta^t(s)\|_{H^{-1}}^2 ds = h(t), \tag{147}$$

for $\varepsilon_0 \in (0, \varepsilon)$ where

$$h(t) = -2\alpha\|\partial_t u(t)\|^2 + 2\varepsilon\|\partial_t u(t)\|_{H^{-1}}^2 - 2\varepsilon \int_0^\infty \nu'(s)(u(t), A_N^{-1}\eta^t(s))ds$$
$$- 2\varepsilon_0(F'(u(t))u(t) - F(u(t)), 1) - 2(\varepsilon - \varepsilon_0)(F'(u(t)), u(t)) + \varepsilon_0\|\eta^t\|_{\mathcal{M}_{-1}}^2$$
$$- (2\varepsilon - \varepsilon_0)\|\|u(t)\|\|_{W_0^{\beta,2}}^2 + \varepsilon_0\varepsilon\alpha\|u(t)\|^2 - 2\varepsilon_0\varepsilon\int_0^\infty \nu(s)(u(t), A_N^{-1}\eta^t(s))ds + \varepsilon_0 C. \tag{148}$$

From (42) and (43) (with $M = 0$), it follows that

$$-2\varepsilon_0(F'(u(t))u(t) - F(u(t)), 1) - 2(\varepsilon - \varepsilon_0)(F'(u(t)), u(t))$$
$$\leq -(\varepsilon - \varepsilon_0)(|F(u)|, 1) + \varepsilon_0 C\|\|u\|\|_{W_0^{\beta,2}}^2. \tag{149}$$

Next, using assumption (K4) and the embeddings $H^{-1}(\Omega) \hookrightarrow L^2(\Omega) \hookrightarrow W_0^{\beta,2}(\Omega)$, we find

$$-2\varepsilon \int_0^\infty \nu'(s)(u, A_N^{-1}\eta^t(s))ds = -2\varepsilon \int_0^\infty \nu'(s)(A_N^{-1/2}u, A_N^{-1/2}\eta^t(s))ds$$
$$\leq -\varepsilon \int_0^\infty \nu'(s)\left(\frac{1}{\nu_0}|||u|||_{W_0^{\beta,2}}^2 + C\nu_0\|\eta^t(s)\|_{H^{-1}}^2\right)ds$$
$$\leq \varepsilon|||u|||_{W_0^{\beta,2}}^2 - \varepsilon C \int_0^\infty \nu'(s)\|\eta^t(s)\|_{H^{-1}}^2 ds, \tag{150}$$

and, with (K3) and (87) (without the index n),

$$-2\varepsilon_0\varepsilon \int_0^\infty \nu(s)(u, A_N^{-1}\eta^t(s))ds \leq \varepsilon_0\varepsilon C|||u|||_{W_0^{\beta,2}}^2 + \varepsilon_0\varepsilon\|\eta^t\|_{\mathcal{M}_{-1}}^2. \tag{151}$$

Together, (148)–(151) make the following estimate

$$h \leq -2\alpha\|\partial_t u\|^2 + 2\varepsilon\|\partial_t u\|_{H^{-1}}^2 - (\varepsilon - \varepsilon_0(1 + C + \varepsilon\alpha C))|||u|||_{W_0^{\beta,2}}^2 + 2\varepsilon_0\|\eta^t\|_{\mathcal{M}_{-1}}^2$$
$$- \varepsilon C \int_0^\infty \nu'(s)\|\eta^t(s)\|_{H^{-1}}^2 ds + C. \tag{152}$$

Here, we employ assumption (K5) so that from (147) and (152), we are able to fix $\varepsilon \in (0, \lambda)$ and $\varepsilon_0 \in (0, \varepsilon)$ sufficiently small to, in turn, find positive constants $\varepsilon_1, \varepsilon_2, \varepsilon_3$ so that there holds

$$\frac{d}{dt}\mathcal{Y} + \varepsilon_1 \mathcal{Y} + 2\|\eta^t\|_{\mathcal{M}_{-1}}^2 + \varepsilon_2\alpha\|\partial_t u\|^2 + \varepsilon_3|||u|||_{W_0^{\beta,2}}^2 \leq C. \tag{153}$$

It is important to note that C on the right-hand side of (153) is independent of t and ϕ_0. One can readily show (see (73), (76)–(77)) that there holds, for all $t \geq 0$,

$$C_1\|\phi(t)\|_{\mathcal{H}_{\beta,0}^M}^2 - C_2 \leq \mathcal{Y}(t) \leq Q(\|\phi_0\|_{\mathcal{H}_{\beta,0}^M}), \tag{154}$$

for some positive constants C_1, C_2, and for some monotone nondecreasing function Q independent of t. Finally, by applying a Grönwall type inequality to (153) (see, e.g., [34] (Lemma 2.5)), then integrating the result and applying (154) yield the claim (144). This finishes the proof. □

We immediately deduce the existence of a bounded absorbing set from Lemma 1.

Proposition 3. *Let the assumptions of Lemma 1 hold. Additionally, assume (N4) holds. Then, there exists $R_0 > 0$, independent of t and ϕ_0, such that $\mathcal{S}(t)$ possesses an absorbing ball $\mathcal{B}_{\beta,0}^M(R_0) \subset \mathcal{H}_{\beta,0}^M$, bounded in $\mathcal{H}_{\beta,0}^M$. Precisely, for any bounded subset $B \subset \mathcal{H}_{\beta,0}^M$, there exists $t_0 = t_0(B) > 0$ such that $\mathcal{S}(t)B \subset \mathcal{B}_{\beta,0}^M(R_0)$, for all $t \geq t_0$. Moreover, for every $R > 0$, there exists $C_* = C_*(R) \geq 0$, such that, for any $\phi_0 \in \mathcal{B}_{\beta,0}^M(R)$,*

$$\sup_{t \geq 0} \|\mathcal{S}(t)\phi_0\|_{\mathcal{H}_{\beta,0}^M} + \int_0^\infty \|\partial_t u(\tau)\|^2 d\tau \leq C_*, \tag{155}$$

where $\mathcal{B}_{\beta,0}^M(R)$ denotes the ball in $\mathcal{H}_{\beta,0}^M$ of radius R, centered at $\mathbf{0}$.

Throughout the remainder of the article, we simply write $\mathcal{B}_{\beta,0}^M$ in place of $\mathcal{B}_{\beta,0}^M(R_0)$ to denote the bounded absorbing set admitted by the semigroup of solution operators $\mathcal{S}(t)$. For the rest of this section, our aim is to prove the following.

Theorem 3. *Let the assumptions of Lemma 1 hold. Additionally, assume (N4) holds. The dynamical system $(\mathcal{X}_{\beta,0}^M, \mathcal{S}(t))$ (see Corollary 2) possesses a connected global attractor $\mathcal{A}_{\beta,0}^M$ in $\mathcal{H}_{\beta,0}^M$. Precisely:*

1. For each $t \geq 0$, $\mathcal{S}(t)\mathcal{A}_{\beta,0}^M = \mathcal{A}_{\beta,0}^M$;
2. For every nonempty bounded subset B of $\mathcal{H}_{\beta,0}^M$,

$$\lim_{t\to\infty} \text{dist}_{\mathcal{H}_{\beta,0}^M}(\mathcal{S}(t)B, \mathcal{A}_{\beta,0}^M) := \lim_{t\to\infty} \sup_{\zeta\in B} \inf_{\xi\in\mathcal{A}_{\beta,0}^M} \|\mathcal{S}(t)\zeta - \xi\|_{\mathcal{H}_{\beta,0}^M} = 0.$$

Additionally:

3. The global attractor is the unique maximal compact invariant subset in $\mathcal{H}_{\beta,0}^M$ given by

$$\mathcal{A}_{\beta,0}^M := \omega(\mathcal{B}_{\beta,0}^M) := \bigcap_{s\geq 0} \overline{\bigcup_{t\geq s} \mathcal{S}(t)\mathcal{B}_{\beta,0}^M}^{\mathcal{H}_{\beta,0}^M}.$$

Furthermore:

4. The global attractor $\mathcal{A}_{\beta,0}^M$ is connected and given by the union of the unstable manifolds connecting the equilibria of $\mathcal{S}(t)$.
5. For each $\zeta_0 = (\phi_0, \theta_0)^{tr} \in \mathcal{H}_{\beta,0}^M$, the set $\omega(\zeta_0)$ is a connected compact invariant set, consisting of the fixed points of $\mathcal{S}(t)$.

With the existence of a bounded absorbing set $\mathcal{B}_{\beta,0}^M$ (in Lemma 1), the existence of a global attractor now depends on the precompactness of the semigroup of solution operators $\mathcal{S}$. To this end we show there is a $t_* > 0$ such that the map $\mathcal{S}(t_*)$ is a so-called α-contraction on $\mathcal{B}_{\beta,0}^M$; that is, there exist a time $t_* > 0$, a constant $0 < \kappa < 1$, and a precompact pseudometric M_* on $\mathcal{B}_{\beta,0}^M$ such that, for all $\phi_{01}, \phi_{02} \in \mathcal{B}_{\beta,0}^M$,

$$\|\mathcal{S}(t_*)\phi_{01} - \mathcal{S}(t_*)\phi_{02}\|_{\mathcal{H}_{\beta,0}^M} \leq \kappa\|\phi_{01} - \phi_{02}\|_{\mathcal{H}_{\beta,0}^M} + M_*(\phi_{01}, \phi_{02}). \tag{156}$$

Such a contraction is commonly used in connection with phase-field-type equations as an alternative to establish the precompactness of a semigroup; for some particular recent results see [16,48,49].

Lemma 2. *Under the assumptions of Proposition 2 where $\phi_{01}, \phi_{02} \in \mathcal{B}_{\beta,0}^M$, there are positive constants κ_2, C_1, and $C_{2\alpha} \sim \alpha^{-1}$, each depending on Ω but independent of t and ϕ_{01}, ϕ_{02}, such that, for all $t \geq 0$,*

$$\|\phi_1(t) - \phi_2(t)\|_{\mathcal{H}_{\beta,0}^M}^2 \leq C_1 e^{-\kappa_2 t}\|\phi_1(0) - \phi_2(0)\|_{\mathcal{H}_{\beta,0}^M}^2$$
$$+ C_{2\alpha} \int_0^t \left(\|\nabla\mu_1(\tau) - \nabla\mu_2(\tau)\|^2 + \|u_1(\tau) - u_2(\tau)\|^2\right) d\tau. \tag{157}$$

Proof. The proof is based on the proof of Proposition 2. We begin by recovering (140) by multiplying (136) and (137) by μ and $\partial_t u$, respectively, in $L^2(\Omega)$, and multiplying (138) by $A_N^{-1}\eta^t$ in $\mathcal{M}_0$, then adding the obtained relations together to find

$$\frac{1}{2}\frac{d}{dt}\{\|\|u\|\|_{W_0^{\beta,2}}^2 + \|\eta^t\|_{\mathcal{M}_{-1}}^2\} + \alpha\|\partial_t u\|^2 - \int_0^\infty v'(s)\|\eta^t(s)\|_{H^{-1}}^2 ds + (F'(u_1) - F'(u_2), \partial_t u) = 0. \tag{158}$$

Recall $\phi_1 = (u_1, \eta_1)$, $\phi_2 = (u_2, \eta_2)$ are the unique weak solutions corresponding to the initial data ϕ_{01} and ϕ_{02}, respectively; also, $u = u_1 - u_2$ and $\eta^t = \eta_1^t - \eta_2^t$ formally satisfy (136) and (137). Applying Assumption (K5) and the estimate based on (N4),

$$|(F'(u_1) - F'(u_2), \partial_t u)| \leq \|F'(u_1) - F'(u_2)\| \|\partial_t u\|$$
$$\leq C\|(1 + |u_1|^{\rho-2} + |u_2|^{\rho-2})u\| \|\partial_t u\|$$
$$\leq C(1 + \|u_1\|_{L^{2(\rho-2)}}^{\rho-2} + \|u_2\|_{L^{2(\rho-2)}}^{\rho-2})\|u\|_{L^\infty}\|\partial_t u\|$$
$$\leq Q_\alpha(\|(u_{0i}, \eta_{0i})\|_{\mathcal{H}_{\beta,0}^M})\|u\|_{W_0^{\beta,2}}^2 + \frac{\alpha}{2}\|\partial_t u\|^2 \qquad (159)$$
$$\leq Q_\alpha(\|(u_{0i}, \eta_{0i})\|_{\mathcal{H}_{\beta,0}^M}) + \frac{\alpha}{2}\|\partial_t u\|^2, \qquad (160)$$

where the positive monotone increasing function $Q_\alpha(\cdot) \sim \alpha^{-1}$, and we find the differential inequality

$$\frac{1}{2}\frac{d}{dt}\{\|u\|_{W_0^{\beta,2}}^2 + \|\eta^t\|_{\mathcal{M}_{-1}}^2\} + \frac{\alpha}{2}\|\partial_t u\|^2 + \lambda\|\eta^t\|_{\mathcal{M}_{-1}}^2 \leq Q_\alpha(\|(u_{0i}, \eta_{0i})\|_{\mathcal{H}_{\beta,0}^M}). \qquad (161)$$

In addition, we now multiply (137) by u in $L^2(\Omega)$ to obtain

$$\|u\|_{W_0^{\beta,2}}^2 + (F'(u_1) - F'(u_2), u) + \frac{\alpha}{2}\frac{d}{dt}\|u\|^2 = (\mu, u). \qquad (162)$$

Estimating the first product above using (N1) yields

$$(F'(u_1) - F'(u_2), u) \geq -c_F\|u\|^2. \qquad (163)$$

We also estimate with Young's inequality

$$(\mu, u) \leq \frac{1}{2}\|\mu\|^2 + \frac{1}{2}\|u\|^2. \qquad (164)$$

Combining (161)–(164) yields

$$\frac{1}{2}\frac{d}{dt}\left\{\|u\|_{W_0^{\beta,2}}^2 + \|\eta^t\|_{\mathcal{M}_{-1}}^2 + \frac{\alpha}{2}\|u\|^2\right\} + \frac{\alpha}{2}\|\partial_t u\|^2 + \|u\|_{W_0^{\beta,2}}^2 + \lambda\|\eta^t\|_{\mathcal{M}_{-1}}^2$$
$$\leq \frac{1}{2}\|\mu\|^2 + Q_\alpha(\|(u_{0i}, \eta_{0i})\|_{\mathcal{H}_{\beta,0}^M})\|u\|_{W_0^{\beta,2}}^2. \qquad (165)$$

Then, adding $\frac{\alpha}{2}\|u\|^2$ to each side of (165), we find

$$\frac{d}{dt}\mathcal{N} + c\mathcal{N} + \alpha\|\partial_t u\|^2 \leq \|\mu\|^2 + Q_\alpha(\|(u_{0i}, \eta_{0i})\|_{\mathcal{H}_{\beta,0}^M}), \qquad (166)$$

where $c = \min\{2, 2\lambda, \alpha\}$ and

$$\mathcal{N}(t) := \|u(t)\|_{W_0^{\beta,2}}^2 + \|\eta^t\|_{\mathcal{M}_{-1}}^2 + \frac{\alpha}{2}\|u(t)\|^2. \qquad (167)$$

Applying Grönwall's inequality to (166) after omitting the term $\alpha\|\partial_t u\|^2$, we obtain the claim (157). □

Consequently, we deduce the following precompactness result for the semigroup $\mathcal{S}$.

Proposition 4. Let the assumptions of Lemma 2 hold. There is $t_* > 0$ such that the operator $\mathcal{S}(t_*)$ is a strict contraction up to the precompact pseudometric on $\mathcal{B}_{\beta,0}^M$, in the sense of (156), where

$$M_*(\phi_{01}, \phi_{02}) := C_{2\alpha} \left(\int_0^{t_*} \left(\|\nabla \mu_1(\tau) - \nabla \mu_2(\tau)\|^2 + \|u_1(\tau) - u_2(\tau)\|^2 \right) d\tau \right)^{1/2}, \quad (168)$$

with $C_\alpha \sim \alpha^{-1}$. Furthermore, $\mathcal{S}$ is precompact on $\mathcal{B}_{\beta,0}^M$.

Proof. Naturally, we follow from the conclusion of Lemma 2. Clearly, there is a $t_* > 0$ so that $C_1 e^{-\kappa_2 t_*/2} < 1$. Thus, the operator $\mathcal{S}(t_*)$ is a strict contraction up to the pseudometric M_* defined by (168). The pseudometric M_* is precompact thanks to the Aubin–Lions compact embedding (99). This completes the proof. □

Proof of Theorem 3. The precompactness of the solution operators $\mathcal{S}$ follows via the method of precompact pseudometrics (see Proposition 4). With the existence of a bounded absorbing set $\mathcal{B}_{\beta,0}^M$ in $\mathcal{H}_{\beta,0}^M$ (Lemma 1), the existence of a global attractor in $\mathcal{H}_{\beta,0}^M$ is well-known and can be found in [50,51] for example. Additional characteristics of the attractor follow thanks to the gradient structure of Problem **P** (Remark 8). In particular, the first three claims in the statement of Theorem 3 are a direct result of the existence of an absorbing set, a Lyapunov functional $\mathcal{E}$, and the fact that the system $(\mathcal{X}_{\beta,0}^M, \mathcal{S}(t), \mathcal{E})$ is a gradient. The fourth property is a direct result of [51] (Theorem VII.4.1), and the fifth follows from [52] (Theorem 6.3.2). This concludes the proof. □

Author Contributions: E.Ö. and J.L.S. have contributed equally to the development of the manuscript. All authors have read and agreed to the published version of the manuscript.

Funding: This research received no external funding.

Institutional Review Board Statement: Not applicable.

Informed Consent Statement: Not applicable.

Data Availability Statement: Not applicable.

Acknowledgments: The authors are indebted to the generosity of Professor Ciprian G. Gal, whose enthusiasm and insight into this project proved indispensable and enlightening.

Conflicts of Interest: The authors declare no conflict of interest.

Appendix A

The following is reported from [1] (Theorem 2.5).

Theorem A1. Let $0 < \beta < 1$. For $K \in \{E, D\}$, the following assertions hold:

(a) The operator $-A_{K,\beta}$ generates a submarkovian semigroup $(e^{-A_{K,\beta}})_{t \geq 0}$ on $L^2(\Omega)$ and hence can be extended to a strongly continuous contraction semigroup on $L^p(\Omega)$ for every $p \in [1, \infty)$, and to a contraction semigroup on $L^\infty(\Omega)$.

(b) The operator $A_{K,\beta}$ has a compact resolvent, and hence has a discrete spectrum. The spectrum of $A_{K,\beta}$ may be ordered as an increasing sequence of real numbers $0 \leq \lambda_1 < \lambda_2 < \cdots < \lambda_k < \cdots$ that diverges to $+\infty$. Moreover, 0 is not an eigenvalue for $A_{K,\beta}$, and if ϕ_k is an eigenfunction associated with the eigenvalue λ_k, then $\phi_k \in D(A_{K,\beta}) \cap L^\infty(\Omega)$.

(c) Denoting the generator of the semigroup on $L^p(\Omega)$ by $A_{K,p}$ so that $A_K = A_{K,2}$, then the spectrum of $A_{K,p}$ is independent of p for every $p \in [1, \infty]$.

(d) There holds $D(A_{K,\beta}) \subset L^\infty(\Omega)$ provided that $N < 4\beta$. Let $p \in (2, \infty)$ and assume that $N < 4\beta p/(p-2)$. Then, $D(A_{K,\beta}) \subset L^p(\Omega)$.

Remark A1. *From [1] (page 1284, after Equation (2.3))), we know the following embedding is compact*

$$W_0^{\beta,2}(\Omega) \hookrightarrow L^p(\Omega) \quad \text{when} \quad 1 \leq p < \star \quad \text{for} \quad \star = \begin{cases} \dfrac{2N}{N-2\beta} & \text{if } N > 2\beta \\ +\infty & \text{if } N = 2\beta. \end{cases} \tag{A1}$$

Furthermore,

$$W_0^{\beta,2}(\Omega) \hookrightarrow C^{0,h}(\overline{\Omega}) \quad \text{with} \quad h := \beta - \frac{N}{2} \quad \text{if} \quad N < 2\beta \quad \text{and} \quad 2 < p < \infty.$$

The following result is the classical Aubin–Lions Lemma, reported here for the reader's convenience (see [53], and, e.g., [54] (Lemma 5.51) or [52] (Theorem 3.1.1)).

Lemma A1. *Let X, Y, Z be Banach spaces where $Z \hookrightarrow Y \hookrightarrow X$ with continuous injections, the second being compact. Then, the following embeddings are compact:*

$$W := \{\chi \in L^2(0,T;X), \, \partial_t \chi \in L^2(0,T;Z)\} \hookrightarrow L^2(0,T;Y),$$

and

$$W' := \{\chi \in L^\infty(0,T;X), \, \partial_t \chi \in L^2(0,T;Z)\} \hookrightarrow C([0,T];Y).$$

Here, we recall the notion of α-contraction and provide the main propositions which guarantee the existence of a global attractor for the semigroup of solution operators $\mathcal{S}(t)$.

Definition A1. *Let X be a Banach space and α be a measure of compactness in X (see, e.g., [49] (Definition A.1)). Let $B \subset X$. A continuous map $T : B \to B$ is an α-contraction on B, if there exists a number $q \in (0,1)$ such that for every subset $A \subset B$, $\alpha(T(A)) \leq q\alpha(A)$.*

Proposition A1. *Assume that $B \subset X$ is closed and bounded, and that $T : B \to B$ is an α-contraction on B. Define the semigroup generated by the iterations of T, i.e., $S := (T^n)_{n \in \mathbb{N}}$. Then, the set*

$$\omega(B) := \bigcap_{n \geq 0} \overline{\bigcup_{m \geq n} T^m(B)}^X$$

is compact, invariant, and attracts B.

Proposition A2. *Assume that S is a continuous semigroup of operators on X admitting a bounded, positively invariant absorbing set B, and that there exists $t_* > 0$ such that the operator $S_* := S(t_*)$ is an α-contraction on B. Let*

$$A_* := \bigcap_{n \geq 0} \overline{\bigcup_{m \geq n} S_*^m(B)}^X = \omega_*(B)$$

be the ω-limit set of B under the map S_*, and set

$$A := \bigcup_{0 \leq t \leq t_*} S(t) A_*.$$

Assume further that for all $t \in [0, t_*]$, the map $x \to S(t)x$ is Lipschitz continuous from B to B, with Lipschitz constant $L(t)$, $L : [0, t_*] \to (0, +\infty)$ being a bounded function. Then, $A = \omega(B)$, and this set is the global attractor of S in B.

Theorems 3.1 and 3.2 are motivated by [55] (Sections II.2 and III.2), but appear in the above form in [49] (Appendix A) and [56] (Sections II.7). We also rely on the following.

Definition A2. *A pseudometric d in X is precompact in X if every bounded sequence has a subsequence which is a Cauchy sequence relative to d.*

Proposition A3. *Let $B \subset X$ be bounded, let d be a precompact pseudometric in X, and let $T : B \to B$ be a continuous map. Suppose T satisfies the estimate*

$$\|Tx - Ty\|_X \leq q\|x - y\|_X + d(x, y)$$

for all $x, y \in B$ and some $q \in (0, 1)$ independent of x and y. Then, T is an α-contraction.

References

1. Gal, C.G.; Warma, M. Reaction-diffusion equations with fractional diffusion on non-smooth domains with various boundary conditions. *Discret. Contin. Dyn. Syst.* **2016**, *36*, 1279–1319.
2. Warma, M. The fractional relative capacity and the fractional Laplacian with Neumann and Robin boundary conditions on open sets. Potential Analysis (to appear). *Potential Anal.* **2015**, *42*, 499–547.
3. Bucur, C.; Valdinoci, E. *Nonlocal Diffusion and Applications*; Lecture Notes of the Unione Matematica Italiana; Springer: Bologna, Italy, 2016; Volume 20.
4. Caffarelli, L.A.; Roquejoffre, J.-M.; Sire, Y. Variational problems with free boundaries for the fractional laplacian. *J. Eur. Math. Soc.* **2010**, *12*, 1151–1179.
5. Gal, C.G. Non-local Cahn–Hilliard equations with fractional dynamic boundary conditions. *Eur. J. Appl. Math.* **2017**, *28*, 736–788.
6. Cahn, J.W.; Hilliard, J.E. Free energy of a nonuniform system i. interfacial energy. *J. Chem. Phys.* **1958**, *28*, 258–267.
7. Giacomin, G.; Lebowitz, J.L. Phase segregation dynamics in particle systems with long range interactions. i. macroscopic limits. *J. Statist. Phys.* **1997**, *87*, 37–61.
8. Gal, C.G. *Doubly Nonlocal Cahn–Hilliard Equations*; Annales de l'Institut Henri Poincaré (C) Analyse Non Linéaire: Berlin, Germany, 2016.
9. Gal, C.G. On the strong-to-strong interaction case for doubly nonlocal Cahn–Hilliard equations. *Discret. Contin. Dyn. Syst.* **2017**, *37*, 131–167.
10. Andreu-Vaillo, F.; Mazón, J.M.; Rossi, J.D.; Toledo-Melero, J.J. *Nonlocal Diffusion Problems*; Mathematical Surveys and Monographs; American Mathematical Society, Real Sociedad Matemática Española: Providence, RI, USA, 2010; Volume 165.
11. Bates, P.; Han, J. The Neumann Boundary Problem for a Nonlocal Cahn–Hilliard Equation. *J. Differ. Equ.* **2005**, *212*, 235–277.
12. Colli, P.; Frigeri, S.; Grasselli, M. Global existence of weak solutions to a nonlocal Cahn–Hilliard–Navier–Stokes system. *J. Math. Anal. Appl.* **2012**, *386*, 428–444.
13. Frigeri, S.; Grasselli, M. Global and trajectory attractors for a nonlocal Cahn–Hilliard–Navier–Stokes system. *J. Dynam. Differ. Equ.* **2012**, *24*, 827–856.
14. Frigeri, S.; Grasselli, M.; Rocca, E. A diffuse interface model for two-phase incompressible flows with non-local interactions and non-constant mobility. *Nonlinearity* **2015**, *28*, 1257–1293.
15. Gal, C.G.; Grasselli, M. Longtime behavior of nonlocal Cahn–Hilliard equations. *Discret. Contin. Dyn. Syst.* **2014**, *34*, 145–179.
16. Grasselli, M.; Schimperna, G. Nonlocal phase-field systems with general potentials. *Discret. Contin. Dyn. Syst.* **2013**, *33*, 5089–5106.
17. Porta, F.D.; Grasselli, M. Convective nonlocal cahn-hilliard equations with reaction terms. *Discret. Contin. Dyn. Syst. Ser. B* **2015**, *20*, 1529–1553.
18. Shomberg, J.L. Upper-Semicontinuity of the Global Attractors for a Class of Nonlocal Cahn–Hilliard Equations. *arXiv* **2018**, arXiv:1805.06320.
19. Shomberg, J.L. Well-posedness and global attractors for a non-isothermal viscous relaxation of nonlocal Cahn–Hilliard equations. *AIMS Math. Nonlinear Evol. PDEs Interfaces Appl.* **2016**, *1*, 102–136.
20. Akagi, G.; Schimperna, G.; Segatti, A. Fractional Cahn–Hilliard, Allen–Cahn and Porous Medium Equations. *J. Differ. Equ.* **2016**, *261*, 2935–2985.
21. Conti, M.; Pata, V.; Squassina, M. Singular limit of differential systems with memory. *Indiana Univ. Math. J.* **2006**, *55*, 169–215.
22. Gal, C.G.; Shomberg, J.L. Coleman-Gurtin type equations with dynamic boundary conditions. *Phys. D* **2015**, *292/293*, 29–45.
23. Giorgi, C.; Pata, V.; Marzocchi, A. Asymptotic behavior of a semilinear problem in heat conduction with memory. *NoDEA Nonlinear Differ. Equ. Appl.* **1998**, *5*, 333–354.
24. Giorgi, C.; Pata, V.; Marzocchi, A. Uniform attractors for a non-autonomous semilinear heat equation with memory. *Quart. Appl. Math.* **2000**, *58*, 661–683.
25. Shomberg, J.L. Robust exponential attractors for Coleman–gurtin equations with dynamic boundary conditions possessing memory. *Electron. J. Differ. Equ.* **2016**, *2016*, 1–35.
26. Cavaterra, C.; Grasselli, M.; Grasselli, M. Cahn–Hilliard equations with memory and dynamic boundary conditions. *Asymptot. Anal.* **2011**, *71*, 123–162.
27. Conti, M.; Mola, G. 3-D viscous Cahn–Hilliard equation with memory. *Math. Models Methods Appl. Sci.* **2008**, *32*, 1370–1395.
28. Gal, C.G.; Grasselli, M. Singular limit of viscous Cahn–Hilliard equations with memory and dynamic boundary conditions. *DCDS-B* **2013**, *18*, 1581–1610.

29. Gatti, S.; Grasselli, M.; Miranville, A.; Pata, V. Memory relaxation of first order evolution equations. *Nonlinearity* **2005**, *18*, 1859–1883.
30. Gatti, S.; Grasselli, M.; Pata, V.; Squassina, M. Robust exponential attractors for a family of nonconserved phase-field systems with memory. *Discret. Contin. Dyn. Syst.* **2005**, *12*, 1019–1029.
31. Giorgi, C.; Grasselli, M.; Pata, V. Well-posedness and longtime behavior of the phase-field model with memory in a history space setting. *Quart. Appl. Math.* **2001**, *59*, 701–736.
32. Grasselli, M. On the large time behavior of a phase-field system with memory. *Asymptot. Anal.* **2008**, *56*, 229–249.
33. Grasselli, M.; Pata, V. Robust exponential attractors for a phase-field system with memory. *J. Evol. Equ.* **2005**, *5*, 465–483.
34. Grasselli, M.; Pata, V.; Vegni, F. Longterm dynamics of a conserved phase-field system with memory. *Asymptot. Anal.* **2003**, *33*, 261–320.
35. Gatti, S.; Miranville, A.; Pata, V.; Zelik, S. Continuous families of exponential attractors for singularly perturbed equations with memory. *Proc. R. Soc. Edinb. Sect. A* **2010**, *140*, 329–366.
36. Grasselli, M.; Schimperna, G.; Segatti, A.; Zelik, S. On the 3D Cahn–Hilliard equation with inertial term. *J. Evol. Equ.* **2009**, *9*, 371–404.
37. Grasselli, M.; Pata, V. *Uniform Attractors of Nonautonomous Dynamical Systems with Memory*; Evolution Equations, Semigroups and Functional Analysis; Birkhäuser: Boston, MA, USA, 2002; Volume 50.
38. Adams, D.; Hedberg, L.I. *Function Spaces and Potential Theory*; Grundlehren der Mathematischen Wissenschaften; Springer: Berlin, Germay, 1996; Volume 314.
39. Bogdan, K.; Burdzy, K.; Chen, Z.-Q. Censored stable processes. *Probab. Theory Relat. Fields* **2003**, *127*, 89–152.
40. Pata, V.; Zucchi, A. Attractors for a damped hyperbolic equation with linear memory. *Adv. Math. Sci. Appl.* **2001**, *11*, 505–529.
41. Pazy, A. *Semigroups of Linear Operators and Applications to Partial Differential Equations*; Applied Mathematical Sciences; Springer: New York, NY, USA, 1983; Volume 44.
42. Gal, C.G.; Miranville, A. Uniform global attractors for non-isothermal viscous and non-viscous Cahn–Hilliard equations with dynamic boundary conditions. *Nonlinear Anal. Real World Appl.* **2009**, *10*, 1738–1766.
43. Temam, R. *Navier-Stokes Equations—Theory and Numerical Analysis*; AMS Chelsea Publishing: Providence, RI, USA, 2001.
44. Barbu, V. *Nonlinear Semigroups and Differential Equations in Banach Spaces*; Noordhoff International Publishing: Bucharest, Romania, 1976.
45. Colli, P.; Krejčí, P.; Rocca, E.; Sprekels, J. Nonlinear evolution inclusions arising from phase change models. *Czechoslov. Math. J.* **2007**, *57*, 1067–1098.
46. Conti, M.; Zelati, M.C. Attractors for the non-viscous Cahn–Hilliard equation with memory in 2D. *Nonlinear Anal.* **2010**, *72*, 1668–1682.
47. Grasselli, M.; Schimperna, G.; Zelik, S. On the 2D Cahn–Hilliard equation with inertial term. *Comm. Part. Differ. Equ.* **2009**, *34*, 707–737.
48. Grasselli, M. Finite-dimensional global attractor for a nonlocal phase-field system. *Ist. Lomb. (Rend. Sci.) Math.* **2012**, *146*, 113–132.
49. Zheng, S.; Milani, A. Global attractors for singular perturbations of the Cahn–Hilliard equations. *J. Differ. Equ.* **2005**, *209* 101–139.
50. Babin, A.V.; Vishik, M.I. *Attractors of Evolution Equations*; North-Holland: Amsterdam, The Netherlands, 1992.
51. Temam, R. *Infinite-Dimensional Dynamical Systems in Mechanics and Physics*; Applied Mathematical Sciences; Springer: New York, NY, USA, 1988; Volume 68.
52. Zheng, S. *Nonlinear Evolution Equations*; Monographs and Surveys in Pure and Applied Mathematics; Chapman & Hall/CRC: Boca Raton, FL, USA, 2004; Volume 133.
53. Lions, J.L. *Quelques Méthodes de Résolution des Problèmes aux Limites Non Linéaires*; Dunod: Paris, France, 1969.
54. Tanabe, H. *Equations of Evolution*; Pitman: London, UK, 1979.
55. Hale, J.K. *Asymptotic Behavior of Dissipative Systems*; Mathematical Surveys and Monographs—No. 25; American Mathematical Society: Providence, RI, USA, 1988.
56. Milani, A.J.; Koksch, N.J. *An Introduction to Semiflows*; Monographs and Surveys in Pure and Applied Mathematics; Chapman & Hall/CRC: Boca Raton, FL, USA, 2005; Volume 134.

 *fractal and fractional*

Article

Hybridization of Block-Pulse and Taylor Polynomials for Approximating 2D Fractional Volterra Integral Equations

Davood Jabari Sabegh [1], Reza Ezzati [2], Omid Nikan [3], António M. Lopes [4] and Alexandra M. S. F. Galhano [5,*]

[1] Department of Mathematics, Bonab Branch, Islamic Azad University, Bonab 55517-85176, Iran; davood.jabari@bonabiau.ac.ir
[2] Department of Mathematics, Karaj Branch, Islamic Azad University, Karaj 31499-68111, Iran; ezzati@kiau.ac.ir
[3] School of Mathematics, Iran University of Science and Technology, Narmak, Tehran 16846-13114, Iran; omidnikan77@yahoo.com
[4] Institute of Mechanical Engineering, Faculty of Engineering, University of Porto, 4200-465 Porto, Portugal; aml@fe.up.pt
[5] Faculdade de Ciências Naturais, Engenharias e Tecnologias, Universidade Lusófona do Porto, Rua Augusto Rosa 24, 4000-098 Porto, Portugal
* Correspondence: alexandra.galhano@ulp.pt

Abstract: This paper proposes an accurate numerical approach for computing the solution of two-dimensional fractional Volterra integral equations. The operational matrices of fractional integration based on the Hybridization of block-pulse and Taylor polynomials are implemented to transform these equations into a system of linear algebraic equations. The error analysis of the proposed method is examined in detail. Numerical results highlight the robustness and accuracy of the proposed strategy.

Keywords: two dimensional Volterra integral equation; operational matrix; block pulse; operational matrix; Taylor polynomials

1. Introduction

Fractional calculus (FC) generalizes the classical differential calculus [1,2]. The FC has been applied to model several anomalous phenomena having nonlocal dynamics and involving long memory [3,4]. Indeed, the models based on classical calculus often fail to explain the genetic and inheritance properties of many complex systems having anomalous dynamics, whereas the fractional derivatives and integrals allow for a simpler and more accurate representation of their features. Due to the above-mentioned properties, fractional order integral equations (FOIEs) have been used in many engineering and physics fields to investigate complex systems, for instance, viscoelasticity and traffic models, temperature and motor control, and solid mechanics [4–8]. However, FOIEs pose difficulties in achieving their accurate analytical solution and numerical techniques have to be used in order to derive useful result [9–19].

In this work, we study a robust computational scheme based on two-dimensional (2D) Hybridization of block pulse and Taylor polynomials (2D-HBTs) for computing the approximate solution of 2D fractional Volterra integral Equations (2DFVIEs) as

$$f(x,y) - \frac{1}{\Gamma(\lambda_1)\Gamma(\lambda_2)} \int_0^x \int_0^y \frac{f(s,t)k(x,y,s,t)}{(y-t)^{1-\lambda_2}(x-s)^{1-\lambda_1}} dt ds = g(x,y), \quad (x,y) \in \Omega, \quad (1)$$

where $(\lambda_1, \lambda_2) \in (0, +\infty) \times (0, +\infty)$, $f(s,t)$ is an unknown function to be calculated, $\Omega = [0,1] \times [0,1]$ denotes the spatial domain, and $g(x,y)$ and $k(x,y,s,t)$ represent prescribed smooth functions. Over past years, for approximating 2D fractional integral Equations (2DFIEs) and 2D fractional integro-differential Equations (2DFIDEs), different basic functions have been employed. For example, Najafalizadeh and Ezzati [20] used 2D block pulse functions, while Jabari et al. [21] studied 2D orthogonal triangular functions for solving the 2DFIEs. Maleknejad et al. [22] used the Hybrid functions to simulate general nonlinear 2DFIDEs. Maleknejad and Hoseingholipour [23] implemented Laguerre functions for singular integral equation in unbounded domain. Kumar and Gupta [24] analyzed an operational matrix based 2D fractional-order Lagrange polynomials for approximating nonlinear 2DFIDEs. Mirzaee and Samadyar [25] obtained an operational matrix based on 2D hat basis functions for stochastic 2DFIEs. Asgari and Ezzati [26] employed the Bernstein polynomials and Rashidinia et al. [27] implemented shifted Jacobi polynomials for approximating 2DFIEs. Heydari et al. [28] presented an iterative multistep kernel based scheme for solving the 2DFIEs. Ardabili and Talaei [29] adopted a new Chelyshkov polynomials collocation method to solve the 2DFIEs. Hesameddini and Shahbazi [30] applied 2D shifted Legendre polynomials to estimate 2DFIEs. Asgari et al. [31] adopted the Bernstein polynomials to approximate the 2DFVIEs. Abdollahi et al. [32] presented an operational matrix scheme based 2D Haar wavelets, whereas Wang et al. [33] used 2D Euler polynomials combined with Gauss-Jacobi quadrature technique to simulate the 2DFVIEs. Liu et al. [34] employed the Bivariate barycentric rational interpolation for the 2DFVIEs. Khan et al. [35] implemented 2D Bernstein's approximation to approximate the 2DFVIEs. Wang et al. [33] applied the modified block-by-block technique, while Mohammad et al. [36] proposed an efficient approach based on Framelets for solving the 2DFVIEs. Ahsan et al. [37] used optimal Homotopy asymptotic scheme and Fazeli et al. [38] considered the Chebyshev polynomials for approximating the 2DFVIEs. Laib et al. [39] applied a numerical approach based on Taylor polynomials for the 2DFVIEs.

The main motivation of this paper is to propose an accurate numerical approach for finding the approximate solution of 2DFVIEs. The operational matrices of fractional integration based on the Hybridization of block-pulse and Taylor polynomials (2D-HBTs) are adopted to transform 2DFVIEs into a system of linear algebraic equations. The error analysis of the proposed method is examined in detail. Numerical results show the robustness and accuracy of the proposed method.

This paper includes seven sections as follows. Section 2 introduces the notation and basic definitions of FC. Section 3 derives an operational matrix of fractional integration of 2D-HBTs. Section 4 approximates the 2DFVIEs by employing the obtained operational matrix of fractional integration. Section 5 performs convergence analysis of the proposed strategy. Section 6 highlights the efficiency and accuracy of the proposed method by means of the results of numerical experiments. Finally, Section 7 contains the concluding remarks.

2. Preliminaries and Notations

In this section, we provide the basic concepts and definitions [1,2] needed in the follow-up.

Definition 1. The Riemann-Liouville fractional integration (RLFI) of order $\alpha \geq 0$ of a function $f(t) \in L^1(I)$ is defined by

$$I^\alpha f(t) = \frac{1}{\Gamma(\alpha)} \int_0^t (t-\tau)^{(\alpha-1)} f(\tau) \, d\tau \qquad \alpha > 0, \tag{2}$$

in which $\Gamma(\theta)$ represents the Euler's gamma function described as $\Gamma(\theta) = \int_0^{+\infty} s^{\theta-1} e^{-s} ds$.

The RLFI has the following properties:

- $I^0 f(x) = f(x)$,
- $I^\alpha I^\beta f(x) = I^\beta I^\alpha f(x) = I^{\alpha+\beta} f(x)$,
- $I^\alpha (x-a)^\beta = \frac{\Gamma(\beta+1)}{\Gamma(\alpha+\beta+1)} (x-a)^{\alpha+\beta}$.

Definition 2. The left-sided mixed RLFI of order r of f can be represented as [1]

$$I_\theta^r f(x,y) = \frac{1}{\Gamma(\lambda_1)\Gamma(\lambda_2)} \int_0^x \int_0^y (x-s)^{\lambda_1-1}(y-t)^{\lambda_2-1} f(s,t)\,dtds, \quad (3)$$

where $\theta = (0,0)$ and $r = (\lambda_1, \lambda_2) \in (0,\infty) \times (0,\infty)$.

Here, we list some notations of the left-sided mixed RLFI [1,2] as follows:

- $I_\theta^\alpha f(x,y) = \int_0^x \int_0^y (f(s,t))\,dtds$, $\alpha = (1,1)$, $(x,y) \in \Omega$,
- $I_\theta^r x^p y^q = \frac{\Gamma(p+1)\Gamma(q+1)}{\Gamma(p+1+\lambda_1)\Gamma(q+1+\lambda_2)} x^{p+\lambda_1} y^{q+\lambda_2}$, $-1 < p,q < \infty$,
- $I_\theta^\theta f(x,y) = f(x,y)$.

3. Hybrid Functions

3.1. The 2D-HBTs

First, we introduce the 1D-HBTs, $h_{i,j}(x)$, $1 \leq i \leq N$, $0 \leq j \leq M$, on the interval $[0,1]$ as [40,41]

$$h_{i,j}(x) = \begin{cases} T_j(Nx - i + 1) & \frac{i-1}{N} \leq x \leq \frac{i}{N}, \\ 0 & \text{otherwise,} \end{cases} \quad (4)$$

in which j and i represent the order of the Taylor polynomials and block-pulse functions, respectively, and $T_j(x) = x^j$.

We can approximate a function $f(x) \in L^2[0,1]$ in the form of 1D-HBT by

$$f(x) \simeq \sum_{i=1}^N \sum_{j=0}^{M-1} f_{ij} h_{ij}(x) = C^T H(x), \quad (5)$$

in which

$$C = [f_{10}, \ldots, f_{1(M-1)}, \ldots, f_{N0}, \ldots, f_{N(M-1)}]^T, \quad (6)$$

and

$$H(x) = [h_{10}(x), \ldots, h_{1(M-1)(x)}, h_{20}(x), \ldots, h_{2(M-1)}(x), \ldots, h_{N0}(x), \ldots, h_{N(M-1)}(x)]^T. \quad (7)$$

Obviously, we can obtain the hybrid coefficients f_{ij} computed by

$$f_{ij} = \frac{\langle f(x), h_{ij}(x) \rangle}{\langle h_{ij}(x), h_{ij}(x) \rangle} = \frac{1}{j!N!}\left(\frac{d^j f(x)}{dx^j}\right)\Big|_{x=\frac{i-1}{M}}, \quad (8)$$

where $\langle \cdot, \cdot \rangle$ denotes the inner product.

Orthogonal 2D-HBTs functions $h_{i_1 j_1 i_2 j_2}(x,y)$, $0 \leq j_1, j_2 \leq M$, $1 \leq i_1, i_2 \leq N$, on the region $\Omega = [0,1] \times [0,1]$, are defined as

$$h_{i_1 i_2 j_1 j_2}(x,y) = \begin{cases} T_{j_1}(Nx - i_1 + 1)T_{j_2}(Ny - i_2 + 1) & (x,y) \in [\frac{i_1-1}{N}, \frac{i_1}{N}] \times [\frac{i_2-1}{N}, \frac{i_2}{N}] \\ 0 & \text{otherwise.} \end{cases}$$

Let S be a set of 2D-HBTs as follows:

$$S = \{h_{1010}(x,y), \ldots, h_{101(M-1)}(x,y), h_{1020}(x,y), \ldots,$$
$$h_{102(M-1)}(x,y), \ldots, h_{N(M-1)N0}(x,y), \ldots, h_{N(M-1)N(M-1)}(x,y)\}.$$

Since S is a finite dimensional subspace of $L^2(\Omega)$ for an arbitrary $f(x,y) \in L^2(\Omega)$, it has the unique best approximation outside of S, therefore, there exist unique coefficients $f_{i_1 j_1 i_2 j_2}$, $0 \leq j_1, j_2 \leq M-1, 1 \leq i_1, i_2 \leq N$, so that

$$f(x,y) = \sum_{i_1=1}^{N} \sum_{j_1=0}^{M-1} \sum_{i_2=1}^{N} \sum_{j_2=0}^{M-1} f_{i_1 j_1 i_2 j_2} h_{i_1 i_2 j_1 j_2}(x,y) = F^T H(x,y), \qquad (9)$$

in which

$$F = [f_{1010}, \ldots, f_{101(M-1)}, f_{1020}, \ldots, f_{102(M-1)}, \ldots, f_{N(M-1)N0}, \ldots, f_{N(M-1)N(M-1)}]^T, \quad (10)$$

and

$$H(x,y) = [h_{1010}(x,y), \ldots, h_{101(M-1)}(x,y), h_{1020}(x,y), \ldots,$$
$$h_{102(M-1)}(x,y), \ldots, h_{N(M-1)N0}(x,y), \ldots, h_{N(M-1)N(M-1)}(x,y)]^T = H(x) \otimes H(y), \qquad (11)$$

in which the superscript T is transposition and $\otimes$ denotes the Kronecker product. Clearly 2D-HBTs coefficients, $f_{i_1 j_1 i_2 j_2}$, can be determined by

$$f_{i_1 j_1 i_2 j_2} = \frac{\langle h_{i_1 j_1}(x), \langle f(x,y), h_{i_2 j_2}(y) \rangle \rangle}{\langle h_{i_1 j_1}(x), h_{i_1 j_1}(x) \rangle \cdot \langle h_{i_2 j_2}(y), h_{i_2 j_2}(y) \rangle}$$
$$= \frac{1}{N^{i_1+j_2} j_1! j_2!} \left(\frac{\partial^{i_1+j_2} f(x,y)}{\partial x^{j_1} \partial y^{j_2}} \right) \bigg|_{(x,y)=(\frac{i_1}{N}, \frac{i_2}{N})}.$$

Similarly, we expand the functions $k(x,y,s,t) \in L^2(\Omega \times \Omega)$ in terms of the 2D-HBTs in the following form:

$$K(x,y,s,t) = H^T(x,y) K H(s,t), \qquad (12)$$

in which K represents a $(MN)^2 \times (MN)^2$ matrix:

$$K = \begin{pmatrix} K_{0000} & \cdots & K_{000(MN-1)} & K_{0010} & \cdots & K_{00(MN-1)(MN-1)} \\ K_{0100} & \cdots & K_{010(MN-1)} & K_{0110} & \cdots & K_{01(MN-1)(MN-1)} \\ \vdots & \vdots & & \cdot & & \vdots \\ K_{(MN-1)(MN-1)00} & \cdot & & \cdot & \cdot & K_{(MN-1)(MN-1)(MN-1)(MN-1)} \end{pmatrix},$$

in which

$$K_{i_1 j_1 i_2 j_2} = \frac{1}{N^{z+u+v+w} z! u! v! w!} \left(\frac{\partial^{z+u+v+w} K(x,y,s,t)}{\partial x^z \partial y^u \partial s^v \partial t^w} \right) \bigg|_{(x,y,s,t)=(\frac{i_1}{N}, \frac{j_1}{N}, \frac{i_2}{N}, \frac{j_2}{N})},$$

$i_1, j_1, i_2, j_2 = 0, 1, 2, \ldots, (NM-1)$, $z = i_1 - [\frac{i_1}{M}]M$, $u = j_1 - [\frac{j_1}{M}]M$, $v = i_2 - [\frac{i_2}{M}]M$, $w = j_2 - [\frac{j_2}{M}]M$,

in which $[\cdot]$ represents the integer part of the number. We use the product of two vectors $H(x,y)$ and $H^T(x,y)$ as follows

$$H(x,y) H^T(x,y) b = \hat{b} H(x,y), \qquad (13)$$

in which b represents a $(MN)^2$-vector, and $\hat{b}$ is a $(MN)^2 \times (MN)^2$ product operational matrix given as

$$\hat{b} = \begin{pmatrix} \hat{b}_{10} & 0 & \cdots & 0 \\ 0 & \hat{b}_{11} & \cdots & 0 \\ \vdots & \vdots & \ddots & \vdots \\ 0 & 0 & \cdots & \hat{b}_{N(M-1)} \end{pmatrix}_{(MN)^2 \times (MN)^2},$$

in which $\hat{b}_{ij}$, $1 \leq i \leq N$, $0 \leq j \leq M$, are $NM \times NM$ matrices given as

$$\hat{b}_{ij} = \begin{pmatrix} b_{ij10} & b_{ij11} & \cdots & b_{ijN(M-1)} \\ 0 & b_{ij10} & \cdots & b_{ij(N-1)(M-1)} \\ \vdots & \vdots & \ddots & \vdots \\ 0 & 0 & \cdots & b_{ij10} \end{pmatrix}.$$

3.2. Operational Matrix of Fractional Integration of 2D-HBTs

Here, we construct an operational matrix for fractional integration of the 2D-HBTs. Following [42], the operational matrix of fractional integration of 1D-HBT can be derived as follows:

$$I^\alpha H(x) \simeq P^\alpha H(x), \tag{14}$$

in which $H(x)$ is a vector of 1D-HBT defined in (11), and P^α represents an operational matrix of 1D-HBT. It is proved that [42]:

$$P^\alpha = \Phi F^\alpha \Phi^{-1}, \tag{15}$$

where Φ represents the projection matrix which converts the hybrid functions onto block pulse functions and

$$F^\alpha = \frac{1}{\Gamma(\alpha+2)NM^\alpha} \begin{pmatrix} 1 & \xi_1 & \xi_2 & \xi_3 & \cdots & \xi_{NM-1} \\ 0 & 1 & \xi_1 & \xi_2 & \cdots & \xi_{NM-2} \\ 0 & 0 & 1 & \xi_1 & \cdots & \xi_{NM-3} \\ \vdots & \vdots & \vdots & \vdots & \ddots & \vdots \\ 0 & 0 & 0 & 0 & \cdots & \xi_1 \\ 0 & 0 & 0 & 0 & \cdots & 1 \end{pmatrix},$$

with $\xi_k = (k+1)^{\alpha+1} - 2k^{(\alpha+1)} + (k-1)^{\alpha+1}$. By means of Equations (3) and (14), we have:

$$\begin{aligned} &\frac{1}{\Gamma(\lambda_1)\Gamma(\lambda_2)} \int_0^x \int_0^y (x-s)^{\lambda_1-1}(y-t)^{\lambda_2-1} H(s,t) \, dt ds \\ &= \frac{1}{\Gamma(\lambda_1)\Gamma(\lambda_2)} \int_0^x \int_0^y (x-s)^{\lambda_1-1}(y-t)^{\lambda_2-1} H(s) \otimes H(t) \, dt ds \\ &= \frac{1}{\Gamma(\lambda_1)} \int_0^x (x-s)^{\lambda_1-1} H(s) \, ds \otimes \frac{1}{\Gamma(\lambda_2)} \int_0^y (y-t)^{\lambda_2-1} H(t) \, dt \\ &= p^{\lambda_1} H(x) \otimes p^{\lambda_2} H(y) \\ &= (p^{\lambda_1} \otimes p^{\lambda_2})(H(x) \otimes H(y)) \\ &= (p^{\lambda_1} \otimes p^{\lambda_2}) H(x,y) = p^{\lambda_1,\lambda_2} H(x,y). \end{aligned}$$

Hence,

$$I^{(\lambda_1,\lambda_2)} H(x,y) = \frac{1}{\Gamma(\lambda_1)\Gamma(\lambda_2)} \int_0^x \int_0^y (x-s)^{\lambda_1-1}(y-t)^{\lambda_2-1} H(s,t) \, dt ds = p^{\lambda_1,\lambda_2} H(x,y), \tag{16}$$

in which p^{λ_1,λ_2} is called the operational matrix of fractional integration of the 2D-HBTs, that is,

$$p^{\lambda_1,\lambda_2} = (p^{\lambda_1} \otimes p^{\lambda_2}).$$

4. Numerical Solution of the 2DFVIEs

This section employs the 2D-HBTs to approximate the 2DFVIEs (1). For this purpose, we expand $g(x,y)$, $k(x,y,s,t)$, and $f(x,y)$ functions in terms of 2D-HBTs in the following forms

$$\begin{aligned} g(x,y) &= G^T H(x,y), \\ k(x,y,s,t) &= H(x,y)^T K H(x,y)), \\ f(x,y) &= F^T H(x,y), \end{aligned} \tag{17}$$

in which $H(x,y)$ is introduced in Equation (11), and vector g, and matrix G and vector F denote 2D-HBTs coefficients of $g(x,y)$, $k(x,y,s,t)$, and $f(x,y)$, respectively.

Meanwhile, substituting relation (17) into relation (1), we arrive at

$$F^T H(x,y) - \frac{1}{\Gamma(\lambda_1)\Gamma(\lambda_2)} \int_0^x \int_0^y \frac{H^T(x,y) K H(s,t) H^T(s,t) F}{(x-s)^{1-\lambda_1}(y-t)^{1-\lambda_2}} dt ds \simeq H^T(x,y) G. \quad (18)$$

With the help of Equation (13), we can obtain

$$H^T(x,y) F - \frac{H^T(x,y) K \hat{F}}{\Gamma(\lambda_1)\Gamma(\lambda_2)} \int_0^x \int_0^y (y-t)^{\lambda_2-1}(x-s)^{\lambda_1-1} H(s,t) \, dt ds \simeq H^T(x,y) G. \quad (19)$$

Applying Equation (16), we arrive at

$$H^T(x,y) F - H^T(x,y) K \hat{F} P^{\lambda_1,\lambda_2} H(x,y) = H^T(x,y) G. \quad (20)$$

In order to find F, we collocate the relation (20) in $(MN)^2$ Newton-Cotes points as

$$(x_i, y_j) = \left(\frac{2i-1}{2(MN)^2}, \frac{2j-1}{2(MN)^2}\right), i = j = 1, 2, \ldots, (MN)^2. \quad (21)$$

Therefore, we obtain a system of $(MN)^2$ linear equations. After solving this system, we can determine F. Consequently, the approximate solution of (1) can be represented as below:

$$f(x,y) = F^T H(x,y). \quad (22)$$

5. Convergence Analysis

In this section, we discuss the convergence of the proposed strategy based on 2D-HBTs. For this aim, suppose that $(C[\Omega], \|.\|)$ is the Banach space of all continuous functions in the region Ω, including norm $\|f\| = \max_{(x,y)\in\Omega} |f(x,y)|$, and let $\|K\| = C$. Moreover, the functions $f(x,y)$ and $f_{MN}(x,y)$ represent the analytic and numerical solutions, respectively.

Theorem 1. *For $0 < \alpha < 1$ the numerical solution of (1) in terms of 2D-HBTs is convergent so that $\alpha = \frac{C}{\Gamma(\lambda_1+1)\Gamma(\lambda_2+1)}$.*

Proof.

$$\|f - f_{MN}\|_\infty = \max_{(x,y)\in\Omega} |f(x,y) - f_{MN}(x,y)|$$

$$= \max_{(x,y)\in\Omega} \left| \frac{1}{\Gamma(\lambda_1)\Gamma(\lambda_2)} \int_0^x \int_0^y \frac{k(x,y,s,t)(f(s,t) - f_{MN}(s,t))}{(x-s)^{1-\lambda_1}(y-t)^{1-\lambda_2}} dt ds \right|$$

$$\leq \max_{(x,y)\in\Omega} \frac{1}{\Gamma(\lambda_1)\Gamma(\lambda_2)} \int_0^x \int_0^y \left| \frac{k(x,y,s,t)(f(s,t) - f_{MN}(s,t))}{(x-s)^{1-\lambda_1}(y-t)^{1-\lambda_2}} \right| dt ds$$

$$\leq \max_{(x,y)\in\Omega} \frac{C}{\Gamma(\lambda_1)\Gamma(\lambda_2)} \int_0^x \int_0^y \left| \frac{(f(s,t) - f_{MN}(s,t))}{(y-t)^{1-\lambda_2}(x-s)^{1-\lambda_1}} \right| dt ds$$

$$\leq \frac{C}{\Gamma(\lambda_1)\Gamma(\lambda_2)} \|f - f_{MN}\|_\infty \int_0^x \frac{ds}{(x-s)^{1-\lambda_1}} \int_0^y \frac{dt}{(y-t)^{1-\lambda_2}}$$

$$= C\|f - f_{MN}\|_\infty I^{\lambda_1}(1) I^{\lambda_2}(1)$$

$$= C\|f - f_{MN}\|_\infty \frac{x^{\lambda_1} y^{\lambda_2}}{\Gamma(\lambda_1+1)\Gamma(\lambda_2+1)}$$

$$\leq \frac{C\|f - f_{MN}\|_\infty}{\Gamma(\lambda_1+1)\Gamma(\lambda_2+1)}$$

$$= \alpha \|f - f_{MN}\|_\infty$$

$$\Rightarrow \|f - f_{MN}\|_\infty \leq \alpha \|f - f_{MN}\|_\infty.$$

Since $0 < \alpha < 1$, we conclude that:
$$\lim_{MN \to \infty} \|f - f_{MN}\|_\infty = 0. \tag{23}$$

□

6. Numerical Experiments

This section provides four numerical test problems to illustrate that the proposed strategy is more accurate, applicable and effective than other techniques reported in the literature.

Example 1. First, we consider the 2DFVIE [20] as

$$f(x,y) - \frac{1}{\Gamma(\frac{7}{2})\Gamma(\frac{7}{2})} \int_0^x \int_0^y (x-s)^{\frac{5}{2}}(y-t)^{\frac{5}{2}} xy\sqrt{t} f(s,t) \, dt \, ds = \frac{2362}{4725} xy.$$

The theoretical solution of the above problem is $f(x,y) = \frac{1}{2} yx$.

Table 1 reports the exact and the approximate solutions by using selected nodes in the computational region $\Omega = [0,1] \times [0,1]$ and compares the results with the scheme described in [20]. Numerical results indicate that the proposed strategy based on 2D-HBTs is considerably more accurate than the technique presented in [20].

Table 1. Numerical results of Example 1.

	2D-HBTs	Ref. [20]	Exact Solution
$x = y$	$M = 5, N = 5$	$M = 16$	
0	0.000011	0.0011458	0
0.1	0.005072	−0.011725	0.005
0.2	0.195430	0.030901	0.02
0.3	0.043278	0.02872	0.045
0.4	0.080007	0.0892319	0.08
0.5	0.127394	0.99179	0.125
0.6	0.180027	0.187449	0.18
0.7	0.244633	0.219189	0.245
0.8	0.319782	0.329976	0.32
0.9	0.406851	0.381779	0.405

Example 2. We consider the 2DFVIE [26] as:

$$f(x,y) - \frac{1}{\Gamma(\frac{7}{2})\Gamma(\frac{5}{2})} \int_0^x \int_0^y (x-s)^{\frac{5}{2}}(y-t)^{\frac{3}{2}} (y^2+s)e^{-t} f(s,t) \, dt \, ds$$
$$= x^2 e^y - \frac{1024 x^{\frac{11}{2}} y^{\frac{5}{2}} (6x + 13y^2)}{2027025\pi}.$$

This example has the theoretical solution $f(x,y) = x^2 e^y$.

Table 2 exhibits the maximum norm errors of $f(x,y)$ by the proposed strategy based on 2D-HBTs and compares the results with the technique described in [26].

Table 2. The maximum norm errors of Example 2.

	2D-HBTs		Ref. [26]	
$x = y$	$M = N = 3$	$M = N = 4$	$M = N = 3$	$M = N = 4$
0.0	5.466×10^{-6}	7.023×10^{-6}	3.046×10^{-4}	4.086×10^{-4}
0.1	5.604×10^{-6}	6.886×10^{-6}	3.157×10^{-4}	4.181×10^{-4}
0.2	3.673×10^{-7}	7.509×10^{-6}	3.509×10^{-4}	4.471×10^{-4}
0.3	3.701×10^{-6}	7.006×10^{-6}	3.834×10^{-4}	4.970×10^{-4}
0.4	4.778×10^{-6}	5.756×10^{-6}	3.912×10^{-4}	5.656×10^{-4}
0.5	2.425×10^{-6}	4.613×10^{-6}	4.001×10^{-4}	6.474×10^{-4}
0.6	7.164×10^{-6}	4.092×10^{-6}	4.698×10^{-4}	7.316×10^{-4}
0.7	3.425×10^{-5}	4.416×10^{-6}	6.143×10^{-4}	7.086×10^{-4}
0.8	3.371×10^{-5}	4.867×10^{-6}	6.501×10^{-4}	6.788×10^{-4}
0.9	1.483×10^{-5}	7.554×10^{-6}	3.592×10^{-5}	1.004×10^{-4}

Example 3. Finally, we consider the following 2DFVIE:

$$f(x,y) - \frac{1}{\Gamma(\frac{1}{2})\Gamma(\frac{1}{2})} \int_0^x \int_0^y (x-s)^{-\frac{1}{2}}(y-t)^{-\frac{1}{2}} f(s,t)\,dtds = (x^2 - y^2)\left(1 - \frac{32}{15}\sqrt{xy}\right).$$

The analytic solution of the aforesaid problem is $f(x,y) = x^2 - y^2$.
Table 3 reports the maximum norm errors for various values of N and M with the help of the proposed strategy based on 2D-HBTs.

Table 3. The maximum norm errors of Example 3.

$y = x$	$N = 3, M = 3$	$N = 4, M = 4$
0.1	0	9.8482×10^{-19}
0.2	1.9745×10^{-19}	8.9765×10^{-18}
0.3	7.6763×10^{-19}	7.6538×10^{-18}
0.4	5.7461×10^{-16}	5.7461×10^{-17}
0.5	4.8877×10^{-16}	3.5534×10^{-16}
0.6	4.5511×10^{-17}	4.8549×10^{-17}
0.7	1.6695×10^{-16}	5.9879×10^{-16}
0.8	2.3340×10^{-16}	2.3340×10^{-16}
0.9	8.4997×10^{-16}	8.2781×10^{-16}

Example 4. Finally, we consider the following 2DFIE studied in [26]:

$$f(x,y) - \frac{1}{\Gamma(\lambda_1)\Gamma(\lambda_2)} \int_0^x \int_0^y (x-s)^{\lambda_1-1}(y-t)^{\lambda_2-1} \sqrt{xy} st f(s,t)\,dtds$$
$$= x^3(y^2 - y) - \frac{1}{60} x^{\frac{11}{2}} y^{\frac{7}{2}} (3y - 4).$$

We adopt the proposed method for various values of M, N for solving this example. For $\lambda_1 = \lambda_2 = 1$, the exact solution is given as $f(x,y) = x^3(y^2 - y)$. Tables 4 and 5 show the maximum absolute errors of $f(x,y)$ by the proposed method and compare the results with the method reported in [26].

Table 4. The maximum absolute errors for $\lambda_1 = \lambda_2 = 0.8$ in Example 4.

	2D-HBTs		Ref. [26]	
$x = y$	$M = N = 2$	$M = N = 3$	$M = N = 2$	$M = N = 3$
0.1	8.355×10^{-4}	6.084×10^{-5}	1.388×10^{-3}	1.440×10^{-3}
0.2	9.734×10^{-5}	4.746×10^{-5}	8.772×10^{-4}	3.097×10^{-3}
0.3	4.230×10^{-4}	5.449×10^{-5}	1.407×10^{-3}	4.872×10^{-3}
0.4	6.328×10^{-4}	7.149×10^{-5}	1.153×10^{-3}	6.606×10^{-3}
0.5	8.036×10^{-4}	9.043×10^{-6}	5.673×10^{-3}	8.179×10^{-3}
0.6	9.301×10^{-4}	6.643×10^{-5}	9.748×10^{-3}	9.379×10^{-3}
0.7	2.731×10^{-4}	5.708×10^{-5}	1.089×10^{-2}	9.822×10^{-3}
0.8	4.550×10^{-4}	3.531×10^{-5}	7.730×10^{-3}	8.922×10^{-3}
0.9	2.936×10^{-4}	3.892×10^{-5}	1.222×10^{-3}	5.918×10^{-3}

Table 5. The maximum absolute errors for $\lambda_1 = \lambda_2 = 0.95$ in Example 4.

	2D-HBTs		Ref. [26]	
$x = y$	$M = N = 2$	$M = N = 3$	$M = N = 2$	$M = N = 3$
0.1	2.480×10^{-4}	4.913×10^{-5}	1.021×10^{-3}	9.073×10^{-4}
0.2	4.609×10^{-4}	3.320×10^{-6}	1.592×10^{-3}	1.950×10^{-3}
0.3	5.002×10^{-4}	7.049×10^{-6}	2.535×10^{-3}	3.065×10^{-3}
0.4	2.436×10^{-4}	5.819×10^{-5}	4.268×10^{-4}	4.161×10^{-3}
0.5	5.712×10^{-4}	4.007×10^{-5}	3.633×10^{-3}	5.143×10^{-3}
0.6	6.913×10^{-4}	4.573×10^{-5}	7.262×10^{-3}	5.794×10^{-3}
0.7	4.320×10^{-4}	6.413×10^{-5}	7.991×10^{-2}	5.704×10^{-3}
0.8	3.651×10^{-4}	8.472×10^{-5}	4.471×10^{-3}	4.241×10^{-3}
0.9	3.825×10^{-4}	2.732×10^{-5}	2.332×10^{-3}	5.881×10^{-4}

7. Conclusions

This work derived a general technique for computing the solution of 2DFVIEs (1). The operational matrices of 2D-HBTs and their properties were employed to convert the 2DFVIEs into a system of algebraic equations that can be solved. It was shown that the proposed strategy is convergent. Numerical experiments illustrated its superior efficiency and performance when compared with other alternative methods found in the literature.

Author Contributions: Conceptualization, D.J.S. and R.E.; data curation, D.J.S. and R.E.; formal analysis, D.J.S., O.N. and R.E.; investigation, D.J.S. and O.N.; methodology, D.J.S. and R.E.; software, D.J.S. and R.E.; supervision, A.M.L. and A.M.S.F.G.; validation, R.E., O.N. and A.M.S.F.G.; visualization, D.J.S. and O.N.; writing—original draft, D.J.S. and O.N.; writing—review and editing, A.M.S.F.G and A.M.L. All authors have read and agreed to the published version of the manuscript.

Funding: This research received no external funding.

Institutional Review Board Statement: Not applicable.

Informed Consent Statement: Not applicable.

Data Availability Statement: Not applicable.

Conflicts of Interest: The authors declare no conflict of interest.

References

1. Podlubny, I. *Fractional Differential Equations, Mathematics in Science and Engineering*; Academic Press: New York, NY, USA, 1999.
2. Milici, C.; Drăgănescu, G.; Machado, J.T. *Introduction to Fractional Differential Equations*; Springer: Cham, Switzerland, 2018; Volume 25.
3. Biswas, K.; Bohannan, G.; Caponetto, R.; Lopes, A.M.; Machado, J.A.T. *Fractional-Order Devices*; Springer: Cham, Switzerland, 2017.

4. Sabatier, J.; Agrawal, O.P.; Machado, J.T. *Advances in Fractional Calculus*; Springer: Dordrecht, The Netherlands, 2007; Volume 4.
5. Ionescu, C.; Lopes, A.; Copot, D.; Machado, J.T.; Bates, J.H. The role of fractional calculus in modeling biological phenomena: A review. *Commun. Nonlinear Sci. Numer. Simul.* **2017**, *51*, 141–159. [CrossRef]
6. Tenreiro Machado, J.; Lopes, A.M. Relative fractional dynamics of stock markets. *Nonlinear Dyn.* **2016**, *86*, 1613–1619. [CrossRef]
7. Ababneh, O. Adaptive synchronization and anti-synchronization of fractional order chaotic optical systems with uncertain parameters. *J. Math. Comput. Sci.* **2021**, *23*, 302–314. [CrossRef]
8. Prasad, R.; Kumar, K.; Dohare, R. Caputo fractional order derivative model of Zika virus transmission dynamics. *J. Math. Comput. Sci.* **2023**, *28*, 145–157. [CrossRef]
9. Aghdam, Y.E.; Mesgarani, H.; Moremedi, G.; Khoshkhahtinat, M. High-accuracy numerical scheme for solving the space-time fractional advection-diffusion equation with convergence analysis. *Alex. Eng. J.* **2022**, *61*, 217–225. [CrossRef]
10. Rakhshan, S.A.; Effati, S. Fractional optimal control problems with time-varying delay: A new delay fractional Euler–Lagrange equations. *J. Frankl. Inst.* **2020**, *357*, 5954–5988. [CrossRef]
11. Nikan, O.; Avazzadeh, Z.; Machado, J.T. Numerical approach for modeling fractional heat conduction in porous medium with the generalized Cattaneo model. *Appl. Math. Model.* **2021**, *100*, 107–124. [CrossRef]
12. Nikan, O.; Avazzadeh, Z. Numerical simulation of fractional evolution model arising in viscoelastic mechanics. *Appl. Numer. Math.* **2021**, *169*, 303–320. [CrossRef]
13. Qiao, L.; Qiu, W.; Xu, D. A second-order ADI difference scheme based on non-uniform meshes for the three-dimensional nonlocal evolution problem. *Comput. Math. Appl.* **2021**, *102*, 137–145. [CrossRef]
14. Qiao, L.; Xu, D.; Qiu, W. The formally second-order BDF ADI difference/compact difference scheme for the nonlocal evolution problem in three-dimensional space. *Appl. Numer. Math.* **2022**, *172*, 359–381. [CrossRef]
15. Qiao, L.; Guo, J.; Qiu, W. Fast BDF2 ADI methods for the multi-dimensional tempered fractional integrodifferential equation of parabolic type. *Comput. Math. Appl.* **2022**, *123*, 89–104. [CrossRef]
16. Huang, Q.; Qi, R.j.; Qiu, W. The efficient alternating direction implicit Galerkin method for the nonlocal diffusion-wave equation in three dimensions. *J. Appl. Math. Comput.* **2021**, 1–21. [CrossRef]
17. Yang, Y.; Chen, Y.; Huang, Y.; Wei, H. Spectral collocation method for the time-fractional diffusion-wave equation and convergence analysis. *Comput. Math. Appl.* **2017**, *73*, 1218–1232. [CrossRef]
18. Yang, Y.; Huang, Y.; Zhou, Y. Numerical simulation of time fractional Cable equations and convergence analysis. *Numer. Methods Partial Differ. Equ.* **2018**, *34*, 1556–1576. [CrossRef]
19. Yang, Y.; Huang, Y.; Zhou, Y. Numerical solutions for solving time fractional Fokker–Planck equations based on spectral collocation methods. *J. Comput. Appl. Math.* **2018**, *339*, 389–404. [CrossRef]
20. Najafalizadeh, S.; Ezzati, R. Numerical methods for solving two-dimensional nonlinear integral equations of fractional order by using two-dimensional block pulse operational matrix. *Appl. Math. Comput.* **2016**, *280*, 46–56. [CrossRef]
21. Jabari Sabeg, D.; Ezzati, R.; Maleknejad, K. A new operational matrix for solving two-dimensional nonlinear integral equations of fractional order. *Cogent Math.* **2017**, *4*, 1347017. [CrossRef]
22. Maleknejad, K.; Rashidinia, J.; Eftekhari, T. Operational matrices based on hybrid functions for solving general nonlinear two-dimensional fractional integro-differential equations. *Comput. Appl. Math.* **2020**, *39*, 103. [CrossRef]
23. Maleknejad, K.; Hoseingholipour, A. Numerical treatment of singular integral equation in unbounded domain. *Int. J. Comput. Math.* **2021**, *98*, 1633–1647. [CrossRef]
24. Kumar, S.; Gupta, V. An approach based on fractional-order Lagrange polynomials for the numerical approximation of fractional order non-linear Volterra-Fredholm integro-differential equations. *J. Appl. Math. Comput.* **2022**, 1–22. [CrossRef]
25. Mirzaee, F.; Samadyar, N. Application of hat basis functions for solving two-dimensional stochastic fractional integral equations. *Comput. Appl. Math.* **2018**, *37*, 4899–4916. [CrossRef]
26. Asgari, M.; Ezzati, R. Using operational matrix of two-dimensional Bernstein polynomials for solving two-dimensional integral equations of fractional order. *Appl. Math. Comput.* **2017**, *307*, 290–298. [CrossRef]
27. Rashidinia, J.; Eftekhari, T.; Maleknejad, K. Numerical solutions of two-dimensional nonlinear fractional Volterra and Fredholm integral equations using shifted Jacobi operational matrices via collocation method. *J. King Saud Univ. Sci.* **2021**, *33*, 101244. [CrossRef]
28. Heydari, M.; Shivanian, E.; Azarnavid, B.; Abbasbandy, S. An iterative multistep kernel based method for nonlinear Volterra integral and integro-differential equations of fractional order. *J. Comput. Appl. Math.* **2019**, *361*, 97–112. [CrossRef]
29. Ardabili, J.S.; Talaei, Y. Chelyshkov collocation method for solving the two-dimensional Fredholm–Volterra integral equations. *Int. J. Appl. Comput. Math.* **2018**, *4*, 25. [CrossRef]
30. Hesameddini, E.; Shahbazi, M. Two-dimensional shifted Legendre polynomials operational matrix method for solving the two-dimensional integral equations of fractional order. *Appl. Math. Comput.* **2018**, *322*, 40–54. [CrossRef]
31. Asgari, M.; Ezzati, R.; Jafari, H. Solution of 2D Fractional Order Integral Equations by Bernstein Polynomials Operational Matrices. *Nonlinear Dyn. Syst. Theory* **2019**, *19*, 10–20.
32. Abdollahi, Z.; Mohseni Moghadam, M.; Saeedi, H.; Ebadi, M. A computational approach for solving fractional Volterra integral equations based on two-dimensional Haar wavelet method. *Int. J. Comput. Math.* **2022**, *99*, 1488–1504. [CrossRef]
33. Wang, Z.Q.; Liu, Q.; Cao, J.Y. A Higher-Order Numerical Scheme for Two-Dimensional Nonlinear Fractional Volterra Integral Equations with Uniform Accuracy. *Fractal Fract.* **2022**, *6*, 314. [CrossRef]

34. Liu, H.; Huang, J.; He, X. Bivariate barycentric rational interpolation method for two dimensional fractional Volterra integral equations. *J. Comput. Appl. Math.* **2021**, *389*, 113339. [CrossRef]
35. Khan, F.; Omar, M.; Ullah, Z. Discretization method for the numerical solution of 2D Volterra integral equation based on two-dimensional Bernstein polynomial. *AIP Adv.* **2018**, *8*, 125209. [CrossRef]
36. Mohammad, M.; Trounev, A.; Cattani, C. An efficient method based on framelets for solving fractional Volterra integral equations. *Entropy* **2020**, *22*, 824. [CrossRef] [PubMed]
37. Ahsan, S.; Nawaz, R.; Akbar, M.; Nisar, K.S.; Baleanu, D. Approximate solutions of nonlinear two-dimensional Volterra integral equations. *Math. Methods Appl. Sci.* **2021**, *44*, 5548–5559. [CrossRef]
38. Fazeli, S.; Hojjati, G.; Kheiri, H. A piecewise approximation for linear two-dimensional volterra integral equation by chebyshev polynomials. *Int. J. Nonlinear Sci.* **2013**, *16*, 255–261.
39. Laib, H.; Boulmerka, A.; Bellour, A.; Birem, F. Numerical solution of two-dimensional linear and nonlinear Volterra integral equations using Taylor collocation method. *J. Comput. Appl. Math.* **2022**, *417*, 114537. [CrossRef]
40. Abbas, S.; Benchohra, M. Fractional order integral equations of two independent variables. *Appl. Math. Comput.* **2014**, *227*, 755–761. [CrossRef]
41. Mirzaee, F.; Hoseini, A.A. A computational method based on hybrid of block-pulse functions and Taylor series for solving two-dimensional nonlinear integral equations. *Alex. Eng. J.* **2014**, *53*, 185–190. [CrossRef]
42. Maleknejad, K.; Mahmoudi, Y. Numerical solution of linear Fredholm integral equation by using hybrid Taylor and block-pulse functions. *Appl. Math. Comput.* **2004**, *149*, 799–806. [CrossRef]

Article

Analysis of a Fractional Variational Problem Associated with Cantilever Beams Subjected to a Uniformly Distributed Load

Apassara Suechoei [1,2], Parinya Sa Ngiamsunthorn [1,*], Waraporn Chatanin [1], Chainarong Athisakul [3], Somchai Chucheepsakul [3] and Danuruj Songsanga [1]

1   Department of Mathematics, Faculty of Science, King Mongkut's University of Technology Thonburi, Bangkok 10140, Thailand; apassara.sue@gmail.com (A.S.); waraporn.chat@kmutt.ac.th (W.C.); danuruj.ice@gmail.com (D.S.)
2   Learning Institute, King Mongkut's University of Technology Thonburi, Bangkok 10140, Thailand
3   Department of Civil Engineering, Faculty of Engineering, King Mongkut's University of Technology Thonburi, Bangkok 10140, Thailand; chainarong.ath@kmutt.ac.th (C.A.); somchai.chu@kmutt.ac.th (S.C.)
*   Correspondence: parinya.san@kmutt.ac.th

Abstract: In this paper, we investigate the existence and uniqueness of minimizers of a fractional variational problem generalized from the energy functional associated with a cantilever beam under a uniformly distributed load. We apply the fractional Euler–Lagrange condition to formulate the minimization problem as a boundary value problem and obtain existence and uniqueness results in both L^2 and L^∞ settings. Additionally, we characterize the continuous dependence of the minimizers on varying loads in the energy functional. Moreover, an approximate solution is derived via the homotopy perturbation method, which is numerically demonstrated in various examples. The results show that the deformations are larger for smaller orders of the fractional derivative.

Keywords: cantilever beam; existence and uniqueness of minimizers; fractional boundary value problem; Euler–Lagrange theorem; homotopy perturbation method

1. Introduction

Fractional calculus is a branch of mathematics concerned with derivatives and integrals of non-integer order. It has been applied in various fields including chemistry, biology, engineering, epidemic modeling, and viscoelasticity [1–4]. Several researchers have investigated differential equations of arbitrary order, beginning with the existence and uniqueness of solutions and moving on to analytical and computational techniques to find solutions [5–8].

Although there are several engineering applications for the construction of bridges and buildings, attentive analyses of elastic beam equations are required to ensure the stability of the structure. A cantilever beam is a rigid structural element that is rigidly fixed at a single point on one side while the other side is free. In structural engineering, the behavior of cantilever beams is often analyzed using classical beam theory, which is based on the assumptions of small deformations and linear elastic material behavior. In the context of a cantilever beam, fractional calculus can be used to analyze the response of the beam to external loads and predict its dynamic behavior under different conditions [9,10]. For example, the motion of a cantilever beam subjected to a harmonic load can be described using fractional differential equations. In addition, fractional calculus can be used to study the beam's natural frequencies and mode shapes, which are important characteristics that influence its behavior [11,12].

Overall, employing fractional calculus in the analysis of cantilever beams can provide more accurate predictions of the behavior of these structures under various load conditions. By considering the effects of fractional derivatives on the stiffness and strength of a cantilever beam, it is possible to better understand and predict its response to external loads. This can be useful for the design and optimization of cantilever beams in a variety of applications. For example, the existence and uniqueness of solutions to the boundary value problem of the cantilever beam were studied in the framework of quantum calculus in [13] and the ψ−Hilfer derivative in [14]. In addition, the deflection of the cantilever beam based on fractional calculus was also studied in [15,16]. Moreover, there are several methods available for solving fractional differential equations including integral transform techniques such as the Laplace and Fourier transforms, fixed-point techniques, and the Adomian decomposition method. These methods can be used to analyze the behavior of cantilever beams with fractional calculus and obtain the corresponding solutions.

One significant method for determining an elastica's equilibrium forms is to derive the condition for stationary of the total energy. Then, the corresponding boundary value problems associated with ordinary differential equations are used to determine the equilibrium shapes. Della et al. [17] analyzed the equilibrium configuration of an elastica with one end clamped under a uniformly distributed load, which is depicted in Figure 1.

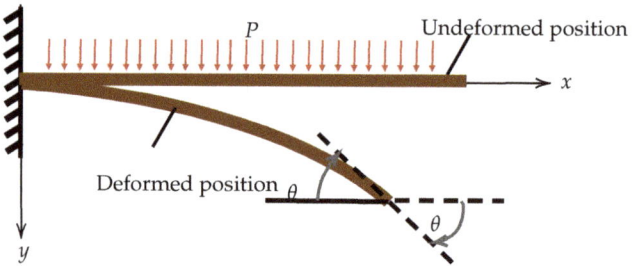

Figure 1. Undeformed and deformed positions of a cantilever beam subjected to a uniformly distributed load.

They investigated the sufficient conditions for the stability and instability of the equilibrium shape of the elastica obtained from the minimization problem of the total energy functional described by

$$\begin{cases} \min E(\theta) = \dfrac{1}{2}\int_0^L |\theta'(s)|^2 ds - P\int_0^L (L-s)\sin\theta(s) ds, \\ \theta(0) = \theta'(L) = 0, \end{cases} \quad (1)$$

where P, L, s, and θ denote the concentrated load, the length of the beam, the arc length, and the tangent angle, respectively.

It is possible to use fractional calculus to analyze the behavior of cantilever beams. In this approach, the beam is modeled as a dynamic system with memory and the governing equations of motion are described by fractional calculus operators. The solutions of these equations can provide insights into the response of the beam under various loading conditions and can be used to design and optimize the beam's structural performance.

Motivated by previous works, we consider the generalization of the potential energy associated with the cantilever beam under the framework of fractional calculus and determine the shape that minimizes the functional E and satisfies the boundary conditions:

$$\begin{cases} \min E(\theta) = \dfrac{1}{2}\int_0^L \left|{}^C_0\mathcal{D}_s^\alpha \theta(s)\right|^2 ds - \dfrac{P}{\Gamma(\alpha+1)}\int_0^L (L-s)^\alpha \sin\theta(s) ds, \\ \theta(0) = {}^C_0\mathcal{D}_s^\alpha \theta(s)\Big|_{s=L} = 0, \end{cases} \quad (2)$$

where $P > 0$ and $\dfrac{1}{2} < \alpha < 1$ is the order of the Caputo fractional derivative. The properties of the minimizers of the total energy can be characterized by the corresponding Euler–Lagrange conditions.

The aim of this paper is to use Euler–Lagrange conditions for Problem (2) to characterize the boundary value problem. Then, the well-known fixed-point theorems of Schaefer and Banach are used to establish the existence and uniqueness of the solutions for these boundary value problems. Different load values are analyzed for continuous dependence. Finally, we approximate the analytical solution for various loads and fractional orders to demonstrate the theoretical results. The main contribution of this paper is to provide an analysis of the deflection of the cantilever beam through the fractional energy functional derived from the physical and geometrical aspects in terms of the tangent angle or curvature, which is complementary to [8,16]. This technique can be applied to analyze the deformation of the cantilever beam under different load types.

The rest of the paper is organized as follows. In Section 2, we introduce some notations and essential theoretical results on fractional calculus and calculus of variations. In Section 3, the total energy is reformulated as a boundary value problem using Euler–Lagrange conditions. The existence and uniqueness results are proved via fixed-point techniques in Section 4. Based on techniques from nonlinear functional analysis, we analyze the continuous dependence of minimizers on the different loads in Section 5. Finally, the analytical solution is approximated by the homotopy perturbation method in Section 6. We also present numerical examples to support the validity of the analytical results.

2. Preliminary Background of Fractional Calculus and Calculus of Variations

In this section, we first give some essential definitions and properties of fractional differential operators and fractional integral operators.

Further details on this subject and its applications can be found, in [3,18,19].

2.1. Fractional Calculus

Let u be a real valued function defined on the interval $[a, b]$ and $\text{Re}(\alpha) > 0$.

Definition 1 (Fractional integral in the sense of Riemann–Liouville, [3]). *The left and right Riemann–Liouville fractional integral operators of order α of function u are defined, respectively, by*

$$(_a\mathcal{I}_x^\alpha u)(x) = \frac{1}{\Gamma(\alpha)} \int_a^x (x-s)^{\alpha-1} u(s) ds$$

and

$$(_x\mathcal{I}_b^\alpha u)(x) = \frac{1}{\Gamma(\alpha)} \int_x^b (s-x)^{\alpha-1} u(s) ds,$$

for all $x \in [a, b]$.

Definition 2 (Fractional derivative in the sense of Riemann–Liouville [3]). *The left and right Riemann–Liouville fractional derivatives of order α of a function u are defined, respectively, by*

$$(_a\mathcal{D}_x^\alpha u)(x) = \frac{1}{\Gamma(1-\alpha)} \frac{d}{dx} \int_a^x (x-s)^{-\alpha} u(s) ds$$

and

$$(_x\mathcal{D}_b^\alpha u)(x) = -\frac{1}{\Gamma(1-\alpha)} \frac{d}{dx} \int_x^b (s-x)^{-\alpha} u(s) ds,$$

for all $x \in [a, b]$.

We denote by $AC([a, b])$ the space of the functions defined on $[a, b]$, which are absolutely continuous.

Definition 3 (Fractional derivative in the sense of Caputo, [3]). *Let $u \in AC([a,b])$. The left and right Caputo fractional derivatives are defined, respectively, by*

$$\left({}_a^C\mathcal{D}_x^\alpha u\right)(x) = \frac{1}{\Gamma(1-\alpha)}\int_a^x (x-s)^{-\alpha} u'(s)ds$$

and

$$\left({}_x^C\mathcal{D}_b^\alpha u\right)(x) = -\frac{1}{\Gamma(1-\alpha)}\int_x^b (s-x)^{-\alpha} u'(s)ds,$$

for all $x \in [a,b]$.

Remark 1. *For $0 < \alpha < 1$, the Riemann–Liouville and Caputo fractional derivatives satisfy the following relations:*

$$\left({}_a^C\mathcal{D}_x^\alpha u\right)(x) = \left({}_a\mathcal{D}_x^\alpha u\right)(x) - \frac{u(a)}{\Gamma(1-\alpha)}(x-a)^{-\alpha}$$

and

$$\left({}_x^C\mathcal{D}_b^\alpha u\right)(x) = \left({}_x\mathcal{D}_b^\alpha u\right)(x) - \frac{u(b)}{\Gamma(1-\alpha)}(b-x)^{-\alpha}.$$

Lemma 1 (Fundamental Theorem of Caputo Calculus, [3]). *Let $0 < \alpha < 1$ and let f be a differentiable function on $[a,b]$. We have*

$$_a\mathcal{I}_x^\alpha\left({}_a^C\mathcal{D}_x^\alpha u\right)(x) = u(b) - u(a)$$

and

$$_x\mathcal{I}_b^\alpha\left({}_x^C\mathcal{D}_b^\alpha u\right)(x) = u(a) - u(b).$$

2.2. Fractional Calculus of Variations

The fractional calculus of variations involves finding a function y that optimizes (minimizes or maximizes) a certain functional that depends on y and its fractional derivatives. Consider the optimization problem for the functional given by

$$\mathcal{J}[y] = \int_a^b \mathcal{L}\left(x, y, {}_a^C\mathcal{D}_x^\alpha y\right) dx \qquad (3)$$

with a Lagrangian $\mathcal{L} \in C^1\left([a,b] \times \mathbb{R}^2\right)$ depending on y, which is a function of the independent variable x and its left Caputo fractional derivative of order $0 < \alpha < 1$. For $\xi_a, \xi_b \in \mathbb{R}$ given, we impose the boundary conditions:

$$y(a) = \xi_a, \quad y(b) = \xi_b. \qquad (4)$$

Notice that $\mathcal{J}$ becomes a functional for the classical calculus of variations when $\alpha = 1$. We next state the Euler–Lagrange equation for the above problem.

Theorem 1 (The Euler–Lagrange Equation for a Functional with Caputo Derivatives, [20]). *Consider the optimization problem of the functional (3), where the Lagrangian $\mathcal{L}$ belongs to $C^2\left([a,b] \times \mathbb{R}^2\right)$ under the boundary conditions (4). If $y \in C^1[a,b]$ is an optimal solution, the fractional Euler–Lagrange condition*

$$\frac{\partial \mathcal{L}\left(x, y, {}_a^C\mathcal{D}_x^\alpha y\right)}{\partial y} + {}_x^C\mathcal{D}_b^\alpha \frac{\partial \mathcal{L}\left(x, y, {}_a^C\mathcal{D}_x^\alpha y\right)}{{}_a^C\mathcal{D}_x^\alpha y} = 0.$$

holds.

3. Boundary Value Problem Associated with Minimizers

To reformulate the minimization problem (2), we apply the Euler–Lagrange condition in Theorem 1, where the Lagrangian has the form

$$\mathcal{L}\left(s,\theta, {}^C_0\mathcal{D}^\alpha_s\theta\right) := \frac{1}{2}\left|{}^C_0\mathcal{D}^\alpha_s\theta(s)\right|^2 - \frac{P}{\Gamma(\alpha+1)}(L-s)^\alpha \sin\theta(s).$$

Then, the extremum of the energy functional in Equation (2) is as follows:

$${}^C_s\mathcal{D}^\alpha_L\left({}^C_0\mathcal{D}^\alpha_s\theta(s)\right) = \frac{P}{\Gamma(\alpha+1)}(L-s)^\alpha \cos\theta(s). \tag{5}$$

To study the nonlinear problem (5), we first reformulate it into an integral equation in the following section.

Lemma 2. *The solution of (5) satisfies*

$$\theta(s) = \theta(0) + P\left({}^C_0\mathcal{I}^\alpha_s{}^C_s\mathcal{I}^\alpha_L(L-s)^\alpha \cos\theta(s)\right)$$
$$+ \left(\frac{s}{L}\right)^\alpha \left(\theta(L) - \theta(0) - \frac{P}{\Gamma(\alpha+1)}\left({}^C_0\mathcal{I}^\alpha_s{}^C_s\mathcal{I}^\alpha_L(L-s)^\alpha \cos\theta(s)\Big|_{s=L}\right)\right).$$

Moreover, if $\theta(0) = 0$ and $\theta(L) = c$, we have that

$$\theta(s) = \frac{P}{\Gamma(\alpha+1)}\left({}^C_0\mathcal{I}^\alpha_s{}^C_s\mathcal{I}^\alpha_L(L-s)^\alpha \cos\theta(s) - \left(\frac{s}{L}\right)^\alpha {}^C_0\mathcal{I}^\alpha_s{}^C_s\mathcal{I}^\alpha_L(L-s)^\alpha \cos\theta(s)\Big|_{s=L}\right) + \left(\frac{s}{L}\right)^\alpha \theta(L)$$
$$= \frac{P}{\Gamma(\alpha+1)}\left(\frac{1}{(\Gamma(\alpha))^2}\int_0^s (s-x)^{\alpha-1}\int_x^L (\tau-x)^{\alpha-1}(L-\tau)^\alpha \cos\theta(\tau)d\tau dt\right.$$
$$\left. - \left(\frac{s}{L}\right)^\alpha \frac{1}{(\Gamma(\alpha))^2}\int_0^L (L-t)^{\alpha-1}\int_x^L (\tau-x)^{\alpha-1}(L-\tau)^\alpha \cos\theta(\tau)d\tau dt\right)$$
$$+ \left(\frac{s}{L}\right)^\alpha \theta(L).$$

Proof. We integrate (5) twice by applying the right fractional integral operator followed by the left fractional integral operator to obtain

$${}^C_0\mathcal{I}^\alpha_s\left({}^C_s\mathcal{I}^\alpha_L\left({}^C_s\mathcal{D}^\alpha_L\left({}^C_0\mathcal{D}^\alpha_s\theta(s)\right)\right)\right) - \frac{P}{\Gamma(\alpha+1)}{}^C_0\mathcal{I}^\alpha_s\left({}^C_s\mathcal{I}^\alpha_L(L-s)^\alpha \cos\theta(s)\right) = 0.$$

Next, we apply the composition rule and property from Lemma 1 on $[s, L]$ to obtain

$${}^C_0\mathcal{I}^\alpha_s\left({}^C_0\mathcal{D}^\alpha_s\theta(s) - {}^C_0\mathcal{D}^\alpha_s\theta(s)\Big|_{s=L}\right) = \frac{P}{\Gamma(\alpha+1)}{}^C_0\mathcal{I}^\alpha_s\left({}^C_s\mathcal{I}^\alpha_L(L-s)^\alpha \cos\theta(s)\right).$$

Since the value ${}^C_0\mathcal{D}^\alpha_s\theta(s)\Big|_{s=L}$ is a constant, this yields that

$$\theta(s) - \theta(0) - {}^C_0\mathcal{D}^\alpha_s\theta(s)\Big|_{s=L}\frac{s^\alpha}{\Gamma(\alpha+1)} = \frac{P}{\Gamma(\alpha+1)}{}^C_0\mathcal{I}^\alpha_s\left({}^C_s\mathcal{I}^\alpha_L(L-s)^\alpha \cos\theta(s)\right). \tag{6}$$

In the above equation, we see that the unknown value ${}^C_0\mathcal{D}^\alpha_s\theta(s)\Big|_{s=L}$ can be determined due to the boundary condition. We substitute $s = L$ into (6) to give

$${}^C_0\mathcal{D}^\alpha_s\theta(s)\Big|_{s=L} = \frac{\Gamma(\alpha+1)}{L^\alpha}\left(\theta(L) - \theta(0) - \frac{P}{\Gamma(\alpha+1)}\left({}^C_0\mathcal{I}^\alpha_s{}^C_s\mathcal{I}^\alpha_L(L-s)^\alpha \cos\theta(s)\Big|_{s=L}\right)\right). \tag{7}$$

As a consequence of (7) and (6), we obtain the integral form of (5) in the following:

$$\theta(s) = \theta(0) + P\left({}^C_0\mathcal{I}^\alpha_s {}^C_s\mathcal{I}^\alpha_L (L-s)^\alpha \cos\theta(s)\right)$$
$$+ \left(\frac{s}{L}\right)^\alpha \left(\theta(L) - \theta(0) - \frac{P}{\Gamma(\alpha+1)}\left({}^C_0\mathcal{I}^\alpha_s {}^C_s\mathcal{I}^\alpha_L (L-s)^\alpha \cos\theta(s)\Big|_{s=L}\right)\right).$$

Hence, the proof is complete. □

Corollary 1. *The solution of (5) subject to $\theta(0) = {}^C_0\mathcal{D}^\alpha_s \theta(s)\big|_{s=L} = 0$ satisfies the integral equation*

$$\theta(s) = \frac{P}{\Gamma(\alpha+1)} \int_0^L \mathcal{H}(s,\tau)(L-\tau)^\alpha \cos\theta(\tau)d\tau,$$

where

$$\mathcal{H}(s,\tau) = \frac{1}{(\Gamma(\alpha))^2} \times \begin{cases} \int_0^\tau (s-x)^{\alpha-1}(\tau-x)^{\alpha-1}dt, & 0 \leq \tau \leq s \leq L, \\ \int_0^s (s-x)^{\alpha-1}(\tau-x)^{\alpha-1}dt, & 0 \leq s \leq \tau \leq L. \end{cases}$$

Proof. From Equation (6) in Lemma 2, we obtain

$$\theta(s) = \frac{P}{\Gamma(\alpha+1)}\left({}^C_0\mathcal{I}^\alpha_s {}^C_s\mathcal{I}^\alpha_L (L-s)^\alpha \cos\theta(s)\right) \qquad (8)$$
$$= \frac{P}{(\Gamma(\alpha))^2} \int_0^s (s-\sigma)^{\alpha-1} \int_\sigma^L (\sigma'-\sigma)^{\alpha-1}(L-\sigma')^\alpha \cos\theta(\sigma')d\sigma'd\sigma.$$

Applying the Fubini's theorem, we obtain

$$\theta(s) = \frac{P}{(\Gamma(\alpha))^2} \int_0^s \int_0^\tau (s-x)^{\alpha-1}(\tau-x)^{\alpha-1}(L-\tau)^\alpha \cos\theta(\tau)dxd\tau$$
$$+ \frac{P}{(\Gamma(\alpha))^2} \int_s^L \int_0^s (s-x)^{\alpha-1}(\tau-x)^{\alpha-1}(L-\tau)^\alpha \cos\theta(\tau)dxd\tau.$$

Then, we obtain its solution in terms of a Green function. □

Remark 2. *When the load P is small, we may consider the behavior of the solution of the following boundary value problem*

$$\begin{cases} {}^C_s\mathcal{D}^\alpha_L \left({}^C_0\mathcal{D}^\alpha_s \theta(s)\right) = \frac{P}{\Gamma(\alpha+1)}(L-s)^\alpha, & 0 < s < L, \\ \theta(0) = {}^C_0\mathcal{D}^\alpha_s \theta(s)\big|_{s=L} = 0. \end{cases}$$

Here, we approximate $\cos\theta$ by 1, which is a legitimate approximation when P is small. For this problem, we obtain

$$\theta(s) = \frac{P}{(\Gamma(\alpha))^2} \int_0^s (s-\sigma)^{\alpha-1} \int_\sigma^L (\sigma'-\sigma)^{\alpha-1}(L-\sigma')^\alpha d\sigma'd\sigma$$
$$= \frac{\alpha P}{\Gamma(2\alpha+1)} \int_0^s (s-\sigma)^{\alpha-1}(L-\sigma)^{2\alpha}d\sigma.$$

Lemma 3. *The function $\mathcal{H}$ is continuous, non-negative and*

$$\mathcal{H}(s,\tau) \leq \frac{L^{2\alpha-1}}{(2\alpha-1)(\Gamma(\alpha))^2}, \qquad \text{for all } s,\tau \in [0,L].$$

4. Existence and Uniqueness Results

This section is devoted to proving the existence and uniqueness of the solutions for the following problem:

$$\begin{cases} {}^C_s\mathcal{D}^\alpha_L\left({}^C_0\mathcal{D}^\alpha_s\theta(s)\right) = \dfrac{P}{\Gamma(\alpha+1)}(L-s)^\alpha \cos\theta(s), & 0 < s < L, \\ \theta(0) = {}^C_0\mathcal{D}^\alpha_s\theta(s)\Big|_{s=L} = 0 \end{cases} \quad (9)$$

where $\frac{1}{2} < \alpha < 1$. We apply Corollary 1 to define the integral operator $\mathcal{K}$ from $C[0, L]$ to $C[0, L]$ as

$$(\mathcal{K}\theta)(s) = \frac{P}{\Gamma(\alpha+1)(\Gamma(\alpha))^2} \int_0^s (s-x)^{\alpha-1} \int_x^L (\tau-x)^{\alpha-1}(L-\tau)^\alpha \cos\theta(\tau) d\tau dx$$

$$= \frac{P}{\Gamma(\alpha+1)} \int_0^L \mathcal{H}(s,\tau)(L-\tau)^\alpha \cos\theta(\tau) d\tau. \quad (10)$$

Theorem 2. *The initial value problem (9) attains at least one solution θ in $C[0, L]$.*

Proof. Schaefer's fixed-point theorem is used to show that the operator $\mathcal{K}$ given by (10) has a fixed point. We outline the proof in the following steps.

Step 1: $\mathcal{K}$ is a continuous operator.

Let $\{\theta_m\}$ be a convergent sequence with $\theta_m \to \theta$ in $C[0, L]$. For each $s \in [0, L]$, we have

$$|(\mathcal{K}\theta_m)(s) - (\mathcal{K}\theta)(s)| \leq \frac{P}{\Gamma(\alpha+1)} \int_0^L |\mathcal{H}(s,\tau)||(L-\tau)^\alpha(\cos\theta(\tau) - \cos\theta_m(\tau))| d\tau$$

$$\leq \frac{P}{\Gamma(\alpha+1)} \sup_{\tau \in [0,L]} |(L-\tau)^\alpha(\cos\theta(\tau) - \cos\theta_m(\tau))| \int_0^L |\mathcal{H}(s,\tau)| d\tau$$

$$\leq \frac{P}{\Gamma(\alpha+1)} L^\alpha \sup_{\tau \in [0,L]} |\theta(\tau) - \theta_m(\tau)| \int_0^L \frac{L^{2\alpha-1}}{(2\alpha-1)(\Gamma(\alpha))^2} d\tau$$

$$\leq \frac{P}{(2\alpha-1)\Gamma(\alpha+1)(\Gamma(\alpha))^2} L^{3\alpha} \sup_{\tau \in [0,L]} |\theta(\tau) - \theta_m(\tau)|.$$

It follows that

$$\|\mathcal{K}\theta_m - \mathcal{K}\theta\|_\infty \leq \frac{P}{(2\alpha-1)\Gamma(\alpha+1)(\Gamma(\alpha))^2} L^{3\alpha} \|\theta - \theta_m\|_\infty$$

which implies that

$$\|\mathcal{K}\theta_m - \mathcal{K}\theta\|_\infty \to 0 \quad \text{as} \quad m \to \infty.$$

Step 2: The image of a bounded set in $C[0, L]$ under $\mathcal{K}$ is also a bounded set.

We show that there is a positive constant $\ell > 0$ such that

$$\forall \theta \in B_{\eta^*} = \{\theta \in C[0, L] : \|\theta\|_\infty \leq \eta^*\},$$

and $\|\mathcal{K}\theta\|_\infty \leq \ell$ for $\eta^* > 0$. Indeed, for any $s \in [0, L]$, by the boundedness of the nonlinear term we have

$$|(\mathcal{K}\theta)(s)| \leq \frac{P}{\Gamma(\alpha+1)} \int_0^L \mathcal{H}(s,\tau)(L-\tau)^\alpha |\cos\theta(\tau)| d\tau$$

$$\leq \frac{PL^\alpha}{\Gamma(\alpha+1)} \int_0^L \mathcal{H}(s,\tau) d\tau$$

$$\leq \frac{PL^{3\alpha}}{(2\alpha-1)\Gamma(\alpha+1)(\Gamma(\alpha))^2},$$

thus,

$$\|\mathcal{K}\theta\|_\infty \leq \ell$$

where

$$\ell = \frac{PL^{3\alpha}}{(2\alpha-1)\Gamma(\alpha+1)(\Gamma(\alpha))^2}.$$

Step 3: The image of a bounded set in $C[0, L]$ under $\mathcal{K}$ is an equicontinuous set.

Let $s_1, s_2 \in [0, L]$ such that $s_1 < s_2$ and $\theta \in B_{\eta^*}$, which is a bounded set of $C[0, L]$, as above. Then, we see that

$$
\begin{aligned}
&|(\mathcal{K}\theta)(s_2) - (\mathcal{K}\theta)(s_1)| \\
&\leq \frac{P}{\Gamma(\alpha+1)} \int_0^L |(\mathcal{H}(s_2, \tau) - \mathcal{H}(s_1, \tau))(L-\tau)^\alpha \cos\theta(\tau)| d\tau \\
&\leq \frac{PL^\alpha}{\Gamma(\alpha+1)} \int_0^L |\mathcal{H}(s_2, \tau) - \mathcal{H}(s_1, \tau)| d\tau \\
&= \frac{PL^\alpha}{\Gamma(\alpha+1)} \left(\int_0^{s_1} |\mathcal{H}(s_2, \tau) - \mathcal{H}(s_1, \tau)| d\tau + \int_{s_1}^{s_2} |\mathcal{H}(s_2, \tau) - \mathcal{H}(s_1, \tau)| d\tau \right. \\
&\quad \left. + \int_{s_2}^L |\mathcal{H}(s_2, \tau) - \mathcal{H}(s_1, \tau)| d\tau \right) \\
&= \frac{PL^\alpha}{\Gamma(\alpha+1)(\Gamma(\alpha))^2} \left(\int_0^{s_1} \left| \int_0^\tau \left[(s_2-t)^{\alpha-1} - (s_1-t)^{\alpha-1} \right] (\tau-t)^{\alpha-1} dt \right| d\tau \right. \\
&\quad + \int_{s_1}^{s_2} \left| \int_0^\tau (s_2-t)^{\alpha-1}(\tau-t)^{\alpha-1} dt - \int_0^{s_1} (s_1-t)^{\alpha-1}(\tau-t)^{\alpha-1} dt \right| d\tau \\
&\quad \left. + \int_{s_2}^L \left| \int_0^{s_2} (s_2-\tau)^{\alpha-1}(\tau-t)^{\alpha-1} dt - \int_0^{s_1} (s_1-\tau)^{\alpha-1}(\tau-t)^{\alpha-1} dt \right| d\tau \right) \\
&\leq \frac{PL^\alpha}{\Gamma(\alpha+1)(\Gamma(\alpha))^2} \left(\int_0^{s_1} \int_0^\tau \left((s_1-t)^{\alpha-1} - (s_2-t)^{\alpha-1} \right)(\tau-t)^{\alpha-1} dt\, d\tau \right. \\
&\quad + \int_{s_1}^L \int_0^{s_1} \left((s_1-t)^{\alpha-1} - (s_2-t)^{\alpha-1} \right)(\tau-t)^{\alpha-1} dt\, d\tau \\
&\quad + \int_{s_1}^{s_2} \int_{s_1}^\tau (s_2-t)^{\alpha-1}(\tau-t)^{\alpha-1} dt\, d\tau \\
&\quad \left. + \int_{s_2}^L \int_{s_1}^{s_2} (s_2-t)^{\alpha-1}(\tau-t)^{\alpha-1} dt\, d\tau \right) \\
&\leq \frac{PL^\alpha}{\Gamma(\alpha+1)(\Gamma(\alpha))^2} \left(\frac{(1-\alpha)(s_2-s_1)s_1^{2\alpha-1}}{(2\alpha-2)(2\alpha-1)} + \frac{(1-\alpha)(s_2-s_1)(L-s_1)s_1^{2\alpha-2}}{2\alpha-2} \right. \\
&\quad \left. + \frac{(s_2-s_1)^{2\alpha-1}(L-s_2)}{(2\alpha-1)} + \frac{(s_2-s_1)^{2\alpha}}{2\alpha(2\alpha-1)} \right).
\end{aligned}
$$

As $s_1 \to s_2$, the right-hand side of the above inequality tends to zero. Following Step 1 to Step 3 and the Arzelá–Ascoli theorem, $\mathcal{K} : C[0, L] \to C[0, L]$ is completely continuous.

Step 4: A priori bounds. Let $\varepsilon = \{\theta \in C[0, L] : \theta = \lambda\mathcal{K}\theta \text{ for some } 0 < \lambda < 1\}$. We claim that ε is bounded. Let $\theta \in \varepsilon$, then $\theta = \lambda\mathcal{K}\theta$ for some $0 < \lambda < 1$. Hence, $\forall s \in [0, L]$,

$$\theta = \lambda\mathcal{K}\theta = \lambda\left(\frac{P}{\Gamma(\alpha+1)} \int_0^L \mathcal{H}(s, \tau)(L-\tau)^\alpha \cos\theta(\tau) d\tau \right).$$

By the condition in Step 2, we obtain

$$|\theta(s)| \leq \frac{L^{3\alpha} P}{(2\alpha - 1)\Gamma(\alpha + 1)(\Gamma(\alpha))^2}$$

and hence for every $s \in [0, L]$,

$$\|\theta\|_\infty \leq \frac{L^{3\alpha} P}{(2\alpha - 1)\Gamma(\alpha + 1)(\Gamma(\alpha))^2} := R.$$

This implies the boundedness of the set ε.

Consequently, Schaefer's fixed-point theorem assures that $\mathcal{K}$ attains a fixed point, which is a solution of the boundary value problem (9). □

Theorem 3. *Problem (9) has a unique solution θ in $C[0, L]$ if*

$$\frac{PL^{3\alpha}}{\Gamma(2\alpha + 1)} < 1.$$

Proof. We show that $\mathcal{K}$ is a contraction. For any $\theta, \tilde{\theta} \in C[0, L]$ and $s \in [0, L]$, we have

$$|(\mathcal{K}\theta)(s) - (\mathcal{K}\tilde{\theta})(s)|$$
$$= \frac{P}{\Gamma(\alpha + 1)(\Gamma(\alpha))^2} \left| \int_0^s (s - x)^{\alpha - 1} \int_x^L (\tau - x)^{\alpha - 1}(L - \tau)^\alpha (\cos \theta(\tau) - \cos \tilde{\theta}(\tau)) d\tau dx \right|$$
$$\leq \frac{P}{\Gamma(\alpha + 1)(\Gamma(\alpha))^2} \int_0^s (s - x)^{\alpha - 1} \int_x^L (\tau - x)^{\alpha - 1}(L - \tau)^\alpha |\theta(\tau) - \tilde{\theta}(\tau)| d\tau dx$$
$$\leq \frac{P}{\Gamma(\alpha + 1)(\Gamma(\alpha))^2} \|\theta - \tilde{\theta}\|_\infty \int_0^s (s - x)^{\alpha - 1} \int_x^L (\tau - x)^{\alpha - 1}(L - \tau)^\alpha d\tau dx$$
$$= \frac{PB(\alpha, \alpha + 1)}{\Gamma(\alpha + 1)(\Gamma(\alpha))^2} \|\theta - \tilde{\theta}\|_\infty \int_0^s (s - x)^{\alpha - 1}(L - t)^{2\alpha} dt$$
$$\leq \frac{\alpha P}{\Gamma(2\alpha + 1)} \|\theta - \tilde{\theta}\|_\infty L^{2\alpha} \int_0^s (s - x)^{\alpha - 1} dt$$
$$= \frac{\alpha P}{\Gamma(2\alpha + 1)} \|\theta - \tilde{\theta}\|_\infty L^{2\alpha} \left(\frac{s^\alpha}{\alpha} \right)$$
$$\leq \frac{PL^{3\alpha}}{\Gamma(2\alpha + 1)} \|\theta - \tilde{\theta}\|_\infty.$$

It follows that $\quad \|\mathcal{K}\theta - \mathcal{K}\tilde{\theta}\|_\infty \leq \frac{PL^{3\alpha}}{\Gamma(2\alpha + 1)} \|\theta - \tilde{\theta}\|_\infty.$ □

We also establish the existence and uniqueness results with respect to the L^2 norm.

Theorem 4. *Problem (9) has a unique solution θ in $L^2[0, L]$ if*

$$\frac{PL^{3\alpha}}{2\alpha\Gamma(\alpha + 1)(\Gamma(\alpha))^2} \sqrt{\frac{\Gamma(2\alpha + 1)\Gamma(2\alpha - 1)}{2(2\alpha - 1)\Gamma(4\alpha)}} < 1. \quad (11)$$

Proof. It is obvious that $\mathcal{K}$ is self-mapping on $L^2[0, L]$. We show that $\mathcal{K}$ is a contraction. For any $\theta, \tilde{\theta} \in L^2[0, L]$ and $s \in [0, L]$, we use Hölder's inequality to obtain

$$|(\mathcal{K}\theta)(s) - (\mathcal{K}\tilde{\theta})(s)|$$
$$= \frac{P}{\Gamma(\alpha + 1)(\Gamma(\alpha))^2} \left| \int_0^s (s - x)^{\alpha - 1} \int_x^L (\tau - x)^{\alpha - 1}(L - \tau)^\alpha (\cos \theta(\tau) - \cos \tilde{\theta}(\tau)) d\tau dx \right|$$

$$\leq \frac{P}{\Gamma(\alpha+1)(\Gamma(\alpha))^2} \int_0^s (s-x)^{\alpha-1} \int_x^L (\tau-x)^{\alpha-1}(L-\tau)^\alpha |\theta(\tau) - \tilde{\theta}(\tau)| d\tau dx$$

$$\leq \frac{P}{\Gamma(\alpha+1)(\Gamma(\alpha))^2} \int_0^s (s-x)^{\alpha-1} \left(\int_x^L (\tau-x)^{2\alpha-2}(L-\tau)^{2\alpha} d\tau \right)^{\frac{1}{2}}$$

$$\times \left(\int_x^L |\theta(\tau) - \tilde{\theta}(\tau)|^2 d\tau \right)^{\frac{1}{2}} dx$$

$$\leq \frac{P\|\theta - \tilde{\theta}\|_{L^2[0,L]}}{\Gamma(\alpha+1)(\Gamma(\alpha))^2} \sqrt{\frac{\Gamma(2\alpha+1)\Gamma(2\alpha-1)}{\Gamma(4\alpha)}} \int_0^s (s-x)^{\alpha-1}(L-t)^{2\alpha-\frac{1}{2}} dx$$

$$\leq \frac{P\|\theta - \tilde{\theta}\|_{L^2[0,L]}}{\Gamma(\alpha+1)(\Gamma(\alpha))^2} \sqrt{\frac{\Gamma(2\alpha+1)\Gamma(2\alpha-1)}{\Gamma(4\alpha)}} \left(\int_0^s (s-x)^{2\alpha-2} dx \right)^{\frac{1}{2}} \left(\int_0^s (L-x)^{4\alpha-1} dx \right)^{\frac{1}{2}}$$

$$= \frac{P}{\Gamma(\alpha+1)(\Gamma(\alpha))^2} \sqrt{\frac{\Gamma(2\alpha+1)\Gamma(2\alpha-1)}{\Gamma(4\alpha)}} \left(\frac{L^{4\alpha}}{4\alpha} \right)^{\frac{1}{2}} \left(\frac{s^{2\alpha-1}}{2\alpha-1} \right)^{\frac{1}{2}} \|\theta - \tilde{\theta}\|_{L^2[0,L]}.$$

It follows that

$$\|\mathcal{K}\theta - \mathcal{K}\tilde{\theta}\|_{L^2[0,L]}$$

$$= \left(\int_0^L |(\mathcal{K}\theta)(s) - (\mathcal{K}\tilde{\theta})(s)|^2 ds \right)^{\frac{1}{2}}$$

$$\leq \left(\int_0^L \left| \frac{P}{\Gamma(\alpha+1)(\Gamma(\alpha))^2} \sqrt{\frac{\Gamma(2\alpha+1)\Gamma(2\alpha-1)}{\Gamma(4\alpha)}} \left(\frac{L^{4\alpha}}{4\alpha} \right)^{\frac{1}{2}} \left(\frac{s^{2\alpha-1}}{2\alpha-1} \right)^{\frac{1}{2}} \|\theta - \tilde{\theta}\|_{L^2[0,L]} \right|^2 ds \right)^{\frac{1}{2}}$$

$$= \frac{PL^{2\alpha}}{\Gamma(\alpha+1)(\Gamma(\alpha))^2} \sqrt{\frac{\Gamma(2\alpha+1)\Gamma(2\alpha-1)}{4\alpha\Gamma(4\alpha)}} \left(\int_0^L \frac{s^{2\alpha-1}}{2\alpha-1} ds \right)^{\frac{1}{2}} \|\theta - \tilde{\theta}\|_{L^2[0,L]}$$

$$= \frac{PL^{2\alpha}}{\Gamma(\alpha+1)(\Gamma(\alpha))^2} \sqrt{\frac{\Gamma(2\alpha+1)\Gamma(2\alpha-1)}{4\alpha\Gamma(4\alpha)}} \left(\frac{L^{2\alpha}}{(2\alpha-1)2\alpha} \right)^{\frac{1}{2}} \|\theta - \tilde{\theta}\|_{L^2[0,L]}$$

$$= \frac{PL^{3\alpha}}{2\alpha\Gamma(\alpha+1)(\Gamma(\alpha))^2} \sqrt{\frac{\Gamma(2\alpha+1)\Gamma(2\alpha-1)}{2(2\alpha-1)\Gamma(4\alpha)}} \|\theta - \tilde{\theta}\|_{L^2[0,L]}.$$

This implies that $\mathcal{K}$ is a contraction satisfying (11). Hence, the uniqueness of a fixed point of the map $\mathcal{K}$ in $L^2[0,L]$ follows from the Banach contraction principle. □

5. Continuous Dependence of Minimizers on Varying Loads

To study the continuity of minimizers when the load P changes, we begin with a definition in terms of the branch of solutions.

Definition 4. *Let us denote by θ_P a solution of (5) with $P = \bar{P}$, $\theta(0) = 0$ and $\left. {}_0^C \mathcal{D}_s^\alpha \theta(s) \right|_{s=L} = 0$. We say that the set of minimizers θ_P for $P \in [0,B]$, with $B > 0$ is a branch of solutions if the maps from $[0,B]$ to $L^2[0,L]$ given by $P \mapsto \theta_P$ and $P \mapsto {}_0^C \mathcal{D}_s^\alpha \theta_P$ are continuous functions of P.*

According to the defined problem of the cantilever beam subjected to the downward uniformly distributed load, the deflection shape of the beam is a concave down. Consequently, the angle on $[0,L]$ will be in the range of 0 to $\frac{\pi}{2}$ according to the deflection shape. Then, we obtain the following results.

Lemma 4. *Let θ_P be a minimizer of the energy functional (explicitly depends on P). The function $P \mapsto E_P(\theta_P)$ is a decreasing function.*

Proof. Let be $P_2 > P_1$. Then, we have

$$E_{P_2}(\theta_{P_2}) - E_{P_1}(\theta_{P_1}) = E_{P_2}(\theta_{P_2}) - E_{P_2}(\theta_{P_1}) + E_{P_2}(\theta_{P_1}) - E_{P_1}(\theta_{P_1})$$
$$\leq \frac{P_1 - P_2}{\Gamma(\alpha+1)} \int_0^L (L-s)^\alpha \sin\theta_{P_1}(s)ds.$$

which implies that $E_{P_2}(\theta_{P_2}) - E_{P_1}(\theta_{P_1})$ is negative because $\sin\theta_{P_1}$ is positive on $[0, L]$ (see Figure 1). □

Proposition 1. *The set of minimizers for the functional (2) forms a branch of solutions.*

Proof. By Theorem 4, there exist P and P_0, which satisfy (11) and provide the existence and uniqueness of the minimizers for E_P and E_{P_0}, respectively. We prove that $\{\theta_P\}$ is a minimizing sequence for E_{P_0} if $P \to P_0$.

For every ψ such that ψ and $^C_0\mathcal{D}^\alpha_s \psi$ in $L^2[0,L]$, we have

$$E_P(\psi) - E_{P_0}(\psi) = \frac{P - P_0}{\Gamma(\alpha+1)} \int_0^L (L-s)^\alpha \sin\psi(s)ds \leq \frac{L^{\alpha+1}}{(\alpha+1)\Gamma(\alpha+1)}|P - P_0|.$$

Since θ_P is the minimizer of E_P, it follows that

$$E_{P_0}(\psi) = E_P(\psi) + E_{P_0}(\psi) - E_P(\psi)$$
$$\geq E_P(\theta_P) - \frac{L^{\alpha+1}}{(\alpha+1)\Gamma(\alpha+1)}|P - P_0|$$
$$= E_P(\theta_P) - E_{P_0}(\theta_P) + E_{P_0}(\theta_P) - \frac{L^{\alpha+1}}{(\alpha+1)\Gamma(\alpha+1)}|P - P_0|$$
$$\geq E_{P_0}(\theta_P) - \frac{2L^{\alpha+1}}{(\alpha+1)\Gamma(\alpha+1)}|P - P_0|.$$

As the result holds for every ψ such that ψ and $^C_0\mathcal{D}^\alpha_s \psi$ in $L^2[0,L]$, this yields that

$$E_{P_0}(\theta_P) \leq E_{P_0}(\theta_{P_0}) + \frac{2L^{\alpha+1}}{(\alpha+1)\Gamma(\alpha+1)}|P - P_0|$$

or equivalently,

$$E_{P_0}(\theta_P) - E_{P_0}(\theta_{P_0}) \leq \frac{2L^{\alpha+1}}{(\alpha+1)\Gamma(\alpha+1)}|P - P_0|.$$

It follows that $\{\theta_P\}$ is a minimizing sequence for E_{P_0}.

Now, we consider the difference $E_{P_0}(\theta_P) - E_{P_0}(\theta_{P_0})$ and $^C_0\mathcal{D}^\alpha_s \theta_P(s) - ^C_0\mathcal{D}^\alpha_s \theta_{P_0}(s)$ as

$$E_{P_0}(\theta_P) - E_{P_0}(\theta_{P_0})$$
$$= \frac{1}{2}\int_0^L \left(\left|^C_0\mathcal{D}^\alpha_s \theta_P(s)\right|^2 - \left|^C_0\mathcal{D}^\alpha_s \theta_{P_0}(s)\right|^2\right)ds - \frac{P_0}{\Gamma(\alpha+1)}\int_0^L (L-s)^\alpha (\sin\theta_P(s) - \sin\theta_{P_0}(s))ds$$

and

$$^C_0\mathcal{D}^\alpha_s \theta_P(s) - ^C_0\mathcal{D}^\alpha_s \theta_{P_0}(s)$$
$$= \frac{1}{\Gamma(\alpha+1)}\left(^C_s\mathcal{I}^\alpha_L(L-s)^\alpha \left(P\cos\theta_P(s) - P_0\cos\theta_{P_0}(s)\right)\right)$$
$$= \frac{P - P_0}{\Gamma(\alpha+1)}\left(^C_s\mathcal{I}^\alpha_L(L-s)^\alpha (\cos\theta_P(s))\right) + \frac{P_0}{\Gamma(\alpha+1)}\left(^C_s\mathcal{I}^\alpha_L(L-s)^\alpha (\cos\theta_P(s) - \cos\theta_{P_0}(s))\right)$$
$$= \frac{P - P_0}{\Gamma(\alpha+1)\Gamma(\alpha)}\int_s^L (\tau-s)^{\alpha-1}(L-\tau)^\alpha \cos\theta_P(\tau)d\tau$$

$$+ \frac{P_0}{\Gamma(\alpha+1)\Gamma(\alpha)} \int_s^L (\tau-s)^{\alpha-1}(L-\tau)^\alpha \big(\cos\theta_P(\tau) - \cos\theta_{P_0}(\tau)\big) d\tau.$$

Then, by direct calculation and using the dominated convergence theorem, we obtain

$$\left\| {}_0^C\mathcal{D}_s^\alpha(\theta_P - \theta_{P_0}) \right\|_{L^2[0,L]}^2$$

$$= 2\big(E_{P_0}(\theta_P) - E_{P_0}(\theta_{P_0})\big) - 2\int_0^L \big({}_0^C\mathcal{D}_s^\alpha\theta_{P_0}(s)\big)\big({}_0^C\mathcal{D}_s^\alpha(\theta_P - \theta_{P_0})\big) ds$$

$$+ \frac{2P_0}{\Gamma(\alpha+1)} \int_0^L (L-s)^\alpha \big(\sin\theta_P(s) - \sin\theta_{P_0}(s)\big) ds$$

$$\leq \frac{4L^{\alpha+1}}{(\alpha+1)\Gamma(\alpha+1)} |P - P_0|$$

$$- \frac{2}{\Gamma(\alpha+1)} \int_0^L \big({}_0^C\mathcal{D}_s^\alpha\theta_{P_0}(s)\big)\big({}_s^C\mathcal{I}_L^\alpha(L-s)^\alpha P\cos\theta_P(s) - {}_s^C\mathcal{I}_L^\alpha(L-s)^\alpha P_0\cos\theta_{P_0}(s)\big) ds$$

$$+ \frac{2P_0}{\Gamma(\alpha+1)} \int_0^L (L-s)^\alpha \big(\sin\theta_P(s) - \sin\theta_{P_0}(s)\big) ds \to 0$$

as $P \to P_0$, which completes the proof. □

6. Approximate Solutions and Numerical Examples

The homotopy perturbation method (HPM) was pioneered and developed by He [21]. This technique involves the introduction of an expanding parameter, which serves as an alternative approach. Let A be a differential operator and B be a boundary operator. In general, the HPM can be applied to nonlinear differential equations of the form

$$A(u) - f(r) = 0, \quad r \in \Omega \tag{12}$$

with boundary conditions

$$B\left(u(r), \frac{\partial u(r)}{\partial n}\right) = 0, \quad r \in \Gamma$$

where Γ denotes the boundary of the domain Ω and f is a given analytical function.

The basic idea of the HPM is to split the operator A into linear and nonlinear parts denoted by L and N, respectively, so that (12) can be rewritten as

$$L(u)(r) + N(u)(r) - f(r) = 0, \quad r \in \Omega.$$

Consider a homotopy $v(r,p) : \Omega \times [0,1] \to \mathbb{R}$ satisfying

$$H(v,p) = p[A(v) - f(r)] + (1-p)[L(v) - L(u_0)] = 0 \tag{13}$$

or

$$H(v,p) = p[N(v) - f(r)] + L(v) - L(u_0) + pL(u_0) = 0 \tag{14}$$

where u_0 is the first approximation of (12) in correspondence with the boundary conditions and $p \in [0,1]$ is an embedding parameter. It can be readily seen from (13) or (14) that

$$H(v,0) = L(v) - L(u_0) = 0$$
$$H(v,1) = A(v) - f(r) = 0.$$

Clearly, when $p = 0$, (13) or equivalently, (14), is a linear equation, whereas when $p = 1$, it is the original nonlinear problem. Hence, changing the embedding parameter p

from 0 to 1 is equivalent to $L(v) - L(u_0) = 0$ with $A(v) - f(r) = 0$. The basic idea of the HPM is thus to continuously deform a simpler problem into the more difficult original one.

We write the solution of (13) or (14) in terms of a power series in p:

$$v = v_0 + pv_1 + p^2 v_2 + \cdots \tag{15}$$

By choosing $p = 1$, we obtain an approximate solution of Equation (12):

$$u = \lim_{p \to 1} v = v_0 + v_1 + v_2 + \cdots.$$

The power series (15) converges in most circumstances. Nonetheless, the rate of convergence depends on the nonlinear operator $A(v)$.

To illustrate this method, we solve the boundary value problem (9) with $L = 1$. We set the following homotopy:

$${}^C_s D_1^\alpha \left({}^C_0 D_s^\alpha \theta(s) \right) - p \left[\frac{P}{\Gamma(\alpha + 1)} (L - s)^\alpha \cos \theta(s) \right] = 0. \tag{16}$$

If we expand the nonlinear term in (16) using the Taylor series, we obtain

$$\cos \theta = 1 - \frac{\theta^2}{2!} + \frac{\theta^4}{4!} - \frac{\theta^6}{6!} + \frac{\theta^8}{8!} - \cdots$$

and

$$(1-s)^{\alpha+1} = 1 - (\alpha+1)s + \frac{(\alpha+1)\alpha}{2!} s^2 - \frac{(\alpha+1)\alpha(\alpha-1)}{3!} s^3 + \frac{(\alpha+1)\alpha(\alpha-1)(\alpha-2)}{4!} s^4 + \cdots$$

Hence, we can approximate (16) as follows:

$${}^C_s D_1^\alpha \left({}^C_0 D_s^\alpha \theta(s) \right) = p \left[\frac{P}{\Gamma(\alpha+1)} (1-s)^\alpha \left(1 - \frac{\theta^2}{2!} + \frac{\theta^4}{4!} - \frac{\theta^6}{6!} \right) \right].$$

Substituting (15) into the homotopy (16) and applying the initial conditions, we obtain a set of linear differential equations from the coefficients of terms with equal powers of p as follows:

$$p^0 : {}^C_s D_1^\alpha \left({}^C_0 D_s^\alpha \theta_0(s) \right) = 0, \quad \theta_0(0) = {}^C_s D_1^\alpha \theta_0(1) = 0,$$

$$p^1 : {}^C_s D_1^\alpha \left({}^C_0 D_s^\alpha \theta_1(s) \right) = \frac{P}{\Gamma(\alpha+1)} (1-s)^\alpha \left(1 - \frac{1}{2}\theta_0^2 + \frac{1}{24}\theta_0^4 - \frac{1}{720}\theta_0^6 \right), \quad \theta_1(0) = {}^C_s D_1^\alpha \theta_1(1) = 0,$$

$$p^2 : {}^C_s D_1^\alpha \left({}^C_0 D_s^\alpha \theta_2(s) \right) = \frac{P}{\Gamma(\alpha+1)} (1-s)^\alpha \left(-\theta_0 \theta_1 + \frac{1}{6}\theta_0^3 \theta_1 - \frac{1}{120}\theta_0^5 \theta_1 \right),$$
$$\theta_2(0) = {}^C_s D_1^\alpha \theta_2(1) = 0,$$

$$p^3 : {}^C_s D_1^\alpha \left({}^C_0 D_s^\alpha \theta_3(s) \right) = \frac{P}{\Gamma(\alpha+1)} (1-s)^\alpha \left(-\frac{1}{2}\theta_1^2 + \frac{1}{4}\theta_0^2 \theta_1^2 - \frac{1}{48}\theta_0^4 \theta_1 - \theta_0 \theta_2 + \frac{1}{6}\theta_0^3 \theta_2 - \frac{1}{120}\theta_0^5 \theta_2 \right),$$
$$\theta_3(0) = {}^C_s D_1^\alpha \theta_3(1) = 0,$$

$$p^4 : {}^C_s D_1^\alpha \left({}^C_0 D_s^\alpha \theta_4(s) \right) = \frac{P}{\Gamma(\alpha+1)} (1-s)^\alpha \left(\frac{1}{6}\theta_0 \theta_1^3 - \frac{1}{36}\theta_0^3 \theta_1^3 - \theta_1 \theta_2 + \frac{1}{2}\theta_0^2 \theta_1 \theta_2 - \frac{1}{24}\theta_0^4 \theta_1 \theta_2 \right.$$
$$\left. -\theta_0 \theta_3 + \frac{1}{6}\theta_0^3 \theta_3 - \frac{1}{120}\theta_0^5 \theta_3 \right), \quad \theta_4(0) = {}^C_s D_1^\alpha \theta_4(1) = 0,$$

$\vdots$

By applying Corollary 1 to the above equation, we obtain

$$\theta_0 = 0,$$
$$\theta_1 = \frac{Ps^\alpha}{\Gamma(2\alpha+1)} \text{Hypergeometric}_2F_1(1, -2\alpha; \alpha+1; s)$$
$$\theta_2 = 0$$
$$\theta_3 = -\frac{P}{2(\Gamma(\alpha))^2\Gamma(\alpha)} \int_0^s (s-\sigma)^{\alpha-1} \int_\sigma^1 (\sigma'-\sigma)^{\alpha-1}(1-\sigma')^\alpha (\theta_1(\sigma'))^2 d\sigma' d\sigma$$
$$\theta_4 = 0\ldots,$$

so that the approximate solution of the problem is given by

$$\theta(s) = \lim_{p \to 1} \sum_{i=0}^\infty p^i \theta_i(s)$$
$$= \frac{Ps^\alpha}{\Gamma(2\alpha+1)} \text{Hypergeometric}_2F_1(1, -2\alpha; \alpha+1; s)$$
$$- \frac{P}{2(\Gamma(\alpha))^2} \int_0^s (s-\sigma)^{\alpha-1} \int_\sigma^1 (\sigma'-\sigma)^{\alpha-1}(1-\sigma')^\alpha \theta_1(\sigma') d\sigma' d\sigma + \cdots$$

From the tangent angle θ of a cantilever beam, we can calculate the deflection shape of a cantilever beam at the equilibrium position in xy-coordinates based on the following equations:

$$\frac{dx}{ds} = \cos\theta \quad \text{and} \quad \frac{dy}{ds} = \sin\theta.$$

Example 1. *Consider Problem (9), with $L = 1$, $P = 0.73$, and taking values of $\alpha_1 = 0.6$, $\alpha_2 = 0.75$, and $\alpha_3 = 0.95$.*

This example corresponds to a cantilever beam with a uniformly distributed load $P = 0.73$. Then, we obtain for $\varphi_\alpha = \frac{L^{3\alpha}}{\Gamma(2\alpha+1)}$ and $\gamma_\alpha = \frac{L^{3\alpha}}{2\alpha\Gamma(\alpha+1)(\Gamma(\alpha))^2}\sqrt{\frac{\Gamma(2\alpha+1)\Gamma(2\alpha-1)}{2(2\alpha-1)\Gamma(4\alpha)}}$ as follows:

$$P\varphi_{\alpha_1} \approx 0.6626 < 1,$$
$$P\varphi_{\alpha_2} \approx 0.5491 < 1,$$
$$P\varphi_{\alpha_3} \approx 0.3995 < 1,$$
$$P\gamma_{\alpha_3} \approx 0.9795 < 1,$$
$$P\gamma_{\alpha_2} \approx 0.3827 < 1,$$
$$P\gamma_{\alpha_3} \approx 0.1772 < 1.$$

Then, by Theorems 2 and 3, we conclude that there is a unique tangent angle $\theta(s)$ in $C[0,1]$ that minimizes the energy functional of the beam. Furthermore, in light of Theorem 4, the boundary value problem has a unique solution in $L^2[0,1]$.

Applying the HPM, the approximate solution for the tangent angle is shown in Figure 2. Furthermore, the deflection shape of the beam under a uniformly distributed load at the equilibrium position can be depicted, as shown in Figure 3. It is highlighted that the curvature of the beam is larger for smaller orders of the fractional derivative.

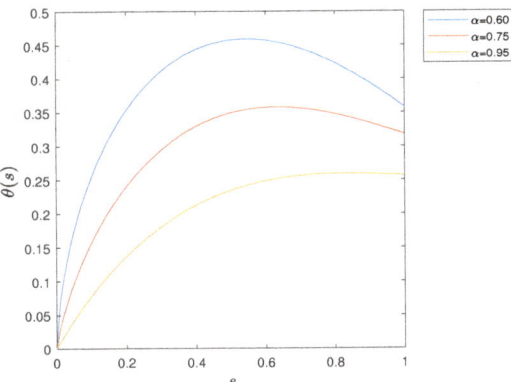

Figure 2. Approximated solutions for θ (tangent angle) of a cantilever beam with a uniformly distributed load $P = 0.73$ for $\alpha = 0.6, 0.75$, and 0.95.

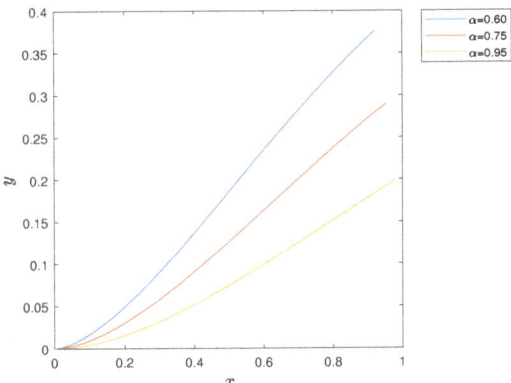

Figure 3. Deflection shapes of a cantilever beam under a uniformly distributed load $P = 0.73$ at the equilibrium position for $\alpha = 0.6, 0.75$, and 0.95.

Example 2. *Consider Problem* (9) *with* $L = 1$, $\alpha = 0.85$, *and P taking the values* $P_1 = 0.5$, $P_2 = 1.6, P_3 = 1.7, P_4 = 1.8$, *and* $P_5 = 2.8$.

This example corresponds to a cantilever beam with a uniformly distributed load with $\alpha = 0.85$.

We obtain $\gamma_\alpha = \dfrac{L^{3\alpha}}{2\alpha\Gamma(\alpha+1)(\Gamma(\alpha))^2}\sqrt{\dfrac{\Gamma(2\alpha+1)\Gamma(2\alpha-1)}{2(2\alpha-1)\Gamma(4\alpha)}}$ as follows:

$$P_1\gamma_\alpha \approx 0.1742 < 1,$$
$$P_2\gamma_\alpha \approx 0.5574 < 1,$$
$$P_3\gamma_\alpha \approx 0.5923 < 1,$$
$$P_4\gamma_\alpha \approx 0.6271 < 1,$$
$$P_5\gamma_\alpha \approx 0.9755 < 1.$$

It follows from Theorem 4 that there is a unique tangent angle $\theta(s)$ in $L^2[0,1]$ that minimizes the energy functional of the beam. Applying the homotopy perturbation method, the approximate solution of the tangent angle can be determined, as shown in Figure 4. Furthermore, the deflection shape of the beam subjected to a uniformly distributed load at the equilibrium position can be depicted, as shown in Figure 5. It can be seen that the minimizers behave continuously when the loads P_2 and P_4 are close to P_3, inducing continuous dependence on the loads, which is in agreement with Proposition 1. It is highlighted that the curvature of the beam depends on the load.

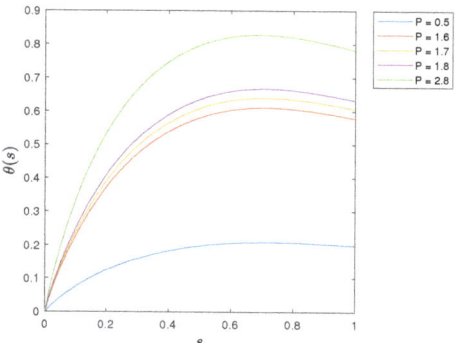

Figure 4. Approximated solutions for θ (tangent angle) of a cantilever beam with a uniformly distributed load $P = 0.5, 1.7,$ and 2.8 when $\alpha = 0.85$.

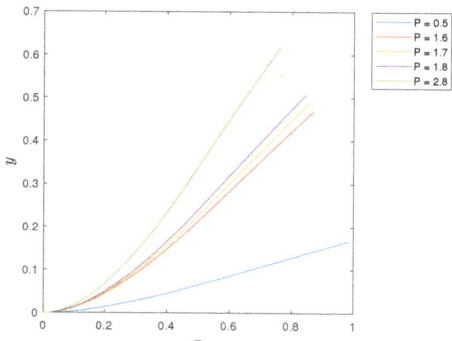

Figure 5. Deflection shapes of a cantilever beam under a uniformly distributed load $P = 0.5, 1.6, 1.7, 1.8,$ and 2.8 at the equilibrium position when $\alpha = 0.85$.

7. Conclusions

We apply the Euler–Lagrange condition for the minimization problem of the energy functional describing the deflection shape of a cantilever beam at the equilibrium position in the fractional calculus framework. By considering boundary value problems, we represent the minimizers in an integral form involving a Green's function and prove the existence and uniqueness of the minimizers using the Banach contraction principle and Schaefer's fixed-point theorem. When the load parameters in the energy functional are varied, the set of minimizers forms a branch of solutions with continuous dependence on the load parameters. Finally, the analytical solution is numerically approximated by the homotopy perturbation method to illustrate the deflection shape of cantilever beams at the equilibrium position when various loads and fractional orders are applied. Moreover, the results illustrate that the deformations are larger for smaller orders of the fractional derivative, which is in agreement with [16].

Author Contributions: W.C. was the project leader. S.C. and C.A. introduced the problem and provided the physical and engineering explanations. The main idea of this paper was proposed and partially proved by P.S.N. and A.S. performed the main proofs and provided some examples. W.C. performed the literature review. D.S. worked on the numerical examples. W.C. and P.S.N. reviewed the final draft of the manuscript. All authors have read and agreed to the published version of the manuscript.

Funding: This research was financially supported by the FSci Highly Impact Research project, Faculty of Science and Faculty of Engineering, King Mongkut's University of Technology Thonburi, Bangkok, Thailand.

Institutional Review Board Statement: Not applicable.

Informed Consent Statement: Not applicable.

Data Availability Statement: Not applicable.

Acknowledgments: The authors would like to thank the referees for their valuable comments, which helped to improve the manuscript.

Conflicts of Interest: The authors declare no conflicts of interest. The funders had no role in the design of the study; in the collection, analyses, or interpretation of data; in the writing of the manuscript; or in the decision to publish the results.

References

1. Miller, K.S.; Ross, B. *An Introduction to the Fractional Calculus and Fractional Differential Equations*; Wiley: Hoboken, NJ, USA, 1993.
2. Hilfer, R. *Applications of Fractional Calculus in Physics*; World Scientific: Singapore, 2000.
3. Kilbas, A.A.; Srivastava, H.M.; Trujillo, J.J. *Theory and Applications of Fractional Differential Equations*; Elsevier: Amsterdam, The Netherlands, 2006; Volume 204.
4. Chen, W.; Sun, H.; Li, X. *Fractional Derivative Modeling in Mechanics and Engineering*; Springer: Singapore, 2022.
5. Furati, K.M.; Kassim, M.D.; Tatar, N.E. Existence and uniqueness for a problem involving Hilfer fractional derivative. *Comput. Math. Appl.* **2012**, *64*, 1616–1626. [CrossRef]
6. Khaminsou, B.; Sudsutad, W.; Thaiprayoon, C.; Alzabut, J.; Pleumpreedaporn, S. Analysis of impulsive boundary value Pantograph problems via Caputo proportional fractional derivative under Mittag–Leffler functions. *Fractal Fract.* **2021**, *5*, 251. [CrossRef]
7. Owolabi, K.M. Modelling and simulation of a dynamical system with the Atangana-Baleanu fractional derivative. *Eur. Phys. J. Plus* **2018**, *133*, 15. [CrossRef]
8. Valério, D.; Da Costa, J.S. Variable-order fractional derivatives and their numerical approximations. *Signal Process.* **2011**, *91*, 470–483. [CrossRef]
9. Stempin, P.; Sumelka, W. Dynamics of space-fractional Euler–Bernoulli and Timoshenko beams. *Materials* **2021**, *14*, 1817. [CrossRef] [PubMed]
10. Hao, Y.; Zhang, M.; Cui, Y.; Cheng, G.; Xie, J.; Chen, Y. Dynamic analysis of variable fractional order cantilever beam based on shifted Legendre polynomials algorithm. *J. Comput. Appl. Math.* **2023**, *423*, 114952. [CrossRef]
11. Bahraini, S.M.S.; Eghtesad, M.; Farid, M.; Ghavanloo, E. Large deflection of viscoelastic beams using fractional derivative model. *J. Mech. Sci. Technol.* **2013**, *27*, 1063–1070. [CrossRef]
12. Sumelka, W.; Blaszczyk, T.; Liebold, C. Fractional Euler–Bernoulli beams: Theory, numerical study and experimental validation. *Eur. J. Mech.-A/Solids* **2015**, *54*, 243–251. [CrossRef]
13. Etemad, S.; Hussain, A.; Imran, A.; Alzabut, J.; Rezapour, S.; Selvam, A.G.M. On a fractional cantilever beam model in the q-difference inclusion settings via special multi-valued operators. *J. Inequalities Appl.* **2021**, *2021*, 174. [CrossRef]
14. Kotsamran, K.; Sudsutad, W.; Thaiprayoon, C.; Kongson, J.; Alzabut, J. Analysis of a nonlinear ψ-Hilfer fractional integro-differential equation describing cantilever beam model with nonlinear boundary conditions. *Fractal Fract.* **2021**, *5*, 177. [CrossRef]
15. Villa-Morales, J.; Rodríguez-Esparza, L.J.; Ramírez-Aranda, M. Deflection of Beams Modeled by Fractional Differential Equations. *Fractal Fract.* **2022**, *6*, 626. [CrossRef]
16. Lazopoulos, K.; Lazopoulos, A. On fractional bending of beams. *Arch. Appl. Mech.* **2016**, *86*, 1133–1145. [CrossRef]
17. Della Corte, A.; dell'Isola, F.; Esposito, R.; Pulvirenti, M. Equilibria of a clamped Euler beam (Elastica) with distributed load: Large deformations. *Math. Model. Methods Appl. Sci.* **2017**, *27*, 1391–1421. [CrossRef]
18. Podlubny, I. *Fractional Differential Equations, Mathematics in Science and Engineering*; Academic Press: New York, NY, USA, 1999.
19. Samko, S.G.; Kilbas, A.A.; Marichev, O.I. *Fractional Integrals and Derivatives*; Gordon and Breach Science Publishers: Yverdon Yverdon-les-Bains, Switzerland, 1993; Volume 1.
20. Lazo, M.J.; Torres, D.F. The DuBois–Reymond fundamental lemma of the fractional calculus of variations and an Euler–Lagrange equation involving only derivatives of Caputo. *J. Optim. Theory Appl.* **2013**, *156*, 56–67. [CrossRef]
21. He, J.H. Homotopy perturbation method: A new nonlinear analytical technique. *Appl. Math. Comput.* **2003**, *135*, 73–79. [CrossRef]

Disclaimer/Publisher's Note: The statements, opinions and data contained in all publications are solely those of the individual author(s) and contributor(s) and not of MDPI and/or the editor(s). MDPI and/or the editor(s) disclaim responsibility for any injury to people or property resulting from any ideas, methods, instructions or products referred to in the content.

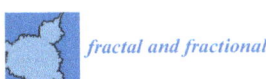

Article

A General Return-Mapping Framework for Fractional Visco-Elasto-Plasticity

Jorge L. Suzuki [1], Maryam Naghibolhosseini [2] and Mohsen Zayernouri [3,*]

[1] Department of Mechanical Engineering & Computational Mathematics, Science and Engineering, Michigan State University, East Lansing, MI 48824, USA
[2] Department of Communicative Sciences and Disorders, Michigan State University, East Lansing, MI 48824, USA
[3] Department of Mechanical Engineering & Statistics and Probability, Michigan State University, East Lansing, MI 48824, USA
* Correspondence: zayern@egr.msu.edu

Citation: Suzuki, J.L.; Naghibolhosseini, M.; Zayernouri, M. A General Return-Mapping Framework for Fractional Visco-Elasto-Plasticity. *Fractal Fract.* **2022**, *6*, 715. https://doi.org/10.3390/fractalfract6120715

Academic Editors: Angelo B. Mingarelli, Leila Gholizadeh Zivlaei and Mohammad Dehghan

Received: 20 September 2022
Accepted: 8 November 2022
Published: 1 December 2022

Publisher's Note: MDPI stays neutral with regard to jurisdictional claims in published maps and institutional affiliations.

Copyright: © 2022 by the authors. Licensee MDPI, Basel, Switzerland. This article is an open access article distributed under the terms and conditions of the Creative Commons Attribution (CC BY) license (https:// creativecommons.org/licenses/by/ 4.0/).

Abstract: We develop a fractional return-mapping framework for power-law visco-elasto-plasticity. In our approach, the fractional viscoelasticity is accounted for through canonical combinations of Scott-Blair elements to construct a series of well-known fractional linear viscoelastic models, such as Kelvin–Voigt, Maxwell, Kelvin–Zener, and Poynting–Thomson. We also consider a fractional quasi-linear version of Fung's model to account for stress/strain nonlinearity. The fractional viscoelastic models are combined with a fractional visco-plastic device, coupled with fractional viscoelastic models involving serial combinations of Scott-Blair elements. We then develop a general return-mapping procedure, which is fully implicit for linear viscoelastic models, and semi-implicit for the quasi-linear case. We find that, in the correction phase, the discrete stress projection and plastic slip have the same form for all the considered models, although with different property and time-step-dependent projection terms. A series of numerical experiments is carried out with analytical and reference solutions to demonstrate the convergence and computational cost of the proposed framework, which is shown to be at least first-order accurate for general loading conditions. Our numerical results demonstrate that the developed framework is more flexible and preserves the numerical accuracy of existing approaches while being more computationally tractable in the visco-plastic range due to a reduction of 50% in CPU time. Our formulation is especially suited for emerging applications of fractional calculus in bio-tissues that present the hallmark of multiple viscoelastic power-laws coupled with visco-plasticity.

Keywords: power-law visco-elasto-plasticity; time-fractional integration; fractional quasi-linear viscoelasticity

1. Introduction

Power-law behavior has been observed in living cells [1,2] and bio-tissues [3–5]. This stems from the ubiquitous self-similar and scale-free nature of the tissue/cell microstructure, which can be physically and mathematically scaled up to continuum level, manifesting in the power-law behavior in the lumped sense. Such power-law relationships have been seen in auditory hair cells, positioned in the sensory organ of hearing, cochlea [6], vocal fold tissues [7], and bladder tissues [5]. Experimental evidence suggests that complex material behavior may possess more than a single power-law scaling in the viscoelastic regime, particularly in multi-fractal structures, such as in cells [8] and biological tissues [9], due to their complex, hierarchical, and heterogeneous microstructures. For such cases, a single fractional rheological element is not sufficient to capture the observed behavior even if the data suggest a linear viscoelastic behavior. Stamenović et al. [8] measured the complex shear modulus of cultured human airway smooth muscle and observed two distinct power-law regimes, separated by an intermediate *plateau*. Kapnistos et al. [10]

found an unexpected tempered power-law relaxation response of entangled polystyrene ring polymers compared with the usual relaxation plateau of linear chain polymers. Such behavior was interpreted through self-similar conformations of double-folded loops in the ring polymer, instead of the repetition observed in linear chains.

In addition to multiple viscoelastic power-law behaviors, there also exists evidence of bio-plasticity in soft media [11,12]. The creep behavior of human embryonic stem cells under differentiation was studied by Pajerowski et al. [11] through micro-aspiration experiments at different pressures. The cell nucleus demonstrated distinguished visco-elasto-plastic power-law scalings, with $\alpha = 0.2$ for the plastic regime, independent of the applied pressure. It is discussed that such low power-law exponent arises due to the fractal arrangement of chromatin inside the cell nucleus. Studies on force-induced mechanical plasticity of mouse embryonic fibroblasts were performed by Bonadkar et al. [12]. They found that the viscoelastic relaxation and the permanent deformations followed a stochastic, normally distributed, power-law scaling $\beta(\omega)$ with values ranging from $\beta \approx 0$ to $\beta \approx 0.6$. The microstructural mechanism of plastic deformation in the cytoskeleton is due to the combination of permanent stretching and buckling of actin fibers.

Regarding existing modeling approaches of anomalous plasticity, several works employed fractional calculus to account for the visco-plastic regimes of different classes of materials [13]. Three of the main approaches include: time-fractional, space-fractional, and stress-fractional modeling. The time-fractional approaches focus on introducing memory effects into non-equilibrium viscous variables [14,15] and consequently modeling power-laws in both viscoelastic and visco-plastic regimes, which is applied for polymers, cells, and tissues. Suzuki et al. [14] developed a fractional visco-elasto-plastic model that provides a constitutive interpolation between rate-independent plasticity and Perzyna's visco-plasticity by introducing a Scott-Blair (SB) model acting the plastic regime. This model utilizes a rate-dependent-yield function, which was later proved to be thermodynamically consistent in a further extension of the model to account for continuum damage mechanics [16]. A three-dimensional space-fractional approach to elasto-plasticity was also developed by Sumelka [17] in order to consider the spatial nonlocalities. The model is based on rate-independent elasto-plasticity, and nonlocal effects are modeled using a fractional continuum mechanics approach, where the strains are defined through a space-fractional Riesz–Caputo derivative of the displacements. Finally, the stress-fractional models for plasticity have been found to be applicable for modeling the soil mechanics and geomaterials that follow a non-associated plastic flow [18,19], i.e., in which the yield surface expansion in the stress space does not follow the usual normality rule and may be non-convex. Sumelka [18] proposed a three-dimensional fractional visco-plastic model, where a fractional flow-rule with the order $0 < \alpha < 1$ in the stress domain naturally modeled the non-associative plasticity. This model recovers the classical Perzyna visco-plasticity as $\alpha \to 1$, and the effect of the fractional flow rule can be a compact descriptor of microstructure anisotropy. Later on, Sun and Sumelka [19] developed a similar stress-fractional model, which was successfully applied for soils under compression. We refer the reader to the Sun et al. review work on fractional calculus applications in plasticity [20].

In this work, we develop a generalized fractional visco-elasto-plastic model, where the visco-plastic device can be coupled with several existing fractional linear/nonlinear viscoelastic representations. More specifically, we utilize a fractional visco-plastic device developed in [14,16], which is then coupled with a series of linear fractional models, such as Scott-Blair (SB), Kelvin–Voigt (FKV), Maxwell (FM), Kelvin–Zener (FKZ), Poynting–Thomson (FPT); also a fractional quasi-linear viscoelastic (FQLV) model for large strains Figure 1. Then, a generalized fractional return-mapping algorithm is proposed, which overcomes existing difficulties in previous developments by first fully discretizing all fractional operators and then performing the predictor–corrector procedure. More specifically, the existing approaches are built on the notion of employing the predictor–corrector approach before the full discretization of fractional operators while treating trial states for stress and internal variables as continuous functions of time. This prevents models with serial combinations of SB elements to be incorporated in associated yield functions in a straightforward fashion. The main features of the proposed framework are:

- We perform a full discretization of fractional viscoelastic models prior to the definition of trial states, which allows a linear decomposition between final and trial stresses regardless of the employed models.
- The fractional return-mapping algorithm is fully implicit for linear viscoelastic rheology and semi-implicit for quasi-linear viscoelasticity.
- Due to the full-discretization before the return-mapping procedure, the operations involving the plastic-slip are memoryless, which resembles return-mapping steps from the classical elasto-plasticity.
- The correction (return-mapping) step has the same structure regardless of the employed viscoelastic models.

We carry out a number of numerical experiments involving fabricated and reference solutions under monotone and general loading conditions and observe a global accuracy ranging from $\mathcal{O}(\Delta t)$ to $\mathcal{O}(\Delta t^{2-\beta})$, according to the regularity induced by the associated fractional differential equations (FDEs) and loading conditions.

This work is organized as follows. In Section 2, we present the mathematical definitions employed in this work. In Section 3, we describe the considered linear/quasi-linear fractional viscoelastic models, coupled with fractional visco-elasto-plasticity as explained in Section 4. All corresponding models are discretized and posed in a unified fractional return-mapping form in Section 5. Convergence analyses and computational performance evaluation of presented models and return-mapping algorithms are performed in Section 6, followed by the concluding remarks in Section 7.

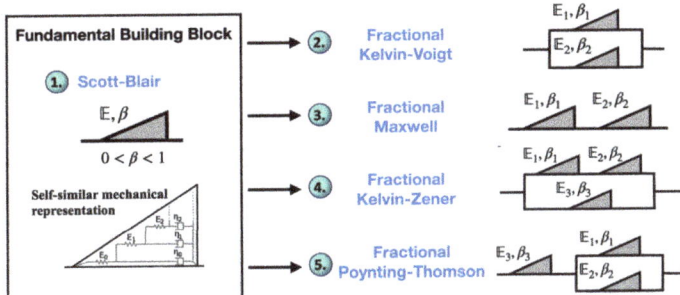

Figure 1. Fractional linear viscoelastic models employed in this work, constructed from serial/parallel combinations of "building block" SB elements. The SB building blocks naturally account for an infinite fractal arrangement of Hookean/Newtonian elements. The employed fractional quasi-linear model is not represented by a mechanical analogue although the time-dependent component of the relaxation function has an SB-like representation.

2. Definitions of Fractional Calculus

We start with some preliminary definitions of fractional calculus [21]. The left-sided Riemann–Liouville integral of order $\beta \in (0,1)$ is defined as

$$\left({}^{RL}_{t_L}\mathcal{I}^{\beta}_t f\right)(t) = \frac{1}{\Gamma(\beta)} \int_{t_L}^{t} \frac{f(s)}{(t-s)^{1-\beta}} ds, \quad t > t_L, \tag{1}$$

where Γ represents the Euler gamma function, and t_L denotes the lower integration limit. The corresponding inverse operator, the left-sided fractional derivative of order β, is then defined based on (1) as

$$\left({}^{RL}_{t_L}\mathcal{D}^{\beta}_t f\right)(t) = \frac{d}{dt}\left({}^{RL}_{t_L}\mathcal{I}^{1-\beta}_t f\right)(t) = \frac{1}{\Gamma(1-\beta)} \frac{d}{dt} \int_{t_L}^{t} \frac{f(s)}{(t-s)^{\beta}} ds, \quad t > t_L. \tag{2}$$

The left-sided Caputo derivative of order $\beta \in (0,1)$ is obtained as

$$({}^C_{t_L}\mathcal{D}^\beta_t f)(t) = ({}^{RL}_{t_L}\mathcal{I}^{1-\beta}_t \frac{df}{dt})(t) = \frac{1}{\Gamma(1-\beta)} \int_{t_L}^t \frac{f'(s)}{(t-s)^\beta} ds, \quad t > t_L. \tag{3}$$

The definitions of Riemann–Liouville and Caputo derivatives are linked by the following relationship:

$$({}^{RL}_{t_L}\mathcal{D}^\beta_t f)(t) = \frac{f(t_L)}{\Gamma(1-\beta)(t+t_L)^\beta} + ({}^C_{t_L}\mathcal{D}^\beta_t f)(t), \tag{4}$$

which can be obtained through integration by parts followed by the application of the Leibniz rule on (2). We should note that the aforementioned derivatives coincide when dealing with homogeneous Dirichlet initial/boundary conditions. Finally, we define the two-parameter Mittag–Leffler function $E_{a,b}(z)$ [22] as:

$$E_{a,b}(z) = \sum_{k=0}^\infty \frac{z^k}{\Gamma(ak+b)}, \quad Re(a) > 0, \quad b \in \mathbb{C}, \quad z \in \mathbb{C}. \tag{5}$$

3. Fractional Viscoelasticity

We present the linear and quasi-linear fractional viscoelastic models that we couple with the visco-plastic return-mapping procedure.

3.1. Linear Viscoelasticity

Scott-Blair (SB) Model: The rheological *building block* for our framework is the fractional SB viscoelastic element, which compactly represents an anomalous viscoelastic constitutive law relating the stresses and strains:

$$\sigma(t) = \mathbb{E} \, {}^C_0\mathcal{D}^\beta_t \varepsilon(t), \quad t > 0, \quad \varepsilon(0) = 0, \tag{6}$$

with pseudo-constant $\mathbb{E}_1 \, [Pa.s^\beta] \geq 0$, and constant fractional order $0 < \beta < 1$, which provides a material interpolation between the Hookean ($\beta \to 0$) and Newtonian ($\beta \to 1$) elements. The pair $(\beta, \mathbb{E})$ uniquely represents the SB constants, where the *pseudo-constant* $\mathbb{E} \, [Pa.s^\beta]$ compactly describes textural properties, such as the firmness of the material [23,24]. In this sense, $\mathbb{E}$ is interpreted as a snapshot of a non-equilibrium dynamic process instead of an equilibrium state. The corresponding rheological symbol for the SB model represents a fractal-like arrangement of springs and dashpots [25,26], which we interpret as a compact, upscaled representation of a fractal-like microstructure. Regarding the thermodynamic admissibility, we refer the reader to Lion [27] for the SB model and Suzuki et al. [16] for the combination of the SB element with more complex mechanisms of visco-plasticity and damage. The relaxation function $G(t) \, [Pa]$ for the SB model is given by the following inverse power-law form:

$$G^{SB}(t) := \frac{\mathbb{E}}{\Gamma(1-\alpha)} t^{-\beta}, \tag{7}$$

which is the convolution kernel of the differ-integral form in (6).

Fractional Kelvin–Voigt (FKV) Model: Through a parallel combination of SB elements, we obtain the following stressd–strain relationship [25]:

$$\sigma(t) = \mathbb{E}_1 \, {}^C_0\mathcal{D}^{\beta_1}_t \varepsilon(t) + \mathbb{E}_2 \, {}^C_0\mathcal{D}^{\beta_2}_t \varepsilon(t), \quad t > 0, \quad \varepsilon(0) = 0, \tag{8}$$

with fractional orders $0 < \beta_1, \beta_2 < 1$, and associated pseudo-constants $\mathbb{E}_1 \, [Pa.s^{\beta_1}] \geq 0$, and $\mathbb{E}_2 \, [Pa.s^{\beta_2}] \geq 0$. The corresponding relaxation modulus $G(t) \, [Pa]$ is also an additive form of two SB elements:

$$G^{FKV}(t) := \frac{\mathbb{E}_1}{\Gamma(1-\beta_1)} t^{-\beta_1} + \frac{\mathbb{E}_2}{\Gamma(1-\beta_2)} t^{-\beta_2}, \tag{9}$$

which has a response characterized by two power-law regimes with a transition from faster to slower relaxation. Assuming $\beta_2 > \beta_1$, the asymptotic responses for small and large time-scales are given by $G^{FKV} \sim t^{-\beta_2}$ as $t \to 0$ and $G^{FKV} \sim t^{-\beta_1}$ as $t \to \infty$.

Fractional Maxwell (FM) Model: Through a serial combination of SB elements, we obtain the fractional Maxwell (FM) model [24], given by:

$$\sigma(t) + \frac{\mathbb{E}_2}{\mathbb{E}_1} {}_0^C\mathcal{D}_t^{\beta_2-\beta_1}\sigma(t) = \mathbb{E}_2 {}_0^C\mathcal{D}_t^{\beta_2}\varepsilon(t), \quad t > 0, \tag{10}$$

with pseudo-constants $\mathbb{E}_1[Pa.s^{\beta_1}] > 0$ and $\mathbb{E}_2[Pa.s^{\beta_1}] \geq 0$, fractional orders $0 < \beta_1 < \beta_2 < 1$ with $0 < \beta_2 - \beta_1 < 1$ and two sets of initial conditions for strains $\varepsilon(0) = 0$ and stresses $\sigma(0) = 0$. We should note that in the case of non-homogeneous initial conditions, there needs to be a compatibility condition [22] between stresses and strains at $t = 0$. The corresponding relaxation function for this building block model assumes a more complex Miller–Ross form [24]:

$$G^{FM}(t) := \mathbb{E}_1 t^{-\beta_1} E_{\beta_2-\beta_1,1-\beta_1}\left(-\frac{\mathbb{E}_1}{\mathbb{E}_2}t^{\beta_2-\beta_1}\right). \tag{11}$$

The presence of a Mittag–Leffler function in (11) leads to a stretched exponential relaxation for smaller times and a power-law behavior for longer times. We also observe that the limit cases are given by $G^{FM} \sim t^{-\beta_1}$ as $t \to 0$ and $G^{FM} \sim t^{-\beta_2}$ as $t \to \infty$, indicating that the FM model provides a behavior transitioning from slower-to-faster relaxation. We refer the reader to [5,24,28] for a number of applications of the aforementioned models. We should notice that both FKV and FM models are able to recover the SB element with a convenient set of pseudo-constants and $\beta_1 = \beta_2$.

Fractional Kelvin–Zener (FKZ) model: The fractional generalization of the standard linear solid (SLS) model is given by an FM branch in parallel with a third SB element, given by the following FDE:

$$\left[1 + \frac{\mathbb{E}_2}{\mathbb{E}_1} {}_0^C\mathcal{D}_t^{\beta_2-\beta_1}\right]\sigma(t) = \left[\mathbb{E}_2 {}_0^C\mathcal{D}_t^{\beta_2} + \mathbb{E}_3 {}_0^C\mathcal{D}_t^{\beta_3} + \frac{\mathbb{E}_2\mathbb{E}_3}{\mathbb{E}_1} {}_0^C\mathcal{D}_t^{\beta_2+\beta_3-\beta_1}\right]\varepsilon(t), \tag{12}$$

with fractional orders $0 < \beta_1 < \beta_2 < 1$ and conditions $0 < \beta_2 - \beta_1 < 1$ and $0 < \beta_2 + \beta_3 - \beta_1 < 1$, pseudo-constants $\mathbb{E}_1[Pa.s^{\beta_1}] > 0$, $\mathbb{E}_2[Pa.s^{\beta_2}] \geq 0$ and $\mathbb{E}_3[Pa.s^{\beta_3}] \geq 0$, and the same initial conditions as in the FM model. We should note that the FM model is recovered when $\mathbb{E}_3 = 0$, and the FKV model is recovered when setting $\mathbb{E}_1 = 0$. The relaxation function is obtained in a straightforward fashion as the summation of the relaxation functions from the SB and FM models:

$$G^{FKZ}(t) := \mathbb{E}_1 t^{-\beta_1} E_{\beta_2-\beta_1,1-\beta_1}\left(-\frac{\mathbb{E}_1}{\mathbb{E}_2}t^{\beta_2-\beta_1}\right) + \frac{\mathbb{E}_3}{\Gamma(1-\beta_3)}t^{-\beta_3}, \tag{13}$$

which leads to three inverse power-law regimes for short, intermediate, and long times with particular relationships between β_1, β_2, β_3 [29].

Fractional Poynting–Thomson (FPT) Model: Finally, we introduce our last fractional linear viscoelastic model, given by the serial combination between an FKV model and an SB element:

$$\left[1 + \frac{\mathbb{E}_1}{\mathbb{E}_3} {}_0^C\mathcal{D}_t^{\beta_1-\beta_3} + \frac{\mathbb{E}_2}{\mathbb{E}_3} {}_0^C\mathcal{D}_t^{\beta_2-\beta_3}\right]\sigma(t) = \left[\mathbb{E}_1 {}_0^C\mathcal{D}_t^{\beta_1} + \mathbb{E}_2 {}_0^C\mathcal{D}_t^{\beta_2}\right]\varepsilon(t), \tag{14}$$

with $0 < \beta_3 < \beta_1 < 1$ and $0 < \beta_3 < \beta_2 < 1$, additional conditions $0 < \beta_1 - \beta_3 < 1$ and $0 < \beta_2 - \beta_3 < 1$, and pseudo-constants $\mathbb{E}_1[Pa.s^{\beta_1}] \geq 0$, $\mathbb{E}_2[Pa.s^{\beta_2}] \geq 0$, and $\mathbb{E}_3[Pa.s^{\beta_3}] > 0$ and homogeneous initial conditions $\sigma(0) = 0$ and $\varepsilon(0) = 0$. Similar to the FKZ model, we recover the FM model when setting either $\mathbb{E}_1$ or $\mathbb{E}_2$ to zero; although the FKV model cannot be recovered except for a trivial case when $\sigma(t) = 0$.

3.2. Quasi-Linear Fractional Viscoelasticity

Although fractional linear viscoelastic models provide suitable relaxation functions that describe the anomalous viscoelastic dynamics of a number of soft materials, at times, complex microstructural deformation mechanisms and large strains induce material non-linearities; hence, the relaxation function itself depends on the applied strain levels. To incorporate this additional effect, we also consider the following FQLV model [30,31]:

$$\sigma(t,\varepsilon) = \int_0^t G(t-s) \frac{\partial \sigma^e(\varepsilon)}{\partial \varepsilon} \dot{\varepsilon} \, ds, \quad (15)$$

where the convolution kernel is given by a multiplicative decomposition of a reduced relaxation function $G(t)$ and an instantaneous nonlinear elastic tangent response with stress σ^e. In the work by Craiem et al. [31], the reduced relaxation function has a fractional Kelvin–Voigt-like form with one of the SB replaced with a Hookean element. Here, we assume a simpler rheology and adopt an SB-like reduced relaxation in the form:

$$G(t) = E t^{-\alpha} / \Gamma(1-\alpha) \quad (16)$$

with the pseudo-constant E with units $[s^\alpha]$. We adopt the same two-parameter exponential nonlinear elastic part as in [31]:

$$\sigma^e(\varepsilon) = A\left(e^{B\varepsilon} - 1\right), \quad (17)$$

with A having units of $[Pa]$. Plugging in (16) and (17) into (15), we obtain:

$$\sigma(t,\varepsilon) = \frac{EAB}{\Gamma(1-\alpha)} \int_0^t \frac{e^{B\varepsilon(s)} \dot{\varepsilon}(s)}{(t-s)^\alpha} \, ds, \quad (18)$$

which differs slightly from the linear SB model (6) in the sense that an additional exponential factor multiplies the function being convoluted.

4. Fractional Visco-Elasto-Plasticity

With all fractional viscoelastic models defined in Section 3, we can couple any of them, subject to a viscoelastic strain $\varepsilon^{ve}(t)$, to the fractional visco-plastic device, illustrated in Figure 2. The visco-plastic device is composed of a parallel combination of a Coulomb element with initial yield stress σ^Y $[Pa]$, an SB element with pseudo-constant $\mathbb{K}$ $[Pa.s^{\beta_K}]$, and fractional order β_K, and a Hookean spring with constant H $[Pa]$. The entire visco-plastic part is subject to a visco-plastic strain $\varepsilon^{vp}(t) : \mathbb{R}^+ \to \mathbb{R}$. In order to obtain the kinematic equations for the internal variables, we start with an additive decomposition of the total logarithmic strain $\varepsilon(t) : \mathbb{R}^+ \to \mathbb{R}$ acting on the visco-elasto-plastic device:

$$\varepsilon(t) = \varepsilon^{ve}(t) + \varepsilon^{vp}(t) \quad (19)$$

The visco-plastic effects are accounted for through the definition of a memory- and rate-dependent-yield function $f(\sigma, \alpha) : \mathbb{R} \times \mathbb{R}^+ \to \mathbb{R}^- \cup \{0\}$ in the following form [14]:

$$f(\sigma, \alpha) := |\sigma| - \left[\sigma^Y + \mathbb{K} \, {}_0^C \mathcal{D}_t^{\beta_K}(\alpha) + H\alpha\right]. \quad (20)$$

where $\alpha \in \mathbb{R}^+$ represents the internal hardening variable, and the above form accounts for the isotropic hardening. The set of admissible stresses lie in a closed convex space, where the associated boundary respects the yield condition of classical plasticity (see [16], Lemma 4.1, setting the damage as $D = 0$). From the defined yield function (20) and the principle of maximum plastic dissipation [32], the following properties hold: (i) associativity of the flow rule, (ii) associativity in the hardening law, (iii) Kuhn–Tucker complimentary conditions, and (iv) convexity. The set of evolution equations for the internal variables ε^{vp} and α is obtained by:

$$\dot{\varepsilon}^{vp} = \frac{\partial f}{\partial \sigma}\dot{\gamma}, \quad \dot{\alpha} = -\frac{\partial f}{\partial R}\dot{\gamma}, \qquad (21)$$

where $\dot{\gamma}(t) : \mathbb{R}^+ \to \mathbb{R}^+$ denotes the plastic slip rate. Evaluating the above equations using (20), we obtain the evolution for visco-plastic strains and hardening [14]:

$$\dot{\varepsilon}^{vp} = \text{sign}(\tau)\dot{\gamma}, \qquad (22)$$

$$\dot{\alpha} = \dot{\gamma}. \qquad (23)$$

Proposition 1. *The closure for the plastic slip rate $\dot{\gamma}(t) \in \mathbb{R}^+$ with an SB viscoelastic part of constants $(\mathbb{E}, \beta_E)$, $(\mathbb{K}, \beta_K)$, and H (model M1 [14]) with homogeneous initial conditions for the internal variables and their respective rates, i.e., $\varepsilon^{vp}(0) = \alpha(0) = \gamma(0) = 0$, $\dot{\gamma}(0) = 0$, and $\dot{\varepsilon}^{vp}(0) = \dot{\alpha}(0) = \dot{\gamma}(0) = 0$, is given by the following fractional Cauchy problem:*

$$\mathbb{E}\,{}^C_0\mathcal{D}^{\beta_E}_t \dot{\gamma}(t) + \mathbb{K}\,{}^C_0\mathcal{D}^{\beta_K}_t \dot{\gamma}(t) + H\dot{\gamma}(t) = \text{sign}(\sigma)\mathbb{E}\left[\frac{\dot{\varepsilon}(0)t^{-\beta_E}}{\Gamma(1-\beta_E)} + {}^C_0\mathcal{D}^{\beta_E}_t \dot{\varepsilon}(t)\right] \qquad (24)$$

Proof. See Appendix A. □

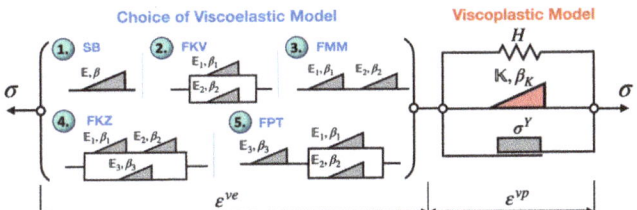

Figure 2. Fractional visco-elasto-plastic model subject to a uniaxial stress σ. Here, any of the linear and quasi-linear (not illustrated) fractional viscoelastic models under strains ε^{ve} can be chosen and then coupled with a fractional viscoplastic rheological device under strains ε^{vp}.

5. A Class of Return-Mapping Algorithms for Fractional Visco-Elasto-Plasticity

Given the presented viscoelastic and visco-plastic models, respectively, in Sections 3 and 4, we now demonstrate how to solve each resulting system of nonlinear equations according to the choice of viscoelastic models. The considered fractional return-mapping approach in this work is fully discrete, i.e., we first discretize all fractional derivatives using a finite-difference approach and then employ trial states for the internal variables in a predictor–corrector scheme.

We discretize the fractional Caputo derivatives in (6)–(10) through an implicit L1 finite-difference scheme [33]. Extensions to account for fast time-stepping approaches [34] are straightforward, since they mostly affect the history terms computation. Let $\Omega = (0, T]$ be decomposed into a uniform time grid with N time steps of size Δt, such that $t_n = n\Delta t$, with $n = 0, 1, \ldots, N$. The time-fractional Caputo derivative of a real-valued function $u(t) \in C^2(\Omega)$ at time $t = t_{n+1}$ is therefore discretized as [33]:

$${}^C_0\mathcal{D}^{\beta}_t u(t)\big|_{t=t_{n+1}} = \frac{1}{\Delta t^{\beta}\Gamma(2-\beta)}[u_{n+1} - u_n + \mathcal{H}^{\alpha}u] + \mathcal{O}(\Delta t^{2-\beta}), \qquad (25)$$

with the history term $\mathcal{H}^{\nu}u$ given by the following form:

$$\mathcal{H}^{\beta}u = \sum_{j=1}^{n} b^{\beta}_j [u_{n+1-j} - u_{n-j}] \qquad (26)$$

with weights $b_j^\beta := (j+1)^{1-\beta} - j^{1-\beta}$.

5.1. Time-Fractional Integration of Viscoelastic Models

In the following, we present the discretized forms for each considered fractional viscoelastic model from Section 3, which are represented in a fully implicit fashion.

Scott-Blair Model: Evaluating both sides of (6) at $t = t_{n+1}$, we obtain:

$$\sigma_{n+1} = \mathbb{E}_1 \, {}_0^C\mathcal{D}_t^{\beta_1} \varepsilon(t) \big|_{t=t_{n+1}} \tag{27}$$

in which by applying (25), we directly obtain:

$$\sigma_{n+1} = C_1^{SB} \left[\varepsilon_{n+1} - \varepsilon_n + \mathcal{H}^{\beta_1} \varepsilon \right] \tag{28}$$

with the strain history $\mathcal{H}^{\beta_1} \varepsilon$ and constant C_1^{SB}, shown in Appendix B for the SB and the following model discretizations.

Fractional Kelvin–Voigt Model: Evaluating both sides of (8) at $t = t_{n+1}$, we obtain:

$$\sigma_{n+1} = \mathbb{E}_1 \, {}_0^C\mathcal{D}_t^{\beta_1} \varepsilon(t) \big|_{t=t_{n+1}} + \mathbb{E}_2 \, {}_0^C\mathcal{D}_t^{\beta_2} \varepsilon(t) \big|_{t=t_{n+1}}, \tag{29}$$

which, applying (25) for the fractional derivatives of order β_1 and β_2, leads to:

$$\sigma_{n+1} = C_1^{KV} \left[\varepsilon_{n+1} - \varepsilon_n + \mathcal{H}^{\beta_1} \varepsilon \right] + C_2^{KV} \left[\varepsilon_{n+1} - \varepsilon_n + \mathcal{H}^{\beta_2} \varepsilon \right]. \tag{30}$$

Fractional Maxwell Model: Evaluating both sides of (10) at $t = t_{n+1}$, we obtain:

$$\sigma_{n+1} + \frac{\mathbb{E}_2}{\mathbb{E}_1} \, {}_0^C\mathcal{D}_t^{\beta_2-\beta_1} \sigma(t) \big|_{t=t_{n+1}} = \mathbb{E}_2 \, {}_0^C\mathcal{D}_t^{\beta_2} \varepsilon(t) \big|_{t=t_{n+1}} \tag{31}$$

in which applying (25) for the fractional derivatives of strains and stresses leads to:

$$\sigma_{n+1} = \frac{C_1^M \left[\varepsilon_{n+1} - \varepsilon_n + \mathcal{H}^{\beta_2} \varepsilon \right] + C_2^M \left[\sigma_n - \mathcal{H}^{\beta_2-\beta_1} \sigma \right]}{1 + C_2^M}, \tag{32}$$

with the emergence of a stress history term $\mathcal{H}^{\beta_2-\beta_1} \sigma$.

Fractional Kelvin–Zener Model: Evaluating both sides of (12) at $t = t_{n+1}$, we obtain:

$$\sigma_{n+1} + \frac{\mathbb{E}_2}{\mathbb{E}_1} \, {}_0^C\mathcal{D}_t^{\beta_2-\beta_1} \sigma(t) \big|_{t=t_{n+1}} = \mathbb{E}_2 \, {}_0^C\mathcal{D}_t^{\beta_2} \varepsilon(t) \big|_{t=t_{n+1}} + \mathbb{E}_3 \, {}_0^C\mathcal{D}_t^{\beta_3} \varepsilon(t) \big|_{t=t_{n+1}}$$
$$+ \frac{\mathbb{E}_2 \mathbb{E}_3}{\mathbb{E}_1} \, {}_0^C\mathcal{D}_t^{\beta_2+\beta_3-\beta_1} \varepsilon(t) \big|_{t=t_{n+1}},$$

which after applying (25) for the fractional derivatives of strains and stresses leads to:

$$\sigma_{n+1} = (1 + C_4^{KZ})^{-1} \Big[C_1^{KZ} \left(\Delta\varepsilon_{n+1} + \mathcal{H}^{\beta_2} \varepsilon \right) + C_2^{KZ} \left(\Delta\varepsilon_{n+1} + \mathcal{H}^{\beta_3} \varepsilon \right)$$
$$+ C_3^{KZ} \left(\Delta\varepsilon_{n+1} + \mathcal{H}^{\beta_2+\beta_3-\beta_1} \varepsilon \right) + C_4^{KZ} \left(\sigma_n - \mathcal{H}^{\beta_2-\beta_1} \sigma \right) \Big] \tag{33}$$

with $\Delta\varepsilon_{n+1} = \varepsilon_{n+1} - \varepsilon_n$.

Fractional Poynting–Thomson Model: Finally, we evaluate both sides of (14) and obtain:

$$\sigma_{n+1} + \frac{\mathbb{E}_1}{\mathbb{E}_3} \, {}_0^C\mathcal{D}_t^{\beta_1-\beta_3} \sigma(t) \big|_{t=t_{n+1}} + \frac{\mathbb{E}_2}{\mathbb{E}_3} \, {}_0^C\mathcal{D}_t^{\beta_2-\beta_3} \sigma(t) \big|_{t=t_{n+1}} = \mathbb{E}_1 \, {}_0^C\mathcal{D}_t^{\beta_1} \varepsilon(t) \big|_{t=t_{n+1}}$$
$$+ \mathbb{E}_2 \, {}_0^C\mathcal{D}_t^{\beta_2} \varepsilon(t) \big|_{t=t_{n+1}},$$

which after applying (25) for the fractional derivatives of strains and stresses, leads to:

$$\sigma_{n+1} = (1 + C_3^{PT} + C_4^{PT})^{-1} \left[C_1 \left(\Delta \varepsilon_{n+1} + \mathcal{H}^{\beta_1} \varepsilon \right) + C_2^{PT} \left(\Delta \varepsilon_{n+1} + \mathcal{H}^{\beta_2} \varepsilon \right) \right.$$
$$\left. + C_3^{PT} \left(\sigma_{n+1} + \mathcal{H}^{\beta_1 - \beta_3} \sigma \right) + C_4^{PT} \left(\sigma_n - \mathcal{H}^{\beta_2 - \beta_3} \sigma \right) \right]. \quad (34)$$

Fractional Quasi-Linear Viscoelastic Model: The discretization for the FQLV model (18) has a slightly different development than the preceding models. It involves a slight modification of the fully implicit L1 difference approach by a trapezoidal rule, taken on the exponential factor. More specifically, we evaluate the FQLV operator as:

$$\sigma_{n+1} = \frac{EAB}{\Gamma(1-\beta)} \sum_{k=0}^{n} \int_{t_k}^{t_{k+1}} (t_{n+1} - s)^{-\beta} \exp(B\varepsilon_{k+\frac{1}{2}}) \left(\frac{\varepsilon_{k+1} - \varepsilon_k}{\Delta t} \right) ds \quad (35)$$

with $\varepsilon_{i+\frac{1}{2}} = (\varepsilon_i + \varepsilon_{i+1})/2$. Following similar steps as in [33], we obtain the following discretized stresses at $t = t_{n+1}$ for the FQLV model:

$$\sigma_{n+1} = C_1^{QLV} \left[\exp(B\varepsilon_{n+\frac{1}{2}})(\varepsilon_{n+1} - \varepsilon_n) + \mathcal{H}^\alpha \left(\varepsilon, \frac{\partial \sigma^e}{\partial \varepsilon} \right) \right] \quad (36)$$

with constant $C_1^{QLV} = EAB/(\Delta t^\alpha \Gamma(2-\alpha))$. The discretized history load in this case is given by:

$$\mathcal{H}^\alpha \left(\varepsilon, \frac{\partial \sigma^e}{\partial \varepsilon} \right) = \sum_{k=1}^{n} \exp(B\varepsilon_{n-k+\frac{1}{2}})(\varepsilon_{n-k+1} - \varepsilon_{n-k}) b_k \quad (37)$$

with weights $b_k = (k+1)^{1-\alpha} - k^{1-\alpha}$. Since the trapezoid approximation of the strains in the exponential term are second-order accurate, the overall accuracy of the viscoelastic models is still bounded by the native L1-difference approach and, therefore, should be of $\mathcal{O}(\Delta t^{2-\alpha})$.

Remark 1. *We note that except for the FQLV model, any of the aforementioned discretizations for the linear models can recover the existing classical counterparts by properly setting $\beta_i \to 0$ or $\beta_i \to 1$. In these cases, to achieve a comparable performance to the integer-order models, history terms can be selectively disregarded, and the corresponding discretization constants can be adjusted to their integer-order counterparts.*

5.2. Time-Fractional Integration of Visco-Plasticity

We start with the discretization of internal variables. Following [14], we assume a strain-driven process with known total strains ε_{n+1} at time t_{n+1}. The strain decomposition becomes:

$$\varepsilon_{n+1} = \varepsilon_{n+1}^{ve} + \varepsilon_{n+1}^{vp}. \quad (38)$$

The flow rule (22) is discretized through a first-order backward-Euler approach, which yields:

$$\varepsilon_{n+1}^{vp} = \varepsilon_n^{vp} + \text{sign}(\sigma_{n+1}) \Delta \gamma_{n+1} \quad (39)$$

with $\Delta \gamma_{n+1} = \gamma_{n+1} - \gamma_n$ representing the plastic slip increment in the interval $[t_n, t_{n+1}]$. Similarly, the discretization of the hardening law (23) is given by

$$\alpha_{n+1} = \alpha_n + \Delta \gamma_{n+1}. \quad (40)$$

Evaluating the yield function (20) at t_{n+1} and employing discretization (25) for the hardening variable, we obtain:

$$f_{n+1} = |\sigma_{n+1}| - \left[\sigma^Y + \mathbb{K}\,{}_0^C\mathcal{D}_t^{\beta_K}(\alpha)\big|_{t=t_{n+1}} + H\alpha_{n+1}\right]$$
$$= |\sigma_{n+1}| - \left[\sigma^Y + \mathbb{K}^*\left(\alpha_{n+1} - \alpha_n + \mathcal{H}^{\beta_K}\alpha\right) + H\alpha_{n+1}\right] \quad (41)$$

with $\mathbb{K}^* = \mathbb{K}/(\Delta t^{\beta_K}\Gamma(2-\beta_K))$.

The next step is to define the trial states for the stress and yield functions, which is the core idea to define the viscoelastic prediction phase, and the correction step after solving the internal visco-plastic variables. Therefore, we freeze the internal variables for the prediction step at t_{n+1}. Accordingly, the trial visco-plastic strains and hardening are given by:

$$\varepsilon_{n+1}^{vp\,trial} = \varepsilon_n^{vp}, \quad \alpha_{n+1}^{trial} = \alpha_n. \quad (42)$$

In this token, the trial yield function is given by setting the above relationship for the hardening variable into (41) to obtain:

$$f_{n+1}^{trial} = |\sigma_{n+1}^{trial}| - \left[\sigma^Y + \mathbb{K}^*\left(\mathcal{H}^{\beta_K}\alpha\right) + H\alpha_n\right]. \quad (43)$$

In order to complete the return-mapping procedure, we need an explicit relationship between the stresses σ_{n+1} in terms of the known total strains ε_{n+1}. To achieve this, we solve for the plastic slip $\Delta\gamma$ using a discrete consistency condition $f_{n+1} = 0$. We start with the trial stresses for each presented fractional viscoelastic model by substituting the visco-plastic trial strain (42) and (38) into (28)–(36), where we obtain the following for each discretized model:

Scott-Blair:

$$\sigma_{n+1}^{trial} = C_1^{SB}\left[\varepsilon_{n+1} - \varepsilon_n + \mathcal{H}^{\beta_1}(\varepsilon - \varepsilon^{vp})\right] \quad (44)$$

Fractional Kelvin–Voigt:

$$\sigma_{n+1}^{trial} = C_1^{KV}\left[\varepsilon_{n+1} - \varepsilon_n + \mathcal{H}^{\beta_1}(\varepsilon - \varepsilon^{vp})\right] + C_2^{KV}\left[\varepsilon_{n+1} - \varepsilon_n + \mathcal{H}^{\beta_2}(\varepsilon - \varepsilon^{vp})\right] \quad (45)$$

Fractional Maxwell:

$$\sigma_{n+1}^{trial} = \frac{C_1^M\left[\varepsilon_{n+1} - \varepsilon_n + \mathcal{H}^{\beta_2}(\varepsilon - \varepsilon^{vp})\right] + C_2^M\left[\sigma_n - \mathcal{H}^{\beta_2-\beta_1}\sigma\right]}{1 + C_2^M} \quad (46)$$

Fractional Kelvin–Zener:

$$\sigma_{n+1}^{trial} = (1 + C_4^{KZ})^{-1}\left[C_1^{KZ}\left(\Delta\varepsilon_{n+1} + \mathcal{H}^{\beta_2}(\varepsilon - \varepsilon^{vp})\right) + C_2^{KZ}\left(\Delta\varepsilon_{n+1} + \mathcal{H}^{\beta_3}(\varepsilon - \varepsilon^{vp})\right)\right.$$
$$\left. + C_3^{KZ}\left(\Delta\varepsilon_{n+1} + \mathcal{H}^{\beta_2+\beta_3-\beta_1}(\varepsilon - \varepsilon^{vp})\right) + C_4^{KZ}\left(\sigma_n - \mathcal{H}^{\beta_2-\beta_1}\sigma\right)\right] \quad (47)$$

Fractional Poynting–Thomson:

$$\sigma_{n+1}^{trial} = (1 + C_3^{PT} + C_4^{PT})^{-1}\left[C_1^{PT}\left(\Delta\varepsilon_{n+1} + \mathcal{H}^{\beta_1}(\varepsilon - \varepsilon^{vp})\right) + C_2^{PT}\left(\Delta\varepsilon_{n+1} + \mathcal{H}^{\beta_2}(\varepsilon - \varepsilon^{vp})\right)\right.$$
$$\left. + C_3^{PT}\left(\sigma_{n+1} + \mathcal{H}^{\beta_1-\beta_3}\sigma\right) + C_4^{PT}\left(\sigma_n - \mathcal{H}^{\beta_2-\beta_3}\sigma\right)\right] \quad (48)$$

Fractional Quasi-Linear Viscoelastic Model:

For this model, we follow a similar procedure of substituting the viscoelastic strains into (36), however, we evaluate the exponential term explicitly in time for all stages of the return-mapping algorithm. Therefore, the corresponding trial state becomes:

$$\sigma_{n+1}^{trial} = C_1^{QLV}\left[\exp(B(\varepsilon_n - \varepsilon_n^{vp}))(\varepsilon_{n+1} - \varepsilon_n) + \mathcal{H}^\alpha\left(\varepsilon - \varepsilon^{vp}, \frac{\partial \sigma^e}{\partial \varepsilon}\right)\right]. \quad (49)$$

5.3. Generalized Fractional Return-Mapping Algorithm (Algorithm 1)

From the aforementioned trial states, each discretized viscoelastic constitutive laws (28)–(36) and recalling (39), one can show the following stress correction onto the yield surface:

$$\sigma_{n+1} = \sigma_{n+1}^{trial} - \text{sign}(\sigma_{n+1}^{trial}) C_{RM}^{ve}(\mathbb{E}, \Delta t, \varepsilon) \Delta \gamma_{n+1}, \quad (50)$$

where all discretized aforementioned viscoelastic models change the return-mapping procedure by a scaling factor $C_{RM}^{ve}(C, \varepsilon_n, \varepsilon_n^{vp}) \in \mathbb{R}^+$ acting on the Lagrange multiplier $\Delta \gamma$, which is given by the following for each model:

$$C_{RM}^{ve} = \begin{cases} C_1^{SB} & (\text{Scott-Blair}) \\ C_1^{KV} + C_2^{KV} & (\text{Fractional Kelvin–Voigt}) \\ C_1^M / (1 + C_2^M) & (\text{Fractional Maxwell}) \\ (C_1^{KZ} + C_2^{KZ} + C_3^{KZ}) / (1 + C_4^{KZ}) & (\text{Fractional Kelvin–Zener}) \\ (C_1^{PT} + C_2^{PT}) / (1 + C_3^{PT} + C_4^{PT}) & (\text{Fractional Poynting–Thomson}) \\ C_1^{QLV} \exp(B(\varepsilon_n - \varepsilon_n^{vp})) & (\text{Fractional Quasi-Linear-Viscoelastic}) \end{cases} \quad (51)$$

We show the derivation of (50) for the fractional Kelvin–Zener model in Appendix C, from which the Scott-Blair, fractional Maxwell, and fractional Kelvin–Voigt models can be directly recovered; note that the derivation for the fractional Poynting–Thomson and quasi-linear viscoelasticity follow similarly in a straightforward fashion. Substituting the updated stresses (50) into the discrete yield function (41) and recalling (43), we obtain:

$$f_{n+1} = f_{n+1}^{trial} - (C_{RM}^{ve} + \mathbb{K}^* + H)\Delta \gamma. \quad (52)$$

Enforcing the discrete yield condition $f_{n+1} = 0$, we obtain the solution for the discrete plastic slip:

$$\boxed{\Delta \gamma_{n+1} = \frac{f_{n+1}^{trial}}{C_{RM}^{ve} + \mathbb{K}^* + H}.} \quad (53)$$

Algorithm 1 Fractional return-mapping algorithm.

1: Database for ε, ε^{vp}, σ, α, and total strain ε_{n+1}.
2: $\varepsilon_{n+1}^{vp\,trial} = \varepsilon_n^{vp}$, $\alpha_{n+1}^{trial} = \alpha_n$
3: Compute σ_{n+1}^{trial} from (28)–(36) according to the selected fractional viscoelastic model.
4: $f_{n+1}^{trial} = |\sigma_{n+1}^{trial}| - [\sigma^Y + \mathbb{K}^*(\mathcal{H}^{\beta_K}\alpha) + H\alpha_n]$
5: **if** $f_{n+1}^{trial} \leq 0$ **then**
6: $\quad \varepsilon_{n+1}^{vp} = \varepsilon_n^{vp}$, $\alpha_{n+1} = \alpha_n$, $\sigma_{n+1} = \sigma_{n+1}^{trial}$.
7: **else**
8: $\quad$ Return-Mapping:
9: $\quad$ Compute C_{RM}^{ve} from (51) according to the selected fractional viscoelastic model.
10: $\quad \Delta \gamma_{n+1} = f_{n+1}^{trial} / (C_{RM}^{ve} + \mathbb{K}^* + H)$
11: $\quad \sigma_{n+1} = \sigma_{n+1}^{trial} - \text{sign}(\sigma_{n+1}^{trial}) C_{RM}^{ve} \Delta \gamma$
12: $\quad \varepsilon_{n+1}^{vp} = \varepsilon_n^{vp} + \text{sign}(\tau_{n+1}) \Delta \gamma$
13: $\quad \alpha_{n+1} = \alpha_n + \Delta \gamma$
14: **end if**

Comparison of the Return-Mapping Algorithm to the Existing Approaches

In [14], trial states were defined prior to the discretization of fractional operators, and the corresponding trial variables were taken as continuous functions of time, therefore making the return-mapping procedure "semi-discrete." Let the quantities with bars, $(\bar{\cdot})$, be the corresponding solutions for the procedure developed in [14]. For the SB viscoelastic case, one has the following trial stresses at $t = t_{n+1}$:

$$\bar{\sigma}_{n+1}^{\text{trial}} = \mathbb{E} \, {}_0^C\mathcal{D}_t^{\beta_E}(\varepsilon - \bar{\varepsilon}^{vp\,\text{trial}})\big|_{t=t_{n+1}} \tag{54}$$

in which, after employing the discretized plastic flow rule, the following relationship between the corrected and trial stresses is obtained:

$$\bar{\sigma}_{n+1} = \bar{\sigma}_{n+1}^{\text{trial}} - \mathbb{E}\,\text{sign}(\bar{\sigma}_{n+1})\, {}_0^C\mathcal{D}_t^{\beta_E}(\Delta\gamma)\big|_{t=t_{n+1}}. \tag{55}$$

This equation can be explicitly inserted into the discrete yield function to solve for the plastic slip rate. While such a procedure is straightforward for SB and FKV viscoelastic elements, it is non-trivial for the serial combinations such as the FM, FKZ, and FPT models. For instance, if we follow the same procedure for the FM model, we obtain:

$$\bar{\sigma}_{n+1}^{\text{trial}} + \frac{\mathbb{E}_2}{\mathbb{E}_1}\, {}_0^C\mathcal{D}_t^{\beta_2-\beta_1}(\bar{\sigma}^{\text{trial}})\big|_{t=t_{n+1}} = \mathbb{E}_2\, {}_0^C\mathcal{D}_t^{\beta_2}(\varepsilon - \bar{\varepsilon}^{vp\,\text{trial}})\big|_{t=t_{n+1}}, \tag{56}$$

which yields the following relationship between $\bar{\sigma}$ and $\bar{\sigma}^{\text{trial}}$:

$$\left(\bar{\sigma}_{n+1} - \bar{\sigma}_{n+1}^{\text{trial}}\right) + \frac{\mathbb{E}_2}{\mathbb{E}_1}\, {}_0^C\mathcal{D}_t^{\beta_2-\beta_1}(\bar{\sigma} - \bar{\sigma}^{\text{trial}})\big|_{t=t_{n+1}} = -\mathbb{E}_2\, {}_0^C\mathcal{D}_t^{\beta_2}(\varepsilon - \bar{\varepsilon}^{vp\,\text{trial}})\big|_{t=t_{n+1}}. \tag{57}$$

Except for the SB case, a fractional viscoelastic model involving a serial combination of SB elements cannot be incorporated into the yield function in a differential form unless a full discretization is performed at this stage. This happens since the discretized yield function (41) requires a closed description of σ_{n+1}, needing an equivalent Boltzmann representation for such models, which is impractical due to complex forms of relaxation kernels. Therefore, our approach in this work already carries the trial states with fully discretized fractional operators, which closely and completely resembles classical elasto-plastic approaches.

Regarding the obtained discretizations in this work, we note that the plastic slip (53) assumes a simple form similar to the rate-independent elasto-plasticity. As discussed above, in the return-mapping procedure developed in [14], the trial states and plastic slip were assumed to have memory in the discretization procedure; therefore, a fractional relaxation equation in the following form was obtained:

$$\Delta\bar{\gamma}_{n+1} = \frac{\mathbb{E}^*\left(\Delta\bar{\gamma}_n - \mathcal{H}^{\beta_E}\Delta\bar{\gamma}\right) + \mathbb{K}^*\left(\Delta\bar{\gamma}_n - \mathcal{H}^{\beta_K}\Delta\bar{\gamma}\right) + \bar{f}_{n+1}^{\text{trial}}}{\mathbb{E}^* + \mathbb{K}^* + H}. \tag{58}$$

Furthermore, we observe that the obtained plastic slip discretization in this work has two less history terms to be evaluated. Although this does not influence the computational complexity of the original scheme, we show in the numerical examples that this fact still leads to about 50% less CPU time. Regarding the difference in the stress solutions, let $t = t_p$ be the time step of onset of plasticity for the first time. Therefore, we have the following estimate:

$$|\sigma_{p+1} - \bar{\sigma}_{p+1}| = \frac{\mathbb{E}^*}{\mathbb{E}^* + \mathbb{K}^* + H}\left[\mathbb{K}^*\left(\mathcal{H}^{\beta_E}\Delta\bar{\gamma} - \mathcal{H}^{\beta_K}\Delta\bar{\gamma}\right) - H\left(\Delta\bar{\gamma}_p - \mathcal{H}^{\beta_E}\Delta\bar{\gamma}\right)\right], \tag{59}$$

which shows that at such stage both discretizations coincide when $\beta_E = \beta_K$ and $H = 0$. In the following Section, we verify such an estimate by obtaining an analytical solution with the aid of Proposition 1.

6. Numerical Tests

We present three convergence examples with different loading conditions to verify the employed fractional viscoelastic models, the validity of the new fractional visco-plastic return-mapping algorithm, and the full visco-elasto-plastic response of the models. For the convergence analyses, let $\mathbf{u}^*$ and $\mathbf{u}^\delta$ be, respectively, the reference and approximate solutions in $\Omega = (0, T]$, for a specific time-step size Δt. We define the following relative error measures:

$$\mathrm{err}_N(\Delta t) = \frac{|u_N^* - u_N^\delta|}{|u_N^*|}, \quad \mathrm{err}(\Delta t) = \frac{||\mathbf{u}^* - \mathbf{u}^\delta||_{L^2(\Omega)}}{||\mathbf{u}^*||_{L^2(\Omega)}}, \quad \mathrm{Order} = \log_2\left[\frac{\mathrm{err}(\Delta t)}{\mathrm{err}(\Delta t/2)}\right]. \tag{60}$$

We consider homogeneous initial conditions for all model variables in all cases. The presented algorithms were implemented in MATLAB R2020b and were run in a system with Intel Core i7-8850H CPU with 2.60 GHz, 32 GB RAM and MacOS 11.5 operating system.

Example 1 (Convergence of fractional viscoelastic algorithms). *We perform a convergence study of the fractional viscoelastic component of our framework under the stress relaxation and monotone loading experiments. For this example, we set $(\mathbb{E}_1, \mathbb{E}_2, \mathbb{E}_3) = (1, 1, 1)$ and $(\beta_1, \beta_2, \beta_3) = (0.3, 0.7, 0.1)$ for fractional linear viscoelastic models, ensuring all fractional derivatives are taken with an "equivalent order" $\beta \in (0, 1)$, i.e., the sum of fractional orders arising in the fractional derivatives of each linear viscoelastic model. For the FQLV model, we set $E = 1$, $A = 1$, and $B = 1$, and varying fractional order β.*

For the stress relaxation test, we impose a step strain $\varepsilon(t) = H(t)\varepsilon_0$ with $\varepsilon_0 = 1$ for $T = 1000$ [s], where $H(t)$ denotes the Heaviside step function. We compare the obtained solutions at $t = T$ for the SB, FKV, FM, and FKZ models to their corresponding relaxation functions (7), (9), (11) and (13). The FPT and QLV models are not analyzed in this step since their time-dependent stress relaxation functions are not readily available, and they are instead analyzed under the monotone strains. The obtained results are illustrated in Figure 3a, where an expected linear convergence behavior is obtained for all models when the error is evaluated at the end point, given the non-smooth nature of the applied step strain in the stress relaxation solution.

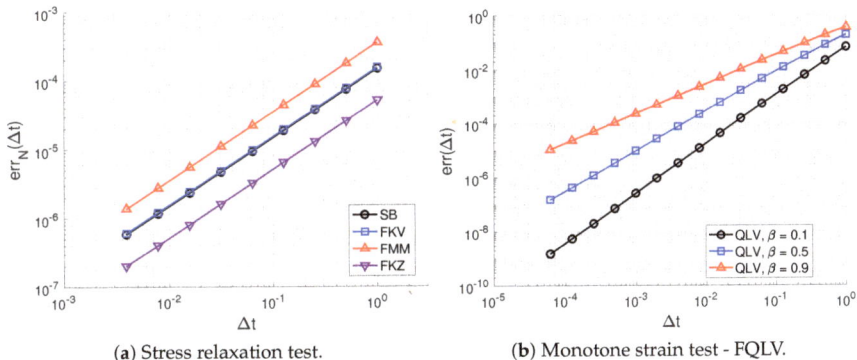

(**a**) Stress relaxation test. (**b**) Monotone strain test - FQLV.

Figure 3. Convergence analysis for the fractional viscoelastic models with known analytical solutions: (**a**) a stress relaxation test with non-smooth step-strains and material parameters $(\mathbb{E}_1, \mathbb{E}_2, \mathbb{E}_3) = (1,1,1)$ and $(\beta_1, \beta_2, \beta_3) = (0.3, 0.7, 0.1)$ yielding first-order convergence; (**b**) convergence for the FQLV model with a fabricated solution of linearly increasing strains and material properties $(E, A, B) = (1, 1, 1)$ and varying β. The slopes of the error curves are $q \approx 2 - \beta$.

For the monotone strain case, we set $T = 1$ and fabricate a solution for strains in the form $\varepsilon(t) = \varepsilon_T(t/T)$ with the total applied strain fixed at $\varepsilon_f = 1$. Since analytical solutions for all fractional viscoelastic models are difficult to obtain, we compute a reference solution for each model with $\Delta t = 2^{-17}$ [s]. Particularly for the FQLV model, we utilize the fabricated strain function $\varepsilon(t)$ to obtain the following analytical stress solution:

$$\sigma^{QLV^*}(t) = EAB^\beta \exp(Bt) \left[1 - \frac{\Gamma(1-\beta, Bt)}{\Gamma(1-\beta)} \right], \quad (61)$$

where $\Gamma(\cdot, \cdot)$ denotes the upper incomplete gamma function. The convergence results for all fractional viscoelastic models with respect to the reference numerical solution are presented in Figure 4, while the results for the FQLV model with the analytical solution are illustrated in Figure 3b. We observe for both cases that the accuracy of the implemented and developed schemes is of order $\mathcal{O}(\Delta t^{2-\beta})$. We note that although we have employed a trapezoid rule for the exponential term in the FQLV model, we do not obtain a second-order convergence, since the accuracy is limited by the L1 approach. The difference in error slopes among models in Figure 4 is due to the highest fractional order assigned to each model. For the SB and FQLV models, the fractional order is set as $\beta = 0.3$, and therefore, the observed slope is $q \approx 1.7$. For all remaining models and choice of fractional orders, the error slopes are determined by the fractional derivative of the highest order, which is $\beta_2 = 0.7$ in this example, yielding $q \approx 1.3$.

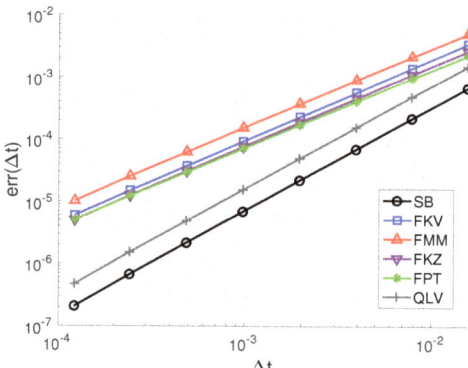

Figure 4. Convergence analysis for all fractional viscoelastic models with $(\mathbb{E}_1, \mathbb{E}_2, \mathbb{E}_3) = (1,1,1)$ and $(\beta_1, \beta_2, \beta_3) = (0.3, 0.7, 0.1)$. A cubic strain function was employed with a reference solution using the time step size $\Delta t = 2^{-17}$. A monotone loading test with the convergence rate of $q \approx 1.3$ was applied for all models.

Example 2 (Convergence of fractional visco-plastic algorithms). *The purpose of this example is to demonstrate the conditions where the presented plastic slip discretization (53), the form (58) from [14] and their associated return-mapping algorithms are equivalent, and also provide a numerical estimate for their difference when such conditions are not satisfied. For this purpose, we test a monotone load where an analytical solution is available and a case with a cyclic load under high strain rates. For both cases, we set an SB viscoelastic part with $\mathbb{E} = 50 \, [Pa.s^{\beta_E}]$, and $\mathbb{K} = 5 \, [Pa.s^{\beta_K}]$.*

For the monotone strain case, we start with a fabricated solution for strains in the form $\varepsilon(t) = At^3$ with $A = \varepsilon_T/T^3 \, [s^{-3}]$. Here, ε_f denotes the total applied stress, and T represents the final simulation time. Utilizing the result of Proposition 1 and setting $\beta_E = \beta_K = 0$ and $\sigma^Y = H = 0$, we obtain the following analytical solution for stresses:

$$\sigma^*(t) = \frac{6 A \mathbb{E} \mathbb{K}}{\mathbb{E} + \mathbb{K}} \frac{t^{3-\beta_E}}{\Gamma(4-\beta_E)}. \quad (62)$$

We should note that the proposed fabricated solution ensures no internal variable is a linear function and, therefore, not computed exactly by the L1 discretization. We set $\varepsilon_T = 1$ and $T = 1\,[s]$, and therefore, $A = 1\,[s^{-3}]$. Table 1 presents the obtained convergence results for the fabricated solution (62) for both return-mapping algorithms and under the same fractional-orders β_E and β_K. We observe that the errors coincide for this particular case, while the accuracy of order $\mathcal{O}(\Delta t^{2-\beta})$ of the L1 approach is also achieved. The computational times are illustrated in Figure 5, where the developed fractional return-mapping approach, when using an SB viscoelastic element, is about 50% faster than the original return-mapping approach from [14] since about half of the history terms need to be computed.

Table 1. Convergence behavior for the return-mapping Algorithm 1 obtained in this work and the original approach from [14] for an FVEP device with an SB element.

	$\beta_E = \beta_K = 0.1$		$\beta_E = \beta_K = 0.5$		$\beta_E = \beta_K = 0.9$	
Δt	err(Δt)	Order	err(Δt)	Order	err(Δt)	Order
2^{-9}	3.2426×10^{-6}	–	9.2971×10^{-5}	–	1.3246×10^{-3}	–
2^{-10}	9.1853×10^{-7}	1.8197	3.3109×10^{-5}	1.4895	6.1875×10^{-4}	1.0981
2^{-11}	2.5845×10^{-7}	1.8294	1.1763×10^{-5}	1.4929	2.8884×10^{-4}	1.0991
2^{-12}	7.2323×10^{-8}	1.8374	4.1731×10^{-6}	1.4951	1.3479×10^{-4}	1.0995
2^{-13}	2.0145×10^{-8}	1.8440	1.4788×10^{-6}	1.4966	6.2895×10^{-5}	1.0998
2^{-14}	5.5891×10^{-9}	1.8497	5.2369×10^{-7}	1.4977	2.9344×10^{-5}	1.0999

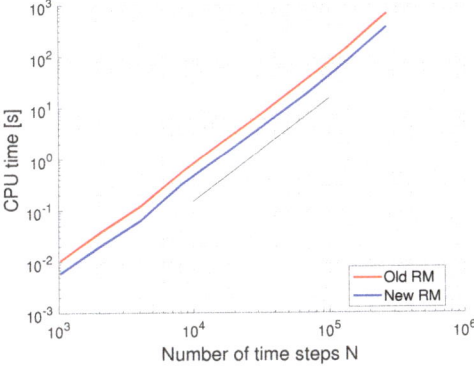

Figure 5. CPU times for the developed fractional return-mapping algorithm and the original one [14] for an SB viscoelastic part. The black line has slope $q = 2$.

Similar results are obtained for the monotone loading condition; however, this is not the case under general loadings. To demonstrate the difference between the visco-elasto-plastic discretization σ_{n+1} developed in this work and $\tilde{\sigma}_{n+1}$ from [14], we take the latter as a reference solution with $\Delta t = 2^{-19}\,[s]$, and $T = 1\,[s]$. We also consider $\sigma^Y = 10\,[Pa]$, $\beta_E = 0.3$, and $\beta_K = 0.7$ with the same pseudo-constants as in the previous test case. A constant rate loading/unloading cyclic strain test of the following form is employed:

$$\varepsilon(t) = \frac{2\varepsilon_A}{\pi} \arcsin(\sin(2\pi\omega t)), \tag{63}$$

where we consider a strain amplitude $\varepsilon_A = 0.25$ and two strain frequencies of $\omega = 1\,[Hz]$, and $\omega = 60\,[Hz]$. The difference between both approaches is illustrated in Figure 6. Here, higher frequencies result in higher strain rates and consequently a significant plastic strain history even after a number of hysteresis cycles. The obtained results confirm the estimates from (59), which is already valid at the onset of plasticity. Furthermore, we observe that a tenfold increase in strain rates approximately leads to a tenfold increase in the difference between both algorithms.

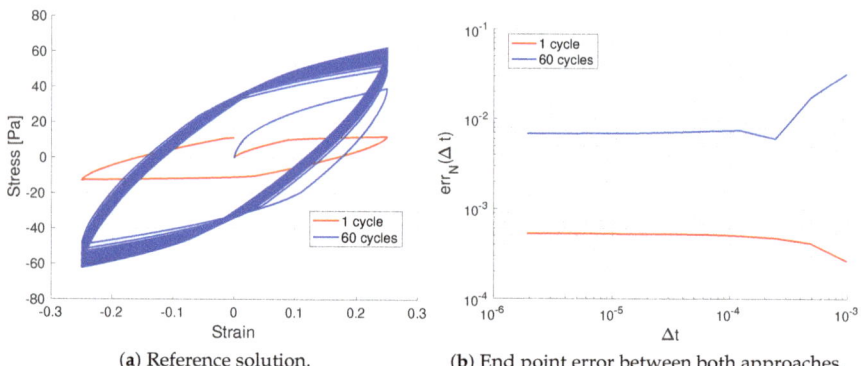

(a) Reference solution.   (b) End point error between both approaches.

Figure 6. Comparison between the presented return-mapping algorithm and the reference approach from [14] under low- and high-frequency loading.

Example 3 (Convergence of fractional visco-elasto-plasticity). *Finally, we perform a verification on the entire fractional visco-elasto-plastic framework under cyclic strain. Since no fabricated solutions are available, we employ reference solutions with time step size $\Delta t = 2^{-18}$ [s]. Let $T = 1$ [s] with the same applied strains (63) as in the previous example. The viscoelastic material parameters are set to $(\mathbb{E}_1, \mathbb{E}_2, \mathbb{E}_3) = (50, 50, 50)$, and $(\beta_1, \beta_2, \beta_3) = (0.3, 0.7, 0.1)$. In addition, the visco-plastic parameters are taken as $\mathbb{K} = 5$, $\beta_K = 0.7$, $H = 0$, and $\sigma^Y = 1$. Figures 7 and 8 illustrates the obtained convergence results, where all models except the FKV one showed a convergence rate of order $q \approx 1.3$, which is compatible with the employed L1 discretization scheme and given $\beta_2 = \beta_K = 0.7$. The FKV model achieved linear asymptotic convergence for the considered example, which is the expected worst case scenario from the backward-Euler discretization of internal variables. We believe the difference in convergence behavior between the FKV model and the others could be due to the sharper response of the FKV model because of the stiffer rheology combined with the nonlinear loading/unloading response. This combination of effects could result in a lower solution regularity and therefore, a lower convergence rate.*

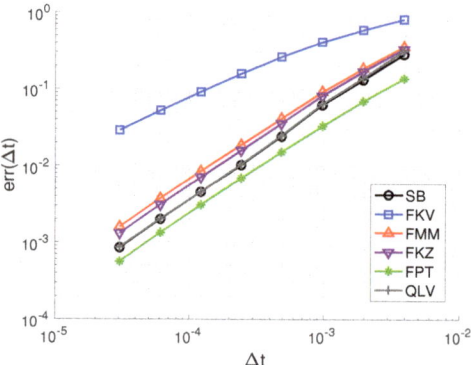

Figure 7. Convergence analysis for the fractional visco-elasto-plastic models under cyclic loads. Due to the particular choice of fractional orders (with $\beta_2 = \beta_K = 0.7$ being dominant), we observed the convergence rate of $q \approx 1.3$ for all models except for the FKV. In the latter case, we observed a linear convergence to the reference solution.

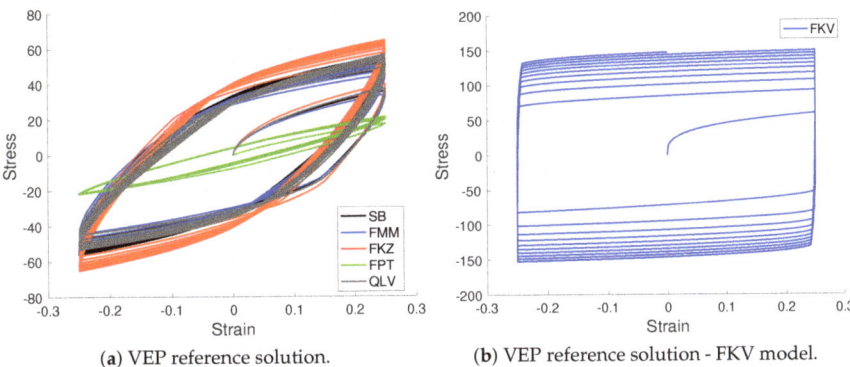

Figure 8. Visco-elasto-plastic reference solutions for the employed models for the first 30 loading cycles. We noticed a similar behavior for most models under the choice of material parameters except for the FPT and FKV models. The FKV particularly yielded a very stiff response due to the combination of high fractional order values and high strain rates.

7. Conclusions

We proposed a general return-mapping procedure for multiple power-law, time-fractional visco-elasto-plastic materials. The developed framework provided a flexible way to integrate multiple known fractional viscoelastic models that are representative of soft materials rheology to power-law visco-plastic hardening and permanent strains. Furthermore, a nonlinear viscoelasticity, suitable for bio-tissues, was considered through a fractional quasi-linear Fung's model, which allowed the possibility of plasticity onset after substantial amounts of viscoelastic strains. The main features of the proposed framework are:

- The trial states were taken after full discretization of stress and internal variables, which allowed a straightforward decomposition of the yield function into the final and trial states.
- The developed return-mapping procedure is fully implicit for linear viscoelastic models and semi-implicit for quasi-linear viscoelasticity. For simplicity, the chosen numerical discretization for fractional derivatives was an L1 finite-difference approach.
- Our correction step for visco-plasticity had the same structure for all viscoelastic models with the only difference being a scaling discretization constant.
- We carried out numerical experiments with analytical and reference solutions that demonstrated the $\mathcal{O}(\Delta t^{2-\beta})$ global accuracy, surprisingly even in some instances with general loading/unloading conditions.
- The developed return-mapping discretization was compared to an existing approach, and the difference between discretizations relied on cases with extensive plastic history and high strain rates.

Regarding the computational costs, the framework is computationally tractable since it does not involve history calculations for the plastic slip and is therefore about 50% faster than the existing fractional frameworks, regardless of the employed numerical discretization for fractional derivatives. Extensions on fast numerical schemes of order $\mathcal{O}(N \log N)$ for the employed time-fractional derivatives would be straightforward to implement. We also note that the thermodynamics of all models in the developed framework can be analyzed through the approach developed in [16].

The modeling framework developed here could be applied to simulate the self-similar structures and memory-dependent behavior in human bio-tissues [3,35,36]. The visco-elasto-plastic characteristics can be observed in different bio-tissues in the human body, specifically due to the process of aging. Aging results in the oxidation or loss of elastin, which leads to the loss of tissue elasticity such as in the vocal fold tissues [37,38]. Furthermore, in terms of multi-scale modeling, the lumped plastic behavior introduced here could potentially be coupled with existing discrete dislocation dynamics (DDD) models [39,40]. The models developed in this work uniquely qualify for simulating such characteristics, which will be undertaken in our future work.

Author Contributions: Conceptualization, J.L.S. and M.Z.; Methodology, J.L.S., M.N. and M.Z.; Investigation, M.N. and M.Z.; Resources, M.N. and M.Z.; Data curation, J.L.S.; Writing—original draft, J.L.S., M.N. and M.Z.; Visualization, J.L.S.; Supervision, M.N. and M.Z.; Project administration, M.N. and M.Z.; Funding acquisition, J.L.S. and M.Z. All authors have read and agreed to the published version of the manuscript.

Funding: This work was supported by the ARO YIP Award (W911NF-19-1-0444), the NSF Award (DMS-1923201), the MURI/ARO Award (W911NF-15-1-0562), the AFOSR YIP Award (FA9550-17-1-0150), and NIH NIDCD K01DC017751 and R21DC020003.

Institutional Review Board Statement: Not applicable.

Informed Consent Statement: Not applicable.

Data Availability Statement: Not applicable.

Conflicts of Interest: The authors declare no conflict of interest. The funders had no role in the design of the study; in the collection, analyses, or interpretation of data; in the writing of the manuscript, or in the decision to publish the results.

Appendix A. Proof of Proposition 1

Proof. Similar to the derivation of the tangent elasto-plastic modulus in classical plasticity [32], we start by taking the time derivative of the yield function to enforce the persistency condition:

$$\dot{f}(\sigma, \alpha) = \frac{d}{dt}\left\{|\sigma(t)| - \left[\sigma^Y + \mathbb{K}\,{}_0^C\mathcal{D}_t^{\beta_K}\alpha(t) + H\alpha(t)\right]\right\} \quad (A1)$$

$$= \text{sign}(\sigma)\dot{\sigma}(t) - \left[\mathbb{K}\frac{d}{dt}{}_0^C\mathcal{D}_t^{\beta_K}\alpha(t) + H\dot{\alpha}(t)\right].$$

Using the SB stress–strain relationship (6), we obtain:

$$\dot{f}(\sigma, \alpha) = \text{sign}(\sigma)\mathbb{E}\left[\frac{d}{dt}{}_0^C\mathcal{D}_t^{\beta_E}\varepsilon(t) - \frac{d}{dt}{}_0^C\mathcal{D}_t^{\beta_E}\varepsilon^{vp}(t)\right] - \left[\mathbb{K}\frac{d}{dt}{}_0^C\mathcal{D}_t^{\beta_K}\alpha(t) + H\dot{\alpha}(t)\right]. \quad (A2)$$

Employing definition (3) for the Caputo derivative, performing integration by parts and employing the Leibniz integral rule, we obtain:

$$\frac{d}{dt}{}_0^C\mathcal{D}_t^{\beta}u(t) = \frac{1}{\Gamma(1-\beta)}\frac{d}{dt}\int_0^t \frac{\dot{u}(s)}{(t-s)^\beta}ds \quad (\text{from}(3))$$

$$= \frac{1}{\Gamma(1-\beta)}\frac{d}{dt}\left[\dot{u}(s)\frac{(t-s)^{1-\beta}}{1-\beta}\Big|_t^0 + \int_0^t \frac{(t-s)^{1-\beta}\ddot{u}(s)}{1-\beta}ds\right]$$

$$= \frac{\dot{u}(0)t^{-\beta}}{\Gamma(1-\beta)} + \frac{1}{\Gamma(1-\beta)}\int_0^t \frac{\ddot{u}(s)}{(t-s)^\beta}ds$$

$$= \frac{\dot{u}(0)t^{-\beta}}{\Gamma(1-\beta)} + {}_0^C\mathcal{D}_t^{\beta}\dot{u}(t). \quad (A3)$$

Substituting (A3) into (A2), setting $\dot{\gamma}(0) = 0$, and therefore $\dot{\alpha}(0) = 0$ from (23) and $\dot{\varepsilon}^{vp}(0) = 0$ from (22), we obtain:

$$\dot{f}(\sigma, \alpha) = \text{sign}(\sigma)\mathbb{E}\left[\frac{\dot{\varepsilon}(0)t^{-\beta_E}}{\Gamma(1-\beta_E)} + {}_0^C\mathcal{D}_t^{\beta_E}\dot{\varepsilon}(t) - {}_0^C\mathcal{D}_t^{\beta_E}\dot{\varepsilon}^{vp}(t)\right] - \mathbb{K}\,{}_0^C\mathcal{D}_t^{\beta_K}\dot{\alpha}(t) - H\dot{\alpha}(t). \quad (A4)$$

Finally, substituting (23) and (22) into (A4), and enforcing the persistency condition $\dot{f}(\sigma, \alpha) = 0$, we obtain:

$$\mathbb{E} \,{}_0^C\mathcal{D}_t^{\beta_E}\dot{\gamma}(t) + \mathbb{K} \,{}_0^C\mathcal{D}_t^{\beta_K}\dot{\gamma}(t) + H\dot{\gamma}(t) = \text{sign}(\sigma)\mathbb{E}\left[\frac{\dot{\varepsilon}(0)t^{-\beta_E}}{\Gamma(1-\beta_E)} + {}_0^C\mathcal{D}_t^{\beta_E}\dot{\varepsilon}(t)\right]. \quad (A5)$$

□

Appendix B. Discretization Constants and Terms for Fractional Viscoelastic Models

Scott-Blair:
$$C_1^{SB} = \frac{\mathbb{E}}{\Delta t^{\beta_1}\Gamma(2-\beta_1)} \quad (A6)$$

Fractional Kelvin–Voigt:
$$C_1^{KV} = \frac{\mathbb{E}_1}{\Delta t^{\beta_1}\Gamma(2-\beta_1)}, \quad C_2^{KV} = \frac{\mathbb{E}_2}{\Delta t^{\beta_2}\Gamma(2-\beta_2)} \quad (A7)$$

Fractional Maxwell:
$$C_1^{M} = \frac{\mathbb{E}_2}{\Delta t^{\beta_2}\Gamma(2-\beta_2)}, \quad C_2^{M} = \frac{\mathbb{E}_2/\mathbb{E}_1}{\Delta t^{\beta_2-\beta_1}\Gamma(2-\beta_2+\beta_1)} \quad (A8)$$

Fractional Kelvin–Zener:
$$C_1^{KZ} = \frac{\mathbb{E}_2}{\Delta t^{\beta_2}\Gamma(2-\beta_2)}, \quad C_2^{KZ} = \frac{\mathbb{E}_3}{\Delta t^{\beta_3}\Gamma(2-\beta_3)} \quad (A9)$$

$$C_3^{KZ} = \frac{\mathbb{E}_2\mathbb{E}_3/\mathbb{E}_1}{\Delta t^{\beta_2+\beta_3-\beta_1}\Gamma(2-\beta_1-\beta_3+\beta_2)}, \quad C_4^{KZ} = \frac{\mathbb{E}_2/\mathbb{E}_1}{\Delta t^{\beta_2-\beta_1}\Gamma(2-\beta_2+\beta_1)} \quad (A10)$$

Fractional Poynting–Thomson:
$$C_1^{PT} = \frac{\mathbb{E}_1}{\Delta t^{\beta_1}\Gamma(2-\beta_1)}, \quad C_2^{PT} = \frac{\mathbb{E}_2}{\Delta t^{\beta_2}\Gamma(2-\beta_2)} \quad (A11)$$

$$C_3^{PT} = \frac{\mathbb{E}_1/\mathbb{E}_3}{\Delta t^{\beta_1-\beta_3}\Gamma(2-\beta_1+\beta_3)}, \quad C_4^{PT} = \frac{\mathbb{E}_2/\mathbb{E}_3}{\Delta t^{\beta_2-\beta_3}\Gamma(2-\beta_2+\beta_3)} \quad (A12)$$

Fractional Quasi-Linear viscoelastic:
$$C_1^{QLV} = \frac{EAB}{\Delta t^{\beta}\Gamma(2-\beta)} \quad (A13)$$

Appendix C. Return-Mapping Derivation for the Fractional Kelvin–Zener Model

Recalling the discretized FKV model (33) employed as the viscoelastic part of the visco-elasto-plastic model:

$$\sigma_{n+1} = (1+C_4^{KZ})^{-1}\left[C_1^{KZ}\left(\Delta\varepsilon_{n+1}^{ve} + \mathcal{H}^{\beta_2}\varepsilon\right) + C_2^{KZ}\left(\Delta\varepsilon_{n+1}^{ve} + \mathcal{H}^{\beta_3}\varepsilon^{ve}\right)\right.$$
$$\left. + C_3^{KZ}\left(\Delta\varepsilon_{n+1}^{ve} + \mathcal{H}^{\beta_2+\beta_3-\beta_1}\varepsilon^{ve}\right) + C_4^{KZ}\left(\sigma_n - \mathcal{H}^{\beta_2-\beta_1}\sigma\right)\right], \quad (A14)$$

where with the kinematic relationship (38) and the viscoplastic strain evolution (39), we note that $\Delta\varepsilon_{n+1}^{ve} = \Delta\varepsilon_{n+1} - \Delta\gamma_{n+1}\,\text{sign}(\sigma_{n+1})$. Therefore, (A14) becomes:

$$\sigma_{n+1} = (1 + C_4^{KZ})^{-1} \Big[C_1^{KZ}\left(\Delta\varepsilon_{n+1} + \mathcal{H}^{\beta_2}\varepsilon\right) + C_2^{KZ}\left(\Delta\varepsilon_{n+1} + \mathcal{H}^{\beta_3}\varepsilon^{ve}\right)$$
$$+ C_3^{KZ}\left(\Delta\varepsilon_{n+1} + \mathcal{H}^{\beta_2+\beta_3-\beta_1}\varepsilon^{ve}\right) + C_4^{KZ}\left(\sigma_n - \mathcal{H}^{\beta_2-\beta_1}\sigma\right)$$
$$- \left(C_1^{KZ} + C_2^{KZ} + C_3^{KZ}\right)\Delta\gamma_{n+1}\,\mathrm{sign}(\sigma_{n+1}) \Big]. \tag{A15}$$

Recalling the trial state for the FKZ model:

$$\sigma_{n+1}^{trial} = (1 + C_4^{KZ})^{-1} \Big[C_1^{KZ}\left(\Delta\varepsilon_{n+1} + \mathcal{H}^{\beta_2}(\varepsilon - \varepsilon^{vp})\right) + C_2^{KZ}\left(\Delta\varepsilon_{n+1} + \mathcal{H}^{\beta_3}(\varepsilon - \varepsilon^{vp})\right)$$
$$+ C_3^{KZ}\left(\Delta\varepsilon_{n+1} + \mathcal{H}^{\beta_2+\beta_3-\beta_1}(\varepsilon - \varepsilon^{vp})\right) + C_4^{KZ}\left(\sigma_n - \mathcal{H}^{\beta_2-\beta_1}\sigma\right) \Big] \tag{A16}$$

which, by combining the above two equations, we find:

$$\sigma_{n+1} = \sigma_{n+1}^{trial} - \mathrm{sign}(\sigma_{n+1})\left(\frac{C_1^{KZ} + C_2^{KZ} + C_3^{KZ}}{1 + C_4^{KZ}}\right)\Delta\gamma_{n+1}. \tag{A17}$$

Finally, we obtain the loading/unloading sign consistency by following standard plasticity procedures:

$$\mathrm{sign}(\sigma_{n+1})|\sigma_{n+1}| = \mathrm{sign}(\sigma_{n+1}^{trial})|\sigma_{n+1}^{trial}| - \mathrm{sign}(\sigma_{n+1})\left(\frac{C_1^{KZ} + C_2^{KZ} + C_3^{KZ}}{1 + C_4^{KZ}}\right)\Delta\gamma_{n+1}, \tag{A18}$$

therefore,

$$\mathrm{sign}(\sigma_{n+1})\left[|\sigma_{n+1}| + \left(\frac{C_1^{KZ} + C_2^{KZ} + C_3^{KZ}}{1 + C_4^{KZ}}\right)\Delta\gamma_{n+1}\right] = \mathrm{sign}(\sigma_{n+1}^{trial})|\sigma_{n+1}^{trial}|, \tag{A19}$$

since both terms multiplying the sign functions on the left and right sides of the above equation are positive, we therefore conclude that $\mathrm{sign}(\sigma_{n+1}) = \mathrm{sign}(\sigma_{n+1}^{trial})$, and hence (A17) becomes:

$$\sigma_{n+1} = \sigma_{n+1}^{trial} - \mathrm{sign}(\sigma_{n+1}^{trial})\left(\frac{C_1^{KZ} + C_2^{KZ} + C_3^{KZ}}{1 + C_4^{KZ}}\right)\Delta\gamma_{n+1}, \tag{A20}$$

which completes the derivation.

References

1. Okajima, T. Nanorheology of Living Cells. In *The World of Nano-Biomechanics*; Ikai, A., Ed.; Elsevier: Amsterdam, The Netherlands, 2017; pp. 249–265.
2. De Sousa, J.; Freire, R.; Sousa, F.; Radmacher, M.; Silva, A.; Ramos, M.; Monteiro-Moreira, A.; Mesquita, F.; Moraes, M.; Montenegro, R.; et al. Double power-law viscoelastic relaxation of living cells encodes motility trends. *Sci. Rep.* **2020**, *10*, 4749. [CrossRef]
3. Naghibolhosseini, M.; Long, G.R. Fractional-order modelling and simulation of human ear. *Int. J. Comput. Math.* **2018**, *95*, 1257–1273. [CrossRef]
4. Guo, J.; Yin, Y.; Peng, G. Fractional-order viscoelastic model of musculoskeletal tissues: correlation with fractals. *Proc. R. Soc. A* **2021**, *477*, 20200990. [CrossRef]
5. Suzuki, J.L.; Tuttle, T.G.; Roccabianca, S.; Zayernouri, M. A data-driven memory-dependent modeling framework for anomalous rheology: Application to urinary bladder tissue. *Fractal Fract.* **2021**, *5*, 223. [CrossRef]
6. Martin, P.; Hudspeth, A. Compressive nonlinearity in the hair bundle's active response to mechanical stimulation. *Proc. Natl. Acad. Sci. USA* **2001**, *98*, 14386–14391. [CrossRef]
7. Choi, J.S.; Kim, N.J.; Klemuk, S.; Jang, Y.H.; Park, I.S.; Ahn, K.H.; Lim, J.Y.; Kim, Y.M. Preservation of viscoelastic properties of rabbit vocal folds after implantation of hyaluronic acid-based biomaterials. *Otolaryngol. Head Neck Surg.* **2012**, *147*, 515–521. [CrossRef]
8. Stamenović, D.; Rosenblatt, N.; Montoya-Zavala, M.; Matthews, B.; Hu, S.; Suki, B.; Wang, N.; Ingber, D. Rheological Behavior of Living Cells Is Timescale-Dependent. *Biophys. J.* **2007**, *93*, L39–L41. [CrossRef]

9. Vincent, J. *Structural Biomaterials*; Princeton University Press: Princeton, NJ, USA, 2012.
10. Kapnistos, M.; Lang, M.; Vlassopoulos, D.; Pyckhout-Hintzen, D.; Richter, D.; Cho, D.; Chang, T.; Rubinstein, M. Unexpected power-law stress relaxation of entangled ring polymers. *Nat. Mater.* **2008**, *7*, 997–1002. [CrossRef]
11. Pajerowski, J.; Dahl, K.; Zhong, F.; Sammak, P.; Discher, D. Physical plasticity of the nucleus in stem cell differentiation. *Proc. Natl. Acad. Sci. USA* **2007**, *40*, 15619–15624. [CrossRef]
12. Bonadkar, N.; Gerum, R.; Kuhn, M.; Sporer, M.; Lippert, A.; Schneider, W.; Aifantis, K.; Fabry, B. Mechanical plasticity of cells. *Nat. Mater.* **2016**, *15*, 1090–1094.
13. Suzuki, J.L.; Gulian, M.; Zayernouri, M.; D'Elia, M. Fractional modeling in action: A survey of nonlocal models for subsurface transport, turbulent flows, and anomalous materials. *J. Peridynamics Nonlocal Model.* **2022**, 1–68. [CrossRef]
14. Suzuki, J.; Zayernouri, M.; Bittencourt, M.; Karniadakis, G. Fractional-order uniaxial visco-elasto-plastic models for structural analysis. *Comput. Methods Appl. Mech. Eng.* **2016**, *308*, 443–467. [CrossRef]
15. Xiao, R.; Sun, H.; Chen, W. A finite deformation fractional viscoplastic model for the glass transition behavior of amorphous polymers. *Int. J. Nonlinear Mech.* **2017**, *93*, 7–14. [CrossRef]
16. Suzuki, J.; Zhou, Y.; D'Elia, M.; Zayernouri, M. A thermodynamically consistent fractional visco-elasto-plastic model with memory-dependent damage for anomalous materials. *Comput. Methods Appl. Mech. Eng.* **2021**, *373*, 113494. [CrossRef]
17. Sumelka, W. Application of fractional continuum mechanics to rate independent plasticity. *Acta Mech.* **2014**, *225*, 3247–3264. [CrossRef]
18. Sumelka, W. Fractional Viscoplasticity. *Mech. Res. Commun.* **2014**, *56*, 31–36. [CrossRef]
19. Sun, Y.; Sumelka, W. Fractional viscoplastic model for soils under compression. *Acta Mech.* **2019**, *230*, 3365–3377. [CrossRef]
20. Sun, H.; Zhang, Y.; Baleanu, D.; Chen, W.; Chen, Y. A new collection of real world applications of fractional calculus in science and engineering. *Commun. Nonlinear Sci. Numer. Simul.* **2018**, *64*, 213–231. [CrossRef]
21. Podlubny, I. *Fractional Differential Equations: An Introduction to Fractional Derivatives, Fractional Differential Equations, to Methods of Their Solution and Some of Their Applications*; Elsevier: Amsterdam, The Netherlands, 1998.
22. Mainardi, F.; Spada, G. Creep, Relaxation and Viscosity Properties for Basic Fractional Models in Rheology. *arXiv* **2011**, arXiv:1110.3400v1.
23. Blair, G.; Veinoglou, B.; Caffyn, B. Limitations of the Newtonian time scale in relation to non-equilibrium rheological states and a theory of quasi-properties. *Proc. R. Soc. A Math. Phys. Eng. Sci.* **1947**, *189*, 69–87.
24. Jaishankar, A.; McKinley, G. Power-law rheology in the bulk and at the interface: Quasi-properties and fractional constitutive equations. *Proc. R. Soc. A* **2013**, *469*, 20120284. [CrossRef]
25. Schiessel, H.; Blumen, A. Hierarchical analogues to fractional relaxation equations. *J. Phys. A Math. Gen.* **1993**, *26*, 5057–5069. [CrossRef]
26. McKinley, G.; Jaishankar, A. Critical Gels, Scott Blair and the Fractional Calculus of Soft Squishy Materials. In Proceedings of the Bingham Lecture, 85th Annual Meeting of the Society of Rheology, Montréal, QC, Canada, 13–17 October 2013.
27. Lion, A. On the thermodynamics of fractional damping elements. *Contin. Mech. Thermodyn.* **1997**, *9*, 83–96. [CrossRef]
28. Bonfanti, A.; Kaplan, J.L.; Charras, G.; Kabla, A.J. Fractional viscoelastic models for power-law materials. *Soft Matter* **2020**, *16*, 6002–6020. [CrossRef]
29. Schiessel, H. Generalized viscoelastic models: Their fractional equations with solutions. *J. Phys. A Math. Gen.* **1995**, *28*, 6567–6584. [CrossRef]
30. Fung, Y.C. *Biomechanics: Mechanical Properties of Living Tissues*; Springer Science & Business Media: Berlin/Heidelberg, Germany, 2013.
31. Craiem, D.; Rojo, F.; Atienza, J.; Armentano, R.; Guinea, G. Fractional-order viscoelasticity applied to describe uniaxial stress relaxation of human arteries. *Phys. Med. Biol* **2008**, *53*, 4543. [CrossRef]
32. Simo, J.; Hughes, T. *Computational Inelasticity*; Springer: Berlin/Heidelberg, Germany, 1998.
33. Lin, Y.; Xu, C. Finite difference/spectral approximations for the time-fractional diffusion equation. *J. Comput. Phys.* **2007**, *225*, 1533–1552. [CrossRef]
34. Zeng, F.; Turner, I.; Burrage, K. A stable fast time-stepping method for fractional integral and derivative operators. *J. Sci. Comput.* **2018**, *77*, 283–307. [CrossRef]
35. Naghibolhosseini, M. *Estimation of Outer-Middle Ear Transmission Using DPOAEs and Fractional-Order Modeling of Human Middle Ear*; City University of New York: New York, NY, USA, 2015.
36. Suzuki, J.L.; Kharazmi, E.; Varghaei, P.; Naghibolhosseini, M.; Zayernouri, M. Anomalous nonlinear dynamics behavior of fractional viscoelastic beams. *J. Comput. Nonlinear Dyn.* **2021**, *16*, 111005. [CrossRef]
37. Branco, A.; Todorovic Fabro, A.; Gonçalves, T.M.; Garcia Martins, R.H. Alterations in extracellular matrix composition in the aging larynx. *Otolaryngol. Head Neck Surg.* **2015**, *152*, 302–307. [CrossRef]
38. Ferster, A.P.; Malmgren, L.T. Cellular and Molecular Mechanisms of Aging of the Vocal Fold. In *Voice Science*; Sataloff, R.T., Ed.; Plural Publishing Inc.: San Diego, CA, USA, 2017; pp. 157–167.
39. de Moraes, E.A.B.; Suzuki, J.L.; Zayernouri, M. Atomistic-to-meso multi-scale data-driven graph surrogate modeling of dislocation glide. *Comput. Mater. Sci.* **2021**, *197*, 110569. [CrossRef]
40. de Moraes, E.A.B.; D'Elia, M.; Zayernouri, M. Nonlocal Machine Learning of Micro-Structural Defect Evolutions in Crystalline Materials. *arXiv* **2022**, arXiv:2205.05729.

Article

Multiplicity of Solutions for Fractional-Order Differential Equations via the $\kappa(x)$-Laplacian Operator and the Genus Theory

Hari M. Srivastava [1,2,3,4,*] **and Jose Vanterler da Costa Sousa** [5]

1. Department of Mathematics and Statistics, University of Victoria, Victoria, BC V8W 3R4, Canada
2. Department of Medical Research, China Medical University Hospital, China Medical University, Taichung 40402, Taiwan
3. Department of Mathematics and Informatics, Azerbaijan University, 71 Jeyhun Hajibeyli Street, Baku AZ1007, Azerbaijan
4. Section of Mathematics, International Telematic University Uninettuno, 00186 Rome, Italy
5. Center for Mathematics, Computing and Cognition, Federal University of ABC-UFABC, 5001 Bangú, Santo André 09210-580, SP, Brazil; jose.vanterler@ufabc.edu.br
* Correspondence: harimsri@math.uvic.ca

Abstract: In this paper, we investigate the existence and multiplicity of solutions for a class of quasi-linear problems involving fractional differential equations in the χ-fractional space $\mathcal{H}^{\gamma,\beta;\chi}_{\kappa(x)}(\Delta)$. Using the Genus Theory, the Concentration-Compactness Principle, and the Mountain Pass Theorem, we show that under certain suitable assumptions the considered problem has at least k pairs of non-trivial solutions.

Keywords: fractional differential equations; $\kappa(x)$-Laplacian; χ-Hilfer fractional derivative; existence; multiplicity of solutions; genus theory; Concentration-Compactness Principle; Mountain Pass Theorem; variable exponents; variational methods

MSC: Primary 26A33, 34A08; Secondary 35A15, 35J20, 35J66, 35J92

1. Introduction

Let $I = [a,b]$ $(-\infty < a < b < \infty)$ denote a finite interval on the real axis $\mathbb{R}$. In the theory and application of fractional integrals and fractional derivatives, it is known that the right-sided Hilfer fractional derivative ${}^H\mathcal{D}^{\gamma,\beta}_{a+}$ and the left-sided Hilfer fractional derivative ${}^H\mathcal{D}^{\gamma,\beta}_{b-}$ of order γ $(0 < \gamma < 1)$ and type β $(0 \leqq \beta \leqq 1)$ reduce, when $\beta = 0$ and $\beta = 1$, to the corresponding relatively more familiar Riemann-Liouville fractional derivatives and Liouville-Caputo fractional derivatives, respectively (see [1–4] for details, along with several other related recent works [5–9]). For $n - 1 < \gamma < n$ $(n \in \mathbb{N})$, let $f, \chi \in C^n(I \subset \mathbb{R})$, where the function χ is increasing and $\chi'(x) \neq 0$ in the interval I. Then, we have the right-sided χ-H ${}^H\mathcal{D}^{\gamma,\beta;\chi}_{a+}$ and the left-sided χ-Hilfer fractional derivative ${}^H\mathcal{D}^{\gamma,\beta;\chi}_{b-}$ of order γ $(0 < \gamma < 1)$ and type β $(0 \leqq \beta \leqq 1)$.

Let

$$\theta = (\theta_1, \theta_2, \cdots, \theta_N), \quad d = (d_1, d_2, \cdots, d_N) \quad \text{and} \quad \gamma = (\gamma_1, \gamma_2, \cdots, \gamma_N),$$

where $0 < \gamma_1, \gamma_2, \cdots, \gamma_N < 1$ with $\theta_j < d_j$ for all $j \in \{1, 2, \cdots, N\}$ and $N \in \mathbb{N}$, and use

$$\Delta = I_1 \times I_2 \times \cdots \times I_N = [\theta_1, d_1] \times [\theta_2, d_2] \times \cdots \times [\theta_N, d_N],$$

where $T_1, d_2, \cdots, T_N$ and $\theta_1, \theta_2, \cdots, \theta_N$ are positive constants. We consider $\chi(\cdot)$ to be an increasing and positive monotone function on $(\theta_1, d_1), (\theta_2, d_2), \cdots, (\theta_N, d_N)$ having

a continuous derivative $\chi'(\cdot)$ on $(\theta_1, d_1], (\theta_2, d_2], \cdots, (\theta_N, d_N]$. The χ-Riemann-Liouville fractional integral of order γ and of N variables $\varphi = (\varphi_1, \varphi_2, \cdots, \varphi_N) \in L^1(\Delta)$, denoted by $\mathcal{I}_{\theta,x_j}^{\gamma;\chi}(\cdot)$, is defined as follows (see [10–12]):

$$\mathcal{I}_{\theta,x_j}^{\gamma;\chi} \varphi(x_j) := \frac{1}{\Gamma(\gamma_j)} \int\int\cdots\int_\Delta \chi'(s_j)[\chi(x_j) - \chi(s_j)]^{\gamma_j - 1} \varphi(s_j)\, ds_j$$

with

$$\chi'(s_j)[\chi(x_j) - \chi(s_j)]^{\gamma_j - 1} = \chi'(s_1)[\chi(x_1) - \chi(s_1)]^{\gamma_1 - 1} \chi'(s_2)[\chi(x_2) - \chi(s_2)]^{\gamma_2 - 1} \cdots \chi'(s_N)[\chi(x_N) - \chi(s_N)]^{\gamma_N - 1},$$

where

$$\Gamma(\gamma_j) := \Gamma(\gamma_1)\Gamma(\gamma_2)\cdots\Gamma(\gamma_N),$$
$$\varphi(s_j) := \varphi(s_1)\varphi(s_2)\cdots\varphi(s_N)$$

and

$$ds_j := ds_1\, ds_2 \cdots ds_N$$

for all $j \in \{1, 2, \cdots, N\}$. We can then define $\mathcal{I}_{d,x_j}^{\gamma;\chi}(\cdot)$ by analogy.

Furthermore, we let $\varphi, \chi \in C^n(\Delta)$ be two functions such that χ is increasing, $\chi'(x_j) \neq 0$ ($j \in \{1, 2, \cdots, N\}$), and $x_j \in \Delta$. The χ-Hilfer fractional partial derivative (χ-H) of functions of N variables, denoted by ${}^H\mathcal{D}_{\theta,x_j}^{\gamma,\beta;\chi}(\cdot)$, of order γ ($n-1 < \gamma < n$) and type β ($0 \leq \beta \leq 1$), is defined as follows (see [10–12]):

$${}^H\mathcal{D}_{\theta,x_j}^{\gamma,\beta;\chi} \varphi(x_j) := \mathcal{I}_{\theta,x_j}^{\beta(1-\gamma),\chi} \left(\frac{1}{\chi'(x_j)} \left(\frac{\partial^N}{\partial x_j} \right) \right) \mathcal{I}_{\theta,x_j}^{(1-\beta)(1-\gamma);\chi} \varphi(x_j) \quad (1)$$

with

$$\partial x_j = \partial x_1 \partial x_2 \cdots \partial x_N \quad \text{and} \quad \chi'(x_j) = \chi'(x_1)\chi'(x_2)\cdots\chi'(x_N)$$

for all $j \in \{1, 2, \cdots, N\}$. We can then define ${}^H\mathcal{D}_{T,x_j}^{\gamma,\beta;\chi}(\cdot)$ by analogy.

Throughout this work, we use the following notations:

$$\mathcal{I}_-^{\gamma;\chi}(\cdot) := \mathcal{I}_{T,x_j}^{\gamma;\chi}(\cdot),$$

$$\mathcal{I}_+^{\gamma;\chi}(\cdot) := \mathcal{I}_{\theta,x_j}^{\gamma;\chi}(\cdot),$$

$${}^H\mathcal{D}_+^{\gamma,\beta;\chi}(\cdot) := {}^H\mathcal{D}_{\theta,x_j}^{\gamma,\beta;\chi}(\cdot)$$

and

$${}^H\mathcal{D}_-^{\gamma,\beta;\chi}(\cdot) := {}^H\mathcal{D}_{T,x_j}^{\gamma,\beta;\chi}(\cdot).$$

In the present paper, we consider the following class of quasi-linear fractional-order problems with variable exponents:

$$\begin{cases} {}^H\mathcal{D}_-^{\gamma,\beta;\chi}\left(\left|{}^H\mathcal{D}_+^{\gamma,\beta;\chi}\varphi\right|^{\kappa(x)-2} {}^H\mathcal{D}_+^{\gamma,\beta;\chi}\varphi \right) = \lambda|\varphi|^{n(x)-2}\varphi + \mathbf{F}(x,\varphi) \\ \varphi = 0, \end{cases} \quad (2)$$

where $\Delta := [0, T] \times [0, T] \times [0, T]$ is a bounded domain with a smooth boundary, and (for simplicity) ${}^H\mathcal{D}_+^{\gamma,\beta;\chi}(\cdot)$ and ${}^H\mathcal{D}_-^{\gamma,\beta;\chi}(\cdot)$ are the χ-H of order γ $\left(\frac{1}{\kappa(x)} < \gamma < 1\right)$ and type β ($0 \leq \beta \leq 1$), $\lambda > 0$; $\kappa, n : \overline{\Delta} \to \mathbb{R}$ are Lipschitz functions such that:

- (**p₁**) $1 < \kappa_- \leqq \kappa(x) \leqq \kappa_+ < 3, \kappa_+ < n_- \leqq n(x) \leqq \kappa_\gamma^*(x)$ for all $x \in \overline{\Delta}$;
- (**p₂**) The set $A = \left\{ x \in \overline{\Delta} : n(x) = \kappa_\gamma^*(x) \right\}$ is not empty.

We now make several assumptions which are detailed below.
Let $f : \overline{\Delta} \times \mathbb{R} \to \mathbb{R}$ be a function provided by

$$f(x,t) = \zeta(x)|t|^{\kappa(x)-2}t + \psi(x,t)$$

with $\zeta \in L^\infty(\Delta)$ and the function $\psi : \overline{\Delta} \times \mathbb{R} \to \mathbb{R}$ satisfying the following conditions:
- (**g₁**) The function g is odd with respect to t, that is, $\psi(x,-t) = -\psi(x,t)$ for all $(x,t) \in \overline{\Delta} \times \mathbb{R}$;
  $\psi(x,t) = o(|t|^{\kappa(x)-1})$ when $|t| \to 0$ uniformly in x;
  $\psi(x,t) = o(|t|^{n(x)-1})$ when $|t| \to \infty$ uniformly in x.
- (**g₂**) $\psi(x,t) \leqq \frac{1}{\kappa_+}\psi(x,t)t$ for all $t \in \mathbb{R}$, and at almost every point $x \in \Delta$, where

$$\psi(x,t) = \int_0^t \psi(x,s)\,ds.$$

In addition, consider the following:
- (**H₁**) There exists $\overline{\gamma} > 0$ such that

$$\int_\Delta \left(\frac{1}{\kappa(x)} \left|{}^H\mathcal{D}_+^{\gamma,\beta;\chi}\varphi\right|^{\kappa(x)-2} - \zeta(x)|\varphi|^{n(x)} \right) dx \geqq \overline{\gamma} \int_\Delta \frac{1}{\kappa(x)} |\varphi|^{\kappa(x)}\,dx.$$

- (**H₂**) $\kappa(x) = \kappa_+$ for all $x \in \Gamma = \{x \in \Delta : \zeta(x) > 0\}$.

The derivative operator

$${}^H\mathcal{D}_-^{\gamma,\beta;\chi}\left(\left|{}^H\mathcal{D}_+^{\gamma,\beta;\chi}\varphi\right|^{\kappa(x)-2}\; {}^H\mathcal{D}_+^{\gamma,\beta;\chi}\varphi\right)$$

is a natural generalization of the operator

$${}^H\mathcal{D}_-^{\gamma,\beta;\chi}\left(\left|{}^H\mathcal{D}_+^{\gamma,\beta;\chi}\varphi\right|^{\kappa-2}\; {}^H\mathcal{D}_+^{\gamma,\beta;\chi}\varphi\right),$$

with $\kappa(x) = \kappa > 1$ being a real constant.

In recent years, there has been growing interest in the study of equations with growth conditions involving variable exponents. The study of such problems has been stimulated by their applications in elasticity [13], electro-rheological fluids [14,15] and image restoration [16]. Lebesgue spaces with variable exponents appeared for the first time as early as 1931 in the work of Orlicz [17]. Applications of this work include clutches, damper and rehabilitation equipment, and more [18–21].

Zhikov [13] was the first to work with the Lavrentiev phenomenon involving variational problems with variable exponents. His work motivated a great deal of research worldwide into variational and differential equations with variable exponent problems, including the works of, among others, Acerbi and Mingione [14], Alves [22,23], Alves and Ferreira [24,25], Antontsev and Shmarev [26], Bonder and Silva [27], Fu [28], Kovacik and Rakosnik [29], and Fan et al. [30,31].

In 2005, Chabrowski and Fu [32] considered the following $\kappa(x)$-Laplacian problem:

$$\begin{cases} -\mathrm{div}\left(\zeta(x)|\nabla\varphi|^{\kappa(x)-2}\nabla\varphi\right) + b(x)|\varphi|^{\kappa(x)-2}\varphi = \mathbf{F}(x,\varphi) & \text{in } \Delta \\ \varphi = 0 & \text{on } \partial\Delta, \end{cases}$$

where $1 < \kappa_1 \leqq b(x) \leqq \kappa_2 < n$, $\Delta \subset \mathbb{R}^n$ is bounded, $0 < \zeta_0 \leqq \zeta(x) \in L^\infty(\Delta)$ and $0 \leqq b_0 \leqq b(x) \in L^\infty(\Delta)$. In fact, Chabrowski and Fu [32] investigated the existence of solutions in $W_0^{1,\kappa(x)}(\Delta)$ in the superlinear and sublinear cases using the Mountain Pass Theorem (MPT). Subsequently, in 2016, Alves and Ferreira [25] discussed the existence of solutions for a class of quasi-linear problems involving variable exponents by applying the Ekeland variational principle and the Mountain Pass Theorem (MPT).

In 2022, Taarabti [33] investigated the existence of positive solutions of the following equation:

$$\begin{cases} \Delta_{\kappa(x)}\varphi + v|\varphi|^{\kappa(x)-2}\varphi = \lambda k(x)|\varphi|^{\gamma(x)-2} + s(x)|\varphi|^{\beta(x)-2}\varphi & \text{in } \Delta \\ \varphi = 0 \text{ on } \partial\Delta. \end{cases} \quad (3)$$

For further details about the parameters and functions of problem (3), see [33].

Over the years, interest in fractional differential equations involving variational techniques has been gaining remarkable popularity and attention from researchers. However, works in this direction remain very limited, especially those involving the χ-Hilfer fractional derivative operators (see [34–36]). The pioneering work involving the χ-Hilfer fractional derivative operator, the m-Laplacian, and the Nehari manifold was conducted by da Costa Sousa et al. [37] in 2018. We mention here that classical variational techniques have been applied in partial differential equations involving fractional derivatives; see, for example, [38–41].

Recently, Zhang and Zhang [42] investigated the properties of the following problem:

$$\begin{cases} (-\Delta_{\kappa(x)})^s \varphi = f(x) & \text{in } \Delta \\ \varphi = 0 \text{ on } \partial\Delta, \end{cases}$$

where $0 < s < 1$, $\kappa : \overline{\Delta} \times \overline{\Delta} \to (1, \infty)$ is a continuous function with $s\kappa(x,y) < N$ for any $(x,y) \in \overline{\Delta} \times \overline{\Delta}$ and $0 \leqq f \in L^1(\Delta)$.

Research on fractional Laplacian operators has been fairly productive in recent years. For example, in 2019 Xiang et al. [41] carried out interesting work on a multiplicity of solutions for the variable-order fractional Laplacian equation with variable growth using the MPT and Ekeland's variational principle. For other interesting results on multiplicity of solutions, see the works by Ayazoglu et al. [43], Xiang et al. [44], Colasuono et al. [45], and Mihailescu and Radulescu [46], as well as the references cited in each of these publications.

In 2021, Rahmoune and Biccari [47] investigated a multiplicity of solutions for the fractional Laplacian operator involving variable exponent nonlinearities of the type

$$(-\Delta)_{q(\cdot)}^{s(\cdot)}\varphi + \lambda V\varphi = \gamma|\varphi|^{p(\cdot)-2}\varphi + \beta|\varphi|^{p(\cdot)-2}u, \in \Delta,$$

with $\varphi = 0$ in $\mathbb{R}^n/\Delta$. Their results were obtained using the MPT and Ekeland's variational principle. Finally, several open and interesting problems about the existence and multiplicity of solutions were highlighted at the end of their paper [47] (see of the aforementioned recent related works [41,43–46] on the same subject).

In the year 2020, da Costa Sousa et al. [48] considered a mean curvature type problem involving a χ-H operator and variable exponents provided by

$$\begin{cases} {}^H\mathcal{L}_T^{\gamma,\beta;\chi}\xi(x) = \lambda f(x)|\xi(x)|^{n(x)-2}\xi(x) + g(x)|\xi(x)|^{s(x)-2}\xi(x) & \text{in } \Delta \\ \mathcal{I}_{0+}^{\beta(\beta-1);\chi}\xi(0) = \mathcal{I}_T^{\beta(\beta-1);\chi}\xi(T) = 0 & \text{on } \partial\Delta, \end{cases} \quad (4)$$

where

$$^H\mathcal{L}_T^{\gamma,\beta;\chi}\xi(x) := {}^H\mathcal{D}_T^{\gamma,\beta;\chi}\left[\left(1 + \frac{|{}^H\mathcal{D}_{0+}^{\gamma,\beta;\chi}\xi(x)|^{\kappa(x)}}{\sqrt{1 + |{}^H\mathcal{D}_{0+}^{\gamma,\beta;\chi}\xi(x)|^{2\kappa(x)}}}\right) \cdot \left|{}^H\mathcal{D}_{0+}^{\gamma,\beta;\chi}\xi(x)\right|^{\kappa(x)-2} {}^H\mathcal{D}_{0+}^{\gamma,\beta;\chi}\xi(x)\right]. \tag{5}$$

For further details about the parameters and functions of problem (5), see [48].

Motivated by the above-mentioned works, our main object in this paper is to investigate the multiplicity of solutions to problem (2) by applying the Concentration-Compactness Principle (CCP), the Mountain Pass Theorem (MPT) for paired functionals, and the genus theory. More precisely, we present the following theorem.

Theorem 1. *Suppose that a function g satisfies the conditions* (g_1) *and* (g_2) *and that the conditions* (p_1), (p_2), (H_1), *and* (H_2) *are satisfied. Then there exists a sequence* $\{\lambda_k\} \subset (0,+\infty)$ *with* $\lambda_k > \lambda_{k+1}$ *for all* $k \in \mathbb{N}$ *such that, for* $\lambda \in (\lambda_{k+1}, \lambda_k)$, *the problem* (2) *has at least k pairs of non-trivial solutions.*

The rest of this paper is organized as follows. In Section 2, we present important definitions results needed for the further development of the paper. In Section 3, we present technical lemmas and discuss the main result of the paper, that is, the multiplicity of solutions for a class of quasi-linear fractional-order problems in (2) via the Genus Theory, the Concentration-Compactness Principle, and the Mountain Pass Theorem (MPT). Finally, in Section 4, we conclude the paper by presenting several closing remarks and observations.

2. Mathematical Background and Auxiliary Results

Consider the space $L_+^\infty(\Delta)$ provided by

$$L_+^\infty(\Delta) := \left\{\varphi \in L^\infty(\Delta) : \operatorname*{ess\,inf}_{x \in \Delta} \varphi \geqq 1\right\}$$

and we assume that $s \in L_+^\infty(\Delta)$. For each $s \in L_+^\infty(\Delta)$, consider the numbers s_- and s_+ by

$$s_- = \operatorname*{ess\,inf}_\Delta h \quad \text{and} \quad s_+ = \operatorname*{ess\,sup}_\Delta h.$$

The Lebesgue space with the variable exponent $L^{s(x)}(\Delta)$ is defined as follows (see [27]):

$$L^{s(x)}(\Delta) = \left\{\varphi : \Delta \to \mathbb{R} \text{ is mensurable}: \int_\Delta |\varphi|^{s(x)}\,dx < \infty\right\},$$

which the norm

$$\|\varphi\|_{L^{s(x)}(\Delta)} = \inf\left\{\lambda > 0 : \int_\Delta \left|\frac{\varphi}{\lambda}\right|^{s(x)} dx \leqq 1\right\}. \tag{6}$$

On the space $L^{s(x)}(\Delta)$, we consider the modular function $\rho : L^{s(x)}(\Delta) \to \mathbb{R}$ defined by

$$\rho(\varphi) = \int_\Delta |\varphi|^{s(x)}\,dx.$$

Definition 1. *Let* $0 < \gamma \leqq 1, 0 \leqq \beta \leqq 1$ *and* $p \in C^+(\overline{\Delta})$. *The right-sided χ-fractional derivative space provided by* $\mathcal{H}_{\kappa(x)}^{\gamma,\beta;\chi} := \mathcal{H}_{\kappa(x)}^{\gamma,\beta;\chi}(\Delta)$ *is the closure of* $C_0^\infty(\Delta)$ *with the following norm:*

$$\|\varphi\|_{\mathcal{H}_{\kappa(x)}^{\gamma\beta;\chi}} = \inf\left\{\lambda > 0 : \int_\Delta \left|\frac{\varphi}{\lambda}\right|^{\kappa(x)} + \left|\frac{{}^H\mathcal{D}_+^{\gamma,\beta;\chi}\varphi}{\lambda}\right|^{\kappa(x)} dx \leqq 1\right\}$$

where ${}^H\mathcal{D}_+^{\gamma,\beta;\chi}(\cdot)$ is the right-sided χ-H with $0 < \gamma \leq 1$ and type $0 \leq \beta \leq 1$ as in (1), which is provided by

$$\mathcal{H}_{\kappa(x)}^{\gamma,\beta;\chi} := \left\{ \varphi \in L^{\kappa(x)}(\Delta) : {}^H\mathcal{D}_+^{\gamma,\beta;\chi} \varphi \in L^{\kappa(x)}(\Delta) \text{ and } \varphi(\Delta) = 0 \right\},$$

where the space $\mathcal{H}_{\kappa(x)}^{\gamma,\beta;\chi}(\Delta)$ is the closure of $C_0^\infty(\Delta)$.

Proposition 1 (see [37,49]). *Let $0 < \gamma \leq 1$, $0 \leq \beta \leq 1$ and $1 < \kappa(x) < \infty$. Then, for all $\varphi \in \mathcal{H}_{\kappa(x)}^{\gamma,\beta;\chi}(\Delta,\mathbb{R})$,*

$$\|\varphi\|_{L^{\kappa(x)}} \leq \frac{(\chi(T) - \chi(0))^\gamma}{\Gamma(\gamma+1)} \left\| {}^H\mathcal{D}_+^{\gamma,\beta;\chi} \varphi \right\|_{L^{\kappa(x)}}. \tag{7}$$

Remark 1. *In view of Inequality (7), we can consider the space $\mathcal{H}_{\kappa(x)}^{\gamma,\beta;\chi}(\Delta,\mathbb{R})$ with respect to the following equivalent norm:*

$$\|\varphi\| = \left\| {}^H\mathcal{D}_+^{\gamma,\beta;\chi} \varphi \right\|_{L^{\kappa(x)}}. \tag{8}$$

Proposition 2 (see [37,49]). *Let $0 < \gamma \leq 1$, $0 \leq \beta \leq 1$ and $1 < \kappa(x) < \infty$. Then, the space $\mathcal{H}_{\kappa(x)}^{\gamma,\beta;\chi}(\Delta;\mathbb{R})$ is a separable Banach space and is reflexive.*

Proposition 3 (see [27]). *Let $\varphi \in L^{s(x)}(\Delta)$. Then, each of the following assertions holds true:*
(1) *If $u \neq 0$, then $\|\varphi\|_{L^{s(x)}(\Delta)} = \lambda$ if and only if $\rho\left(\frac{\varphi}{\lambda}\right) = 1$;*
(2) *$\|\varphi\|_{L^{s(x)}(\Delta)} < 1 (= 1, > 1)$ if and only if $\rho(\varphi) < 1 (= 1, > 1)$;*
(3) *If $\|\varphi\|_{L^{s(x)}(\Delta)} > 1$, then $\|\varphi\|_{L^{s(x)}(\Delta)}^{s_-} \leq \rho(\varphi) \leq \|\varphi\|_{L^{s(x)}(\Delta)}^{s_+}$;*
(4) *If $\|\varphi\|_{L^{s(x)}(\Delta)} < 1$, then $\|\varphi\|_{L^{s(x)}(\Delta)}^{s_+} \leq \rho(\varphi) \leq \|\varphi\|_{L^{s(x)}(\Delta)}^{s_-}$.*

Proposition 4 (see [37,49]). *Let $\mathcal{H}_{\kappa(x)}^{\gamma,\beta;\chi}(\Delta)$ and $\{\varphi_n\} \subset \mathcal{H}_{\kappa(x)}^{\gamma,\beta;\chi}(\Delta)$. Then, the same conclusion as in* Proposition 3 *occurs when considering $\|\cdot\|$ and ρ_0.*

Corollary 1 (see [27]). *Let $\{\varphi_n\} \subset L^{s(x)}(\Delta)$. Then,*
(1) $\lim_{n \to \infty} \|\varphi\|_{L^{s(x)}(\Delta)} = 0$ *if and only if* $\lim_{n \to \infty} \rho(\varphi_n) = 0$.
(2) $\lim_{n \to \infty} \|(\varphi_n)\|_{L^{s(x)}(\Delta)} = \infty$ *if and only if* $\lim_{n \to +\infty} \rho(\varphi_n) = \infty$.

Proposition 5 (see [25,28], Hölder-Type Inequality). *Let $f \in L^{\kappa(x)}(\Delta)$ and $g \in L^{p'(x)}(\Delta)$. Then, the following holds true:*

$$\int_\Delta |f(x)g(x)|\, dx \leq C_p \|f\|_{L^{\kappa(x)}(\Delta)} \|g\|_{L^{p'(x)}(\Delta)}.$$

Lemma 1 (see [25,28]). *Let $h,r \in L_+^\infty(\Delta)$, with $s(x) \leq r(x)$ at almost every point $x \in \Delta$ and $\varphi \in L^{r(x)}(\Delta)$. Then, $|\varphi|^{s(x)} \in L^{\frac{r(x)}{s(x)}}(\Delta)$ and*

$$\left\| |\varphi|^{s(x)} \right\|_{L^{\frac{r(x)}{s(x)}}(\Delta)} \leq \|\varphi\|_{L^{r(x)}(\Delta)}^{s_+} + \|\varphi\|_{L^{r(x)}(\Delta)}^{s_-}$$

or equivalently,

$$\left\| |\varphi|^{s(x)} \right\|_{L^{\frac{r(x)}{s(x)}}(\Delta)} \leq \max\left\{ \|\varphi\|_{L^{r(x)}(\Delta)}^{s_+}, \|\varphi\|_{L^{r(x)}(\Delta)}^{s_-} \right\}.$$

Lemma 2 (see [25,28], Brezis-Lieb Lemma). *Let $\{\Psi_n\} \subset L^{s(x)}(\Delta,\mathbb{R}^m)$ with $m \in \mathbb{N}$. Then,*

(1) $\Psi_n(x) \to \Psi(x)$ at almost every point in $x \in \Delta$;
(2) $\sup_{n\in\mathbb{N}} |\Psi_n|_{L^{s(x)}(\Delta,\mathbb{R}^m)} < \infty$.

Furthermore, $\Psi \in L^{s(x)}(\Delta, \mathbb{R}^m)$ and

$$\int_\Delta \left(|\Psi_n|^{s(x)} - |\Psi_n - \Psi|^{s(x)} - |\Psi|^{s(x)} \right) dx = o_n(1).$$

Remark 2. In the space $\mathcal{H}^{\gamma,\beta;\chi}_{s(x)}(\Delta)$, we consider $\rho_1 : \mathcal{H}^{\gamma,\beta;\chi}_{s(x)}(\Delta) \to \mathbb{R}$ (modular function) provided by

$$\rho_1(\varphi) = \int_\Delta \left(\left|{}^{\mathrm{H}}\mathcal{D}^{\gamma,\beta;\chi}_+ \varphi\right|^{s(x)} + |\varphi|^{s(x)} \right) dx.$$

Remark 3. If we define

$$\|\varphi\|_1 := \inf \left\{ \int_\Delta \frac{\left(\left|{}^{\mathrm{H}}\mathcal{D}^{\gamma,\beta;\chi}_+ \varphi\right|^{s(x)} + |\varphi|^{s(x)} \right)}{t^{s(x)}} dx \leq 1 \right\}$$

then $\|\cdot\|_{\mathcal{H}^{\gamma,\beta;\chi}_{s(x)}(\Delta)}$ and $\|\cdot\|_1$ are equivalent norms in the space $\mathcal{H}^{\gamma,\beta;\chi}_{s(x)}(\Delta)$.

We now present several definitions and a version of the Lions' Compactness-Concentration Principle in the setting of the χ-H operator.

Definition 2 (see [50]). *A finite measure μ on Δ is a continuous linear functional over $C_0(\Delta)$, and the respective norm is defined by*

$$\|\mu\| := \sup_{\substack{\Phi \in C_0(\Delta) \\ \|\Phi\|_\infty = 1}} |\langle \mu, \Phi \rangle|,$$

with

$$\langle \mu, \Phi \rangle = \int_\Delta \Phi \, d\mu.$$

We denote by $\mathcal{M}(\Delta)$ and $\mathcal{M}^+(\Delta)$ the spaces of finite measures and positive finite measures over Δ, respectively. There are two important convergence properties in $\mathcal{M}(\Delta)$, as detailed below.

Definition 3 (see [50]). *A sequence $\mu_n \to \mu$ in $\mathcal{M}(\Delta)$ (strongly converges), if $\|\mu_n - \mu\| \to 0$.*

Definition 4 (see [50]). *A sequence $\mu_n \to \mu$ in $\mathcal{M}(\Delta)$ (weakly converges), if $\langle \mu_n, \Phi \rangle \to \langle \mu, \Phi \rangle$ for all $\Phi \in C_0(\Delta)$.*

Lemma 3 (see [20], Simon Inequality). *Let $x, y \in \mathbb{R}^N$. Then, there is a constant $C = C(\kappa)$ such that*

$$\left\langle |x|^{\kappa-2} x - |y|^{\kappa-2} y, x - y \right\rangle \geq \begin{cases} C \frac{|x-y|^2}{(|x|+|y|)^{2-\kappa}} & \text{if } 1 < \kappa < 2 \\ C|x-y|^\kappa & \text{if } \kappa \geq 2, \end{cases}$$

where $\langle \cdot, \cdot \rangle$ denotes the usual inner product in $\mathbb{R}^N$.

Lemma 4 (see [51], Strauss Compactness Lemma). *Let $\mathcal{P} : \mathbb{R}^N \times \mathbb{R} \to \mathbb{R}$ and $\mathcal{Q} : \mathbb{R}^N \times \mathbb{R} \to \mathbb{R}$ be continuous functions such that*

$$\sup_{x \in \mathbb{R}^N, |t| \leq a} |\mathcal{P}(x,t)| < \infty \quad \text{and} \quad \sup_{x \in \mathbb{R}^N, |t| \leq a} |\mathcal{Q}(x,t)| < \infty$$

for each $a > 0$. In addition, let $\lim_{|s| \to \infty} \frac{\mathcal{P}(x,s)}{\mathcal{Q}(x,s)} = 0$ uniformly in $x \in \mathbb{R}^N$. Suppose that $\{(\varphi_n)\}$ and v are measurable functions on $\mathbb{R}^N$ such that

$$\sup_n \int_{\mathbb{R}^N} |\mathcal{Q}(x, (\varphi_n))| \, dx < \infty$$

and

$$\lim_n \mathcal{P}(x, (\varphi_n)) = v \quad \text{at almost every point} \quad \text{in} \quad \mathbb{R}^N.$$

Then, for every bounded Borel set $\mathcal{B} \subset \mathbb{R}^N$,

$$\lim_n \int_{\mathcal{B}} |\mathcal{P}(x, (\varphi_n)) - v| \, dx = 0.$$

Moreover, if

$$\lim_{|s| \to \infty} \frac{\mathcal{P}(x,s)}{\mathcal{Q}(x,s)} = 0$$

uniformly in $x \in \mathbb{R}^N$ and

$$\lim_{|x| \to \infty} (\varphi_n) = 0$$

uniformly in n, then $\mathcal{P}(x, (\varphi_n)) \to v$ in $L^1(\mathbb{R}^N)$.

Lemma 5 (see [27]). *Let μ and ν be two non-negative and bounded measures on $\overline{\Delta}$ such that for $1 \leqq \kappa(x) < r(x) < \infty$ there exists a constant $c > 0$ satisfying the following inequality:*

$$\|\Xi\|_{L^{r(x)}_\nu(\Delta)} \leqq c \|\Xi\|_{L^{\kappa(x)}_\mu(\Delta)}.$$

Then, there exist $\{x_j\}_{j \in J} \subset \overline{\Delta}$ and $\{\nu_j\}_{j \in J} \subset (0, \infty)$ such that

$$\nu = \sum_i \nu_i \delta_{x_i}.$$

Proposition 6. *Let $m, n \in C(\overline{\Delta})$ such that $1 \leqq n(x) \leqq \kappa^*_\gamma(x)$ for all $x \in \overline{\Delta}$, and let the functions κ and n be log-Hölder continuous. Then, there is a continuous embedding $\mathcal{H}^{\gamma,\beta;\chi}_{\kappa(x)}(\Delta) \hookrightarrow L^{\kappa(x)}(\Delta)$.*

Lemma 6 (see [27]). *Let $\Xi_n \to \Xi$ a.e. and $\Xi_n \to \Xi$ in $L^{\kappa(x)}(\Delta)$. Then,*

$$\lim_{n \to \infty} \left(\int_\Delta |\Xi(x)|^{\kappa(x)} \, dx - \int_\Delta |\Xi(x) - \Xi_n(x)|^{\kappa(x)} \, dx \right) = \int_\Delta |\Xi(x)|^{\kappa(x)} \, dx.$$

Lemma 7 (sse [27]). *For the sequence $\{\nu_j\}_{j \in \mathbb{N}}$, let ν be a non-negative and finite Radon measure in Δ such that $\nu_j \to \nu$ weakly $*$ in the sense of measurement. Then,*

$$\|\Xi\|_{L^{n(x)}_{\nu_j}(\Delta)} \to \|\Xi\|_{L^{n(x)}_\nu(\Delta)} \quad \text{as} \quad j \to \infty$$

for all $\Xi \in C^\infty(\overline{\Delta})$.

Considering $\Xi \in C^\infty(\overline{\Delta})$, from the Poincaré inequality for variable exponents we obtain

$$\left\|\Xi(\varphi_j)\right\|_{L^{n(x)}(\Delta)} S \leqq \left\|{}^H\mathcal{D}_+^{\gamma,\beta;\chi}(\Xi(\varphi_j))\right\|_{L^{\kappa(x)}(\Delta)}. \quad (9)$$

If we take the limit as $j \to \infty$ in (9), from Lemma 7 we have

$$\|\Xi\|_{L^{n(x)}_\nu(\Delta)} S \leqq \|\Xi\|_{L^{\kappa(x)}_\mu(\Delta)}. \quad (10)$$

Theorem 2. *Let $q, r \in C(\Delta)$ be such that*

$$1 < n_- \leqq n_+ < N \quad \text{and} \quad 1 \leqq n(x) \leqq r^*(x)$$

in Δ with bounded domain of $\mathbb{R}^N$ with a smooth border. Also let $\{(\varphi_n)\}$ be a weakly convergent sequence in the space $\mathcal{H}^{\gamma,\beta;\chi}_{s(x)}(\Delta)$ with a weak limit φ such that

(1) $\left|{}^H\mathcal{D}_+^{\gamma,\beta;\chi}(\varphi_n)\right|^{r(x)} \rightharpoonup \mu$ *in* $\mathcal{M}(\Delta)$;

(2) $|(\varphi_n)|^{n(x)} \rightharpoonup \nu$ *in* $\mathcal{M}(\Delta)$.

Suppose further that $\varphi = \{x \in \Delta : n(x) = r^*(x)\}$ is non-empty. Then, for some countable set Λ,

$$\nu = |\varphi|^{n(x)} + \sum_{j \in \Lambda} \nu_j \delta_{x_j}, \quad \nu_j > 0,$$

$$\mu \geqq |{}^H\mathcal{D}_+^{\gamma,\beta;\chi}\varphi|^{r(x)} + \sum_{j \in \Lambda} \mu_j \delta_{x_j}, \quad \mu_j > 0$$

and

$$S\nu_j^{\frac{1}{r^*(x_j)}} \leqq S\mu_j^{\frac{1}{r(x_j)}} \quad \forall j \in \Lambda,$$

where $\{x_j\}_{j \in \Lambda} \subset \varphi$ and S is the best constant provided by

$$S = \inf_{\Xi \in C_0^\infty(\Delta)} \frac{\left\|{}^H\mathcal{D}_+^{\gamma,\beta;\chi}\Xi\right\|_{L^{r(x)}(\Delta)}}{\|\Xi\|_{L^{n(x)}(\Delta)}}.$$

Proof. Let $\Xi \in C^\infty(\Delta)$ and let $v_j = (\varphi_j) - \varphi$. Then, by using Lemma 6, we have

$$\lim_{j \to \infty} \left(\int_\Delta |\Xi|^{n(x)} |(\varphi_j)|^{n(x)} \, dx - \int_\Delta |\Xi|^{n(x)} |v_j|^{n(x)} \, dx \right) = \int_\Delta |\Xi|^{n(x)} |\varphi|^{n(x)} \, dx.$$

Moreover, by using the Hölder measure inequality (10) and Lemma 5 and after taking limits, we obtain the following representation:

$$\nu = |\varphi|^{n(x)} + \sum_{j \in I} \nu_j \delta_{x_j}.$$

Suppose that $x_1 \in \Delta / A$. Let $B = B(x_1, r) \subset\subset \Delta - A$. Then,

$$n(x) < \kappa_\gamma^*(x) - \delta$$

for some $\delta > 0$ in $\overline{B}$. Using Proposition 6, the embedding $\mathcal{H}^{\gamma,\beta;\chi}_{\kappa(x)}(B) \hookrightarrow L^{n(x)}(B)$ is compact. Therefore, $(\varphi_j) \to \varphi$ strongly in $L^{n(x)}(B)$, and thus $|(\varphi_j)|^{n(x)} \hookrightarrow |x|^{n(x)}$ strongly in $L^1(B)$. This is a contradiction to our assumption that $x_1 \in B$.

Next, by applying (9) to $\Xi(\varphi_j)$ and taking into account the fact that $(\varphi_j) \to \varphi$ in $L^{\kappa(x)}(\Delta)$, we find that

$$S\|\Xi\|_{L_v^{n(x)}(\Delta)} \leqq \|\Xi\|_{L_\mu^{n(x)}(\Delta)} + \left\|\left({}^H\mathcal{D}_+^{\gamma,\beta;\chi}\Xi\right)\varphi\right\|_{L^{\kappa(x)}(\Delta)}.$$

We consider $\Xi \in C_0^\infty(\mathbb{R}^N)$ such that $0 \leqq \Xi \leqq 1$ and assume that it is supported in the unit ball of $\mathbb{R}^N$. For a fixed $j \in I$, we let $\varepsilon > 0$ be arbitrary. We set $\Xi_{i_0,\varepsilon}(x) := \varepsilon^{-n}\Xi((x-x_j)\varepsilon)$. Then, decomposition of v yields

$$\rho_v(\Xi_{i_0,\varepsilon}) := \int_\Delta |\Xi_{i_0,\varepsilon}|^{n(x)}\,dx = \int_\Delta |\Xi_{i_0,\varepsilon}|^{n(x)}|\varphi|^{n(x)}\,dx + \sum_{i\in I} v_i \Xi_{i_0,\varepsilon}(x_i)^{q(x_i)} \geqq v_{i_0}.$$

We use

$$q_{i,\varepsilon}^+ := \sup_{B_\varepsilon(x_i)} n(x), \quad q_{i,\varepsilon}^- := \inf_{B_\varepsilon(x_i)} n(x), \quad p_{i,\varepsilon}^+ := \sup_{B_\varepsilon(x_i)} \kappa(x) \quad \text{and} \quad p_{i,\varepsilon}^- := \inf_{B_\varepsilon(x_i)} \kappa(x).$$

Then, if

$$\rho_v(\Xi_{i_0,\varepsilon}) < 1 \quad \text{and} \quad \rho_v(\Xi_{i_0,\varepsilon}) > 1,$$

it follows that

$$\|\Xi_{i_0,\varepsilon}\|_{L_v^{n(x)}(\Delta)} \geqq \rho_v(\Xi_{i_0,\varepsilon})^{\frac{1}{q_{i,\varepsilon}^-}} \geqq v_{i_0}^{\frac{1}{q_{i,\varepsilon}^-}}$$

and

$$\|\Xi_{i_0,\varepsilon}\|_{L_v^{n(x)}(\Delta)} \geqq \rho_v(\Xi_{i_0,\varepsilon})^{\frac{1}{q_{i,\varepsilon}^+}} \geqq v_{i_0}^{\frac{1}{q_{i,\varepsilon}^+}},$$

respectively. Consequently, we have

$$\max\left\{v_{i_0}^{\frac{1}{q_{i,\varepsilon}^-}}, v_{i_0}^{\frac{1}{q_{i,\varepsilon}^+}}\right\} S \leqq \|\Xi_{i,\varepsilon}\|_{L_\mu^{n(x)}(\Delta)} + \left\|\left({}^H\mathcal{D}_+^{\gamma,\beta;\chi}\Xi_{i,\varepsilon}\right)\varphi\right\|_{L^{\kappa(x)}(\Delta)}.$$

Thus, by means of Proposition 3 and Corollary 1, we have

$$\left\|\left({}^H\mathcal{D}_+^{\gamma,\beta;\chi}\Xi_{i,\varepsilon}\right)\varphi\right\|_{L^{\kappa(x)}(\Delta)}$$
$$\leqq \max\left\{\rho\left(\left({}^H\mathcal{D}_+^{\gamma,\beta;\chi}\Xi_{i,\varepsilon}\right)\varphi\right)^{\frac{1}{\kappa_-}}, \rho\left(\left({}^H\mathcal{D}_+^{\gamma,\beta;\chi}\Xi_{i,\varepsilon}\right)\varphi\right)^{\frac{1}{\kappa_+}}\right\}.$$

meaning that by using the Hölder inequality (see Proposition 5), it follows that

$$\rho\left(\left({}^H\mathcal{D}_+^{\gamma,\beta;\chi}\Xi_{i,\varepsilon}\right)\varphi\right) = \int_\Delta \left|{}^H\mathcal{D}_+^{\gamma,\beta;\chi}\Xi_{i,\varepsilon}\right|^{\kappa(x)} \|\varphi\|^{\kappa(x)}\,dx$$
$$\leqq \left\|\|\varphi\|^{\kappa(x)}\right\|_{L^{\gamma(x)}(B_\varepsilon(x_i))} \left\|\left|{}^H\mathcal{D}_+^{\gamma,\beta;\chi}\Xi_{i,\varepsilon}\right|^{\kappa(x)}\right\|_{L^{\gamma'(x)}(B_\varepsilon(x_i))},$$

where

$$\gamma(x) = \frac{n}{n-\kappa(x)} \quad \text{and} \quad \gamma'(x) = \frac{n}{\kappa(x)}.$$

Next, by applying the relation

$${}^H\mathcal{D}_+^{\gamma,\beta;\chi}(\Xi_{i,\varepsilon}) = {}^H\mathcal{D}_+^{\gamma,\beta;\chi}\Xi_{i,\varepsilon}\left(\frac{x-x_i}{\varepsilon}\right)\frac{1}{\varepsilon},$$

it follows that

$$\left\| \left| {}^H\mathcal{D}_+^{\gamma,\beta;\chi} \Xi_{i,\varepsilon} \right|^{\kappa(x)} \right\|_{L^{\gamma'(x)}(\mathcal{B}_\varepsilon(x_i))} \leq \max\left\{ \rho\left(\left| {}^H\mathcal{D}_+^{\gamma,\beta;\chi} \Xi_{i,\varepsilon} \right|^{\kappa(x)} \right)^{\frac{p^+}{n}}, \rho\left(\left| {}^H\mathcal{D}_+^{\gamma,\beta;\chi} \Xi_{i,\varepsilon} \right|^{\kappa(x)} \right)^{\frac{p^-}{n}} \right\}$$

and

$$\rho\left(\left| {}^H\mathcal{D}_+^{\gamma,\beta;\chi} \Xi_{i,\varepsilon} \right|^{\kappa(x)} \right) = \int_{\mathcal{B}_\varepsilon(x_i)} \left| {}^H\mathcal{D}_+^{\gamma,\beta;\chi} \Xi_{i,\varepsilon}\left(\frac{x - x_i}{\varepsilon}\right) \right|^n \frac{1}{\varepsilon^n} dx$$
$$= \int_{B_1(0)} \left| {}^H\mathcal{D}_+^{\gamma,\beta;\chi} \Xi_{i,\varepsilon}(y) \right|^n dy.$$

Thus, clearly, we have

$$ {}^H\mathcal{D}_+^{\gamma,\beta;\chi} \Xi_{i,\varepsilon} \varphi \to 0 $$

in $L^{\kappa(x)}(\Delta)$ (strongly). We note here that

$$\int_\Delta |\Xi_{i,\varepsilon}|^{\kappa(x)} d\mu \leq \mu(\mathcal{B}_\varepsilon(x_i)).$$

Therefore, we obtain

$$\|\Xi_{i,\varepsilon}\|_{L^{\kappa(x)}(\Delta)} \leq \max\left\{ \mu(\mathcal{B}_\varepsilon(x_i))^{\frac{1}{p_{i,\varepsilon}^+}}, \mu(\mathcal{B}_\varepsilon(x_i))^{\frac{1}{p_{i,\varepsilon}^-}} \right\},$$

meaning that

$$S \min\left\{ v_i^{\frac{1}{q_{i,\varepsilon}^+}}, v_i^{\frac{1}{q_{i,\varepsilon}^-}} \right\} \leq \max\left\{ \mu(\mathcal{B}_\varepsilon(x_i))^{\frac{1}{p_{i,\varepsilon}^+}}, \mu(\mathcal{B}_\varepsilon(x_i))^{\frac{1}{p_{i,\varepsilon}^-}} \right\}.$$

As κ and n are continuous functions and $n(x_i) = \kappa_\gamma^*(x_i)$, upon letting $\varepsilon \to \infty$, we obtain

$$S v_i^{\frac{1}{\kappa_\gamma^*(x_i)}} \leq \mu_i^{\frac{1}{p(x_i)}},$$

where

$$\mu_i := \lim_{\varepsilon \to \infty} \mu(\mathcal{B}_\varepsilon(x_i)).$$

Finally, we prove that

$$\mu \geq \left| {}^H\mathcal{D}_+^{\gamma,\beta;\chi} \varphi \right|^{\kappa(x)} + \sum \mu_i \delta_{x_i}.$$

In fact, we have $\mu \geq \sum \mu_i \delta_{x_i}$. As $(\varphi_j) \rightharpoonup \varphi$ in $\mathcal{H}_{\kappa(x)}^{\gamma,\beta;\chi}(\Delta)$ (weakly), ${}^H\mathcal{D}_+^{\gamma,\beta;\chi}(\varphi_j) \rightharpoonup {}^H\mathcal{D}_+^{\gamma,\beta;\chi} \varphi$ weakly in $L^{\kappa(x)}(\varphi)$ for all $U \subset \Delta$. From the weakly lower semi-continuity of the norm, we find that

$$d\mu \geq \left| {}^H\mathcal{D}_+^{\gamma,\beta;\chi} \varphi \right|^{\kappa(x)}.$$

As $\left| {}^H\mathcal{D}_+^{\gamma,\beta;\chi} \varphi \right|^{\kappa(x)}$ is orthogonal to μ, we arrive at the desired result. This completes the proof of Theorem 2. □

Definition 5. When E is an abstract Banach space and $\mathcal{I} \in C^1(E, \mathbb{R})$, we say that a sequence $\{v_n\}$ in E is a Palais-Smale (PS) sequence for $\mathcal{I}$ at level c. We denote this by (PS)$_c$ when $\mathcal{I}(v_n) \to c$

and $\mathcal{I}'(v_n) \to c$ in E^* as $n \to \infty$. We say that $\mathcal{I}$ satisfies the PS condition at level c when every sequence $(PS)_c$ has a subsequence convergent in E.

Theorem 3 (see [52]). *Let $\mathbf{U}$ and $\mathbf{V}$ be an infinite-dimensional space and a finite-dimensional space ($\mathbf{U}$ being a Banach space), respectively, with*

$$\mathbf{U} = \mathbf{V} \oplus \mathbf{W} \quad \text{and} \quad \mathcal{I} \in C^1(\mathbf{U}, \mathbb{R})$$

being an even functional with $\mathcal{I}(0) = 0$ satisfying the following conditions:
- $(\mathbf{I_1})$ *There are constants $\delta, \sigma > 0$ such that $\mathcal{I}(\varphi) \geqq \delta > 0$ for each $\varphi \in \partial B_\sigma \cap \mathbf{W}$;*
- $(\mathbf{I_2})$ *There exists $\varphi > 0$ such that $\mathcal{I}$ satisfies the condition $(PS)_c$ for $0 < c < \varphi$;*
- $(\mathbf{I_3})$ *For each subspace, $\widetilde{\mathbf{U}} \subset \mathbf{U}$ exists with*

$$\mathbf{R} = \mathbf{R}(\widetilde{\mathbf{U}}) > 0$$

such that

$$\mathcal{I}(\varphi) \leqq 0 \quad (\forall \, \varphi \in \widetilde{\mathbf{U}} \setminus B_{\mathbf{R}}(0)).$$

Suppose that $\{e_1, \cdots, e_k\}$ is a basis for the vector space $\mathbf{V}$. For $m \geq k$, choose inductively $e_{m+1} \notin \mathbf{U}_m := \operatorname{span}\{e_1, \cdots, e_m\}$. Let $\mathbf{R}_m = \mathbf{R}(\mathbf{U}_m)$ and $D_m = B_{\mathbf{R}_m}(0) \cap \mathbf{U}_m$. Define the following sets:

$$G_m := \{s \in C(D_m, \mathbf{U}) : h \text{ is odd and } s(\varphi) = \varphi, \, \forall \varphi \in \partial B_{\mathbf{R}_m}(0) \cap \mathbf{U}_m\}$$

and

$$\Gamma_j := \left\{ s(\overline{D_m \setminus \Xi}) : s \in G_m, m \geqq j, \Xi \in \Sigma \text{ and } q(\Xi) \leqq m - j \right\},$$

where Σ is the family of the sets $\Xi \subset \mathbf{U} \setminus \{0\}$ such that Ξ is closed in $\mathbf{U}$ and symmetric with respect to 0; that is,

$$\Sigma = \{\Xi \subset \mathbf{U} \setminus \{0\} : \Xi \text{ is closed in } \mathbf{U} \text{ and } \Xi = -\Xi\}$$

and $q(\Xi)$ is the gender of $\Xi \in \Sigma$. For each $j \in \mathbb{N}$, define

$$\epsilon_j := \inf_{K \in \Gamma_j} \max_{\varphi \in K} I(\varphi).$$

If $0 < \beta \leqq \epsilon_j \leqq \epsilon_{j+1}$ for $j > k$ and, if $j > k$ and $\epsilon_j < \varphi$, then ϵ_j is a critical value for $\mathcal{I}$. Furthermore, if

$$\epsilon_j = \epsilon_{j+1} = \cdots = \epsilon_{j+l} = \epsilon < \varphi \quad (j > k),$$

then $q(K_\epsilon) \geqq l + 1$, where

$$K_\epsilon := \{\varphi \in \mathbf{U} : \mathcal{I}(\varphi) = \epsilon \text{ and } I'(\varphi) = 0\}.$$

3. Main Results

Consider the following energy functional of (2) provided by

$$\mathcal{E}_\lambda : \mathcal{H}_{\kappa(x)}^{\gamma,\beta;\chi}(\Delta) \to \mathbb{R},$$

which is defined by

$$\mathcal{E}_\lambda(\varphi) = \int_\Delta \frac{1}{\kappa(x)} \left| {}^H\mathcal{D}_+^{\gamma,\beta;\chi} \varphi \right|^{\kappa(x)} dx - \lambda \int_\Delta \frac{1}{n(x)} |\varphi|^{n(x)} \, dx - \int_\Delta \frac{\zeta(x)}{\kappa(x)} |\varphi|^{\kappa(x)} \, dx - \int_\Delta \psi(x, \varphi) \, dx.$$

Thus, using condition $(\mathbf{g_1})$, it is shown that

$$\mathcal{E}_\lambda \in C^1\left(\mathcal{H}_{\kappa(x)}^{\gamma,\beta;\chi}(\Delta), \mathbb{R}\right)$$

with

$$\mathcal{E}'_\lambda(\varphi)v = \int_\Delta \left|{}^H\mathcal{D}_+^{\gamma,\beta;\chi}\varphi\right|^{\kappa(x)-2} {}^H\mathcal{D}_+^{\gamma,\beta;\chi}\varphi \, {}^H\mathcal{D}_+^{\gamma,\beta;\chi}v \, dx$$
$$- \lambda \int_\Delta |\varphi|^{n(x)-2}\varphi v \, dx - \int_\Delta \zeta(x)|\varphi|^{\kappa(x)-2}\varphi v \, dx$$
$$- \int_\Delta \psi(x,\varphi)v \, dx$$

for all $\varphi, v \in \mathcal{H}_{\kappa(x)}^{\gamma,\beta;\chi}(\Delta)$. Therefore, the critical points of the energy functional $\mathcal{E}_\lambda(\cdot)$ are solutions to problem (2).

In our first result in this section (Lemma 8 below), we prove that the functional $\mathcal{E}_\lambda(\cdot)$ satisfies the first geometry of the MPT for even functionals.

Lemma 8. *Under conditions* $(\mathbf{H_1})$ *and* $(\mathbf{g_1})$, $\mathcal{E}_\lambda(\cdot)$ *satisfies hypothesis* $(\mathbf{I_1})$ *of Theorem* 3.

Proof. Given $\delta > 0$, we obtain

$$\int_\Delta \frac{1}{\kappa(x)} \left(\left|{}^H\mathcal{D}_+^{\gamma,\beta;\chi}\varphi\right|^{\kappa(x)} - \zeta(x)|\varphi|^{\kappa(x)} \right) dx$$
$$= \frac{1}{1+\delta} \int_\Delta \frac{1}{\kappa(x)} \left(\left|{}^H\mathcal{D}_+^{\gamma,\beta;\chi}\varphi\right|^{\kappa(x)} - \zeta(x)|\varphi|^{\kappa(x)} \right) dx$$
$$+ \frac{\delta}{1+\delta} \int_\Delta \frac{1}{\kappa(x)} \left|{}^H\mathcal{D}_+^{\gamma,\beta;\chi}\varphi\right|^{\kappa(x)} dx - \frac{\delta}{1+\delta} \int_\Delta \frac{1}{\kappa(x)} \zeta(x)|\varphi|^{\kappa(x)} \, dx.$$

From condition $(\mathbf{H_1})$, it follows that

$$\int_\Delta \frac{1}{\kappa(x)} \left(\left|{}^H\mathcal{D}_+^{\gamma,\beta;\chi}\varphi\right|^{\kappa(x)} - \zeta(x)|\varphi|^{\kappa(x)} \right) dx$$
$$\geq \frac{\overline{\gamma}}{1+\delta} \int_\Delta \frac{|\varphi|^{\kappa(x)}}{\kappa(x)} + \frac{\delta}{1+\delta} \int_\Delta \frac{1}{\kappa(x)} \left|{}^H\mathcal{D}_+^{\gamma,\beta;\chi}\varphi\right|^{\kappa(x)} dx$$
$$- \frac{\delta}{1+\delta} \int_\Delta \frac{1}{\kappa(x)} \zeta(x)|\varphi|^{\kappa(x)} \, dx$$
$$\geq \frac{\delta}{1+\delta} \int_\Delta \frac{1}{\kappa(x)} \left|{}^H\mathcal{D}_+^{\gamma,\beta;\chi}\varphi\right|^{\kappa(x)} dx + \frac{1}{1+\delta} \int_\Delta \left(\frac{\overline{\gamma}}{\kappa_+} - \frac{\delta \zeta(x)}{\kappa_-} \right) |\varphi|^{\kappa(x)} \, dx.$$

For a sufficiently small δ, provided that $\zeta(x) \in L^\infty(\Delta)$, we can assume that

$$\frac{1}{1+\delta} \left(\frac{\overline{\gamma}}{\kappa_+} - \frac{\delta \zeta(x)}{\kappa_-} \right) \geq \frac{1}{1+\delta} \left(\frac{\overline{\gamma}}{\kappa_+} - \frac{\delta \|\zeta\|_{L^\infty(\Delta)}}{\kappa_-} \right) = \overline{\gamma}_0 > 0.$$

Therefore, for all $\varphi \in \mathcal{H}_{\kappa(x)}^{\gamma,\beta;\chi}(\Delta)$, we find that

$$\int_\Delta \frac{1}{\kappa(x)} \left(\left|{}^H\mathcal{D}_+^{\gamma,\beta;\chi}\varphi\right|^{\kappa(x)} - \zeta(x)|\varphi|^{\kappa(x)} \right) dx$$
$$\geq \frac{\delta}{1+\delta} \int_\Delta \frac{1}{\kappa(x)} \left|{}^H\mathcal{D}_+^{\gamma,\beta;\chi}\varphi\right|^{\kappa(x)} dx + \overline{\gamma}_0 \int_\Delta |\varphi|^{\kappa(x)} \, dx. \tag{11}$$

For the sake of verifying the above developments, given $\varepsilon > 0$, there exists $C_\varepsilon > 0$ such that

$$|\psi(x,t)| \leq \frac{\varepsilon}{\kappa(x)}|t|^{\kappa(x)} + \frac{C_\varepsilon}{n(x)}|t|^{n(x)} \; \forall \, (x,t) \in \overline{\Delta} \times \mathbb{R}. \tag{12}$$

Indeed, from hypothesis (g_1) we know that

$$\psi(x,t) = o(|t|^{n(x)-1}) \quad \text{when} \quad |t| \to \infty$$

uniformly in x. Thus, given $\varepsilon > 0$, there is a number $R = R(\varepsilon) > 0$ such that $|\psi(x,t)| \leq \varepsilon |t|^{n(x)-1}$ for all $x \in \overline{\Delta}$ and $|t| \geq R$.

By continuity and from the inequalities above, there exists $\mathbf{M} > 0$ such that

$$|\psi(x,t)| \leq \mathbf{M} + \varepsilon |t|^{n(x)-1} \ \forall \ (x,t) \in \overline{\Delta} \times \mathbb{R}.$$

Again, it follows from condition (g_1) that, given $\varepsilon > 0$, $\exists \delta = \delta(\varepsilon) > 0$, satisfying

$$|\psi(x,t)| \leq \varepsilon |t|^{n(x)-1} \ \forall \ (x,t) \in \overline{\Delta} \times [-\delta, \delta]. \tag{13}$$

We can now assume that $\delta < 1$. Therefore, for $|t| \geq \delta$, we have $|t|^{n(x)-1} \geq \delta^{n_+ - 1}$, such that

$$\frac{|\psi(x,t)|}{|t|^{n(x)-1}} \leq \frac{\mathbf{M}}{|t|^{n(x)-1}} + \varepsilon \leq \frac{\mathbf{M}}{|\delta|^{n_+ - 1}} + \varepsilon = C_\varepsilon \ \forall \ x \in \overline{\Delta} \text{ and } |t| \geq \delta. \tag{14}$$

Thus, from Inequalities (13) and (14) we obtain

$$|\psi(x,t)| \leq \varepsilon |t|^{\kappa(x)-1} + C_\varepsilon |t|^{n(x)-1} \ \forall \ (x,t) \in \overline{\Delta} \times \mathbb{R},$$

which leads to the statement to be verified.

Next, using the definition of $\mathcal{E}_\lambda(\cdot)$ and the Equations (11) and (12), we obtain

$$\mathcal{E}_\lambda(\varphi) \geq \frac{\delta}{(1+\delta)\kappa_+} \int_\Delta \left|{}^H\mathcal{D}_+^{\gamma,\beta;\chi}\varphi\right|^{\kappa(x)} dx + \left(\gamma_0 - \frac{\varepsilon}{\kappa_-}\right) \int_\Delta |\varphi|^{\kappa(x)} dx$$
$$- \frac{(\lambda + C_\varepsilon)}{n_-} \int_\Delta |\varphi|^{n(x)} dx.$$

Consequently, if ε is small enough and $\|\varphi\| \leq 1$, from Proposition 4 we find that

$$\mathcal{E}_\lambda(\varphi) \geq \frac{\delta}{(1+\delta)\kappa_+} \left\|{}^H\mathcal{D}_+^{\gamma,\beta;\chi}\varphi\right\|_{L^{\kappa(x)}(\Delta)}^{\kappa_+} - \frac{(\lambda + C_\varepsilon)}{n_-} \int_\Delta |\varphi|^{n(x)} dx.$$

Using Sobolev embeddings, there exists $\epsilon_1 > 0$ such that

$$\|\varphi\|_{L^{n(x)}(\Delta)} \leq \epsilon_1 \|\varphi\|_{\mathcal{H}_{\kappa(x)}^{\gamma,\beta;\chi}(\Delta)}, \ \forall \ \varphi \in \mathcal{H}_{\kappa(x)}^{\gamma,\beta;\chi}(\Delta).$$

Thus, if we apply Proposition 3, we obtain

$$\mathcal{E}_\lambda(\varphi) \geq c_3 \|\varphi\|_{\mathcal{H}_{\kappa(x)}^{\gamma,\beta;\chi}(\Delta)}^{\kappa_+} - c_4 \|\varphi\|_{\mathcal{H}_{\kappa(x)}^{\gamma,\beta;\chi}(\Delta)}^{n_-}$$

for the positive constants ϵ_2, c_3, and c_4. Because $\kappa_+ < n_-$ if $\|\varphi\|_{\mathcal{H}_{\kappa(x)}^{\gamma,\beta;\chi}(\Delta)} = \sigma > 0$ is sufficiently small, $\exists \widetilde{\beta} > 0$ such that

$$\mathcal{E}_\lambda(\varphi) \geq \widetilde{\beta} > 0, \ \forall \ \varphi \in \partial B_\sigma(0).$$

We have thus completed the proof of Lemma 8. □

Lemma 9. *Under the conditions ($\mathbf{H_1}$) and (g_1), $\mathcal{E}_\lambda(\cdot)$ satisfies the condition ($\mathbf{I_3}$).*

Proof. Let $\widetilde{E}$ be a sub-space of $\mathcal{H}_{\kappa(x)}^{\gamma,\beta;\chi}(\Delta)$ of a finite dimension.

For verification of the above statement, given $\varepsilon > 0$, there is a constant $\mathbf{M} > 0$ satisfying
$$\mathbf{F}(x,t) \geq -\mathbf{M} - \varepsilon |t|^{n(x)} \quad \forall \, (x,t) \in \overline{\Delta} \times \mathbb{R}. \tag{15}$$

In fact, we have
$$\frac{f(x,t)}{|t|^{n(x)-1}} \leq |\zeta(x)| \frac{|t|^{\kappa(x)-1}}{|t|^{n(x)-1}} + \frac{|\psi(x,t)|}{|t|^{n(x)-1}} \to 0$$

when $|t| \to \infty$. Hence, given $\varepsilon > 0$, $\exists R_0 > 0$ such that $|f(x,t)| \leq \varepsilon |t|^{n(x)-1}$ for all $x \in \overline{\Delta}$ and $|t| \geq R_0$. Moreover, because f is continuous, it follows that
$$|f(x,t)| \leq \mathbf{M} + \varepsilon |t|^{n(x)-1} \quad \forall \, x \in \overline{\Delta} \times \mathbb{R}$$

for some positive constant $\mathbf{M}_0$. Thus, we have
$$\frac{|\mathbf{F}(x,t)|}{|t|^{n(x)}} \leq \frac{\mathbf{M}_0}{|t|^{n(x)-1}} + \frac{\varepsilon}{n_-} = o(1) \text{ with } |t| \to \infty.$$

Furthermore, given $\varepsilon > 0$, $\exists R > 0$ such that
$$|\mathbf{F}(x,t)| \leq \varepsilon |t|^{n(x)} \quad \forall \, x \in \overline{\Delta} \text{ and } |t| \geq R.$$

By continuity, there is a constant $\mathbf{M} > 0$ such that $\mathbf{F}(x,t) \geq -\mathbf{M}$ for all $x \in \overline{\Delta}$ and $|t| \leq R$. Therefore, we obtain
$$\mathbf{F}(x,t) \geq -\mathbf{M} - \varepsilon |t|^{n(x)} \quad \forall \, (x,t) \in \overline{\Delta} \times \mathbb{R},$$

thereby proving the claim.

Using Inequality (15) and $\mathcal{E}_\lambda(\cdot)$, we have
$$\mathcal{E}_\lambda(\varphi) \leq \frac{1}{\kappa_-} \int_\Delta \left|{}^{\mathrm{H}}\mathcal{D}_+^{\gamma,\beta;\chi} u\right|^{\kappa(x)} dx - \frac{\lambda}{n_+} \int_\Delta |\varphi|^{n(x)} dx + \varepsilon \int_\Delta |\varphi|^{n(x)} dx + \mathbf{M}|\Delta|.$$

Now, upon setting
$$\varepsilon = \frac{\lambda}{2n_+},$$

we can conclude that
$$\mathcal{E}_\lambda(\varphi) \leq \frac{1}{\kappa_-} \int_\Delta \left|{}^{\mathrm{H}}\mathcal{D}_+^{\gamma,\beta;\chi} \varphi\right|^{\kappa(x)} dx - \frac{\lambda}{2n_+} \int_\Delta |\varphi|^{n(x)} dx + \mathbf{M}|\Delta|.$$

By applying Proposition 3, it follows that
$$\mathcal{E}_\lambda(\varphi) \leq \frac{1}{\kappa_-} \max\left\{\|\varphi\|_{\mathcal{H}_{\kappa(x)}^{\gamma,\beta;\chi}(\Delta)}^{\kappa_-}, \|\varphi\|_{\mathcal{H}_{\kappa(x)}^{\gamma,\beta;\chi}(\Delta)}^{\kappa_+}\right\} - \frac{\lambda}{2n_+} \min\left\{\|\varphi\|_{\mathcal{H}_{\kappa(x)}^{\gamma,\beta;\chi}(\Delta)}^{n_-}, \|\varphi\|_{\mathcal{H}_{\kappa(x)}^{\gamma,\beta;\chi}(\Delta)}^{n_+}\right\} + \mathbf{M}|\Delta|.$$

Because $\dim \widetilde{E} < \infty$, any two norms in $\widetilde{E}$ are equivalent, and thus $\exists c > 0$ (constant) such that
$$\mathcal{E}_\lambda(\varphi) \leq \frac{1}{\kappa_-} \max\left\{\|\varphi\|_{\mathcal{H}_{\kappa(x)}^{\gamma,\beta;\chi}(\Delta)}^{\kappa_-}, \|\varphi\|_{\mathcal{H}_{\kappa(x)}^{\gamma,\beta;\chi}(\Delta)}^{\kappa_+}\right\} - \frac{\lambda c}{2n_+} \min\left\{\|\varphi\|_{\mathcal{H}_{\kappa(x)}^{\gamma,\beta;\chi}(\Delta)}^{n_-}, \|\varphi\|_{\mathcal{H}_{\kappa(x)}^{\gamma,\beta;\chi}(\Delta)}^{n_+}\right\} + \mathbf{M}|\Delta|.$$

Moreover, as $\kappa_+ < n_-$, we have
$$\Psi(s) = \frac{s^{\kappa_+}}{\kappa_-} - \frac{\lambda c s^{q_-}}{2n_+} \to -\infty$$

when $s \to \infty$. Consequently, for a sufficiently large $R > 0$, the last inequality implies that

$$\mathcal{E}_\lambda(\varphi) \leqq \frac{\|\varphi\|^{m_+}_{\mathcal{H}^{\gamma,\beta;\chi}_{\kappa(x)}(\Delta)}}{\kappa_-} - \frac{\lambda c \|\varphi\|^{n_-}_{\mathcal{H}^{\gamma,\beta;\chi}_{\kappa(x)}(\Delta)}}{2n_+} + \mathbf{M}|\Delta| < 0$$

for all $\varphi \in \widetilde{E}$ with $\|\varphi\| \geqq R$. Hence, $\mathcal{E}_\lambda(\cdot) < 0$ over $\widetilde{E} \setminus B_R(0)$. □

We now establish a compactness condition for the functional $\mathcal{E}_\lambda(\cdot)$. We prove that the (PS) condition holds true below a certain level, provided that the parameter λ is less than 1.

Lemma 10. *Let the conditions* $(\mathbf{H_1})$, $(\mathbf{g_1})$, *and* $(\mathbf{g_2})$ *be satisfied. Then, every sequence (PS) for the functional* $\mathcal{E}_\lambda(\cdot)$ *is bounded in* $\mathcal{H}^{\gamma,\beta;\chi}_{\kappa(x)}(\Delta)$.

Proof. Let $\{(\varphi_n)\}$ be a sequence $(PS)_c$ for the functional $\mathcal{E}_\lambda(\cdot)$. Then,

$$\mathcal{E}_\lambda(\varphi_n) \to c \text{ and } \mathcal{E}'_\lambda(\varphi_n) \to 0 \text{ when } n \to \infty. \tag{16}$$

We note that

$$\lambda \int_\Delta \left(\frac{1}{\kappa_+} - \frac{1}{n(x)}\right) |(\varphi_n)|^{n(x)}\, dx$$
$$= \mathcal{E}_\lambda(\varphi_n) - \frac{1}{\kappa_+}\mathcal{E}'_\lambda(\varphi_n)(\varphi_n) + \int_\Delta \left(\frac{1}{\kappa_+} - \frac{1}{\kappa(x)}\right) \left|{}^H\mathcal{D}^{\gamma,\beta;\chi}_+(\varphi_n)\right|^{\kappa(x)}\, dx$$
$$+ \int_\Delta \left(\frac{1}{\kappa(x)} - \frac{1}{\kappa_+}\right) \zeta(x) |(\varphi_n)|^{\kappa(x)}\, dx$$
$$- \int_\Delta \left(G(x,(\varphi_n)) - \frac{1}{\kappa_+} g(x,(\varphi_n))(\varphi_n)\right) dx.$$

In the above equality, using the hypotheses $(\mathbf{g_2})$ and (16), we obtain

$$\lambda \int_\Delta \left(\frac{1}{\kappa_+} - \frac{1}{n_-}\right) |(\varphi_n)|^{n(x)}\, dx$$
$$\leqq \lambda \int_\Delta \left(\frac{1}{\kappa_+} - \frac{1}{n(x)}\right) |(\varphi_n)|^{n(x)}\, dx$$
$$\leqq c + 1 + \|(\varphi_n)\|_{\mathcal{H}^{\gamma,\beta;\chi}_{\kappa(x)}(\Delta)} + \|a\|_\infty \int_\Delta \left(\frac{1}{\kappa_-} - \frac{1}{\kappa_+}\right) |(\varphi_n)|^{\kappa(x)}\, dx \tag{17}$$

for sufficiently large n. Provided $\varepsilon > 0$, note that $\exists C_\varepsilon > 0$ such that

$$|t|^{\kappa(x)} \leqq \varepsilon |t|^{n(x)} + C_\varepsilon \ \forall \ (x,t) \in \Delta \times \mathbb{R}.$$

Upon combining the last inequality with (17), we obtain

$$\lambda \left(\frac{1}{\kappa_+} - \frac{1}{n_-}\right) \int_\Delta |(\varphi_n)|^{n(x)}\, dx$$
$$\leqq c + 1 + \|(\varphi_n)\|_{\mathcal{H}^{\gamma,\beta;\chi}_{\kappa(x)}(\Delta)} + \varepsilon \|a\|_\infty \left(\frac{1}{\kappa_-} - \frac{1}{\kappa_+}\right) \int_\Delta |(\varphi_n)|^{n(x)}\, dx$$
$$+ \|a\|_\infty \left(\frac{1}{\kappa_-} - \frac{1}{\kappa_+}\right) C_\varepsilon |\Delta|,$$

which implies that

$$\left[\lambda \left(\frac{1}{\kappa_+} - \frac{1}{n_-}\right) - \|a\|_\infty \left(\frac{1}{\kappa_-} - \frac{1}{\kappa_+}\right) \varepsilon\right] \int_\Delta |(\varphi_n)|^{n(x)}\, dx \leqq c + 1 + \|(\varphi_n)\|_{\mathcal{H}^{\gamma,\beta;\chi}_{\kappa(x)}(\Delta)} + c_5,$$

where c_5 is a positive constant. If we set

$$\varepsilon = \frac{\lambda}{2}\left(\frac{1}{\kappa_+} - \frac{1}{n_-}\right)\left[\|a\|_\infty\left(\frac{1}{\kappa_-} - \frac{1}{\kappa_+}\right)\right]^{-1},$$

we obtain

$$\frac{\lambda}{2}\left(\frac{1}{\kappa_+} - \frac{1}{q_-}\right)\int_\Delta |(\varphi_n)|^{n(x)}\, dx \leqq c + 1 + \|(\varphi_n)\|_{\mathcal{H}^{\gamma,\beta;\chi}_{\kappa(x)}(\Delta)} + c_5,$$

which yields

$$\int_\Delta |(\varphi_n)|^{n(x)}\, dx \leqq c_6\left(1 + \|(\varphi_n)\|_{\mathcal{H}^{\gamma,\beta;\chi}_{\kappa(x)}(\Delta)}\right).$$

Now, using the definition of $\mathcal{E}_\lambda(\cdot)$ together with (11), we obtain

$$\frac{\delta}{(1+\delta)\kappa_+}\int_\Delta \left|{}^H\mathcal{D}^{\gamma,\beta;\chi}_+(\varphi_n)\right|^{\kappa(x)}\, dx \leqq \mathcal{E}_\lambda(\varphi_n) + \lambda\int_\Delta \frac{|(\varphi_n)|^{n(x)}}{n(x)}\, dx + \int_\Delta G(x,(\varphi_n))\, dx.$$

Of the growth conditions over g, given $\varepsilon > 0$, there exists $C_\varepsilon > 0$ such that

$$|\psi(x,t)| \leqq \varepsilon|t|^{n(x)} + C_\varepsilon$$

for all $x \in \overline{\Delta}$ and $t \in \mathbb{R}$, meaning that

$$\frac{\delta}{(1+\delta)\kappa_+}\int_\Delta \left|{}^H\mathcal{D}^{\gamma,\beta;\chi}_+(\varphi_n)\right|^{\kappa(x)}\, dx$$

$$\leqq c + o_n(1) + \frac{\lambda}{n_-}\int_\Delta |(\varphi_n)|^{n(x)}\, dx + \varepsilon\int_\Delta |(\varphi_n)|^{n(x)}\, dx + C_\varepsilon|\Delta|$$

$$\leqq c + o_n(1) + \left(\frac{\lambda}{n_-} + \varepsilon\right)c_6(1 + \|(\varphi_n)\|_{\mathcal{H}^{\gamma,\beta;\chi}_{\kappa(x)}(\Delta)}) + C_\varepsilon|\Delta|.$$

Therefore, for sufficiently large n, we have

$$\int_\Delta \left|{}^H\mathcal{D}^{\gamma,\beta;\chi}_+(\varphi_n)\right|^{\kappa(x)}\, dx \leqq c_7\left(1 + \|(\varphi_n)\|_{\mathcal{H}^{\gamma,\beta;\chi}_{\kappa(x)}(\Delta)}\right),$$

where c_7 is a positive constant. If

$$\|(\varphi_n)\|_{\mathcal{H}^{\gamma,\beta;\chi}_{\kappa(x)}(\Delta)} > 1,$$

then it follows from Proposition 4 that

$$\|(\varphi_n)\|^{\kappa_-}_{\mathcal{H}^{\gamma,\beta;\chi}_{\kappa(x)}(\Delta)} \leqq c_7\left(1 + \|(\varphi_n)\|_{\mathcal{H}^{\gamma,\beta;\chi}_{\kappa(x)}(\Delta)}\right).$$

Finally, as $\kappa_- > 1$, the above inequality implies that $\{(\varphi_n)\}$ is bounded in $\mathcal{H}^{\gamma,\beta;\chi}_{\kappa(x)}(\Delta)$. We have thus completed the proof of Lemma 10. □

From the reflexivity of $\mathcal{H}^{\gamma,\beta;\chi}_{\kappa(x)}(\Delta)$, if $\{(\varphi_n)\}$ is a sequence (PS)$_c$ for $\mathcal{E}_\lambda(\cdot)$, then up to subsequence $(\varphi_n) \rightharpoonup \varphi$ in $\mathcal{H}^{\gamma,\beta;\chi}_{\kappa(x)}(\Delta)$. As the immersion of $\mathcal{H}^{\gamma,\beta;\chi}_{\kappa(x)}(\Delta)$ in $L^{n(x)}(\Delta)$ is continuous, $(\varphi_n) \rightharpoonup \varphi$ in $L^{n(x)}(\Delta)$. On the other hand, the immersion $\mathcal{H}^{\gamma,\beta;\chi}_{\kappa(x)}(\Delta)$ in $L^{r(x)}(\Delta)$ is compact for $1 < r_- \leqq r \ll \kappa^*_\gamma$.

Consequently, $(\varphi_n) \to \varphi$ in $L^{\kappa(x)}(\Delta)$. From the CCP, for Lebesgue spaces with variable exponents (see Theorem 2) there are two non-negative measures $\mu, \nu \in \mathcal{M}(\Delta)$, a countable set Λ, points $\{x_j\}_{j \in J}$ in Λ, and sequences $\{\mu_j\}_{j \in J}$ and $\{\nu_j\}_{j \in J} \subset [0, \infty)$, and thus we have

$$|{}^H\mathcal{D}_+^{\gamma,\beta;\chi}(\varphi_n)|^{\kappa(x)} \rightharpoonup \mu \geqq |{}^H\mathcal{D}_+^{\gamma,\beta;\chi}\varphi|^{r(x)} + \sum_{j \in \Lambda} \mu_j \delta_{x_j} \text{ in } \mathcal{M}(\Delta),$$

$$|(\varphi_n)|^{n(x)} \to \nu = |\varphi|^{n(x)} + \sum_{j \in \Lambda} \nu_j \delta_{x_j} \text{ in } \mathcal{M}(\Delta)$$

and

$$S\nu_j^{\frac{1}{q(x_j)}} \leqq \mu_j^{\frac{1}{m(x_j)}} \quad \forall\, j \in \Lambda.$$

Our objective is now to establish a lower estimate for $\{\nu_j\}$. For this purpose, we need to prove the following lemma.

Lemma 11. *Let $\Xi \in C_0^\infty(\Delta)$, satisfying the following conditions:*

$$\Xi(x) = 1 \text{ in } B_1(0), \quad \sup p\,\Xi \subset B_2(0) \text{ and } 0 \leqq \Xi(x) \leqq 1 \; \forall\, x \in \Delta.$$

Then, for $\varepsilon > 0$, $z \in \overline{\Delta}$ and $\varphi \in L^{\kappa(x)}(\Delta)$, it is asserted that

$$\int_\Delta \left| \varphi\, {}^H\mathcal{D}_+^{\gamma,\beta;\chi}\Xi_\varepsilon(x-z)\right|^{\kappa(x)} dx \leq C\left(\|\varphi\|_{L^{\kappa_\gamma^*(x)}(B_{2\varepsilon}(z))}^{\kappa_+} + \|\varphi\|_{L^{\kappa_\gamma^*(x)}(B_{2\varepsilon}(z))}^{\kappa_-}\right), \tag{18}$$

where

$$\Xi_\varepsilon(x) = \Xi\left(\frac{x}{\varepsilon}\right)$$

for all $x \in \Delta$ and for a constant C independent of ε and z.

Proof. We note that

$$\int_\Delta \left| \varphi\, {}^H\mathcal{D}_+^{\gamma,\beta;\chi}\Xi_\varepsilon(x-z)\right|^{\kappa(x)} dx$$

$$= \int_{B_{2\varepsilon}(z)} |\varphi|^{\kappa(x)} \left|\frac{1}{\varepsilon}\, {}^H\mathcal{D}_+^{\gamma,\beta;\chi}\Xi\left(\frac{x-z}{\varepsilon}\right)\right|^{\kappa(x)} dx$$

$$\leqq c_p \left\||\varphi|^{\kappa(x)}\right\|_{L^{\frac{p_\gamma^*(x)}{\kappa(x)}}(B_{2\varepsilon}(z))} \left\|\left|\frac{1}{\varepsilon}\, {}^H\mathcal{D}_+^{\gamma,\beta;\chi}\Xi\left(\frac{\cdot-z}{\varepsilon}\right)\right|^{\kappa(x)}\right\|_{L^{\frac{\kappa_\gamma^*(x)}{\kappa_\gamma^*(x)-\kappa(x)}}(B_{2\varepsilon}(z))},$$

where c_p is the constant provided by the Hölder inequality (see Proposition 5). Thus, upon changing the variable, we have

$$\int_{B_{2\varepsilon}(z)} \left|\frac{1}{\varepsilon}\, {}^H\mathcal{D}_+^{\gamma,\beta;\chi}\Xi\left(\frac{x-z}{\varepsilon}\right)\right|^{\frac{\kappa(x)\kappa_\gamma^*(x)}{\kappa_\gamma^*(x)-\kappa(x)}} dx$$

$$= \int_{B_2(0)} \left|\frac{1}{\varepsilon}\, {}^H\mathcal{D}_+^{\gamma,\beta;\chi}\Xi(y)\right|^N \varepsilon^N dx$$

$$= \int_{B_2(0)} \left|{}^H\mathcal{D}_+^{\gamma,\beta;\chi}\Xi(y)\right|^N dx.$$

Now, the result follows from Proposition 3 and Lemma 1. We have thus completed the proof of Lemma 11. □

Lemma 12. *Under the conditions of* Lemma 10, *let* $\{(\varphi_n)\}$ *be a sequence* (PS) *for the functional* $\mathcal{E}_\lambda(\cdot)$ *and* $\{\nu_j\}$. *Then, for each* $j \in \Lambda$,

$$\nu_j \geqq \frac{S^N}{\lambda^{\frac{N}{\kappa(x_j)}}} \quad \text{or} \quad \nu_j = 0.$$

Proof. First, for each $\varepsilon > 0$ let $\Xi_\varepsilon \in C_0^\infty(\Delta)$, as in Lemma 11. Therefore, we have

$$\{\Xi_\varepsilon(\cdot - x_j)(\varphi_n)\} \subset \mathcal{H}_{\kappa(x)}^{\gamma,\beta;\chi}(\Delta)$$

for any $j \in \Lambda$. In addition, by direct calculation we can see that $\{\Xi_\varepsilon(\cdot - x_j)(\varphi_n)\}$ is bounded in $\mathcal{H}_{\kappa(x)}^{\gamma,\beta;\chi}(\Delta)$. Thus, we obtain

$$\mathcal{E}_\lambda'(\varphi_n)\big(\Xi_\varepsilon(\cdot - x_j)(\varphi_n)\big) = o_n(1)$$

or equivalently,

$$\int_\Delta \left|{}^H\mathcal{D}_+^{\gamma,\beta;\chi}(\varphi_n)\right|^{\kappa(x)} \Xi_\varepsilon(x - x_j)\, dx$$
$$+ \int_\Delta \left|{}^H\mathcal{D}_+^{\gamma,\beta;\chi}(\varphi_n)\right|^{\kappa(x)-2}(\varphi_n)\, {}^H\mathcal{D}_+^{\gamma,\beta;\chi}(\varphi_n)\, {}^H\mathcal{D}_+^{\gamma,\beta;\chi}\Xi_\varepsilon(x - x_j)\, dx + o_n(1)$$
$$= \lambda \int_\Delta |(\varphi_n)|^{n(x)} \Xi_\varepsilon(x - x_j)\, dx + \int_\Delta \zeta(x)|(\varphi_n)|^{\kappa(x)} \Xi_\varepsilon(x - x_j)\, dx$$
$$+ \int_\Delta g(x,(\varphi_n))\,(\varphi_n)\, \Xi_\varepsilon(x - x_j)\, dx. \tag{19}$$

Now, for each $\delta > 0$, by applying the Cauchy-Schwartz and Young inequalities, we obtain

$$\int_\Delta \left|\left|{}^H\mathcal{D}_+^{\gamma,\beta;\chi}(\varphi_n)\right|^{\kappa(x)-2}(\varphi_n)\, {}^H\mathcal{D}_+^{\gamma,\beta;\chi}(\varphi_n)\, {}^H\mathcal{D}_+^{\gamma,\beta;\chi}\Xi_\varepsilon(x - x_j)\right| dx$$
$$\leqq \delta \int_\Delta \left|{}^H\mathcal{D}_+^{\gamma,\beta;\chi}(\varphi_n)\right|^{\kappa(x)} dx + C_\delta \int_\Delta \left|(\varphi_n)\,{}^H\mathcal{D}_+^{\gamma,\beta;\chi}(\varphi_n)\right|^{\kappa(x)} dx. \tag{20}$$

Thus, by the Lebesgue Dominated Convergence Theorem and the limit of $\{(\varphi_n)\}$, we can conclude that

$$\limsup_{n\to\infty} \int_\Delta \left|\left|{}^H\mathcal{D}_+^{\gamma,\beta;\chi}(\varphi_n)\right|^{\kappa(x)-2}(\varphi_n)\, {}^H\mathcal{D}_+^{\gamma,\beta;\chi}(\varphi_n)\, {}^H\mathcal{D}_+^{\gamma,\beta;\chi}\Xi_\varepsilon(x - x_j)\right| dx$$
$$\leqq \delta\epsilon_1 + C_\delta \int_\Delta \left|\varphi\,{}^H\mathcal{D}_+^{\gamma,\beta;\chi}\Xi_\varepsilon(x - x_j)\right|^{\kappa(x)} dx. \tag{21}$$

Therefore, by applying Lemma 11, it follows that

$$\limsup_{n\to\infty} \int_\Delta \left|\left|{}^H\mathcal{D}_+^{\gamma,\beta;\chi}(\varphi_n)\right|^{\kappa(x)-2}(\varphi_n)\, {}^H\mathcal{D}_+^{\gamma,\beta;\chi}(\varphi_n)\, {}^H\mathcal{D}_+^{\gamma,\beta;\chi}\Xi_\varepsilon(x - x_j)\right| dx$$
$$\leqq \delta\epsilon_1 + CC_\delta \left(\|\varphi\|_{L^{p_\gamma^*(x)}(B_{2\varepsilon}(x_j))}^{\kappa_+} + \|\varphi\|_{L^{p_\gamma^*(x)}(B_{2\varepsilon}(x_j))}^{\kappa_-}\right). \tag{22}$$

Applying the Strauss Lemma (see Lemma 4) with

$$\mathcal{P}(x,t) = \psi(x,t)t \quad \text{and} \quad \mathcal{Q}(x,t) = |t|^{\kappa(x)} + |t|^{n(x)},$$

and using the Lebesgue Dominated Convergence Theorem, we obtain

$$\lim_{n\to\infty} \int_\Delta \zeta(x)|(\varphi_n)|^{\kappa(x)} \Xi_\varepsilon(x-x_j)\,dx = \int_\Delta \zeta(x)\|\varphi\|^{\kappa(x)} \Xi_\varepsilon(x-x_j)\,dx. \tag{23}$$

Next, using Equation (19) and Equations (21) to (23), we obtain

$$\lim_{n\to\infty} \int_\Delta \left|{}^H\mathcal{D}_+^{\gamma,\beta;\chi}(\varphi_n)\right|^{\kappa(x)} \Xi_\varepsilon(x-x_j)\,dx$$
$$\leq \lambda \lim_{n\to\infty} \int_\Delta |(\varphi_n)|^{n(x)} \Xi_\varepsilon(x-x_j)\,dx + \int_\Delta \zeta(x)\|\varphi\|^{\kappa(x)} \Xi_\varepsilon(x-x_j)\,dx$$
$$+ \int_\Delta \psi(x,\varphi)\varphi\, \Xi_\varepsilon(x-x_j)\,dx + \delta\epsilon_1 + CC_\delta \left[\|\varphi\|^{\kappa_+}_{L^{\kappa_\gamma^*(x)}(B_{2\varepsilon}(x_j))} + \|\varphi\|^{\kappa_-}_{L^{\kappa_\gamma^*(x)}(B_{2\varepsilon}(x_j))} \right],$$

where C is a constant independent of ε and j. Because

$$\left|{}^H\mathcal{D}_+^{\gamma,\beta;\chi}(\varphi_n)\right|^{\kappa(x)} \rightharpoonup \mu \quad\text{and}\quad |(\varphi_n)|^{n(x)} \rightharpoonup \nu \text{ in } \mathcal{M}(\Delta),$$

we have

$$\lim_{n\to\infty} \int_\Delta \left|{}^H\mathcal{D}_+^{\gamma,\beta;\chi}(\varphi_n)\right|^{\kappa(x)} \Xi_\varepsilon(x-x_j)\,dx \geq \int_{B_\varepsilon(x_j)} d\mu \geq \mu_j(\{x_j\}) = \mu_j$$

and

$$\lim_{n\to\infty} \int_\Delta |(\varphi_n)|^{n(x)} \Xi_\varepsilon(x-x_j)\,dx = \int_{B_{2\varepsilon}(x_j)} \Xi_\varepsilon(x-x_j)\,d\nu \leq \int_{B_{2\varepsilon}(x_j)} d\nu \leq \nu_j.$$

Consequently, we have

$$\mu_j \leq \lim_{n\to\infty} \int_\Delta \left|{}^H\mathcal{D}_+^{\gamma,\beta;\chi}(\varphi_n)\right|^{\kappa(x)} \Xi_\varepsilon(x-x_j)\,dx$$
$$\leq \lambda \nu_j + \int_{B_{2\varepsilon}(x_j)} \zeta(x)|\varphi|^{\kappa(x)} \Xi_\varepsilon(x-x_j)\,dx + \int_{B_{2\varepsilon}(x_j)} \psi(x,\varphi)\varphi\, \Xi_\varepsilon(x-x_j)\,dx$$
$$+ \delta\epsilon_1 + CC_\delta \left(\|\varphi\|^{\kappa_+}_{L^{\kappa_\gamma^*(x)}(B_{2\varepsilon}(x_j))} + \|\varphi\|^{\kappa_-}_{L^{\kappa_\gamma^*(x)}(B_{2\varepsilon}(x_j))} \right). \tag{24}$$

Upon first letting $\varepsilon \to 0$ and then $\delta \to 0$, we obtain $\mu_j \leq \lambda \nu_j$. Hence,

$$S \nu_j^{\frac{1}{\kappa_\gamma^*(x_j)}} \leq \mu_j^{\frac{1}{\kappa(x_j)}} \leq (\lambda \nu_j)^{\frac{1}{\kappa(x_j)}},$$

and thus

$$\nu_j \geq \frac{S^N}{\lambda^{\frac{N}{\kappa(x_j)}}} \quad\text{or}\quad \nu_j = 0.$$

This evidently concludes our proof of Lemma 12. □

We are now able to demonstrate that the (PS) condition for the functional $\mathcal{E}_\lambda(\cdot)$ holds true below a certain level. More precisely, we can prove the following lemma.

Lemma 13. *Let the conditions* (**H$_1$**), (**H$_2$**), (**g$_1$**), *and* (**g$_2$**) *be satisfied. If* $\lambda < 1$, *then* $\mathcal{E}_\lambda(\cdot)$ *satisfies the condition* (PS)$_d$ *for*

$$d < \lambda^{1-\frac{N}{\kappa_+}} \left(\frac{1}{\kappa_+} - \frac{1}{n_-} \right) S^N.$$

Proof. Let the sequence $\{(\varphi_n)\}$ be $(PS)_d$ for the energy functional $\mathcal{E}_\lambda(\cdot)$ with

$$d < \lambda^{1-\frac{N}{\kappa_+}} \left(\frac{1}{\kappa_+} - \frac{1}{n_-}\right) S^N,$$

that is,

$$\mathcal{E}_\lambda(\varphi_n) = d + o_n(1) \quad \text{and} \quad \mathcal{E}'_\lambda(\varphi_n) = o_n(1).$$

We observe that

$$d = \lim_{n \to \infty} \left[\int_\Delta \left(\frac{1}{\kappa(x)} - \frac{1}{\kappa_+}\right) \left|{}^H\mathcal{D}_+^{\gamma,\beta;\chi}(\varphi_n)\right|^{\kappa(x)} dx + \lambda \int_\Delta \left(\frac{1}{\kappa_+} - \frac{1}{\kappa_\gamma^*(x)}\right) |(\varphi_n)|^{n(x)} dx \right]$$
$$+ \int_\Delta \left(\frac{1}{\kappa_+} - \frac{1}{\kappa(x)}\right) \zeta(x) |(\varphi_n)|^{\kappa(x)} dx - \int_\Delta \left(G(x,(\varphi_n)) - \frac{1}{\kappa_+} g(x,(\varphi_n))(\varphi_n)\right). \quad (25)$$

Then, it follows from conditions $(\mathbf{H_1})$ and $(\mathbf{H_2})$ that

$$d \geq \lambda \left(\frac{1}{\kappa_+} - \frac{1}{n_-}\right) \lim_{n \to \infty} \int_\Delta |(\varphi_n)|^{n(x)} dx. \quad (26)$$

Now, recalling that

$$\lim_{n \to \infty} \int_\Delta |(\varphi_n)|^{n(x)} dx = \int_\Delta |\varphi|^{n(x)} dx + \sum_{j \in \Lambda} v_j \geq v_j,$$

it follows that if $v_j > 0$ for some $j \in \Lambda$, then

$$d \geq \lambda \left(\frac{1}{\kappa_+} - \frac{1}{n_-}\right) v_j \geq \lambda \left(\frac{1}{\kappa_+} - \frac{1}{n_-}\right) \frac{S^N}{\lambda^{\frac{N}{\kappa(x_j)}}}.$$

Thus, for $\lambda < 1$, we find that

$$d \geq \lambda \left(\frac{1}{\kappa_+} - \frac{1}{n_-}\right) \left(\frac{S}{\lambda^{\frac{1}{\kappa_+}}}\right)^N = \lambda^{1-\frac{N}{\kappa_+}} \left(\frac{1}{\kappa_+} - \frac{1}{n_-}\right) S^N, \quad (27)$$

which is absurd. Therefore, we must have $v_j = 0$ for all $j \in \Lambda$, implying that

$$\int_\Delta |(\varphi_n)|^{n(x)} dx \to \int_\Delta |\varphi|^{n(x)} dx. \quad (28)$$

Combining the above limit with Lemma 2, we have

$$\int_\Delta |(\varphi_n) - \varphi|^{n(x)} dx \to 0 \quad \text{when} \quad n \to \infty.$$

Thus, by Proposition 3, $(\varphi_n) \to \varphi$ in $L^{n(x)}(\Delta)$.
Now let us denote by $\{\mathcal{P}_n\}$ the sequence provided by

$$\mathcal{P}_n(x) := \left(\left|{}^H\mathcal{D}_+^{\gamma,\beta;\chi}(\varphi_n)\right|^{\kappa(x)-2} {}^H\mathcal{D}_+^{\gamma,\beta;\chi}(\varphi_n) - \left|{}^H\mathcal{D}_+^{\gamma,\beta;\chi}\varphi\right|^{\kappa(x)-2} {}^H\mathcal{D}_+^{\gamma,\beta;\chi}\varphi \right) {}^H\mathcal{D}_+^{\gamma,\beta;\chi}((\varphi_n) - \varphi). \quad (29)$$

From the above definition of $\mathcal{P}_n$ we find that

$$\int_\Delta \mathcal{P}_n(x)\,dx = \int_\Delta \left|{}^H\mathcal{D}_+^{\gamma,\beta;\chi}(\varphi_n)\right|^{\kappa(x)} dx$$
$$- \int_\Delta \left|{}^H\mathcal{D}_+^{\gamma,\beta;\chi}(\varphi_n)\right|^{\kappa(x)-2} {}^H\mathcal{D}_+^{\gamma,\beta;\chi}(\varphi_n)\, {}^H\mathcal{D}_+^{\gamma,\beta;\chi}\varphi\,dx$$
$$- \int_\Delta \left|{}^H\mathcal{D}_+^{\gamma,\beta;\chi}\varphi\right|^{\kappa(x)-2} {}^H\mathcal{D}_+^{\gamma,\beta;\chi}\varphi\, {}^H\mathcal{D}_+^{\gamma,\beta;\chi}((\varphi_n)-\varphi)\,dx.$$

Because $(\varphi_n) \rightharpoonup \varphi$ in $\mathcal{H}_{\kappa(x)}^{\gamma,\beta;\chi}(\Delta)$, we have

$$\int_\Delta \left|{}^H\mathcal{D}_+^{\gamma,\beta;\chi}\varphi\right|^{\kappa(x)-2} {}^H\mathcal{D}_+^{\gamma,\beta;\chi}\varphi\, {}^H\mathcal{D}_+^{\gamma,\beta;\chi}((\varphi_n)-\varphi)\,dx \to 0 \tag{30}$$

when $n \to \infty$. This implies that

$$\int_\Delta \mathcal{P}_n(x)\,dx = \int_\Delta \left|{}^H\mathcal{D}_+^{\gamma,\beta;\chi}(\varphi_n)\right|^{\kappa(x)} dx - \int_\Delta \left|{}^H\mathcal{D}_+^{\gamma,\beta;\chi}(\varphi_n)\right|^{\kappa(x)-2}$$
$$\times {}^H\mathcal{D}_+^{\gamma,\beta;\chi}(\varphi_n)\,{}^H\mathcal{D}_+^{\gamma,\beta;\chi}\varphi\,dx + o(1).$$

On the other hand, because

$$\mathcal{E}_\lambda'(\varphi_n)(\varphi_n) = o_n(1) \quad \text{and} \quad \mathcal{E}_\lambda'(\varphi_n)\varphi = o_n(1),$$

we have

$$\int_\Delta \mathcal{P}_n(x)\,dx$$
$$= o_n(1) + \lambda \int_\Delta |(\varphi_n)|^{n(x)}\,dx + \int_\Delta \zeta(x)|(\varphi_n)|^{\kappa(x)}\,dx + \int_\Delta g(x,(\varphi_n))\,dx$$
$$- \lambda \int_\Delta |(\varphi_n)|^{n(x)-2}(\varphi_n)\varphi\,dx - \int_\Delta \zeta(x)|(\varphi_n)|^{\kappa(x)-2}\,dx - \int_\Delta g(x,(\varphi_n))\,dx.$$

Combining (28) with the Strauss lemma (see Lemma 4), we can conclude that

$$\int_\Delta \mathcal{P}_n\,dx \to 0 \quad \text{when} \quad n \to \infty. \tag{31}$$

Let us now consider the following sets:

$$\Delta_+ = \{x \in \Delta : \kappa(x) \geqq 2\} \text{ and } \Delta_- = \{x \in \Delta : 1 < \kappa(x) < 2\}. \tag{32}$$

It follows from Lemma 3 that

$$\mathcal{P}_n(x) \geqq \begin{cases} \frac{2^{3-\kappa_+}}{\kappa_+} \left|{}^H\mathcal{D}_+^{\gamma,\beta;\chi}(\varphi_n) - {}^H\mathcal{D}_+^{\gamma,\beta;\chi}\varphi\right|^{\kappa(x)} & \text{if } \kappa(x) \geqq 2 \\ (\kappa_- - 1)\dfrac{\left|{}^H\mathcal{D}_+^{\gamma,\beta;\chi}(\varphi_n) - {}^H\mathcal{D}_+^{\gamma,\beta;\chi}\varphi\right|^2}{\left(\left|{}^H\mathcal{D}_+^{\gamma,\beta;\chi}(\varphi_n)\right| + \left|{}^H\mathcal{D}_+^{\gamma,\beta;\chi}\varphi\right|\right)^{2-\kappa(x)}} & \text{if } 1 < \kappa(x) < 2. \end{cases} \tag{33}$$

Consequently, we obtain

$$\int_{\Delta_+} \left|{}^H\mathcal{D}_+^{\gamma,\beta;\chi}(\varphi_n) - {}^H\mathcal{D}_+^{\gamma,\beta;\chi}\varphi\right|^{\kappa(x)} dx = o_n(1). \tag{34}$$

Now, by applying the Hölder inequality (see Proposition 5), we have

$$\int_{\Delta_-} \left|{}^H\mathcal{D}_+^{\gamma,\beta;\chi}(\varphi_n) - {}^H\mathcal{D}_+^{\gamma,\beta;\chi}\varphi\right|^{\kappa(x)} dx \leq C \|g_n\|_{L^{\frac{2}{\kappa(x)}}(\Delta_-)} \|s_n\|_{L^{\frac{2}{2-\kappa(x)}}(\Delta_-)},$$

where

$$g_n(x) = \frac{\left|{}^H\mathcal{D}_+^{\gamma,\beta;\chi}(\varphi_n) - {}^H\mathcal{D}_+^{\gamma,\beta;\chi}\varphi\right|^{\kappa(x)}}{\left(\left|{}^H\mathcal{D}_+^{\gamma,\beta;\chi}(\varphi_n)\right| + \left|{}^H\mathcal{D}_+^{\gamma,\beta;\chi}\varphi\right|\right)^{\frac{\kappa(x)(2-\kappa(x))}{2}}}$$

and

$$s_n(x) = \left(\left|{}^H\mathcal{D}_+^{\gamma,\beta;\chi}(\varphi_n)\right| + \left|{}^H\mathcal{D}_+^{\gamma,\beta;\chi}\varphi\right|\right)^{\frac{\kappa(x)(2-\kappa(x))}{2}},$$

$C > 0$ (constant). In addition, by direct calculation we can see that

$$\left\{ \|s_n\|_{L^{\frac{2}{2-\kappa(x)}}(\Delta_-)} \right\}$$

is a bounded sequence and

$$\int_{\Delta_-} |g_n|^{\frac{2}{\kappa(x)}} dx \leq C \int_{\Delta_-} \mathcal{P}_n(x)\, dx.$$

Therefore, we have

$$\int_{\Delta} \left|{}^H\mathcal{D}_+^{\gamma,\beta;\chi}(\varphi_n) - {}^H\mathcal{D}_+^{\gamma,\beta;\chi}\varphi\right|^{\kappa(x)} dx \to 0 \quad \text{when } n \to \infty. \tag{35}$$

From Equations (31), (34), and (35), we deduce that $(\varphi_n) \to \varphi$ in $\mathcal{H}_{\kappa(x)}^{\gamma,\beta;\chi}(\Delta)$. We thus conclude the proof of Lemma 13. □

Lemma 14. *Under conditions* ($\mathbf{g_1}$) *and* ($\mathbf{H_1}$), *there is a sequence* $\{\mathbf{M}_m\} \subset (0, \infty)$ *independent of λ with $\mathbf{M}_\lambda \leq \mathbf{M}_{m+1}$ such that, for all $\lambda > 0$,*

$$c_m^\lambda = \inf_{K \in \Gamma_m} \max_{\varphi \in K} \mathcal{E}_\lambda(\varphi) < \mathbf{M}_m.$$

Proof. First, we observe that

$$c_m^\lambda = \inf_{K \in \Gamma_m} \max_{\varphi \in K} \left\{ \int_\Delta \frac{1}{\kappa(x)} \left|{}^H\mathcal{D}_+^{\gamma,\beta;\chi}\varphi\right|^{\kappa(x)} dx - \int_\Delta \frac{\lambda}{n(x)} \|\varphi\|^{\kappa(x)} dx - \int_\Delta F(x,\varphi)\, dx \right\}$$

$$\leq \inf_{K \in \Gamma_m} \max_{\varphi \in K} \left\{ \int_\Delta \frac{1}{\kappa(x)} \left|{}^H\mathcal{D}_+^{\gamma,\beta;\chi}\varphi\right|^{\kappa(x)} dx - \int_\Delta F(x,\varphi)\, dx \right\}.$$

Let

$$\mathbf{M}_m = \inf_{K \in \Gamma_m} \max_{\varphi \in K} \left\{ \int_\Delta \frac{1}{\kappa(x)} \left|{}^H\mathcal{D}_+^{\gamma,\beta;\chi}\varphi\right|^{\kappa(x)} dx - \int_\Delta F(x,\varphi)\, dx \right\} + 1.$$

Then, by the definition of the set Γ_m and by the properties of the infimum of a set, it follows that $\mathbf{M}_m \leq \mathbf{M}_{m+1}$. Therefore, as $F(x,t) \leq c_1 + \epsilon_2 |t|^{n(x)}$, we can conclude that $\mathbf{M}_m < \infty$, proving the result asserted by Lemma 14. □

Finally, we prove the main result (Theorem 1) of this paper.

Proof. Proof of Theorem 1: First, λ_k for each $k \in \mathbb{N}$ such that

$$\mathbf{M}_k < \lambda_k^{1-\frac{N}{\kappa_+}} \left(\frac{1}{\kappa_+} - \frac{1}{n_-} \right) S^N.$$

Thus, for $\lambda \in (\lambda_k, \lambda_{k+1}]$ we have

$$0 < \epsilon_1^\lambda \leqq \epsilon_2^\lambda \leqq \cdots \leqq \epsilon_k^\lambda < \mathbf{M}_k \leqq \lambda_k^{1-\frac{N}{\kappa_+}} \left(\frac{1}{\kappa_+} - \frac{1}{n_-} \right) S^N.$$

Now, by Theorem 3, the levels provided by

$$\epsilon_1^\lambda \leqq \epsilon_2^\lambda \leqq \cdots \leqq c_k^\lambda$$

are the critical values of the functional $\mathcal{E}_\lambda(\cdot)$. Thus, if

$$\epsilon_1^\lambda < \epsilon_2^\lambda < \cdots < \epsilon_k^\lambda,$$

the functional $\mathcal{E}_\lambda(\cdot)$ has at least k critical points, meaning that if $\epsilon_j^k = \epsilon_{j+1}^\lambda$ for some $j = 1, 2, \cdots, k$, it follows from Theorem 3 that $K_{\epsilon_j^\lambda}$ is an infinite set. Consequently, problem (2) has infinite solutions in this case. In either case, therefore, we can see that the problem (2) has at least k pairs of non-trivial solutions. Our proof of Theorem 1 is thus completed. □

4. Application

In this section, we present an application of the investigated result.

First, let us consider $\kappa(x) = 2$, $n(x) = 2$, $\zeta(x) = 2$, $\chi(x) = x$ and $\beta = 1$ in Equation (2). Then, we have the following class of quasi-linear fractional-order problems:

$$\begin{cases} {}^c\mathcal{D}_-^\gamma \left({}^c\mathcal{D}_+^\gamma \varphi \right) = (2+\lambda)\varphi + \psi(x, \varphi) \\ \varphi = 0, \end{cases} \quad (36)$$

where $\Delta := [0, T] \times [0, T] \times [0, T]$ is a bounded domain with a smooth boundary and, for simplicity, ${}^C\mathcal{D}_+^\gamma(\cdot)$, ${}^C\mathcal{D}_-^\gamma(\cdot)$ are the Liouville-Caputo fractional derivatives of order γ $\left(\frac{1}{2} < \gamma < 1 \right)$ and $p, q : \overline{\Delta} \to \mathbb{R}$ are Lipschitz functions such that:

- (p$_1$) $1 < \kappa_- \leqq 2 \leqq \kappa_+ < 3, \kappa_+ < n_- \leqq 2 \leqq \kappa_\gamma^*(x)$ for all $x \in \overline{\Delta}$ and
- (p$_2$) The set $A = \left\{ x \in \overline{\Delta} : 2 = p_\gamma^*(x) \right\}$ is not empty.

We now make several assumptions, which are detailed below.
Let $f : \overline{\Delta} \times \mathbb{R} \to \mathbb{R}$ be a function provided by

$$f(x, t) = 2t + \psi(x, t)$$

with $a \in L^\infty(\Delta)$ and the function $g : \overline{\Delta} \times \mathbb{R} \to \mathbb{R}$ satisfying the following conditions:

- (g$_1$) The function g is odd with respect to t, that is, $\psi(x, -t) = -\psi(x, t)$ for all $(x, t) \in \overline{\Delta} \times \mathbb{R}$, $\psi(x, t) = o(|t|^{\kappa(x)-1})$ when $|t| \to 0$ uniformly in x, and $\psi(x, t) = o(|t|^{n(x)-1})$ when $|t| \to \infty$ uniformly in x;
- (g$_2$) $\psi(x, t) \leqq \frac{1}{\kappa_+} \psi(x, t) t$ for all $t \in \mathbb{R}$ and at almost every point $x \in \Delta$, where

$$\psi(x, t) = \int_0^t \psi(x, s) ds.$$

Furthermore, we make the following assumptions:

- ($\mathbf{H_1}$) There exists $\overline{\gamma} > 0$ such that

$$\int_\Delta \left(\frac{1}{2} - 2|\varphi|^2\right) dx \geqq \overline{\gamma} \int_\Delta \frac{1}{2}|\varphi|^2 \, dx.$$

- ($\mathbf{H_2}$) $2 = \kappa_+$ for all $x \in \Gamma = \{x \in \Delta : 2 > 0\}$.

Theorem 4. *Suppose that a function g satisfies the conditions* ($\mathbf{g_1}$) *and* ($\mathbf{g_2}$) *and that the conditions* ($\mathbf{p_1}$), ($\mathbf{p_2}$), ($\mathbf{H_1}$) *and* ($\mathbf{H_2}$) *are also satisfied. Then there exists a sequence* $\{\lambda_k\} \subset (0, +\infty)$ *with* $\lambda_k > \lambda_{k+1}$ *for all* $k \in \mathbb{N}$ *such that, for* $\lambda \in (\lambda_{k+1}, \lambda_k)$, *the problem* (36) *has at least k pairs of non-trivial solutions.*

Remark 4. We have presented an application of problem (2) in a particular case in the sense of the Liouville-Caputo fractional derivative. However, it is possible for particular choices of β and χ to obtain a new class of particular cases, especially when the limit $\gamma \to 1$.

5. Concluding Remarks and Observations

In the investigations presented in this paper, we have successfully addressed a problem involving the multiplicity of solutions for a class of fractional-order differential equations via the $\kappa(x)$-Laplacian operator and the Genus Theory. We have first presented several definitions, lemmas and other preliminaries related to the problem. Applying these lemmas and other preliminaries, we have then studied the existence and multiplicity of solutions for a class of quasi-linear problems involving fractional differential equations in the χ-fractional space $\mathcal{H}^{\gamma,\beta;\chi}_{\kappa(x)}(\Delta)$ via the Genus Theory, the Concentration-Compactness Principle (CCP) and the Mountain Pass Theorem (MPT). We have considered a number of corollaries and consequences of the main results in this paper. On the other hand, although we have obtained several results in this paper, many open questions remain about the theory involving the χ-Hilfer fractional derivative. As presented in the introduction, the first work with m-Laplacian via the χ-Hilfer derivative was developed in 2019. It should be noted that there have been few further developments thus far. In this sense, several future questions need to be answered, in particular, those that are itemized below:

- Is it possible to discuss the results in Orlicz Spaces and Generalized Orlicz Spaces?
- Would it be possible to obtain the existence and multiplicity of solutions of Equation (2) unified with Kirchhoff's problem?
- Is it possible to extend these results to more general and global fractional-calculus operators?

Yet another possibility is to further extend this work to the distributed-order Hilfer fractional derivative and the ψ-Hilfer fractional derivative operators with variable exponents. For additional details, see [53,54], and (for recent developments) see [55], which is based upon the Riemann-Liouville, the Liouville-Caputo, and the Hilfer fractional derivatives).

As can be seen, it is a new area and there are many questions yet to be answered. Surely, this calls for the attention of researchers toward the discussing of new and complex problems.

Author Contributions: Formal analysis, H.M.S. and J.V.d.C.S.; Investigation, H.M.S. and J.V.d.C.S.; Methodology, J.V.d.C.S.; Supervision, H.M.S.; Validation, J.V.d.C.S.; Writing – original draft, J.V.d.C.S.; Writing – review and editing, H.M.S. All authors have read and agreed to the published version of the manuscript.

Funding: This research received no external funding.

Institutional Review Board Statement: Not applicable

Informed Consent Statement: Not applicable

Data Availability Statement: This article has no associated data.

Conflicts of Interest: The authors declare that they have no conflict of interest.

References

1. Hilfer, R. (Ed.) *Applications of Fractional Calculus in Physics*; World Scientific Publishing Company: Singapore; Hackensack, NJ, USA; London, UK; Hong Kong, China, 2000.
2. Kilbas, A.A.; Trujillo, H.M.S.; Trujillo, J.J. *Theory and Applications of Fractional Differential Equations*; North-Holland Mathematical Studies; Elsevier: Amsterdam, The Netherlands; London, UK; New York, NY, USA, 2006; Volume 204.
3. Srivastava, H.M. An introductory overview of fractional-calculus operators based upon the Fox-Wright and related higher transcendental functions. *J. Adv. Eng. Comput.* **2021**, *5*, 135–166. [CrossRef]
4. Srivastava, H.M. Some families of Mittag-Leffler type functions and associated operators of fractional calculus. *TWMS J. Pure Appl. Math.* **2016**, *7*, 123–145.
5. Tomovski, Ž.; Hilfer, R.; Srivastava, H.M. Fractional and operational calculus with generalized fractional derivative operators and Mittag-Leffler type functions. *Integral Transform. Spec. Funct.* **2010**, *21*, 797–814. [CrossRef]
6. Hilfer, R.; Luchko, Y.; Tomovski, Ž. Operational method for solution of the fractional differential equations with the generalized Riemann-Liouville fractional derivatives. *Fract. Calc. Appl. Anal.* **2009**, *12*, 299–318.
7. Srivastava, H.M. Fractional-order derivatives and integrals: Introductory overview and recent developments. *Kyungpook Math. J.* **2020**, *60*, 73–116.
8. Srivastava, H.M. Some parametric and argument variations of the operators of fractional calculus and related special functions and integral transformations. *J. Nonlinear Convex Anal.* **2021**, *22*, 1501–1520.
9. Srivastava, H.M. A survey of some recent developments on higher transcendental functions of analytic number theory and applied mathematics. *Symmetry* **2021**, *13*, 2294. [CrossRef]
10. da Costa Sousa, J.V.; de Oliveira, E.C. On the χ-Hilfer fractional derivative. *Commun. Nonlinear Sci. Numer. Simul.* **2018**, *60*, 72–91. [CrossRef]
11. da Costa Sousa, J.V.; de Oliveira, E.C. Leibniz type rule: χ-Hilfer fractional operator. *Commun. Nonlinear Sci. Numer. Simul.* **2019**, *77*, 305–311. [CrossRef]
12. da Costa Sousa, J.V.; Frederico, G.; de Oliveira, E.C χ-Hilfer pseudo-fractional operator: New results about fractional calculus. *Comput. Appl. Math.* **2020**, *39*, 254. [CrossRef]
13. Zhikov, V.V. Averaging of functionals of the calculus of variations and elasticity theory. *Izvest. Rossiiskoi Akad. Nauk. Ser. Mat.* **1986**, *50*, 675–710. [CrossRef]
14. Acerbi, E.; Mingione, G. Regularity results for stationary electro-rheological fluids. *Arch. Rational Mech. Anal.* **2002**, *164*, 213–259. [CrossRef]
15. Ruzicka, M. *Electrorheological Fluids: Modeling and Mathematical Theory*; Lecture Notes in Mathematics; Springer: Berlin/Heidelberg, Germany; New York, NY, USA, 2000; Volume 1748; pp. 16–38.
16. Chen, Y.; Levine, S.; Rao, M. Variable exponent, linear growth functionals in image restoration. *SIAM J. Appl. Math.* **2006**, *66*, 1383–1406. [CrossRef]
17. Orlicz, W. Über konjugierte exponentenfolgen. *Studia Math.* **1931**, *3*, 200–211. [CrossRef]
18. Nikitczuk, J.; Weinberg, B.; Canavan, P.K.; Mavroidis, C. Active knee rehabilitation orthotic device with variable damping characteristics implemented via an electrorheological fluid. *IEEE/ASME Trans. Mech.* **2009**, *15*, 952–960. [CrossRef]
19. Simmonds, A.J. Electro-rheological valves in a hydraulic circuit. *IEE Proc. D-Control Theory Appl.* **1991**, *138*, 400–404. [CrossRef]
20. Simon, J. Régularité de la solution d'une équation non linéaire dans $\mathbb{R}^N$. In *Journées d'Analyse Non Linéaire*; Lecture Notes in Mathematics Book Series; Springer: Berlin/Heidelberg, Germany; New York, NY, USA, 1978, Volume 665; pp. 205–227.
21. Stanway, R.; Sproston, J.L.; El-Wahed, A.K. Applications of electro-rheological fluids in vibration control: A survey. *Smart Mater. Struct.* **1996**, *5*, 464–492. [CrossRef]
22. Alves, C.O. Existence of solution for a degenerate $\kappa(x)$-Laplacian equation in $\mathbb{R}^N$. *J. Math. Anal. Appl.* **2008**, *345*, 731–742. [CrossRef]
23. Alves, C.O. Existence of radial solutions for a class of $\kappa(x)$-Laplacian equations with critical growth. *Differ. Integral Equ.* **2010**, *23*, 113–123.
24. Alves, C.O.; Ferreira, M.C. Nonlinear perturbations of a $\kappa(x)$-Laplacian equation with critical growth in $\mathbb{R}^N$. *Math. Nachr.* **2014**, *287*, 849–868. [CrossRef]
25. Alves, C.O.; Ferreira, M.C. Existence of solutions for a class of $\kappa(x)$-Laplacian equations involving a concave-convex nonlinearity with critical growth in $\mathbb{R}^N$. *Topolog. Meth. Nonlinear Anal.* **2015**, *45*, 399–422. [CrossRef]
26. Antontsev, S.N.; Shmarev, S.I. Elliptic equations with anisotropic nonlinearity and nonstandard conditions. In *Handbook of Differential Equations: Stationary Partial Differential Equations*; Chipot, M., Ed.; Elsevier B.V.: Amsterdam, The Netherlands; London, UK; New York, NY, USA, 2006; Volume 3; pp. 1–100.
27. Bonder, J.F.; Silva, A. Concentration-compactness principle for variable exponent spaces and applications. *Electon. J. Differ. Equ.* **2010**, *2010*, 141.
28. Fu, Y. The principle of concentration compactness in $L^{\kappa(x)}$ spaces and its application. *Nonlinear Anal.* **2009**, *71*, 1876–1892. [CrossRef]
29. Kovacik, D.; Rakosnik, J. On spaces $L^{\kappa(x)}$ and $W^{1,\kappa(x)}$. *Czechoslovak Math. J.* **1991**, *41*, 592–618.

30. Fan, X.; Shen, J.; Zhao, D. Sobolev embedding theorems for spaces $W^{k,\kappa(x)}$. *J. Math. Anal. Appl.* **2001**, *262*, 749–760. [CrossRef]
31. Fan, X.; Zhao, Y.; Zhao, D. Compact embedding theorems with symmetry of Strauss-Lions type for the space $W^{1,\kappa(x)}(\mathbb{R}^N)$. *J. Math. Anal. Appl.* **2001**, *255*, 333–348. [CrossRef]
32. Chabrowski, J.; Fu, Y. Existence of solutions for $\kappa(x)$-Laplacian problems on a bounded domain. *J. Math. Anal. Appl.* **2005**, *306*, 604–618. [CrossRef]
33. Taarabti, S. Positive solutions for the $\kappa(x)$-Laplacian: Application of the Nehari method. *Discrete Cont. Dyn. Syst.-S* **2022**, *15*, 229–243. [CrossRef]
34. Sousa, J.V.d.; Tavares, L.S.; Ledesma, C.E.T. A variational approach for a problem involving a χ-Hilfer fractional operator. *J. Appl. Anal. Comput.* **2021**, *11*, 1610–1630.
35. da Costa Sousa, J.V. Nehari manifold and bifurcation for a χ-Hilfer fractional p-Laplacian. *Math. Meth. Appl. Sci.* **2021**, *44*, 9616–9628. [CrossRef]
36. Sousa, J.V.d.; de Oliveira, M.P..E.C.; Existence and regularity of weak solutions for χ-Hilfer fractional boundary value problem. *Mediterr. J. Math.* **2021**, *18*, 1–15. [CrossRef]
37. Sousa, J.V.d.; Zuo, J.; O'Regan, D. The Nehari manifold for a χ-Hilfer fractional p-Laplacian. *Applicable Anal.* **2021**, 1–31. [CrossRef]
38. Ledesma, C.E.; Nemat, N. Impulsive fractional boundary value problem with p-Laplace operator. *J. Appl. Math. Comput.* **2017**, *55*, 257–278. [CrossRef]
39. Nyamoradi, N. The Nehari manifold and its application to a fractional boundary value problem. *Differ. Equ. Dyn. Sys.* **2013**, *21*, 323–340. [CrossRef]
40. Nyamoradi, N.; Zhou, Y. Bifurcation results for a class of fractional Hamiltonian systems with Liouville–Weyl fractional derivatives. *J. Vibration Control* **2016**, *22*, 1358–1368. [CrossRef]
41. Xiang, M.; Zhang, R.; Yang, D. Multiplicity results for variable-order fractional Laplacian equations with variable growth. *Nonlinear Anal. Ser. A Theory Methods Appl.* **2019**, *178*, 190–204. [CrossRef]
42. Zhang, C.; Zhang, X. Renormalized solutions for the fractional $\kappa(x)$-Laplacian equation with L1 data. *Nonlinear Anal.* **2020**, *190*, 111610. [CrossRef]
43. Ayazoglu, R.; Sarac, Y.; Sener, S.S.; Alisoy, G. Existence and multiplicity of solutions for a Schrödinger–Kirchhoff type equation involving the fractional $p(\cdot,\cdot)$-Laplacian operator in $\mathbb{R}^N$. *Collect. Math.* **2021**, *72*, 129–156. [CrossRef]
44. Xiang, M.; Hu, D.; Zhang, R.; Wang, Y. Multiplicity of solutions for variable-order fractional Kirchhoff equations with nonstandard growth. *J. Math. Anal. Appl.* **2021**, *501*, 124269. [CrossRef]
45. Colasuonno, F.; Pucci, P. Multiplicity of solutions for $\kappa(x)$-polyharmonic elliptic Kirchhoff equations. *Nonlinear Anal. Ser. A Theory Methods Anal.* **2011**, *74*, 5962–5974. [CrossRef]
46. Mihăilescu, M.; Radulescu, V. A multiplicity result for a nonlinear degenerate problem arising in the theory of electrorheological fluids. *Proc. Roy. Soc. London Ser. A Math. Phys. Eng. Sci.* **2006**, *462*, 2625–2641. [CrossRef]
47. Rahmoune, R.; Biccari, U. Multiplicity of solutions for fractional $q(\cdot)$-Laplacian equations. *arXiv* **2021**, arXiv:2103.12600.
48. da Costa Sousa, J.V.; Oliveira, D.S.; Tavares, L.S. Solutions for a mean curvature equation involving a χ-Hilfer fractional operator and variable exponents via the Nehari manifold. **2022**, Preprint.
49. Ledesma, C.E.T.; da Costa Sousa, J.V. Fractional integration by parts and Sobolev-type inequalities for χ-fractional operators. *Math. Methods Appl. Sci.* **2022**, 1–22. [CrossRef]
50. Willem, M. *Minimax Theorems, Progress in Nonlinear Differential Equations and Their Applications*; Birkhäuser: Basel, Switzerland, 1996; Volume 24.
51. Chabrowski, J. *Weak Convergence Methods for Semilinear Elliptic Equations*; World Scientific Publishing Company: Singapore; Hackensack, NJ, USA; London, UK; Hong Kong, China, 1999.
52. Rabinowitz, P.H. *Minimax Methods in Critical Point Theory with Applications to Diferential Equations*; CBMS Regional Conference Series in Mathematics; American Mathematical Society: Providence, RI, USA, 1984; Volume 65.
53. Luchko, Y.F. The 1st level general fractional derivatives and some of their Properties. *arXiv* **2022**, arXiv:2206.02154.
54. Fernźmdez-Anaya, G.; Quezada-Téllez, L.A.; Franco-Pxexrez, L. Stability analysis of distributed order of Hilfer nonlinear systems. *Math. Methods Appl. Sci.* **2021**, *44*, 4137–4155. [CrossRef]
55. Srivastava, H.M.; Raghavan, D.; Nagarajan, S. A comparative study of the stability of some fractional-order cobweb economic models. *Rev. Real Acad. Cienc. Exactas Fís. Natur. Ser. A Mat. (RACSAM)* **2022**, *116*, 98. [CrossRef]

Article

Influences of the Order of Derivative on the Dynamical Behavior of Fractional-Order Antisymmetric Lotka–Volterra Systems

Mengrui Xu

Department of Mathematics, Shandong University, Jinan 250100, China; xumr@mail.sdu.edu.cn

Abstract: This paper studies the dynamic behavior of a class of fractional-order antisymmetric Lotka–Volterra systems. The influences of the order of derivative on the boundedness and stability are characterized by analyzing the first-order and $0 < \alpha < 1$-order antisymmetric Lotka–Volterra systems separately. We show that the order does not affect the boundedness but affects the stability. All solutions of the first-order system are periodic, while the $0 < \alpha < 1$-order system has no non-trivial periodic solution. Furthermore, the $0 < \alpha < 1$-order system can be reduced on a two-dimensional space and the reduced system is asymptotically stable, regardless of how close to zero the order of the derivative used is. Some numerical simulations are presented to better verify the theoretical analysis.

Keywords: fractional differential equations; Lotka–Volterra system; boundedness; stability

MSC: 34A08; 34C11; 34D20

Citation: Xu, M. Influences of the Order of Derivative on the Dynamical Behavior of Fractional-Order Antisymmetric Lotka–Volterra Systems. *Fractal Fract.* **2023**, *7*, 360. https://doi.org/10.3390/fractalfract7050360

Academic Editors: Angelo B. Mingarelli, Leila Gholizadeh Zivlaei and Mohammad Dehghan

Received: 6 March 2023
Revised: 24 April 2023
Accepted: 27 April 2023
Published: 28 April 2023

Copyright: © 2023 by the author. Licensee MDPI, Basel, Switzerland. This article is an open access article distributed under the terms and conditions of the Creative Commons Attribution (CC BY) license (https://creativecommons.org/licenses/by/4.0/).

1. Introduction

The classical Lotka–Volterra equations (LVE for short) can be expressed in a compact form as

$$\frac{dx_i(t)}{dt} = x_i(Ax)_i, \quad i = 1, 2, \cdots, n,$$

where $A = (a_{ij})_{n \times n}$ is a real matrix, $x = (x_1, x_2, \cdots, x_n)^T \in \mathbb{R}^n$. It was first introduced by Volterra [1] in the context of predator–prey oscillations in population biology. Under the background of the predator–prey relationship, LVE is used to study the dynamic change of an individual population. The different species are labeled by i (or j) with $i, j = 1, 2, \cdots, n$, $x_i(t)$ represents the density of population of species i at the time of t, and the parameter a_{ij} represents the impact of species j on species i: $a_{ij} > 0$ indicates that species i preys on species j, $a_{ij} < 0$ indicates that species i is the prey of j, and $a_{ij} = 0$ means that species i and j have no predation relationship. The size of a_{ij} is seen as the predatory efficiency. Nowadays it is also of central importance to many other fields of science (e.g., plasma physics and chemical kinetics [2]). Mathematically speaking, many important results on the Lotka–Volterra system have been produced, such as global asymptotic behavior and bifurcation [3–5]. In particular, the three-dimensional antisymmetric LVE is known as the replicator equation of the rock–paper–scissors game [6]. Furthermore, the rock–paper–scissors dynamical system is found to be rather common for biological systems, for example, polymorphic groups of side-blotched lizards [7], microbial laboratory communities [8].

In recent years, fractional calculus has attracted much attention from researchers [9–14]. The fractional derivative at time t is not defined locally and depends on the total effects of the classical integer-order derivatives on the interval $[0, t]$, so it can be used to describe the variation of a system in which the instantaneous change rate depends on the past state, which is called the memory effect in a visualized manner [15–17]. We refer to [18–23] for some interpretations of physical and biological significance of fractional operators by supplying specific examples. Nowadays, many dynamical systems with integer order have been extended to the fractional-order systems. This extension allows us to explore and obtain some new behaviors. From the mathematical viewpoint, many researchers consider the influence of fractional derivatives on dynamic behavior [24–26]. In [27,28], the authors discuss that the chaos in integer-order systems disappears in their fractional-order counterparts with sufficiently small values of fractional order. In [29], the authors extend the classical model of the prey–predator model to a new model based on the Caputo fractional derivatives and propose that the new model is very sensitive to varying the fractional order. Reference [30] considers a three-dimensional fractional-order slow–fast prey–predator model and reveals that the fractional-order exponent has an impact on the stability and the existence of Hopf bifurcations in this model.

In this paper, we consider a fractional-order antisymmetric Lotka–Volterra system composed of three species

$$_0D_t^\alpha x_i(t) = x_i(Ax)_i, \quad i = 1, 2, 3, \tag{1}$$

with the initial value

$$x(0) = b, \tag{2}$$

where $_0D_t^\alpha$ is the Caputo fractional derivative with $\alpha \in (0,1]$, $A = (a_{ij})_{3\times 3}$ is an antisymmetric matrix ($a_{ij} = -a_{ji}$), $x = (x_1, x_2, x_3)^T$ and $b = (b_1, b_2, b_3)^T$. Considering the practical significance, we always assume that $b_i > 0$, $i = 1, 2, 3$. We assume that three species dominate each other according to the popular rock–paper–scissors game rules, as illustrated in Figure 1; that is, $a_{12}, a_{23}, a_{31} > 0$, which means that each predator has an effective predation probability.

The model is an extension of the classical antisymmetric Lotka–Volterra model to a fractional order, but there are essential differences between $\alpha = 1$ and $0 < \alpha < 1$ on the dynamical behavior. Our aim is to characterize the influences of the order of derivative on antisymmetric Lotka–Volterra systems (1).

We first prove that for any $\alpha \in (0,1]$, $\sum_{i=1}^{3} x_i(t)$ is a conserved quantity, and all x_i stays away from zero for all times. Note that in the context of population dynamics, this means that the total number of individuals for all species is conserved and all species coexist independently of the predatory efficiency. We further analyze the influences of the order of derivative on the stability of the system (1). The results show that all solutions of the first-order system are periodic, while the $0 < \alpha < 1$-order system has no non-trivial periodic solution. Furthermore, for any choice of $a_{12}, a_{23}, a_{31} > 0$, all solutions of the $0 < \alpha < 1$-order system starting near equilibrium points go towards a unique equilibrium point on the plane depending on $\sum_{i=1}^{3} b_i$, regardless of how close to zero the order of the derivative used is. This means that in this model if the equilibrium state is slightly disturbed, as long as the total number of species remains unchanged, it will always return to the original equilibrium state after a long time. This may reflect the memory of the fractional-order system. Finally, we give some numerical simulations.

The paper is organized as follows. In Section 2, some basic concepts and preliminary results are presented. In Section 3, the conclusions of the boundedness of solutions are given. In Section 4, the influences of the order of derivative on stability are characterized. Some numerical simulations are provided in Section 5. Section 6 gives the conclusions.

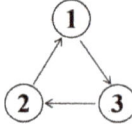

Figure 1. Illustration of the predation interaction rules among species in the rock–paper–scissors model. Arrows from j to i indicate $a_{ij} > 0$, i.e., species i preys on species j in a predator–prey relationship.

2. Preliminaries

This section includes some basic preliminaries. We review some definitions and preliminary results that will be required for our theorems.

Definition 1 ([16]). *The Riemann–Liouville fractional integral $_0I_t^\alpha f$ of order $\alpha > 0$ is defined by*

$$(_0I_t^\alpha f)(t) := \frac{1}{\Gamma(\alpha)} \int_0^t (t-s)^{\alpha-1} f(s)\,ds, \quad t > 0,$$

where $\Gamma(\alpha)$ is the Gamma function.

The Riemann–Liouville fractional derivative $^{RL}_0D_t^\alpha y$ of order $\alpha > 0$ is defined by

$$\left(^{RL}_0 D_t^\alpha y\right)(t) := \left(\frac{d}{dt}\right)^n \left(_0I_t^{n-\alpha} y\right)(t), \quad n = [\alpha] + 1,$$

where $[\alpha]$ means the integer part of α.

Definition 2 ([16]). *The Caputo fractional derivative $_0D_t^\alpha y$ of order $\alpha > 0$ is defined by*

$$(_0D_t^\alpha y)(t) := \left(^{RL}_0 D_s^\alpha \left[y(s) - \sum_{k=0}^{n-1} \frac{y^{(k)}(0)}{k!} s^k\right]\right)(t),$$

where

$$n = [\alpha] + 1 \text{ for } \alpha \notin \mathbb{N}_0; \quad n = \alpha \text{ for } \alpha \in \mathbb{N}_0.$$

Lemma 1 ([16]). *Let $0 \leq \alpha \leq 1$. If $y(t)$ is an absolutely continuous function on $[0,c]$ ($c \in \mathbb{R}+$), then the Caputo fractional derivative $(_0D_t^\alpha y)(t)$ exists almost everywhere on $[0,c]$.*
(a) *If $0 < \alpha < 1$, $(_0D_t^\alpha y)(t)$ is represented by*

$$(_0D_t^\alpha y)(t) = \frac{1}{\Gamma(1-\alpha)} \int_0^t \frac{y'(t)}{(t-s)^\alpha} ds.$$

(b) *If $\alpha = 1$, $(_0D_t^\alpha y)(t) = y'(t)$.*

Definition 3 ([16]). *The Mittag–Leffler function is defined as*

$$E_\alpha(z) = \sum_{k=0}^\infty \frac{z^k}{\Gamma(\alpha k + 1)}, \quad \alpha > 0, \, z \in \mathbb{C}.$$

Lemma 2 ([16]). *The solution to the problem*

$$_0D_t^\alpha u(t) - \lambda u(t) = 0, \, u(0) = c$$

with $0 < \alpha < 1$ and $\lambda, c \in \mathbb{R}$ has the form

$$u(t) = c E_\alpha(\lambda t^\alpha).$$

Lemma 3. *Assume that $0 < \alpha < 1$ and $f : [0, +\infty) \to \mathbb{R}^+$ is continuously differentiable. Then*

$$_0D_t^\alpha \ln f(t) \geq \frac{_0D_t^\alpha f(t)}{f(t)}, \quad t > 0.$$

Proof. According to Definition 2, we only need to show that

$$_0D_t^\alpha f(t) - f(t) \, _0D_t^\alpha \ln f(t) = \int_0^t (t-s)^{-\alpha} \left[f'(s) - \frac{f(t)f'(s)}{f(s)}\right] ds \leq 0, \quad t > 0. \quad (3)$$

By the integration-by-part formula, we conclude that

$$\int_0^t (t-s)^{-\alpha}\left[f'(s) - \frac{f(t)f'(s)}{f(s)}\right]ds$$
$$= \int_0^t (t-s)^{-\alpha} \frac{d}{ds}\left[f(s) - f(t) - f(t)\ln\frac{f(s)}{f(t)}\right]ds$$
$$= \lim_{s\to t}\frac{f(s) - f(t) - f(t)\ln\frac{f(s)}{f(t)}}{(t-s)^{\alpha}} - t^{-\alpha}\left(f(0) - f(t) - f(t)\ln\frac{f(0)}{f(t)}\right)$$
$$- \alpha\int_0^t\left(f(s) - f(t) - f(t)\ln\frac{f(s)}{f(t)}\right)(t-s)^{-\alpha-1}ds. \tag{4}$$

First, by L'Hôpital's rule, we can obtain the first term on the right side of Equation (4) equal to

$$\lim_{s\to t}\frac{f'(s) - f(t)\frac{f'(s)}{f(s)}}{\alpha(t-s)^{\alpha-1}} = 0. \tag{5}$$

Next, we estimate the other two items. It is understood that

$$\xi - \ln\xi - 1 \geq 0, \quad \forall \xi \in \mathbb{R}^+.$$

Then, for any fixed t and τ, we have

$$f(\tau) - f(t) - f(t)\ln\frac{f(\tau)}{f(t)} \geq 0.$$

Therefore, we have that the second term on the right side of Equation (4) is non-positive when $\tau = 0$. For any $s \in (0,t)$, $f(s) - f(t) - f(t)\ln\frac{f(s)}{f(t)} \geq 0$, which shows that the last integral item of Equation (4) is non-positive. Therefore, (4) is non-positive; that is, (3) holds. □

Lemma 4 (Fractional Comparison Principle [16]). *Let $_0D_t^\alpha x(t) \leq {_0D_t^\alpha} y(t)$ and $x(0) = y(0)$, where $0 < \alpha < 1$. Then $x(t) \leq y(t)$.*

Lemma 5. *Let $L(x)$ be a differentiable function defined on an open set U containing x^* in $\mathbb{R}^n$. Suppose that $L(x^*) = 0$ and $L(x) > 0$ if $x \neq x^*$. Then, if $c > 0$ is small enough, each connected component of $L(x) = c$ is a closed surface surrounding x^*.*

Proof. Let $\delta > 0$ be small enough that a closed ball centering at x^* of radius δ lies entirely in U, that is,

$$B_\delta(x^*) = \{x \in \mathbb{R}^n \mid \|x - x^*\| \leq \delta\} \subset U.$$

The boundary of $B_\delta(x^*)$ is the sphere $S_\delta(x^*)$ of radius δ and center x^*, i.e.,

$$S_\delta(x^*) := \{x \in B_\delta(x^*) \mid \|x - x^*\| = \delta\}.$$

By the compactness of $S_\delta(x^*)$ and the continuity of L, there is a minimum $x_* \in S_\delta^*$ of L restricted on the sphere. Let γ be the minimum value of L on the sphere S_δ^*, i.e.,

$$\gamma = \min_{x\in S_\delta(x^*)} L(x) = L(x_*).$$

For any $0 < c < \gamma$, let

$$W_c = \{x \in U \mid L(x) = c\} \subseteq B_\delta(x^*).$$

For any continuous curve $\xi \subseteq B_\delta(x^*)$ connecting x^* and any point on $S_\delta(x^*)$, there exists at least one point $z \in \xi$ satisfying $L(\xi) = c$ by the intermediate value theorem of the continuous function $L|_\zeta$ and $L(x^*) = 0$. Then no curve starting from x^* to $S_\delta(x^*)$ meets the set W_c. Hence, each connected component of W_c is a closed surface. This proves that W_c is a closed surface or a family of closed surfaces surrounding x^*. □

Lemma 6 ([31]). *Let $n > 0$, $r > 0$, $\varphi \in [-\pi, \pi]$ and $\lambda = r\exp(i\varphi)$. Denote $y(t) := E_n(-\lambda t^n)$. Then,*

(a) $\lim_{x \to \infty} y(t) = 0$ if $|\varphi| < n\pi/2$,

(b) $y(t)$ *is unbounded as $x \to \infty$ if $|\varphi| > n\pi/2$.*

Let $0 < \alpha < 1$. The homogeneous linear system is given by

$$_0D_t^\alpha x(t) = Bx(t), \quad x(t) \in \mathbb{R}^n \tag{6}$$

with $x(0) = b$, where B is an $n \times n$ real matrix. The nonlinear system is given by

$$_0D_t^\alpha x(t) = f(x(t)), \quad x(t) \in \mathbb{R}^n \tag{7}$$

with $x(0) = b$, where $f(x)$ is continuous.

Definition 4 ([32]). *The system (6) is said to be asymptotically stable if $\lim_{t \to +\infty} \|x(t)\| = 0$.*

Definition 5 ([32]). *The point e is an equilibrium point of system (7) if and only if $f(e) = 0$.*

Definition 6 ([32]). *Suppose that e is an equilibrium point of system (7) and $Df(e)$ is linearized matrix of f at e. If all the eigenvalues λ of $Df(e)$ satisfy $|\lambda| \neq 0$ and $|\arg(\lambda)| \neq \frac{\pi\alpha}{2}$, then we call e a hyperbolic equilibrium point.*

Lemma 7 ([32]). *If e is a hyperbolic equilibrium point of (7), then vector field $f(x)$ is topologically equivalent with its linearization vector field $Df(e)x$ in the neighborhood of e.*

3. Boundedness Results

In this section, we will find the significantly common property between the first-order and the $0 < 1 < \alpha$-order system (1). The boundedness is independent of the order of derivative. For any choice of $a_{12}, a_{23}, a_{31} > 0$, all solutions of the systems are bounded for all time, and the lower bound is away from zero for each solution.

Lemma 8. *For arbitrary solutions $x = (x_1, x_2, x_3)^T$ of system (1) with initial value (2), $H(x) := \sum_{i=1}^{3} x_i$ is a conserved quantity.*

Proof. From the antisymmetry of A, it can be obtained that x satisfies

$$_0D_t^\alpha \left(\sum_{i=1}^{3} x_i(t) \right) = \sum_{i=1}^{3} {}_0D_t^\alpha x_i(t) = \sum_{i=1}^{3} x_i(Ax)_i = 0, \quad \forall t > 0. \tag{8}$$

If $0 < \alpha < 1$, from Lemma 2, we have

$$\sum_{i=1}^{3} x_i(t) = \sum_{i=1}^{3} x_i(0) \text{ for } t > 0. \tag{9}$$

If $\alpha = 1$, it is clear that (8) implies (9). The proof is complete. □

We next show that $x_i(t)$ remains bounded away from 0. By calculating the $Ar = 0$, we can obtain the kernel of A is

$$\ker(A) = \{r \in \mathbb{R}^3 \mid r = s(a_{23}, a_{31}, a_{12})^T, s \in \mathbb{R}\}.$$

By assumption $a_{12}, a_{23}, a_{31} > 0$, we have $\ker(A) \neq \emptyset$. On the domain $\mathbb{R}^3_+$, we define a function

$$V(z) = \sum_{i=1}^{3}\left(z_i - y_i - y_i \ln \frac{z_i}{y_i}\right) \tag{10}$$

for one fixed $y \in \ker(A)$ with $y = (y_1, y_2, y_3)^T > 0$.

Lemma 9. *For any solution $x(t) = (x_1(t), x_2(t), x_3(t))^T$ of the system (1) with initial value (2), $V(x)$ has the following properties along $x(t)$.*
(i) *If $\alpha = 1$, $V(x(t)) \equiv V(b)$ for all $t > 0$.*
(ii) *If $0 < \alpha < 1$, $V(x(t)) \leq V(b)$ for all $t > 0$.*

Proof. For case (i), considering the time derivative of $V(x(t))$ and employing Equation (1) yields

$$\frac{d}{dt}\left(\sum_{i=1}^{3}\left(x_i(t) - y_i - y_i \ln \frac{x_i(t)}{y_i}\right)\right)$$

$$= \frac{d}{dt}\left(\sum_{i=1}^{3} x_i(t)\right) - \sum_{i=1}^{3}\left(\frac{y_i}{x_i(t)} \frac{dx_i(t)}{dt}\right) \tag{11}$$

$$= \frac{d}{dt}\left(\sum_{i=1}^{3} x_i(t)\right) - \sum_{i=1}^{3} y_i(Ax(t))_i.$$

From Lemma 8, $\frac{d}{dt}\sum_{i=1}^{3} x_i(t) = 0$. According to the antisymmetry of A and $y \in \ker(A)$, we have

$$-\sum_{i=1}^{3} y_i(Ax)_i = \sum_{i=1}^{3} x_i(Ay)_i = 0, \quad \forall x \in \mathbb{R}^3_+.$$

Then (11) implies $\frac{d}{dt}V(x(t)) = 0$. Therefore, case (i) holds.

For case (ii), we consider the Caputo fractional derivative of $V(x(t))$. By (8) and Lemma 3, we deduce that

$$_0D_t^\alpha V(x(t)) = {_0D_t^\alpha}\left(\sum_{i=1}^{3} x_i\right) - {_0D_t^\alpha}\left(\sum_i y_i \ln x_i\right)$$

$$= -\sum_i y_i \, {_0D_t^\alpha}(\ln x_i(t))$$

$$\leq -\sum_i y_i \frac{{_0D_t^\alpha}(x_i(t))}{x_i(t)} \tag{12}$$

$$= -\sum_{i=1}^{3} y_i(Ax)_i.$$

Then, using the antisymmetry of A and definition of y, we have

$$-\sum_{i=1}^{3} y_i(Ax)_i = \sum_{i=1}^{3} x_i(Ay)_i = 0.$$

Therefore, (12) leads to

$$_0D_t^\alpha V(x(t)) \leq 0, \quad \forall t > 0. \tag{13}$$

Let $y(t) \equiv V(x(0))$, $\forall\, t > 0$. Then, by Definition 2, we have $_0D_t^\alpha y(t) = 0$. Therefore, combining (13) with the Fractional Comparison Principle (Lemma 4), we can obtain

$$V(x(t)) \leq V(x(0)) \text{ for all } t > 0. \tag{14}$$

Case (ii) is complete. □

Corollary 1. *For $0 < \alpha < 1$, for any solution $x(t) = (x_1(t), x_2(t), x_3(t))^T$ of the system (1) with initial value (2), if $b \notin \ker(A)$, then $V(x(t)) < V(b)$ for all $t > 0$.*

Proof. For $x(0) = b \notin \ker(A)$, we can obtain $x(t) \not\equiv x(0)$. Then, by the proof of Lemma 3, we have $D_t^\alpha(\ln x_i(t)) \neq \frac{D_t^\alpha(x_i(t))}{x_i(t)}$. Therefore, combining (12), we can derive from (13) that $_0D_t^\alpha V(x(t)) < 0$ for $t > 0$, which implies $V(x(t)) < V(x(0))$ for all $t > 0$. □

Theorem 1. *For arbitrary solutions $x = (x_1, x_2, x_3)^T$ of the system (1) with initial value (2), there exist constants $\delta, \eta > 0$ such that*

$$\delta \leq x_i(t) \leq \eta, \ \forall\, t > 0, \ i = 1, 2, 3. \tag{15}$$

Proof. By Lemma 8, the existence of η is clear. Next, we will show the existence of δ.

On the contrary, if there is no $\delta > 0$ such that $\delta \leq x_i(t)$ for all $t > 0$ and $i = 1,2,3$, then there exists sequence $\{t_n\}$ with $t_n \to \infty$ as $n \to \infty$ satifying

$$\lim_{n \to \infty} x_i(t_n) = 0 \text{ for some } i \in \{1, 2, 3\}.$$

Then, $\lim_{n \to \infty} \ln x_i(t_n) = -\infty$ and $\lim_{n \to \infty} V(x(t_n)) = +\infty$ by (10). This is contradictory with $V(x(t)) \leq V(b) = const.$ by Lemma 9. Therefore, the assumption is false; that is, there exists $\delta > 0$ satisfying (15). The proof is complete. □

4. Stability Results

In this section, we will characterize the effects of order α on the stability of the systems (1) by analyzing the long-time dynamical behaviors of first-order and $0 < \alpha < 1$-order systems, respectively.

We will use the conserved quantity $H(x)$, defined in Lemma 8, to reduce the system (1), so that the dynamics of the original system can be limited to the two-dimensional space. For any constant $c > 0$, denote an open and bounded plane in $\mathbb{R}_+^3$ as

$$S_c := \left\{ v \in \mathbb{R}_+^3 \,\Big|\, v = (v_1, v_2, v_3)^T, \sum_{i=1}^{3} v_i = c \right\}.$$

By Lemma 8, the solution to the system (1) with initial value $b = (b_1, b_2, b_3) \in \mathbb{R}_+^3$ contained in the plane $S_{H(b)}$. For convenience, we reduce the system (1) on the plane S_1. Consider the reduced system

$$\begin{cases} _0D_t^\alpha x_1 = (a_{12}x_2 + a_{13}(1 - x_1 - x_2))x_1 := f_1(x_1, x_2) \\ _0D_t^\alpha x_2 = (-a_{12}x_1 + a_{23}(1 - x_1 - x_2))x_2 := f_2(x_1, x_2) \end{cases} \tag{16}$$

on the domain $Z = \{x \in \mathbb{R}_+^2 \mid x = (x_1, x_2)^T, x_1 + x_2 < 1\}$.

Lemma 10. *If $\alpha = 1$, the system (16) has a unique equilibrium point, and all the solution curves are closed and around the equilibrium point on Z.*

Proof. By assumption $a_{12}, a_{23}, a_{31} > 0$, the two-dimensional system (16) has a unique equilibrium point

$$p = (p_1, p_2) = \left(\frac{a_{23}}{a_{23} + a_{31} + a_{12}}, \frac{a_{31}}{a_{23} + a_{31} + a_{12}}\right).$$

Note that the function V restricted on the plane S can be rewritten as

$$\tilde{V}(w) := -p_1 \ln \frac{w_1}{p_1} - p_2 \ln \frac{w_2}{p_2} - (1 - p_1 - p_2) \ln \frac{1 - w_1 - w_2}{1 - p_1 - p_2}.$$

In addition, $\tilde{V}$ is differentiable on domain Z. By simple calculation, we can find that $\tilde{V}$ satisfies

(a) $\tilde{V}(z) > 0$ if $z \in Z \setminus \{p\}$ and $\tilde{V}(p) = 0$,
(b) $\tilde{V}(z) \to +\infty$ as z goes to the boundary of domain Z.

For any $x_0 \in Z$, there is a unique solution $x(t) = (x_1(t), x_2(t))$ to the system (16) with $x(0) = x_0$ in domain Z. First, we claim that the level set

$$W_{x_0} = \{x \in Z \mid \tilde{V}(x) = \tilde{V}(x_0)\}$$

is actually the orbit $x(t)$ and prove it with two steps.

Step 1. By Theorem 1, there are $0 < \delta < \eta < 1$ such that $\delta < x_1(t), x_2(t) < \eta$ for all $t > 0$. We define a domain

$$Z_{\delta, \eta} = \{x = (x_1, x_2) \in Z \mid \delta < x_1, x_2 < \eta, \; x_1 + x_2 < \max\{1 - \delta, \eta\}\}.$$

Take the minimum value $\gamma_{\delta, \eta}$ of $\tilde{V}$ on the boundary of domain $Z_{\delta, \eta}$. According to property (b), we can choose $\delta > 0$ sufficiently small and $\eta < 1$ sufficiently close to 1 such that $\gamma_{\delta, \eta} > \tilde{V}(x_0)$. Then W_{x_0} is a family of closed curves around p by Lemma 5.

Step 2. Connect the origin and p with the segment $\xi(t) = t(p_1, p_2)$, $t \in [0, 1]$. For any $t \in (0, 1]$, by direct calculation, we obtain

$$\frac{d}{dt} \tilde{V}(\xi(t)) < 0.$$

This means that the function $\tilde{V}$ is monotonic along the segment ξ from p to the origin. Hence, segment ξ meets the set W_{x_0} only one time. In conclusion, W_{x_0} is one closed curve; that is, the solution curve starting from x_0 is a closed curve. The claim is proved.

By the arbitrariness of the initial value $x_0 \in Z$, all the solution curves of the system (16) are closed curves around the equilibrium point. The proof is complete. □

In the following, we describe the entire behavior of the first-order antisymmetric Lotka–Volterra system (1).

Theorem 2. *If $\alpha = 1$, all solutions of the systems (1) are periodic. Moreover, any solution curve is around the unique equilibrium point on one plane parallel with S_1.*

Proof. For any initial value $b \in \mathbb{R}^3_+$, there is a plane $S_{H(b)}$. By Lemma 8, the solution to the system (1) with initial value b is on the plane $S_{H(b)}$. By Lemma 10, the solution curve is closed and around the unique equilibrium point on $S_{H(b)}$. By the arbitrariness of the initial value b, all solutions of the system (1) are periodic. The proof is complete. □

We point out that the behaviors of the fractional system are entirely different from the first-order antisymmetric Lotka–Volterra around the equilibrium point.

Lemma 11. *If $0 < \alpha < 1$, the system (16) is locally asymptotically stable on Z.*

Proof. According to Definition 5, $p = (\frac{a_{23}}{a_{23}+a_{31}+a_{12}}, \frac{a_{31}}{a_{23}+a_{31}+a_{12}})^T$ is the only equilibrium point on Z. The linearization matrix of the vector field $f(x) = (f_1(x_1,x_2), f_2(x_1,x_2))^T$ at point p is given by

$$Df(p) = \begin{pmatrix} a_{31}p_1 & (a_{12}+a_{31})p_1 \\ (-a_{12}-a_{23})p_2 & -a_{23}p_2 \end{pmatrix}.$$

The eigenvalues of $Df(p)$ are $\lambda_1, \lambda_2 = \pm\sqrt{\frac{a_{12}a_{31}a_{23}}{a_{12}+a_{31}+a_{23}}}$ i. From Lemma 6, p is a hyperbolic equilibrium point. According to Lemma 7, the vector field $f(x)$ is topologically equivalent to its linearization vector field $Df(p)x$ in the neighborhood of p. Therefore, it is sufficient to consider the homogeneous linear system

$$_0D_t^\alpha \varepsilon(t) = J_p\,\varepsilon(t), \tag{17}$$

where $J_p = Df(p)$ and $\varepsilon = (\varepsilon_1, \varepsilon_2)^T$. Denote $\Lambda = \text{diag}\{\lambda_1, \lambda_2\}$. Then there exists a matrix Q such that $J_p = Q\Lambda Q^{-1}$, which implies

$$_0D_t^\alpha \varepsilon = (Q\Lambda Q^{-1})\varepsilon,$$

and

$$_0D_t^\alpha(Q^{-1}\varepsilon) = \Lambda(Q^{-1}\varepsilon).$$

Let $z = (z_1, z_2)^T = Q^{-1}\varepsilon$. Then

$$_0D_t^\alpha z_i = \lambda_i z_i, \quad i = 1, 2. \tag{18}$$

By Lemma 2, the solutions of the equations (18) are given by the Mittag–Leffler function

$$z_i(t) = E_\alpha(\lambda_i t^\alpha)z_i(0), \quad i = 1, 2.$$

Since $|\arg(\lambda_i)| = \frac{\pi}{2} > \alpha\frac{\pi}{2}$, we can derive $\lim_{t\to\infty} z_i(t) = 0$ by Lemma 6, and then $\lim_{t\to\infty} \varepsilon_i(t) = 0$. From Definition 4, the system (17) is asymptotically stable, which implies system (16) is locally asymptotically stable in the neighborhood of the equilibrium point p by Lemma 7. The proof is complete. □

Theorem 3. *If $0 < \alpha < 1$, the system (1) has no non-trivial periodic solution and the solution goes towards a unique equilibrium point on the plane $S_{H(b)}$ provided the initial value b closed to $\ker(A)$.*

Proof. From Lemma 9 and Corollary 1, if the initial value $b \notin \ker(A)$, then

$$V(x(T)) \neq V(x(0)) \text{ for any } T > 0$$

along the solution $x(t)$ of the system (16) starting from b. If the initial value $b \in \ker(A)$, then b is the unique equilibrium point on $S_{H(b)}$. Hence, the system (1) has no periodic solution except the equilibrium points.

For any b, restrict the system (1) on the plane $S_{H(b)}$. By Lemma 11, the reduced system has a locally asymptotically stable equilibrium point on $S_{H(b)}$. The proof is complete. □

Remark 1. *The equilibrium points are degenerated and set up the ray from the origin to infinity in $\mathbb{R}_+^3$. Since the quality $H(x)$ is conserved along the solution of system (1), any solution is towards the line on the plane $S_{H(b)}$, which is determined by the initial value near the line. Therefore, there are local asymptotic behaviors. However, it is not a strictly asymptotically stable phenomenon. Furthermore, we find that there are solutions spiraling towards the ray for some $\alpha \in (0, 1)$ and the initial value b by numerical simulation. In Section 5, we give descriptions of this phenomenon in detail.*

5. Numerical Simulations

Consider a system

$$\begin{cases} D_t^\alpha x_1 = (x_2 - x_3)x_1 \\ D_t^\alpha x_2 = (-x_1 + x_3)x_2 \\ D_t^\alpha x_3 = (x_1 - x_2)x_3, \end{cases} \quad (19)$$

with the initial value $x(0) = (0.35, 0.35, 0.3)^T$, where the D_t^α is the Caputo fractional derivative with $\alpha \in (0,1]$, $A = \begin{pmatrix} 0 & 1 & -1 \\ -1 & 0 & 1 \\ 1 & -1 & 0 \end{pmatrix}$. By Lemma 8, $\sum_{i=1}^{3} x_i \equiv 1$; then, the solution to the system (19) with initial value $x(0)$ contained in the plane

$$S_1 := \left\{ v \in \mathbb{R}_+^3 \,\middle|\, v = (v_1, v_2, v_3)^T, \sum_{i=1}^{3} v_i = 1 \right\}.$$

Direct calculations yield that the equilibrium points are

$$\{r \in \mathbb{R}^3 \mid r = (s, s, s)^T, s \in \mathbb{R}\}$$

and $p = (\frac{1}{3}, \frac{1}{3}, \frac{1}{3})^T$ is a unique equilibrium point on plane S_1. For $\alpha = 1$, any solution curve is closed and around p on S_1 by Theorem 2. For $0 < \alpha < 1$, the solution goes towards p on the plane S_1 by Theorem 3.

Next, using Matlab, based on the fractional Adams–Bashforth–Moulton Method (see Appendix C of [31]), numerical simulations are provided to substantiate the theoretical results established in the previous sections of this paper. Next we will monitor the effect of varying order α on the dynamical behavior of the model.

Take the time step as 0.01 and draw the change curve of x with time t in the system (19). Simulations are then run with varying values of α and initial values as in Figures 2–7, where the grid-like plane is $S_{H(b)}$ and $u1 = (2,3,5)^T$, $u2 = (4,3,3)^T$, $u3 = (2,4,4)^T$, $v1 = (0.5, 0.5, 0.3)^T$, $v2 = (1, 0.5, 0.3)^T$, $v3 = (1, 2, 0.3)^T$.

We have the following conclusions.

(i) By Figures 2–5, all $x_i(t)$ have a positive below bound, and all solution curves are on the plane S_1 for all times, no matter what α.
(ii) By Figures 6, all solution curves are on one plane if the totals of $x_i(0)$ are same, no matter what α.
(iii) By Figures 6a and 7a, all solution curves of the first-order system (19) are closed curves and around the equilibrium point.
(iv) By Figures 7b, all solution curves of the 0.95-order system (19) go towards the equilibrium point.

The numerical simulation results show that the order does not affect the boundedness but affects the stability.

In addition, an interesting asymptotic behavior can be seen from the Figures 2–5, 6b and 7b. To be specific, the equilibrium points set up the ray from the origin to infinity in $\mathbb{R}_+^3$, and any solution is towards the line on the plane, which is determined by the initial value near the line. Furthermore, there are solutions spiraling towards the ray for some $\alpha \in (0,1)$.

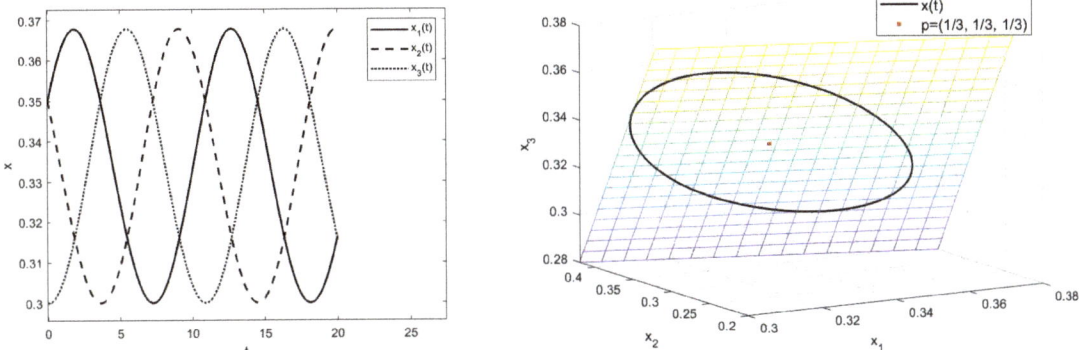

Figure 2. Simulations of system (19) for $\alpha = 1$ with initial value $b = (0.35, 0.35, 0.3)$.

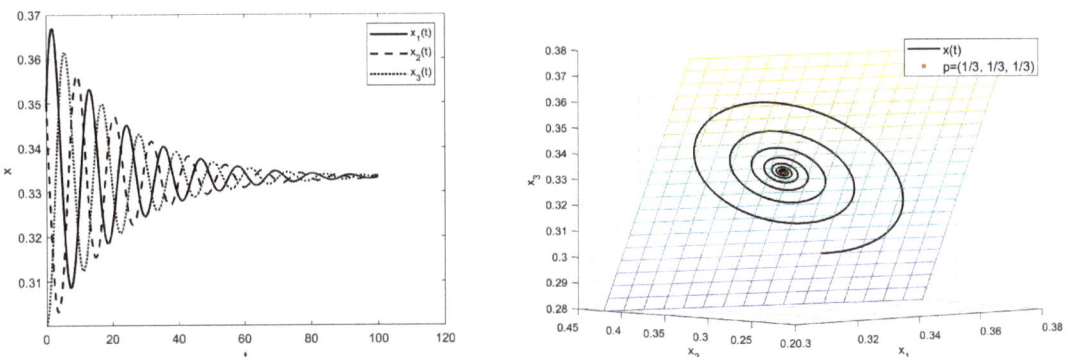

Figure 3. Simulations of system (19) for $\alpha = 0.95$ with initial value $b = (0.35, 0.35, 0.3)$.

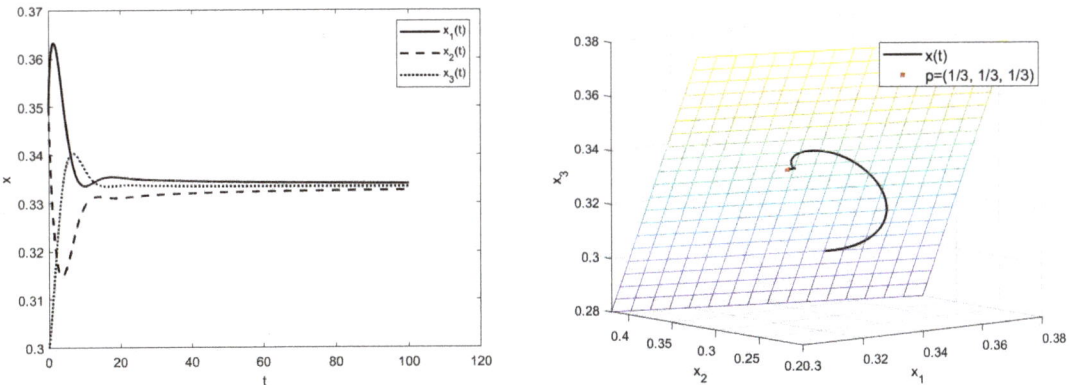

Figure 4. Simulations of system (19) for $\alpha = 0.7$ with initial value $b = (0.35, 0.35, 0.3)$.

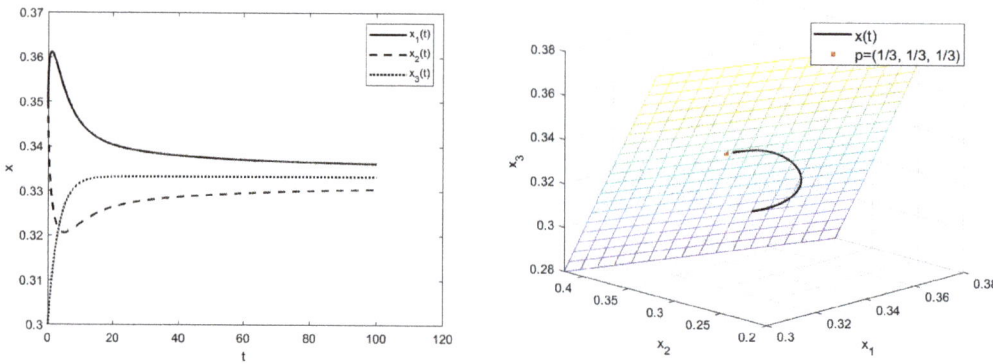

Figure 5. Simulations of system (19) for $\alpha = 0.5$ with initial value $b = (0.35, 0.35, 0.3)$.

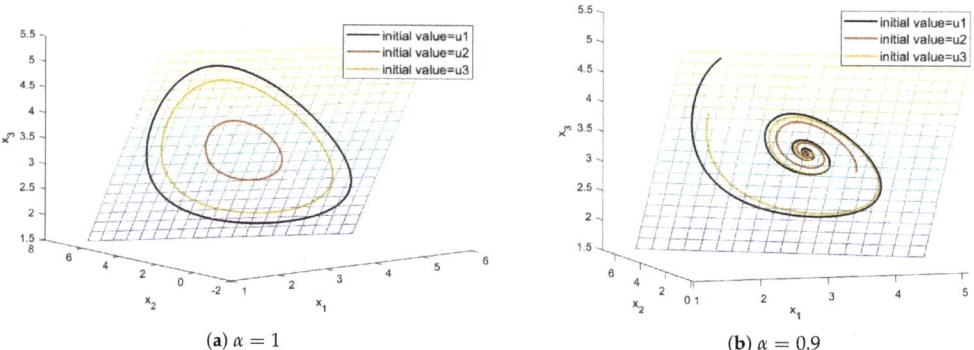

(**a**) $\alpha = 1$ (**b**) $\alpha = 0.9$

Figure 6. Simulations of system (19) for $\alpha = 1$ and $\alpha = 0.9$ with initial values $u1, u2$ and $u3$ separately.

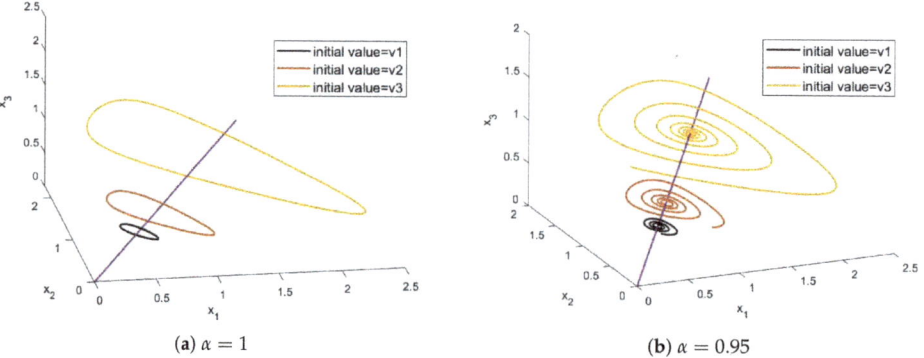

(**a**) $\alpha = 1$ (**b**) $\alpha = 0.95$

Figure 7. Simulations of system (19) for $\alpha = 1$ and $\alpha = 0.95$ with initial values $v1, v2$ and $v3$ separately (where the rays from the origin are degenerate equilibrium points of system (19)).

6. Conclusions

Since biological systems have memory properties, fractional differential equations provide an excellent tool in this respect. Thus, this paper studied a class of fractional antisymmetric Lotka–Volterra equations composed of three species under the rock–paper–scissors game rules. The first-order and $0 < \alpha < 1$-order antisymmetric Lotka–Volterra systems are studied separately. The results show that the order does not affect the boundedness but affects the stability:

(1) For any $\alpha \in (0,1]$, $\sum_{i=1}^{3} x_i(t) = \sum_{i=1}^{3} x_i(0)$ for all times $t > 0$, and all x_i bounded away from zero for all times for any choice of $a_{12}, a_{23}, a_{31} > 0$. In the context of population dynamics, this means that the total number of individuals for all species is conserved and all species coexist independently of the predatory efficiency.

(2) All the solutions of the first-order system are periodic. However, the $0 < \alpha < 1$-order system can be reduced on a two-dimensional space and the reduced system is asymptotically stable, regardless of how close to zero the order of the derivative used is. This implies that if the equilibrium state is slightly disturbed, as long as the total number of species remains unchanged, it will always return to the original equilibrium state after a long time. This may reflect the memory of the fractional-order system.

Funding: This research is supported by the National Natural Science Foundation of China (No. 12071255).

Data Availability Statement: Not applicable.

Acknowledgments: The author sincerely thanks Xijun Hu for his guidance. The author is grateful to Shimin Wang for his discussion and many useful suggestions. The author is grateful to the editor and the anonymous referees for their valuable comments and constructive suggestions, which helped to improve the paper significantly.

Conflicts of Interest: The author declares no conflict of interest.

References

1. Volterra, V. *Leçons sur la Théorie Mathématique de la Lutte pourla Vie*; Gauthier-Villars: Paris, France, 1931.
2. Van Kampen, N.G. *Stochastic Process in Physics and Chemistry*, 3rd ed.; Elsevier: Amsterdam, The Netherlands, 2007.
3. Zhou, P.; Tang, D.; Xiao, D. On Lotka-Volterra competitive parabolic systems: Exclusion, coexistence and bistability. *J. Differ. Equ.* **2021**, *282*, 596–625. [CrossRef]
4. Ahmed, E.; El-Sayed, A.M.A.; El-Saka, H.A.A. Equilibrium points, stability and numerical solutions of fractional-order predator-prey and rabies models. *J. Math. Anal. Appl.* **2007**, *325*, 542–553. [CrossRef]
5. Nowak, M. *Evolutionary Dynamics*; Harvard University Press: Cambridge, MA, USA, 2006.
6. Menezes, J. Antipredator behavior in the rock-paper-scissors model. *Phys. Rev. Lett. E* **2021**, *103*, 052216. [CrossRef] [PubMed]
7. Sinervo, B.; Lively, C. The rock-paper-scissors game and the evolution of alternative male strategies. *Nature* **1996**, *380*, 240–243. [CrossRef]
8. Kirkup, B.; Riley, M. Antibiotic-mediated antagonism leads to a bacterial game of rock-paper-scissors in vivo. *Nature* **2004**, *428*, 412–414. [CrossRef]
9. Wang, Y.; Liu, S. Fractal analysis and control of the fractional Lotka-Volterra model. *Nonlinear Dyn.* **2019**, *95*, 1457–1470. [CrossRef]
10. Zhao, Y.; Sun, S.; Han, Z.; Zhang, M. Positive solutions for boundary value problems of nonlinear fractional differential equations. *Appl. Math. Comput.* **2011**, *217*, 6950–6958. [CrossRef]
11. Elsadany, A.A.; Matouk, A.E. Dynamical behaviors of fractional-order Lotka-Volterra predator-prey model and its discretization. *J. Appl. Math. Comput.* **2015**, *49*, 269–283. [CrossRef]
12. Xu, M.; Sun, S. Positivity for integral boundary value problems of fractional differential equations with two nonlinear terms. *J. Appl. Math. Comput.* **2019**, *59*, 271–283. [CrossRef]
13. Xu, M.; Sun, S.; Han, Z. Solvability for impulsive fractional Langevin equation. *J. Appl. Anal. Comput.* **2020**, *10*, 486–494. [CrossRef]
14. Yavuz, M.; Sene, N. Stability Analysis and Numerical Computation of the Fractional Predator-Prey Model with the Harvesting Rate. *Fractal Fract.* **2020**, *4*, 35. [CrossRef]
15. Podlubny, I. *Fractional Differential Equation*; Academic Press: New York, NY, USA, 1999.
16. Kilbas, A.; Srivastava, H.; Trujillo, J. *Theory and Applications of Fractional Differential Equations*; Elsevier: Amsterdam, The Netherlands, 2006.
17. Tarasov, V.E. Predator-prey models with memory and kicks: Exact solution and discrete maps with memory. *Math. Methods Appl. Sci.* **2021**, *44*, 11514–11525. [CrossRef]
18. Zhou, P.; Ma, J.; Tang, J. Clarify the physical process for fractional dynamical systems. *Nonlinear Dyn.* **2020**, *100*, 2353–2364. [CrossRef]
19. Tarasov, V.E. Applications in Physics, Part A. In *Handbook of Fractional Calculus with Applications*; De Gruyter: Berlin, Germany, 2019; Volume 4.
20. Heymans, N.; Podlubny, I. Physical interpretation of initial conditions for fractional differential equations with Riemann–Liouville fractional derivatives. *Rheol. Acta* **2006**, *45*, 765–771. [CrossRef]

21. Tavassoli, M.H.; Tavassoli, A.; Rahimi, M.R.O. The geometric and physical interpretation of fractional order derivatives of polynomial functions. *Differ. Geom. Dyn. Syst.* **2013**, *15*, 93–104.
22. Ionescu, C.; Lopes, A.; Copot, D.; Machado, J.A.T.; Bates, J.H.T. The role of fractional calculus in modeling biological phenomena: A review. *Commun. Nonlinear Sci. Numer. Simul.* **2017**, *51*, 141–159. [CrossRef]
23. Echenausía-Monroy, J.L.; Gilardi-Velázquez, H.E.; Jaimes-Reátegui, R.; Aboites, V.; Huerta-Cuéllar, G. A physical interpretation of fractional-order-derivatives in a jerk system: Electronic approach. *Commun. Nonlinear Sci. Numer. Simul.* **2020**, *90*, 105413. [CrossRef]
24. Bhalekara, S.; Patilb, M. Singular points in the solution trajectories of fractional order dynamical systems. *Chaos* **2018**, *28*, 113123. [CrossRef]
25. El-Dib, Y.; Elgazery, N. Effect of fractional derivative properties on the periodic solution of the nonlinear oscillations. *Fractals* **2020**, *28*, 2050095. [CrossRef]
26. Monroy, J.; Cuellar, G.; Reategui, R.; García-López, J.H.; Aboites, V.; Cassal-Quiroga, B.B.; Gilardi-Velázquez, H.E. Multistability Emergence through Fractional-Order-Derivatives in a PWL Multi-Scroll System. *Electronics* **2020**, *9*, 880. [CrossRef]
27. Daftardar-Gejji, V.; Bhalekar, S. Chaos in fractional ordered Liu system. *Comput. Math. Appl.* **2010**, *59*, 1117–1127. [CrossRef]
28. Li, C.; Chen, G. Chaos, hyperchaos in the fractional-order Rossler equations. *Phys. A Stat. Mech. Appl.* **2004**, *341*, 55–61. [CrossRef]
29. Moustafa, M.; Abdullah, F.A.; Shafie, S. Dynamical behavior of a fractional-order prey-predator model with infection and harvesting. *J. Appl. Math. Comput.* **2022**, *68*, 4777–4794. [CrossRef]
30. Das, S.; Mahato, S.; Mondal, A.; Kaslik, E. Emergence of diverse dynamical responses in a fractional-order slow-fast pest-predator model. *Nonlinear Dyn.* **2023**, *111*, 8821–8836. [CrossRef]
31. Kai, D. *The Analysis of Fractional Differential Equations*; Springer: Berlin/Heidelberg, Germany, 2010.
32. Li, C.; Ma, Y. Fractional dynamical system and its linearization theorem. *Nonlinear Dyn.* **2013**, *71*, 621–633. [CrossRef]

Disclaimer/Publisher's Note: The statements, opinions and data contained in all publications are solely those of the individual author(s) and contributor(s) and not of MDPI and/or the editor(s). MDPI and/or the editor(s) disclaim responsibility for any injury to people or property resulting from any ideas, methods, instructions or products referred to in the content.

Article

Existence, Stability and Simulation of a Class of Nonlinear Fractional Langevin Equations Involving Nonsingular Mittag–Leffler Kernel

Kaihong Zhao

Department of Mathematics, School of Electronics & Information Engineering, Taizhou University, Taizhou 318000, China; zhaokaihongs@126.com

Abstract: The fractional Langevin equation is a very effective mathematical model for depicting the random motion of particles in complex viscous elastic liquids. This manuscript is mainly concerned with a class of nonlinear fractional Langevin equations involving nonsingular Mittag–Leffler (ML) kernel. We first investigate the existence and uniqueness of the solution by employing some fixed-point theorems. Then, we apply direct analysis to obtain the Ulam–Hyers (UH) type stability. Finally, the theoretical analysis and numerical simulation of some interesting examples show that there is a great difference between the fractional Langevin equation and integer Langevin equation in describing the random motion of free particles.

Keywords: fractional Langevin equation; ML-kernel; existence of solutions; UH-type stability; numerical simulation

MSC: 34A08; 34D20; 37C25

1. Introduction

To expound the random motion of particles in fluid after colliding with each other, Langevin raised the famous Langevin equation in 1908. Afterward, many random phenomena and processes were found to be described by the Langevin Equation [1,2]. However, the integer-order Langevin equation is unable to meet the accuracy requirements in describing complex viscoelasticity. Thereby, the classical Langevin equation has been extended and modified. Kubo [3,4] put forward a general Langevin equation to simulate the complex viscoelastic anomalous diffusion process. Eab and Lim [5] applied a fractional Langevin equation to describe single-file diffusion. Sandev and Tomovski [6] established a fractional Langevin equation model to study the motion of free particles driven by power-law noise. Furthermore, the stability of the system represents the most important dynamics characteristic. Ulam and Hyers [7,8] proposed a concept of system stability called UH-stability in the 1940s. Over the past decade, there have been many works published (some of which can be found in [9–15]) on the UH-stability of a fractional system.

It is worth noting that these works on the fractional Langevin system basically involve Caputo or Riemann–Liouville fractional derivatives. In fact, the Caputo or Riemann–Liouville fractional derivatives can produce singularity under some conditions. This makes them difficult to employ as mathematical models of certain physical phenomena. Consequently, a new nonsingular fractional derivative with exponential kernel was raised by Caputo and Febrizio in [16]. Furthermore, another new nonsingular fractional derivative with ML-kernel was put forward by Atangana and Baleanu in [17]. Since their introduction, these nonsingular fractional derivatives have attracted much attention and research in theory [18–21] and application [22–27]. Some new findings on the fractional Langevin equation have been published in recent papers (see [28–36]). However, there are a paucity of papers on Ulam–Hyers stability of fractional Langevin system with ML-kernel.

Inspired by the aforementioned research, this manuscript focuses on the following nonlinear fractional Langevin equation with ML-kernel of the form

$$\begin{cases} {}^{ML}\mathcal{D}_{0^+}^{\beta}[{}^{ML}\mathcal{D}_{0^+}^{\alpha} - \lambda]u(t) = f(t,u(t)), \ t \in (0,T], \\ u(0) = A, \ {}^{ML}\mathcal{D}_{0^+}^{\alpha} u(0) = B, \end{cases} \quad (1)$$

where $D = [0,T]$, $T > 0$, $0 < \alpha, \beta \leq 1$, $\lambda > 0$, $A, B \in \mathbb{R}$, $f \in C(\mathbb{R}^2, \mathbb{R})$, ${}^{ML}\mathcal{D}_{0^+}^{\alpha}$ and ${}^{ML}\mathcal{D}_{0^+}^{\beta}$ represent the fractional derivative with ML-kernel.

The remaining structure of the manuscript is as follows. Section 2 introduces some fundamental definitions and lemmas. In Section 3, we obtain some criteria on the existence of solutions to the system (1) by using some fixed-point theorems. The UH-type stabilities of (1) are built in Section 4. As applications, we conduct theoretical analysis and numerical simulation on some examples to verify the correctness and effectiveness of our main results in Section 5. Finally, a brief summary is provided in Section 6.

2. Preliminaries

Definition 1. *[27] For $0 < \alpha \leq 1$, $T > 0$ and $u : [0,T] \to \mathbb{R}$, the left-sided α-order Mittag–Leffler fractional integral of function u is defined by*

$$^{ML}\mathcal{I}_{0^+}^{\alpha} u(t) = \frac{1-\alpha}{\mathcal{N}(\alpha)} u(t) + \frac{\alpha}{\mathcal{N}(\alpha)\Gamma(\alpha)} \int_0^t (t-s)^{\alpha-1} u(s) ds,$$

provided the integral exists, here $\Gamma(\alpha)$ is the gamma function, $\mathcal{N}(\alpha) \in C([0,1],(0,1])$ is a normalization constant satisfying $\mathcal{N}(0) = \mathcal{N}(1) = 1$.

Definition 2. *[17] For $0 < \alpha \leq 1$, $T > 0$ and $u \in C^1(0,T)$, the left-sided α-order Mittag–Leffler fractional derivative of function u in sense of Caputo is given by*

$$^{ML}\mathcal{D}_{0^+}^{\alpha} u(t) = \frac{\mathcal{N}(\alpha)}{(1-\alpha)} \int_0^t \mathbb{E}_{\alpha}\left[-\frac{\alpha}{1-\alpha}(t-s)^{\alpha}\right] u'(s) ds,$$

where $\mathbb{E}_{\alpha}(\cdot)$ is single parameter Mittag-Leffer function and defined by

$$\mathbb{E}_{\alpha}(x) = \sum_{k=0}^{\infty} \frac{x^k}{\Gamma(\alpha k + 1)}.$$

Remark 1. *The Caputo fractional derivative of order $0 < \alpha \leq 1$ of a continuous function $u : (0,\infty) \to \mathbb{R}$ is defined by*

$$^C\mathcal{D}_{0^+}^{\alpha} u(t) = \frac{1}{\Gamma(1-\alpha)} \int_0^t (t-s)^{-\alpha} u'(s) ds,$$

provided that the right-hand side is pointwise defined on $(0,\infty)$. From Definition 2 and the Caputo fractional derivative, one finds two differences between them. One is that the coefficients are different. The other is that the kernel function is different. The kernel function $(t-s)^{-\alpha}$ of Caputo fractional derivative is singular at $s = t$, but the kernel function $\mathbb{E}_{\alpha}\left[-\frac{\alpha}{1-\alpha}(t-s)^{\alpha}\right]$ of Mittag–Leffler fractional derivative is nonsingular at $s = t$.

Lemma 1. *[37] Assume that $h \in C[0,T]$. Then, the unique solution of fractional differential equation*

$$\begin{cases} {}^{ML}\mathcal{D}_{0^+}^{\gamma} w(t) = h(t), \ t \in (0,T), \ 0 < \gamma \leq 1, \\ w(0) = w_0, \end{cases}$$

is written as

$$w(t) = w_0 + \frac{1-\gamma}{\mathcal{N}(\gamma)}[h(t) - h(0)] + \frac{\gamma}{\mathcal{N}(\gamma)\Gamma(\gamma)}\int_0^t (t-s)^{\gamma-1} h(s) ds.$$

Remark 2. *It follows from Definition 2 and Lemma 1 that $^{ML}\mathcal{D}_{0^+}^\alpha u(t) \equiv 0$ if and only if $u(t) \equiv$ constant.*

Lemma 2. *Let $T > 0$, $0 < \alpha, \beta \leq 1$, $\lambda > 0$, $A, B \in \mathbb{R}$, $f \in C(\mathbb{R}^2, \mathbb{R})$. If $\delta \triangleq 1 - \frac{\lambda(1-\alpha)}{\mathcal{N}(\alpha)} \neq 0$, then the fractional differential Langevin Equation (1) is equivalent to the following integral equation*

$$\begin{aligned}
u(t) = & A + \frac{1}{\delta}\Bigg\{ \frac{B - \lambda A}{\mathcal{N}(\alpha)\Gamma(\alpha)} t^\alpha + \frac{(1-\alpha)(1-\beta)}{\mathcal{N}(\alpha)\mathcal{N}(\beta)}[f(t, u(t)) - f(0, A)] \\
& + \frac{\lambda \alpha}{\mathcal{N}(\alpha)\Gamma(\alpha)}\int_0^t (t-s)^{\alpha-1} u(s) ds + \frac{(1-\alpha)\beta}{\mathcal{N}(\alpha)\mathcal{N}(\beta)\Gamma(\beta)}\int_0^t (t-s)^{\beta-1} f(s, u(s)) ds \\
& + \frac{\alpha(1-\beta)}{\mathcal{N}(\alpha)\mathcal{N}(\beta)\Gamma(\alpha)}\int_0^t (t-s)^{\alpha-1} f(s, u(s)) ds \\
& + \frac{\alpha\beta}{\mathcal{N}(\alpha)\mathcal{N}(\beta)\Gamma(\alpha+\beta)}\int_0^t (t-s)^{\alpha+\beta-1} f(s, u(s)) ds \Bigg\}, \ t \in D.
\end{aligned} \quad (2)$$

Proof. Assume that the function $u(t) \in C(0, T)$ is a solution of (1), Then, for $t \in D$, we derive from Lemma 1 that

$$\begin{aligned}
\left[^{ML}\mathcal{D}_{0^+}^\alpha - \lambda\right] u(t) = & \ ^{ML}\mathcal{D}_{0^+}^\alpha u(0) - \lambda u(0) + \frac{1-\beta}{\mathcal{N}(\beta)}[f(t, u(t)) - f(0, u(0))] \\
& + \frac{\beta}{\mathcal{N}(\beta)\Gamma(\beta)}\int_0^t (t-\tau)^{\beta-1} f(\tau, u(\tau)) d\tau.
\end{aligned} \quad (3)$$

(3) gives

$$\begin{aligned}
^{ML}\mathcal{D}_{0^+}^\alpha u(t) = & \left(^{ML}\mathcal{D}_{0^+}^\alpha u(0) - \lambda u(0)\right) + \lambda u(t) + \frac{1-\beta}{\mathcal{N}(\beta)}[f(t, u(t)) - f(0, u(0))] \\
& + \frac{\beta}{\mathcal{N}(\beta)\Gamma(\beta)}\int_0^t (t-\tau)^{\beta-1} f(\tau, u(\tau)) d\tau.
\end{aligned} \quad (4)$$

From Lemma 1, $u(0) = A$ and (4), we yield

$$\begin{aligned}
u(t) = & A + \frac{1-\alpha}{\mathcal{N}(\alpha)}\bigg[\lambda[u(t) - A] + \frac{1-\beta}{\mathcal{N}(\beta)}[f(t, u(t)) - f(0, A)] \\
& + \frac{\beta}{\mathcal{N}(\beta)\Gamma(\beta)}\int_0^t (t-\tau)^{\beta-1} f(\tau, u(\tau)) d\tau\bigg] + \frac{\alpha}{\mathcal{N}(\alpha)\Gamma(\alpha)} \\
& \times \int_0^t (t-s)^{\alpha-1}\bigg[(B - \lambda A) + \lambda u(s) + \frac{1-\beta}{\mathcal{N}(\beta)} f(s, u(s)) \\
& + \frac{\beta}{\mathcal{N}(\beta)\Gamma(\beta)}\int_0^s (s-\tau)^{\beta-1} f(\tau, u(\tau)) d\tau\bigg] ds \\
= & \left[1 - \frac{\lambda(1-\alpha)}{\mathcal{N}(\alpha)}\right] A + \frac{\lambda(1-\alpha)}{\mathcal{N}(\alpha)} u(t) + \frac{(1-\alpha)(1-\beta)}{\mathcal{N}(\alpha)\mathcal{N}(\beta)}[f(t, u(t)) - f(0, A)] \\
& + \frac{(1-\alpha)\beta}{\mathcal{N}(\alpha)\mathcal{N}(\beta)\Gamma(\beta)}\int_0^t (t-\tau)^{\beta-1} f(\tau, u(\tau)) d\tau + \frac{B - \lambda A}{\mathcal{N}(\alpha)\Gamma(\alpha)} t^\alpha \\
& + \frac{\lambda \alpha}{\mathcal{N}(\alpha)\Gamma(\alpha)}\int_0^t (t-s)^{\alpha-1} u(s) ds + \frac{\alpha(1-\beta)}{\mathcal{N}(\alpha)\mathcal{N}(\beta)\Gamma(\alpha)}\int_0^t (t-s)^{\alpha-1} f(s, u(s)) ds \\
& + \frac{\alpha\beta}{\mathcal{N}(\alpha)\mathcal{N}(\beta)\Gamma(\alpha)\Gamma(\beta)}\int_0^t (t-s)^{\alpha-1}\bigg[\int_0^s (s-\tau)^{\beta-1} f(\tau, u(\tau)) d\tau\bigg] ds.
\end{aligned} \quad (5)$$

Noting the last integral term of (5), we exchange the order of double integrals to get

$$\frac{\alpha\beta}{\mathcal{N}(\alpha)\mathcal{N}(\beta)\Gamma(\alpha)\Gamma(\beta)} \int_0^t (t-s)^{\alpha-1} \left[\int_0^s (s-\tau)^{\beta-1} f(\tau,u(\tau))d\tau \right] ds$$

$$= \frac{\alpha\beta}{\mathcal{N}(\alpha)\mathcal{N}(\beta)\Gamma(\alpha)\Gamma(\beta)} \int_0^t f(\tau,u(\tau)) \left[\int_\tau^t (t-s)^{\alpha-1}(s-\tau)^{\beta-1} ds \right] d\tau$$

$$= \frac{\alpha\beta}{\mathcal{N}(\alpha)\mathcal{N}(\beta)\Gamma(\alpha+\beta)} \int_0^t (t-\tau)^{\alpha+\beta-1} f(\tau,u(\tau))d\tau. \tag{6}$$

It follows from (5) and (6) that

$$u(t) = A + \frac{1}{\delta} \left\{ \frac{B-\lambda A}{\mathcal{N}(\alpha)\Gamma(\alpha)} t^\alpha + \frac{(1-\alpha)(1-\beta)}{\mathcal{N}(\alpha)\mathcal{N}(\beta)} [f(t,u(t)) - f(0,A)] \right.$$
$$+ \frac{\lambda\alpha}{\mathcal{N}(\alpha)\Gamma(\alpha)} \int_0^t (t-s)^{\alpha-1} u(s) ds + \frac{(1-\alpha)\beta}{\mathcal{N}(\alpha)\mathcal{N}(\beta)\Gamma(\beta)} \int_0^t (t-\tau)^{\beta-1} f(\tau,u(\tau))d\tau$$
$$+ \frac{\alpha(1-\beta)}{\mathcal{N}(\alpha)\mathcal{N}(\beta)\Gamma(\alpha)} \int_0^t (t-s)^{\alpha-1} f(s,u(s)) ds$$
$$\left. + \frac{\alpha\beta}{\mathcal{N}(\alpha)\mathcal{N}(\beta)\Gamma(\alpha+\beta)} \int_0^t (t-\tau)^{\alpha+\beta-1} f(\tau,u(\tau))d\tau \right\}. \tag{7}$$

Thus, Equation (2) holds, that is, $u(t) \in C(0,T)$ is also a solution of integral Equation (2). Furthermore, vice versa, if $u(t) \in C(0,T)$ is a solution of integral Equation (2), then one knows that (4) and (3) hold by finding the fractional derivative $^{Ml}\mathcal{D}_{0+}^\alpha$ at both ends of (2). Next, by finding the fractional derivative $^{Ml}\mathcal{D}_{0+}^\beta$ at both ends of (3), one easily gets the first fractional equation of (1). According to (2) and (3), we have $u(0) = A$ and $^{Ml}\mathcal{D}_{0+}^\alpha u(0) = B$. Thus, we verify that $u(t) \in C(0,T)$ also satisfies system (1). The proof is completed. □

3. Existence of Solutions

In this section, by applying the following important fixed-point theorems, we emphasize to investigate the existence of solutions for system (1).

Lemma 3. *[38] Let $\mathbb{E}$ be a non-empty closed subset of a Banach space $\mathbb{X}$. If $\mathscr{T} : \mathbb{E} \to \mathbb{E}$ is contractive, namely, there is a constant $0 < k < 1$ such that $\|\mathscr{T}u - \mathscr{T}v\| \leq k\|u - v\|$, $\forall u, v \in \mathbb{E}$, then $\mathscr{T}$ has a unique fixed point $u^* \in \mathbb{E}$ such that $\mathscr{T}u^* = u^*$.*

Lemma 4. *(Krasnoselskii's fixed-point theorem [39]) Let $\mathbb{Y}$ be a non-empty closed convex subset of a Banach space $\mathbb{X}$. Assume that $\mathscr{P}$ and $\mathscr{Q}$ are two operators satisfying*
(i) $\mathscr{P}u + \mathscr{Q}v \in \mathbb{Y}, \forall u,v \in \mathbb{Y}$.
(ii) $\mathscr{P}$ is contraction, and $\mathscr{Q}$ is continuous and compact.
Then there is at least a solution $u^* \in \mathbb{Y}$ such that $u^* = \mathscr{P}u^* + \mathscr{Q}u^*$.

By (2), we take $D = [0,T]$, $\mathbb{X} = C(D,\mathbb{R})$. Then $\mathbb{X}$ is a Banach space with the norm $\|u\| = \sup_{t \in D} |u(t)|$. We shall study the existence and stability of the solution of (1) in $(\mathbb{X}, \|\cdot\|)$. In the whole paper, we need the following essential assumption.

(H_1) $T, \alpha, \beta, \lambda, A$ and B are some constants and satisfy $T, \lambda > 0$, $0 < \alpha, \beta \leq 1$, $A, B \in \mathbb{R}$ and $\delta \triangleq 1 - \frac{\lambda(1-\alpha)}{\mathcal{N}(\alpha)} \neq 0$.

Theorem 1. *Assume that (H_1) holds, and further assume that (H_2) and (H_3) are also true.*
(H_2) $f \in C(\mathbb{R}^2, \mathbb{R})$, and there is a constant $M > 0$ such that $|f(t,u)| \leq M, \forall t, u \in \mathbb{R}$.
(H_3) $0 < \kappa \triangleq \frac{\lambda T^\alpha}{|\mathcal{N}(\alpha) - \lambda(1-\alpha)|\Gamma(\alpha)} < 1$.

Then, the system (1) has at least one solution $u^*(t) \in \mathbb{X}$.

Proof. Based on Lemma 2, for all $u \in \mathbb{X}$, we define two operators $\mathscr{P}, \mathscr{Q} : \mathbb{X} \to \mathbb{X}$ as follows:

$$(\mathscr{P}u)(t) = A + \frac{1}{\delta}\left\{ \frac{B - \lambda A}{\mathcal{N}(\alpha)\Gamma(\alpha)}t^\alpha + \frac{\lambda\alpha}{\mathcal{N}(\alpha)\Gamma(\alpha)}\int_0^t (t-s)^{\alpha-1}u(s)ds \right\}, \quad \forall t \in D, u \in \mathbb{X}, \quad (8)$$

and

$$(\mathscr{Q}u)(t) = \frac{1}{\delta}\left\{ \frac{(1-\alpha)(1-\beta)}{\mathcal{N}(\alpha)\mathcal{N}(\beta)}[f(t, u(t)) - f(0, A)] + \frac{(1-\alpha)\beta}{\mathcal{N}(\alpha)\mathcal{N}(\beta)\Gamma(\beta)} \right.$$
$$\times \int_0^t (t-s)^{\beta-1}f(s, u(s))ds + \frac{\alpha(1-\beta)}{\mathcal{N}(\alpha)\mathcal{N}(\beta)\Gamma(\alpha)}\int_0^t (t-s)^{\alpha-1}f(s, u(s))ds$$
$$\left. + \frac{\alpha\beta}{\mathcal{N}(\alpha)\mathcal{N}(\beta)\Gamma(\alpha+\beta)}\int_0^t (t-s)^{\alpha+\beta-1}f(s, u(s))ds \right\}, \quad \forall t \in D, u \in \mathbb{X}. \quad (9)$$

It is easy to see from (8) and (9) that $\mathscr{P}u + \mathscr{Q}v \in \mathbb{X}, \forall u, v \in \mathbb{X}$. Thus, the condition (i) in Lemma 4 holds. In addition, for all $t \in D, u, v \in \mathbb{X}$, we have

$$|(\mathscr{P}u)(t) - (\mathscr{P}v)(t)| = \left| \frac{\lambda\alpha}{\delta\mathcal{N}(\alpha)\Gamma(\alpha)}\int_0^t (t-s)^{\alpha-1}[u(s) - v(s)]ds \right|$$
$$\leq \frac{\mathcal{N}(\alpha)}{|\mathcal{N}(\alpha) - \lambda(1-\alpha)|} \times \frac{\lambda\alpha}{\mathcal{N}(\alpha)\Gamma(\alpha)}\int_0^t (t-s)^{\alpha-1}|u(s) - v(s)|ds$$
$$\leq \frac{\lambda\alpha}{|\mathcal{N}(\alpha) - \lambda(1-\alpha)|\Gamma(\alpha)}\int_0^t (t-s)^{\alpha-1}ds \cdot \|u - v\| = \frac{\lambda t^\alpha}{|\mathcal{N}(\alpha) - \lambda(1-\alpha)|\Gamma(\alpha)}\|u - v\|$$
$$\leq \frac{\lambda T^\alpha}{|\mathcal{N}(\alpha) - \lambda(1-\alpha)|\Gamma(\alpha)}\|u - v\| = \kappa\|u - v\|. \quad (10)$$

(10) implies that

$$\|\mathscr{P}u - \mathscr{P}v\| \leq \frac{\lambda T^\alpha}{|\mathcal{N}(\alpha) - \lambda(1-\alpha)|\Gamma(\alpha)}\|u - v\| = \kappa\|u - v\|. \quad (11)$$

From (H_3) and (11), we know that $\mathscr{P} : \mathbb{X} \to \mathbb{X}$ is contractive.

Next, we shall show that $\mathscr{Q} : \mathbb{X} \to \mathbb{X}$ is a completely continuous operator by using the Arzelá–Ascoli theorem. Indeed, for all $t \in D, u \in \mathbb{X}$, we derive from ($H_2$) that

$$|(\mathscr{Q}u)(t)| \leq \frac{1}{|\delta|}\left\{ \frac{(1-\alpha)(1-\beta)}{\mathcal{N}(\alpha)\mathcal{N}(\beta)}[|f(t, u(t))| + |f(0, A)|] + \frac{(1-\alpha)\beta}{\mathcal{N}(\alpha)\mathcal{N}(\beta)\Gamma(\beta)} \right.$$
$$\times \int_0^t (t-s)^{\beta-1}|f(s, u(s))|ds + \frac{\alpha(1-\beta)}{\mathcal{N}(\alpha)\mathcal{N}(\beta)\Gamma(\alpha)}\int_0^t (t-s)^{\alpha-1}|f(s, u(s))|ds$$
$$\left. + \frac{\alpha\beta}{\mathcal{N}(\alpha)\mathcal{N}(\beta)\Gamma(\alpha+\beta)}\int_0^t (t-s)^{\alpha+\beta-1}|f(s, u(s))|ds \right\}$$
$$\leq \frac{M}{|\delta|}\left\{ \frac{2(1-\alpha)(1-\beta)}{\mathcal{N}(\alpha)\mathcal{N}(\beta)} + \frac{(1-\alpha)\beta}{\mathcal{N}(\alpha)\mathcal{N}(\beta)\Gamma(\beta)}\int_0^t (t-s)^{\beta-1}ds \right.$$
$$\left. + \frac{\alpha(1-\beta)}{\mathcal{N}(\alpha)\mathcal{N}(\beta)\Gamma(\alpha)}\int_0^t (t-s)^{\alpha-1}ds + \frac{\alpha\beta}{\mathcal{N}(\alpha)\mathcal{N}(\beta)\Gamma(\alpha+\beta)}\int_0^t (t-s)^{\alpha+\beta-1}ds \right\}$$
$$\leq \frac{M}{|\delta|}\left\{ \frac{2(1-\alpha)(1-\beta)}{\mathcal{N}(\alpha)\mathcal{N}(\beta)} + \frac{(1-\alpha)T^\beta}{\mathcal{N}(\alpha)\mathcal{N}(\beta)\Gamma(\beta)} + \frac{(1-\beta)T^\alpha}{\mathcal{N}(\alpha)\mathcal{N}(\beta)\Gamma(\alpha)} \right.$$
$$\left. + \frac{\alpha\beta T^{\alpha+\beta}}{\mathcal{N}(\alpha)\mathcal{N}(\beta)\Gamma(\alpha+\beta+1)} \right\} = \varrho M, \quad (12)$$

where $\varrho = \frac{1}{|\delta|}\left\{ \frac{2(1-\alpha)(1-\beta)}{\mathcal{N}(\alpha)\mathcal{N}(\beta)} + \frac{(1-\alpha)T^\beta}{\mathcal{N}(\alpha)\mathcal{N}(\beta)\Gamma(\beta)} + \frac{(1-\beta)T^\alpha}{\mathcal{N}(\alpha)\mathcal{N}(\beta)\Gamma(\alpha)} + \frac{\alpha\beta T^{\alpha+\beta}}{\mathcal{N}(\alpha)\mathcal{N}(\beta)\Gamma(\alpha+\beta+1)} \right\}$. (12) indicates that $\mathscr{Q} : \mathbb{X} \to \mathbb{X}$ is uniformly bounded.

On the other hand, for $\forall u \in \mathbb{X}$, $t_1, t_2 \in D$ with $t_1 < t_2$, it follows from $f \in C(\mathbb{R}^2, \mathbb{R})$ and (H_2) that

$$|(\mathcal{Q}u)(t_2) - (\mathcal{Q}u)(t_1)| = \frac{1}{|\delta|} \left| \frac{(1-\alpha)(1-\beta)}{\mathcal{N}(\alpha)\mathcal{N}(\beta)} [f(t_2, u(t_2)) - f(t_1, u(t_1))] \right.$$

$$+ \frac{(1-\alpha)\beta}{\mathcal{N}(\alpha)\mathcal{N}(\beta)\Gamma(\beta)} \left[\int_0^{t_2} (t_2-s)^{\beta-1} f(s, u(s)) ds - \int_0^{t_1} (t_1-s)^{\beta-1} f(s, u(s)) ds \right]$$

$$+ \frac{\alpha(1-\beta)}{\mathcal{N}(\alpha)\mathcal{N}(\beta)\Gamma(\alpha)} \left[\int_0^{t_2} (t_2-s)^{\alpha-1} f(s, u(s)) ds - \int_0^{t_1} (t_1-s)^{\alpha-1} f(s, u(s)) ds \right]$$

$$+ \frac{\alpha\beta}{\mathcal{N}(\alpha)\mathcal{N}(\beta)\Gamma(\alpha+\beta)} \left[\int_0^{t_2} (t_2-s)^{\alpha+\beta-1} f(s, u(s)) ds \right.$$

$$\left. \left. - \int_0^{t_1} (t_1-s)^{\alpha+\beta-1} f(s, u(s)) ds \right] \right|$$

$$= \frac{1}{|\delta|} \left| \frac{(1-\alpha)(1-\beta)}{\mathcal{N}(\alpha)\mathcal{N}(\beta)} [f(t_2, u(t_2)) - f(t_1, u(t_1))] + \frac{(1-\alpha)\beta}{\mathcal{N}(\alpha)\mathcal{N}(\beta)\Gamma(\beta)} \right.$$

$$\times \left[\int_{t_1}^{t_2} (t_2-s)^{\beta-1} f(s, u(s)) ds + \int_0^{t_1} \left[(t_2-s)^{\beta-1} - (t_1-s)^{\beta-1} \right] f(s, u(s)) ds \right]$$

$$+ \frac{\alpha(1-\beta)}{\mathcal{N}(\alpha)\mathcal{N}(\beta)\Gamma(\alpha)} \left[\int_{t_1}^{t_2} (t_2-s)^{\alpha-1} f(s, u(s)) ds + \int_0^{t_1} \left[(t_2-s)^{\alpha-1} - (t_1-s)^{\alpha-1} \right] \right.$$

$$\left. \times f(s, u(s)) ds \right] + \frac{\alpha\beta}{\mathcal{N}(\alpha)\mathcal{N}(\beta)\Gamma(\alpha+\beta)} \left[\int_{t_1}^{t_2} (t_2-s)^{\alpha+\beta-1} f(s, u(s)) ds \right.$$

$$\left. \left. + \int_0^{t_1} \left[(t_2-s)^{\alpha+\beta-1} - (t_1-s)^{\alpha+\beta-1} \right] f(s, u(s)) ds \right] \right|$$

$$\leq \frac{1}{|\delta|} \left\{ \frac{(1-\alpha)(1-\beta)}{\mathcal{N}(\alpha)\mathcal{N}(\beta)} |f(t_2, u(t_2)) - f(t_1, u(t_1))| + \frac{(1-\alpha)\beta}{\mathcal{N}(\alpha)\mathcal{N}(\beta)\Gamma(\beta)} \right.$$

$$\times \left[\int_{t_1}^{t_2} (t_2-s)^{\beta-1} |f(s, u(s))| ds + \int_0^{t_1} |(t_2-s)^{\beta-1} - (t_1-s)^{\beta-1}| |f(s, u(s))| ds \right]$$

$$+ \frac{\alpha(1-\beta)}{\mathcal{N}(\alpha)\mathcal{N}(\beta)\Gamma(\alpha)} \left[\int_{t_1}^{t_2} (t_2-s)^{\alpha-1} |f(s, u(s))| ds + \int_0^{t_1} |(t_2-s)^{\alpha-1} - (t_1-s)^{\alpha-1}| \right.$$

$$\left. \times |f(s, u(s))| ds \right] + \frac{\alpha\beta}{\mathcal{N}(\alpha)\mathcal{N}(\beta)\Gamma(\alpha+\beta)} \left[\int_{t_1}^{t_2} (t_2-s)^{\alpha+\beta-1} |f(s, u(s))| ds \right.$$

$$\left. \left. + \int_0^{t_1} |(t_2-s)^{\alpha+\beta-1} - (t_1-s)^{\alpha+\beta-1}| |f(s, u(s))| ds \right] \right\}$$

$$\leq \frac{1}{|\delta|} \left\{ \frac{(1-\alpha)(1-\beta)}{\mathcal{N}(\alpha)\mathcal{N}(\beta)} |f(t_2, u(t_2)) - f(t_1, u(t_1))| + \frac{M(1-\alpha)\beta}{\mathcal{N}(\alpha)\mathcal{N}(\beta)\Gamma(\beta)} \left[\int_{t_1}^{t_2} (t_2-s)^{\beta-1} ds \right. \right.$$

$$\left. + \int_0^T |(t_2-s)^{\beta-1} - (t_1-s)^{\beta-1}| ds \right] + \frac{M\alpha(1-\beta)}{\mathcal{N}(\alpha)\mathcal{N}(\beta)\Gamma(\alpha)} \left[\int_{t_1}^{t_2} (t_2-s)^{\alpha-1} ds \right.$$

$$\left. + \int_0^T |(t_2-s)^{\alpha-1} - (t_1-s)^{\alpha-1}| ds \right] + \frac{M\alpha\beta}{\mathcal{N}(\alpha)\mathcal{N}(\beta)\Gamma(\alpha+\beta)} \left[\int_{t_1}^{t_2} (t_2-s)^{\alpha+\beta-1} ds \right.$$

$$\left. \left. + \int_0^T |(t_2-s)^{\alpha+\beta-1} - (t_1-s)^{\alpha+\beta-1}| ds \right] \right\}$$

$$= \frac{1}{|\delta|} \left\{ \frac{(1-\alpha)(1-\beta)}{\mathcal{N}(\alpha)\mathcal{N}(\beta)} |f(t_2, u(t_2)) - f(t_1, u(t_1))| + \frac{M(1-\alpha)\beta}{\mathcal{N}(\alpha)\mathcal{N}(\beta)\Gamma(\beta)} \left[\frac{1}{\beta}(t_2-t_1)^{\beta} \right. \right.$$

$$\left. + \int_0^T |(t_2-s)^{\beta-1} - (t_1-s)^{\beta-1}| ds \right] + \frac{M\alpha(1-\beta)}{\mathcal{N}(\alpha)\mathcal{N}(\beta)\Gamma(\alpha)} \left[\frac{1}{\alpha}(t_2-t_1)^{\alpha} \right.$$

$$\left. + \int_0^T |(t_2-s)^{\alpha-1} - (t_1-s)^{\alpha-1}| ds \right] + \frac{M\alpha\beta}{\mathcal{N}(\alpha)\mathcal{N}(\beta)\Gamma(\alpha+\beta)} \left[\frac{1}{\alpha+\beta}(t_2-t_1)^{\alpha+\beta} \right.$$

$$\left. \left. + \int_0^T |(t_2-s)^{\alpha+\beta-1} - (t_1-s)^{\alpha+\beta-1}| ds \right] \right\} \to 0, \text{ as } t_2 \to t_1. \tag{13}$$

From (13), we conclude that, $\forall \epsilon > 0, \exists \sigma = \sigma(\epsilon) > 0$, for all $t_1, t_2 \in D, u \in \mathbb{X}$, when $|t_2 - t_1| < \sigma$, there is $|(\mathcal{Q}u)(t_2) - (\mathcal{Q}u)(t_1)| < \epsilon$, namely, $\mathcal{Q} : \mathbb{X} \to \mathbb{X}$ is equicontinuous. Thus, we verify that the condition (ii) is true. Therefore, according to Lemmas 2 and 4, one knows that there exists at least a fixed point $u^*(t) \in \mathbb{X}$ such that $u^*(t) = (\mathcal{P}u^*)(t) + (\mathcal{Q}u^*)(t)$, which is a solution of system (1). The proof is completed. □

Theorem 2. *Assume that* (H$_1$) *holds, further assume that* (H$_4$) *and* (H$_5$) *are also true.*

(H$_4$) $f \in C(\mathbb{R}^2, \mathbb{R})$, *and there is a constant* $L > 0$ *such that* $|f(t, u) - f(t, v)| \leq L|u - v|$, $\forall t, u, v \in \mathbb{R}$.

(H$_5$) $0 < \rho < 1$, *here* $\rho = \frac{1}{|\delta|}\{\frac{L(1-\alpha)(1-\beta)}{\mathcal{N}(\alpha)\mathcal{N}(\beta)} + \frac{L(1-\alpha)T^\beta}{\mathcal{N}(\alpha)\mathcal{N}(\beta)\Gamma(\beta)} + \frac{L(1-\beta)T^\alpha}{\mathcal{N}(\alpha)\mathcal{N}(\beta)\Gamma(\alpha)} + \frac{L\alpha\beta T^{\alpha+\beta}}{\mathcal{N}(\alpha)\mathcal{N}(\beta)\Gamma(\alpha+\beta+1)} + \frac{\lambda T^\alpha}{\mathcal{N}(\alpha)\Gamma(\alpha)}\}$.

Then system (1) *has a unique solution* $u^*(t) \in \mathbb{X}$.

Proof. According to Lemma 2, we define an operator $\mathcal{T} : \mathbb{X} \to \mathbb{X}$ as follows:

$$(\mathcal{T}u)(t) = A + \frac{1}{\delta}\left\{\frac{B - \lambda A}{\mathcal{N}(\alpha)\Gamma(\alpha)}t^\alpha + \frac{(1-\alpha)(1-\beta)}{\mathcal{N}(\alpha)\mathcal{N}(\beta)}[f(t, u(t)) - f(0, A)]\right.$$
$$+ \frac{\lambda\alpha}{\mathcal{N}(\alpha)\Gamma(\alpha)}\int_0^t (t-s)^{\alpha-1}u(s)ds + \frac{(1-\alpha)\beta}{\mathcal{N}(\alpha)\mathcal{N}(\beta)\Gamma(\beta)}\int_0^t (t-s)^{\beta-1}f(s, u(s))ds$$
$$+ \frac{\alpha(1-\beta)}{\mathcal{N}(\alpha)\mathcal{N}(\beta)\Gamma(\alpha)}\int_0^t (t-s)^{\alpha-1}f(s, u(s))ds$$
$$\left. + \frac{\alpha\beta}{\mathcal{N}(\alpha)\mathcal{N}(\beta)\Gamma(\alpha+\beta)}\int_0^t (t-s)^{\alpha+\beta-1}f(s, u(s))ds\right\}. \tag{14}$$

Then, for all $u, v \in \mathbb{X}$, we derive from (H$_4$) and (H$_5$) that

$$|(\mathcal{T}u)(t) - (\mathcal{T}v)(t)|$$
$$\leq \frac{1}{|\delta|}\left\{\frac{(1-\alpha)(1-\beta)}{\mathcal{N}(\alpha)\mathcal{N}(\beta)}|f(t,u(t)) - f(t,v(t))| + \frac{\lambda\alpha}{\mathcal{N}(\alpha)\Gamma(\alpha)}\int_0^t (t-s)^{\alpha-1}|u(s) - v(s)|ds\right.$$
$$+ \frac{(1-\alpha)\beta}{\mathcal{N}(\alpha)\mathcal{N}(\beta)\Gamma(\beta)}\int_0^t (t-s)^{\beta-1}|f(s,u(s)) - f(s,v(s))|ds$$
$$+ \frac{\alpha(1-\beta)}{\mathcal{N}(\alpha)\mathcal{N}(\beta)\Gamma(\alpha)}\int_0^t (t-s)^{\alpha-1}|f(s,u(s)) - f(s,v(s))|ds$$
$$\left. + \frac{\alpha\beta}{\mathcal{N}(\alpha)\mathcal{N}(\beta)\Gamma(\alpha+\beta)}\int_0^t (t-s)^{\alpha+\beta-1}|f(s,u(s)) - f(s,v(s))|ds\right\}$$
$$\leq \frac{1}{|\delta|}\left\{\frac{L(1-\alpha)(1-\beta)}{\mathcal{N}(\alpha)\mathcal{N}(\beta)}|u(t) - v(t)| + \frac{\lambda\alpha}{\mathcal{N}(\alpha)\Gamma(\alpha)}\int_0^t (t-s)^{\alpha-1}|u(s) - v(s)|ds\right.$$
$$+ \frac{L(1-\alpha)\beta}{\mathcal{N}(\alpha)\mathcal{N}(\beta)\Gamma(\beta)}\int_0^t (t-s)^{\beta-1}|u(s) - v(s)|ds$$
$$+ \frac{L\alpha(1-\beta)}{\mathcal{N}(\alpha)\mathcal{N}(\beta)\Gamma(\alpha)}\int_0^t (t-s)^{\alpha-1}|u(s) - v(s)|ds$$
$$\left. + \frac{L\alpha\beta}{\mathcal{N}(\alpha)\mathcal{N}(\beta)\Gamma(\alpha+\beta)}\int_0^t (t-s)^{\alpha+\beta-1}|u(s) - v(s)|ds\right\}$$
$$\leq \frac{1}{|\delta|}\left\{\frac{L(1-\alpha)(1-\beta)}{\mathcal{N}(\alpha)\mathcal{N}(\beta)} + \frac{\lambda\alpha}{\mathcal{N}(\alpha)\Gamma(\alpha)}\int_0^t (t-s)^{\alpha-1}ds + \frac{L(1-\alpha)\beta}{\mathcal{N}(\alpha)\mathcal{N}(\beta)\Gamma(\beta)}\int_0^t (t-s)^{\beta-1}ds\right.$$
$$\left. + \frac{L\alpha(1-\beta)}{\mathcal{N}(\alpha)\mathcal{N}(\beta)\Gamma(\alpha)}\int_0^t (t-s)^{\alpha-1}ds + \frac{L\alpha\beta}{\mathcal{N}(\alpha)\mathcal{N}(\beta)\Gamma(\alpha+\beta)}\int_0^t (t-s)^{\alpha+\beta-1}ds\right\}\|u - v\|$$
$$= \frac{1}{|\delta|}\left\{\frac{L(1-\alpha)(1-\beta)}{\mathcal{N}(\alpha)\mathcal{N}(\beta)} + \frac{\lambda t^\alpha}{\mathcal{N}(\alpha)\Gamma(\alpha)} + \frac{L(1-\alpha)t^\beta}{\mathcal{N}(\alpha)\mathcal{N}(\beta)\Gamma(\beta)}\right.$$
$$\left. + \frac{L(1-\beta)t^\alpha}{\mathcal{N}(\alpha)\mathcal{N}(\beta)\Gamma(\alpha)} + \frac{L\alpha\beta t^{\alpha+\beta}}{\mathcal{N}(\alpha)\mathcal{N}(\beta)\Gamma(\alpha+\beta+1)}\right\}\|u - v\|$$
$$\leq \frac{1}{|\delta|}\left\{\frac{L(1-\alpha)(1-\beta)}{\mathcal{N}(\alpha)\mathcal{N}(\beta)} + \frac{\lambda T^\alpha}{\mathcal{N}(\alpha)\Gamma(\alpha)} + \frac{L(1-\alpha)T^\beta}{\mathcal{N}(\alpha)\mathcal{N}(\beta)\Gamma(\beta)} + \frac{L(1-\beta)T^\alpha}{\mathcal{N}(\alpha)\mathcal{N}(\beta)\Gamma(\alpha)}\right.$$
$$\left. + \frac{L\alpha\beta T^{\alpha+\beta}}{\mathcal{N}(\alpha)\mathcal{N}(\beta)\Gamma(\alpha+\beta+1)}\right\}\|u - v\| = \rho\|u - v\|. \tag{15}$$

(15) leads to

$$\|\mathcal{T}u - \mathcal{T}v\| \leq \rho \|u - v\|. \tag{16}$$

By (16) and (H$_5$), we know that $\mathcal{T} : \mathbb{X} \to \mathbb{X}$ is contractive. Thus, it follows from Lemmas 3 and 2 that the operator has a unique fixed point $u^*(t)$, which is a unique solution of system (1). The proof is completed. □

4. Stability of Ulam–Hyers Type

This section mainly discusses the stability of types such as Ulam–Hyers, generalized Ulam–Hyers, Ulam–Hyers–Rassias and generalized Ulam–Hyers–Rassias for system (1).

Let $z \in \mathbb{X}$, $\varepsilon > 0$, $0 < \alpha, \beta \leq 1$ and $\varphi \in C(D, \mathbb{R}^+)$ be non-decreasing. Consider the following two inequalities

$$\begin{cases} |{}^{ML}\mathcal{D}_{0^+}^{\beta}[{}^{ML}\mathcal{D}_{0^+}^{\alpha} - \lambda]z(t) - f(t,z)| \leq \varepsilon, \ 0 < t \leq T, \\ z(0) = A, \ {}^{ML}\mathcal{D}_{0^+}^{\alpha} z(0) = B, \end{cases} \tag{17}$$

and

$$\begin{cases} |{}^{ML}\mathcal{D}_{0^+}^{\beta}[{}^{ML}\mathcal{D}_{0^+}^{\alpha} - \lambda]z(t) - f(t,z)| \leq \varphi(t)\varepsilon, \ 0 < t \leq T, \\ z(0) = A, \ {}^{ML}\mathcal{D}_{0^+}^{\alpha} z(0) = B. \end{cases} \tag{18}$$

Definition 3. *Assume that for each $\varepsilon > 0$ and each solution $z \in \mathbb{X}$ of inequality (17), there is a constant $C_1 > 0$ and a unique solution $u \in \mathbb{X}$ of system (1) such that*

$$\|z(t) - u(t)\| \leq C_1 \varepsilon,$$

then system (1) is called Ulam–Hyers stable (abbreviated as UH-stable).

Definition 4. *Assume that for each $\varepsilon > 0$ and each solution $z \in \mathbb{X}$ of inequality (17), there is a function $\theta(\cdot) \in C(\mathbb{R}, \mathbb{R}^+)$ with $\theta(0) = 0$ and a unique solution $u \in \mathbb{X}$ of system (1) such that*

$$\|z(t) - u(t)\| \leq \theta(\varepsilon),$$

then system (1) is called generalized Ulam–Hyers (GUH) stable (abbreviated as GUH-stable).

Definition 5. *Assume that for each $\varepsilon > 0$ and each solution $z \in \mathbb{X}$ of inequality (18), there is a constant $C_2 > 0$ and a unique solution $u \in \mathbb{X}$ of system (1) such that*

$$\|z(t) - u(t)\| \leq C_2 \varphi(t)\varepsilon, \ t \in D,$$

then system (1) is called Ulam–Hyers–Rassias stable (abbreviated as UHR-stable).

Definition 6. *Assume that for each $\varepsilon > 0$ and each solution $z \in \mathbb{X}$ of inequality (18), there is a constant $C_3 > 0$ and a unique solution $u \in \mathbb{X}$ of system (1) such that*

$$\|z(t) - u(t)\| \leq C_3 \varphi(t), \ t \in D,$$

then system (1) is called generalized Ulam–Hyers–Rassias stable (abbreviated as GUHR-stable).

Obviously, UH-stable $\Rightarrow$ GUH-stable, and UHR-stable $\Rightarrow$ GUHR-stable.

Remark 3. *A function $z \in \mathbb{X}$ is a solution of inequality (17) if and only if there exists a function $\phi \in \mathbb{X}$ such that*
(1) $|\phi(t)| \leq \varepsilon, 0 < t \leq T.$
(2) ${}^{ML}\mathcal{D}_{0^+}^{\beta}[{}^{ML}\mathcal{D}_{0^+}^{\alpha} - \lambda]z(t) = f(t,z) + \phi(t), \ 0 < t \leq T.$

Remark 4. A function $z \in \mathbb{X}$ is a solution of inequality (18) if and only if there exists a function $\psi \in \mathbb{X}$ such that

(1) $|\psi(t)| \leq \varphi(t)\epsilon, 0 < t \leq T.$
(2) $^{ML}\mathcal{D}_{0+}^{\beta}[^{ML}\mathcal{D}_{0+}^{\alpha} - \lambda]z(t) = f(t,z) + \psi(t),\ 0 < t \leq T.$

Theorem 3. *If all the conditions of Theorem 2 hold, then the system (1) is UH-stable and also GUH-stable.*

Proof. Based on Lemma 2 and Remark 3, the solution $z(t)$ of inequality (17) is expressed as

$$z(t) = A + \frac{1}{\delta}\left\{\frac{B - \lambda A}{\mathcal{N}(\alpha)\Gamma(\alpha)}t^{\alpha} + \frac{(1-\alpha)(1-\beta)}{\mathcal{N}(\alpha)\mathcal{N}(\beta)}[f(t,z(t)) - f(0,A) + \phi(t) - \phi(0)]\right.$$
$$+ \frac{\lambda\alpha}{\mathcal{N}(\alpha)\Gamma(\alpha)}\int_0^t (t-s)^{\alpha-1}z(s)ds + \frac{(1-\alpha)\beta}{\mathcal{N}(\alpha)\mathcal{N}(\beta)\Gamma(\beta)}\int_0^t (t-s)^{\beta-1}[f(s,z(s)) + \phi(s)]ds$$
$$+ \frac{\alpha(1-\beta)}{\mathcal{N}(\alpha)\mathcal{N}(\beta)\Gamma(\alpha)}\int_0^t (t-s)^{\alpha-1}[f(s,z(s)) + \phi(s)]ds$$
$$\left.+ \frac{\alpha\beta}{\mathcal{N}(\alpha)\mathcal{N}(\beta)\Gamma(\alpha+\beta)}\int_0^t (t-s)^{\alpha+\beta-1}[f(s,z(s)) + \phi(s)]ds\right\},\ t \in D. \tag{19}$$

By the Theorem 2 and Lemma 2, the unique solution $u^*(t)$ of (1) satisfies

$$u^*(t) = A + \frac{1}{\delta}\left\{\frac{B - \lambda A}{\mathcal{N}(\alpha)\Gamma(\alpha)}t^{\alpha} + \frac{(1-\alpha)(1-\beta)}{\mathcal{N}(\alpha)\mathcal{N}(\beta)}[f(t,u^*(t)) - f(0,A)]\right.$$
$$+ \frac{\lambda\alpha}{\mathcal{N}(\alpha)\Gamma(\alpha)}\int_0^t (t-s)^{\alpha-1}u^*(s)ds + \frac{(1-\alpha)\beta}{\mathcal{N}(\alpha)\mathcal{N}(\beta)\Gamma(\beta)}\int_0^t (t-s)^{\beta-1}f(s,u^*(s))ds$$
$$+ \frac{\alpha(1-\beta)}{\mathcal{N}(\alpha)\mathcal{N}(\beta)\Gamma(\alpha)}\int_0^t (t-s)^{\alpha-1}f(s,u^*(s))ds$$
$$\left.+ \frac{\alpha\beta}{\mathcal{N}(\alpha)\mathcal{N}(\beta)\Gamma(\alpha+\beta)}\int_0^t (t-s)^{\alpha+\beta-1}f(s,u^*(s))ds\right\},\ t \in D. \tag{20}$$

Similar to (15), it follows from (19) and (20) that

$$|z(t) - u^*(t)| \leq \frac{1}{|\delta|}\left\{\frac{(1-\alpha)(1-\beta)}{\mathcal{N}(\alpha)\mathcal{N}(\beta)}[|f(t,z(t)) - f(t,u^*(t))| + |\phi(t)| + |\phi(0)|]\right.$$
$$+ \frac{\lambda\alpha}{\mathcal{N}(\alpha)\Gamma(\alpha)}\int_0^t (t-s)^{\alpha-1}|z(s) - u^*(s)|ds + \frac{(1-\alpha)\beta}{\mathcal{N}(\alpha)\mathcal{N}(\beta)\Gamma(\beta)}\int_0^t (t-s)^{\beta-1}$$
$$\times [|f(s,z(s)) - f(s,u^*(s))| + |\phi(s)|]ds + \frac{\alpha(1-\beta)}{\mathcal{N}(\alpha)\mathcal{N}(\beta)\Gamma(\alpha)}\int_0^t (t-s)^{\alpha-1}$$
$$\times [|f(s,z(s)) - f(s,u^*(s))| + |\phi(s)|]ds + \frac{\alpha\beta}{\mathcal{N}(\alpha)\mathcal{N}(\beta)\Gamma(\alpha+\beta)}$$
$$\left.\int_0^t (t-s)^{\alpha+\beta-1}[|f(s,z(s)) - f(s,u^*(s))| + |\phi(s)|]ds\right\}$$
$$\leq \frac{1}{|\delta|}\left\{\frac{(1-\alpha)(1-\beta)}{\mathcal{N}(\alpha)\mathcal{N}(\beta)}[L\|z(t) - u^*(t)\| + \varepsilon + \varepsilon] + \frac{\lambda\alpha}{\mathcal{N}(\alpha)\Gamma(\alpha)}\int_0^t (t-s)^{\alpha-1}\right.$$
$$\times \|z(s) - u^*(s)\|ds + \frac{(1-\alpha)\beta}{\mathcal{N}(\alpha)\mathcal{N}(\beta)\Gamma(\beta)}\int_0^t (t-s)^{\beta-1}[L\|z(s) - u^*(s)\| + \varepsilon]ds$$
$$+ \frac{\alpha(1-\beta)}{\mathcal{N}(\alpha)\mathcal{N}(\beta)\Gamma(\alpha)}\int_0^t (t-s)^{\alpha-1}[L\|z(s) - u^*(s)\| + \varepsilon]ds$$
$$\left.+ \frac{\alpha\beta}{\mathcal{N}(\alpha)\mathcal{N}(\beta)\Gamma(\alpha+\beta)}\int_0^t (t-s)^{\alpha+\beta-1}[L\|z(s) - u^*(s)\| + \varepsilon]ds\right\}$$
$$\leq \rho\|z(t) - u^*(t)\| + \varrho\varepsilon,$$

which implies that

$$\|z(t) - u^*(t)\| \leq \frac{\varrho}{1-\rho}\varepsilon. \tag{21}$$

Thus, (21) shows that system (1) is UH-stable and also GUH-stable. The proof is completed. □

Theorem 4. *If all the conditions of Theorem 2 hold, then the system (1) is UHR-stable and also GUHR-stable.*

Proof. By applying Lemma 2 and Remark 4, the solution $z(t)$ of inequality (18) is formulated by

$$\begin{aligned}z(t) =& A + \frac{1}{\delta}\bigg\{\frac{B-\lambda A}{\mathcal{N}(\alpha)\Gamma(\alpha)}t^\alpha + \frac{(1-\alpha)(1-\beta)}{\mathcal{N}(\alpha)\mathcal{N}(\beta)}[f(t,z(t))-f(0,A)+\psi(t)-\psi(0)] \\ &+ \frac{\lambda\alpha}{\mathcal{N}(\alpha)\Gamma(\alpha)}\int_0^t(t-s)^{\alpha-1}z(s)ds + \frac{(1-\alpha)\beta}{\mathcal{N}(\alpha)\mathcal{N}(\beta)\Gamma(\beta)}\int_0^t(t-s)^{\beta-1}[f(s,z(s))+\psi(s)]ds \\ &+ \frac{\alpha(1-\beta)}{\mathcal{N}(\alpha)\mathcal{N}(\beta)\Gamma(\alpha)}\int_0^t(t-s)^{\alpha-1}[f(s,z(s))+\psi(s)]ds \\ &+ \frac{\alpha\beta}{\mathcal{N}(\alpha)\mathcal{N}(\beta)\Gamma(\alpha+\beta)}\int_0^t(t-s)^{\alpha+\beta-1}[f(s,z(s))+\psi(s)]ds\bigg\},\ t\in D.\end{aligned} \tag{22}$$

Noting that $\varphi \geq 0$ is non-decreasing and together with (19) and (22), we have

$$\begin{aligned}|z(t)-u^*(t)| \leq & \frac{1}{|\delta|}\bigg\{\frac{(1-\alpha)(1-\beta)}{\mathcal{N}(\alpha)\mathcal{N}(\beta)}[|f(t,z(t))-f(t,u^*(t))|+|\psi(t)-\psi(0)|] \\ &+ \frac{\lambda\alpha}{\mathcal{N}(\alpha)\Gamma(\alpha)}\int_0^t(t-s)^{\alpha-1}|z(s)-u^*(s)|ds + \frac{(1-\alpha)\beta}{\mathcal{N}(\alpha)\mathcal{N}(\beta)\Gamma(\beta)}\int_0^t(t-s)^{\beta-1} \\ &\times[|f(s,z(s))-f(s,u^*(s))|+|\psi(s)|]ds + \frac{\alpha(1-\beta)}{\mathcal{N}(\alpha)\mathcal{N}(\beta)\Gamma(\alpha)}\int_0^t(t-s)^{\alpha-1} \\ &\times[|f(s,z(s))-f(s,u^*(s))|+|\psi(s)|]ds + \frac{\alpha\beta}{\mathcal{N}(\alpha)\mathcal{N}(\beta)\Gamma(\alpha+\beta)} \\ &\int_0^t(t-s)^{\alpha+\beta-1}[|f(s,z(s))-f(s,u^*(s))|+|\psi(s)|]ds\bigg\} \\ \leq & \frac{1}{|\delta|}\bigg\{\frac{(1-\alpha)(1-\beta)}{\mathcal{N}(\alpha)\mathcal{N}(\beta)}[L\|z(t)-u^*(t)\|+\varphi(t)\varepsilon+\varphi(t)\varepsilon|] \\ &+ \frac{\lambda\alpha}{\mathcal{N}(\alpha)\Gamma(\alpha)}\int_0^t(t-s)^{\alpha-1}\|z(s)-u^*(s)\|ds + \frac{(1-\alpha)\beta}{\mathcal{N}(\alpha)\mathcal{N}(\beta)\Gamma(\beta)}\int_0^t(t-s)^{\beta-1} \\ &\times[L\|z(s)-u^*(s)\|+\varphi(t)\varepsilon]ds + \frac{\alpha(1-\beta)}{\mathcal{N}(\alpha)\mathcal{N}(\beta)\Gamma(\alpha)}\int_0^t(t-s)^{\alpha-1} \\ &\times[L\|z(s)-u^*(s)\|+\varphi(t)\varepsilon]ds + \frac{\alpha\beta}{\mathcal{N}(\alpha)\mathcal{N}(\beta)\Gamma(\alpha+\beta)} \\ &\int_0^t(t-s)^{\alpha+\beta-1}[L\|z(s)-u^*(s)\|+\varphi(t)\varepsilon]ds\bigg\} \\ \leq & \rho\|z(t)-u^*(t)\|+\varrho\varphi(t)\varepsilon,\ t\in D,\end{aligned}$$

which implies that

$$\|z(t)-u^*(t)\| \leq \frac{\varrho}{1-\rho}\varphi(t)\varepsilon,\ t\in D. \tag{23}$$

Thus, (23) shows that system (1) is UHR-stable and also GUHR-stable. The proof is completed. □

5. Applications

In this section, we will apply our results to deal with the existence and stability of solutions for two specific systems.

5.1. Theoretical Analysis

Example 1. *Consider the following nonlinear fractional order Langevin equation*

$$\begin{cases} {}^{ML}\mathcal{D}_{0+}^{0.3}[{}^{ML}\mathcal{D}_{0+}^{0.9} - \frac{2}{3}]u(t) = \sin(t) + \arctan(u(t)), \ t \in [0,1], \\ u(0) = 1, \ {}^{ML}\mathcal{D}_{0+}^{0.9}u(0) = 1. \end{cases} \tag{24}$$

Obviously, $T = 1 > 0$, $A = B = 1$, $0 < \alpha = 0.9 \leq 1$, $0 < \beta = 0.3 \leq 1$, $\lambda = \frac{2}{3} > 0$, $f(t, u) = \sin(t) + \arctan(u) \in C(\mathbb{R}^2, \mathbb{R})$. Take $\mathcal{N}(x) = 1 - x + \frac{x}{\Gamma(x)}, 0 < x \leq 1$. By a simple calculation, one has $\mathcal{N}(0) = \mathcal{N}(1) = 1$, $|f(t,u)| \leq M = 1 + \frac{\pi}{2}$ and

$$\delta = 1 - \frac{\lambda(1-\alpha)}{\mathcal{N}(\alpha)} \approx 0.9292 > 0, \quad 0 < \kappa = \frac{\lambda T^\alpha}{|\mathcal{N}(\alpha) - \lambda(1-\alpha)|\Gamma(\alpha)} \approx 0.7125 < 1.$$

Thus, the conditions (H_1)-(H_3) hold. It follows from Theorem 1 that Equation (24) has at least a solution $u^*(t) \in C^1([0,1], \mathbb{R})$.

Example 2. *Consider the following nonlinear fractional order Langevin equation*

$$\begin{cases} {}^{ML}\mathcal{D}_{0+}^{0.8}[{}^{ML}\mathcal{D}_{0+}^{0.6} - \frac{1}{5}]u(t) = \frac{t^2+2u(t)}{10}, \ t \in [0,1], \\ u(0) = 3, \ {}^{ML}\mathcal{D}_{0+}^{0.9}u(0) = -1. \end{cases} \tag{25}$$

Obviously, $T = 1 > 0$, $A = 3$, $B = -1$, $0 < \alpha = 0.6 \leq 1$, $0 < \beta = 0.8 \leq 1$, $\lambda = \frac{1}{5} > 0$, $f(t,u) = \frac{t^2+2u}{10} \in C(\mathbb{R}^2, \mathbb{R})$. Take $\mathcal{N}(x) = 1 - x + \frac{x}{\Gamma(x)}, 0 < x \leq 1$. By a simple calculation, one has $\mathcal{N}(0) = \mathcal{N}(1) = 1$, $|f(t,u) - f(t,v)| \leq \frac{1}{5}|u-v|$, $L = \frac{1}{5}$, $\delta = 1 - \frac{\lambda(1-\alpha)}{\mathcal{N}(\alpha)} \approx 0.9004 > 0$ and

$$\rho = \frac{1}{|\delta|} \left\{ \frac{L(1-\alpha)(1-\beta)}{\mathcal{N}(\alpha)\mathcal{N}(\beta)} + \frac{L(1-\alpha)T^\beta}{\mathcal{N}(\alpha)\mathcal{N}(\beta)\Gamma(\beta)} + \frac{L(1-\beta)T^\alpha}{\mathcal{N}(\alpha)\mathcal{N}(\beta)\Gamma(\alpha)} \right.$$
$$\left. + \frac{L\alpha\beta T^{\alpha+\beta}}{\mathcal{N}(\alpha)\mathcal{N}(\beta)\Gamma(\alpha+\beta+1)} + \frac{\lambda T^\alpha}{\mathcal{N}(\alpha)\Gamma(\alpha)} \right\} \approx 0.3731 < 1.$$

Thus, we verify that the conditions (H_1), (H_4) and (H_5) are true. From Theorem 2, we know that Equation (24) has a unique solution $u^*(t) \in C^1([0,1], \mathbb{R})$. Meanwhile, according to Theorems 3 and 4, we conclude that Equation (24) is stable in the sense of UH, GUH, UHR and GUHR, respectively.

5.2. Numerical Simulation

Let $v(t) = ({}^{ML}\mathcal{D}_{0+}^\alpha - \lambda)u(t)$, then Equation (1) is transformed into a system of equations as follows:

$$\begin{cases} {}^{ML}\mathcal{D}_{0+}^\alpha u(t) = \lambda u(t) + v(t), \ t \in (0, T], \\ {}^{ML}\mathcal{D}_{0+}^\beta v(t) = f(t, u(t)), \ t \in (0, T], \\ u(0) = A, \ v(0) = B - \lambda A. \end{cases} \tag{26}$$

When $\alpha = \beta = 1$, the fractional Langevin Equation (1) is a classical integer-order differential Langevin equation formulated by

$$\begin{cases} [u'(t) - \lambda u(t)]' = f(t, u(t)), \ t \in (0, T], \\ u(0) = A, \ u'(0) = B. \end{cases} \tag{27}$$

The system of equations equivalent to Equation (27) is formed as

$$\begin{cases} u'(t) = \lambda u(t) + v(t), \ t \in (0, T], \\ v'(t) = f(t, u(t)), \ t \in (0, T], \\ u(0) = A, \ v(0) = B - \lambda A. \end{cases} \tag{28}$$

The numerical simulation algorithm in this manuscript is briefly stated as follows: Step 1, by applying Lemma 1, it is similar to the proof of Lemma 2 whereby the fractional Langevin equations (26) are transformed into a system of integral equations; Step 2, by calculating the derivative of integer order and simplifying, this system of integral equations becomes a system of delay differential equations of integer order; Step 3, by using ddesd toolbox in MATLAB, this system of delay differential equations of integer order can be numerically simulated. In addition, the corresponding integer-order Langevin Equations (28) are simulated by ode23 toolbox in MATLAB. Next, based on the above algorithm, we numerically simulate and discuss the solutions of (26) and (28) corresponding to Example 1 and Example 2, respectively.

Discussions. (a) Under the condition of the same values of system parameters, the simulations of solutions of Example 1 and its corresponding integer-order differential equation are shown in Figure 1 and Figure 2, respectively. Through the comparison of Figures 1 and 2, $u(t)$ is very different in two aspects. On the one hand, although the solutions $u(t)$ of fractional-order and integer-order equations increase monotonically in $t \in [0, 1]$, the curvature of $u(t)$ in Figure 1 is much larger than that in Figure 2. On the other hand, when $t \in [0, 1]$, we find that $1 \leq u(t) < 14$ in Figure 1 and $1 \leq u(t) < 3.5$ in Figure 2, which is also very different.

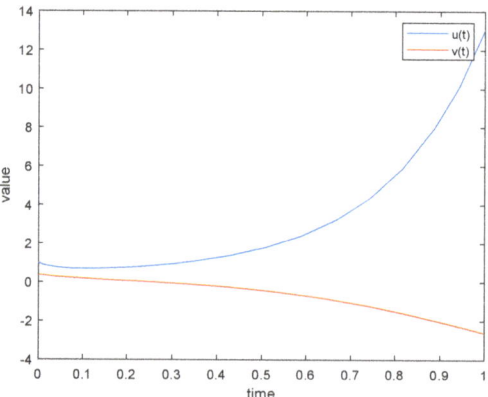

Figure 1. Numerical simulation of solutions of Example 1.

(b) Under the condition of the same values of system parameters, the simulations of solutions of Example 2 and the corresponding integer-order differential equation are shown in Figure 3 and Figure 4, respectively. Through the comparison of Figures 3 and 4, $u(t)$ is greatly different as follows. In Figure 4, the solution $u(t)$ of integer-order equation increases monotonically in $t \in [0, 1]$. However, the solution $u(t)$ of fractional equation is not monotonous and has maxima and minima in $t \in [0, 1]$, shown in Figure 3.

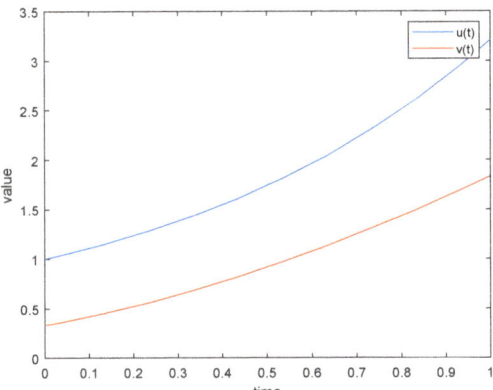

Figure 2. Numerical simulation of the integer-order equation solutions corresponding to Example 1.

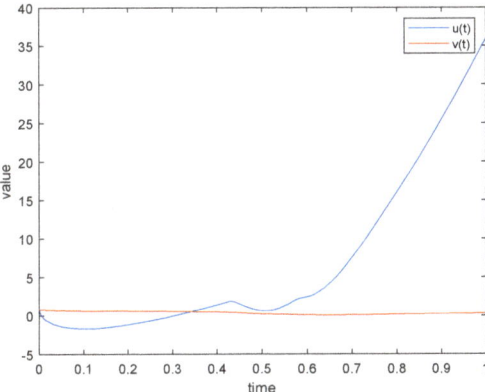

Figure 3. Numerical simulation of solutions of Example 2.

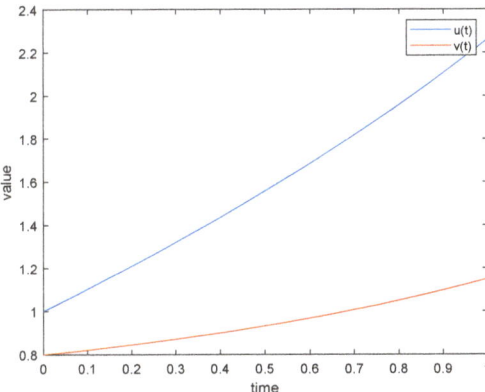

Figure 4. Numerical simulation of the integer-order equation solutions corresponding to Example 2.

(c) Under the condition of the same values of system parameters, the simulations of Ulam–Hyers stability of Example 2 are shown in Figure 5. It follows from the images of $\varepsilon = 0.1$ and $\varepsilon = 0.05$ that, when $\varepsilon \to 0^+$, the solution curve of the inequality (17) almost coincides with that of Equation (25), which shows that Equation (25) is UH-stable.

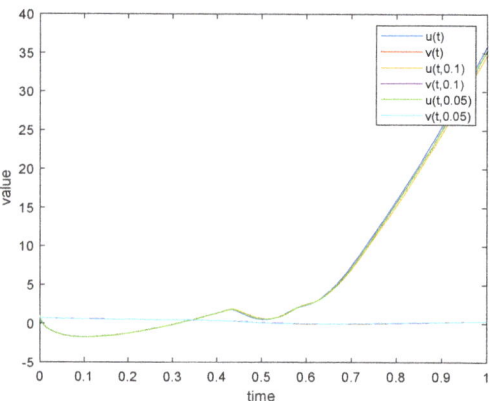

Figure 5. Example 2 numerical simulation of the UH-stability of the solutions with $\varepsilon = 0.1, 0.05$.

6. Conclusions

It is well known that the Langevin equation is a powerful tool in describing the random motion of particles in a fluid. In a particularly complex viscous liquid, the integer-order Langevin equation that describes the motion of particles is no longer accurate. Some scholars have started using the fractional Langevin equation as a model to study this problem, and have achieved good results. However, the research results of these fractional Langevin systems are all centered on Riemann–Liouville or Caputo fractional derivatives. Unfortunately, Riemann–Liouville and Caputo fractional derivatives produce singularities under certain conditions, which renders their application difficult in certain physical fields. Interestingly, the fractional derivative with ML-kernel can eliminate the singularity. In this manuscript, we investigate the existence, uniqueness and UH-stability of solutions for the nonlinear fractional-order Langevin equation with ML-kernel. The theoretical analysis and numerical simulations of two examples verify the correctness and effectiveness of our main conclusions. Furthermore, the mathematical theories and methods employed in this paper can be used as a reference for the study of other fractional differential systems. In addition, considering the fact that the Langevin equation is a classical stochastic differential equation, we can further study the fractional random Langevin equation of nonsingular ML-kernel in future work to reveal the influence of random noise on the motion of free particles.

Funding: The APC was funded by research start-up funds for high-level talents of Taizhou University.

Data Availability Statement: No data were used to support this study.

Acknowledgments: The author would like to express his heartfelt gratitude to the editors and reviewers for their constructive comments.

Conflicts of Interest: The authors declare no conflict of interest.

References

1. Beck, C.; Roepstorff, G. From dynamical systems to the langevin equation. *Physical A* **1987**, *145*, 1–14. [CrossRef]
2. Coffey, W.; Kalmykov, Y.; Waldron, J. *The Langevin Equation*; World Scientific: Singapore, 2004.
3. Kubo, R. The fluctuation-dissipation theorem. *Rep. Prog. Phys.* **1966**, *29*, 255–284. [CrossRef]
4. Kubo, R.; Toda, M.; Hashitsume, N. *Statistical Physics II*; Springer: Berlin/Heidelberg, Germany, 1991.
5. Eab, C.; Lim, S. Fractional generalized Langevin equation approach to single-file diffusion. *Physical A* **2010**, *389*, 2510–2521. [CrossRef]
6. Sandev, T.; Tomovski, Z. Langevin equation for a free particle driven by power law type of noises. *Phys. Lett. A* **2014**, *378*, 1–9. [CrossRef]
7. Ulam, S. *A Collection of Mathematical Problems-Interscience Tracts in Pure and Applied Mathmatics*; Interscience: New York, NY, USA, 1906.
8. Hyers, D. On the stability of the linear functional equation. *Proc. Nat. Acad. Sci. USA* **1941**, *27*, 2222–2240. [CrossRef]

9. Rezaei, H.; Jung, S.; Rassias, T. Laplace transform and Hyers-Ulam stability of linear differential equations. *J. Math. Anal. Appl.* **2013**, *403*, 244–251. [CrossRef]
10. Wang, C.; Xu, T. Hyers-Ulam stability of fractional linear differential equations involving Caputo fractional derivatives. *Appl. Math.* **2015**, *60*, 383–393. [CrossRef]
11. Haq, F.; Shah, K.; Rahman, G. Hyers-Ulam stability to a class of fractional differential equations with boundary conditions. *Int. J. Appl. Comput. Math.* **2017**, *3*, 1135–1147. [CrossRef]
12. Ibrahim, R. Generalized Ulam-Hyers stability for fractional differential equations. *Int. J. Math.* **2014**, *23*, 9. [CrossRef]
13. Yu, X. Existence and β-Ulam-Hyers stability for a class of fractional differential equations with non-instantaneous impulses. *Adv. Differ. Equ.* **2015**, *1*, 104. [CrossRef]
14. Gao, Z.; Yu, X. Stability of nonlocal fractional Langevin differential equations involving fractional integrals. *J. Appl. Math. Comput.* **2017**, *53*, 599–611. [CrossRef]
15. Zhao, K. Local exponential stability of four almost-periodic positive solutions for a classic Ayala-Gilpin competitive ecosystem provided with varying-lags and control terms. *Int. J. Control* **2022**, in press. [CrossRef]
16. Caputo, M.; Fabrizio, M. A new definition of fractional derivative without singular kernel. *Prog. Fract. Differ. Appl.* **2015**, *1*, 73–85.
17. Atangana, A.; Baleanu, D. New fractional derivatives with nonlocal and non-singular kernel: theory and application to heat transfer model. *Therm. Sci.* **2016**, *20*, 763–769. [CrossRef]
18. Sadeghi, S.; Jafari, H.; Nemati, S. Operational matrix for Atangana-Baleanu derivative based on Genocchi polynomials for solving FDEs. *Chaos Solitons Fractals* **2020**, *135*, 109736. [CrossRef]
19. Ganji, R.M.; Jafari, H.; Baleanu, D. A new approach for solving multi variable orders differential equations with Mittag–Leffler kernel. *Chaos Solitons Fractals* **2020**, *130*, 109405. [CrossRef]
20. Tajadodi, H. A Numerical approach of fractional advection-diffusion equation with Atangana-Baleanu derivative. *Chaos Solitons Fractals* **2020**, *130*, 109527. [CrossRef]
21. Khan, H.; Khan, A.; Jarad, F.; Shah, A. Existence and data dependence theorems for solutions of an ABC-fractional order impulsive system. *Chaos Solitons Fractals* **2020**, *130*, 109477. [CrossRef]
22. Khan, H.; Li, Y.; Khan, A.; Khan, A. Existence of solution for a fractional-order Lotka-Volterra reaction-diffusion model with Mittag–Leffler kernel. *Math. Meth. Appl. Sci.* **2019**, *42*, 3377–3387. [CrossRef]
23. Acay, B.; Bas, E.; Abdeljawad, T. Fractional economic models based on market equilibrium in the frame of different type kernels. *Chaos Solitons Fractals* **2020**, *130*, 109438. [CrossRef]
24. Khan, A.; Gómez-Aguilar, J.F.; Khan, T.S.; Khan, H. Stability analysis and numerical solutions of fractional order HIV/AIDS model. *Chaos Solitons Fractals* **2019**, *112*, 119–128. [CrossRef]
25. Khan, H.; Gómez-Aguilar, J.F.; Alkhazzan, A.; Khan, A. A fractional order HIV-TB coinfection model with nonsingular Mittag–Leffler Law. *Math. Meth. Appl. Sci.* **2020**, *43*, 3786–3806. [CrossRef]
26. Koca, I. Modelling the spread of Ebola virus with Atangana-Baleanu fractional operators. *Eur. Phys. J. Plus* **2018**, *133*, 100. [CrossRef]
27. Morales-Delgado, V.; Gómez-Aguilar, J.; Taneco-Hernández, M.; Escobar-Jimenezc, R.F.; Olivares-Peregrino, V.H. Mathematical modeling of the smoking dynamics using fractional differential equations with local and nonlocal kernel. *J. Nonl. Sci. Appl.* **2018**, *11*, 1004–1014. [CrossRef]
28. Seemab, A.; Rehman, M.; Alzabut, J.; Abdo, M.S. Langevin equation with nonlocal boundary conditions involving a ψ-Caputo fractional operators of different orders. *AIMS Math.* **2021**, *6*, 6749–6780. [CrossRef]
29. Dien, N.; Trong, D. On the nolinear generalized Langevin equation involving ψ-Caputo fractional derivatives. *Fractals* **2021**, *29*, 2510128. [CrossRef]
30. Rizwan, R.; Zada, A.; Ahmad, M.; Shah, S.O.; Waheed, H. Existence theory and stability analysis of switched coupled system of nonlinear implicit impulsive Langevin equations with mixed derivatives. *Math. Method Appl. Sci.* **2021**, *44*, 8963–8985. [CrossRef]
31. Matar, M.; Alzabut, J.; Jonnalagadda, J. A coupled system of nonlinear Caputo-Hadamard Langevin equations associated with nonperiodic boundary conditions. *Math. Method Appl. Sci.* **2021**, *44*, 2650–2670. [CrossRef]
32. Dien, N. Existence and continuity results for a nonlinear fractional Langevin equation with a weakly singular source. *J. Integral Equ. Appl.* **2021**, *33*, 349–369. [CrossRef]
33. Boutiara, A.; Abdo, M.; Alqudah, M.; Abdeljawad, T. On a class of Langevin equations in the frame of Caputo function-dependent-kernel fractional derivatives with antiperiodic boundary conditions. *AIMS Math.* **2021**, *6*, 5518–5534. [CrossRef]
34. Abbas, M.; Ragusa, M. Solvability of Langevin equations with two Hadamard fractional derivatives via Mittag–Leffler functions. *Appl. Anal.* **2022**, *101*, 3231–3245. [CrossRef]
35. Heydarpour, Z.; Izadi, J.; George, R.; Ghaderi, M.; Rezapour, S. On a partial fractional hybrid version of generalized Sturm–Liouville–Langevin equation. *Fractal Fract.* **2022**, *6*, 269. [CrossRef]
36. Zhao, K. Stability of a nonlinear ML-nonsingular kernel fractional Langevin system with distributed lags and integral control. *Axioms* **2022**, *11*, 350. [CrossRef]
37. Jarad, F.; Abdeljawad, T.; Hammouch, Z. On a class of ordinary differential equations in the frame of Atangana-Baleanu fractional derivative. *Chaos Solitons Fractals* **2018**, *117*, 16–20. [CrossRef]

38. Guo, D.; Lakshmikantham, V. *Nonlinear Problems in Abstract Cone*; Academic Press: Orlando, FL, USA, 1988.
39. Granas, A.; Dugundji, J. *Fixed Point Theory*; Springer: New York, NY, USA, 2003.

MDPI
St. Alban-Anlage 66
4052 Basel
Switzerland
www.mdpi.com

Fractal and Fractional Editorial Office
E-mail: fractalfract@mdpi.com
www.mdpi.com/journal/fractalfract

Disclaimer/Publisher's Note: The statements, opinions and data contained in all publications are solely those of the individual author(s) and contributor(s) and not of MDPI and/or the editor(s). MDPI and/or the editor(s) disclaim responsibility for any injury to people or property resulting from any ideas, methods, instructions or products referred to in the content.

www.ingramcontent.com/pod-product-compliance
Lightning Source LLC
LaVergne TN
LVHW070240100526
838202LV00015B/2158